Sergt. H. J. Nicholas, V.C., M.M.
1st Battalion

The History of the
Canterbury Regiment, N.Z.E.F.

1914 - 1919

BY

CAPTAIN DAVID FERGUSON, M.C.

(Late of the 2nd Battalion, Canterbury Regiment).

PRINTED BY

WHITCOMBE AND TOMBS LIMITED

AUCKLAND, CHRISTCHURCH, DUNEDIN AND WELLINGTON, N.Z.

MELBOURNE AND LONDON.

1921

To the memory of the officers,
non = commissioned officers, and
men of the Canterbury Regiment
who fell in the Great War of
1914=1918

PREFACE

The object of this book is to give, in a clear and concise manner, a record of the doings of the Canterbury Regiment of the New Zealand Expeditionary Force from its enrolment to its disbandment.

The book consists mainly of a compilation of the War Diaries of the service battalions of the Regiment, and does not pretend to give a vivid picture of the fighting in which those battalions took part. Many of the diaries (and especially the earlier ones) give very little information, and it has been necessary to obtain the missing particulars from brigade and divisional diaries and from personal recollections of various officers. As a general rule, the writer has not attempted to describe the dangers and hardships of war: the members of the Regiment, for whom the book is primarily intended, all have personal experiences of these things; and for the general reader there are many books which purport to picture them.

The writer admits at once that the work is incomplete, and invites members of the Regiment to write down a full account of their own remembrance of any incident to which they consider he has not done justice, and to address it to him, care of the publishers. If this is done faithfully by all readers of the book, the materials will be available for a real history of the Regiment.

Where the official records mention the names of members of the Regiment who especially distinguished themselves, the fact has been recorded in this book; but a glance at the list of Honours and Awards (Appendix "F") will show how many officers and men whose services have obtained them decorations are not mentioned by name in the war diaries. Every soldier knows that not half the men who earn decorations are awarded them; and those whose names deserve to appear in these pages, but do not, would be the last to complain of their being overlooked.

In several places in the following pages, it is recorded that one or other of the Canterbury Battalions was unable to advance on account of the unit on one of its flanks not being sufficiently forward. The writer particularly wishes it to be understood that this is not intended to cast any slur upon the units concerned: it is usually a pure matter of luck that one unit is sent against a weak point in the enemy's line, while another next to it meets determined opposition. To take an actual example:—When the 3rd Army crossed the Canal du Nord on September 4th, 1918, the New Zealand Division was fortunate in being allotted a line of attack over ground where the Canal passed through a tunnel, while the Division on its left had to cross the Canal where it ran through a cutting about eighty feet deep. The reader should therefore bear in mind that where matters of this nature are mentioned, no adverse criticism of other units is intended.

The attention of the reader is drawn to the colours of the binding, which are those of the Regiment.

The writer wishes to place on record the great assistance he has received from Lieutenant-Colonel H. Stewart, C.M.G., D.S.O., M.C., late Commanding Officer of the 2nd Canterbury Battalion, who not only was always ready to discuss matters within his own personal experience, but also freely gave information which was the result of many hours of searching in records of every description. The writer has also had the benefit of Colonel Stewart's perusal of his manuscript, which he has altered considerably as the result of Colonel Stewart's criticisms. Finally, many of the excellent maps which illustrate Colonel Stewart's *The New Zealanders in France* (Whitcombe and Tombs Ltd.) are reproduced here by courtesy of the author and the publishers, and also of the New Zealand Government, by whose draughtsmen they were compiled.

The writer also wishes to express his indebtedness to Lieutenant G. T. Weston, late Intelligence Officer of the 1st Canterbury Battalion, who began the work of writing this record. When the present writer took over the work from Lieutenant Weston, the latter had already prepared a précis of the war diaries up to the beginning of 1918, and had also obtained from various members of the Regiment accounts of their personal experiences.

Lieutenant Weston's work has proved of great assistance to the writer.

To the numerous other officers of the Regiment and of the New Zealand Expeditionary Force and the New Zealand Defence Department who have helped him, the writer also expresses his thanks—particularly to the members of the Regimental History Committee, to Major H. S. Westmacott, O.B.E., and Lieutenant V.G. Jervis, N.Z.S.C., both of the Historical War Records Section, and to Major F. L. Hindley, O.B.E., of the Base Records Office.

CONTENTS

LIST OF MAPS

The Maps marked with an asterisk are reproduced from "The New Zealanders in France" (Whitcombe & Tombs Ltd.), by courtesy of Lieutenant-Colonel H. Stewart, the Government of New Zealand, and the Publishers.

LIST OF ILLUSTRATIONS

The History of the Canterbury Regiment
New Zealand Expeditionary Force
1914 - 1919

CHAPTER I.

THE FORMATION OF THE REGIMENT.

The history of the New Zealand Expeditionary Force begins on August 7th, 1914, when the New Zealand Government cabled to the Imperial Government offering the services of the headquarters staff and personnel of a Division of two brigades—one of mounted rifles and the other of infantry.* This offer was accepted on the 14th, and the mobilisation and concentration of the Division began immediately. Major-General Sir A. J. Godley, K.C.M.G., C.B., was appointed to command the Division; and he continued to command the New Zealand Expeditionary Force after he had been given the command of an Army Corps, and until the Expeditionary Force was disbanded. As far as the infantry brigade was concerned, recruiting proceeded on a Territorial basis, and preference was given to members of the existing Territorial Regiments. It was decided to send two battalions from each island—one from each of the principal provincial districts; and the geographical situation of the Territorial Regimental areas made it possible to allot four Regiments to each battalion, for the purposes of recruiting. Accordingly, recruits for the infantry of the Main Body of the New Zealand Expeditionary Force were obtained from the following Regiments:—

AUCKLAND BATTALION.

3rd (Auckland), 6th (Hauraki), 15th (North Auckland), and 16th (Waikato) Regiments.

---

*One brigade only of artillery, consisting of brigade headquarters, three 18-pounder field batteries (4 guns each), and an ammunition column, accompanied the Main Body; but the infantry brigade had the regular establishment of field ambulance, field company (engineers), supply company (Army Service Corps), etc.

WELLINGTON BATTALION.

7th (Wellington West Coast), 9th (Hawke's Bay), 11th (Taranaki), and 17th (Ruahine) Regiments. The 5th (Wellington) Regiment was not represented, as it had been largely drawn on to provide the Samoan Force.

CANTERBURY BATTALION.

1st (Canterbury), 2nd (South Canterbury), 12th (Nelson), and 13th (North Canterbury and Westland) Regiments.

OTAGO BATTALION.

4th (Otago), 8th (Southland), 10th (North Otago), and 14th (South Otago) Regiments.

Thus came about the peculiar system of numbering the companies of the New Zealand Infantry Brigade (and later of the 1st, 2nd, and 4th Infantry Brigades), which was later on to cause so much mystification to units of other forces. As far as the New Zealand Brigades were concerned, however, this curious system caused no practical inconvenience, and though the Territorial system was not strictly observed in some of the later reinforcements, it was always the aim of battalion commanders to allot new men to the company representing the district of New Zealand from which they had come. There is no doubt that in this way local pride was converted into pride in the company, and so in the Territorial Regiment in New Zealand from which that company had its origin.

It is not, however, with the 1st, 2nd, 12th, and 13th Regiments that this book is concerned, but with what may be termed the "artificial" Canterbury Regiment — the Canterbury Regiment of the New Zealand Expeditionary Force — which was built up from the four Territorial Regiments. There are many officers and men who refer with pride to their association with the Canterbury Regiment, who have never had any service with the Territorials. Yet now the Canterbury Regiment of the New Zealand Expeditionary Force has been disbanded, it is to the Territorial Regiments that belongs the privilege of carrying on its traditions; and it must not be forgotten that it was the Territorials who first made its name as a fighting unit.

Until after the evacuation of the Gallipoli Peninsula, there was only one battalion of the Canterbury Regiment in the field. Then the large number of reinforcements accumulated in Egypt, and the arrival of two battalions of rifles, then called "The Trentham Regiment," made possible the formation of a Division of New Zealand Infantry. The Imperial Government having notified its desire to have infantry rather than mounted troops, the reinforcements for the latter were drawn upon to help to make up a second Infantry Brigade; and a certain number of officers and men were transferred from the Mounted Rifle Brigade to the 2nd Infantry Brigade. The 3rd (Rifle) Brigade was formed with the two battalions of the "Trentham Regiment" as a nucleus; and its fighting strength was completed by the arrival of two more battalions in March, 1916.

The original Brigade now became the 1st Brigade, and few of its personnel were transferred to the 2nd Brigade, the exceptions being senior officers and company commanders of the new battalions, and a stiffening of junior officers and of non-commissioned officers. The 2nd Brigade also consisted of one battalion from each of the four principal provincial districts; and, as in the case of the 1st Brigade, each of the sixteen companies wore the badges of the Territorial Regiment which it represented.

To distinguish the men of the new battalions from those of the old, distinctive patches, to be worn on the back of the tunic, were issued to each battalion of the 2nd Brigade on its formation. The patch of the 2nd Canterbury Battalion was a scarlet triangle above an inverted dark blue triangle, on a square black ground.* The strength of each infantry battalion was now laid down as thirty-three officers and nine hundred and seventy-seven other ranks, and this was maintained till May, 1917. The battalions were then re-organised on a basis of thirty-four officers and nine hundred and ten other ranks, which was the establishment of the infantry battalions till the Armistice of November, 1918. In January of that year, it was found necessary to reduce the strength of infantry in each British

---

*The black ground was chosen for two reasons—one the association of this colour with the New Zealand football team, the "All Blacks," and the other as a compliment to the Brigade's commander, Brigadier-General Braithwaite, of the Royal Welsh Fusiliers, of whose uniform a bunch of black ribbon hanging from the tunic collar is a distinctive feature.

Division from twelve battalions to nine battalions. As the New Zealand Expeditionary Force had a sufficient supply of reinforcements in hand. no such reduction was made in the New Zealand Division.

At the end of 1916. the separation of the battalions of the various regiments having proved inconvenient in practice, chiefly in the matter of reinforcements, and the exchange of officers between battalions, the General Officer Commanding the New Zealand Expeditionary Force decided to reorganize the 1st and 2nd Brigades. On January 1st, 1917, the 2nd Auckland and 2nd Wellington Battalions were transferred from the 2nd Brigade to the 1st, and the 1st Canterbury and 1st Otago Battalions came to the 2nd Brigade. New patches were devised for the 1st Battalion of each regiment, that of the 1st Canterbury Battalion being the same as that of the 2nd Battalion, but worn sideways with the scarlet triangle on the left, instead of on top.

The change in the brigades was not at first welcomed by the battalions; but from the regimental point of view the gain was very great, and if there were some slight feelings of soreness, they quickly passed away. Eventually, the 1st Canterbury Battalion had the honour of having its Commanding Officer (Lieut.-Colonel R. Young) promoted Brigadier-General; and though he was lost to the Regiment for a while, his subsequent appointment to command the 2nd Brigade gave very great satisfaction.

During the winter of 1916-1917, large numbers of reinforcements had accumulated in England, consisting not only of drafts from New Zealand, but also of men of the Division who had been wounded, chiefly at the Somme. At the request of the Imperial Government, these men were formed into a 4th Brigade, consisting of a 3rd Battalion from each of the Auckland, Wellington, Canterbury, and Otago Regiments. These went into camp at Codford at the end of March, 1917, and left for France at the end of May. The new battalions also wore distinguishing patches, that of the 3rd Canterbury Battalion consisting of a dark blue square, with a perpendicular scarlet stripe down the centre.

The arrangements made between the Imperial and New Zealand Governments provided that the latter should not be called upon to provide extra reinforcements to maintain the strength of the 4th Brigade; and that the Brigade should be disbanded in the event of the Division falling below strength, and the drafts from New Zealand being insufficient to supply all the men required by the Division. The heavy losses of the Division at Passchendaele, and during the following winter in the Ypres Salient, drained all its available reinforcements; and in consequence, in February, 1918, the 4th Brigade was disbanded, and the 3rd Battalions of the four regiments ceased to exist as service battalions. Those officers and men who were not immediately required for reinforcing the Division were formed into entrenching battalions. Despite their name, they saw some desperate fighting in the spring of 1918, and did useful work in helping to stop the German advance in Flanders.

Finally, there was the Reserve Battalion of the Regiment, which was called the 3rd or 4th Battalion, according to the number of service battalions for the time being in the field. An account of the system of training and administration of this battalion will be found in Appendix "A."

To return now to the mobilization of the original Canterbury Battalion of the New Zealand Infantry Brigade, the quotas supplied by the Territorial Regiments were assembled at the local Territorial headquarters and medically examined there. They were then concentrated at their regimental headquarters, those of the 1st Regiment at Christchurch, of the 2nd Regiment at Timaru, of the 12th Regiment at Nelson, and the West Coast quota of the 13th Regiment at Greymouth, and were re-examined at those centres. The North Canterbury men of the 13th Regiment went direct to Christchurch, arriving there on August 14th, the same day as the men of the 1st Regiment went into camp at the Addington Show Grounds. The following day the South Canterbury and Westland men arrived, and the Nelson men reached the camp on Sunday, August 16th.

The battalion was organized on the old basis of four double companies, of a strength of two hundred and fifty each, and each divided into four platoons. Each company was commanded by a major, with a captain as second-in-command, and with a subaltern to command each platoon. In addition, the Expeditionary Force took with it its first reinforcement of ten per cent. of its strength. These extra men were included in the quotas supplied by the Territorial Regiments, and were attached to the battalions for training and discipline. Separate rolls of the reinforcement were kept, and the men were not posted to the companies of the four battalions, but when the Main Body sailed for Gallipoli they accompanied it.

In command of the Canterbury Battalion was Lieut.-Colonel D. McB. Stewart, the Commanding Officer of the 1st (Canterbury) Regiment in the Territorial Forces. The complete list of the officers of the Canterbury Battalion at the date of its departure from New Zealand is as follows:—

HEADQUARTERS:

Commanding Officer.—Lieutenant-Colonel D. McB. Stewart.
Second in Command.—Major A. E. Loach.
Adjutant.—Captain A. C. B. Critchley-Salmonson.
Assistant Adjutant.—Captain P. B. Henderson.
Quartermaster.—Hon. Captain F. J. W. Stewart.
Transport Officer.—2nd Lieutenant D. P. Fraser.
Machine-Gun Officer.—Lieutenant A. E. Conway.
Medical Officers (Attached). — Lieutenant-Colonel W. R. Pearless, Lieutenant T. R. Ritchie.
1st Reinforcement Officer.—Lieutenant F. D. Maurice.

1ST (CANTERBURY) COMPANY:

Officer Commanding.—Major R. A. Row.
Second in Command.—Captain K. M. Gresson.
Subalterns. — Lieutenant H. Stewart, Lieutenant D. M. Robertson, Lieutenant H. H. Ffitch, 2nd Lieutenant D. Dobson.

2ND (SOUTH CANTERBURY) COMPANY:

Officer Commanding.—Major D. Grant.
Second in Command.—Captain F. B. Brown.
Subalterns. — Lieutenant J. C. Hill, Lieutenant R. A. R. Lawry, Lieutenant C. C. Barclay, Lieutenant O. H. Mead.

12TH (NELSON) COMPANY:

Officer Commanding.—Major C. B. Brereton.

Second in Command.—Captain G. C. Griffiths.

Subalterns. — Lieutenant V. G. Jarvis, Lieutenant H. Saunders, 2nd Lieutenant F. Starnes, 2nd Lieutenant A. E. Forsythe.

13TH (NORTH CANTERBURY AND WESTLAND) COMPANY:

Officer Commanding.—Major B. S. Jordan.

Second in Command.—Captain C. W. E. Cribb.

Subalterns.—Lieutenant N. F. Shepherd, 2nd Lieutenant W. G. Skelton, 2nd Lieutenant A. D. Stitt, 2nd Lieutenant E. H. S. Batchelor.

CHAPTER II.

TRAINING IN NEW ZEALAND AND EGYPT:
AND THE SUEZ CANAL FIGHTING.

Training began at Addington immediately the troops marched in; and though the parade ground was small, there was room for squad drill and elementary musketry, and there was a route march every day. Equipment such as uniforms, boots, blankets, rifles, and Mill's web (the two latter withdrawn from the Territorials) arrived in small lots, and was issued immediately it became available. Every man was keen, as he realized that if he failed to reach the required standard, there were dozens of men anxiously waiting to take his place.

The bulk of the training was carried out under the tuition of the officers, and non-commissioned officers of the battalion, who quickly proved the value of their Territorial experience. The range at Redcliffs was used for musketry practice. The first field training was carried out at the end of the first week; when the battalion marched against an imaginary force at New Brighton, made an attack, and bivouacked for the night at Wainoni Park.

At the beginning of September, bad weather made the Show Grounds uninhabitable, and the battalion moved to the Metropolitan Trotting Club's Grounds adjoining, where the men had their first experience of billeting, in the tea kiosk, luncheon bar, and other buildings. Here drill proceeded, varied by occasional field work, and route marches by day and night; and the work of equipping the battalion went on slowly but steadily. On September 7th, another move was made, to the Plumpton Park Trotting Ground at Sockburn, where the troops were under canvas again. Here the area available for training was much larger than before, and both battalion and company drill became possible. The results of the good work done were now becoming evident, and the steadiness of the men on parade at a review by the Minister of Defence, on September 14th, showed the high standard of discipline in the battalion.

OFFICERS OF CANTERBURY BATTALION, MAIN BODY, N.Z.E.F, TAKEN AT ADDINGTON, AUGUST, 1914.

Back Row.—2nd. Lieut. D. P. Fraser, Lieut. N. F. Shepherd, Lieut. A. D. Stitt, Lieut. R. Miles, Lieut. J. Parker, Lieut. Temple, 2nd. Lieut. F. Starnes, Lieut. J. C. Hill.

2nd Row.—Lieut. V. G. Jervis, Lieut. F. Maurice, 2nd Lieut. E. H. Batchelor, 2nd Lieut. D. Dobson, Lieut. H. Stewart, Lieut. O. Mead, Lieut. N. Forsythe, Capt. K. M. Gresson, Capt. F. Brown.

3rd Row.—Capt. G. C. Griffiths, Lieut. H. Saunders, Lieut. H. Ffitch, Lieut. A. E. Conway, Lieut. R. A. R. Lawrie, 2nd Lieut. C. Barclay, 2nd Lieut. W. G. Skelton, Rev. T. Taylor (C.F.),

Front Row.—Major C. Brereton, Major D. Grant, Major R. A. Row, Capt. A. Critchley Salmonson, Lieut.-Col. D. Macbean Stewart, Major A. E. Loach, Major B. Jordan, Capt. C. Cribb, Lieut. F. J. Stewart.

The battalion remained at Sockburn till September 23rd, when it entrained there at noon and went straight through to Lyttelton. Very few of the public of Christchurch were aware that the troops were leaving, but a large crowd of Lyttelton people gave the transports a hearty send-off. Battalion headquarters and the 2nd, 12th, and 13th Companies embarked at once on the *Athenic* (H.M.N.Z.T. No. 11), and the 1st Company, the machine-gun section, and the first line transport on the *Tahiti* (H.M.N.Z.T. No. 4). The strength of the battalion (including the 1st Reinforcement of one officer and ninety-nine other ranks) was thirty-four officers and one thousand and seventy-six other ranks: of these, twenty-eight officers and eight hundred and forty-four other ranks were on the *Athenic*, and six officers and two hundred and thirty-two other ranks, as well as sixty horses, were on the *Tahiti*. During the afternoon of October 2nd, the transports left the harbour, and having picked up the Otago transports outside the Lyttelton Heads, entered Wellington harbour at 2 p.m. the following day.

It had been originally intended that the four South Island transports should be joined by the Wellington transports, and then should go straight on, picking up the Auckland transports off the coast. However, orders had now been received that the departure of the Expeditionary Force was to be indefinitely postponed. The reason for the change of plan, no doubt, was the presence in the South Pacific of enemy warships, and the lack of a naval escort sufficiently powerful to protect the transports.

The ships were berthed at the wharves, and the 1st Company and machine-gunners were transferred to the *Arawa*,* while the horses were sent to the Canterbury Mounted Rifles' lines at Lyall Bay. The troops lived on board, but were taken ashore daily for exercise and training on the hills on the outskirts of Wellington; and were also taken by train to the Trentham rifle range. In this way the rest of September and the first fortnight of October were spent. On October 10th, the whole force was inspected by His Excellency the Governor-General, the Earl of Liverpool, at Lower Hutt Park.

---

*These troops were re-transferred to the *Tahiti* on October 13th.

The ships for the escort arrived on October 14th: they were H.M.S. *Minotaur*, and the Japanese warship *Ibuki*. The following day the Auckland transports came into harbour, and during the night the remaining transports left the wharves and joined the Auckland ships in the stream. H.M.S. *Psyche* and *Philomel* completed the escort, and the whole fleet left Wellington harbour at 6 a.m. on the 16th. On clearing Cook Strait the convoy formed up in two columns eight cables (1,600 yards) apart, and with the ships in each column three cables (600 yards) apart. The first column or "division" consisted of H.M.N.Z.T. No. 3, *Maunganui*; No. 9, *Hawke's Bay*; No. 8, *Star of India*; No. 7, *Limerick*; No. 4, *Tahiti*: and the second of H.M.N.Z.T. No. 10, *Arawa*; No. 11, *Athenic*; No. 6, *Orari*; No. 5, *Ruapehu*; No. 12, *Waimana*. The *Minotaur* steamed six miles ahead. the *Ibuki* and *Psyche* were at the same distance on the starboard and port beam respectively, and the *Philomel* as rearguard was four miles astern. At night the escort closed in to 4,000 yards' distance.

The routine established for the Main Body was adopted, in the main, on all the transports which carried troops from New Zealand; though experience showed that it was advisable to devote more time to properly organised amusements than to purely military exercises. In addition to physical training before breakfast, two and a half hours were spent each morning and afternoon in lectures, musketry, rifle exercises, and such drill as the very limited deck-space permitted. It is obvious, however, that drill carried out in such circumstances is of little value, beyond its power to kill time.

The food was good, and was usually much more varied than that supplied in camps; but there is no doubt that, on practically every transport that left New Zealand, food was occasionally spoilt by cooks who had plenty of good intentions but little skill in their art. On the whole, however, the men were as well fed as conditions of life on a transport admit. It is true that there were often complaints; but it is also notorious that the monotony of a long sea-voyage breeds grumbling, and naturally both the Main Body and every reinforcement had its share of grumblers.

The meals were served in a special mess-room, which was not used as sleeping-quarters, though it was usually available in the evening for amusements. Canteens gave the troops a chance to buy a few luxuries and some of the smaller necessities of life: here again, experience was needed to show what was most in demand, and the later reinforcements had better canteens than the Main Body and early reinforcements. The military work of the Y.M.C.A. was also in its infancy when the Expeditionary Force left New Zealand, so that this organization was not in a position to help the men on the early transports in the full way it did later on.

Such was the everyday life on board the transports: it is not necessary to give more than a few details of the voyage of the Main Body, and the movements of subsequent reinforcements cannot be recorded here. On October 21st the fleet called at Hobart, where the troops landed the following day for a route march, and leaving on that day reached Albany on the 28th. Before the fleet left Hobart, H.M.S. *Pyramus* replaced H.M.S. *Psyche* in the escort. On arrival at Albany, the fleet found awaiting it there most of the Australian transports, which formed a large and imposing fleet. The Canterbury troops on the *Athenic*, which was berthed late in the afternoon of arrival, were taken ashore for a route march; and those on the *Tahiti* also had a march with the other troops from their own transport.

On the morning of November 1st the Australian and New Zealand transports put to sea under charge of their escort, in which H.M.A.S. *Sydney* and *Melbourne* had replaced H.M.S. *Pyramus* and *Philomel*. On November 9th H.M.A.S. *Sydney* destroyed the *Emden*, near Cocos Island. H.M.S. *Minotaur* had left the convoy on November 8th, and H.M.A.S. *Melbourne* left on the 12th. A few days later (November 13th) the New Zealand transports and three of the Australian ships received orders to steam ahead of the rest of the fleet, and to pick up H.M.S. *Hampshire*, under whose escort they reached Colombo on the 15th. It took two days to coal and water the ships, and small parties of the troops were allowed on shore under their officers.

Only the faster ships of the convoy (including the *Athenic* and *Tahiti*) called at Aden (on the 25th); and these left the next day to join the remainder of the fleet, which was sailing direct to Suez. At this time orders were received that the Australian and New Zealand Expeditionary Forces were not to go direct to France, but would land at Alexandria and would complete their training in Egypt.

The convoy arrived at Alexandria on December 3rd, and the New Zealand Expeditionary Force was ordered to camp at Zeitoun, four miles out of Cairo. The site was sandy and dirty, and the first troops arrived there at night to find that the camp existed only in name. Disembarkation was slow, and it was not till the 9th that the whole of the New Zealand Expeditionary Force was at Zeitoun. Here the British contingent, which had been training on Salisbury Plain, joined the Force on December 24th.

For administrative purposes, the 1st Australian Light Horse Brigade was grouped with the Divisional headquarters and the two brigades of the New Zealand Expeditionary Force, and the whole became the New Zealand and Australian Division, under the command of Major-General Sir A. J. Godley. Each brigade, however, carried on its training independently of the other two brigades.

The training of the infantry brigade naturally at first consisted mainly of drill, from squad drill up to battalion drill and ceremonial; but as time went on, more and more attention was paid to field training. This was varied by long route marches through the sand, much night work, and entrenching practice. By degrees the men were hardened up, and the condition which they had lost on the sea-voyage was gradually recovered; till an actual experience in a practice attack showed they were capable, if need be, of covering twenty-seven miles in a day, without any bad effects. A great deal of time was spent on the rifle range at Abbassia, with the result that the average of shooting was claimed to be as high as that of any troops in the world.

During this time many ceremonial parades were held. The first was on December 23rd, when the force marched through the streets of Cairo, where Lieutenant-General Sir J. G. Maxwell, K.C.B., C.V.O., C.M.G., D.S.O., commanding the forces in Egypt, took the salute. At the end of the month, it was announced that the Australian and New Zealand forces were to be organized as an Army Corps, and would be commanded by Lieutenant-General Sir W. R. Birdwood, K.C.S.I., K.C.M.G., C.I.E., D.S.O. The arrival in Egypt of the High Commissioner for New Zealand (Sir Thomas Mackenzie) at this time made it a suitable occasion for a review of the New Zealand Expeditionary Force; and on December 30th, General Birdwood inspected the Force, and was accompanied by the High Commissioner. Again on January 9th the whole Force was paraded, and was addressed by the High Commissioner, after which the troops marched past Lieutenant-General Sir J. G. Maxwell.

At the end of January the troops were well advanced in their training; so that on news being received on the 25th that the Turks were advancing on the Suez Canal in three columns, the New Zealand Infantry Brigade was considered fit to support the 11th (Indian) Division, which was holding the defence of the Canal.

The brigade was divided into two portions, headquarters and the Auckland and Canterbury Battalions being sent to Ismailia, on Lake Timsah, midway between Port Said and Suez, and the remaining battalions to El Kubri, near Suez. The troops for Ismailia entrained at Palais de Koubbeh and Helmieh Stations on the afternoon of January 26th, and reaching their destination the same day, became the general reserve of the forces defending the Canal.

The Canterbury Battalion was ordered to garrison certain posts, namely, one at El Ferdan, and another at Battery Post (both north-east of Ismailia), and one at Serapeum (south of Lake Timsah). One company of the battalion was kept in reserve at Ismailia (Ferry Post), and a platoon of one of the other companies was also retained there, to act as an armed patrol under the Assistant Provost Marshal. On February 2nd, there arrived the battalion's draft from the 2nd Reinforcements, consisting of three officers and one hundred and ninety-two other ranks.

The expected attack was made by the Turks early on the morning of February 3rd.

An official report on the fighting, issued for the benefit of the battalions at El Kubri, reads as follows:—

REPORT OF FIGHTING ON CANAL
February 2nd to 4th, 1915.

KANTARA:

Early on the morning of the 3rd an attack was made on our outposts which was repulsed, the enemy retreating leaving 15 killed and wounded and 40 unwounded. Later in the day a partial attack was made from the S.E., but the enemy were stopped 1,200 yards from the position.

EL FERDAN:

At El Ferdan, where the 13th Regiment Company and two platoons of the 1st Regiment Company were stationed, the enemy made an attack. At 7 a.m. a Turkish Battery of four small guns opened fire on the Signal Station, finding the range immediately; they hit the buildings several times. At this juncture H.M.S. *Clio* came up and silenced the batteries, though she was hit three times in so doing. The action was ended at 1 p.m.

BATTERY POST:

North of Ismailia, at the Battery Post, there were two platoons of the 12th Nelson Regiment Company. These men were not actually fired on. But the battery on their left was shelled. Later in the day this post was relieved by two platoons of the 3rd Auckland Regiment Company. These platoons were shelled on their way out to the post but suffered no casualties.

ISMAILIA FERRY:

By Ismailia Ferry Post, where the 2nd South Canterbury Company were stationed under Major Grant as general reserve, the enemy were found to be entrenching about half a mile to the east at daylight. Two battalions (sic) opened fire, and the enemy's guns engaged the *Hardinge, Requin,* and our Mountain Artillery. Though no regular attack was made, intermittent shelling continued throughout the day. The New Zealand platoons actually saw no fighting, but they were exposed to shell fire throughout the day. Some of the shells fired at this point fell within half a mile of the ground where the Auckland and Canterbury Battalions were encamped.

The shipping on Lake Timsah was subjected to shell fire during the day, and also the outskirts of Ismailia at various points.

During the night of the 3rd a half-hearted attack was made, after which the enemy withdrew the bulk of their forces to Kataib El Kheil.

TOUSSUM AND SERAPEUM.

At daylight on the 3rd the enemy were found to be close to Toussum and Serapeum, and their guns opened fire on both posts. At the latter post where our ships and artillery engaged the enemy, there were two platoons of the 12th Nelson Regiment Company under Major Brereton, who took up outposts at 5 p.m. on the night of the 2nd on the west bank of the Canal. On his right was a battery of the Lancashire Artillery, and on his left the 62nd Punjabis Infantry. All was quiet until 3.20 a.m., when heavy machine-gun fire from the enemy commenced to our north. At this time there was no fire to the New Zealanders' front. The Punjabis were reinforced with 30 of our men, who on arrival at once commenced opening fire at a party of Turks attempting to cross the Canal in boats, which movement they effectively stopped. At this the enemy retreated and entrenched on the eastern bank under our fire. Many of the enemy tried to retreat but were stopped by our fire. We were helped by enfilading fire from the rest of the two platoons on our right, who had the command of the enemy's trenches for a distance of 1,200 yards. There were three distinct attempts made to cross the Canal at this point, all of which failed. A counter-attack by the 62nd Punjabis about mid-day produced considerable results. Early in the afternoon orders were received to close on the 22nd Brigade Headquarters. During this move Private Ham was severely wounded and afterwards succumbed to his wounds. The only other New Zealand casualty was that of Sergeant Williams, who was slightly wounded by shrapnel. Outpost duty was resumed at 5 p.m. No more fighting took place except for persistent sniping, the enemy having retired leaving many dead and nearly 300 prisoners.

On the morning of the 4th, troops from Serapeum captured some 150 of the enemy, who were still entrenched on the Canal bank some one and a half miles south of Toussum, after having been treacherously fired on, the white flag having been raised and signs of surrender made.

During the day H.M.S. *Swiftsure*, *Clio*, and *Hardinge*, the French ships *Requin*, *D'Entreastreaux*, as well as torpedo boats and launches engaged the enemy and rendered valuable assistance. The *Hardinge* was struck by two 6 in. shells and had ten men wounded. The *Swiftsure* had one man killed. Military casualties were:—British officers killed, 1; wounded, 4. British, Indian, and Egyptian rank and file killed, 17; wounded, 79. The enemy along the Canal at all points attacked, appear to muster in all some 12,000 men, and at least six batteries. One 6 in. gun was also located, which is thought to have been silenced by the *Requin*.

Throughout the fighting two companies were always kept ready to leave camp at a moment's notice to reinforce any position where they might be required.

Over 500 of the enemy were buried by our troops, and upwards of 500 are prisoners in our hands. It is calculated that on a basis of three wounded to one killed, the enemy must have suffered a loss of at least 1,500 wounded, making total casualties of between 2,500 and 3,000. The enemy is now in retreat all along the line: whether they will make another attack cannot yet be determined. It has been ascertained that General Dyemal Pasha was present during the action with a number of German officers, one of whom has been killed.

On February 3rd a message of congratulation on the three days' fighting was received from the General Officer Commanding in Chief and Lord Kitchener.

A. C. TEMPERLEY,

Major,

Brigade Major,

New Zealand Infantry Brigade.

Ismailia,
    February 12th, 1915.

OFFICERS OF 1ST BN. CANTERBURY INFANTRY REGIMENT, N.Z.E.F., FRANCE, APRIL 22ND, 1917.

Back Row.—2nd Lieut. C. H. Holmes, 2nd Lieut. A. Andrews, 2nd Lieut. F. Comer, Lt. E. H. L. Bernau, 2nd Lieut. E. Haydon, Lieut. S. E. K. Marshall, Hon. Lieut. W. H. Osborne.

2nd Row.—2nd Lieut. J. M. Barton, Lieut. S. Natusch, 2nd Lieut. H. H. Hanna, Lieut. W. F. Brothers, 2nd Lieut. E. C. D. Withell, Lieut. S. G. Smith, Lieut. A. G. Dean, Lieut. J. A. McQueen, Lieut. W. N. Elliott, 2nd Lieut. A. C. C. Hunter, 2nd Lieut. J. W. Fraser, 2nd Lieut. R. L. Wilson.

Front Row.—Capt. S. W. Brooker, Capt. F. N. Johns (M.O.), Capt. T. W. L. Rutherfurd, Capt. J. L. C. Merton, M.C., Capt. A. D. Stitt, M.C., Lieut.-Col. R. Young, C.M.G., D.S.O., Capt. D. Dobson, M.C., Capt. F. J. W. Stewart, Capt. L. G. O'Callaghan, Rev. C. O. H. Tobin (C.F.), Capt. G. H. Gray.

No further attacks were made on the Canal, but the Canterbury Battalion remained in garrison of its posts till February 8th, when it was relieved by troops of the 1st Australian Brigade. On the afternoon of February 5th, the New Zealand Infantry Brigade was ordered to provide a detachment of four hundred rifles and a machine-gun section, to form part of a force under the command of Major-General Younghusband, which was to attack a Turkish force at Katib El Kheil, five miles east of Ismailia. The 2nd Company was detailed as part of this force, and had actually started, when orders were received that the operations had been abandoned.

The battalion remained in the Canal area, manning a few posts north of Ismailia, but continuing training all the while; till it returned to Zeitoun on February 26th. The 4th Australian Infantry Brigade had arrived in Egypt in the meantime, and had been included in the New Zealand and Australian Division. Field practices, on a larger scale than had hitherto been tried, were now frequent. Thus, on March 3rd, the whole Division practised an attack on a skeleton force, representing part of the main Turkish army, which was supposed to have crossed the Canal and to be advancing on Cairo. Again, on the 5th, the Division moved out after dark, took up and entrenched a defensive position, and returned to camp the following morning. The two infantry brigades opposed each other on the 10th, and on the 12th the Division attacked the East Lancashire Territorial Division. On the 17th the Division practised taking over trenches by night, and a night assault on the enemy trench-system opposite it; and returned to camp by daylight.

The Division on February 27th had been warned to hold itself in readiness for active service, and it was guessed that an offensive against the Turks was being planned. A Divisional mobilisation parade was therefore ordered for March 22nd: at this parade the High Commissioner of Egypt, Sir Henry McMahon, was present and took the salute at the subsequent march-past. On the 29th, the Division was inspected by its new Commander-in-Chief, General Sir Ian Hamilton.

At the beginning of April, Divisional Headquarters was notified that the Division would probably begin to embark on the 7th of that month, and an advanced base was established at Mustafa, near Alexandria. Orders were issued to the infantry battalions to reduce their strength to the war establishment of thirty-three officers and nine hundred and seventy-seven other ranks; and each battalion was also ordered to detail an additional body of one officer and ninety-nine other ranks (equivalent to ten per cent. of the strength of a battalion) which was to accompany the battalion as a reinforcement. All the remaining officers and men of the New Zealand Expeditionary Force who were left after the battalions had been reduced in strength to war establishment, and the ten per cent. of reinforcements had been selected, were ordered to remain in the Zeitoun Camp, which was to be made a training depôt.

The infantry battalions were meanwhile being daily exercised in long distance route-marching, with packs brought up to the weight of seventy pounds. This was fifteen pounds above the usual weight carried, the extra weight being necessary to prepare the men to carry on disembarkation an extra eighty rounds of ammunition and three days' rations. To ensure that every man was properly equipped, a preparatory embarkation parade was held on April 5th, when every man, horse and wagon was on parade, and every detail of equipment was carefully checked.

The 12th and 13th Companies left for Alexandria before the rest of the Canterbury Battalion, entraining at Palais de Koubbeh station on April 9th, and embarking on the *Itonus* the same day. Battalion Headquarters and the 1st and 2nd Companies entrained at Helmieh station on the 10th, and embarked on the *Lutzow* the next day. The transport officer and forty men, with horses and vehicles, embarked on the *Katuna*: but though these were taken to Gallipoli, they were not landed, but returned to Alexandria.

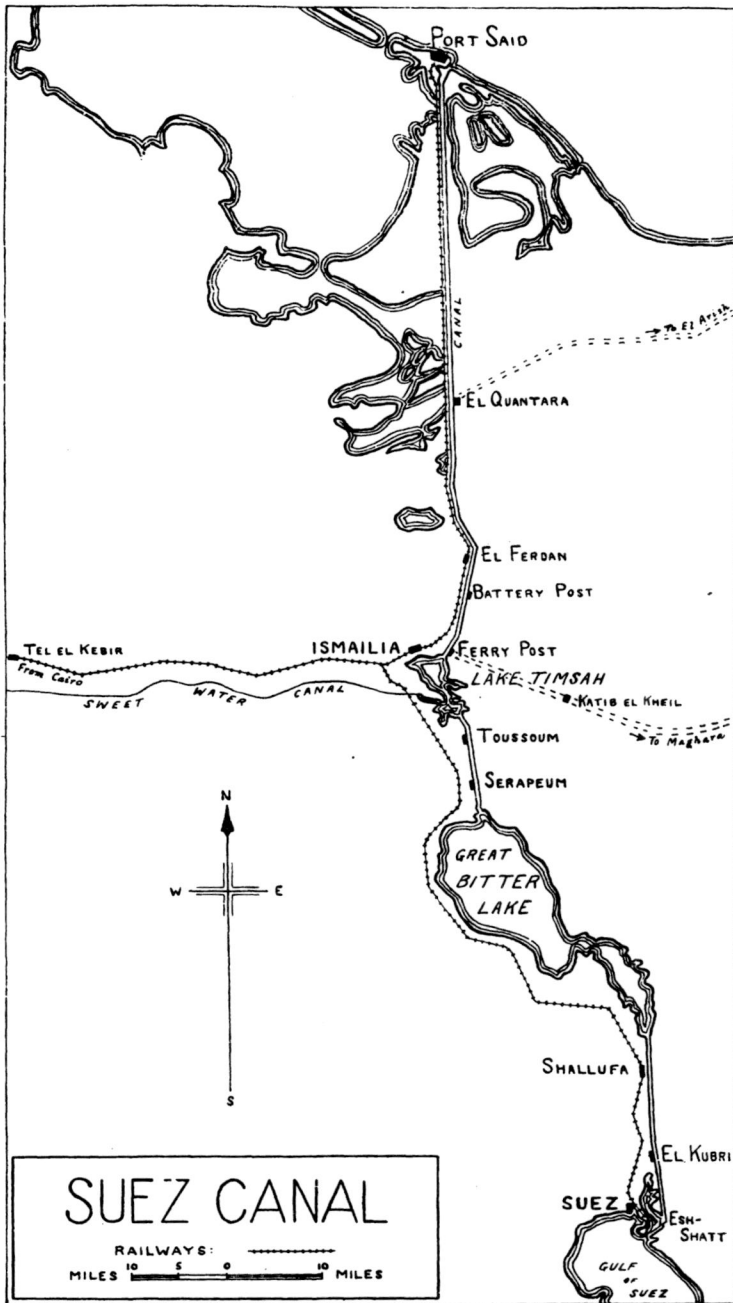

PORT SAID

CANAL

To El Arish

EL QUANTARA

EL FERDAN

BATTERY POST

TEL EL KEBIR

From Cairo

ISMAILIA

FERRY POST

LAKE TIMSAH

KATIB EL KHEIL

SWEET WATER CANAL

TOUSSOUM

To Maghara

SERAPEUM

N
W E
S

GREAT
BITTER
LAKE

SHALLUFA

EL KUBRI

SUEZ

ESH-
SHATT

GULF
OF
SUEZ

SUEZ CANAL

RAILWAYS: ··········
MILES 10 5 0 10 MILES

CHAPTER III.

GALLIPOLI, FROM THE LANDING TO THE END OF JULY; INCLUDING THE CAPE HELLES FIGHTING.

A very full and clear account of the strategical aims of the Gallipoli campaign is to be found in Mr. H. W. Nevinson's *The Dardanelles Campaign*. The aims may be briefly summarised here as:—

    (1) The capture of Constantinople, which would cause Turkey to surrender, and thus remove all anxiety about Egypt and the Suez Canal.

    (2) The attraction of Italy, Bulgaria, and Roumania to the alliance against the Central Powers, leaving the latter entirely surrounded by enemies, and securing the left flank of the Russian armies.

    (3) The opening of a channel for the supply of munitions to Russia by her Allies, and in return, the supply to them of Russian wheat.

It was unfortunate that the British War Council assumed that the Dardanelles could be forced, and Constantinople captured, by the Navy alone. British and French naval forces made attacks on the forts at the end of February, 1915, and in March of the same year, during the course of which landings were made on both the Peninsula and the Asiatic Coast. But these attacks failed to open the Straits; and the interval which elapsed between the attempts and the military landing at the end of April gave the Turks time to put the Peninsula in an elaborate state of defence.

It is not proposed to criticise here the conduct of the campaign, or the causes of its failure: these matters are ably dealt with in Mr. Nevinson's book, to which the reader is referred. Neither will there be any attempt made to convey an impression of the epic nature of the fighting; for a writer of genius has adequately described the tremendous struggles and hardships which made up the daily lives of the troops on Gallipoli.* The

---

*Mr. John Masefield's "Gallipoli."

business of this, and the following chapters, is to follow the doings of the Canterbury Battalion, and to describe its share in the operations.

In order that the connected story of the operations shall not be interrupted by digressions which have no direct bearing on the military situation, it may be mentioned here once and for all that in the Gallipoli campaign, as in all campaigns in the Eastern theatres of war, disease was responsible for a very large proportion of the casualties among the troops; and that so rife was dysentery that had all those who suffered from its less severe forms been evacuated, there would have been practically no troops left in the trenches.

The constricted area held by the Allied troops was responsible to some extent for unavoidable extra suffering to the wounded: collected as they often were under fire and with great difficulty, they were not out of danger from the enemy's shrapnel until they reached the hospital ships; and this always involved their lying in exposed positions for hours (and on some occasions for days) until the lighters arrived to take them from the beach. Delays of this nature were inevitable on account of the nature of the operations; but it is undeniable that the arrangements for the evacuation and care of the wounded on the day of the original landing were hopelessly inadequate.

Even after a secure footing had been established on the Peninsula, the troops in the trenches had constantly to bear hardships which were almost as bad as the sufferings of the sick and wounded. Those men who were sick enough by all ordinary standards, but who could not be evacuated on account of the large number of more serious cases which claimed prior attention to them, had their sufferings increased by the unsuitability of their food. Water was scarce; and the rations issued were ill-suited for troops fighting in a hot climate.

But in fairness to those who were responsible for the feeding of the troops, it must be said that the distance of the firing line from the base made the question of supplies very difficult. On this account and also because of the lack of space in the supply ships, biscuits replaced bread as the staple article of food; and practically all other food was tinned, and naturally consisted mainly of "bully-beef." Though these and other hardships of the campaign will not be continually mentioned, the reader must constantly have them in mind, in order to do full justice to the achievements of the troops who took part in the operations on the Peninsula.

The army entrusted with the attack on the defences of the Dardanelles was placed under the command of Sir Ian Hamilton, G.C.B., D.S.O., A.D.C., and consisted of the 29th and Royal Naval Divisions, the Australian and New Zealand Army Corps, and a French Division. The Australian and New Zealand Army Corps consisted of the Australian Division (1st, 2nd, and 3rd Infantry Brigades) and the New Zealand and Australian Division (the New Zealand Infantry Brigade and the 4th Australian Infantry Brigade), and was commanded by Lieutenant-General Sir W. R. Birdwood. As has been already mentioned, the New Zealand and Australian Division also included the New Zealand Mounted Rifle Brigade and the 1st Australian Light Horse Brigade; but mounted troops were considered unsuitable for the attack, and were therefore left in Egypt for the present. The 29th (Indian) Infantry Brigade was to be attached to the Division, to take the place of the mounted brigades; however, this infantry brigade did not arrive at Gallipoli till May 1st; and then it was landed on the southern part of the Peninsula.

The main fleet of transports carrying the troops of the New Zealand and Australian Division left Alexandria at 6 p.m. on Monday, April 12th, and entered Mudros harbour, in the island of Lemnos, early in the morning of the 15th. The *Lutzow*, which carried Divisional Headquarters, also had on board the Canterbury Battalion, less the 12th and 13th Companies, which travelled by the *Itonus*. The last mentioned transport, and the *Katuna* with one officer and forty-one other ranks of the Battalion and sixty horses, left Alexandria on the 10th, and arrived at Mudros on the 13th. The voyages of both portions of the fleet were uneventful. The harbour of Mudros, large as it was, provided with difficulty anchorages for the ships of war and one hundred and eight transport and supply vessels assembled there.

On arrival at Mudros, the general plan for the attack was given to the Divisional Staff. On account of the previous naval attacks, it was recognised that there was no hope of taking the enemy by surprise; but it was possible to deceive him as to the actual locality of the landing, by means of feints at landing in other places. The main landing was to be made by the 29th Division, at the south-eastern extremity of the Peninsula; and a subsidiary landing was to be made by the Australian and New Zealand Army Corps, about nine miles further north, with the object of threatening the lines of communication and the rear of the Turkish troops opposed to the 29th Division. The feint attacks were to be delivered by the Royal Naval Division near Bulair, at the head of the Gulf of Xeres, and by the French Division, upon the Asiatic entrance to the Straits. It may be said here that no attempt at landing was made by the Royal Naval Division, nor did the Commander-in-Chief intend that its presence near Bulair should be anything more than a diversion, to pin to this ground the enemy troops which were known to be there. At Kum Kale, however, the French landed the 6th Regiment of the Brigade Coloniale, which captured the village and five hundred prisoners, and was re-embarked on the morning of the 26th, having fulfilled its task of assisting the landing of the 29th Division by drawing the fire of the guns on the Asiatic coast.

The time at Mudros was spent in company and battalion training ashore, and in practising boat drill with a view to the landing. It was intended to have a practice of disembarkation of the whole of the New Zealand Brigade, but owing to the weather being unsuitable the attempt was abandoned.

The orders for the attack on the Peninsula provided that the Australian and New Zealand Army Corps should land at "Z" Beach, between Gaba Tepe and Fisherman's Hut, and capture the ridge over which ran the Gallipoli-Maidos and Boghali-Koja Dere roads. The Australian Division was to land before the New Zealand and Australian Division, and was to provide a party, consisting of the 3rd Australian Brigade, to effect the first landing, and to cover the disembarkation of the remainder of the Corps.

The transports carrying the Australian Division sailed out of Mudros Bay on the afternoon of April 24th, and reached the rendezvous, off the coast of the Peninsula, at 1.30 a.m. on the 25th. Here 1,500 troops of the 3rd Australian Brigade, who had

made the voyage on H.M.S. *Queen, London,* and *Prince of Wales,*
were transferred to the boats of those ships and taken in tow
by them. The remaining 2,500 troops of the covering force
were at the same time transferred from their transports to six
destroyers. The battleships and destroyers then proceeded inshore; and when about a mile and a quarter off the coast the
battleships dropped the tows, which moved on towards the beach.

To quote Sir Ian Hamilton's Despatch of May 20th, 1915:—

"All these arrangements worked without a hitch, and were
carried out in complete orderliness and silence. No breath of
wind ruffled the surface of the sea, and every condition was
favourable save for the moon, which, sinking behind the ships,
may have silhouetted them against its orb, betraying them thus
to the watchers on the shore.

"A rugged and difficult part of the coast had been selected
for the landing, so difficult and rugged that I considered the
Turks were not at all likely to anticipate such a descent. Indeed,
owing to the tows having failed to maintain their exact direction,
the actual point of disembarkation was more than a mile north
of that which I had selected, and was more closely overhung by
steeper cliffs. Although this accident increased the initial difficulty of driving the enemy off the heights inland, it has since
proved itself to have been a blessing in disguise, inasmuch as
the actual base of the force of occupation has been much better
defiladed from shell-fire.

"The beach on which the landing was actually effected is a
very narrow strip of sand, about 1,000 yards in length, bounded
on the north and south by two small promontories. At its
southern extremity a deep ravine, with exceedingly steep scrub-
clad sides, runs inland in a north-easterly direction. Near the
northern end of the beach a small but steep gully runs up into
the hills at right angles to the shore. Between the ravine and
the gully the whole of the beach is backed by the seaward face
of the spur which forms the north-western side of the ravine.
From the top of the spur the ground falls almost sheer, except
near the southern limit of the beach, where gentler slopes give
access to the mouth of the ravine behind. Further inland lie in
a tangled knot the under-features of Sari Bair, separated by
deep ravines, which make a most confusing diversity of direction.

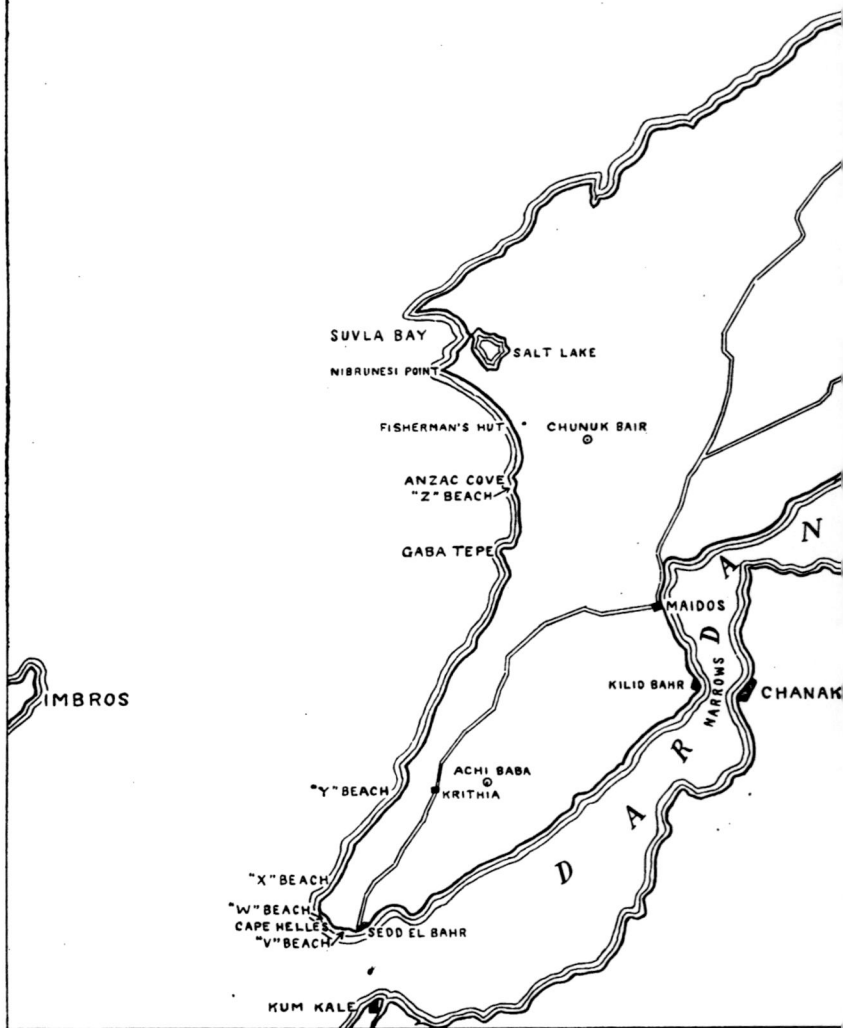

GALLIPOLI

SUVLA BAY

SALT LAKE

NIBRUNESI POINT

FISHERMAN'S HUT   CHUNUK BAIR

ANZAC COVE
"Z" BEACH

GABA TEPE

MAIDOS

KILID BAHR   CHANAK

IMBROS

N

MARROWS

ACHI BABA
"Y" BEACH   KRITHIA

"X" BEACH

"W" BEACH
CAPE HELLES   SEDD EL BAHR
"V" BEACH

D A R D A

KUM KALE

GULF OF XEROS

CAPE XEROS

BULAIR

GALLIPOLI

GALLIPOLI STRAIT

E L L E S

ASIA MINOR

ES 5 4 3 2 1 0   5   10 MILES

Sharp spurs, covered with dense scrub, and falling away in many places in precipitous sandy cliffs, radiate from the principal mass of the mountain, from which they run north-west, west, south-west, and south to the coast.

"The boats approached the land in the silence and the darkness, and they were close to the shore before the enemy stirred. Then about one battalion of the Turks was seen running along the beach to intercept the lines of the boats. At this so critical a moment, the conduct of all ranks was most praiseworthy. Not a word was spoken—everyone remained perfectly orderly and quiet awaiting the enemy's fire, which sure enough opened, causing many casualties. The moment the boats touched land, the Australians' turn had come. Like lightning they leapt ashore, and each man as he did so went straight as his bayonet to the enemy. So vigorous was the onslaught that the Turks made no effort to withstand it and fled from ridge to ridge pursued by the Australian Infantry."*

Directly the boats had landed the first party of 1,500, they returned to the destroyers, which had meanwhile stood further inshore, and disembarked the remaining troops of the 3rd Australian Brigade. The 1st and 2nd Australian Brigades followed, and were all disembarked by 2 p.m.

Meanwhile, the first transports of the New Zealand and Australian Division had not left Lemnos till 1 a.m. on the 25th, and the *Goslar*, carrying the New Zealand Brigade Headquarters, did not leave till 9 a.m. the same day. The *Lutzow*, on which were the Headquarters and the 1st and 2nd Companies of the Canterbury Battalion, arrived at 7 a.m. off Anzac Cove (as the landing place of the Corps was henceforth known); but owing to the confusion caused by the alteration of the place of landing, and the casualties incurred by the Navy, the first troops of the battalion did not leave the ship till 10 a.m. Disembarkation was completed by about 12.30 p.m.; and although the landing was made under shrapnel fire no casualties were incurred.

Owing to the facts that Colonel F. E. Johnston commanding the New Zealand Brigade was temporarily indisposed, and that the *Goslar* with the headquarters' staff of the same brigade had

---

*Naval and Military Despatches, Part II., p. 276.

not yet arrived off the landing-place, Brigadier-General H. B. Walker, D.S.O., Brigadier-General on the General Staff of the Australian and New Zealand Army Corps, took command of the brigade for the time being.

On landing, the 3rd Australian Brigade had spread out fan-wise, and crossing the ridge to the east and south-east of Anzac Cove (MacLagan's Ridge) had fought its way to the south-eastern side of Shrapnel Gully, which lay beyond the ridge. The brigade was reinforced on its right and centre by the two remaining brigades of the Australian Division, and throughout the day a line of posts was being established from the sea, about a mile south of the landing place, along the ridge on the south-east side of Shrapnel Gully as far as Pope's Hill, about fifteen hundred yards east of Ari Burnu. From here to a point on the shore about half a mile north of Ari Burnu, the line was very weakly held by a few troops of the 3rd Australian Brigade; in fact there was a gap of some hundred yards between the left of the line and the sea. The 2nd Australian Battalion of the 1st Brigade apparently went astray, as it took up a position on the lower slopes of Walker's Ridge near the sea, instead of going with the rest of the Brigade to Shrapnel Gully.

The first troops of the New Zealand Brigade to land were the Auckland Battalion, at noon, and the Headquarters and 1st and 2nd Companies of the Canterbury Battalion, at 12.30 p.m. These were immediately ordered to reinforce the left flank of the 3rd Australian Brigade, and to fill the gap between that flank and the sea. While the order was in process of being carried out, the two Canterbury Companies became separated on Plugge's Plateau, a quarter of a mile east of the beach. There was great confusion, as the men of the various companies had not only become mixed with one another, but in some cases had attached themselves to the Auckland and various Australian Battalions; while Aucklanders and Australians were picked up by the officers commanding the various Canterbury parties.

Lieutenant-Colonel Stewart with the 2nd Company got well forward, and took up a position on the upper portion of Walker's Ridge, which ran north-east from near Pope's Hill down to the sea. They immediately became involved in heavy fighting, and

Lieutenant-Colonel Stewart, going back to bring up reinforcements, collected a large party of Australians, and was killed while exposing himself in leading them up to the firing line. There the 2nd Company and the Australian reinforcements repulsed with the bayonet three Turkish attacks, and then withdrew slightly to more suitable ground, where they dug in.

Two platoons of the 1st Company went east from the Plateau and reached the firing line at Quinn's and Courtney's Posts. The other two platoons were held in reserve on the Plateau: one of them, later in the day, was taken by Captain Critchley-Salmonson to fill a gap on the left flank, where Walker's Ridge ran down to the sea coast. Two sections of the remaining platoon were engaged in carrying ammunition to the Australians on the right, and on reaching the firing line were kept there and were very badly cut up.

The transport carrying the 12th and 13th Companies did not arrive at its anchorage off Anzac till 5 p.m., and these companies on landing were immediately dispatched to the lower slopes of Walker's Ridge, which they reached at about 9.30 p.m. The night was spent in consolidating the position under heavy fire and in the face of several infantry attacks.

At the close of the day the question of re-embarkation was seriously discussed at Corps Headquarters; but General Birdwood pointed out the difficulty of the operation, and decided to wait long enough to enable the position to stabilize.

The above is a very bare outline of the day's events; but the whole operation was a very confused one, and the accounts of eye-witnesses do not help to make it clearer. It must be remembered that the elaborate orders to which officers were accustomed later in France, assigning a definite rôle to each company, and even to each platoon, could not be issued in an undertaking of this nature. In the absence of previous reconnaissance of the country, which was of course impossible, elaborate plans would have led to confusion rather than they would have helped those entrusted with the task of carrying them out. In any case, owing to the landing taking place further north than was intended, such plans would have proved useless. All that could be done was for the Divisional Commanders on the spot to issue their orders to meet the needs of the moment.

The orderly landing of five brigades on a beach but a thousand yards long, backed by precipitous hills two hundred feet high, would even under peace conditions prove a difficult feat: when it is considered that this was done in the face of the enemy, it is not surprising that a great deal of confusion arose. Again, after the landing was successfully carried out, the troops had to attack, over precipitous country totally strange to them. an enemy who was invisible to them, and who was established in formidable defensive positions.

The difficult nature of the country is testified to by the fact that many who took part in the fighting were unable afterwards to recognise the routes over which they had travelled, in spite of the fact that the area of the country occupied at Anzac for the first three months was under a mile and a half long, and twelve hundred and fifty yards across at its broadest.

The casualties of the Canterbury Battalion, for the day of the landing alone, show the desperate nature of the fighting. They are:—

	Officers.	Other Ranks.
Killed	3*	21
Wounded	2	87
Missing	1†	100
Total	6	198

*Lieutenant-Colonel D. McB. Stewart, Major D. Grant, Lieutenant H. Ffitch.

†Lieutenant C. C. Barclay.

During the afternoon of the 25th, the Otago Battalion landed and was held in Brigade support on Plugge's Plateau; and the Wellington Battalion and three battalions of the 4th Australian Brigade came ashore during the night of the 25th/26th. Two Australian battalions were sent to reinforce the firing line on the right of the New Zealand Brigade, where the 3rd Australian Brigade troops were present in such small numbers that there was practically a gap in the lines. A company and a half of the Wellingtons were sent to Walker's Ridge, and the remainder of the battalion, with the 13th Australian Battalion, were held in Divisional reserve on the beach.

Up till this time the infantry had had as artillery support, beyond the guns of the warships, only one mountain battery (the 21st) and one field gun of the Australian Divisional Artillery. Neither these few field guns nor the naval guns were able, on account of their flat trajectory, to bring their fire to bear on the enemy artillery, most of which was firing from deep gullies inaccessible to the fire of anything but howitzers. The result was that, though the guns of the fleet and the few guns ashore were able to give valuable assistance in repulsing enemy infantry attacks, they could not silence the enemy howitzers, which continually harassed our firing line. So serious were the effects of the enemy shell-fire that the Commander of the New Zealand Brigade informed the Divisional Commander that if the line was to be held more field guns would have to be landed during the night of the 25th/26th. The situation was improved by the landing of the New Zealand Howitzer Battery on the 26th.

On the morning of the 26th, the enemy's guns again opened an accurate fire on the firing line, Plugge's Plateau, and the beach. The guns of the Mountain Battery on shore replied, and the bursts of their shrapnel enabled the *Queen Elizabeth* to pick up their targets. The effect of the gunfire from the battleship was to silence the enemy's batteries for several hours.

During the morning the whole of the Canterbury Battalion was concentrated on Walker's Ridge, and the companies were re-organised as well as possible, though there were still numbers of the men of the battalion astray with other battalions. At 2 p.m., the Commanding Officer of the 2nd Australian Battalion asked for reinforcements to be sent to his left flank, which was being attacked. The 12th Company was sent; but while advancing to the required position it was checked by the withdrawal of two Australian platoons from the Ridge. The 12th Company went forward and by 6.30 p.m. had re-established the line. During the night the position was strengthened by hard digging.

The following day (the 27th) the Canterbury Battalion was ordered to take over the remainder of Walker's Ridge from the 2nd Australian Battalion. The Otago Battalion came into the front line on the right of the Canterbury Battalion, and the 12th Company was withdrawn to its original position at the foot of Walker's Ridge. An officer's patrol, under Lieutenant R. A. R. Lawry, went out to the north of the Ridge and found the Fisherman's Hut on the beach unoccupied, though there was an enemy post on the hill above the hut. During the afternoon orders were received from Brigade Headquarters to send a strong company to support the Wellington Battalion, which had reinforced the Australians on the right of the Otago Battalion, and was being attacked. The Battalion War Diary does not say whether the company was sent; apparently it was not. The day passed quietly in the Canterbury Battalion's sector; though enemy snipers were very active, and could not be located.

On the morning of April 28th, the 1st Company relieved the 13th Company, a platoon of which was sent out to bury about fifty Australians, whose bodies were lying on the beach near Fisherman's Hut. Immediately the platoon left the trenches it came under heavy and accurate fire from enemy snipers. and having lost two killed and three wounded, it was ordered by the Commanding Officer of the Battalion to return. In the evening two battalions of Royal Marines (1st Naval Brigade) landed, and went into the right of the Australian Division's line, and the following day two battalions of the 3rd Naval Brigade came ashore.

At 2 a.m. on April 29th, a false alarm of an enemy attack along the beach, on the left flank, roused the whole battalion. Otherwise the day passed without incident, beyond the arrival of a party of reinforcements of an officer and twenty other ranks. On the 30th, the 12th Company was ordered to take up a position on the ridge north-east of Walker's Ridge, in order to cover a section of 18-pounder guns, which was to be dug in on the beach. The battalion scouts reached the position during the day, and finding it clear of the enemy, remained there until dusk, when the 12th Company joined them without opposition. Fire trenches were dug and communications established by a telephone to Battalion Headquarters behind Walker's Ridge. Three posts were established, afterwards known as No. 1, No. 2, and No. 3 Posts.*

The 29th Indian Infantry Brigade, which had been attached to the New Zealand and Australian Division in order to bring it up to normal Divisional strength, was expected to arrive on the 30th, but it was sent to Cape Helles instead.

In summing up the position at the end of the month, the Divisional War Diary comments on the fact that, during the last few days, enemy artillery fire had practically ceased. It was believed that the enemy had withdrawn the bulk of his guns and infantry to reinforce the troops defending the southern part of the Peninsula, and was using only a small force to hold his position at Anzac. Unfortunately, it was imposssible for us to take advantage of the position, as even if we had made a successful attack, we had no troops in reserve to enable us to hold a larger area than we then had.

On May 1st, Major Loach was wounded while reconnoitring, and Major B. Jordan of the 13th Company assumed command of the Canterbury Battalion. During the night the 1st Company was sent down to the gully north-east of Walker's Ridge to cover the construction of emplacements for the 18-pounders, which had been taken along the beach during the day, but had been temporarily abandoned on account of the enemy sniping. The work was completed without mishap.

Reports from our airmen had led the Staff to believe that the enemy were placing guns on the hill above Nibrunesi Point, south of the salt lake at Suvla Bay, and the Canterbury Battalion was ordered to supply a party to destroy the emplacements and guns. At 4.40 a.m. on May 2nd, Captain Cribb with two subalterns and fifty men of the 13th Company, and Captain F. Waite and two sappers of the New Zealand Engineers, embarked on the destroyer *Colne* and were landed at the Point.

The force was divided into three parties, of which one worked round each side of the hill and a third went straight up a nullah towards the top. About two hundred yards from the top this party came on a trench containing a party of sleeping Turks,

---

*Not to be confused with "Old No. 3" Post, which was on higher ground and further inland. This post was established by the New Zealand Mounted Rifle Brigade on May 28th and lost again by that Brigade three days later.

who on awaking attempted to resist. Three were killed and four wounded, and the remainder surrendered. The locality was then thoroughly searched, but no sign of guns or emplacements was found. The force thereupon re-embarked with fifteen prisoners, and returned to Anzac without having suffered any casualties.

The general position at Anzac was now much the same as on the day of the landing, except for the establishment of new posts (Nos. 1, 2, and 3) near Fisherman's Hut, and similar minor alterations of the line on other parts of the Corps front. Numerous Turkish counter-attacks had failed to break the line at any point; but many of the positions hastily taken up on the day of the landing were not well sited or suitable either for defence or for jumping-off places for new attacks. The trenches of the Australian Division, in particular, being sited on the south-eastern side of Shrapnel and Monash Gullies, were difficult and dangerous to approach, as they were enfiladed from a hill to the north-east, known as Baby 700. It was from this hill that most of the Turkish counter-attacks had been launched; while numerous machine-guns in its strong defences swept the top of the ridge, on the south-west slopes of which lay the Australian trenches.

The Commander-in-Chief had at first intended that a general advance should be made by all the troops at Anzac on May 1st, the New Zealand and Australian Division having been reinforced by a brigade of Royal Marine Light Infantry (less one battalion). But as the Divisional Commanders considered that such an advance would weaken still more the weakest point in the line —the junction of the two Divisions near Pope's Hill—the Commander of the Australian and New Zealand Army Corps obtained leave to abandon the idea of a general advance. His new plan of attack provided that the Australian Division should not move, but that the New Zealand and Australian Division should attack and capture Baby 700. Should this operation prove successful, his intention was that the Australian Division should, on a later date, cross the ridge in front of their trenches and establish a new line on the forward slope of the ridge.

The new attack was timed to begin at 7.15 p.m. on May 2nd. The capture of Baby 700 was assigned to the New Zealand

OFFICERS OF 2ND BN. CANTERBURY REGIMENT, N.Z. DIVISION, MAY, 1917.

Back Row.—Lieut. D. Ferguson, 2nd Lieut. W. M. Hocking, Lieut. H. A. Woolf, Capt. A. W. Duncan, 2nd Lieut. C. A. S. Hind, Lieut. H. S. Gabites, 2nd Lieut. H. Henderson, 2nd Lieut. J. F. O'Leary.

2nd Row.—Capt. E. J. Fawcett, 2nd Lieut. J. M. C. McLeod, Lieut. J. P. Hanratty, Lieut. F. A. Anderson, Lieut. T. S. Gillies, Lieut. F. W. French, Lieut. H. E. McGowan, 2nd Lieut. A. E. Talbot, Lieut. C. R. Rawlings, Lieut. A. C. Wilson.

Sitting.—Lieut. M. R. Walker (Adj.), Capt. L. J. Ford, Capt. N. R. Wilson, Major G. C. Griffiths, Lieut.-Col. H. Stewart, Capt. K. F. Gordon, Capt. C. W. Free, Capt. M. J. Morrison, Capt. L. F. Jones.

Front Row.—2nd Lieut. J. V. Wilson, 2nd Lieut. W. P. Thompson, Hon. 2nd Lieut. M. Brunette.

(Photograph taken at Setques, prior to the Battle of Messines.)

Brigade, and the task of the 4th Australian Brigade was to make good a line connecting Baby 700 with the left flank of Quinn's Post—the latter being the left flank of the Australian Division. The Naval Brigade was held in reserve. The Otago Battalion was ordered to lead the attack of the New Zealand Brigade, with the Canterbury Battalion in support and the Auckland Battalion in reserve. The Wellington Battalion was to hold the trenches of the Brigade on Walker's Ridge.

At 7 p.m. the Turkish positions were heavily bombarded by the guns of the fleet and the guns on shore. This bombardment lasted for a quarter of an hour. At 7.15 p.m., the 16th Battalion, on the right of the 4th Australian Brigade, advanced under heavy enfilade machine-gun fire to the objectives assigned to it, and dug in there. On its left, the 13th Battalion also advanced; but as it had received orders to move in touch with the Otago Battalion, and the latter had not yet arrived, the left flank of the 13th Battalion was held back, while its right advanced.

The Otago Battalion had left Walker's Ridge at 4.30 p.m. and had moved along the beach with the object of advancing up Shrapnel and Monash Gullies and attacking from Pope's Hill. The time allowed for this movement would seem to be ample; but three reasons were given by the Commanding Officer of the Battalion to account for the delay :—

(a) The fire of enemy snipers in the trenches at the head of Monash Gully delayed movement up the gully.

(b) Stretcher parties coming down the track obstructed the troops moving up.

(c) Reserve troops of the Naval Brigade blocked the road in Monash Gully.

Whatever the reasons, the battalion did not reach Pope's Hill till an hour and a half late, on an occasion where punctuality was essential for success.

The Otago Battalion attacked Baby 700 at once; but it had lost the benefit not only of the artillery bombardment, but also of the co-operation of the 4th Australian Brigade. It was met by a withering fire from machine-guns and rifles in the trenches on Baby 700, and was held up one hundred yards from its objective. There the battalion lay down, opened fire, and began to dig in. Troops of the 4th Australian Brigade moved up and established touch with Otago's right flank; and one Australian company actually reached the Turkish trenches, but could not hold them, and had to return to the general line established by its Brigade. The firing line on the Divisional front at 11 p.m. had its right flank resting on Quinn's Post, and from there curved towards the enemy till it was three hundred yards forward of Pope's Hill. From this point the line curved back again towards our line, the left flank of the Otago Battalion being a hundred and fifty yards forward of Pope's Hill.

The Canterbury Battalion, though in support of Otago, had been ordered to assemble at 7.5 p.m. at the headquarters of the Wellington Battalion, on the south-west slopes of Walker's Ridge. The 1st Company, in the lead, was ordered to move up to the advanced trenches of the Wellington Battalion, and to hold itself in readiness to move up on the left of the Otago Battalion, when the latter had taken its objective. On Otago arriving and moving forward, the 1st Company also advanced, but found the slopes from Baby 700 to Walker's Ridge strongly held by the enemy.

The ground was at this time covered with heavy scrub (which was afterwards cut clean away by small-arms fire), and the only approach from Walker's Ridge against Baby 700 was a saddle called "The Nek," a razor-edge over which only one man could cross at a time. Captain Gresson, in command of the company, went back to make a personal report to the Brigadier and received direct orders to advance no further. The company was in an exposed position, and on the moon beginning to rise, Captain Gresson decided to withdraw to the Wellington trenches. The company reached the trenches without casualties.

In consequence of the reports received from the 1st Company, the Brigadier ordered the remainder of the battalion to stand by and await further instructions. It therefore remained behind Walker's Ridge till 3 a.m. on the 3rd, when it was ordered to dig communication trenches up to the Otago Battalion's new positions. Very few tools were available, but about 4 a.m. Captain Critchley-Salmonson reported to the Commanding Officer of the Otago Battalion with about fifty men, and was ordered to prolong the left of the line. The remainder of the working parties went astray: some of the 1st Company

under Lieutenant H. Stewart, and a platoon of the 13th Company
under Lieutenant Shepherd, eventually reached the Otago line;
but a party of two hundred and fifty men under Lieutenant
Stitt was held in Monash Gully by order of the Officer Commanding the 4th Australian Brigade, who forbade any more troops
to come down the Gully, owing to the approach being enfiladed
by machine-guns. This party apparently also reached the firing
line later: at all events Lieutenant Stitt and a number of men
joined forces with Lieutenant Stewart's party.

Dawn was now approaching, and the enemy, who had brought
up machine-guns during the night, opened a heavy enfilade fire
with rifles and machine-guns upon the trenches of the Otago
Battalion. Two companies of the Nelson Battalion (Royal Naval
Division) had by this time reinforced Otago; but about 5 a.m.
most of the garrison of the line had to withdraw to the trenches
from which the attack was launched. Small parties of the Otago
Battalion still held on in the advanced trenches, but they were
compelled to retire during the day; although one party held out
for two days, until it was ordered to cut its way out. The 13th
Australian Battalion also held its trenches till nightfall on the
3rd, when it was withdrawn to the old line.   .

Thus the result of the attack was no ground gained: and
though it was claimed that heavy casualties were inflicted on
the enemy, it seems highly improbable that these were as great
as our loss of forty-four officers and eight hundred other ranks.
Of these, the Canterbury Regiment's casualties were:—

				Officers.	Other Ranks.
Killed	..	..	..	1*	1
Wounded	..	..	..	—	33
Wounded and Missing	..		..	—	3
Missing	..	..	..	—	13
				—	—
Total	..	..	..	1	50

*Second Lieutenant W. G. Skelton.

The Canterbury Battalion began to re-assemble on the beach
at 8.30 a.m. on May 3rd, with a view to another attack. This
attempt was abandoned, however, and the battalion spent the
whole of the day and the following night on the beach. Next

day (the 4th). the 13th Company relieved the 12th Company at No. 1, No. 2, and No. 3 Posts, where the latter had remained during the operations of the night of the 2nd and 3rd, and the 12th Company went into battalion support. The 1st and 2nd Companies went into the trenches at the beach end of Walker's Ridge.

That night orders were issued that the New Zealand and 2nd Australian Brigades were to embark the following night for Cape Helles, to take part in a big attack by the forces operating at the southern end of the Peninsula.

The general position at Cape Helles at the moment was that on April 28th the 29th Division. the 2nd Naval Brigade, and the 1st French Division had advanced from the positions established on the day of landing. and had reached a line approximately straight across the Peninsula, from nearly a mile north of Point Eski Hissarlik (on the Dardanelles coast) to a point on the Ægean coast half way between "Y" Beach and Gully Beach (the mouth of the Saghir Dere or Gully Ravine). This line was afterwards known as the Eski line.

On the night of May 1st the Turks had attacked this line, and a general Allied counter-attack on the morning of the 2nd had advanced the British lines about a quarter of a mile to the north. On account of the French having made no progress, the new line was rendered untenable by enfilade machine-gun fire; and our troops were forced to withdraw to the Eski line. The Turks, however, still remained in their prepared positions, about half a mile north of the Eski line.

Sir Ian Hamilton determined to make another attack at once, in order to seize as much as he could of "No-Man's-Land" between the opposing lines; for, in his opinion, "several hundred yards, whatever it might mean to the enemy, was a matter of life and death to a force crowded together under gun fire on so narrow a tongue of land."[*]

The 29th Indian Infantry Brigade, originally intended to complete the establishment of the New Zealand and Australian Division, had landed on Cape Helles on May 1st; and the Lancashire Fusilier Brigade, of the 42nd Division, arrived on

---

*Despatch of August 26th, 1915: Naval and Military Despatches, Part IIII., p. 338.

the 5th. These two brigades were added to the 29th Division,
which had suffered many casualties, and the remnant of the 86th
Brigade was divided between the 87th and 88th Brigades and
used as reinforcements by these brigades.

During daylight on the 5th, the New Zealand Brigade was
relieved in the trenches at Anzac by two battalions of the 2nd
Naval Brigade; and the Canterbury Battalion assembled in
Mule Gully, south-west of Walker's Ridge. Lieutenant-Colonel
C. H. J. Brown (who afterwards commanded the 1st New
Zealand Infantry Brigade in France, and was killed in the
Battle of Messines) took command of the battalion, being temporarily transferred from Divisional Headquarters for that purpose. The Canterbury Battalion was now the strongest in the
Brigade, having twenty-six officers and seven hundred and
seventy-eight other ranks, out of a brigade strength of eighty-
eight officers and two thousand seven hundred and twenty-four
other ranks.

The embarkation for Cape Helles was timed to begin at
8.30 p.m. on May 5th, but the destroyers which were to carry
the New Zealand Brigade did not arrive in time, and the troops
had a long wait on the beach. When the destroyers eventually
arrived the troops were taken on board by lighters, and were
very hospitably treated by the ships' companies. The voyage
was uneventful, and the warships arrived at Cape Helles about
2 a.m. on the 6th.

The Canterbury Battalion landed in the dark on "V"
Beach, west of the village of Sedd El Bahr, and after a pause
there for reorganization, and the issue of picks and shovels, left
the beach as day was breaking. Leaving the village on the right,
the battalion marched two miles to its bivouac area at Stone
Bridge (by which the Krithia-Sedd El Bahr road crossed the
Krithia Nullah) to the left of and behind a line of ruined water-
towers which ended at the Achi Baba Nullah.

The New Zealand and 2nd Australian Brigades, with two
battalions of the 2nd Naval Brigade, had been formed into a
composite division, under the command of Major-General A.
Paris, C.B., the General Officer commanding the Royal Naval
Division. The new division was held in reserve for the attack,
which was timed for 11 a.m. on May 6th.

After arrival at the bivouac area, the New Zealand troops dug shrapnel-proof trenches, and rested there the following night and until the afternoon of the 7th. They found themselves in country very different from the jungle-covered mountains of Anzac. The southern end of the Peninsula consisted of a plateau, with cliffs at the water's edge, except at "W" and "V" beaches. As one went inland from the top of the cliffs, the land sloped downwards slightly, so as to form a spoon-shaped depression. To the north of the depression, the land sloped up to the peak of Achi Baba, with the village of Krithia on its lower slopes. Almost exactly down the centre of the depression ran the Achi Baba Nullah (or gully), with the Krithia-Sedd El Bahr Road close to the west of it. Running parallel to, and about half a mile to the west of Achi Baba Nullah was a larger gully, the Krithia Nullah. West again, and about a quarter of a mile east of the Ægean coast, lay the Saghir Dere, a wide and deep nullah better known as the Gully Ravine. Mid-way between "X" and "Y" beaches, this nullah turned towards the sea, and breaking the cliffs, came out at a small beach known as Gully Beach.

Much of the land on the plateau had been cultivated, and was dotted with small clumps of trees. Water was abundant — so much so that it interfered at times with the digging of the trenches — but men fresh from the waterless heights of Anzac could appreciate the benefits of an unlimited water supply.

The attack on the Turkish trenches had begun on the morning of the 6th. The Allied forces were disposed with the 1st French Division on the right, and the 29th Division on the left, with the Plymouth and Drake Battalions of the Royal Naval Division astride Krithia Road between them to keep touch. On that morning the 29th Division, which the New Zealand Brigade was called upon to support on the 8th, attacked with the 29th (Indian) and 88th Brigades on its right, between the Krithia Nullah and the Gully Ravine (exclusive), and the 89th and Lancashire Fusilier Brigades on its left, from the west bank of the Gully Ravine to the sea.

The preliminary and covering bombardments by the guns of the fleet had little effect on the deep and narrow enemy trenches, and the advance was made under heavy and accurate machine-gun and rifle fire as well as shrapnel and high explosive shells. The attacking troops had to fight for every yard of ground against an invisible enemy, and over country which gave little protection from fire of any kind. The 88th Brigade and the Indians were held up by strong resistance from a wood of fir trees, on the left of the western branch of the Krithia Nullah, and about three hundred yards north of the Eski Line. On their left the advance of the rest of the Division was checked by machine-guns posted on the bluff above "Y" Beach (afterwards called Ghurka Bluff), and by snipers and machine-guns in the Gully Ravine.

By 4.30 in the afternoon it was plain that the troops engaged could go no further, and they were ordered to dig in. The result of the day's fighting was an average advance of two to three hundred yards beyond the starting point—the Eski Line— and the Turkish positions had not yet been reached.

The attack was resumed at 10 a.m. on the 7th, but little progress was made. On the right, the 88th Brigade continued the advance, and the 5th Royal Scots reached the Fir Wood, but were forced to withdraw early in the afternoon, as it had been rendered untenable by enfilade machine-gun and rifle fire. On the other side of the Gully Ravine, the machine-guns on the Ghurka Bluff prevented the Lancashire Fusiliers from making any progress.

Sir Ian Hamilton thereupon decided to make a general attack at 4.15 p.m. and ordered the whole of the 87th Brigade to reinforce the 88th Brigade, and the New Zealand Brigade to support the two. After a short and violent bombardment, the whole line, French and British, rose together and rushed forward. The Fir Wood was again captured, and all along the line, except on the east of the Gully Ravine, another two to three hundred yards was gained, and the first line of Turkish trenches was taken. The line was consolidated for the night, and orders were issued for the resumption of the attack the next day.

In the meantime, the New Zealand Brigade, to carry out its rôle of brigade in support, had left the Stone Bridge at 2.45 p.m. on May 7th and had moved towards the mouth of the Gully Ravine. The brigade dug in on the slope to the south of the

Ravine, but at 8.20 p.m. the Auckland and Wellington Battalions moved forward to support the 87th and 88th Brigades. The remaining battalions passed the night in the trenches they had dug during the afternoon.

Orders were now received that the New Zealand Brigade was to attack Krithia and the trenches covering it, on the morning of the 8th. The front to be covered extended from the Krithia Nullah on the right to the Gully Ravine on the left; and the brigade was ordered to pass through, at 10.30 a.m., the front line established by the 88th Brigade on the afternoon of the 7th. The Canterbury, Auckland, and Wellington Battalions were ordered to make the attack, the Otago Battalion being held in reserve.

The front covered by the Canterbury Battalion was bounded on the right by the Krithia Nullah, and on the left by the eastern edge of the Fir Wood, which had caused so much trouble the previous day. On its left was the Auckland Battalion, with the Wellington Battalion extending to the Gully Ravine on the left flank.

The Canterbury Battalion advanced to the attack in two lines with the 12th Company (right) and 2nd Company (left) in the front line, and the 1st Company (right) and 13th Company (left) in reserve. The battalion deployed behind the front line trenches held by the 4th Worcester Battalion, and advanced over the open under heavy fire. On the right, towards the Krithia Nullah, and in advance of the Worcester's trenches, were entrenched the remnants of the 1st Battalions of the Royal Dublin Fusiliers and the Royal Munster Fusiliers, which had suffered such heavy casualties in the early days of the campaign that they had been amalgamated into one battalion known as the "Dubsters."

The firing line met with strong resistance and made slow progress, and the majority of the troops did not get beyond the "Dubsters'" trench. But two platoons of the 12th Company, in the face of murderous fire from machine-guns and rifles, pushed forward over the open space afterwards known as the "Daisy Patch." The survivors of these platoons reached a point about two hundred yards beyond the "Dubsters'"

trench, and there lay down in a small depression, unable either
to move forward or to return. This was the position of the firing
line at 2 p.m.

During this time the reserve companies had moved up just
behind the Worcester's trenches. where they dug in and prepared
to bivouac for the night. At 4.30 p.m., however, orders had been
issued for a general advance at 5.30 p.m. along the whole line;
the 2nd Australian Brigade being ordered to advance on the east
of the Krithia Nullah. The attack was preceded by a preliminary
bombardment for a quarter of an hour by the guns of the warship and the "heavies" ashore; and was also supported by the
field guns shelling the ground in front of the advancing infantry.
But guns were few and ammunition scarce, so that the field
artillery support was practically negligible.

The 13th Company and the two remaining platoons of the
12th Company advanced with great dash over the open, under
heavy rifle and machine-gun fire. for a distance of three hundred yards. This was rendered possible by the good support
given by the fire of our own machine-gunners and those of the
"Dubsters' "; but in spite of this support the firing line could
advance no further, as casualties had been very heavy. Moreover, the Auckland Battalion, in the centre, had been badly cut
up, and was well behind except for a few men who were a long
way forward and unsupported; and although the Wellington
Battalion on the left flank of the brigade had advanced level
with Canterbury, the Fir Wood in the centre threatened the
inner flanks of both the right and left battalions.

The right flank company of the Canterbury Battalion had
used the Krithia Nullah for cover, and was facing almost due
west, at right angles to its proper direction of advance. After
darkness fell, the troops in the Nullah set to work to join up
with the left flank company, and by daylight there was a continuous line of trench from the Nullah to the eastern edge of
the Fir Wood.

The first warning to the reserve companies of the impending
attack came to them after five o'clock, when they were ordered
to rush by platoons to the "Dubsters' " trenches. The machine-
gun fire which covered the advance of the leading companies also
served to help the forward rush of the reserves; but the latter

also came in for the enemy small-arms fire, directed against our firing line, and suffered some casualties.

After reaching the "Dubsters'" trenches the reserve companies were witnesses of what has been described as one of the most spectacular advances in the war — the attack of the 2nd Australian Brigade to the west of the Krithia Nullah. But after resting ten minutes in the trenches, the 1st Company was ordered to reinforce the firing line; and the 2nd Company was shortly afterwards sent to defend the left flank, which the failure of the advance of the Auckland Battalion had left "in the air." On the right the Canterbury Battalion was in touch with the Australians, but could not find the Auckland line.

The whole night was spent in consolidating the positions gained, and though the main body of the enemy to the immediate front was estimated to have retired six hundred yards, a certain amount of rifle and machine-gun fire was exchanged during the night. The collection of the wounded was extremely difficult, and many spent the night where they had fallen. The night was wet, and as most of the packs had been shed by the men before the advance, there were no overcoats in the trenches.

Considering the small gains in ground, the casualties of the battalion for the day had been very severe, being:—

				Officers.	Other Ranks.
Killed	..	..	..	1*	49
Wounded	..	..	..	4†	131
Missing	..	..	..	–	21
Total	..	..	..	5	201

*Lieutenant A. E. Forsythe.

†Subsequently died of wounds, Lieutenant F. D. Maurice, Acting 2nd Lieutenant Burnard: the latter had been recommended for a commission, but died before he was actually gazetted.

The morning of May 9th was fine, and the day was spent in improving the trenches, and in obtaining superiority in sniping over the enemy. Water and food were scarce; but rations came up late that night, together with the battalion's quota of the 3rd Reinforcements — two officers and thirty-eight other ranks.

These had landed at Cape Helles on the morning of the previous day, but had not reached brigade headquarters when the attack began. However, they were under fire throughout the day, and helped to collect the wounded after dark. Burial parties were sent out at dusk, and all our dead within reach were buried. The lack of water was remedied by digging small wells in and about the trenches.

The battalion remained in the trenches without being attacked till the night of May 11th / 12th, when the brigade was relieved by the 127th (Manchester) Brigade of the 42nd Division. The relief was a slow one: as each company was relieved it moved back to the former bivouac area at the Stone Bridge. The night was very wet and dark; nobody had any clear idea of the direction of the Stone Bridge, and the information given to the companies was extremely vague. The experience of most of the parties appears to have been, that exhausted by the ardours of the previous three days, and loaded with packs and wet overcoats, they trudged on till they were "dead beat," and then lay down in their tracks and slept till daylight. By noon on the 12th the battalion was assembled at its old bivouacs.

The New Zealand Brigade was now in reserve, and was not called upon to do any more fighting in the southern part of the Peninsula. The first three days were spent in rest, sea-bathing, reorganisation and refitting; but from May 15th onwards the brigade was employed on road-making and other work about "W" Beach. The strength of the Canterbury Battalion on coming out of the line is stated in the war diary as thirty-two officers and eight hundred and twenty other ranks; but these figures cannot be reconciled with the strength on embarkation at Anzac on May 5th, and the casualties in the Krithia fighting.

Meanwhile the position at Anzac was critical, for on the afternoon of May 19th, the Turks launched a general and violent attack on our positions there. The battle raged from 3.30 a.m. till nearly 11 a.m. when the last assault was beaten off. Everywhere the line stood firm, and the defenders' casualties were only one hundred killed and five hundred wounded. The Turks' losses were far greater: over three thousand bodies lay in heaps in the narrow strip of neutral ground between the opposing trenches.

In consequence of this attack, the New Zealand Infantry Brigade* was hurriedly recalled to Anzac on the evening of the 19th, and had embarked before midnight. By daylight the transports were off Anzac, and disembarkation began at 9.30 a.m. and was complete by noon. As the troops went ashore in pinnaces, they came under fire from enemy snipers; and between leaving the ship and arriving at its bivouac in Reserve Gully (north side of Plugge's Plateau), the Canterbury Battalion had two men wounded. The battalion remained in Reserve Gully till the evening, but at 8 p.m. received orders to bivouac at the seaward end of Walker's Ridge. Large numbers of Turks had been reported to be massing at Biyuk Anafarta, east of Suvla Bay, and in anticipation of another attack the battalion stood to arms at 3 a.m. on the 21st; but everything was quiet, and the troops returned to their bivouacs at 5.30 a.m.

The New Zealand Brigade remained in Reserve Gully, in general reserve to the New Zealand and Australian Division, till May 29th. During this period, an armistice was arranged, by request of the Turks, for the purpose of burying the dead lying in No-Man's-Land. The duration of the armistice was from 7.30 a.m. to 4.30 p.m. on May 24th, and during that period the neutral ground was divided into two portions, the central line being marked by delimitation parties from each of the opposing forces. In addition, each side provided parties which collected the dead of the opposite side, and carried the bodies to the central line; and each side then buried its own dead. The Canterbury Battalion provided a bearer party of five officers and a hundred other ranks, and a delimitation party of one officer and thirteen other ranks. Several bodies of those killed on April 25th were recognized by these parties. Everybody was greatly impressed by the clearance of the dense scrub about the Nek, which had been completely shot away by machine-gun and rifle fire.

On the 29th the battalion received orders to move to Monash Gully, and to send one company to relieve a company of the 15th Australian Battalion at Quinn's Post. The 1st Company was detailed for this purpose and went up to the post in the

---

*The New Zealand Mounted Rifle Brigade (without its horses) had arrived at Anzac on May 12th, while the Infantry Brigade was at Cape Helles.

evening, the remainder of the battalion returning to Reserve Gully. The battalion came under the orders of Colonel Chauvel, of the 1st Australian Light Horse Brigade, who was in command of No. 3 Section of the Anzac front.

The post took its name from an Australian officer — Major Quinn — who had established it on the day of the landing, and who was killed there the day the 1st Company joined its garrison. The position was considered the most critical and exciting point in the Anzac line, being closer to the Turkish trenches than any other part of the line. On its right, and immediately adjoining it, was Courtney's Post; while in the rear and to the left, a hundred yards away, lay the post known as Pope's Hill. Directly to the left was Dead Man's Ridge, the scene of the New Zealand and Australian Division's unsuccessful attack of May 2nd.

At the extreme right and left flanks of the post, the enemy trenches were thirty to forty yards away; but in the centre of the position the opposing trenches approached each other, and at numbers 3 and 4 posts were only seven yards apart. The use of hand-grenades, which had first been tried by the Turks on May 2nd, had by now become a common practice on both sides, though the bombs were nearly all "home-made," and lighted by a match or cigarette. By reason of the nearness of the two lines, Quinn's was naturally a favourable spot for bombing; and when the 1st Company arrived there the engineers were busy with the erection of bomb-proof shelters.

Both sides were also constantly engaged in mining and counter-mining; and it was on account of part of No. 4 post having been blown in the previous night, and occupied for a while by the enemy, that the 1st Company had been sent there. There had been several Turkish attacks on Quinn's during the early part of the morning; and though these had ceased by 9 a.m., the enemy kept up a continual heavy fire, which interfered very much with the work of restoring the position. The fire trench at No. 4 post could not be occupied, owing to the ease with which the Turks could throw bombs into the crater made by the explosion of the mine. The trench had therefore to be held by sentries in sap-heads, with overcoats lying handy to smother any bombs which might drop near them.

The following day (May 30th) the 13th Company was also sent to Quinn's Post, where it relieved another company of the 15th Battalion. At 1 p.m. two small parties of volunteers from the 1st Company and Australian Light Horse attacked two enemy sap-heads, which had been pushed forward close to Quinn's. The attack seems to have been hastily arranged and badly organized, with the result that when the parties occupied the Turkish trenches they did not put them in defensive condition. Enfilade fire from enemy machine-guns forced the parties to return, and some wounded were left in a mine crater in No-Man's-Land. It was then decided to dig a tunnel out to the crater, so that the wounded might be brought in, and the crater occupied.

The work proceeded slowly; and at 10 p.m. Lieutenant Le Mottee and six other volunteers from the 13th Company made a dash to the crater and began to dig back towards our lines. The parties met at 11.30 p.m., and by midnight the wounded and dead had been brought back to Quinn's. The party in the crater then began to make the crater bomb-proof; but while they were doing so a Turkish bomb killed two of them and wounded three others, including Lieutenant Le Mottee. It was decided that the crater was untenable, and it was therefore abandoned.

May 30th was an anxious day altogether, as there were heavy enemy attacks on the left section of Anzac and a general attack was expected during the afternoon. However, the night passed quietly.

The remaining companies of the battalion moved to Monash Gully on the 30th, and occupied bivouacs to the west of Quinn's Post. The following day the 1st and 13th Companies were relieved in the trenches by the 2nd and 12th Companies, and the latter became the local reserve for the post. The casualties for the month, since the return from Cape Helles, had been four other ranks killed and one officer and twenty-six other ranks wounded, leaving an effective strength of thirty officers and seven hundred and sixty-five other ranks, according to the battalion diary.

On June 1st the New Zealand Brigade took over Quinn's and Courtney's Posts, but the two battalions in the post came under the command of Colonel Chauvel of the 1st Australian

Light Horse Brigade. Arrangements for the garrisoning of the posts were made on the 3rd, under which Courtney's was held by the Wellington Battalion, with half its strength in the line for forty-eight hours at a time, and the remainder in local reserve; and the front line at Quinn's was held for twenty-four hours alternately by the Canterbury Battalion (less half a company) and by the Auckland Battalion, strengthened by the loan of half a company of the Canterbury Battalion. The local reserve at Quinn's consisted of whichever of these two battalions was out of the front trenches. The Otago Battalion was held in brigade reserve. As far as periods of relief were concerned, these arrangements were not strictly carried out.

No events of importance took place till the 4th, when there was a joint sortie by parties from the Auckland and Canterbury Battalions against the Turkish trenches opposite Quinn's Post. This operation was one of several minor operations on that day at Anzac, all designed as demonstrations to assist a big attack at Cape Helles, which was delivered the same day. The assaulting party on the right was composed of volunteers from the Canterbury Battalion, and consisted of two smaller parties each of fifteen men commanded by a non-commissioned officer, which together were led by Lieutenant H. Stewart. All these troops were from the 1st Company. On their left were two assaulting parties of one non-commissioned officer and fourteen men and one non-commissioned officer and ten men of the Auckland Battalion, under Lieutenant Vear.

The scheme was a simple one—to capture the enemy's front line trenches opposite Nos. 3 and 4 Posts, erect loop-holed traverses at each end of the captured portion, and transpose the parapet of the trench so that it could be used as our front line. The traverses were to be built by two working parties, each of ten unarmed men, the right party to be supplied by the Canterbury Battalion, and the left party by the Auckland Battalion. To assist these working parties, by passing out of the trenches filled sandbags, tools, and material, each battalion was to supply a further party of ten unarmed men. Finally, the Canterbury Battalion was ordered to provide two parties of three men each, to dig on each flank a communication trench from our front line to the captured trench. The whole operation was under the command of Lieutenant Stewart, and the

Canterbury working parties were selected from volunteers from the 12th Company.

The 1st Australian Brigade had been ordered to help the sortie at Quinn's Post, by making a raid on an enemy machine-gun near German Officer's Trench, which enfiladed the ground in front of Quinn's Post. This raid was timed for 10.55 p.m.— five minutes before the sortie by Lieutenant Stewart's party— and was to be assisted by rifle fire from Courtney's Post.

The attacking party left the trenches at Quinn's Post at 11 p.m., and immediately came under heavy fire, which had been opened by the Turks in answer to the firing from Court-ney's Post five minutes earlier. So well was the enemy's front trench provided with overhead cover, that the assaulting party on the right, under Sergeant W. J. Rodger, missed it altogether, and ran over it on to the support trench in its rear. There they surprised a party of about ten of the enemy, most of whom they killed. The other Canterbury party, with which was Lieutenant Stewart, found the firing trench without difficulty, and bayonetted about a dozen Turks.

Lieutenant Stewart then found that he was in touch with neither Sergeant Rodger nor the Auckland party; but on going to look for them, he found the sergeant and his party in the Turkish support trench, together with the first working party, which had already begun to dig a traverse in the same trench.

Some of the enemy in the firing line, who had been overrun by Sergeant Rodger's party, now came into the open between the two trenches, and were shot; the remainder opened fire on our men at the support trench, and on the second working party, which had begun to carry material to the support trench. Lieutenant Stewart thereupon returned to the firing trench (where his party was now in touch with the Auckland parties), and led an attack on the Turks who were firing on Sergeant Rodger's party. These surrendered at once, and twenty-eight prisoners were sent back to our lines.

A tunnel between the Turkish firing line and support trenches had now been discovered; and Lieutenant Stewart decided to hold both trenches, since the support trench com-manded a large part of the valley to the north-east of it. Blocks were built on both flanks of the firing and support

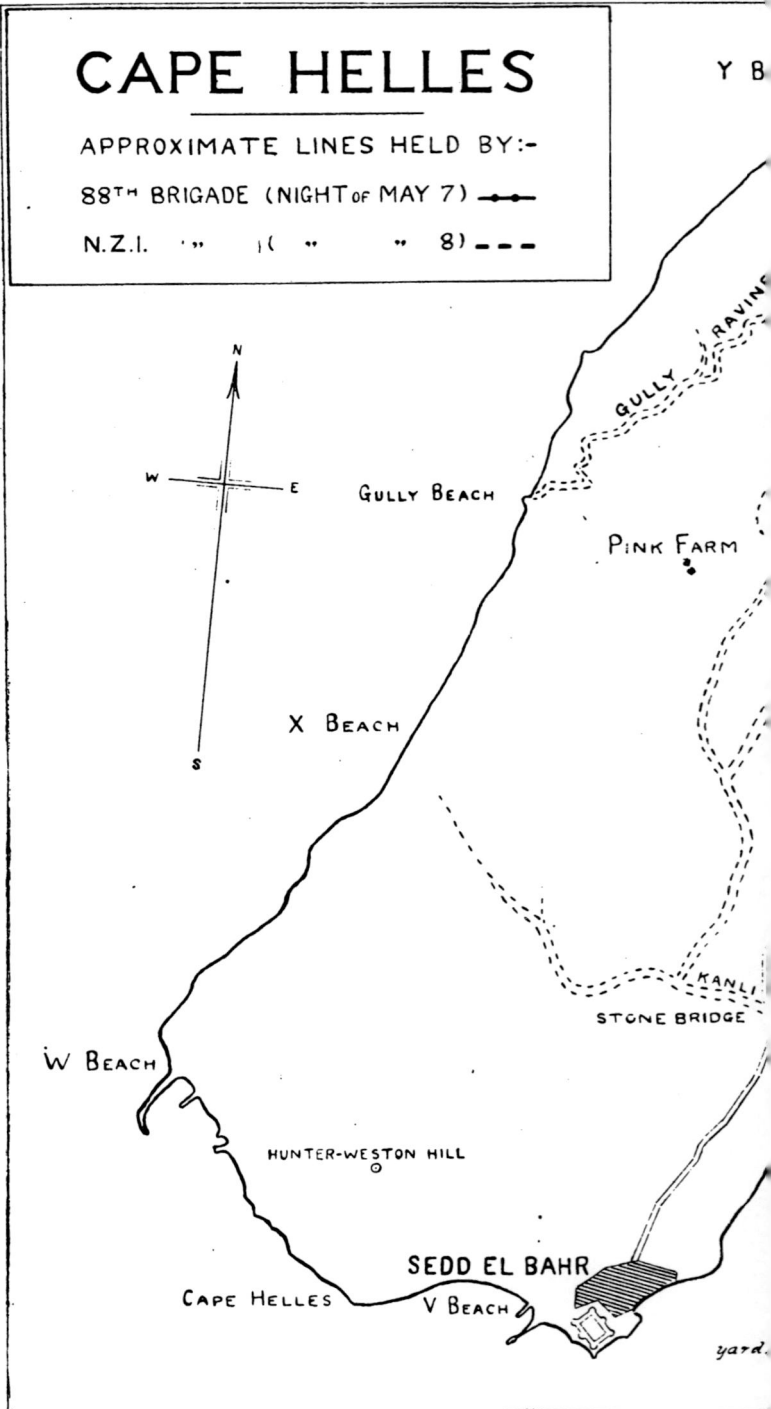

CAPE HELLES

APPROXIMATE LINES HELD BY:-

88TH BRIGADE (NIGHT OF MAY 7) ━●━

N.Z.I. '' ᵢ('' '' 8) ━ ━ ━

Y B

N

W — E

S

GULLY RAVINE

GULLY BEACH

PINK FARM

X BEACH

KANLI

STONE BRIDGE

W BEACH

HUNTER-WESTON HILL
○

SEDD EL BAHR

CAPE HELLES

V BEACH

yard.

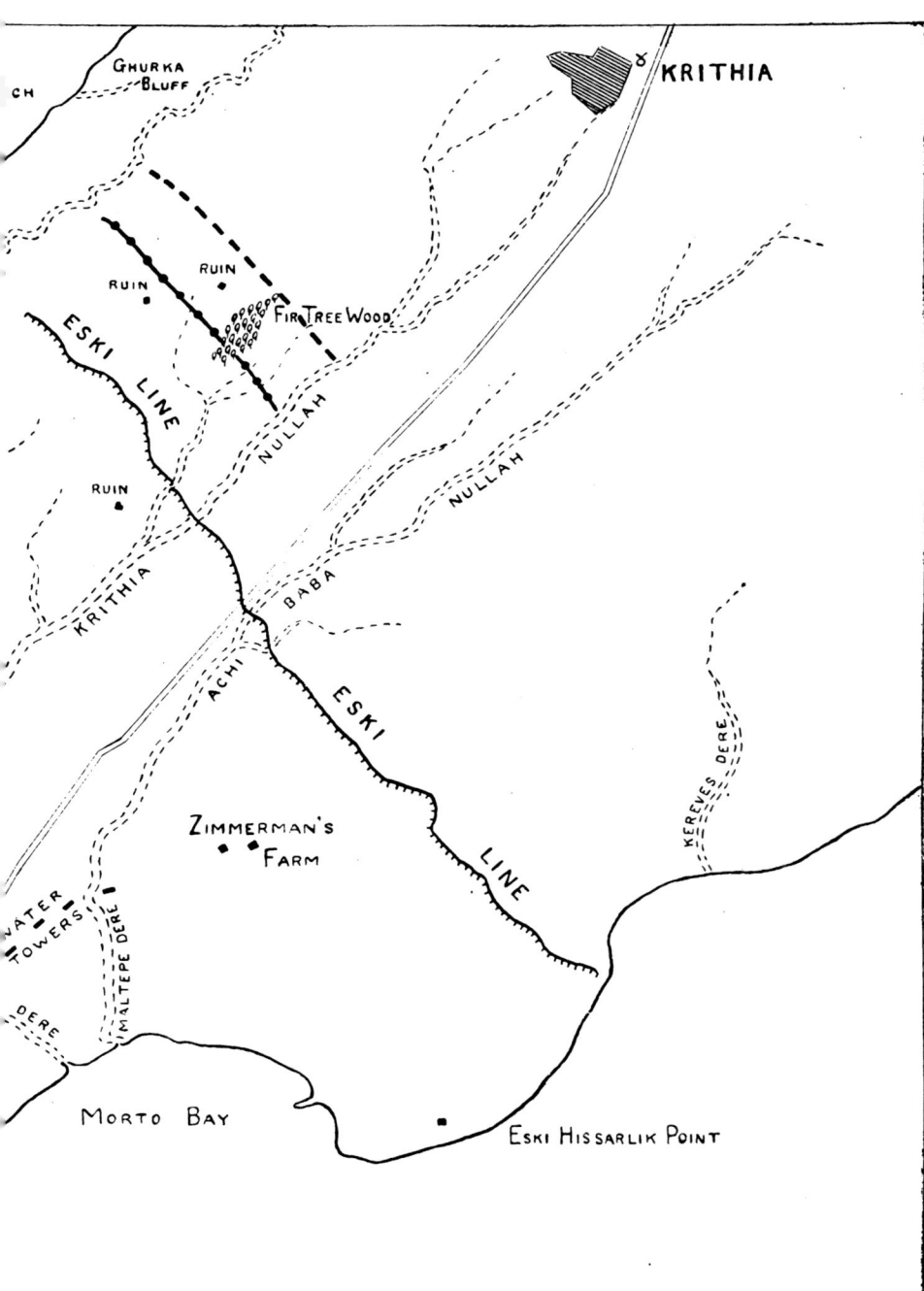

CH

GHURKA
BLUFF

γ KRITHIA

RUIN

RUIN

ESKI
LINE

FIR TREE WOOD

RUIN

NULLAH

NULLAH

KRITHIA

BABA

ACHI

ESKI

KEREVES DERE

LINE

ZIMMERMAN'S
FARM

WATER
TOWERS

MALTEPE DERE

DERE

MORTO   BAY

ESKI HISSARLIK POINT

0   500   0   1000   2000   3000
                                                                          yards

trenches; and attempts by the enemy to enter the support trench by the communication trenches leading to it, or to work along the firing trench from the right, were repulsed.

During the whole of the operations there had been enemy machine-gun fire from Dead Man's Ridge, on the left; and also from the direction of German Officer's Trench, on the right, where the Australians' raid had failed. This fire had been harmless to the men in the trenches, but had interfered considerably with the working and carrying parties. But by dawn communication trenches had been cut through to Quinn's Post, reinforcements had arrived, and the new positions seemed firmly established.

About seventy or eighty yards of the enemy's support trench, and about a hundred yards of his firing line were now in our hands. Shortly afterwards, however, the Turks made an attack on the support trench, relying chiefly on bombs. The Auckland parties (which had meanwhile been reinforced also) were unable to defend themselves, owing to a shortage of bombs, and were forced to retire. Their withdrawal compelled the Canterbury parties to retire also, to avoid being cut off; though the new communication trenches across No-Man's-Land were still held by us.

The operation was over by 7 a.m. on the 5th; and in spite of the fact that our troops were compelled to withdraw, it may fairly be claimed that the losses of the Turks were far greater than ours. In addition to twenty-eight Turkish prisoners being taken, over fifty enemy dead were counted in the captured trenches; while the casualties of the Auckland and Canterbury Battalions, though over a hundred, included only twelve killed and twelve missing. The losses of the Canterbury Battalion were :—

				Officers.	Other Ranks.
Killed	..	..	..	1*	8
Wounded	..	..	..	5	37
Missing	..	..	..	–	4
				6	49

*Captain J. H. Goulding.

Among the wounded were Lieutenant-Colonel Brown and Lieutenant Stewart, both of whom were hit by splinters from bombs.* On the battalion again coming into local reserve to Quinn's Post, on the 7th, Lieutenant-Colonel J. G. Hughes, D.S.O, took over the command. The same night, another sortie from Quinn's Post was attempted by the Auckland Battalion, with the object of destroying the portion of the enemy's firing trench which our troops had occupied on the night of June 4th/5th. One party from the Auckland Battalion reached the Turkish trenches on the left; but everywhere else the attackers were unable to face the enemy's fire. A party of a non-commissioned officer and twenty men from the 1st Company, which had been sent up to act as supports if required, was then sent forward, but could do no better. The attempt was abandoned; and the Canterbury party was sent back to the gully, having lost three wounded and one missing.

The battalion remained in local reserve till June 9th, when a relief by the Wellington Battalion was begun. The relief was completed by 10 a.m. on the 10th, and as the Canterbury companies were relieved they moved to new bivouacs in Canterbury Gully† north of Shrapnel Valley and east of Plugge's Plateau. The 4th Reinforcements, which included a draft of five officers and two hundred and fourteen other ranks for the battalion, had arrived on June 8th, and the newcomers brought the companies up to full strength again.‡ The weather continued fine, and there were no enemy attacks and little shell fire; so the period spent in reserve was comparatively peaceful, and enabled the troops to rest after their hard fighting and digging at Quinn's Post.

The arrangements for the garrisoning of Quinn's and Courtney's Posts had now been altered. Lieutenant-Colonel Malone, the Commanding Officer of the Wellington Battalion, was made permanent commander of Quinn's Post, which was henceforth manned alternately by his battalion and by the Canterbury Battalion. The Auckland and Otago Battalions now garrisoned Courtney's Post. On the evening of June 17th, the head-

---

*Lieutenant-Colonel Brown was evacuated, and did not return again to the Canterbury Regiment.

†Also called "Rest Gully."

‡The strength of the battalion on June 18th was thirty officers and eight hundred and ninety-four other ranks.

quarters and the 1st and 2nd Companies of the Canterbury Battalion relieved the Wellington Battalion at Quinn's Post. The 12th and 13th Companies remained in Canterbury Gully until the following day, when they relieved the 1st and 2nd Companies in the firing trenches, and the latter went into local reserve in Shrapnel Gully. The system of daily inter-company reliefs was henceforward adopted on every occasion when the battalion manned this post.

The post was found to have been greatly improved by the Wellington garrison, which had taken advantage of a quiet week to build bomb-proof shelters, loopholes, and firing embrasures. The Wellington snipers had also established superiority over those of the enemy, and it was now possible to use a periscope without the certainty of its being smashed by a bullet. The Canterbury Battalion carried on the work of improving the trenches, with little interference by the enemy. Supplies of bombs by this time had become plentiful; our men were becoming more expert in their use, and were beginning to hold their own in this respect against the Turks. For the time being, the opposing forces at Anzac had settled down to trench warfare conditions.

No offensive operations by either side occurred while the battalion was in Quinn's Post; and on June 25th the companies in the firing trenches and battalion headquarters were relieved by the Wellington Battalion. The 1st and 2nd Companies remained in local reserve to the post; but were relieved the following day, and rejoined the rest of the battalion at Canterbury Gully. There the battalion was engaged in making a road from that gully to Reserve Gully. north of Plugge's Plateau, and also accommodation terraces in Canterbury Gully— both for the use of fresh troops who were expected to arrive. The battalion stood to arms at 5 a.m. on the 27th, in consequence of heavy bombing and artillery fire against Walker's Ridge, but no enemy attack followed.

On the night of June 29th/30th, however, a determined attack was made against the same portion of our line. A prisoner who was taken during this attack stated that Enver Pasha had addressed the assaulting troops on the previous day, and had ordered them to drive the British troops at Anzac into the sea. Certainly the attack was delivered with great determination, and pressed with obstinate perseverance: nevertheless, the 8th and 9th Regiments of the 3rd Australian Light Horse Brigade, and the 6th Squadron of the Wellington Mounted Rifles Regiment, who were holding the Ridge, beat off all attacks.

The month of July was spent chiefly under trench warfare conditions, the Canterbury Battalion being the garrison of Quinn's Post from the 4th to the 12th, and from the 20th to the 28th. The skill of our bombers had greatly increased, and they had now obtained the same superiority over the Turkish bombers as our snipers enjoyed with the rifle. On the 7th and 11th they succeeded in setting fire to the overhead cover of the Turkish trenches opposite No. 4 Post, and were specially congratulated in the "Anzac Intelligence Bulletin."

The remainder of the month was spent in general reserve at Canterbury Gully, with the exception of a short period at Imbros for rest and training — the battalion embarking at Anzac about 4 a.m. on the 15th and leaving Imbros on the evening of the 19th. Most of the time at Imbros was spent in rest and recreation, though on the 17th the battalion practised a night march and attack over rough and hilly ground. This had been specially ordered by the Divisional Commander, in view of the projected operations in August. An attack in force by the Turks was expected on the 23rd, but the day passed without incident. The casualties for the month were very light, being six other ranks killed and two officers and forty-four other ranks wounded, and leaving a strength of twenty-seven officers and eight hundred and twenty-three other ranks.

CHAPTER IV.

THE SUVLA BAY AND SARI BAIR OPERATIONS.

After the fighting at the beginning of May, Sir Ian Hamilton realized that neither the forces at Cape Helles, nor those at Anzac, were strong enough to fight their way to the Narrows. The chief object of the campaign was to open the way for the fleet to Constantinople; and this involved the capture of the southern part of the peninsula as far as the Narrows, as the unsuccessful attempts of the fleet to force a passage had clearly shown. Sir Ian Hamilton accordingly asked for additional troops for this purpose. Ultimately he was promised three additional Regular Divisions and the infantry of two Territorial Divisions, all of which would be available early in August.

There were various ways in which the Commander-in-Chief might have used these fresh troops: he decided to strike at Maidos from the positions already held at Anzac, and by means of a landing at Suvla Bay, north of Anzac, to protect the flank of the main attacking forces, as well as to secure for them a winter base free from the dangers and difficulties of the original landing places. A successful advance from Anzac would also cut off the Turkish forces opposed to our troops at Cape Helles; and Sir Ian's plans included an attack in the southern theatre, with the object of deceiving the enemy as to his main attack, as well as preventing the Turkish troops in the south from striking at the flank of the troops advancing from Anzac.

Our positions at Anzac at the beginning of August were on the lower spurs of the main Sari Bair ridge, which runs in a north easterly direction from Anzac Cove, and reaches its highest point at Koja Chemen Tepe (Hill 305),* about two miles north east of Russell's Top, the highest post in our lines. Between this post and Koja Chemen Tepe were the peaks known as Baby 700, Battleship Hill, Chunuk Bair, and Hill "Q." From the main ridge, which lies almost parallel to the

---

*i.e.. 305 metres in height.

sea, there runs down to the coast a series of spurs, separated from one another by deep and steep-sided gullies choked up with dense jungle. Two of these, leading up to Chunuk Bair, are called Chailak Dere* and Sazli Beit Dere: another deep ravine, called Aghyl Dere, branches into two, and gives access on the right to Chunuk Bair and on the left to Koja Chemen Tepe. These gullies were all north of our positions at Anzac.

The capture of the Sari Bair Ridge, dominating as it did the whole of the country between Anzac and the Narrows, was an essential part of the plan of attack. But before the ridge could be attacked, it was necessary for the attacking force to be in possession of the sea-coast and foot-hills, from Anzac to the mouth of Aghyl Dere. Between Sazli Beit and Chailak Dere, and near the sea, stood the Old No. 3 Post, which formed the apex of a triangular piece of hill sloping gradually down to our No. 2 and No. 3 posts on the beach. Since its recapture from the New Zealand Mounted Rifle Brigade by the Turks on May 30th, it had been made into a very formidable redoubt, dominating the approaches to both the Deres.

Behind this post, and connected with it by a razor back, lay Table Top—a precipitous-sided, flat-topped hill, about four hundred feet above sea-level. Its summit was a small plateau, a maze of trenches, from which a communication-trench ran to Rhododendron Spur, which in turn sloped up to the peak of Chunuk Bair. Between the Chailak and Aghyl Deres, the prominent features were Bauchop Hill and Little Table Top; and beyond the Aghyl Dere a low hill called Damakjelik Bair commanded the entrance to the last named ravine, and also the beaches south of Nibrunesi Point. It was therefore necessary that there should be preliminary operations to seize the foothills dominating the entrances to the ravines, and for this purpose two covering forces were to be provided.

After this work was done, the attacks on the crest of the Sari Bair ridge were to be made by two fresh assaulting columns. To support the attacks of the two covering forces and the assaulting columns, and to mislead the enemy as to the exact point of our main attack, frontal assaults were also to be made from the existing Anzac positions, against the

---

* Gully or ravine.

Turkish trenches known as Lone Pine, German Officer's Trench, The Nek, and Baby 700. Though these attacks were intended primarily as diversions to draw the enemy's attention and reserves from the chief attack on the Sari Bair ridge, yet their success would be valuable in itself; for the capture of these positions would give us the command of the southern end of the ridge, upon which our existing positions gave us little more than a bare foothold.

The preliminary arrangements for an attack on a large scale presented peculiar difficulties. The area behind our trenches at Anzac was unduly restricted even for the requirements of the normal garrison: but now large bodies of additional troops had to be landed and accumulated; and —what was still more important and difficult—their presence had to be hidden from the enemy, who by day had an uninterrupted view of our landing places, and whose aeroplanes were constantly reconnoitring and photographing our positions. Before a single man or gun, or the extra supplies necessary for either could be landed, extra accommodation had to be constructed, and camouflaged against aerial observation. All the work involved fell, of course, on the garrison. In his (final) Despatch of 11th December, 1915, Sir Ian Hamilton, speaking of these preparations, says:—

"All these local preparations were completed by August 6th in a way which reflects the greatest credit, not only on the Corps Commander and his staff, but also upon the troops themselves, who had to toil like slaves to accumulate food, drink, and munitions of war. Alone the accommodation for the extra troops to be landed necessitated an immense amount of work in preparing new concealed bivouacs, in making interior communications, and in storing water and supplies; for I was determined to put on shore as many fighting men as our modest holding at Anzac could possibly accommodate or provision. All the work was done by Australian and New Zealand soldiers almost entirely by night, and the uncomplaining efforts of these much-tried troops in preparation are in a sense as much to their credit as their heroism in the battles that followed."*

*Naval and Military Despatches, Part IV., page 12.

And in another place in the same despatch:—

"As to water, that element of itself was responsible for a whole chapter of preparations. An enormous quantity had to be collected secretly, and as secretly stowed away at Anzac, where a high-level reservoir had to be built, having a holding capacity of thirty thousand gallons, and fitted out with a regular system of pipes and distribution tanks. A stationary engine was brought over from Egypt to fill that reservoir. Petroleum tins, with a carrying capacity of eighty thousand gallons were got together, and fixed up with handles, etc., but the collision of the *Moorgate* with another vessel delayed the arrival of a great number of these, just as a break down in the stationary engine upset for a while the well-laid plan of the high-level reservoir. But Anzac was ever resourceful in face of misadventures, and when the inevitable accidents arose it was not with folded hands that they were met."[*]

The reinforcing troops were landed at Anzac on the nights of August 4th, 5th, and 6th. Of these, the available fighting troops consisted of the following:—

13th Division (Major-General F. C. Shaw):
> 38th Infantry Brigade (Brigadier-General A. H. Baldwin).
> 6th Royal Lancashire, 6th East Lancashire, 6th South Lancashire, and 6th North Lancashire Battalions.
> 39th Infantry Brigade (Brigadier-General W. de S. Cayley).
> 9th Royal Warwick, 7th Gloucester, 9th Worcester, and 7th North Stafford Battalions.
> 40th Infantry Brigade (Brigadier-General J. H. du B. Travers).
> 4th South Wales Borderers, 8th Royal Welsh Fusiliers, 8th Cheshire, and 5th Wiltshire Battalions.
> 69th Brigade (Howitzer) Royal Field Artillery.
> 8th Battalion Welsh Regiment (Divisional Pioneers).
> 72nd Field Company Royal Engineers.

---

[*]Ibid, page 9.

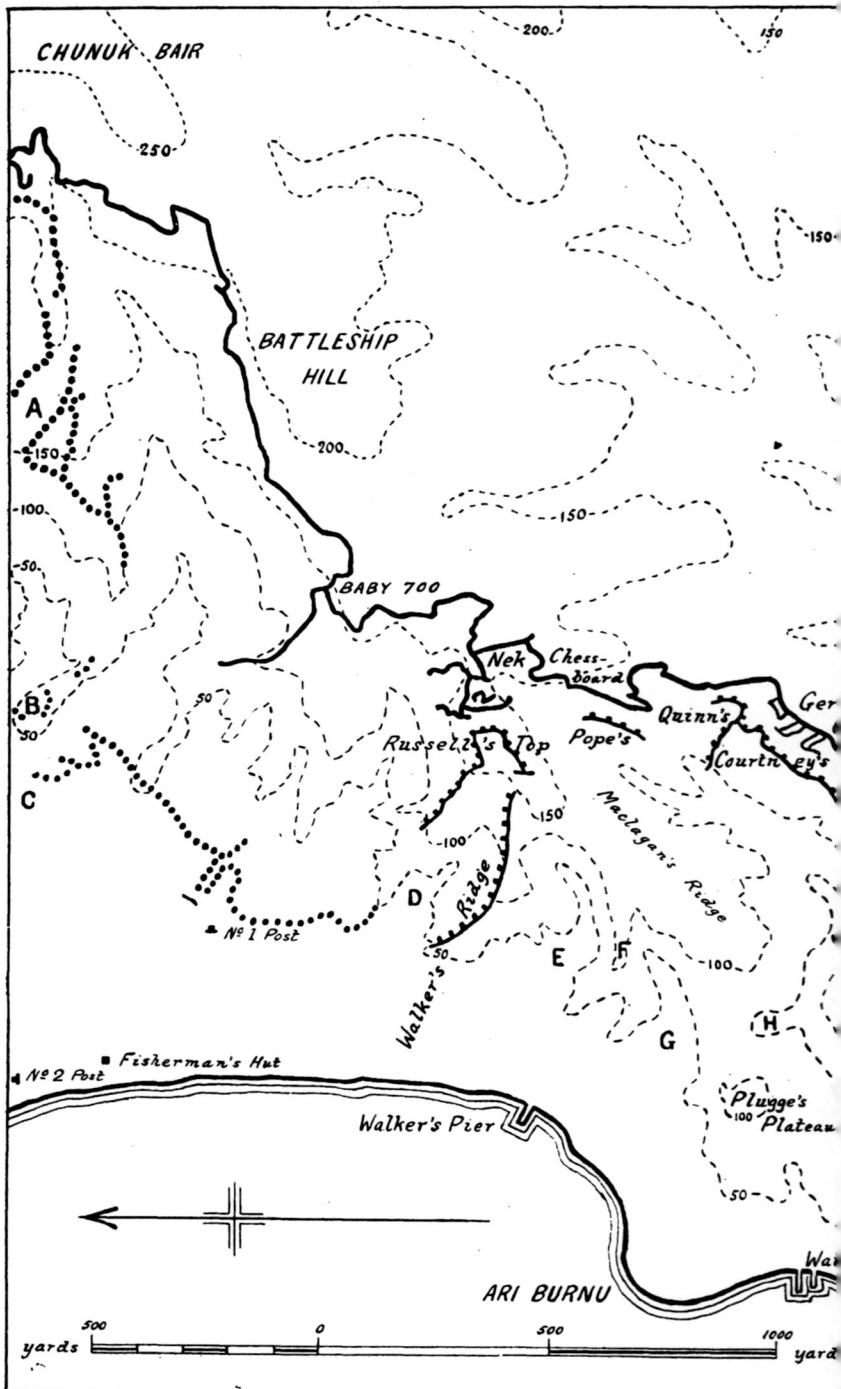

CHUNUK BAIR

200

150

250

BATTLESHIP
HILL

A

150

200

150

100

50

BABY 700

Nek

Chess-
board

Quinn's

Ger

B

50

Russell's Top

Pope's

Courtney's

C

50

Maclagan's Ridge

150

100

D

Walker's Ridge

50

E

F

100

Nº 1 Post

G

H

Nº 2 Post

Fisherman's Hut

Plugge's
Plateau

100

Walker's Pier

50

Wa

ARI BURNU

yards   500   0   500   1000   yard

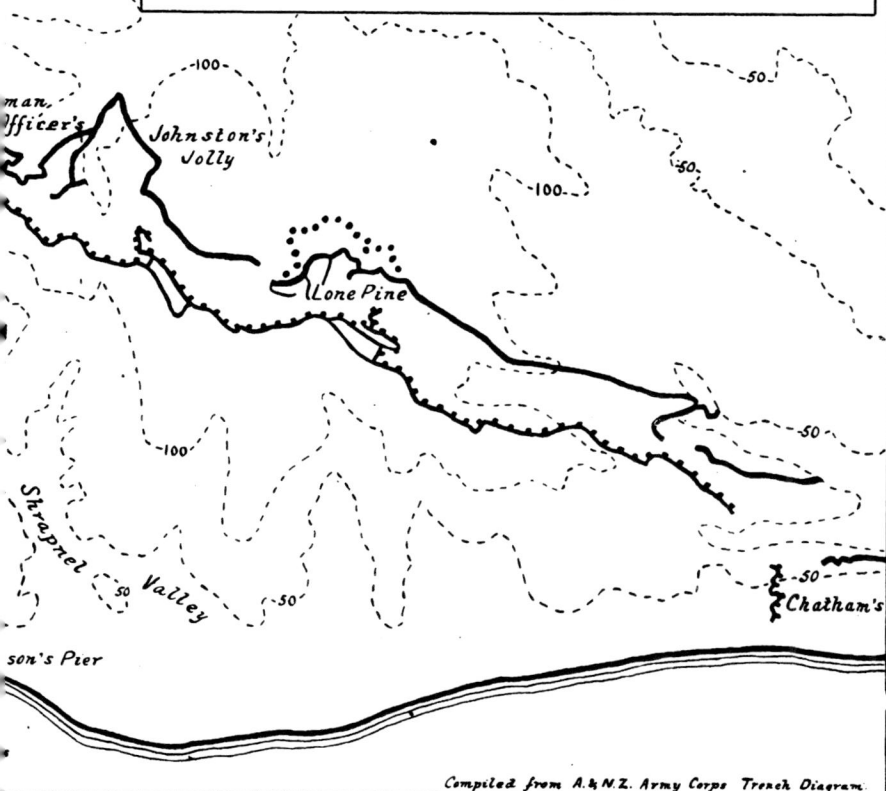

ANZAC

British Front Trenches, April   ·········

New British Positions, August   ··········

Turkish Front Trenches

50 metre contours   – – – – – –

REFERENCE

A Rhododendron Spur   E Mule Gully

B Destroyer Hill   F The Sphinx

C Sazli Beit Dere   G Reserve Gully

D Happy Valley   H Rest Gully

J Monash Gully

-150-

-100-

-100-

man,
Officer's

Johnston's
Jolly

-50-

-50-

-100-

Lone Pine

Shrapnel 50 Valley

-100-

-50-

-50-

-50-

Chatham's

son's Pier

Compiled from A. & N.Z. Army Corps Trench Diagram.

29th Brigade (10th Division) (Brigadier-General R. J.
Cooper).
10th Hampshire, 6th Royal Irish Rifles, 5th
Connaught Rangers, and 6th Leinster Battalions.
29th Indian Infantry Brigade (Brigadier-General H.
V. Cox).
14th Sikhs, 5th, 6th, and 10th Gurkha Rifles
Battalions.

These troops brought the strength of the Australian and New
Zealand Army Corps (Lieutenant-General Sir W. R. Birdwood)
up to thirty-seven thousand rifles and seventy-two guns.

The plans for the attack divided the forces into two parts.
The task of holding the existing positions at Anzac, and of
making the frontal assaults from them, to divert the enemy's
attention from the main flanking attack, was allotted to the
Australian Division, to which were attached the 1st and 3rd
Australian Light Horse Brigades, and the 8th Battalion Royal
Welsh Fusiliers and the 8th Battalion Cheshire Regiment, both
of the 40th Brigade. The main attack was entrusted to Major-
General Godley, whose New Zealand and Australian Division,
reduced to three brigades (the New Zealand Infantry, New
Zealand Mounted Rifle, and 4th Australian Brigades) by the
detachment of the Light Horse Brigades, was strengthened by
the addition of the headquarters and remaining two battalions
of the 40th Brigade (4th Battalion South Wales Borderers and
5th Battalion Wiltshire Regiment), the whole of the 29th Indian
and 39th Brigades, the 6th Battalion South Lancashire Regiment
(38th Brigade), the 8th Battalion Welsh Regiment (13th
Division Pioneers), the 72nd Field Company Royal Engineers,
and the Indian Mountain Artillery Brigade (less one section).

As mentioned above, before the main attack on the Sari Bair
ridge could be made, the coast and foothills to the north of Anzac
had to be captured. General Godley therefore divided his forces
into four bodies, of which two were to act as covering forces and
to make good the entrance to the ravines, by which the other two
columns were to assault the ridge. The troops were organized
into columns and allotted their tasks as under:—

1. RIGHT COVERING FORCE, under Brigadier-General A. H.
Russell (New Zealand Mounted Rifle Brigade).

New Zealand Mounted Rifle Brigade (Auckland, Canterbury, and Wellington Regiments).

Otago Mounted Rifles Regiment (New Zealand and Australian Divisional troops).

The Maori Contingent* (about four hundred and fifty strong).

New Zealand Engineers Field Troop.

The task of this force was to seize Old No. 3 Post, Table Top, and Bauchop Hill, and so open up the Chailak and Sazli Beit Deres for the assaulting columns.

2. RIGHT ASSAULTING COLUMN, under Brigadier-General F. E. Johnston (New Zealand Infantry Brigade).

New Zealand Infantry Brigade.

26th Indian Mountain Battery (less one section).

No. 1 Company, New Zealand Engineers.

This column was to move up the Chailak and Sazli Beit Deres, and capture Chunuk Bair, on the Sari Bair Ridge; and eventually to attack the Chessboard from the rear.

3. LEFT COVERING FORCE, under Brigadier-General J. H. du B. Travers (40th Brigade).

4th South Wales Borderers and 5th Battalion Wiltshire Regiment.

Half of the 72nd Field Company, Royal Engineers.

The task of this force was to seize Damakjelik Bair, so as to open up the Aghyl Dere for the left assaulting column, and to protect the latter's left flank, especially against attacks from troops assembling in the Anafarta Valley. Its presence on Damakjelik Bair would also facilitate the landing of the 9th Corps at Nibrunesi Point.

4. LEFT ASSAULTING COLUMN, under Brigadier-General H. V. Cox (29th Indian Infantry Brigade).

29th Indian Infantry Brigade.

4th Australian Infantry Brigade.

21st Indian Mountain Battery (less one section).

No. 2 Company, New Zealand Engineers.

This column was to move up the Aghyl Dere, and capture Koja Chemen Tepe, the highest point of the Sari Bair Ridge,

---

*This unit had landed on July 3rd, and had then been attached to the New Zealand Mounted Rifle Brigade.

joining up with the right assaulting column at Chunuk Bair. It was also the duty of this column, after it had cleared the left covering force, to protect the left flank against enemy attacks.

    5. RESERVE, under Major-General Shaw, C.B. (G.O.C. 13th Division).

      13th Divisional Headquarters.

      39th Infantry Brigade.

      6th Battalion South Lancashire Regiment (38th Brigade).

      8th Battalion Welsh Regiment (Divisional Pioneers).

(The headquarters and remaining three battalions of the 38th Brigade, which had originally been kept in Corps Reserve, were returned to their Division on the 7th, and became available as reserves for General Godley's forces).

The Canterbury Battalion had been detailed as the right assaulting section of the right assaulting column, and on August 5th had moved from its bivouacs in Canterbury Gully to others in Happy Valley (north-west of Walker's Ridge). There it remained till the evening of the 6th, when at 10.30 p.m. it moved to the attack by way of Sazli Beit Dere. Meanwhile the right covering force had attacked Old No. 3 Post, which was completely in its hands by 10.50 p.m.; and captured Big Table Top an hour later, and Bauchop's Hill by 1.10 a.m. on the 7th.

The task of the Canterbury Battalion was to advance up Sazli Beit Dere and attack the Turkish trenches on Rhododendron Spur from the west; and to picquet the right of the ravine, so as to meet Turkish counter-attacks from Battleship Hill. The remainder of the New Zealand Infantry Brigade, moving up the Chailak Dere, was to attack the trenches on Rhododendron Spur from the north-west. After these trenches were captured, and the two columns of the brigade were in touch, the Canterbury and Wellington Battalions were to attack the summit of the Sari Bair Ridge, on a frontage of about 500 yards each, with the peak of Chunuk Bair inclusive to Wellington and on the latter's extreme right.

The time necessary for the Mounted Rifle Brigade to clear the entrances to the ravines having been under-estimated, there was considerable congestion and confusion in the saps on the beach; so that it was 1 a.m. before the Canterbury Battalion was in the Sazli Beit Dere, whereas, according to the time-table for the attack, the leading troops of the battalion should have reached the Dere before 11 p.m. The 1st Company acted as advanced guard to the battalion.

There had been no opportunity for reconnoitring the ground over which the advance was to be made, save for a distant view of the country from No. 2 Post, by the Commanding Officer and company commanders, on the afternoon of the 6th. Consequently the advance up the Dere was difficult, and the difficulty was increased by the darkness of the night. The battalion lost its way completely in a branch of the main ravine, and had to retrace its steps. About this time a party of the enemy was found on Destroyer Hill, and was attacked with the bayonet—the only weapon permitted to the assaulting and covering columns—and fifty prisoners were taken.

On the battalion turning about, the 12th and 13th Companies, at the rear of the column, received a garbled version of the Commanding Officer's orders to return to the main ravine, and thinking they had been ordered to go right back to Happy Valley, did so. The remainder of the battalion picked up its bearings again and moved up the Dere to Rhododendron Spur. A great deal of time had been lost, and it was now beginning to get light. Pushing on up Rhododendron Spur, the battalion about 5.45 a.m. came in touch with the Otago Battalion, which, in spite of the fact that it had already been heavily engaged at Table Top and Bauchop's Hill, had taken three lightly held Turkish trenches on the Spur.

The 12th and 13th Companies left Happy Valley at dawn, and finding the Dere clear of troops, had little difficulty in re-joining the battalion on Rhododendron Spur. By 8 a.m. the New Zealand Infantry Brigade had reached positions which were practically on the site of the front line of the trench system held by us on the Spur till the evacuation of the Peninsula—Wellington on the north, Otago at the eastern point, and Canterbury on the south.* Here the brigade dug in, under very heavy rifle and machine-gun fire, especially from Battleship Hill, and from a trench on a spur north-east of Chunuk Bair.

General Cox's left assaulting column, having been delayed by the resistance at Bauchop's Hill, was not so far forward as the

---

*The Auckland Battalion was in brigade reserve.

New Zealand Infantry Brigade, which in consequence attracted the fire of the enemy on its left flank, as well as to its immediate front. Some of the 10th Battalion of Gurkhas, who had lost direction, joined the New Zealand Infantry Brigade at this stage of the battle.

At about 9.30 a.m. the brigade was ordered to assault Chunuk Bair; and as neither the Auckland Battalion nor the 10th Gurkhas had been heavily engaged up till now, these battalions were selected for the attack. On their advancing at 11 a.m., they immediately came under heavy fire; and though the Auckland Battalion reached a Turkish trench about a hundred and fifty yards east of our most advanced positions, its casualties were so heavy that it could get no further. The Gurkhas did not advance as far as the Auckland Battalion, which reached the point afterwards called the "the Apex."

At 12.30 p.m. the Canterbury Battalion received orders to hold its trenches with half the battalion, and with the remaining half to support Auckland in a new attack. The 1st Company was left to garrison the trenches (having had the responsible task of advanced guard during the attack) and the remainder of the battalion moved forward and lay down in the open. It at once came under heavy shrapnel fire from the left flank and suffered severe casualties, losing one officer killed and six badly wounded, in addition to three officers previously wounded.

The attack was not made; but an hour later orders were received that half the battalion was to move to the Apex, to make an attack in conjunction with Wellington. The Commanding Officer with three other officers and fifty men (representing half the battalion) moved to the Apex, leaving the remainder of the battalion to garrison Rhododendron Spur; but this attack was abandoned, as the Brigadier received orders from General Godley that no further advance was to be attempted till the following morning. The Canterbury troops detailed for the attack accordingly returned to Rhododendron Spur at 4.30 p.m.

The general position of the Australian and New Zealand Army Corps on the afternoon of August 7th was as follows:—

At Anzac proper, the Australian Division had, on the afternoon of the 6th, after severe fighting, captured the Turkish trenches known as Lone Pine, but could advance no further.

The attacks against German Officer's trenches, Dead Man's Ridge, and the Nek and Baby 700 trenches, during the night of the 6th/7th, had failed to make good any ground, though they had undoubtedly pinned to the positions at Anzac large enemy forces which would otherwise have been used against our troops attacking Sari Bair.

The Indian Brigade of the left assaulting column had reached the open slope known as "the Farm."* east of Chunuk Bair, and north of the Apex, and had also occupied positions on the spurs north-east of the Farm; while the 4th Australian Brigade, of the same force, was holding the line of the Asma Dere, on a front of about one thousand yards, with its right flank on a point due north of Chunuk Bair. The left of this brigade was in touch with the left covering force, entrenched on and around Damakjelik Bair. The right covering force held Big Table Top, Old No. 3 Post, and Bauchop's Hill with two regiments of the New Zealand Mounted Rifle Brigade as garrison; and the remainder of this force was in readiness to move as required.

At Cape Helles, there had been fierce fighting on August 6th and 7th, with scanty gain of ground and heavy casualties; but here again large Turkish forces were engaged, which otherwise would have become available further north. The landing at Suvla Bay had been effected on the morning of the 7th with small losses; but the lack of enterprise shown by the landing force had defeated the expectations that the attack there would lighten the task of the columns assaulting Sari Bair.

THE SECOND ASSAULT ON SARI BAIR (AUGUST 8TH).

On account of the exhaustion of the troops who had taken part in the first assault upon the Sari Bair Ridge, and the casualties they had sustained, General Godley obtained permission to break off the action till the following morning. In preparation for the new attack, he organised his forces into two columns— one to advance on the right, and the other in the centre and on the left. The new columns and their objectives were:—

RIGHT COLUMN, under Brigadier-General F. E. Johnston.

Auckland Mounted Rifles Regiment.

New Zealand Infantry Brigade.

7th Battalion Gloucestershire Regiment (39th Brigade).

---

*So called on account of the buildings there, which had stood out clearly before the attack.

8th Battalion Welsh Regiment.

26th Indian Mountain Battery (less one section).

No. 1 Company, New Zealand Engineers.

Maori Contingent.

OBJECTIVE : the summit of the Sari Bair Ridge from a point about four hundred yards to the south-west of Chunuk Bair to a point about three hundred yards to the north-east of that peak.

CENTRE AND LEFT COLUMN, under Brigadier-General H. V. Cox.

4th Australian Infantry Brigade.

39th Infantry Brigade (less 7th Gloucester Battalion) with 6th South Lancashire Battalion attached.

29th (Indian) Infantry Brigade.

21st Indian Mountain Battery (less one section).

No. 2 Company, New Zealand Engineers.

OBJECTIVE : from the left flank of the right column to Koja Chemen Tepe (inclusive). This column was to attack at two points. The 4th Australian Brigade was to advance up the lower slopes of the Abd El Rahman Bair (a spur running down in a northerly direction from Koja Chemen Tepe) and then to wheel to its right and advance up the spur to Koja Chemen Tepe. The other two infantry brigades were to advance directly against the main ridge between Koja Chemen Tepe and Chunuk Bair.

The attack, which was preceded by what was at that time considered a heavy artillery bombardment, began at 4.15 a.m. on August 8th. General Johnston's right column was headed by the Wellington Infantry Battalion (on the right) and the 7th Gloucestershire Battalion ; with the 8th Welsh Pioneers in the second line, and the Auckland Mounted Rifles (on the right) and the Maori Contingent in the third line. Half the Canterbury Battalion (represented again by four officers and fifty men) was ordered to support the attack, and moved to the Apex ; but it was not called upon to advance, and rejoined the rest of the battalion on Rhododendron Spur during the day.

The Wellington Battalion, advancing with great dash, gained the south-western slopes of the main knoll of Chunuk Bair, on

the summit of Sari Bair Ridge. On its left, however, the Gloucester Battalion came under heavy enfilade fire, lost its direction,
and edged off to the right. It eventually dug itself in, in shallow
trenches, in the rear of the Wellington Battalion; though about
two companies later reached the Wellington's firing line. This
was at first in a Turkish trench; but bombing attacks drove out
our garrison, which had to dig in new trenches west of the Turkish trench, that is, slightly behind the Turkish trench. Here it
hung on all day, in spite of serious enfilade rifle and machine-gun
fire, bombs and shell-fire. Late in the afternoon, it was reinforced
on the right by two squadrons of the Auckland Mounted Rifles.
Just after their arrival, the Commanding Officer of the Wellington Battalion, Lieutenant-Colonel W. G. Malone, who had been
the leading spirit in the attack, was killed.

Meanwhile, the Wellington Mounted Rifles Regiment had
come up to reinforce General Johnston's column; and, together
with the Otago Battalion, was ordered to reinforce the firing line
at dusk. By this time the strength of the Wellington Battalion
was reduced to three officers and under sixty men, while the
Gloucesters had lost all their officers. On the arrival of the reinforcements, the remnants of the Wellington and Gloucester
Battalions withdrew, having erroneously assumed that they were
relieved, instead of merely being reinforced.

The attacks of the other column had not resulted in the gain
of much ground. The central attack had made no progress across
the open ground in front of the Farm; but further to the left the
leading troops had crept further up towards the saddle on the
left of Chunuk Bair. The attack of the Australians further again
to the left had been held up by machine-guns, and the brigade
had been strongly counter-attacked and virtually surrounded by
superior numbers. After losing over a thousand men, the Australians had to retire to their trenches on the south-west of the
Asma Dere, which they reached before 9 a.m. For the rest of
the day they were heavily engaged in a defensive struggle. Once
again the expected support from Suvla Bay had been found
wanting; but the footing gained on Chunuk Bair encouraged
General Godley to issue orders for a third attack on the ridge
to be made the following morning, and to call a halt for the day.

OFFICERS OF III BN. CANTERBURY REGIMENT AT CODFORD, 8TH MAY, 1917.

Back Row.—Lieut. W. Johnston, 2nd Lieut. A. O. Ponder, Capt. H. W. Kennedy, 2nd Lieut. J. Maloney, 2nd Lieut. McKee, Lieut. J. G. C. Wales, 2nd Lieut. F. Richardson.

2nd Row.—Lieut. A. G. Bryan, Lieut. G. M. Lucas, 2nd Lieut. F. G. Painter, Capt. J. MacMorran, 2nd Lieut. C. Quartley, 2nd Lieut. T. Glass, 2nd Lieut. A. Deans, 2nd Lieut. M. O'Connor.

3rd Row.—Rev. G. S. Bryan-Brown (C.F), Capt. J. F. Tonkin, Major O. H. Mead, Major W. L. Robinson, Lieut.-Col. R. A. Row, Lieut H. M. Foster, Major D. A. Dron, Capt. A. F. R. Rohloff, Capt. R. D. Barron (M.O.).

Front Row.—2nd Lieut. A. S. Tonkin, 2nd Lieut. F. Foord, 2nd Lieut. M. Scott, Lieut. J. W. Langridge.

THE THIRD ASSAULT ON SARI BAIR (AUGUST 9TH).

The troops at the disposal of General Godley had now been reinforced by the arrival of the headquarters of the 29th (British) Infantry Brigade, under Brigadier-General R. J. Cooper, and the 10th Battalion Hampshire Regiment and the 6th Battalion Irish Rifles of that Brigade, which had been sent up from the Army Corps Reserve.* The new assault on the ridge was to be made by three columns, with the following constitution and objectives:—

No. 1 COLUMN, under Brigadier-General F. E. Johnston.
Auckland and Wellington Mounted Rifles Regiments.
New Zealand Infantry Brigade.
7th Battalion Gloucester Regiment (39th Brigade).
8th Battalion Welsh Regiment.
26th Indian Mountain Battery (less one section).
No. 1 Company, New Zealand Engineers.

OBJECTIVE: The consolidation of our positions on Chunuk Bair, the pivotal point of the attack; to be followed by an advance to the south-eastern spur of Chunuk Bair, should the attacks of the other columns prove successful.

No 2 COLUMN, under Brigadier-General H. V. Cox.
4th Australian Infantry Brigade.
39th Infantry Brigade (less 7th Gloucester Battalion) with 6th South Lancashire Battalion attached.
29th Indian Infantry Brigade.
21st Indian Mountain Battery (less one section).
No. 2 Company New Zealand Engineers.

OBJECTIVE: Hill "Q" (midway between Koja Chemen Tepe and Chunuk Bair).

No 3 COLUMN, under Brigadier-General A. H. Baldwin (Commanding 38th Infantry Brigade).
6th East Lancashire Battalion (38th Brigade).
6th Loyal North Lancashire Battalion (38th Brigade).
10th Hampshire Battalion (29th Brigade).
6th Royal Irish Rifles Battalion (29th Brigade).
5th Wiltshire Battalion (40th Brigade).

---

*The remaining battalions of this brigade (5th Connaught Rangers and 6th Leinsters) were sent from Corps Reserve to General Godley during the 9th.

OBJECTIVE: Hill "Q," attacking from the south-west and moving
on the eastern side of the Farm. This column was to make
the main attack, and the other columns were ordered to co-
operate with it.

The attack was timed for 5.15 a.m., but at that hour General
Baldwin's column, which had lost its way among the gullies
during the night, and had been hampered by the congestion in
the approaches to Rhododendron Ridge, had not arrived. For
three quarters of an hour before zero, the heights were bombarded
by our artillery; and when the guns lengthened their range the
assaulting troops of the second column went forward, without
waiting for General Baldwin's column. As the operations of
the first column were entirely dependent on the success of the
other two columns, no forward movement was made by General
Johnston's column.

The 6th Battalion Gurkha Rifles gained a footing on the col
(or saddle) between Chunuk Bair and Hill "Q," whence it
looked down upon the Dardanelles; but no fresh troops were
near enough to support it, and a strong counter-attack by the
enemy drove the Gurkhas down the hill again. The leading
troops of General Baldwin's column, the 10th Hampshire Brigade
and two companies of the 6th East Lancashire Battalion, arriving
shortly afterwards, gained the high ground west of the peak of
Chunuk Bair; but were met by the same counter-attack, and were
pressed down to the Farm.

The garrison of the firing line of General Johnston's column
held their position throughout daylight on the 9th, in spite of
persistent Turkish attacks and harassing fire of all kinds. After
dark that night, the New Zealand troops were relieved by the
6th Loyal North Lancashire Battalion, with the 5th Wiltshire
Battalion in support. At dawn on the 10th, a very strong
counter-attack, by a force variously estimated at a division and
at "several thousands," advancing in seven or eight lines
shoulder to shoulder, overwhelmed the firing line, and the Wilt-
shires below, and was with great difficulty checked by the
garrison of Rhododendron Spur and the Apex. When the
attack was broken, the enemy attempted to retreat, but was
cut to pieces by our rifle, machine-gun, and artillery fire, and
very few succeeded in escaping over the ridge.

While this struggle was in progress on the right, strong enemy attacks were delivered against the centre of the line, especially round the farm. Our lines were broken in several places, but by 10 a.m. the position had been restored and the Turks were retreating. Later in the day, enemy attacks were beaten off by the garrison of Asma Dere and Damakjelik Bair.

During the whole of the operations of August 8th, 9th, and 10th, the Canterbury Battalion remained in its trenches on the south of Rhododendron Spur, consolidating the position and linking up the posts into a continuous trench system: though, as mentioned above, four officers and fifty men were sent to the Apex for a time to support the Wellington Battalion's attack. Again, on the loss of the trenches on Chunuk Bair on the 10th, half the battalion was sent up the Apex, to take part in an attempt to recover the position; but the attack did not take place, and the party was sent back very soon after its arrival at the Apex.

The battalion's casualties during the four days' fighting had been very heavy, as the list below shows:—

				Officers.	Other Ranks.
Killed	..	..	..	4*	65
Wounded	..	..	..	8	258
Missing	..	..	..	—	11
				——	——
				12	334

*Major C. W. E. Cribb, Major J. Houlker, Lieutenant H. M. Wright, Lieutenant A. F. L. Priest.

During the fighting the 5th Reinforcement arrived, and was used as a separate unit in reserve. A party of sixty-five of them was sent to carry supplies to the Wellington Battalion on Chunuk Bair, on the 8th; and of these only four returned. The rest of the Canterbury draft was employed behind the firing line for various purposes, and came on several occasions under heavy machine-gun and artillery fire. The result was that the great majority of the draft became casualties. A draft of two officers and thirty-eight other ranks of the same reinforcement arrived separately, and joined the battalion on August 11th.

In the New Zealand Infantry Brigade's sector there were no serious attacks by either side after August 10th, and the opposing forces settled down to trench warfare. Minor operations on the left flank of the new Anzac positions, on the nights of August 12th/13th and 13th/14th, gained some ground, and improved the tactical position on that flank; although the left of our front line still remained out of touch with the forces at Suvla Bay.

The achievements of the New Zealand and Australian Division in the August fighting are referred to thus in Sir Ian Hamilton's Special Order of September 7th, 1915:—

"The troops under the command of Major-General Sir A. J. Godley, and particularly the New Zealand and Australian Division, were called upon to carry out one of the most difficult military operations that has ever been attempted—a night march and assault by several columns in intricate mountainous country, strongly entrenched and held by a numerous and determined enemy. Their brilliant conduct during this operation and the success they achieved have won for them a reputation as soldiers of whom any country must be proud.

"To the Australian and New Zealand Army Corps, therefore, and to those who were associated with that famous Corps in the battle of Sari Bair—the Maoris, Sikhs, Gurkhas, and the new troops of the 10th and 13th Divisions from the Old Country— Sir Ian Hamilton tenders his appreciation of their efforts, his admiration of their gallantry, and his thanks for their achievements. It is an honour to command a force which numbers such men as these in its ranks, and it is the Commander-in-Chief's high privilege to acknowledge that honour."

The 9th Corps, at Suvla Bay, continued its attacks till the 15th, but with practically no success; and Sir Ian Hamilton then appealed to the War Office for further reinforcements to bring his Divisions up to strength, and also for an additional fifty thousand fresh troops, besides extra supplies and munitions. These were refused him, so he determined to make a final effort at Suvla with the troops then available; and for this purpose he broke off operations till August 21st. The attack on this day failed also; though a supporting attack by troops of the Australian and New Zealand Army Corps gained further ground on the left of the Anzac positions, where the Kaiajik Dere was crossed.

Finally, on August 27th, 28th, and 29th, a force under Brigadier-General Russell, consisting of troops of the New Zealand Mounted Rifle Brigade, the 9th and 10th Regiments of the Australian Light Horse, the 4th and 5th Australian Infantry Brigades, and the 5th Battalion Connaught Rangers, stormed the knoll known as Hill 60. This hill lay north of Kaiajik Aghala, north-east of Damakjelik Bair, and between the Kaiajik and Asma Deres. The fighting was almost entirely hand to hand, with bayonet and bomb, and was of a severe nature: the New Zealand Mounted Rifles were particularly singled out for praise by the Divisional Commander. As a result of the operation, the communications along the beach between Anzac and Suvla were much improved, and our new positions commanded the valley between Biyuk Anafarta and the sea.

The New Zealand Infantry Brigade took no part in this fighting; but confined its energies to strengthening its positions on Rhododendron Spur and at the Apex. The Canterbury Battalion remained in garrison of the southern defences of the spur till August 18th, when it relieved the Wellington Battalion and the 8th Royal Welsh Fusiliers at the Apex. The same night (18th/19th) at 12.30 a.m., Lieutenant D. Dobson took out a party of thirty men of the 1st Company, with the object of destroying a Turkish redoubt known as "the Pinnacle," east of the Apex. On reconnoitring the position, the leader of the party found the Turks prepared for an attack; and coming under fire, he withdrew his men, with a loss of one killed and three wounded.

The following night, at 8.30 p.m., a party of twenty men of the 13th Company, under Lieutenant J. B. Le Mottee, made another attempt on the same redoubt, and in spite of heavy fire succeeded in entering it. After remaining there for half an hour, during which time it partially demolished the defences, the party was forced to withdraw. Before the party regained our trenches half its strength had become casualties—three killed and eight wounded.

On 20th August the battalion was relieved by the Otago Battalion,* and went into brigade reserve in bivouacs at Otago Gully, east of No. 3 Post and close to the beach.† Here it remained till the 23rd, when it was ordered to garrison the inner defences — Camel's Hump, Destroyer Ridge, Big Table Top, Bauchop's Hill, and Old No. 3 Post. During the next two days, the battalion was relieved in all these posts except Big Table Top and Old No. 3 Post, but remained in the two last-named posts till the 28th. In the meantime, the Maori Contingent had been attached to the Infantry Brigade, and a platoon was allotted to each battalion. The strength of the Canterbury Battalion was thus increased by one officer and forty other ranks.

The 4th South Wales Borderers took over Big Table Top and Old No. 3 Post on the afternoon of August 28th; and the Canterbury Battalion thereupon moved to the Apex and relieved the 8th Cheshire Battalion, which had been assisting the Wellington Battalion to garrison that post. The Wellington Battalion remained, coming under the orders of Lieutenant-Colonel Hughes. The one noteworthy incident of the battalion's spell in the line was the shelling of the Pinnacle, by a gun from the 26th Indian Mountain Battery, which was brought up into the Apex trenches for the purpose. The gun fired nine rounds, destroying the redoubt, and was got away before the enemy's guns could open fire on it. The battalion was relieved by the Auckland Battalion on September 8th, and went into bivouacs in Chailak Dere, north of Big Table Top and close to brigade headquarters. Here it remained till the 12th, when it moved to bivouacs at Bauchop's Hill.

The troops which had taken part in the original landing at Anzac had now spent nearly five months on the Peninsula, under conditions of great hardship and continual danger. The arrival at the Peninsula of the 2nd Australian Division made it possible to give these troops a rest at Lemnos, and the New Zealand Infantry Brigade received orders to embark on the transport *Osmanieh* on September 14th. The Canterbury Battalion left its bivouacs at Bauchop's Hill on the evening of that

---

*It may be noted that Major H. Stewart commanded the Otago Battalion from August 11th to 24th, and from August 27th to 31st.
†This gully shortly afterwards became the headquarters of the New Zealand and Australian Division.

day, and was on board by 11 p.m. Each battalion had been ordered to leave behind a proportion of its freshest officers and men, to assist the relieving brigade (the 7th Australian Brigade) which was now to come under fire for the first time. The Canterbury Battalion therefore left behind it three officers and eighty-two other ranks, including thirty Maoris and twenty-eight machine-gunners, and embarked with a strength of nine officers and two hundred and thirty other ranks.

The brigade landed at Mudros about 2 p.m. on the following day (September 15th), and marched to the rest camp at Sarpi. This was a camp in name only, as very few tents were there, and the majority of the brigade slept in the open for several days. No training was done during the first week, but the brigade was inspected on the 17th by Lieutenant-General A. E. Altham, General Officer Commanding Lines of Communication, and by the Admiral commanding the French Mediterranean Fleet. This was followed by an inspection by General Godley on September 21st.

Training began on September 20th, and was planned on progressive lines. The syllabus for the first week provided for only two hours' drill and marching daily, so as to smarten up the men, and gradually harden them after the relaxing life on the Peninsula. The work for the following week was increased to four hours daily; and thereafter four and a half hours' work a day was laid down, of which four hours were to be spent in field operations, including two night operations each week. Thus the remainder of September and the whole month of October was spent. At the end of September the 1st and 2nd Companies were quarantined, on account of an outbreak of scarlet fever and diphtheria. On October 4th Lieutenant-Colonel Hughes went to hospital*, and Major R. A. Row assumed the command of the battalion.

In spite of sickness, which during October alone caused the evacuation of one officer and a hundred and fifteen other ranks, the strength of the battalion began to mount up. The arrival of two drafts of the 6th Reinforcements, on September 29th and October 1st, strengthened the battalion by four officers and two hundred and fifty-four other ranks; and early

---

*Lieutenant-Colonel Hughes at this date finally severed his connection with the Canterbury Regiment.

in October the details left at Anzac arrived at Lemnos. The arrival of other details from hospital brought up the strength of the battalion at the end of October to twenty-one officers and six hundred and four other ranks.

It had been intended that the brigade should leave for Anzac at the end of October, but owing to unfavourable weather, it could not embark till November 8th. At 7 a.m. on that date, the Canterbury Battalion left the camp at Sarpi, and embarking on the *Osmanieh* at 9 a.m., landed at Anzac at 6.30 p.m., and bivouacked for the night in a gully off Chailak Dere, below Durant's Post. This post was at the junction of the trenches called Upper and Lower Cheshire Ridges, and was about five hundred yards north-west of the Apex. The following day (the 9th) the 13th Company took over part of the Upper Cheshire Ridge trench from the 27th Australian Battalion; and on the 10th the rest of the battalion took over the remainder of the section from the Australians.

The enemy was not offensive, so the battalion was able to do much useful work in the trenches. Owing to the possibility of the enemy bringing up much heavier artillery than he had hitherto used, it was necessary to dig very deep shelters; and it was on work of this nature that the battalion was employed during its spell in the line. The firing-trench was divided into three sections, and garrisoned by the 13th, 1st, and 12th Companies with the 2nd Company in reserve. On November 20th Lieutenant-Colonel R. Young, originally of the Wellington Regiment but in command of the Auckland Battalion since May, took over the command of the battalion.

The inactivity of the enemy continued during the month, though on the 22nd and 28th small parties of Turks made half-hearted attempts against the Apex. These may possibly have been sent out to discover whether we were still holding our trenches in strength; as our intelligence staff had learnt that the enemy thought we were going to evacuate the Peninsula. In order to encourage the enemy in this belief, and to try to make him attack,* orders were given on the 24th that there should be no firing for 48 hours. This period was eventually extended to midnight of November 27th/28th; but the enemy not only

---

*This was the reason given at the time: it appears that the real reason was to prepare the enemy for the evacuation.

declined to rise to the bait, but also took advantage of our inactivity to repair his parapets and otherwise improve his trenches.

It was at this time that the weather broke, and added another discomfort to the lot of the Gallipoli forces. Heavy rain fell on the night of the 26th/27th, and again during the following afternoon and night, with snow in the early morning of the 28th. Mud made progress in the trenches difficult, but heavy frosts followed, and brought with them fine weather. Throughout the month dysentery had been rife; and though the only casualties caused by enemy action were one other rank killed and six other ranks wounded, the strength of the battalion had sunk again to nineteen officers and five hundred and twelve other ranks.

CHAPTER V.

THE EVACUATION.

The evacuation of the Peninsula had long been urged by a section of English critics and their press: but the first definite sign that the War Council was contemplating withdrawing the Expeditionary Force from there, came in the form of a telegram from Lord Kitchener to Sir Ian Hamilton, on October 11th, 1915. In this, Lord Kitchener asked for an estimate of the losses which would be involved in an evacuation of the Peninsula. To quote Sir Ian's own words:—"On the 12th October I replied in terms showing that such a step was to me unthinkable."[*] He stated that the probable loss was estimated at fifty per cent; but as Mr. Nevinson points out, "No estimate could be anything but a guess, as all depended on incalculable weather and incalculable Turks."

The War Council thereupon decided to obtain "a fresh unbiassed opinion from a responsible commander, upon the question of early evacuation."[*] On October 16th it recalled Sir Ian Hamilton, and appointed in his place General Sir Charles C. Monro, K.C.B. The instructions given to the new commander were:—

(a) To report on the military situation on the Peninsula.

(b) To express an opinion whether on purely military grounds the Peninsula should be evacuated, or another attempt made to carry it.

(c) To state what he considered to be the number of troops that would be required,
   (1) To carry the Peninsula,
   (2) to keep the Straits open, and
   (3) to take Constantinople.

Pending the arrival of the new Commander-in-Chief, General Birdwood was placed in command on the Peninsula, General Godley becoming commander of the Australian and New

---

[*]Naval and Military Despatches, Part IV., p. 47.

Zealand Army Corps, and General Russell of the New Zealand Mounted Rifle Brigade taking over the New Zealand and Australian Division.

General Monro arrived at Gallipoli on October 30th; and his report to the War Council left no room for doubt that he considered evacuation to be urgently required. In particular, he reported that:—"The positions occupied by our troops presented a military situation unique in history. The mere fringe of the coast-line had been secured. The beaches and piers upon which they depended for all requirements in personnel and material were exposed to registered and observed artillery fire. Our entrenchments were dominated almost throughout by the Turks. The possible artillery positions were insufficient and defective. The force, in short, held a line possessing every possible military defect. The position was without depth, the communications were insecure and dependent on the weather. No means existed for the concealment and deployment of fresh troops destined for the offensive—whilst the Turks enjoyed full powers of observation, abundant artillery positions, and they had been given the time to supplement the natural advantages which the position presented by all the devices at the disposal of the field engineer."* He also laid stress upon the exhaustion of the garrison, caused by the lack of rest areas out of range of fire, and their sufferings from disease; and stated that the heavy casualties had caused many units to be short of competent officers.

On receiving this report, the War Council sent Lord Kitchener out to visit the Peninsula, and he left England on November 5th. He was no advocate of evacuation; for apart from the difficulty and risk of the operation, he recognised how serious a blow it would deal to British prestige in the East. He had time to pay only a flying visit to the Peninsula, and was at Anzac on November 13th, but not in the New Zealand trenches.

Whether, having in mind the efficiency of the German artillery on the Western front, he considered that to remain in the tiny area we had on the Peninsula was to run too great

---

*General Sir C. C. Monro's Despatch of March 6th, 1916—Naval and Military Despatches, Part V., p. 153.

a risk; or whether he feared the difficulties of a winter campaign, with all communications at the mercy of wind and sea; or whether his decision was influenced by the fact that the chief political object of the campaign had been frustrated by the entry of Bulgaria into the war as an ally of the Central Powers; for some or all of these reasons Lord Kitchener advised evacuation.

His return to England by way of Salonika and Italy delayed his report to the War Council; so that it was not till December 8th that General Birdwood received orders to proceed with the evacuation of Anzac and Suvla. These orders had been anticipated by General Monro, who now commanded the whole of the Mediterranean Expeditionary Forces, and who towards the end of November had directed General Birdwood, in command at Gallipoli, to perfect a scheme for evacuation, so that no time should be wasted.

General Monro had also suggested that the operation should be divided into three periods or stages:—

(1) The withdrawal of all troops, animals, and supplies not required for a defensive winter campaign, as opposed to an offensive one.

(2) The withdrawal of all troops, guns, animals, and supplies, except the bare minimum required to hold the trenches, in the event of the weather becoming so bad as to interfere temporarily with the evacuation.

(3) The final stage, in which the troops on shore should be embarked with all possible speed, abandoning the guns, animals, and stores which had been kept on shore for the use of the final garrison.

The first stage had actually been in progress before the orders of December 8th were issued: as far as the New Zealand Infantry Brigade was concerned, the only effect of this stage was the retention at Alexandria of reinforcements, which would otherwise have arrived at the Peninsula about the end of November. In this brigade, therefore, matters went on as usual. The Canterbury Battalion remained at Cheshire Ridge, where the building of dugouts continued, and wire was erected in front of some of the trenches.

It was not till December 12th that it was guessed in the battalion that evacuation was to take place at an early date: the publication on the 9th of a Divisional Order directing special precautions to be taken against spies, and the stoppage of outward mails on the 13th, tended to support these guesses. Consequently, when orders came on the 13th that the whole of the Otago Battalion, together with the Maoris attached to the other battalions, and the brigade band and other details, were to leave for a "rest" at Mudros, there were few who did not understand that these troops would not return to the Peninsula. Owing to shortage of transport, this party did not get away till the night of the 14th/15th.

The departure of the Otago Battalion made necessary a redistribution of the sector held by the New Zealand Infantry Brigade; and the 1st Company took over the additional part of the front line allotted to the Canterbury Battalion (on the right of the sector already held by the battalion), with its right flank in the left post of the Apex. Each of the four companies now had some of its own men in the firing-trenches. A small advance party from the battalion left for Mudros on the 15th.

Divisional orders issued on December 15th laid down that the final stage of evacuation would be divided into two nights, and that all but two thousand of the New Zealand and Australian Division would leave the first night. The number of troops from the New Zealand Infantry Brigade to be embarked on the first night was laid down by Division as 741, and 800 of the brigade were left for the final night. The corresponding figures compiled from the brigade states are 555 and 801. The first night of the final stage was originally ordered to be the 17th/18th, but on the 17th the operations were postponed for a day.

Meanwhile, every precaution had been taken to ensure that, to the Turks' eyes, life behind our lines was absolutely normal. For some time before any of the guns were removed, a new system of firing them had been adopted, by which the enemy became accustomed to long intervals of silence. The troops who remained were ordered to show themselves and to move about freely, the usual number of periscopes showed above the parapets, and the diminished garrisons of the trenches were kept busy discharging rifles from various points, so as to maintain the normal rate of fire.

The night of December 17th/18th saw the departure of the 2nd and 12th Companies, the former embarking at 10.30 p.m. and the latter at midnight. There remained now only the 1st and 13th Companies (reduced in strength to about 270 in all) to hold the battalion front; but that night and the following day passed quietly.   ,

As on the previous day, the troops were divided for the purposes of embarkation into three parties — "A," "B," and "C." Shortly after 5 p.m., the "A" party, consisting of ninety-four of all ranks, drawn in equal numbers from the two companies, left for the beach; and with them went all the machine-guns except one. The "B" party, of a hundred and twenty-nine of all ranks, left at 8.45 p.m. There was now left the "C" party of about forty picked officers and men, under Major H. Stewart, to hold the battalion front, and to keep up the appearance of normal conditions.

To quote the report of the General Officer Commanding the Division on the evacuation: — "To give an appearance of numbers to the "C" parties to assist their withdrawal and to hinder the enemy should he endeavour to follow up quickly, various devices were adopted. The men moved rapidly but quietly up and down the trenches, and fired shots from the various points from which fire was usually delivered. To continue fire after the last men had left the trenches, rifles were fixed at loopholes, with an arrangement which fired them after a certain interval of time. The essential of this arrangement was either a tin full of water which leaked, or a time fuse which burnt through a string, and in both cases released a weight which pulled the trigger. Trip wires which withdrew the pins from Mills' bombs, bombs concealed in discarded blankets; wire gates to be dropped in communication trenches and other similar devices were prepared. Everything that could be of use to the enemy was as far as possible removed, destroyed, or buried."

After the departure of the "B" party, the "C" party had been told off in fours along the whole of the firing trench; and at 1.50 a.m. on the 20th, the men numbered "one" (*i.e.* every fourth man along the line) left for the beach, taking with them the remaining machine gun. Ten minutes later the line was further thinned by the departure of the "number threes": each of the men remaining was now holding double the frontage he had held before 1.50 a.m. Major Stewart and the remaining party left the trenches at 2.15 a.m., closed the gap in the entanglement at the head of Salzi Beit Dere. and made their way to the beach.

The time given to this party to reach the pier had been reduced to the absolute minimum, and it had to move at a trot to arrive in time. Passing through the "keep," or inner line round the piers, held by Australian troops under the command of Colonel J. Paton, of the 2nd Australian Division, the "C" party arrived without casualties at the beach. There it joined the "C" parties from the rest of the brigade, and Lieutenant-Colonel Young, who was in command of all the brigade rear parties. As the Canterbury "C" party left the front line, the Turks could be heard putting up wire entanglements, and clearly had no suspicion of what was going on. But when the party reached the beach, they could see Turkish flares going up in quite unusual numbers. The "C" party was not kept waiting long before its members embarked on lighters, from which they were transferred to warships—the majority to H.M.S. *Heroic*, though a few under Lieutenant Gray were put on board another vessel.

This was the last party of the Canterbury Battalion to leave Anzac: the names of the officers were Lieutenant-Colonel R. Young, Major H. Stewart, Captain F. N. Johns (medical officer), Lieutenants A. D. Stitt, D. P. Fraser. D. A. Dron, A. L. Gray, and A. R. Curtis (machine-gun officer); but the names of the thirty-seven other ranks (all except three or four of whom belonged to the 13th Company) are not on record. Before dawn the remaining troops of the Corps had been safely embarked, save for a few stragglers who were picked up by the navy early in the morning.

The rear party joined the rest of the battalion at a camp near Mudros, on the afternoon of December 20th. and the majority spent Christmas there; though an advance party of one officer and thirty-six other ranks left for Egypt on the

23rd, and seven officers and seventy other ranks left the next day. The remainder embarked on the *Ascania* on the 26th, reached Alexandria on the 29th, and left the following day for Ismailia. There the battalion bivouacked behind the Moascar Camp railway station, and was joined by the advance parties and transport. The latter, together with men who had returned from hospital during the month, brought up the battalion strength to nineteen officers and five hundred and sixty-four other ranks. Apart from cases of sickness, the casualties for the month had been very light, being:—

	Officers.	Other Ranks.
Killed	1*	2
Wounded	–	9
Sick	3	80
	4	91

*2nd Lieutenant V. Blake.

The following is a summary of the casualties of the Canterbury Regiment, as shown in the official casualty lists, for the period between the formation of the New Zealand Expeditionary Force and May 14th, 1916 (inclusive). The writer is aware that it differs from the official summary, but after discovering the discrepancy, has checked his figures very carefully, and found no reason to alter them.

	Officers.	Other Ranks.
Killed in Action	7	203
Died of Wounds	5	93
Died of Disease	2	43
Died from Unknown Cause	2	24
Drowned	–	1
Died from Other Causes	–	5
Wounded	33	893*
Total	49	1.262

*Includes no doubt a certain number who subsequently died.

BRIG.-GENERAL R. YOUNG, C.B., C.M.G., D.S.O.

BRIG.-GENERAL C. BROWN, D.S.O, N.Z.S.C.

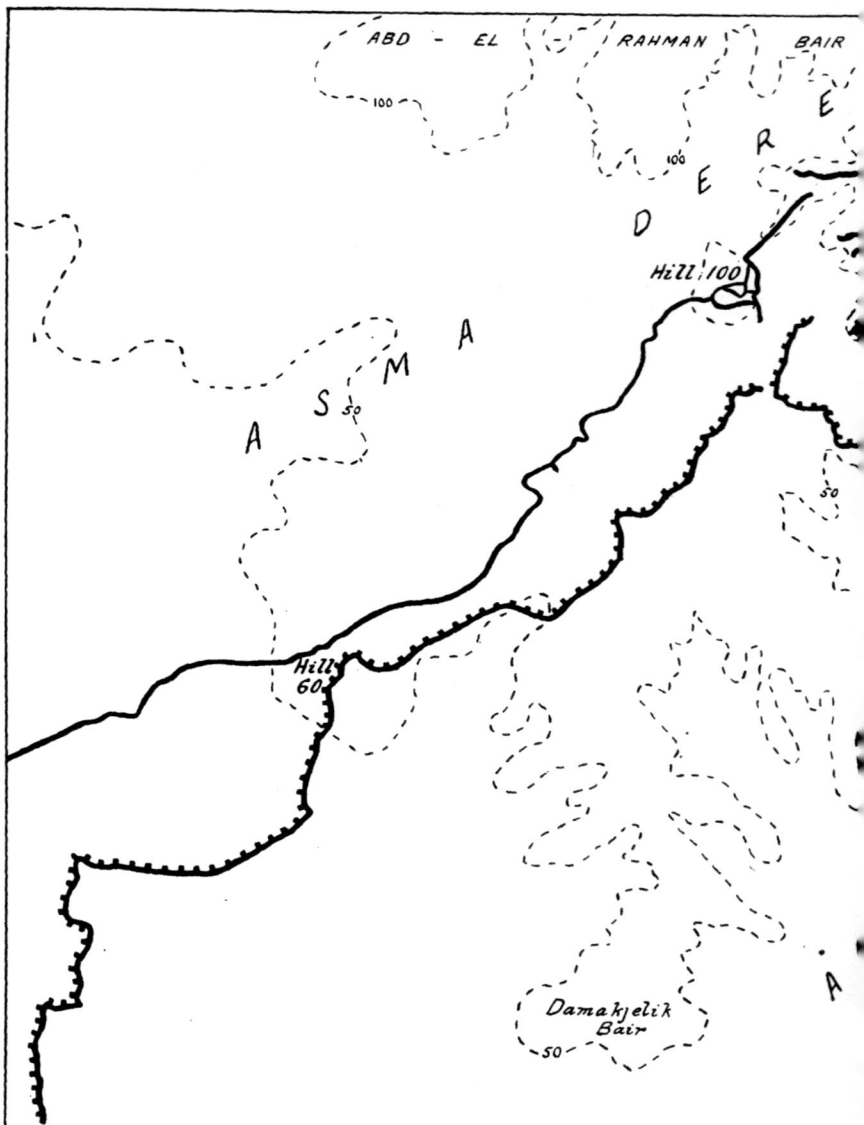

ABD - EL   RAHMAN   BAIR

100

100

D E R E

Hill 100

A S M A

50

50

Hill 60

50

Damakjelik Bair

50

NORTHERN ANZAC

British Front Trenches ......

Turkish Front Trenches ▬▬▬

50 metre contours ‒ ‒ ‒ ‒ ‒ ‒

compiled from A. & N.Z. Army Corps Trench Diagram.

500
yards

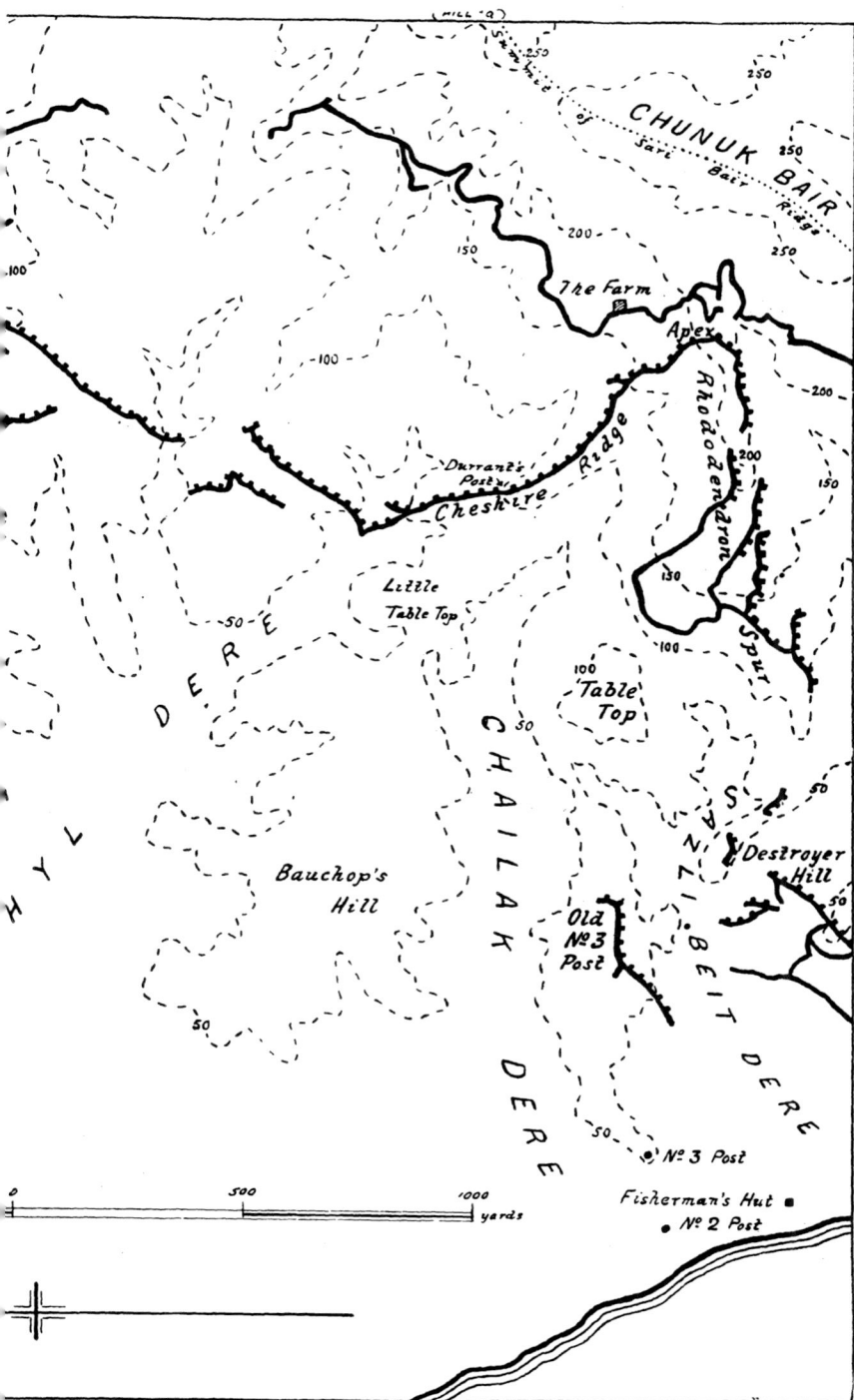

HILL "Q"

CHUNUK BAIR

250

250

Sari

Bair

Ridge

250

250

100

150

200

The Farm

Apex

100

200

Rhododendron

200

Durrant's
Post

Cheshire

Ridge

150

Little
Table Top

130

100

Spur

50

100

DERE

100

Table
Top

50

CHAILAK

50

S

50

A

N

Destroyer
Hill

L

I

Bauchop's
Hill

Old
Nº 3
Post

50

B

E

I

T

DERE

50

HYL

50

DERE

50

Nº 3 Post

Fisherman's Hut

Nº 2 Post

0   500   1000
                                          yards

CHAPTER VI.

FROM EGYPT TO FRANCE:
TRENCH WARFARE AT ARMENTIÈRES.

The New Zealand and Australian Division was now one of the Divisions available for the defence of the Suez Canal, but being in reserve had only a very few active duties to perform. After supplying guards for the reservoir, railway bridge. and aerodrome, the Division was free to devote the whole of its energies to re-organization and re-equipment (badly needed after the rigours of the Gallipoli campaign) and training. In this way January and February passed.

Meanwhile, arrangements were being completed for the establishment of a New Zealand Division, and the 2nd Infantry Brigade came into being on March 1st. One of the new battalions created for the new brigade was the 2nd Canterbury Battalion, commanded by Major H. Stewart, who was now promoted to the rank of Lieutenant-Colonel. He brought with him from the 1st Battalion Major G. C. Griffiths (second in command of the new battalion), Lieutenants A. L. Ford, D. P. Fraser. N. F. Shepherd, F. Starnes, and N. R. Wilson, and Second Lieutenants H. Campbell. M. W. Duncan, H. S. Gabites. and W. J. Marriott, and thirty-seven non-commissioned officers. The whole of the Canterbury draft of the 7th Reinforcements (which had been delayed in Cairo on guard duty over Turkish prisoners) was posted to the new battalion; and this and other drafts, including a number of officers* and men from the Mounted Rifles Regiments brought up the strength of the battalion to thirty officers and seven hundred and thirty-five other ranks on March 21st.

The New Zealand Division had now been allotted a portion of the Canal defences, and accordingly on March 6th the 2nd Canterbury Battalion had moved to Ferry Post. At this date

---

*These officers were Captain R. Logan, Lieutenant C. W. Free, and Second Lieutenant T. S. Gillies. At the same time the following officers were transferred from the New Zealand Mounted Rifle Brigade to the 1st Canterbury Battalion: Major D. B. Blair, Lieutenants J. R. Loudon and M. J. Morrison, and Second Lieutenants L. W. Bishop, L. H. Marshall, and K. S. Williams.

the battalion strength was only eleven officers and thirty-seven other ranks, but drafts arrived quickly and training was carried on briskly: the Turks had retreated from the Canal area, and the garrison's duties consisted of little more than manning the defences at night. The battalion was in reserve living in camp and performing no trench duties. On the 21st of the month, the battalion returned to Moascar.

Definite orders that the Division was soon to go to France were received in March. On the 21st, His Royal Highness the Prince of Wales visited the Canal area, and saw the Division at work; but there was no ceremonial parade in his honour. The last parade of this nature held in Egypt was on April 3rd, when General Sir Archibald Murray, Commander-in-Chief of the Egyptian Expeditionary Force, inspected the Division in full marching order.

On April 6th, the 1st Canterbury Battalion (with the exception of its first line transport personnel and horses) entrained at Ismailia, and on arrival at Port Said the same day, embarked on the *Franconia*. The first line transport went by train to Alexandria and embarked there on the *Cestrian*, the whole operation being completed in one day—the 6th. The 2nd Battalion entrained at Ismailia on the 7th, and embarked the following day on the *Canada* (thirteen officers and five hundred and five other ranks), *Ascania* (ten officers and one hundred and fifty other ranks), and *Haverford* (four officers and one hundred and fifty other ranks).

The transports did not sail in a single fleet. Thus the *Franconia* sailed on April 8th and arrived at Marseilles on the 11th; and the 1st Battalion disembarked the following day. The 2nd Battalion's transports sailed later, and arrived at Marseilles between April 14th and 16th.

On arrival, the troops of both battalions entrained immediately for Steenbecque, three miles south-west of Hazebrouck. The journey was a long one, the troops being in the train for between sixty and seventy hours; but its tediousness was relieved by the beauty of the French countryside, which was all the more welcome to men who had spent so many months on the edge of the desert. The 1st Canterbury Battalion on arrival at Steenbecque marched to a camp at Morbecque, two miles from Hazebrouck; and it did not exchange its tents for billets in the same village till April 19th. Part of the 2nd Battalion detrained at Steenbecque on April 17th, and the remainder detrained at Hazebrouck on the 20th; and both had a very long and tiring march to their billets at Roquetoire, west of the St. Omer-Aire road and three miles north-west of the latter town. The transport personnel and animals of both battalions went direct by train to Abbeville, where harness, vehicles, and all necessary equipment were issued to them. The experience of the transport is an interesting illustration of the good organization of the Army Ordnance at Abbeville. On a given date the number of horses was made up to the establishment of an infantry battalion, and harness for all the horses was issued. The transport officers were then instructed to report at another place, at a certain time on another day, with all their animals ready harnessed. On arrival there, they found all the limbers, G.S.* waggons, field kitchens, and other vehicles on the establishment of an infantry battalion ranged up in proper order, with all equipment in its proper place, and loaded with the rations required for man and beast. After being asked to satisfy themselves that everything they should have was in its place, the officers were asked to sign for what they had received, and then were given in succession the orders to yoke up, to mount, and to march off on trek to join their battalions.

Meanwhile, the artillery, field companies, supply companies, and field ambulances of the Division were being equipped in a similar manner; and pending the completion of its equipment, the Division was of necessity held in Corps Reserve. It had much to learn in the new methods of warfare which had been evolved in France: the infantry was drawn upon for the establishment of Light Trench Mortar companies, and selected officers and non-commissioned officers were sent to army schools to learn the use of grenades and Lewis guns, the protective measures to be taken against gas attacks, and the most effective employment of snipers and observers. The remaining officers and men of the battalions were busy practising musketry, bayonet fighting in the latest fashion, and the new style of fighting which trench warfare had for the time being substituted

---

*General Service.

for the old methods of open warfare. The army school pupils, coming back as fully qualified instructors, passed on to the officers and men of their battalions the knowledge which they had obtained in their special subjects.

While the Division was occupied in this fashion, its equipment had been completed, so that at the end of April it was ready to take its turn in the front line. On April 30th, orders were received that the Division was to remain in reserve for the meantime, but would go into the line about May 20th. It was warned at the same time, however, that a gas attack by the enemy was expected before that date; and that when the attack was made, it was highly likely that the Division would be required to move up at very short notice, to support the troops attacked. It may be noted here that this attack did actually take place; but that the British anti-gas protection proved so efficient that the losses inflicted on the troops in the line were very slight, and consequently the New Zealand Division was not called upon to move.

Early in May, the Division prepared for its move to the line, by sending the 2nd Brigade to the Doulieu area and the 3rd Brigade to the Estaires area (both south-west of Armentières), the 1st Brigade remaining for the meantime near Morbecque. In consequence of these moves, the 2nd Canterbury Battalion (2nd Brigade) marched from Roquetoire, on May 1st, to billets at Neuf Berquin—a distance of twenty miles; but the 1st Battalion (1st Brigade) remained at Morbecque till the 9th.

The I Anzac Army Corps at this time consisted very largely of troops who had never been under fire; and while every battalion of the 1st and 2nd New Zealand Brigades had a considerable stiffening of officers, non-commissioned officers, and men who had seen much active service on Gallipoli, none had any experience of the different conditions of trench warfare in France. Two battalions of the 3rd (Rifle) Brigade had had a small experience of guerilla warfare, against the Senussi in north-west Egypt; but the remainder of this brigade had seen no active service at all. The two Australian Divisions, which made up the remainder of the Corps, were in a similar state.

The Corps had therefore been assigned what was then a very quiet sector of the line—-part of the Armentières Salient.

The New Zealand Division's portion of the Corps sector extended from a point about two miles due west of Pérenchies and a mile south-west of Chappelle d'Armentières (south of the Armentières-Lille Railway) to the left (or northern) flank of the Corps sector on the River Lys, midway between Houplines and Frélinghien. The 2nd Australian Division was in the portion of the line to the immediate right of the New Zealand Division.

The distance between the enemy's lines and ours here averaged about three hundred yards; but at certain points, notably on the Division's left flank, and at Pont Ballot in its centre. No-Man's-Land was only a hundred yards in width. The whole of the front line was not to be garrisoned: various lengths of line, known as "localities," were held strongly, and between these were "gaps" (of an average length of two hundred yards with a straight parapet and dummy parados) which were not held at all; but were patrolled at frequent intervals by the garrisons of the adjoining localities, and were enfiladed by the flank trenches of these localities.

The support trenches (usually about two hundred yards behind the front line) were also held on the locality system, though the trenches were capable of being manned and defended throughout their whole length, and were not broken by gaps, as was the front line. Behind the line at various points, determined by the natural lie of the ground, were constructed "strong-points" — small earth-work forts which were capable of holding out for some hours, in the event of the enemy overwhelming the garrisons of the localities; or which could, by their commanding positions, render our trenches untenable, in the event of the enemy gaining a footing there. About six hundred yards behind the support trenches there was another continuous system of defences, known as the "subsidiary line."

The style of the trenches themselves was quite different from that to which the "old hands" had been used on Gallipoli. From the high ground seven miles north of Armentières, on which stood the village of Messines, and for many miles away to the south, stretched the Plain of Flanders; which was not only practically level, but owing to the heaviness of the annual rainfall, was water-logged nearly all the year round. Experience had proved that trenches below ground-level were uninhabitable: the only thing to be done was to build a continuous breast-work for a parapet, and a smaller breast-work behind for a parados.

Such was the nature of the trenches which the New Zealand Division was ordered to hold: they had been built many months before, and had not been kept in good repair. In addition to the great amount of labour required to put the trenches in proper condition, there was much work to be done before the wire in front of the trenches could be considered an effective protection against a sudden rush by the enemy.

The New Zealand Division received orders early in May that it was to relieve the 17th Division in the line, and that the relief was to be completed by the 20th. The 2nd Brigade received orders on the 10th to relieve the 52nd Brigade, on the nights of May 14th/15th and 15th/16th, on a four-battalion frontage in the left (or northern) portion of the New Zealand Division's sector.

After moving to Neuf Berquin the 2nd Canterbury Battalion had continued its training, while all its officers in turn visited the sector which the battalion was to take over. Marching out of the billets at Neuf Berquin on May 14th, the battalion reached Armentières in the evening, and went into billets there. The following day, advance parties went up to the trenches and took over the signal stations and observation posts by daylight. In the evening the rest of the battalion relieved the 9th Battalion Northumberland Fusiliers in the sections of the front line trench numbered 79 to 81 inclusive, and called the "Pont Ballot" Sector, after the farm-house of that name in the German lines opposite.* This was the right centre portion of the 2nd Brigade's sector, which was held by all four battalions, each distributed over the front, support, and subsidiary lines in its own sub-sector.

The 1st New Zealand Infantry Brigade relieved the 51st Brigade on May 13th, on a two-battalion frontage in the right portion of the New Zealand Division's sector, and consequently

---

*For positions of companies, see Appendix "B."

to the south of the 2nd Brigade. The 1st Canterbury Battalion did not go into the line, but remained for the time being in billets in Armentières, continuing its training by day. At this time the town was shelled only occasionally, and many civilians continued to do business — not without profit to themselves, but also to the great convenience of the troops. It was not until after the Battle of Messines (June, 1917) that the enemy began to shell the town so consistently that the civilian population had to be sent away.

Since leaving Morbecque on May 9th, the 1st Battalion had been billeted at Estaires, where it was inspected on the 12th by General Birdwood, the General Officer Commanding the I Anzac Army Corps; and it left there to march to Armentières on the 13th. It was not until the night of May 20th/21st that the battalion went into the line, when it relieved the 1st Wellington Battalion on the extreme right of the New Zealand Division's sector, in trenches numbered 67 to 72 inclusive. This sub-sector included a salient known as "the Mushroom," of evil memory, of which more will be heard later.

It is not proposed to follow in detail the various reliefs of the two battalions: the records are incomplete, but so far as they exist, they will be found tabulated in Appendix "B."

At first the general system of holding the line was that a battalion should hold a short sector in depth, i.e., a small portion of the front line, with the corresponding length of support and subsidiary lines. The 1st Brigade held two such sectors; and the two battalions which were not in the line formed a brigade reserve, and lived in billets at Armentières, spending their time either in training or in improving the defences. On the left of the 1st Brigade, the 2nd Brigade held four sectors, all four battalions therefore being in the line, and its only reserve being the New Zealand Pioneer Battalion, which was attached to the brigade for this purpose. The 3rd Brigade, in Divisional reserve, lived in Armentières and in Houplines, the eastern suburb of the town. Reliefs took place every eight days, when the line battalions of the 1st Brigade exchanged places with the reserves in Armentières; and the 2nd and 3rd Brigades also changed places.

This system was found unsatisfactory, not only on account of the obvious unsoundness of having either the 2nd or the 3rd Brigade spread over a long line, with only slight reserves of its own to meet any sudden emergency, but also because the whole of the 1st Brigade was never out of the front line at one time. Accordingly, the method of holding the line was changed on June 5th, when the Divisional sector was divided into two equal portions, each of which was held by one brigade; while the remaining brigade was held in Divisional reserve.

The frontage of each brigade in the line was again divided into two battalion frontages, extending as far back as, and including, the support line. Another battalion held the whole of the subsidiary line on the brigade frontage, while the fourth battalion was kept as a brigade reserve, and was housed in billets behind the subsidiary line. In consequence, a new inter-brigade boundary was established immediately north of L'Epinette; and the 2nd Canterbury Battalion took over the right half of the 2nd Brigade's sector.

The following memorandum, issued by Divisional Headquarters at the time of the change, shows the distribution of the battalions of the two brigades holding the front line:—

DISTRIBUTION OF BATTALIONS IN FRONT SYSTEM.

RIGHT SECTOR—

Unit.	Front Line Localities.		Supports.		Supporting Points		Localities in Subsidiary Line.			Remarks
								Nor-mal	Nu-cleus	
Right Bat-talion	No. 1. Piggots Farm	1 Pn.	S. 68 ... 69 ...	3 Pns.			No. I, Cemet'ry	1 Co.	1Pn.	
	No. 2 Mush-room No. 3	2 Pns.	S. 71 ...	2 Pns.	5 Dug-outs	1 Pn.	No. II, Lille Railway	1Pn.	1Pn.	
							No. III, Port Egale Av.	1Pn.	½Pn.	
	No. 4a No. 4 Port Egale	1 Pn.	S. 72 ... 73 ...	3 Pns.	Pt.Egale Redoubt	1 Pn.	No. IV., Lunatic Lane	1Pn.	½Pn.	
Left Bat-talion	No. 5a No. 5b No. 5c Epinette	3 Pns.	S. 74 75. 77.	5 Pns.	S.P.X. S.P.Y.	1 Pn. 1 Pn.	No. V., Buterne	1Pn. 3Pn.	1Pn.	2 Pns. i Quality Row

LEFT SECTOR—

Right Battalion	No. 6, Dominion	...	S. 78 } 79 }	2 Pns.	S.P.Z.	1 Pn.	No. VI. Spain Aven.	1 Co.	1 Pn.
	No. 6a, Fiji	2 Pns.							
	No. 7, Pt. Ballot	2 Pns.	Orchard	1 Pn.	Fry Pan	1 Pn.	No. VII. Glouces-ter Av.	1 Pn.	½ Pn.
	No. 8, Afrikander	2 Pns.	S.82 } 83 } ...	1 Pn.			No. VIII. Wessex Av.		
	No. 9, Cury	1 Pn.			Vancou-ver	3 Pns.		1 Pn.	½ Pn.
Left Battalion	No. 10, Edmeads Farm ...	2 Pns.	S. 84 85	1 Pn. 1 Pn.			No. IX. Edme'ds Av. ...	1. Pn	1 Pn.
	No. 11) No. 12a } Hobbs Farm	3 Pns.	S. 86	1 Pn.	S.S. 88	1 Coy.	No. X. Cam-bridge & Irish Av.	3 Pn.	1 Pn.
	No. 12, River Post	3 Pns.	S. 87	1 Pn.					
			River House	1 Pn.	Neither Compl'te				

It has been stated that the trenches and wire were in a very bad condition: there was unlimited work in sight, and there began for the Division a period of unremitting toil, such as later reinforcements never dreamed of, except those who helped in the preparations for the Battle of Messines. When the Division left this sector at the beginning of August, 1916, it was able to hand over to the relieving Division trenches in perfect repair, amply protected by belts of wire of its own erecting. Nor must it be supposed that the brigade in reserve had a much easier time than those in the line; for large working parties were provided every day and night, many as far forward as the front line. Preparations for gas attacks on the enemy involved the carrying of many hundreds of heavy cylinders to the front line, and this work fell to the share of the reserve troops.

So much for its defensive work. The more important side of a soldier's life — his offensive against the enemy — received even more thought, which bore fruit in ceaseless activity. The Division found the sector a quiet one when it arrived, but it was not in the character of the General Officer Commanding the Division to continue a ''live and let live'' policy. The name of No-Man's-Land must be made true. so far at any rate as the enemy was concerned; and to ensure this, a system of vigorous patrolling was instituted at once. Every means possible was used to annoy the enemy—shell-fire, trench mortar bombs. rifle grenades, sniping. and machine-gun, Lewis gun, and rifle fire— and he naturally retaliated; with the result that the sector rapidly became anything but a peaceful one. The British attack at the Somme on July 1st, and the unsuccessful attack of the 5th Australian Division on July 19th, on the right of the New Zealand Division, naturally increased the enemy's activity on the latter's front.

The daily routine of trench warfare, familiar as it is to those who have experienced it, may be described here for the benefit of other readers. The routine varied in detail, according to the personal views of battalion commanders; but in essentials it was much the same throughout the Division.

The two periods of the day most favoured for making attacks, and accordingly the two periods when the garrison of a trench needs to be best prepared to meet the enemy without delay, are from just before dawn till broad daylight, and from dusk till after dark. It is therefore laid down in all modern armies that, when in the face of the enemy, all troops must stand to their arms at these two periods at least during the day. In the British Army, these periods (called ''stand-to'') are fixed at an hour each, but are subject to extension at the discretion of the responsible officer on the spot, in the event of a fog or other circumstances making a longer ''stand-to'' advisable. The actual times when the morning and evening ''stand-to'' began and ended, varied, of course, according to the season of the year. On these periods, when every officer and man in the trench had to be in his fighting station, with all his equipment on and his bayonet fixed, the daily routine was built up.

The main considerations on which the routine depended were; first, the necessity of rendering it impossible that the enemy should at any time of day or night surprise the garrison; second, the necessity of ensuring that every man should get enough sleep to enable him to carry on his duties properly;

third, the proper feeding of the garrison; fourth, the amount of work required to be done to keep the trenches in fightable order.

In describing the routine of a day of trench-warfare. it is better to begin with the evening, as in this form of warfare the night is the most important period of the twenty-four hours. During this period precautions against surprise obviously need to be much more elaborate than during daylight. They consist firstly of the evening "stand-to," when everyone of the garrison is in his battle position. In the middle of 1916, the front-line garrisons were much larger than they were later on, and the trenches were unduly crowded. It was often necessary to put the whole of a section into one bay of the trench; and it was the duty of the section commander, being responsible for the protection of the men under him, to see that sentries were posted, and personally to change the sentries at the end of their watches. Later on, when experience had shown that trenches were best defended by a deep series of comparatively weak lines, rather than by two or three stronger ones, a section usually occupied two bays: but the same precautions against surprise were taken in each occupied bay.

It was laid down that there must always be two sentries on duty at night, but only one of these need be looking out over the parapet; the other, however, had to be so near the man on the look-out, that the latter could attract his attention by touching him, and without speaking to him. The sentries were relieved, as a rule, every two hours; but in very cold weather reliefs took place every hour. The remaining men of the garrison of the bay were allowed to sleep if they could, but, of course, were forbidden to remove either boots or equipment. So the night passed, till the whole garrison turned out at morning "stand-to." At the end of "stand-to," if there was a ration of rum on issue it was distributed to the men; and breakfast was, as a rule, ready immediately after "stand-down."

Further precautions against surprise by night were effected by means of listening posts and patrols. A listening post usually was garrisoned by six men under a non-commissioned officer; their post was in No-Man's-Land, and was any distance from ten yards upwards in front of our trenches, according to the width of No-Man's-Land and the activity of the enemy. The post was generally a shell-hole, and was sometimes protected by a little wire; but as concealment was essential, it could not be made an elaborate work. Two men only occupied it at a time, one of whom was on the look-out, while the other sat down. The rest of the garrison of the post were accommodated in a bay of the front line trench, and usually kept in touch with their sentries in No-Man's-Land by means of a piece of cord, over which signals were passed by the sentry making an agreed number of pulls. The non-commissioned officer in charge visited the post and changed the sentries—hourly as a rule. This work was particularly trying in cold and wet weather, as practically no movement on the part of the sentry was possible.

Patrols were employed both in our own trenches and in No-Man's-Land. In our own trenches, besides the officers and non-commissioned officers on trench duty, who visited the posts to see that all the sentries were alert, patrols were also sent out at frequent intervals during the night, from the posts on the flank of each company in the front line to the flank posts of the two adjoining companies. Also, where the line was held on the "locality" system, and there was a "gap" between two companies, one of the two was definitely made responsible for the defence of the gap; and its duty was to supply a patrol to report to its neighbour's post on the other side of the gap, at frequent intervals.

No-Man's-Land patrols were also of two kinds, fighting patrols and patrols sent out merely to watch the enemy. At Armentières, in 1916, where our object was to drive the enemy out of No-Man's-Land, fighting patrols were common; their duty was to seek out and attack the enemy, and their strength of numbers was large accordingly. As a rule, however, a patrol was sent out with instructions to obtain some definite piece of information about the enemy's doings, and in order that it should be as inconspicuous as possible, its numbers rarely exceeded three men. Such a patrol had instructions that it was not to get itself involved in a fight, unless it was absolutely impossible to do anything else. Three patrols of this kind were usually sent out on each company's front every night, and the period between the evening "stand-down" and the morning "stand-to" was divided equally between them; so that at no period of the night was No-Man's-Land free of patrols. The officer on trench duty was responsible for seeing that the patrols went out at the proper times and by the proper routes, and for keeping the sentries in the trench informed of their probable movements.

The meal-times of the garrison were usually — breakfast immediately after morning "stand-down," lunch at twelve, and tea just before "stand-to." In the long cold winter nights (after the Division had returned from the Somme) soup or cocoa was issued at midnight.

It was difficult to prevent the hours of sleep and work clashing, except in the summer months, when the day was a very long one. If the work was within a few yards of the front line, it was possible to set the garrison of each bay a definite task to be done during the night. The men were only too glad of some occupation to pass the time; for sleep was not easy, and was broken at every relief. If the work had to be done in the day-time, and each man had to do six hours' good work every day (the standard task when the Division first went to Armentières), the conflicting claims of work and sleep were hard to adjust, and the day's routine varied from time to time.

Besides the daily task of work allotted to each battalion, there were other things which had to be done, but which did not count as "work" from the military point of view. For instance, rations had to be carried by the trench garrison from the point beyond which the horse transport was unable to come. The distance over which rations had to be man-handled usually depended upon the quietness of the sector; but in some sectors the saps leading from the nearest tracks available for limbers were very long ones, and the labour of bringing up rations was increased accordingly.

It was the rule that a man must shave every morning; and though a few men actually found this a hardship, and a rather larger number affected to do so, there can be no doubt that the rule was a good one. For two reasons: firstly, an unshaven man loses his self-respect, and with it no small portion of his morale; and secondly, when a man has shaved he almost invariably has the wash which, but for the act of shaving, might easily slip his memory. In the wet season, another detail of the day's routine was rubbing one's feet with whale-oil, and changing one's socks. These were highly important precautions against trench feet, and were the subject of frequent enquiry by the Commanding Officers of battalions when on their daily rounds of inspection—another feature of the day's routine.

Among the distinctive features of trench warfare was the minor operation known as a "raid," which was carried out by a party of selected officers and other ranks. A party of this kind, after special training, would make an attack on a short portion of the enemy trenches opposite its own; and after killing or capturing the garrison, return to its own trenches. The intelligence branch of General Headquarters did all it could to encourage troops in all parts of the line to initiate minor operations of this nature. It is obvious that, if we were in the habit of taking prisoners frequently in every part of the line, we could keep ourselves informed of the movement of enemy divisions from one part of the line to another, or of the arrival of troops from another front. To move large bodies of troops is a troublesome operation, and it is seldom done without a pretty strong reason; so it follows that our intelligence service could generally rely on deductions which they had made from the movement of the enemy's divisions.

The main object of a raid was, therefore, to get prisoners: raiding parties usually tried to capture documents as well; but documents might be sometimes misleading, while it was very seldom indeed that some detail of uniform, badges, pay-book, identity-disc or even marks on boots or clothing did not show with certainty the unit to which a prisoner belonged. Also, prisoners frequently were willing to talk: if they would not talk to our intelligence officers, they sometimes unthinkingly gave away valuable information to our "agents," disguised as other prisoners.

The first raid in which troops of the New Zealand Division were engaged took place on the night of June 16th/17th, when a party consisting of four officers and eighty-three other ranks, drawn from all four battalions of the 2nd Brigade, raided a new enemy work known as "the Breakwater." This work (as its name suggests) was a sap which curved out from the enemy's front trenches, west of "Les 4 Hallots" Farm, which lay just inside the enemy's lines. The party from the 2nd Canterbury Battalion consisted of 2nd Lieutenant H. G. de F. Garland and sixteen other ranks. As all subsequent raids differed from this one only in matters of detail (though, as a rule, a raiding party was not so large as on this occasion), it may be described rather more fully than its actual importance warrants.

The enemy's new work was about two hundred and fifty yards long; and this work, together with thirty-five yards of his original trench on each side of its junction with the Breakwater, formed the objective of the raid. The main object of the raid was to find out why the enemy was building this work — whether merely to cut off a re-entrant in his line, or to provide a position of assembly from which he might attack our line — but another important object was to identify the enemy unit opposed to the Division, preferably by the capture of prisoners. The raid also had the minor aims of causing loss to the enemy and lowering his morale. The party had carefully rehearsed the operation over a model of No-Man's-Land and the enemy's trenches.

The force was divided into several smaller parties, each of which had its own definite task allotted to it. Thus, some parties were to cut gaps in our own wire, other parties were to act as scouts, to protect the movement of the rest across No-Man's-Land; and there were larger parties whose task was to assault the new work, and after capturing it, to protect other parties engaged in searching for identifications. There was no intention to hold the enemy position after it had been captured, or even to remain there for more than a few minutes: there was, therefore, no need for the members of the party to be encumbered by heavy clothing, equipment, or ammunition. All that anyone carried was a rifle, with bayonet fixed, and with an electric torch firmly bound to the stock, so as to illuminate, if need be, any object at which the bayonet was pointed. A "knobkerry" (or club), hung from the wrist by a lanyard, was designed to serve as an emergency weapon, in the event of a man losing his rifle. Faces and hands were blackened, all marks of identification were removed from clothing, and no papers of any kind were carried.

The night of the 16th was a calm one, and the sky was clear. The wire-cutting parties left the trenches at 11 p.m., and had cut the necessary gaps in our own wire before 11.15 p.m., when our artillery began to bombard the objective and the enemy's wire in front of it. Under cover of the bombardment, which lasted twenty minutes, the remaining parties passed through our wire, and formed up in No-Man's-Land, as near to the enemy's trenches as our artillery fire would allow. At 11.35 p.m., the artillery lifted from the enemy's wire and the Breakwater, and came down on the main trench behind; while certain guns still continued to fire on the flanks of the objective, with the result that the latter was isolated in a semi-circle of fire—known in technical language as a "box-barrage."

The scouting parties then dashed forward to find whether the enemy's wire had been cut by the artillery fire; and on their reporting that the way was clear, the main parties assaulted the Breakwater in the centre, and began to work their way along the sap towards either end. The work was found to be unfinished, and evidently only lightly manned. There were only two of the enemy found there, and these were bayoneted by the left assaulting party; but identifications were obtained from their bodies. The sappers attached to this party demolished with gun-cotton a listening post, which was found at the forward end of the sap. The right assaulting party, working down the sap, found it effectually blocked at a point fifteen yards short of its junction with the main trench. As the time fixed for rallying had almost arrived, this party did not attempt to enter the main trench by going across country.

The raid was a successful one, and set a standard for the many raids which followed it. Its good results were due, in great measure, to the artillery, which not only thoroughly cut the enemy's wire and barraged the raiding party against infantry attacks, but also did such good counter-battery work that the enemy's retaliation was very weak. Indeed, nearly all the losses of the party—one officer and one other rank killed and three officers and five other ranks wounded—were caused by the attacking troops getting too close to our own barrage.

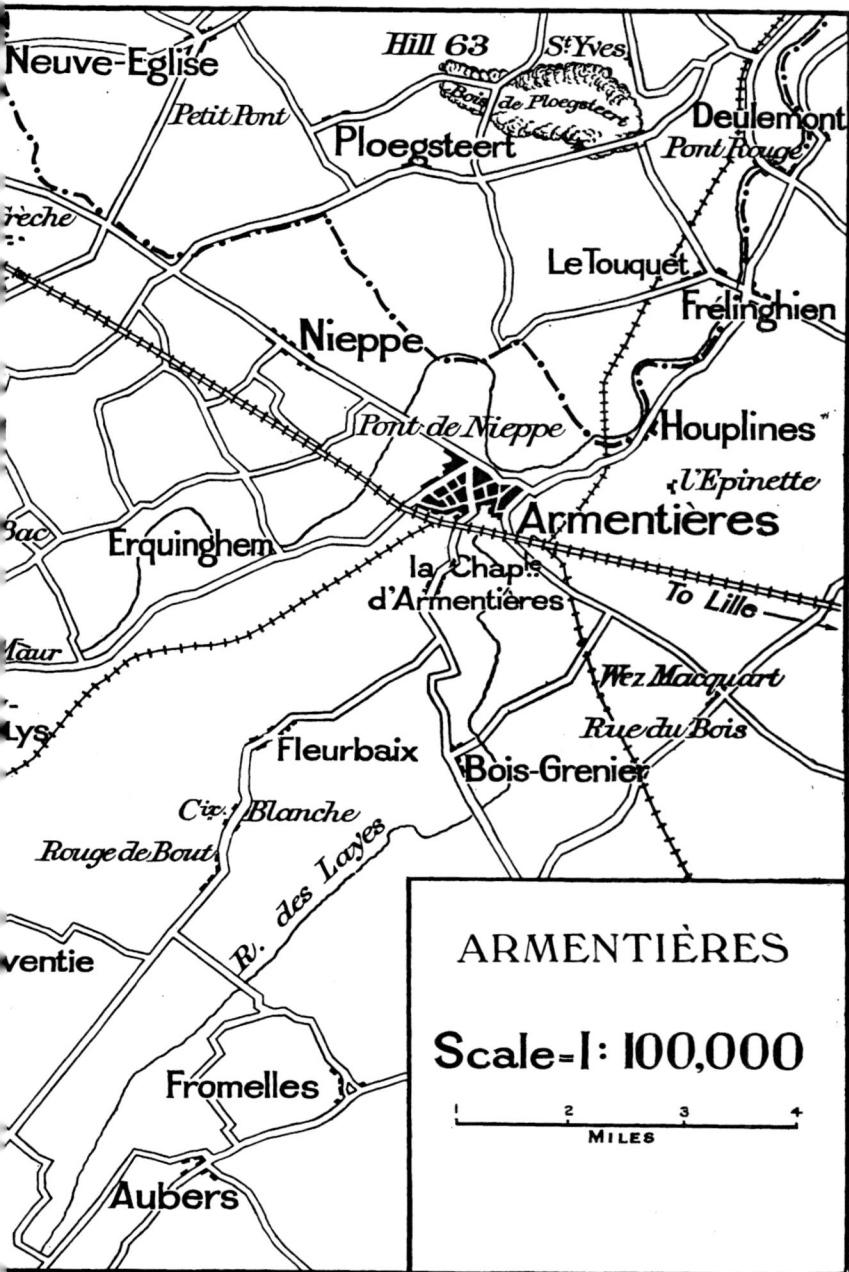

Neuve-Eglise

Hill 63   St Yves

Petit Pont   Bois de Ploegsteert

Ploegsteert   Deulemont

Pont Rouge

reche

Le Touquet

Frelinghien

Nieppe

Pont de Nieppe   Houplines

l'Epinette

Erquinghem   Armentières

Bac   la Chaplle d'Armentières   To Lille

Maur   Wez Macquart

Lys   Rue du Bois

Fleurbaix   Bois-Grenier

Cité Blanche

Rouge de Bout   R. des Layes

ventie

ARMENTIÈRES

Scale=1: 100,000

Fromelles   1   2   3   4
             MILES

Aubers

LIEUT.-COLONEL D. MACBEAN STEWART.

LIEUT.-COLONEL A. E. LOACH

The enemy was also fully aware of the possibilities of raiding, and on July 3rd unsuccessfully raided the 1st Auckland Battalion. The 1st Canterbury Battalion's turn came on the 8th: it had come into the line on the 3rd, and in the interval the enemy had been busy "registering" our trenches—i.e., ascertaining, by observing the fire of single guns, the exact elevation and direction necessary to hit the target, and recording the information for further use. This "registration" had borne fruit in heavy bombardments of our positions, on the nights of the 4th/5th and 6th/7th, by artillery and trench-mortars (minnenwerfer)* of all calibres.

At 9.15 p.m. on July 8th, the enemy opened a still heavier bombardment on all our positions, but concentrated particularly on the centre of the 1st Canterbury Battalion's front line trenches. On the right centre (known as No. 2 Locality, with the strong point called "the Mushroom" in advance of the front line) was part of the 1st Company, the remainder of which was in No. 1 Locality (on the right flank of the battalion) and in the support trenches of the two localities. Part of the 12th Company was in No. 3 Locality, in the left centre.

In the light of subsequent experience, all the British front line trenches were at this time far too strongly garrisoned, and it was impossible for any shell to land in a trench without causing several casualties. The Mushroom had a garrison of one officer and forty other ranks, of which the bombardment which began at 9.15 p.m. killed the officer, his platoon sergeant, and five men, besides severely wounding several others.

When the bombardment lifted off the Mushroom, about fifty of the enemy attacked the strong-point. The survivors of the garrison, under Sergeant S. G. Brister, repelled this attack, but were immediately attacked from both flanks by enemy bombing parties. Fighting desperately, the garrison on the right was driven back up the communication-trench leading back to No. 2 Locality. This party was commanded by Sergeant Brister, who, though wounded, refused to surrender, and established a block in the communication trench, which he held till our counter-attack had been delivered. On the left, the remainder of the garrison was forced to fall back across country.

*Translation: "mine-thrower."

H

Meanwhile, the garrison of No. 2 Locality had suffered even more severely from the bombardment than the platoon in the Mushroom, and almost all had been either killed or wounded. In No. 3 Locality, things were not so desperate, but the officer commanding the garrison had been killed. Here, Lieutenant E. H. T. Kibblewhite, of the 1st Machine-Gun Company, took charge of the position, and organized a counter-attack which he led against the Mushroom. He met with no opposition; on reaching the strong-point he found that the enemy had removed his dead and wounded, and had abandoned the trenches. Apparently our dead had not been searched; no wounded had been taken prisoner, nor was there anything missing from the dugouts.

Working parties were organized at once; and several men who had been buried alive were rescued. All the trenches occupied by the battalion had been badly damaged, and the next few days were spent in repairing the defences, the work being occasionally interfered with by enemy bombardments. The battalion had suffered very severely indeed from the enemy's artillery fire, which was responsible for the bulk of the month's casualties. These were:—

				Officers.	Other Ranks.
Killed	..	..	..	2*	37
Wounded	..	..	..	4	169†
Missing	..	..	..	–	5
Sick	..	..	..	–	67
				–	—
				6	278

*2nd Lieutenants A. F. Cormody and R. P. Herman.
†Including eight died of wounds.

Orders for the relief of the New Zealand Division by the 51st Division were received early in August: the New Zealand Division upon relief was to go to the Somme, where the battle had been raging since July 1st. The relieving division had been engaged in the battle, and was resting and refitting in the back areas near Armentières for some time before it relieved the New Zealanders. During this period some of the officers of the 54th Brigade lectured the officers of the New Zealand Division on their experiences at the Somme.

On the night of August 7th/8th the 1st Battalion completed its last tour of duty in the front line in this sector, and the 2nd Battalion was relieved the following night by the 2nd Auckland Battalion. Both Canterbury Battalions moved to the subsidiary line.

The 1st and 2nd Canterbury Battalions were relieved by the 4th and 1st/5th Battalions respectively of the Gordon Highlanders on August 15th. and moved to billets in Armentières. Marching out with their respective brigades on the 16th, the two battalions entrained at Steenwerck and left train at Eblinghem, midway between Hazebrouck and St. Omer. The 1st Battalion then marched to billets at Wardrecques (three miles away), while the 2nd Battalion marched to Blaringhem, about the same distance from the railway, and four miles south-east of the 1st Battalion's billets. Both battalions remained at these villages for three days, carrying on training. and while there received a draft of reinforcements.

Leaving its billets on August 21st, the Division entrained at Arques, two miles south-east of St. Omer. The 1st Canterbury Battalion left the train at Abbeville, near the mouth of the Somme, on the 21st, and arrived at Merelessart on the evening of the same day, after a march of twelve and a half miles—a long march for men who had so recently left the trenches. The 2nd Brigade detrained the same day at Pont Remy (five miles south-east of Abbeville), and the 2nd Canterbury Battalion marched to Allery, seven miles due south of Pont Remy.

The following summary shows the total casualties of the two Canterbury Battalions during the trench warfare at Armentières :—

1st Battalion.	Officers.	Other Ranks.
Killed in Action and Died of Wounds ..	2*	71
Wounded	6	238
Total	8	309

*Lieutenant A. F. Cormody and 2nd Lieutenant R. P. Herman (8th July).

	Officers.	Other Ranks.
2nd Battalion.		
Killed in Action and Died of Wounds	2†	27
Wounded	4	118
Total	6	145

Total for Regiment—4 officers and 98 other ranks killed; 10 officers and 356 other ranks wounded.

†Lieutenant N. S. Joyce (Died of Wounds 8th June), Lieutenant G. S. Lavie (11th June).

The Division now temporarily ceased to belong to the I Anzac Army Corps, and came under the orders of the General Officer Commanding the X Corps of the First Army. The men needed much training to bring them into good physical condition again after their long stay in the trenches; and this kept everyone very busy during the following ten days, in spite of the wet weather which prevailed at the end of the month.

Owing to the progress which had already been made in the battle, the new methods of attack which had been introduced in its first stages had even now been considerably modified. While the ground gained by the more recent attacks was considerable, it could not compare in extent with that wrested from the enemy in the early stages of the battle. Conditions had settled down into what had been given the name of "semi-trench-warfare."

On a front of twenty miles the enemy had lost his elaborate first and second defensive system, on which he had worked for nearly two years and which he considered impregnable.* The further defences on which he had now fallen back were not nearly so formidable: in certain places where our attacks had met with the greatest success, his front line consisted merely of a series of lines of shell holes, hastily joined together to form trenches. Under cover of these the enemy was working hard on defensive systems further to his rear; but the time at his disposal alone ensured the impossibility of his building any defences of which the strength could in any way compare with that of his old front line.

---

*For a description of these defences, see Sir D. Haig's Despatch of 23rd December, 1916, quoted on page 108 Chapter VII.

Up to now, the chief novelty of the new warfare was the use of a "creeping" artillery barrage. The idea of a stationary barrage was borrowed from the French; but the "creeping" barrage was a British idea, and in the first battle of the Somme had been elaborated to an extent which had not hitherto been thought practicable. In former British offensives, the artillery had been used to bombard the enemy trenches before the attack; but it had not had at its disposal the unlimited ammunition upon which it could now rely. On many occasions, too, the enemy had evaded our bombardment by sheltering in shell-holes in No-Man's-Land, and had then surprised our infantry as it moved to the assault.

The new method of using artillery was to combine a stationary barrage of heavy artillery and 4·5-inch field-howitzers with a "creeping" barrage of 18-pounder field-guns. The stationary barrage rested on the enemy's trenches. till the attacking troops had advanced as close to it as safety allowed, when it was lifted back to the next trench towards the rear. The "creeping" barrage (as its name implies) moved forward in front of the infantry, beginning just in front of their assembly positions. so that it thoroughly swept all the ground over which they had to advance. The rate at which the infantry could be expected to advance governed the rate of the "creep" of the barrage.

It should be explained, however, that the word "creeping" is not a very good one to describe the action of the artillery: unless a gun is practically new, it is almost impossible to lengthen its range by less than a hundred yards at a time. When a "creeping" barrage was in progress, each gun therefore fired on a given line for a period of three or four minutes, or even a longer time (according to the rate at which the infantry were expected to move), and at the end of that period the range was lengthened a hundred yards. The infantry then moved forward at a walking pace, as far as they could go without coming under our own shells, and then halted and knelt down; and so the process was repeated till the infantry had captured the objective which they had been ordered to take.

It must be borne in mind that the area swept by the "creeping" barrage was a deep one. so that the guns engaged were not by any means all firing on a line directly in advance of the infantry, but that the majority were sweeping a broad belt of country well in front of the assaulting troops. It was therefore not unduly complicating the task of the gunners to arrange lifts of fifty yards only, by making the lines on which half the barrage guns were to fire fifty yards in advance of what would normally have been their targets. By lifting half the guns at a time, at the same time halving the rate of lift. the "creep" of the barrage could be reduced to fifty yards at a time; and, of course, the "creep" could be further reduced by more elaborate arrangement of targets and times of lifts. Where the enemy positions were very strong, and concrete shelters protected his troops, the "creep" of the barrage was reduced in this way. As a general rule, however, fifty yards lifts were found to be the most suitable.

The "limited objective" was a second new feature of the Somme fighting. The range of field guns is limited, and also barrage firing is a great strain on the gunners: the infantry advance was therefore made by definite stages, from one line to another, strictly according to time-table. As a result, even if the infantry saw there was no enemy in front of them, they were forbidden to advance beyond the spot on which the time-table showed they should be. The necessity for this is clear; for where a great number of scattered batteries of artillery are working in unison, a considerable time must elapse before information from the firing line can reach them all. in its final shape of orders from the various divisions under which they are working. Infantry units were therefore forbidden to advance beyond the objectives assigned to them, since they would thereby come under the fire of our own guns when the attack was continued.

The training of the New Zealand Division was mainly devoted to the study of the new methods of fighting; and in particular advancing under a barrage was continually practised. the limit of the ground on which our shells were imagined to be falling being represented by lines of men waving flags, and running forward by stages of a hundred yards every three or four minutes. No opportunity was lost by the senior and junior officers of getting in touch with officers who had been engaged in the fighting, and the valuable information so gained was circulated as widely as possible.

Standing orders during an offensive operation now issued by General Headquarters laid down that no more than twenty officers and six hundred and eighty other ranks of a battalion were to go into action. The remainder of the battalion was called "the B team": it included the second in command of the battalion, either the commander or second in command of each company, all other officers in excess of twenty strong, and a certain number of non-commissioned officers and of the specialists —experienced Lewis gunners, signallers, bombers, and so on. When the New Zealand Division went into the battle, the "B teams" from all the battalions were retained in a special camp near Fricourt, and were not allowed to be recalled to their units, except by permission of the brigadier under whose command their particular unit came.

The Division left its training area on September 2nd, when the 1st Battalion left Merelessart, and moving with the remainder of the 1st Brigade, marched to Airaines, five miles to the east. After spending the night in billets there, it marched to La Chaussée (on the main Abbeville-Amiens road, seven miles west of Amiens), where it remained in billets until the 7th. On that day the battalion marched to Coisy (fifteen miles north of Amiens), spent the night there, and on the 8th, after marching east fifteen miles to Dernancourt (south of Albert) bivouacked at "Area 'A'" near there, from that afternoon till the morning of September 10th. It then marched three and a half miles north-east to another bivouac area near Fricourt, where it remained till it was ordered into the line, in the meantime supplying working parties and carrying parties for the front line and also digging assembly trenches for the 3rd (Rifle) Brigade's attack of September 15th.

The 2nd Brigade also left its training area on September 2nd, and on that day the 2nd Canterbury Battalion marched out from its billets at Allery, passed through Airaines, and was billeted for the night in Le Mesge, two and a half miles south of Hangest-sur-Somme. Moving on next morning, the battalion the same day reached Picquigny (on the opposite bank of the Somme from La Chaussée), and remained in billets there for the following three days. The time was spent in training, and a brigade attack was practised. As the method adopted was the same as was afterwards used against the enemy, a description may be found interesting. The final practice took place in the presence of the General Officer Commanding the Division, who expressed his approval of the way in which the operation was carried out.

The scheme of the attack was that the brigade, being part of the garrison of a system of trenches, with a No-Man's-Land three hundred yards in width between it and the enemy's trench system, had received orders to attack and hold seven hundred yards' frontage of the enemy's trench system, which consisted of firing-line, support, and reserve trenches.

The attack was divided into three phases, each of which ended at a limited objective — the first objective being the enemy's firing-trench, the second his supports, and the third (and final) his subsidiary, or reserve, trenches. Every part of the advance was to be supported by stationary and creeping barrages, which were represented by officers with flags. The creeping barrage moved forward at the rate of fifty yards per minute — a rate quite suitable for practice on good ground, but too rapid for an advance over country which has been badly shelled. Two battalions only, the 2nd Otago and 2nd Wellington, were to take part in the assault and to take all the objectives, the 2nd Auckland Battalion being in brigade reserve, while the 2nd Canterbury Battalion was detailed to carry out special duties and to await orders.

The assaulting battalions assembled each with two companies in our support trenches and the reserve battalion occupied our reserve trenches, with orders to move up to the front line and supports directly these were vacated by the assaulting battalions. At "Zero" hour (i.e., the exact moment fixed for the attack), the leading companies of each battalion advanced in three "waves,"* the leading "wave" keeping as close up to the barrage as possible, and the others following at a distance of fifty yards between "waves." The artillery time-table, which of course also was timed from "Zero," was a very simple one, but is quoted here to give the reader an idea of the principles which applied to the co-operation between infantry and artillery in all

---

*A wave consisted of one or more lines of men advancing in extended order.

attacks from now onwards. At this time it was usual for all attacks to be preceded by an intense and continuous artillery bombardment of all objectives for several days before the actual attack of the infantry; but continuous preliminary bombardments were not the rule from the Battle of Messines onwards.

The orders for the artillery ran thus:—"The bombardment of heavy artillery and howitzers, and the double barrage of shrapnel will be as under:—

0.00* Bombardment lifts from enemy's front line to 2nd objective.

First shrapnel barrage continues on enemy's front line.

Second shrapnel barrage opens 50 yards in front of our 1st line.

0.01 Second shrapnel barrage lifts 50 yards.

0.02 .. .. ., ,,

0.03 ,, ,, .. ,.

0.04 .. .. ., .,

0.05 ,, ., .. on to the 1st objective.

0.06 Bombardment lifts on to 3rd objective.

First shrapnel barrage lifts on to 2nd objective.

Second ., .. 50 yards.

0.08 ., ... on to 2nd objective.

0.09 First .. ., ,. 3rd .,

Second ., .. 50 yards.

0.11 Bombardment lifts on to second line system.†

Second shrapnel barrage lifts 50 yards.

0.13 .. ., ,. ,,

0.15 .. ,. ., on to 3rd objective.

0.17 Both shrapnel barrages lift 50 yards.

0.18 ,, ,, ,. ,,

As the shrapnel barrage lifted. the leading wave of the assaulting troops kept moving forward to within forty yards of it, the other waves following at the prescribed distance of fifty yards. At "Zero plus 5" (*i.e.*. 5 minutes after the beginning of the attack), this barrage was on the first objective, and the second wave was closing in on the leading wave. At "Zero

---

*"Zero" hour.
†*i.e.*, the next series of trenches of the enemy's defences. which, like ours, consisted of several trench systems, one behind the other.

plus 6," on both shrapnel barrages lifting off the first objective, the leading wave charged the trenches, and just before reaching them was reinforced by the second wave. The third wave reached the trenches immediately on the heels of the second wave.

Meanwhile, the remaining companies of the assaulting battalions had moved out of our support trenches, and were extended across No-Man's Land, each in two waves; and on the capture of the first objective the third company of each battalion at once crossed the captured trench without entering it, and "hugged" the barrage preparatory to attacking the enemy's support line. It followed up the barrage in the same way as the original leading waves had done; and on its capturing the support trenches, the last remaining company, which had been close on its heels, crossed these trenches, and following the barrage closely, captured the enemy's reserve trenches. This system of attack was called "leap-frogging."

On referring to the barrage time-table, the reader will see that at the time fixed for the capture of the third objective (zero plus 17), the infantry came within fifty yards of both the first and second shrapnel barrages; and that at zero plus 18 the barrages moved on another fifty yards. Here the barrages remained, protecting the leading infantry while it dug in; and when ample time had been given for this to be done, the barrages gradually died away. But, in accordance with the rule that every body of troops, no matter how large or how small, is responsible for its own protection against surprise, the leading company of each battalion, directly it reached the final objective, pushed forward Lewis guns to protect the troops engaged in digging, and sent out patrols to traverse the area between the captured trench and the barrage and to watch for enemy counterattacks.

A feature of the practice was co-operation with aeroplanes, which were supplied by the 3rd Squadron of the Royal Flying Corps. Co-operation of this nature was another successful experiment of the Somme Battle: low-flying aeroplanes, recognizable by a distinctive mark, were ordered to fly over the objectives at defined times; and it was then the duty of the front-line troops to light flares to mark the limit of their advance. In this way, reports of the progress of the attack could be sent to the

commanders of brigades, divisions, and higher formations much
earlier and with more certainty of arrival than by any system
of runners or signallers.

The 2nd Brigade resumed its march on September 7th: the
2nd Canterbury Battalion spent that night in billets at Cardon-
nette, two miles south-east of Coisy. Next day the battalion
marched *viâ* Querrieu and along the Amiens-Albert road to a
camp south of the road and west of Dernancourt. At this camp
the battalion remained till early in the afternoon of the 10th,
and then marched through Dernancourt, Méaulte, and Fricourt,
and bivouacked in Fricourt Wood.

CHAPTER VII.

THE BATTLE OF THE SOMME.

The Battle of the Somme had opened on July 1st, 1916, while the New Zealand Division was at Armentières; and by the time the Division arrived on the battlefield the enemy's defences had been penetrated to a maximum depth of about four miles, on a front of about twenty miles.

The enemy's position in this part of the front is described in Sir Douglas Haig's Despatch of the 23rd December, 1916, as being

"of a very formidable character, situated on a high, undulating tract of ground, which rises to more than 5,000 feet above sea-level, and forms the watershed between the Somme on the one side and the rivers of south-western Belgium on the other. On the southern face of this watershed, the general trend of which is from east-south-east to west-north-west, the ground falls in a series of long irregular spurs and deep depressions to the valley of the Somme. Well down the forward slopes of this face the enemy's first system of defence, starting from the Somme near Curlu, ran at first northwards for 3,000 yards, then westwards for 7,000 yards to near Fricourt, where it turned nearly due north, forming a great salient angle in the enemy's line.

"Some 10,000 yards north of Fricourt the trenches crossed the river Ancre, a tributary of the Somme, and still running northwards passed over the summit of the watershed, about Hébuterne and Gommecourt, and then down its northern spurs to Arras.

"On the 20,000 yards front between the Somme and the Ancre the enemy had a strong second system of defence, sited generally on or near the southern crest of the highest part of the watershed, at an average distance of 3,000 to 5,000 yards behind his first system of trenches.

"During nearly two years' preparation he had spared no pains to render these defences impregnable. The first and second systems each consisted of several lines of deep trenches, well provided with bomb-proof shelters and with numerous communication trenches connecting them. The front of the trenches in each system was protected by wire entanglements, many of them in two belts forty yards broad, built of iron stakes interlaced with barbed wire, often almost as thick as a man's finger.

"The numerous woods and villages in and between these systems of defence had been turned into veritable fortresses. The deep cellars, usually to be found in the villages, and the numerous pits and quarries common to a chalk country were used to provide cover for machine-guns and trench mortars. The existing cellars were supplemented by elaborate dug-outs, sometimes in two stories, and these were connected up by passages as much as thirty feet below the surface of the ground. The salients in the enemy's line, from which he could bring enfilade fire across his front, were made into self-contained forts, and often protected by mine fields; while strong redoubts and concrete machine-gun emplacements had been constructed in positions from which he could sweep his own trenches should these be taken. The ground lent itself to good artillery observation on the enemy's part, and he had skilfully arranged for cross fire by his guns.

"These various systems of defence with the fortified localities and other supporting points between them, were cunningly sited to afford each other mutual assistance and to admit of the utmost possible development of enfilade and flanking fire by machine-guns and artillery. They formed, in short, not merely a series of successive lines, but one composite system of enormous depth and strength.

"Behind this second system of trenches, in addition to woods, villages, and other strong points prepared for defence, the enemy had several other lines already completed; and we had learnt from aeroplane reconnaissance that he was hard at work improving and strengthening these and digging fresh ones between them and still further back.

"North of the Ancre, where the opposing trenches ran transversely across the main ridge, the enemy's defences were equally elaborate and formidable."

The Commander-in-Chief divides the period of active operations at the Somme into three phases:—

"The first phase opened with the attack of 1st July, the success of which evidently came as a surprise to the enemy, and caused considerable confusion and disorganisation in his ranks. The advantages gained on that date and developed during the first half of July may be regarded as having been rounded off by the operations of the 14th July and three following days, which gave us possession of the southern crest of the main plateau between Delville Wood and Bazentin-le-Petit.

"We then entered upon a contest lasting for many weeks, during which the enemy, having found his strongest defences unavailing, and now fully alive to his danger, put forth his utmost efforts to keep his hold on the main ridge. This stage of the battle constituted a prolonged and severe struggle for mastery between the contending armies, in which, although progress was slow and difficult, the confidence of our troops in their ability to win was never shaken. Their tenacity and determination proved more than equal to their task, and· by the first week in September they had established a fighting superiority that has left its mark on the enemy, of which possession of the ridge was merely the visible proof."

On September 13th, the British front line ran from south-west of Combles (still held by the enemy), between Leuze and Bouleaux Woods, round the east and through the north-western end of the village of Ginchy, on the enemy side of Delville Wood, through High Wood (part of which was still held by the enemy), thence west midway between Martinpuich (in enemy hands) and Pozières (in ours) and across the Albert-Bapaume road to the head of the valley south-east of Thiepval. Turning there towards the south-west, the line ran along the spur on the south-east side of the valley, and then crossed the latter to a point five or six hundred yards east of Authuille. Thence it ran north again, midway between the river Ancre and Thiepval, to Hamel, where it crossed the river. From Authuille northwards the attack had gained no ground.

When this line had been gained, Sir Douglas Haig considered that "the way was then opened for the third phase, in which our advance was pushed down the forward slopes of the ridge and further extended on both flanks until, from Morval to Thiepval, the whole plateau and a good deal of ground beyond were in our possession. Meanwhile, our gallant Allies, in addition to great successes south of the Somme, had pushed their advance, against equally determined opposition and under most difficult tactical conditions, up the long slopes on our immediate right, and were now preparing to drive the enemy from the summit of the narrow and difficult portion of the main ridge which lies between the Combles Valley and the river Tortille, a stream flowing from the north into the Somme just below Peronne.''

Such was the position when, on the night of September 8th/ 9th, the New Zealand Division was placed under the command of the XV Corps of the Fourth Army (General Sir Henry Rawlinson). Two nights later, the 3rd New Zealand (Rifle) Brigade relieved part of the 55th and 1st Divisions in the front line, between Longueval and High Wood. The trenches taken over ran from a point about six hundred yards north of the northern end of the village of Longueval, thence almost due west to a sunken road which ran down the north-eastern edge of High Wood towards Longueval; and from there the front line turned at right angles and ran up the road for about five hundred yards, eventually swinging away to the east of the road till it met another trench (called Cork Alley) which ran through High Wood. The New Zealand Division's front ended at Cork Alley, and in consequence its left boundary was a hundred and fifty yards east of the eastern corner of High Wood. On account of the presence of the enemy in the northern part of High Wood, however, the line was not held as far as Cork Alley; but a defensive flank was formed, facing the south-eastern edge of the wood, and distant from it about two thousand yards.

The 3rd Brigade remained in the line till the night of the 12th/13th, and dug a line of posts across the angular re-entrant in the line, and also made them into a continuous new front line by joining up the posts by shallow saps. On the 2nd Brigade relieving the 3rd Brigade on the night of the 12th/13th, the 2nd Auckland and 2nd Otago Battalions took over the front line. The 2nd Canterbury Battalion, seven hundred strong (including twenty officers), was with the 2nd Wellington Battalion in brigade reserve; and bivouacked in Savoy and Carlton Trenches, midway between Longueval and Bazentin-le-Grand. The remaining details of the battalion returned to the transport lines near Fricourt. On the 13th and 14th the reserve battalions completed the new front line (Otago Trench) and dug communication trenches to it.

The opening attack of the third phase of the Somme Battle took place on September 15th. On the right of the British, the French had begun an attack on the 13th, which continued until the 18th. On the British front, the whole of the Fourth Army attacked, with the I Canadian Corps of the Reserve Army (afterwards known as the Fifth Army), also attacking on its left. The objective of the Fourth Army was the enemy's third system of defences, on a front which included the villages of Morval, Les Boeufs, Gueudecourt, and Flers, and extended beyond that village to north of High Wood. The attack was preceded by three days' continuous bombardment. A detailed account of the operations of this day is unnecessary, as neither of the Canterbury Battalions took part in the fighting. The first objective, half a mile of the German switch trench,* with its left flank half a mile from High Wood, was taken by the 2nd Auckland and 2nd Otago Battalions; and the 3rd Brigade then went through, and by the end of the day had dug in north and west of Flers.

Upon the 3rd Brigade getting clear of the switch trench, the 2nd Canterbury Battalion moved forward to Otago, Fern, and Tea trenches, the front line and support trenches from which the attack had been launched. Shortly after the battalion had arrived there, large parties were detailed for carrying forward ammunition, and for work under the Engineers near Flers. The rest of the battalion was sent to complete the digging of the new switch trench, which had been sited about fifty yards in advance of the German trench; and also to dig a series of strong points on the left flank, facing High Wood. The latter works were required to protect the flank, as it was not until late in the afternoon that the wood was definitely reported cleared of the enemy.

At about 5.30 p.m., the battalion was ordered to relieve the 2nd Auckland and 2nd Otago Battalions in the switch line. At this time the company working at Flers had not returned; and

---

*A switch line is a trench connecting diagonally two parallel trenches. This particular switch connected the second and third main German defensive positions, and ran south of Flers, through High Wood to Pozières.

LIEUT.-COLONEL H. STEWART, C.M.G., D.S.O., M.C.

LIEUT.-COLONEL G. A. KING, D.S O

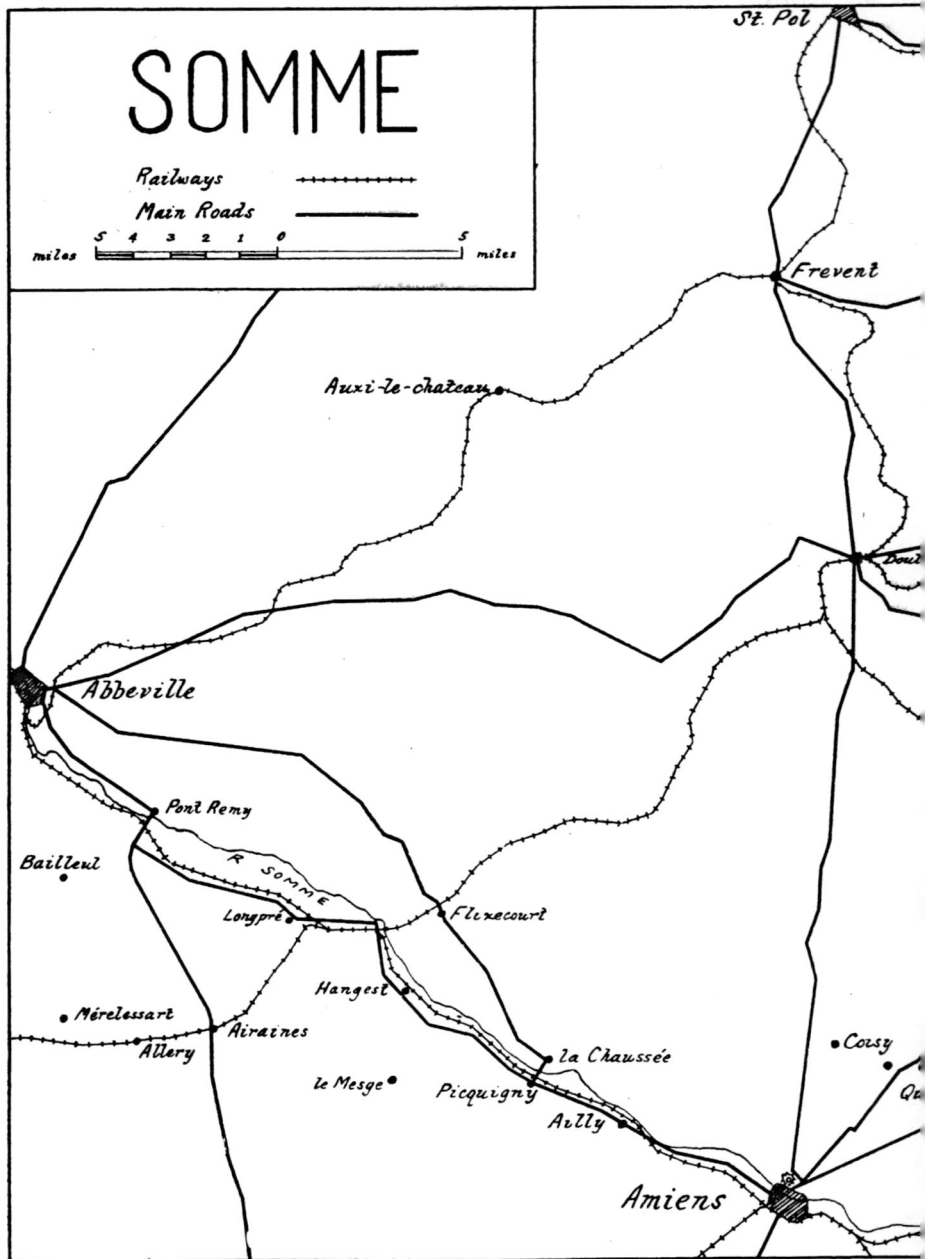

Vimy

To BÉTHUNE   To LENS   FROM LENS

To DOUAI

Arras

To DOUAI

To CAMBRAI

To CAMBRAI

Ablainzeville   Ervillers

oulers

Pas

Couin   Gommecourt   Bucquoy

Sarton   Hébuterne   Achiet-le-Grand   To CAMBRAI

Authie   Sailly-au-bois   Puisieux   Bapaume   To CAMBRAI

Colincamps   Miraumont   To PÉRONNE

Louvencourt   Gueudecourt

Mailly   Hamel   Flers

Englebelmer   Thiepval

Hédauville   Pozières   Longueval

Albert   Fricourt

Mametz   Hardecourt

Dernancourt   Méault   To PÉRONNE

Ville-sous-Corbie   R. SOMME

Cardonette   Morlancourt   Bray

Querrieu   Pont-   R. ANCRE

Noyelles   Sailly-Lorette

Corbie   Chipilly

R. SOMME

was completely out of touch with the rest of the battalion. It was therefore arranged that the Otago Battalion should be relieved; but that the Auckland Battalion, which preferred to postpone its relief rather than to be only partially relieved, should remain in the right of the switch line. The Canterbury Battalion therefore relieved the Otago Battalion at 7 p.m. on the 15th; but did not relieve the Auckland Battalion till 7 a.m. on the 16th. Besides digging a continuous trench through to the troops on the right flank, the battalion worked hard deepening the new front line. This work was done under incessant shell-fire, and the losses were heavy.

The casualties for the two days had been :—

				Officers.	Other Ranks.
15th	Killed	..	..	1*	14
	Wounded	..	..	2	35
				–	——
				3	49
				–	——
16th	Killed	..	..	–	28
	Wounded	..	..	1	91
	Missing	..	..	–	1
				–	——
				1	120

*2nd Lieutenant R. G. Hickmott.

The battalion continued to dig hard during the whole of the 17th, and was reinforced by the arrival of the details which had been left at the transport lines on the 12th. The trenches were very heavily bombarded during the day with high-explosive shells of large calibre; but the troops were now so well dug in that the casualties were light.

Meanwhile, the 1st Brigade had been in Divisional reserve, and the 1st Canterbury Battalion had on the 14th moved from Fricourt to bivouacs at Mametz Wood. During the morning of the 15th, it provided parties for carrying to the forward dumps: but in the afternoon it moved forward to Carlton Trench, and in the evening still further forward to Worcester, Seaforth, and Rifles trenches, between the two Longueval-High Wood roads, where it was in support to the 2nd Brigade. The following morning the battalion was ordered forward to the trenches north-west of Flers preparatory to making an attack on Goose Alley* in the afternoon. On arrival at Flers, however, these orders were cancelled, and the battalion relieved the 3rd Battalion of the 3rd Brigade and the 2nd Wellington Battalion in the trenches north and north-west of Flers. During the morning, the 1st Wellington Battalion had continued the advance and captured Grove Alley, from a point on the Flers-Ligny Thilloy road seven hundred yards north of Flers, to a point on the Abbey road (Flers-Eaucourt l'Abbaye) five hundred yards west of that village. It had been intended that the 1st Brigade should make a further advance to Goose Alley the same day, but the failure of the 41st Division (on the right) to gain its first objective led to the cancellation of the 1st Brigade's orders for the second attack.

The 1st Canterbury Battalion spent the afternoon of the 16th in digging a trench from the right flank of the Wellingtons to its own right flank in the work known as "Box and Cox," on the east of the Flers-Ligny Thilloy road. The battalion remained in front of Flers throughout the 17th, being shelled during the afternoon and right up to the following dawn. It was relieved on the afternoon of the 18th in Box and Cox by troops of the 41st Division, since these trenches formed part of that Division's area, but had been occupied by troops of the 3rd New Zealand (Rifle) Brigade on the 16th, as the troops of the 41st Division were not then far enough advanced to occupy them. On the night of September 18th/19th the 2nd Brigade took over the front line, and shortly after midnight the 2nd Wellington Battalion relieved the 1st Canterbury Battalion, which then moved back to Savoy Trench.

Early on the night of September 18th/19th the 2nd Battalion relieved part of the 1st Auckland Battalion in the Flers Line and Flers Support trench, west of Flers village, and with its left extending almost as far to the north-west as Grove Alley. The following day orders were received for a minor operation to be undertaken by the battalion against a German communication trench called Goose Alley, which ran roughly parallel to and from two hundred and fifty to three hundred and fifty yards

---

*For position of this trench, see below.

east of the High Wood-Le Barque road. The southern part of
this trench, after it had crossed the Flers Line, was called Drop
Alley, since it ended in a strong-point called the Cough Drop.
The portion of the trench which the battalion was ordered to
take extended for about two hundred and fifty yards to the
north-east of Flers Support, for a hundred yards between Flers
Support and Flers Line, and for three hundred yards to the
south-west of Flers Line. The 1st Battalion of the Black Watch
(1st Brigade of 1st Division), which held the Cough Drop, was
ordered to co-operate with our troops by making a bombing
attack up Drop Alley.

On September 19th, the 47th Division had been ordered to
take the Flers Line as far as its junction with Goose Alley, and
to hand it over to the New Zealand Division; but the attack had
not been a success. The 2nd Auckland Battalion, however, by
the night of the 20th/21st, was in occupation of the Flers Line
up to within two hundred yards of Goose Alley.

About half a mile to the north-west of Flers, the Abbey Road
was crossed by the North road, which continued on towards
Longueval, but forked into two branches before crossing the
Flers Line. About 8 p.m. on September 20th, the 1st, 2nd, and
13th Companies of the 2nd Canterbury Battalion, which had
been detailed for the assault, left their trenches and formed up
on the two branches of the North Road. At 8.30 p.m. they advanced to the attack without any barrage. Under cover of the
darkness, they crept up to within fifty yards of Goose Alley
before they were detected. The enemy then immediately opened
heavy machine-gun and rifle fire; but in spite of heavy casualties
our men rushed the trench, cleared it of the enemy, and established blocks beyond it in both Flers Trench and Flers Support,
and also on the north-east of the captured junction of Goose
Alley. On their left flank they were joined by bombing parties
of the Black Watch, who had worked their way up Drop Alley.
Punctually at 8.45 p.m., our artillery placed a box barrage round
the captured positions, in accordance with the arrangements that
had been made. Twenty prisoners and four machine-guns were
taken by the battalion.

In spite of the barrage, at 10 p.m. the enemy launched a
determined counter-attack down all the trenches leading to the

position. Armed with the new light "egg" bomb, his bombers outranged ours; and the Black Watch bombing parties, which had not been reinforced, were driven back down Drop Alley. At the same time, the Canterbury men were pushed from the blocks they had established, and a party of the enemy penetrated into Flers Trench, in the rear of our left flank. Two platoons of the 12th Company were sent up to support the line; but owing to the darkness, and the confused hand-to-hand fighting, they could do very little to help, and soon became mixed up in the general melee. The enemy had now encircled both flanks, and there was grave danger of the battalion being cut off.

At this juncture Captain F. Starnes arrived with the remaining platoons of the 12th Company. Finding men of all companies mixed together, and in many cases without leaders, he organized small parties and set them to clear the enemy out of definite areas. Captain Starnes personally led party after party, and after some very desperate fighting he at length cleared the trench from our original right flank to the northern end of Drop Alley. He then led attacks on Drop Alley, till by 4 a.m. the whole of it was in our hands, and he was able to hand it over to the Black Watch.

There was no rest for the garrison, however, as much hard digging was required to fit the position for defence. Nor was the enemy content to leave the trench in our hands; for at 5.30 p.m. on the 21st he made a most determined counter-attack. Altogether about two hundred of his men worked up Goose Alley on the right flank, and up Flers Support and Flers Trench in the centre and on the left. The enemy bombers were well organized. bold and expert, and were much fresher than our men, who had been fighting all night and digging all day. The attack penetrated our line in several places; but the rest of the line stood firm, in spite of heavy fighting. Finally, led again by Captain Starnes, our men got out of the trenches, and from the open bombed the enemy parties which were still holding out in our trenches. Taking advantage of the confusion caused by this unexpected attack, our men charged with the bayonet, and cleared the trenches. During the fighting, a party from the 2nd Auckland Battalion, led by a private, without orders came overland from the North road to assist our right flank.

Besides the captures mentioned above, the battalion had counted three hundred enemy dead in and about Goose Alley in the morning; and at a very moderate estimate it had killed another hundred in repulsing the counter-attack on the evening of the 21st. For his gallantry in the operations, Captain Starnes was recommended for the V.C., and received the "immediate award" of the D.S.O. The cost to the battalion had been very heavy. Out of eighteen officers and five hundred and twenty-three other ranks engaged, the casualties were:—

	Officers.	Other Ranks.
Killed	8*	32
Wounded	4	156
Missing	—	49
	12	237

*Captain D. P. Fraser, Lieutenants A. J. W. Birdling, W. J. Marriott, 2nd Lieutenants R. H. Kember (M.M.), F. G. McKee, H. F. J. Monson, N. C. Swinard, and H. Gowdy.

Any comment that the writer of this record might make would be impertinent beside the following unique telegrams of congratulation, sent as an acknowledgement of the 2nd Battalion's fine achievement::—

FROM THE III CORPS COMMANDER:

"The Lieutenant-General Commanding III Corps has requested the Corps Commander to convey to the New Zealand Division his appreciation of the good work done by them on the right of the III Corps, and of the assistance rendered by them to the III Corps during the last few days."

FROM THE FOURTH ARMY COMMANDER:

"Please congratulate the New Zealand Division from me on their excellent work in Flers Line and Drop Alley. They deserve every credit for their gallantry and perseverance."

FROM THE XV CORPS COMMANDER:

"The Corps Commander congratulates Major-General A. H. Russell and the New Zealand Division on the success gained last night (20th/21st inst.) by the 2nd Battalion Canterbury Regiment. The repeated attacks, renewed and delivered with such energy and determination speak highly of the fine fighting qualities displayed by all ranks. The Corps Commander particularly desires to express to Lieutenant-Colonel Stewart his high appreciation of the sound conception of the plan, and to Captain Starnes his admiration of his gallant and courageous leading."

On the night of September 21st/22nd the 2nd Canterbury Battalion was relieved by the 1st Battalion Munster Fusiliers, and went back to trenches just north of the Longueval-Bazantin le Grand road, with headquarters at Thistle Dump. The weather was wet, but there was little rest, as working parties had to be supplied to repair the roads. In the period during which the battalion was at Thistle Dump (September 22nd to 28th) it received from the base reinforcements of five officers and ninety-four other ranks.

The 1st Brigade remained in Divisional reserve till the evening of September 24th, and during this period the 1st Canterbury Battalion, in Savoy Trench, received one hundred and thirty reinforcements from the base. On the night of the 24th/25th, the Brigade relieved the 3rd (Rifle) Brigade in the front line, with orders to take part in the Fourth Army's attack the following day. The Army objectives, from right to left, were the villages of Morval, Les Boeufs and Gueudecourt, and from the north-west of Gueudecourt a line running through the junction of the Flers-Ligny Thilloy and Gueudecourt-Eaucourt l' Abbaye roads (Factory Corner) along a spur, which ran in a north-easterly direction between Flers and Eaucourt l'Abbaye, to the junction of the High Wood-Le Barque road with the Flers Line. From here the line of the objectives ran generally west across the forward spurs of the high ground to Courcelette, where the Fourth Army joined the Reserve (or Fifth) Army. The task allotted to the XV Corps was the capture of these objectives from Gueudecourt (inclusive) to the junction of the Flers Line with the High Wood-Le Barque road; and the New

Zealand Division's objectives extended from Factory Corner (inclusive) to the left flank of the Corps.

The 1st Brigade was ordered to capture the Division's objectives, the 3rd Brigade being in support and the 2nd Brigade in reserve. The attack was divided into two stages, during the first of which the three leading battalions, the 1st Canterbury (on the right), the 1st Auckland (in the centre), and the 1st Otago (on the left), were to capture Factory Corner and the general line of the North Road (leading from Factory Corner and west of Flers to Longueval) as far as Flers Support. During the second stage the 1st Otago Battalion was to capture Abbey road* as far to the north-west as its junction with Goose Alley, and also the uncaptured portion of Goose Alley south-west of Abbey road. On the completion of the two stages, a line of outposts was to be established on the high ground between Factory Corner and the junction of Goose Alley and Abbey road, and between the latter point and the junction of the High Wood-Le Barque road and Flers Trench. These posts, situated as they were on the Corps' final objective, were to be connected during the night into a continuous front line.

The 1st Canterbury Battalion assembled with its first line for the attack in Grove Alley, to the left of the Flers-Ligny Thilloy road, and its second line in a trench about two hundred yards to the rear. The weather was now fine. The attack was preceded by a bombardment which began on September 24th; but, unlike previous bombardments, it was not increased in intensity immediately before the attack. The 1st Light Trench Mortar Battery assisted in the preliminary bombardment by shelling the enemy strong-point at the junction of Grove Alley and the Flers-Ligny Thilloy road, inflicting heavy casualties and putting out of action two enemy machine-guns. . These guns were captured by the 1st Canterbury Battalion during the advance, and used later against the enemy.

The attack was launched at 12.35 p.m. on September 25th, under cover of a strong creeping barrage. The Canterbury Battalion met with slight opposition from the sunken road on its right flank; but the majority of those of the enemy who had escaped the barrage did not wait for the bayonet. By 1.5 p.m. the

*See page 114.

battalion had captured all its objectives, with only slight casualties; and it then began to dig in on the reverse slope, a little way beyond the objectives, with a covering line of troops out in front. Though the 55th Division, on the right, had got well forward, it had lost direction, and its left flank was five hundred yards from Factory Corner, instead of resting on it as it should have done. The Canterbury Battalion therefore protected its own right flank by establishing two strong-points—one inside the fork of the roads leading from Factory Corner to Gueudecourt and to Ligny-Thilloy, and the other in Grove Alley to the southeast of the Corner.

The rest of the 1st Brigade also gained their objectives; and the night of the 25th and the whole of the next day were spent in consolidating the new line. Patrols were sent forward after dark on the 26th to examine the wire in front of Gird Trench: that in front of the Canterbury Battalion was found to be destroyed, but the Auckland patrols reported that the wire on their front was practically intact. During the same night, the Canterbury Battalion handed over the strong-points on its right flank to troops of the Royal Irish Rifles (55th Division).

The village of Gueudecourt, which had held out against the attacks of September 25th, was captured by the 21st Division on the following day. This prepared the way for an advance by the remainder of the XV Corps against the German main fourth defensive line, which ran north-west from Gueudecourt and crossed the Albert-Bapaume road between Le Sars and Warlencourt-Eaucourt. The line consisted of two trenches, called in this locality Gird Line and Gird Support, and was protected by a thick belt of wire.

The 55th and New Zealand Divisions were ordered to capture this line from west of Gueudecourt to its junction with the right fork of Goose Alley, about a quarter of a mile east of the High Wood-Le Barque road. The boundary between the two Divisions was the Flers-Ligny Thilloy road, which was inclusive to the 55th Division. The 1st Brigade was again detailed to perform the task of the New Zealand Division, and the Canterbury, Auckland, and Otago Battalions were ordered to attack, in the same relative positions as before. The 1st Canterbury Battalion's objectives were Gird Trench and Gird Support, between the two

Iles
Miraumont
Warlencourt
Eaucourt
Pys
Le Sars
Auchonvillers
Beaucourt
Beaumont-
Hamel
Grandcourt
St. Pierre-
Divion
Courcelette
Hamel
Thiepval
Martinpuich
Mesnil
AVELUY
WOOD
Authuille
Pozières
Ovillers
Bazentin-
le-Petit
Aveluy
Contalmaison
Bazentin-
le-Grand
Le
MAMETZ
WOOD
Bécourt
Montauban
ALBERT
Fricourt
Mametz
FROM AMIENS
Méaulte
ANCRE RIVER
Maricourt
FROM AMIENS
TO BRAY

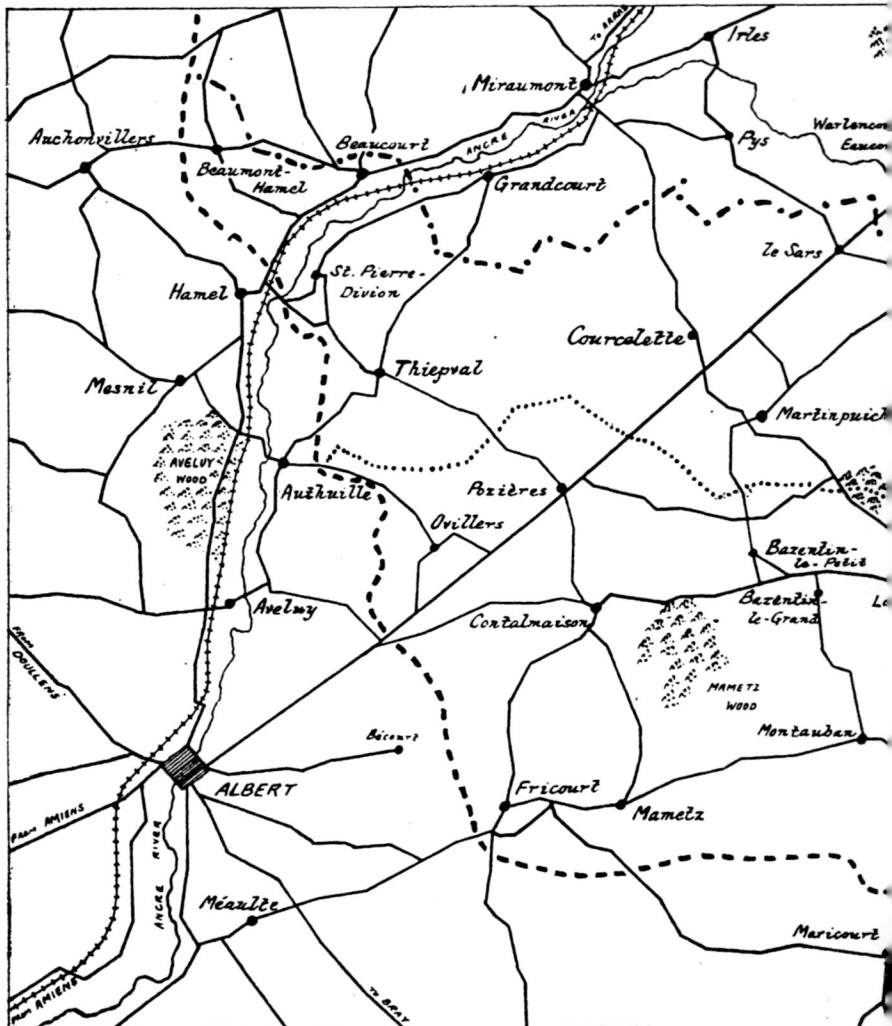

SOMME BATTLEFIELD, 1916

British Line before 1st July   - - - - - -
"   "   13th September   ....
"   "   30th November   -·-·-·-·-
Railways ——— Roads ——— Canals ═══

1 3/4 1/2 1/4 0   1   2   (MILES) 3

Suzanne

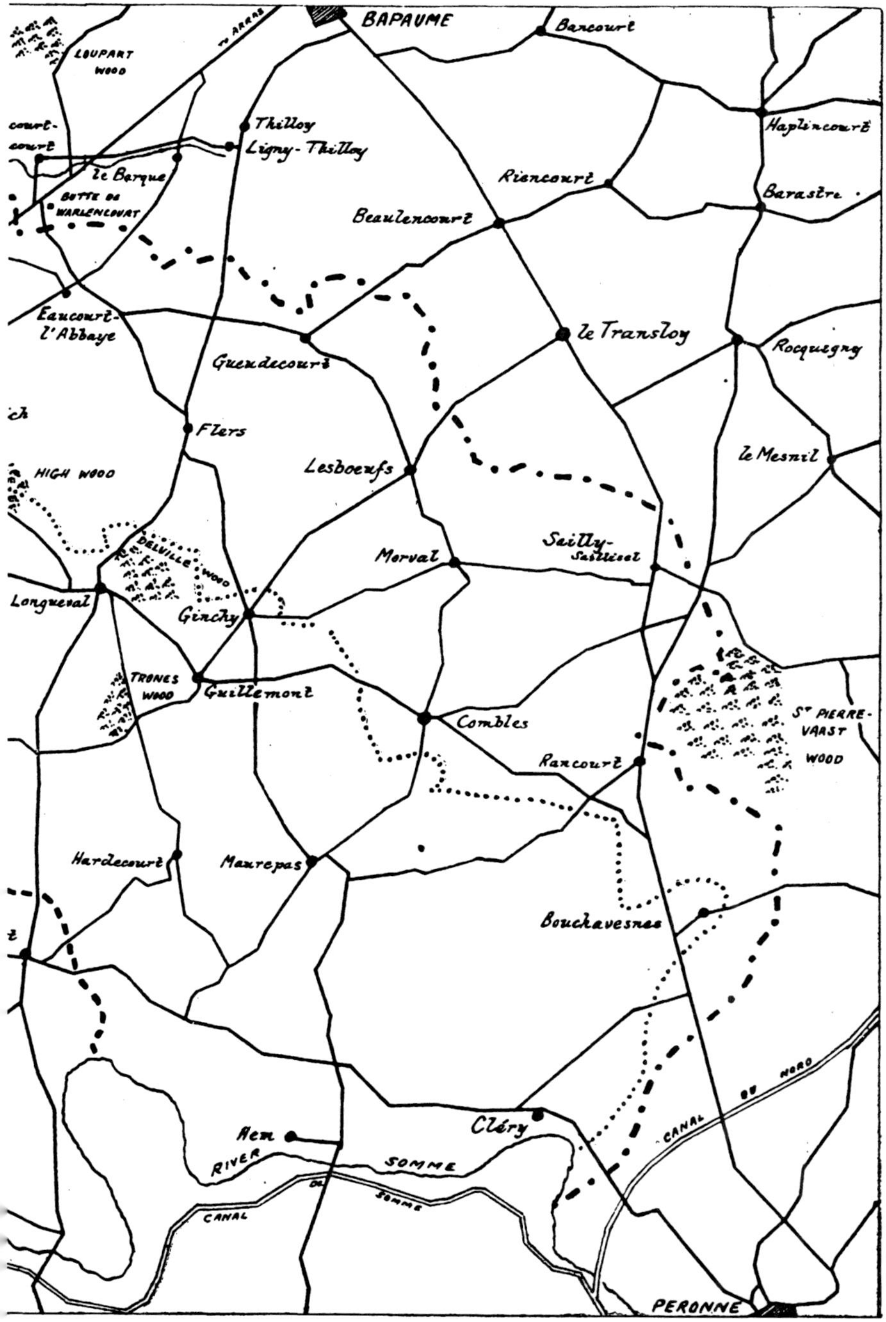

BAPAUME
Bancourt
to ARRAS
LOUPART WOOD
Thilloy
Ligny-Thilloy
Le Barque
BUTTE DE WARLENCOURT
Haplincourt
Riencourt
Barastre
Beaulencourt
Eaucourt-l'Abbaye
Gueudecourt
Le Transloy
Rocquigny
Flers
Le Mesnil
Lesboeufs
HIGH WOOD
DELVILLE WOOD
Morval
Sailly-Saillisel
Longueval
Ginchy
TRONES WOOD
Guillemont
Combles
ST PIERRE-VAAST WOOD
Rancourt
Hardecourt
Maurepas
Bouchavesnes
Hem
Cléry
RIVER SOMME
CANAL DE SOMME
CANAL DU NORD
PERONNE

roads which led up to Ligny-Thilloy from the Gueudecourt-Eau-court l' Abbaye road, one on the east and the other on the west of Factory Corner. The western road was inclusive to the bat- talion. On the brigade's left flank, the 1st Otago Battalion had to take Goose Alley, from where that trench crossed the Abbey Road to its junction with Gird Support, and to form a defensive flank along Goose Alley, facing west. The 1st Auck- land Battalion's task was the capture of the Gird Line and Support, between the inner flanks of the Canterbury and Otago Battalions.

The attack was preceded by an artillery bombardment, and was made under a creeping barrage. At 2.15 p.m. (on the 27th) the 1st Canterbury Battalion advanced behind the barrage, with the 12th and 13th Companies in the first wave and the 1st and 2nd Companies in the second wave. The right company overran the objective, but was withdrawn later to its proper position. On the left, the attacking company was held up for a short while by bombers and machine-guns; but the latter were silenced by our Lewis gunners, and all the objectives of the battalion were captured by 2.38 p.m., with slight casualties. The right flank was in touch with the 55th Division, which had taken its objectives.

On the left, however, the rest of the 1st Brigade did not have so easy a task as the Canterbury Battalion. The Auckland Bat- talion was held up by the wire, the existence of which it had reported the previous day, but which had not been cut; but it finally gained its objective. Three companies of the Otago Battalion came under a very heavy artillery and machine-gun barrage while advancing, suffered very severe casualties, and were unable to capture their objectives. The remaining com- pany captured Goose Alley to a distance of six hundred yards north of Abbey Road, and with the help of a company of the reserve battalion built strong-points there. It was not till the 28th, however, that the front line was joined up with the left flank by a company of the reserve battalion.

During the interval, several unsuccessful attempts had been made to capture the junction of Gird Trench and Gird Support with Goose Alley; but the ground at this point formed a saucer- shaped depression, a hundred feet deep and a hundred yards across, but open on the north-east, which was not shown on the map, and which rendered the trenches in it untenable without the possession of the high ground beyond them. A new trench was therefore dug round the south-east rim of the saucer. joining the Auckland Battalion's left, in Gird Trench and Gird Support, with the Otago-Wellington Battalions' right in Goose Alley. This trench denied to the enemy the trench junction which our troops had found untenable.

The 1st Canterbury Battalion consolidated its new position unmolested, and remained there till the night of September 28th/29th, when the 2nd Brigade relieved the 1st Brigade. On relief by the 2nd Wellington Battalion at 1 a.m., the 1st Canterbury Battalion moved back to Savoy Trench — the 1st Brigade being now in Divisional reserve. There the battalion remained till the night of October 2nd, supplying working parties for road repairs; and then it relieved the 1st Battalion of the 3rd (Rifle) Brigade in trenches south-west of Flers (the "Brown Line"), on the 1st Brigade relieving the 3rd Brigade in Divisional support. The battalion was not called on to move again from its trenches, and on the relief of the Division by the 41st Division on the night of the 3rd/4th, handed over to the 32nd Battalion Royal Fusiliers and marched back to bivouacs at Pommiers Redoubt.

The 2nd Canterbury Battalion had gone into the line on the night of September 28th/29th, and being the reserve battalion of the brigade, had occupied Grove Alley. Orders were issued on September 29th for the capture of Eaucourt l'Abbaye by the 47th Division (III Corps), on the New Zealand Division's left flank; and the New Zealand Division was ordered to co-operate, by establishing a line from its westernmost positions in Gird Trench to a German strong-point, known as "the Circus" by reason of its circular shape, about five hundred yards north-east of Eaucourt l'Abbaye. After passing Goose Alley, the Gird Line swung away to the north-west, so that the New Zealand Division's objectives included a small portion only of this line, and consisted mainly of a general line running due west from the junction of Goose Alley and Gird Support to the German strong-point near Eaucourt l'Abbaye mentioned above.

The 2nd Brigade, being ordered to take the New Zealand Division's objectives, divided the front into two at the High Wood-Le Barque road, and allotted the right portion to the 2nd Canterbury Battalion and the left portion to the 2nd Otago Battalion, with the 2nd Wellington Battalion in support of Otago. On the right of the 2nd Canterbury Battalion, the 2nd Auckland Battalion was ordered to hold the remainder of the front line, but was not to make any advance. The 2nd and 3rd Battalions of the 3rd (Rifle) Brigade were attached to the 2nd Brigade and were held in reserve.

The objectives assigned to the 2nd Canterbury Battalion included the deep depression at the junction of Goose Alley and Gird Trench, and the strong positions on the high ground to the north and west of the hollow. In places, the steep banks on the enemy side of the hollow in themselves were a formidable obstacle; and beyond them the enemy held his trenches in great strength. The battalion was not asked to do more than obtain a secure footing on the north of the hollow; for here Gird Support began to run in a north-westerly direction. The battalion's objective therefore followed the line of Goose Alley across to Gird Trench, and then followed the line of Gird Trench towards the west for some two hundred yards. Here Gird Trench also turned towards the north-west; but a new trench, which the enemy had hastily dug within the last few days, ran from Gird Trench in a south-westerly direction for about two hundred yards, then turned west and crossed the High Wood-Le Barque road, and finally swept north-west again to the Circus. The brigade objective followed this trench, which had been christened "Circus Trench," but the 2nd Canterbury Battalion's objective stopped on the western side of the High Wood-Le Barque road.

Three companies made the battalion attack—the 12th, 2nd, and 1st Companies — while the 13th Company was held in reserve. The objectives of the assaulting companies were:—

12th Company: Gird Support from the westernmost part already in our hands to its junction with Goose Alley; and Goose Alley to its junction with Gird Trench (inclusive); together with the ground beyond the trench-objectives as far as the crest of the high ground behind the trenches.

2nd Company: Gird Trench from Goose Alley (exclusive) to its junction with Circus Trench (inclusive), together with the high ground beyond.

1st Company: Circus Trench from Gird Trench (exclusive) to the High Wood-Le Barque road (inclusive).

Besides the 13th Company, two other reserve companies, the 15th and 16th Companies of the 2nd Auckland Battalion, were placed at the disposal of Lieutenant-Colonel Stewart.

The assaulting companies assembled in the new trenches on the south-east edge of the hollow, in Gird Trench and in Goose Alley. At 3.15 p.m. on October 1st they advanced under a creeping barrage, and at the same time a special detachment of Royal Engineers discharged oil drums from trench-mortars in the front line trenches. These fell short on the left, but reached the enemy trenches on the right; and besides causing numerous casualties had a great moral effect. In spite of this, however, the 12th Company and the right half of the 2nd Company met some rifle and machine-gun fire as they left the trenches; and while they waited in the hollow for the barrage to lift off the enemy's positions, they were heavily bombed by the garrison. Owing to the inaccuracy of the aim of the bombers, however, few casualties were caused by the bombs; and on the barrage lifting the assaulting troops charged the trenches. The remaining company and a half did not have the advantage of dead ground, and suffered severe casualties from machine-gun fire from their right and front. They reached their objectives; but, probably owing to their losses, they did not cover their whole front, and left a considerable gap between their left flank and the 2nd Otago Battalion.

Consolidation was begun at once—on the right at the top of the high ground, and on the left along Circus Trench. Within half an hour of the opening of the attack, the reserve company had been sent forward to reinforce the attacking companies: two platoons were sent to the junction of Goose Alley and Gird Trench, one platoon to the right of the 1st Company, and one platoon to the extreme left. The 16th Company of the 2nd Auckland Battalion was also sent to the junction of the centre and left companies, at about 4 p.m. Early in the evening a platoon of the 15th Company of the same battalion was used to strengthen the left flank.

During the night, at about 11 p.m., a bombing attack developed down the enemy trenches leading to the junction of Gird and Circus Trenches, but it was not pressed with any determination. However. the 3rd and 5th Companies of the 2nd Auckland Battalion, which had been sent up to support the 2nd Canterbury Battalion during the night, were at 1 a.m. on the 2nd put into the line, and into the trenches in rear of the line at this point. The 2nd Otago and 2nd Wellington Battalions on the left had over-run their objectives, but were brought back to their proper positions.

The morning of October 2nd found the companies of the 2nd Canterbury Battalion very much mixed up; so at 8 a.m. a reorganization was ordered. The front line was thereafter held in the following order from right to left: — 12th Company, 3rd (Auckland) Company, 13th Company, 2nd Company, 1st Company. with 16th (Waikato) Company in support. No enemy counter-attacks were made during day; and during the night of October 3rd/4th the battalion was relieved by the 4th Battalion of the 3rd (Rifle) Brigade. Owing to the heavy state of the ground. the relieving battalion was nine hours late, and the relief was therefore not complete till 5.30 a.m. on the 4th.

The 2nd Canterbury Battalion on relief moved back to Fricourt: the tracks were exceedingly muddy, and the men, who had been tired out before the last attack, were practically exhausted. Here the battalion spent three days, resting and re-equipping itself from the salvage that abounded on the battlefield. Its losses in the last attack had been severe, being:—

				Officers.	Other Ranks.
Killed	..	..	..	7*	26
Wounded	..	..	..	5	111
Missing	..	..	..	—	24
				12	161

*Captain H. S. Harley (M.C.), Lieutenant H. B. Riley, 2nd Lieutenants R. H. Allen, J. M. Donn. F. C. R. Upton (M.C.), W. F. Watt. and J. D. Bowden (Died of Wounds 10th October).

The strength of the battalion engaged in this attack (including forty-nine other ranks who arrived on the 1st), had been nineteen officers and four hundred and eighty-seven other ranks.

The losses inflicted on the enemy, however, were much greater than ours; for, in addition to fifty prisoners (including a battalion commander and several other officers) and four machine-guns, the enemy lost in dead, counted in the captured positions. at least three hundred. Besides these, many more were killed by fire from our rifles, Lewis guns, and machine-guns. while attempting to retire over the open. One alone of the machine-gun sections attached to the battalion claims to have destroyed to a man two retreating parties, one of about fifty and the other of about forty.

This was the last attack in the battle in which the New Zealand infantry took part. The Division had been in the battle area for twenty-three days, and had taken part in every attack made during that period. Its total casualties had been six thousand seven hundred and twenty-eight, of whom one thousand and eighty-seven had been killed. The 2nd Canterbury Battalion had lost more heavily than any other battalion in the Division, the casualties of the two Canterbury Battalions being:—

1st Battalion.				Officers.	Other Ranks.
Killed	..	..	..	—	69
Wounded	..	..	..	11	364
Missing	..	..	..	—	42
				11	475

2nd Battalion.				Officers.	Other Ranks.
Killed	...	..	..	16	109
Wounded	..	..	..	16	531
Missing	..	..	..	1	73
				33	713

Total casualties for the two battalions (out of twelve infantry battalions. one pioneer battalion, artillery, engineers, etc.. engaged)—1.132.

On October 5th the General Officer Commanding the Division received the following message from General Headquarters:—

"A copy of a telegram sent to-day from the Commander-in-Chief to the New Zealand Government is forwarded herewith for your information and communication to the Division. The Commander-in-Chief desires to add his warm congratulations to the Division on the splendid record they have achieved. Message:—'The New Zealand Division has fought with greatest gallantry in the Somme Battle for twenty-three consecutive days, carrying out with complete success every task set, and always doing even more than was asked of it. The Division has won universal confidence and admiration. No praise can be too high for such troops.'"

CHAPTER VIII.

TRENCH WARFARE AFTER THE SOMME; AND PREPARATIONS FOR MESSINES.

The New Zealand Division (less artillery) was now in Corps Reserve, and was under orders to be transferred to the II Anzac Army Corps (Second Army). The 1st Canterbury Battalion accordingly left the Pommiers Redoubt at 6 a.m. on October 7th, marched to Albert, and entrained there for Longpré, where it arrived at 6 a.m. on the 8th and went into billets. After three days spent in reorganizing and training, the battalion entrained again at noon on the 11th, and arrived at Caestre (near Haze-brouck) in the early hours of the morning of the 12th. There motor-lorries were waiting to carry the troops to Estaires, on the Lys, and they reached their billets at 3 a.m. the same day.

The 2nd Battalion left Fricourt at 10.15 a.m. on October 6th and marched by way of Méaulte to Dernancourt, where it en-trained, and arrived at Longpré about 6.30 p.m. After a long and trying march the battalion reached its billets at Bailleul (Somme) late that night. The four following days were spent in reorganization and training; and at 1 a.m. on the 11th the battalion marched to Pont Remy where it entrained for Bailleul (Flanders). Arriving there at 7.30 p.m. the battalion marched to its billets in Strazeele, on the Hazebrouck road.

The 2nd Brigade was now attached for tactical purposes to a body called Franks' Force. This force had been formed as a stop-gap, to hold the portion of the line which had been held by the New Zealand Division before its departure for the Somme. While the New Zealand Division was taking part in the battle, the 51st Division, which had relieved the New Zealand Division at Armentières in August, had been sent back to the Somme; and there being no Division available to take its place, Franks' Force had been organized. It consisted of two brigades only, under the command of Major-General G. McK. Franks, and at

LIEUT.-COLONEL O. MEAD, D.S.O.

LIEUT.-COLONEL R. A. ROW, D.S.O.

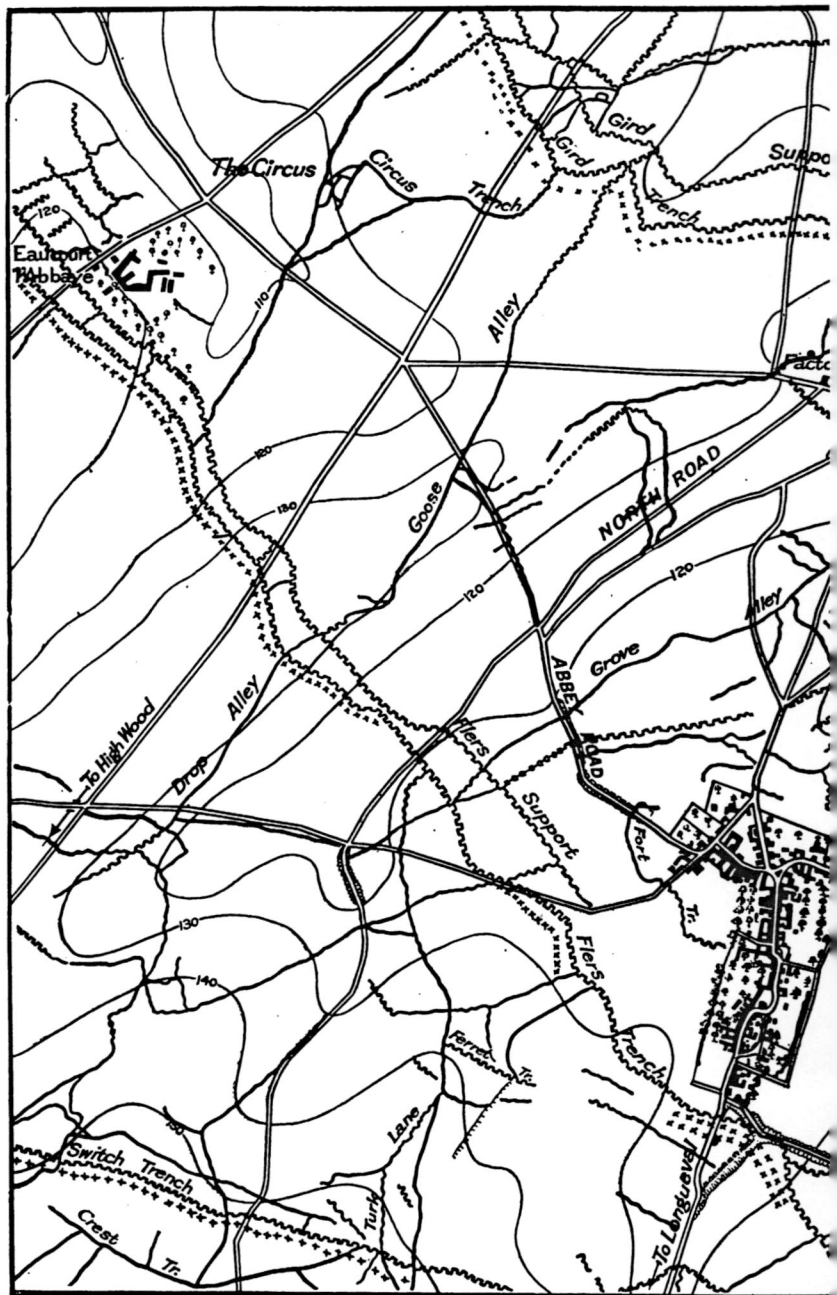

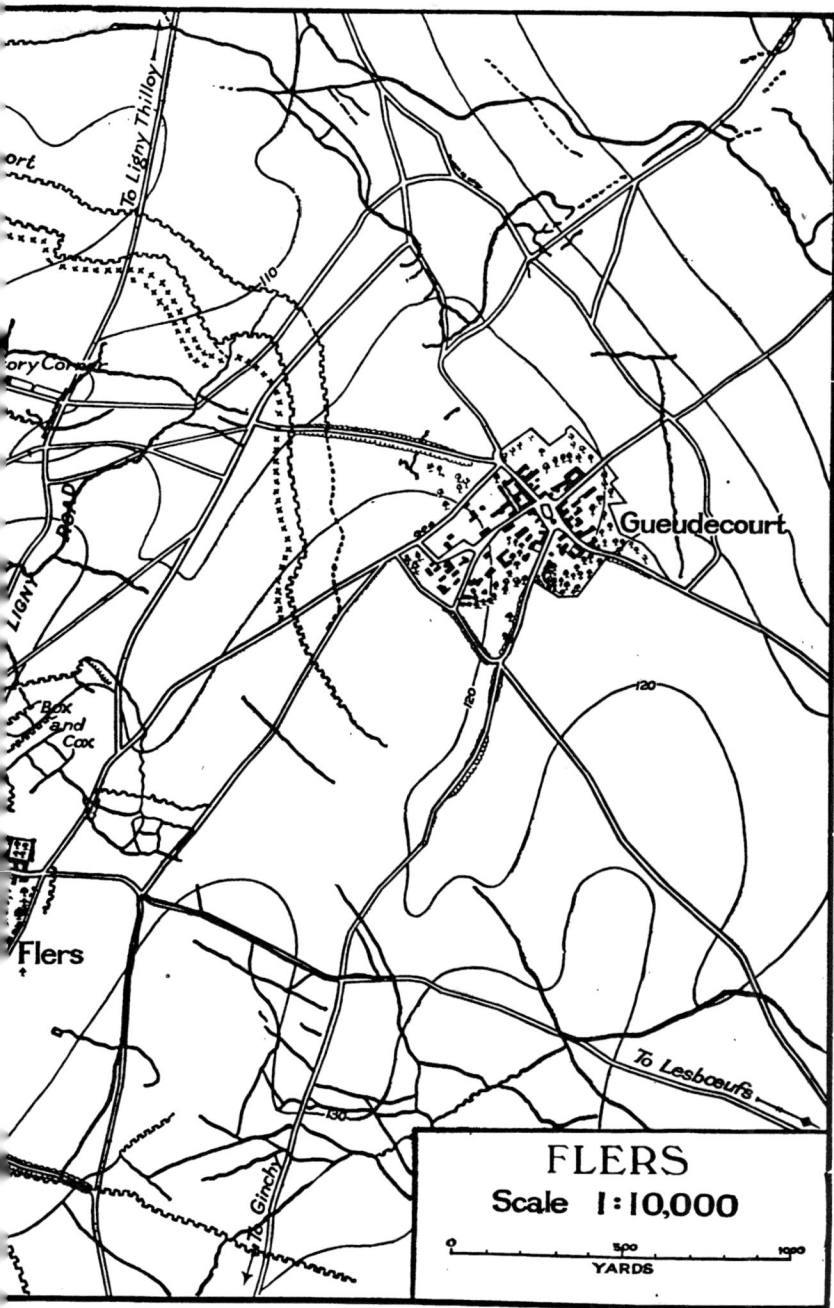

To Ligny Thilloy

To Ligny

ort

ory Corner

110

Gueudecourt

Box
and
Cox

120

120

120

Flers

130

To Lesbœufs

To Ginchy

FLERS

Scale 1:10,000

0   500   1000

YARDS

the beginning of October the two brigades were the 8th Brigade of the 4th Australian Division and the 103rd Brigade of the 34th Division.

The New Zealand Division (reduced by the detachment from it of the 2nd Brigade and the whole of its artillery) was ordered to relieve the 5th Australian Division, which was holding the Sailly Sector. The front line in this sector extended from a point half a mile due east of Picantin, on the Fleurbaix-Neuve Chapelle road to a point on the Bois Grenier-Radinghem road, about a mile south-east of the former village, and was divided into two sub-sectors, the right (or southern) being called Cordonnerie and the left (or northern) Boutillerie.

The country here was low-lying, and very much like that in the Armentières sector; and the defences consisted of breast-works instead of trenches. Only the fire-bays were protected at the back by a parados; at the back of these there ran, in place of the usual travel-trench, a duck-board track, which was protected against fire from in front by the breast-work, but had no protection against shells bursting behind the track. Behind the front line ran a line known, on account of its distance from the former, as the "seventy yards line." This was also a continuous line, but was out of repair, and was not garrisoned. Behind it again was the support line — a series of small posts connected by a continuous breast-work, which could be defended if need be. Further back the ground was rather higher, and the subsidiary line consisted of a trench, which connected a series of defended localities.

The brigades holding the sub-sectors were responsible for the defence of the above lines; but behind them were two other systems of trenches, called General Headquarters lines, for the defence of which the troops in the rear were responsible. The front and support lines were held on the outpost system, with the garrison reduced to a minimum; for the enemy's front line was an average distance of a quarter of a mile away, and it was discovered that it was occupied only at night. The bulk of the garrison was kept in the support and subsidiary lines, whence it could be moved up to hold the front line if an attack were made by the enemy.

K

The New Zealand Division relieved the 5th Australian Division by daylight on October 14th, when the 1st Brigade took over the Cordonnerie sector from the 15th Australian Brigade. The flanking divisions to the New Zealand Division were the 56th, on the right, and the 34th, on the left. The 1st Canterbury Battalion relieved the 60th Battalion Australian Imperial Force in the front line, on the right half of the brigade subsector (a frontage of about one mile), with three companies in the line, each with two platoons in the front trenches and two platoons in support, and one company in reserve. The sector was a very quiet one. After the first tour of eleven days in the line, the battalion settled down to regular reliefs of eight days in the line and eight days in billets in the Rue des Fiefs. a road running south-east from the village of Sailly. Reinforcements arrived steadily, and both the battalions rapidly came up to strength again.

Nothing of importance took place before the end of the year, except a raid on November 21st by Lieutenant E. H. Bernau and fifty other ranks of the 1st Canterbury Battalion, with six sappers from the 1st Field Company, New Zealand Engineers. The point selected for the attack was opposite the Cordonnerie salient, on the battalion's extreme left flank, and the raiding party was ordered to work fifty yards out towards each flank, from the point at which they entered the enemy trench. The objects of the raid were the usual ones, indentification of the enemy unit opposed to us being the chief aim. A feature of the raid was the part played by the light trench mortars (3-inch Stokes) ; these bombarded the objective of the raiders, and also cut the wire in front of it, while the artillery confined its fire to the neighbouring trenches.

The party had no difficulty in entering the enemy's trenches, in which it found no sign of recent occupation except a pair of feet protruding from under a fall of earth. Here was a concrete wall nine feet high, which, the sappers thought, probably concealed a mine shaft, and which they destroyed. The raiders then worked down two communication trenches without meeting any opposition, and returned to their own trenches eight minutes after entering the enemy's line. During the whole raid there was no enemy small-arms fire at all, and the only enemy retaliation took the form of light shelling of our rear area. These facts, and the experiences of the raiding party in the enemy trenches, gave full confirmation of the theory that the enemy had practically vacated his front line. The only casualties to the party were caused by a light trench mortar bomb, which fell short just as the attackers were reaching their objective, and wounded Lieutenant Bernau and twelve other ranks.

As part of the same operation, but later in the night, a patrol from the same battalion, under Lieutenant A. G. Dean, entered the enemy trenches at a point further to the west, and found the line here unoccupied also. From the observations of this patrol, it seemed likely that the enemy front trenches were patrolled regularly by single men, who discharged flares at intervals.

The experiences of the 2nd Brigade during the same period proved to be even less eventful. This brigade had on October 13th and 14th relieved the 8th Australian Brigade, which had then ceased to be attached to Franks' Force, and had returned to the 4th Australian Division. The sector was the identical one which the Brigade had held before it went to the Somme.

The 2nd Canterbury Battalion, which had been carried as far as Armentières in motor-lorries, took over part of the subsidiary line on the 14th, and remained there till the 20th, when it relieved the 2nd Auckland Battalion in the right half of the brigade sector. The battalion front was held by three companies in the front and support lines and one in reserve: every six days it changed places with the 2nd Auckland Battalion, and when out of the line was accommodated in billets in Houplines, and in the factory near "Barbed-wire Square" in Armentières itself.

The sector was now a fairly quiet one; however, there was a great deal of work which called for urgent attention, for apparently the troops who had held the line since the brigade left it for the Somme had made little attempt to keep the trenches in good order. When out of the line, the troops who were not required for working-parties spent their time in drill and training.

On October 31st the Prime Minister of New Zealand (the Honourable Mr. W. F. Massey) and Sir J. G. Ward, accompanied by Lieutenant-General Sir A. J. Godley, commanding the II Anzac Army Corps, visited the New Zealand Division, and inspected the 1st Canterbury Battalion at 11 a.m. and the 2nd Battalion at 12.15 p.m.

The 3rd Australian Division arrived in France during November, and was to be given its first experience in the line in the sector held by Franks' Force. On November 29th and 30th half of the 37th Battalion of the 10th Australian Brigade relieved half of the 2nd Canterbury Battalion in the line, and the troops on relief moved to billets in Armentières. The relief was completed on December 1st, but the Commanding Officer and a number of officers and specialists remained for a few hours to advise the new garrison on the peculiarities of the new sector. The whole of the battalion assembled in Armentières and marched to Estaires the same day.

The 2nd Brigade now ceased to be attached to Franks' Force, and coming again under the orders of the General Officer commanding the New Zealand Division, became brigade in reserve to the Division, and remained in billets in Estaires and Sailly for the best part of December. The 2nd Canterbury Battalion's billets were not good, but training and careful attention to feeding and clothing made a marked improvement in the standard of its health, which had been causing a considerable amount of anxiety.

During this period the battalion was inspected very frequently. Thus on the 17th it was inspected by its Commanding Officer, and on the 18th by the General Officer commanding the Division. On the 22nd the 2nd Brigade was inspected at Sailly by Sir Douglas Haig, Commander-in-Chief of the British Expeditionary Force in France. On December 23rd the 2nd Brigade relieved the 1st Brigade, and the latter came into reserve. The 1st Canterbury Battalion went into billets at Estaires, while the 2nd Battalion moved to billets in the Rue des Fiefs, near Laventie, being one of the battalions in support to the battalions in the line.

The reorganization of the 1st and 2nd Brigades took place on January 1st, 1917, when the 2nd Auckland and 2nd Wellington Battalions were transferred from the 2nd Brigade to the 1st Brigade, and the 1st Canterbury and 1st Otago Battalions went from the 1st Brigade to the 2nd Brigade. On that date the 2nd Canterbury Battalion relieved the 2nd Auckland Battalion in the line, and the latter marched back to its new billets with the 1st Brigade. The 1st Canterbury Battalion took over the billets at Rue des Fiefs vacated that morning by its 2nd Battalion. As the 1st Battalion marched through Sailly, on its way from Estaires, the 1st Wellington Battalion turned out to say good-bye, and its band played the Canterbury Battalion through the village.

From now onward to the Battle of Messines, the two Canterbury Battalions worked together, relieving each other in the front line at regular intervals of eight days. Thus the 2nd Battalion had had two turns in the line and the 1st Battalion one, when the 2nd Brigade's turn to be brigade in reserve came round on January 24th. On that day the 3rd (Rifle) Brigade relieved the 2nd Brigade in the line, and the two Canterbury Battalions marched back to billets in Estaires.

The 1st Battalion seemed fated to have its period of rest snatched from it; for when the 1st Brigade went into Divisional reserve just before Christmas, the reorganization of the brigades had shortened the 1st Battalion's rest to nine days, and now on January 26th the 2nd Brigade was ordered into the line again. This unexpected move was made in consequence of orders which the Division had received to take over the sub-sector held by the right brigade of the 34th Division (on the left of the New Zealand Division) in the Bois Grenier Sector. The whole of the 34th Division had been withdrawn from the line at very short notice and placed in Corps reserve to meet an expected German attack.

The situation appeared to call for urgent measures; and though the 1st Canterbury Battalion did not receive orders till 1 p.m., it had marched the ten miles which lay between Estaires and the trenches, and had relieved the 16th Battalion Royal Scots by 7 p.m., in the right half of the front line. By 10.45 p.m. the relief by the 2nd Brigade was completed. The sector was a quiet one on the whole, though the enemy had many trench mortars, and his artillery was active at times. An interesting point about it is that it was the sector described by Mr. Ian Hay in his "The First Hundred Thousand."

The 2nd Battalion relieved the 15th Battalion Royal Scots in reserve, having battalion headquarters and the 1st and 12th Companies at Rue Delpierre (a mile south of Erquinghem), and the 2nd and 13th Companies at Erquinghem. The expected attack did not take place, and the usual eight days' reliefs were carried out. On February 3rd the Division was notified that it would shortly be relieved by the 57th Division, and on the 4th and 5th some officers and non-commissioned officers of that Division were attached to the battalions in the line. The usual precautions to conceal the relief from the enemy were taken; but on the night of February 18th a patrol, consisting of an officer and non-commissioned officer of the 57th Division, and a non-commissioned officer and four men of the 1st Canterbury Battalion, was surprised, and all save two of its members were captured.

Notwithstanding, the relief by the 57th Division began on the night of February 25th/26th, when the 2nd/9th King's Liverpool Battalion relieved the 1st Canterbury Battalion, which marched to Estaires, was billeted there for the night, and the next day moved to Nieppe, two miles north-west of Armentières. The following night the relief was completed; the 2nd/10th King's Liverpool Battalion relieved the 2nd Canterbury Battalion, and the latter marched to billets in the Rue des Fiefs, near Sailly.

The casualties in the two battalions since the return from the Somme had been:—

1st Battalion.	Officers.	Other Ranks.
Killed in Action and Died of Wounds ..	–	8
Wounded	1	48
Total	1	56

2nd Battalion.	Officers.	Other Ranks.
Killed in Action and Died of Wounds ..	–	19
Wounded	–	35
Total	–	54

Total for both battalions: 27 other ranks killed and 1 officer and 83 other ranks wounded.

The 1st Battalion remained in its billets at Nieppe till March 12th, but on the 5th of that month the 2nd Battalion left the Rue des Fiefs, and marched to a camp at Le Romarin, a small village a mile due north of Nieppe. On the 9th the 2nd Brigade was inspected by the Right Honourable Mr. Walter Long, M.P., Secretary of State for the Colonies, with whom were the General Officers commanding the II Anzac Army Corps and the New Zealand Division. The inspection took place on the Bailleul-Armentières road, and was followed by a march past in column of fours.

The New Zealand Division had now received orders to relieve the 25th Division in the Messines sector, which lay in country very different in character from any in which the Division had up to now been engaged.

The range of low hills on which the village of Messines stood begins at Dixmude, and curving round east of the Forest of Houlthurst and west of Staden, thence runs practically due south, through the villages of Westroosebeke and Passchendaele, a thousand yards east of Zonnebeke to a point about five miles due east of Ypres. From here the ridge runs south-east to Wytschaete, which lies four miles south of Ypres; but at this village it turns again to the west and rises up to Mont Kemmel, the dominant feature of this part of the country, and from there spreads out north, south, and west into a belt of low hills, extending eight miles west of Mont Kemmel with an extreme breadth of about six miles from north to south.

A spur two miles long, and higher than the saddle between Kemmel and Wytschaete, runs south from the latter village. This spur is practically flat on top — almost a plateau — to within half a mile of its southern end, where it descends rather abruptly. The village of Messines, perched on the southern extremity of the plateau, gave the spur its name of "the Messines Ridge."

Commencing between Mont Rouge and Mont Noir in the belt of low hills west of Mont Kemmel, there runs towards the east a broad valley, which is bounded on the north by the southern slopes of Mont Kemmel and the saddle between that hill and Wytschaete. The southern boundary of the valley consists of a chain of low hills, of which the two easternmost are Hill 63* and Neuve Eglise Hill, and which are connected by slightly lower saddles.

Down the centre of the valley there runs a small stream called the Douve, which, flowing east, eventually reaches the River Lys at Warneton. The northern side of the valley of the Douve is broken by a spur running south, the southern half of which is considerably lower than Messines village, and which lies about a mile to the west of Messines Ridge. In the valley between the ridge and the spur there rises a very small stream called the Steenebeek, which joins the Douve between Hill 63 and the southern end of the Messines Ridge.

The height of the range of hills above described is not great: Mont Kemmel is little over five hundred feet high, Neuve Eglise and Wytschaete about half that height, while Hill 63 and Messines are almost exactly the same height of two hundred and ten feet. North of Wytschaete, the highest point of the country is astride the Ypres-Menin road east of Hooge: at no place does its height exceed two hundred feet. Nevertheless, being the only range of hills in the Plain of Flanders, its importance from the military point of view is very great.

In the early fighting of the war, the British had made a great effort to hold Messines, but had found that the capture of the Wytschaete ridge by the enemy had made the village untenable. After the Second Battle of Ypres, the Germans remained in possession of the whole of the ridge, as far as the saddle between Wytschaete and Kemmel; but the British had been able to retain the very important strategical features of Mont Kemmel, Neuve Eglise, and Hill 63, and still held these hills at the beginning of 1917.

At this date the British front line followed the line of the Yser River and Canal from Dixmude to a point on the canal about three miles north of Ypres. Here the line began to swing east and south, till, when a mile east of Zillebeke, it reached its easternmost point, and swung back again towards the west till it reached a point about a mile north-west of Wytschaete. This

---

* So called on account of its height of 63 metres.

point, and the point where the line left the Yser Canal, formed respectively the southern and northern boundaries of the British salient, which was practically semicircular in shape, and on a two mile radius from Ypres.

From the southern end of the Ypres salient, the British line ran virtually due south, crossing the saddle between Kemmel and Wytschaete, and running along the western slopes of the spur above described as running parallel to the Messines Ridge. A quarter of a mile north of the Wulverghem-Messines road, the line took the general direction of south-east. skirted the foot of the Messines Ridge, and ran across to the hamlet of St. Yves, nearly a mile east of Hill 63. From here the line ran south again, along the eastern edge of Ploegsteert ("Plugstreet") Wood, to cross the River Lys at Houplines, north-east of Armentières.

The enemy being entrenched on the high ground, with a ridge at his back, it is clear that he could move about freely without any fear of detection by ourselves. It is true that we held very valuable observation points in Mont Kemmel, Neuve Eglise, and Hill 63; but though these gave us an excellent view of some of his trenches on the west of the ridge, they did not enable us to keep the whole of his trench system with its approaches and back areas under constant observation, as he could keep ours. East of Kemmel or Neuve Eglise, no movement of our troops or transport was possible by day; and even in the trenches there were many places where it was impossible to construct cover from view.

The first sector allotted to the New Zealand Division lay in the low ground south of the River Douve and to the north and east of Ploegsteert Wood. Between March 12th and 16th, however, the Division handed over to the 3rd Australian Division all the portion of the line held by it to the south of St. Yves, and took over from the 36th Division all the front line as far as the point where it crossed the Wulverghem-Wytschaete road. The left of the New Zealand Division's new sector was therefore on the spur which lay to the west of the Messines Ridge, and the River Douve formed the inter-brigade boundary. The relief was carried out by the 3rd New Zealand (Rifle) Brigade side-slipping to the north, and relieving part of the 107th Brigade, and by the 2nd New Zealand Infantry Brigade relieving the remainder of the 107th Brigade and the 108th Brigade. The 1st New Zealand Infantry Brigade, relieved by the 11th Australian Brigade, moved back to the Nieppe-Romarin-De Seule area, and became brigade in reserve to the New Zealand Division.

The relief of the 108th and part of the 107th Brigades was carried out by the 2nd New Zealand Infantry Brigade as follows:—On the night of March 12th/13th, the 1st Canterbury Battalion relieved the 9th Battalion Royal Irish Rifles (107th Brigade) on a seven hundred yards' frontage, with the River Douve (exclusive) on its right flank. The following night, the same battalion took over from the 13th Battalion Royal Irish Rifles (108th Brigade) the part of the front line which lay between the portion of line already held by the 1st Battalion and Boyle's Farm, on the Wulverghem-Messines road. The same night the 1st Otago Battalion relieved the rest of the front line battalions of the 108th Brigade between Boyle's Farm and the Wulverghem-Wytschaete road.

The 2nd Canterbury Battalion on the 14th relieved the 9th Battalion Royal Irish Rifles in a hutted camp at Red Lodge, where Ploegsteert Wood spreads up the southern slopes of Hill 63. It remained there till the 20th, when it relieved the 1st Canterbury Battalion in the line, the latter battalion moving back to Red Lodge. The battalions changed over again on the 28th. After remaining at Red Lodge till April 5th, the 2nd Battalion returned to the camp at Romarin, while the 1st Battalion, on being relieved in the line on April 6th by the 1st Auckland and 2nd Wellington Battalions, marched to billets at Nieppe. During the two battalions' tours in the line, they had been kept fully employed in repairing the trenches, which were in poor order; and while at Red Lodge and in billets, they were engaged on working parties to the front and subsidiary lines, and in laying railway lines and preparing positions for artillery.

The British General Headquarters now estimated that the enemy had sufficient reserves to enable him to make an attack on the British front; and it considered that the point at which the enemy would strike would be the Ypres salient, and that the front of the attack would probably extend as far south as Armentières. It was absolutely imperative that our positions south of the salient should hold out against such an attack; for while the British line in the salient was in an exposed position and liable to be forced back more easily than the line further south, the retirement of our troops from Kemmel and Hill 63 would expose the flank of the troops to their north, and would lead to the destruction of the bulk of the Second Army.

For this reason, special precautions were taken to ensure that the defences were as strong as work could make them, and all officers and senior non-commissioned officers were ordered to reconnoitre thoroughly the whole of the Divisional front, and all approaches from the rear areas.

The trenches between the front system and the subsidiary line, which having long been disused had been allowed to fall into bad repair, and which were ill-provided with covered approaches, were put into fighting order, and were connected with the other defences by proper communication trenches.

The usual standing orders that, in the event of an enemy attack, the troops in the trenches were to hold out against all odds, were repeated with special emphasis; and the impression received by all ranks was that while there might be sectors where the loss of a little ground was unimportant, this was certainly not one of them.

The enemy, however, did not make an attack; but it began to be common knowledge that there was to be a British attack on the Messines and Wytschaete Ridges, and that the New Zealand Division was to take part in it. The almost daily arrival in the back areas of new batteries of artillery—and of heavy artillery especially—showed that the operation was to be on a large scale. The preparation of positions for the newly-arrived batteries called for the assistance of working-parties from the infantry; and both Canterbury Battalions, when out of the line, supplied parties for this purpose. As soon as the guns were put in position, they began a bombardment of the enemy defences, and especially of the ruined village of Messines, which was to continue steadily right up to the day of the attack.

By the middle of April, the plans of the attack were in the hands of brigade commanders. The attack, though complete in itself and on quite a large scale, was but a preliminary to a great attack extending from the Ypres salient to the sea. The enemy's positions from Messines to north of Wytschaete themselves formed a salient in his line; to cut off which would not only shorten our line, but would practically flatten the southern half of our own salient at Ypres, the deep penetration of which into the enemy's country made it vulnerable to flank attacks. Besides reducing this danger, the capture of the Messines and Wytschaete Ridges would take from the enemy much of the ground which gave him his best observation of the Ypres salient; and this would of course make easier the preparations for the main attack from that part of the line.

Though the attack on the ridges was in this sense a subsidiary one, yet it was by no means considered an easy task, or in any sense a minor operation. In the first place, the positions from which our attack was to be made were under full observation by the enemy, who could not fail to be aware of the true reason of the preparations which he saw growing daily under his very eyes. Then the enemy's lines were sited in strong natural defensive positions, and during his long occupation of them he had left nothing undone that military science could devise to improve his defences. He believed them to be impregnable against direct assault. The British preparations to take these positions therefore included a hitherto unprecedented concentration of artillery, which began its work months before the date fixed for the attack; a more elaborate barrage of heavies, field-guns, and machine-guns, to cover the advance of the infantry, than had been employed before; and a very careful and special training of the troops picked for the operation.

The training area of the New Zealand Division was situated south-west of St. Omer, in country that during peace time had been one of the training grounds of the French Army. Consisting of gently rolling downs, broken here and there by deep valleys and lightly cultivated and unfenced, with small woods and villages here and there, it was ideal country for military purposes. The 3rd (Rifle) Brigade had gone to the training area at the beginning of April, and on its return the 2nd Brigade was sent there.

During the period the 2nd Brigade had been in the Messines sector the casualties of the Canterbury Battalion had been:—

1st Battalion.	Officers.	Other Ranks.
Killed in Action and Died of Wounds ..	–	9
Wounded	1	12
Total	1	21

2nd Battalion.	Officers.	Other Ranks.
Killed in Action and Died of Wounds ..	1*	4
Wounded	–	8
Total	1	12

*Major F. B. Brown (accidentally killed 7th March).

Total for both battalions: 1 officer and 13 other ranks killed and 1 officer and 20 other ranks wounded.

The 2nd Brigade marched to the training ground, leaving its back-area camps and billets on April 16th. The first night the 1st Canterbury Battalion spent in billets at Pradelles, and the 2nd Battalion at Grand Sec Bois; and next night the battalions were at Wallon Cappel and Lynde respectively. The following day the march was finished, and the battalions settled down in billets for a period of twelve days — the 1st Battalion at Tatinghem, two miles west of St. Omer, and the 2nd Battalion with its headquarters and three companies at Setques, five miles south-west of the same town, and one company (the 1st) at Quelmes, two miles north-west of Setques.

On arrival at billets, the battalions were re-organized in accordance with recent General Headquarters' orders. The establishment of an infantry battalion was now laid down as thirty-four officers and nine hundred and ten other ranks. Battalion headquarters consisted of ten officers (Commanding Officer, Second in Command, Adjutant, Quartermaster, and Transport, Signalling, Bombing, Lewis-gun, Intelligence, and

Medical Officers) and one hundred and fifty other ranks — seventy on the fighting strength and the remainder engaged on the administration and feeding of the battalion. The strength of each company was to be six officers (company commander, second in command, and four subalterns) and one hundred and ninety other ranks; and of the latter, fourteen were formed into a new section — the company headquarters' section — and the remainder were equally divided among the four platoons. This gave each subaltern a command of forty-four other ranks, of which four were on platoon headquarters, and the remainder provided two sections each of a strength of eleven, and two sections each of a strength of nine.

The training was carried out on progressive lines as usual; though, on account of both battalions having been out of the line for some time before beginning the march, and also on account of the good effect of the three days' marching, little time had to be spent in getting the men into good physical condition. For the first few days, training was carried on by the companies, and the time was spent in rifle exercises and barrack square drill (to smarten everybody up, and thus foster his self-respect and improve his morale), bayonet fighting, gas drill, exercising the platoons in open warfare movements, the siting and digging of communication trenches and strong-points, and night marching by compass.

At the end of the period devoted to company work, the company commanders practised the movement of their commands, in attacks under conditions of open and trench warfare and against villages. Thereafter the companies ceased to work except under the direct control of the Commanding Officer of the battalion. Under his command the battalion practised attacks from trench to trench and in open country, with and without a creeping barrage, moving through enemy country with advance and flank guards, taking up outpost positions, enveloping villages, and street fighting.

In the meanwhile, the Brigade Major, Major H. M. W. Richardson, D.S.O., M.C., (New Zealand Staff Corps) had selected a piece of ground which corresponded closely in contour and area to the ground on which was situated the enemy's defences of the village of Messines. On this he marked out all the enemy's trenches, as shown by aeroplane photographs, the village itself, and the British trenches on the other side of No-Man's-Land. The troops of the brigade then dug shallow trenches and marked the position of streets and houses by scratching lines in the turf, and the result was a replica, to full scale, of the country over which the brigade was to fight.

On this ground the brigade practised the attack again and again, moving forward under a barrage represented by men carrying flags and controlled by the staff captain of the brigade. The time-table laid down in the orders for the operation was strictly adhered to: the time between "zero hour" (*i.e.*, the time the first infantry left the trenches) and the capture of the brigade's last objective was over one and three-quarter hours, so that not more than two complete attacks could be properly carried out in a working day, even though lunch was taken on the field. After each practice, the Brigadier held a conference of officers and criticised the way in which it had been done.

With the exception of the troops detailed to assault the front line trenches, who advanced in extended order across No-Man's-Land, the whole brigade moved in artillery formation, that is, with each platoon in two irregular lines of sections in single file. For the first part of the advance, each line was kept as close up to the preceding one as was safe, so as to enable the rear-most troops to get across No-Man's-Land as quickly as possible. The object of doing this was to get all the attacking troops across No-Man's-Land before the enemy's barrage could be brought down there and on our front line.

The reason for the advance in sections in single file was two-fold; first, this formation prevented loss by artillery fire, and second, experience had proved that it enabled the section to be kept under better control than if it were in extended order, and also that it was the best method of crossing country badly pitted with shell-holes. As each line approached its objective, the platoon commanders gave orders for their sections to extend, and the platoon was then ready to rush in two waves on the enemy trenches. The above brief description of the brigade formation is sufficient in a description of the training for the attack; details of the objectives and the order of battle of the battalions will be found in the description of the actual battle.

Two such practices of the attack took place on April 26th, and two more the next day. The 28th was devoted to an open warfare tactical exercise, in which the brigade, moving under cover of an advanced guard, came in contact with the enemy and attacked him. The enemy was represented by a skeleton force, with gas alarm rattles to represent machine-guns. Next day the brigade marched in the dark to the assembly trenches, and at 5 a.m. carried out another practice attack.

On April 30th the final practice took place, in the presence of General Sir H. Plumer, commanding the Second Army, and the General Officers commanding the II Anzac Army Corps and the Division. A contact aeroplane from the 42nd Squadron of the Royal Flying Corps co-operated with the infantry, and the attack was made more realistic by the use of smoke-bombs and dummy rifle-grenades. The constant practising had made the attack practically a drill movement, and General Plumer expressed his approval of the way in which it was done.

This was the last day of training, and the following day (May 1st) the 2nd Brigade began its return journey to the Divisional sector. The 1st Canterbury Battalion was billeted for the night at Wallon Cappel on May 1st and at Pradelles on the 2nd, and on the afternoon of the 3rd it marched into Bulford Camp on the Neuve Eglise hill. The 2nd Battalion spent the nights of May 1st and 2nd at Lynde and Grand Sec Bois respectively, and arrived at Romarin on the 3rd.

From now on till the 22nd of the month, both battalions, in common with all troops in the sector, worked at a feverish rate. Three hundred men of the 2nd Battalion were engaged for a fortnight on light railway construction, under a Canadian Light Railway Operating Company, while the rest of its available men were employed on work in the forward areas; but after that period it was, like the 1st Battalion, exclusively engaged on work in the front line and the area of assembly for the attack. The brigade dug its own assembly trenches, and though every battalion did not dig the very trench which it occupied on assembling for the attack, each battalion dug an equivalent length of trench for some other battalion. Most of the work was done at night: and owing to the distance of the camps from the line, the working-parties had a march of from one and a half to two hours

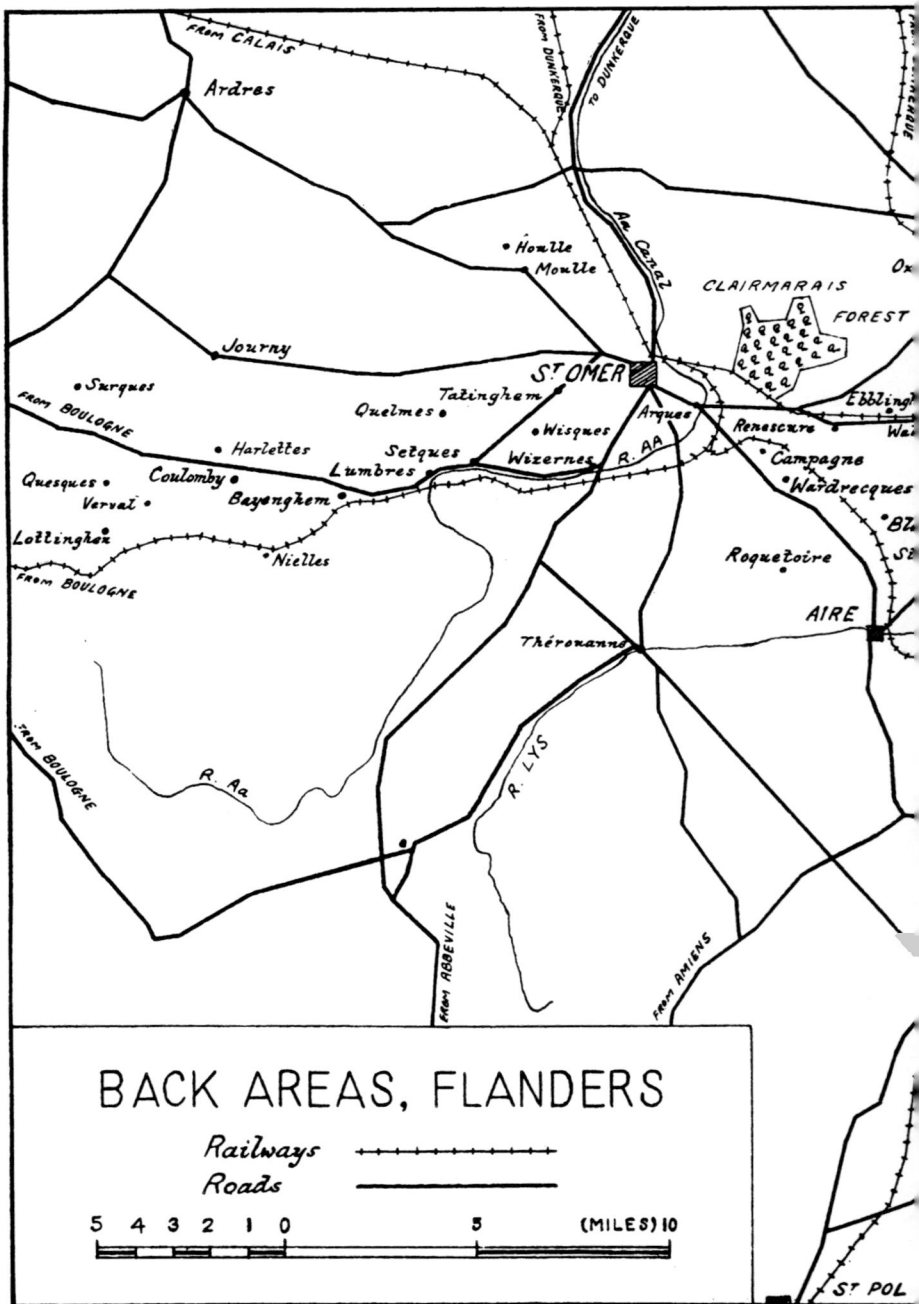

FROM CALAIS

Ardres

FROM DUNKERQUE

TO DUNKERQUE

Ae Canal

• Houlle
Moulle

CLAIRMARAIS

FOREST

Ox

Journy

• Surques

FROM BOULOGNE

Tatingham

Quelmes •

ST OMER

Wisques •

Arques

Renescure

Ebbling

Wa

• Harlettes

Setques

Lumbres •

Wizernes

R. AA

• Campagne

Quesques •
Verval •

Coulomby •

Bayenghem •

• Wardrecques

Lottinghem •

FROM BOULOGNE

• Nielles

Roquetoire •

AIRE

Bl

St

R. Aa

Théronanne

R. LYS

FROM BOULOGNE

FROM ABBEVILLE

FROM AMIENS

ST POL

BACK AREAS, FLANDERS

Railways ++++++++

Roads   ──────

5 4 3 2 1 0   5   (MILES) 10

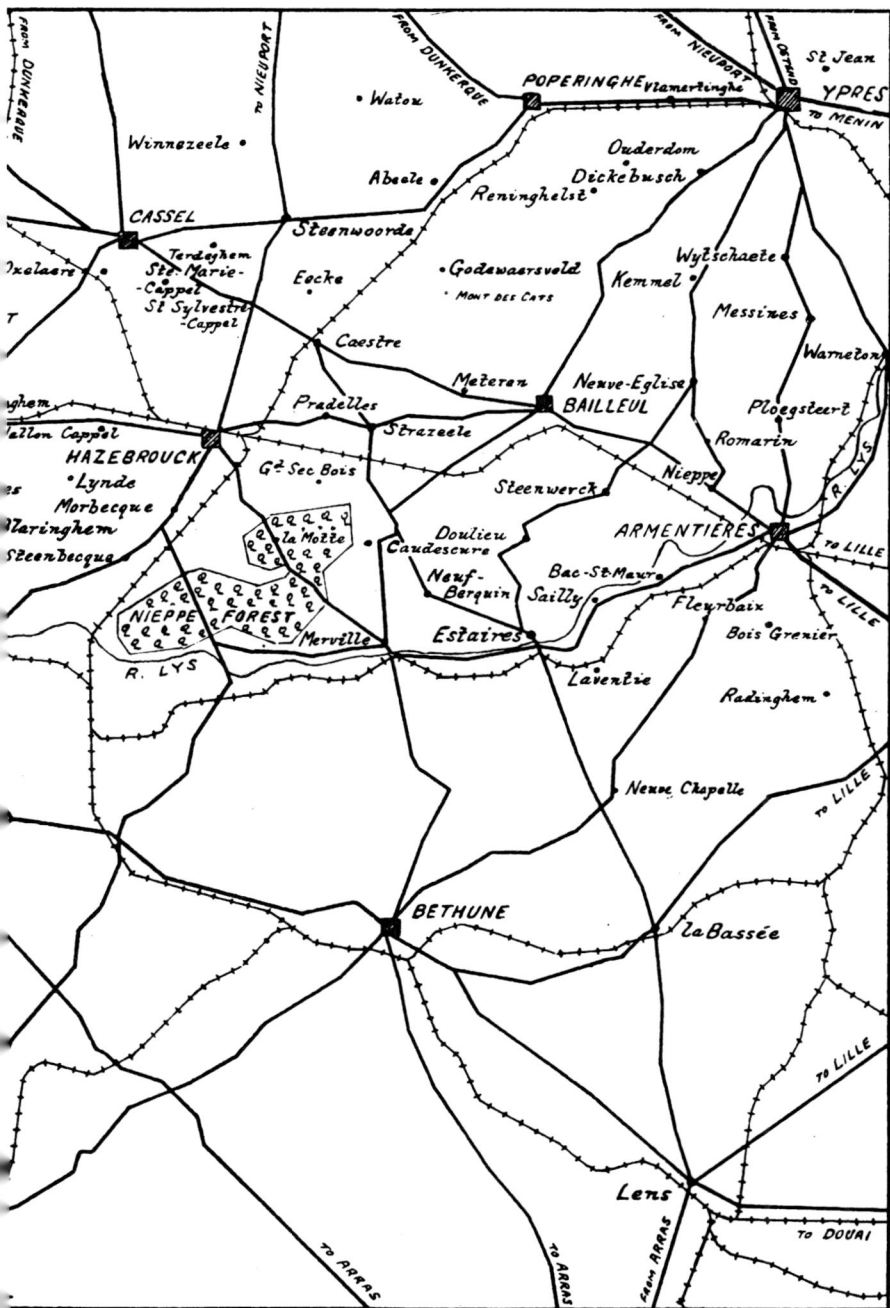

FROM DUNKERQUE
TO NIEUPORT
FROM DUNKERQUE
FROM NIEUPORT
FROM OSTEND

St Jean
POPERINGHE Vlamertinghe
YPRES
TO MENIN
Watou
Winnezeele
Ouderdom
Dickebusch
Abeele
Reninghelst
CASSEL
Steenwoorde
Wytschaete
Ixelaere
Terdeghem
Ste-Marie-
-Cappel
St Sylvestre
-Cappel
Eecke
Godewaersveld
MONT DES CATS
Kemmel
Messines
Warneton
Caestre
Meteren
Neuve-Eglise
Ploegsteert
Pradelles
BAILLEUL
Romarin
Strazeele
Nieppe
HAZEBROUCK
Gd Sec Bois
Steenwerck
ARMENTIÈRES
TO LILLE
Lynde
Morbecque
Wallon Cappel
la Motte
Doulieu
Caudescure
Bac-St-Maur
TO LILLE
Waringhem
Steenbecque
Neuf-
Berquin
Sailly
Fleurbaix
Bois Grenier
NIEPPE FOREST
Merville
Estaires
Lavenzie
Radinghem
R. LYS
Neuve Chapelle
TO LILLE
BETHUNE
la Bassée
TO LILLE
Lens
TO DOUAI
TO ARRAS
TO ARRAS
FROM ARRAS

LIEUT.-COLONEL N. F. SHEPHERD, D.S.O.

LIEUT.-COLONEL G. C. GRIFFITHS, C.M.G.

each way to and from their work, as well as a solid six hours' task of digging.

Casualties were inevitable: but on looking back it is difficult to understand why the enemy did as little as he did to hinder the work, which every morning he must have seen had grown in the night. Certainly it was not because our artillery let him alone: our heavies pounded his defences as long as there was enough daylight for the observers to direct their fire, and all night our field guns hailed shrapnel on his roads and tracks, and our long-range guns shelled his billets. Possibly the enemy was so confident in the strength of his defences, that he considered our attack must end in disaster; and so he wished the attack to be delivered.

However, the enemy did not allow all our activity to go un-checked. On the night of May 5th/6th he shelled our roads and back areas at irregular intervals during the whole of the hours of darkness. The 1st Battalion, at Bulford Camp, was driven out of its quarters three times during the night, as heavy guns shelled the camp between 9.30 and 10 p.m., between 11 and 11.30 p.m., and between 3 and 3.30 a.m. killing one man and wounding one officer and one other rank. The 2nd Battalion's camp was also shelled once during the night: no casualties re-sulted. but one other rank was wounded while on the way back from work in the line. The following night the shelling was re-peated, though not so persistently; but again the 1st Battalion suffered, having one other rank killed and five wounded, as against the 2nd Battalion's loss of one killed and one wounded.

It appears from intelligence subsequently received that the enemy expected to be attacked at this time, and that his artillery fire was directed against the troops he supposed were assembling for that purpose. In consequence of this artillery activity on the part of the enemy, the Second Army arranged a retaliatory shoot on the night of May 7th/8th, when every piece of artillery under the Army's command engaged in a hurricane bombardment between 8.45 and 8.50 p.m., and also between 11 and 11.5 p.m. After this, night fire on our back areas gave very little trouble.

On May 10th the 1st Battalion handed over Bulford Camp to the 9th Battalion Loyal North Lancashire Regiment, and marched to billets at Nieppe. While the battalion was there, it was successful in winning the first prize for battalion transport, at the New Zealand Divisional Horse Show, held on the 13th.

During this period a brigade school was established at Bonanza Lines, between Romarin and Nieppe, and Captain A. D. Stitt was appointed commandant and chief instructor. Platoon commanders and senior non-commissioned officers from all battalions attended for a week's course, which was devoted mainly to the use of maps and compass by day and by night. message writing, and minor tactics. A model platoon was established and billeted at the school, and was used for carrying out the tactical exercises.

The weather during May was wonderfully fine and warm, and enabled preparations for the attack to be pushed forward unceasingly. Besides the preliminary work in which, as has been mentioned, the two Canterbury Battalions took their share, there was very great activity in other directions behind our lines. Our preparations could not be hidden from the enemy: the country swarmed with men building gun positions, new broad- and narrow-gauge railways, light-railway marshalling yards, and dumps for ammunitions, rations, and materials of all kinds, laying buried telephone-cables.* improving old roads and building new ones, and engaged in the hundred other activities which must precede an attack on a large scale.

It would have been waste of labour and time to attempt to hide what we were doing; for while our air force could, and did, keep the bulk of the enemy's aeroplanes from crossing our lines, it could not ensure that single machines, flying at a great height, should not occasionally fly over our back areas. The most elaborate camouflage may succeed in concealing from enemy air-observation single works of first importance; but it is impracticable to attempt to hide work on a large scale. So our preparations went on openly, and with very little interference on the part of the enemy. Yet the element of surprise was not precluded from the attack: for though it was evident to everyone that an attack was going to be made, the secret of the date and hour was successfully kept until the last moment. The evidence of prisoners

---

* Officers and other ranks detached from all battalions of the New Zealand Division were formed into special units for burying cables.

goes to show that the enemy expected us to attack on June 8th, and that our attack on the 7th was a genuine surprise to him.

One of our most important preparations, which no camouflage could possibly conceal, was the work of the artillery. For this battle the General Headquarters Staff had concentrated more guns than had ever before been used in an attack of this size. Except where a battery was to be kept silent till zero hour, as soon as a gun came into position it began to take its share in the destruction of the enemy defences. While the heavies and trench-mortars were engaged by day in cutting the enemy's wire and destroying his trenches, the field-guns spent the night in harassing fire; making the roads their principal targets, with the object of preventing the enemy from bringing up material to renew his defences.

The guns of the larger calibres concentrated their fire on the points where the enemy was known or suspected to have built strong concrete works: in the New Zealand sector their chief target was the village of Messines, which before the attack had been reduced to practically the level of the ground. The enemy retaliated chiefly by counter-battery work; and as the whole face of the country was covered with small ammunition dumps, fires and explosions were frequent.

In order to make the enemy disclose the position of his guns, our artillery carried out very heavy bombardments of Messines on June 2nd and 3rd. There was no continuous bombardment, such as had occurred in previous battles, immediately preceding the assault; heavy concentrations at irregular intervals, followed by periods of silence, were the rule, and on the morning of the attack our guns were comparatively silent from 12.30 a.m. till zero hour.

To support the attack of the infantry, the staff had arranged a most elaborate barrage, consisting of standing barrages by the heavy artillery, laid on certain dangerous areas and continued until the infantry approached the danger zone of the shells, and a creeping barrage by the field guns and machine guns. Some idea of the amount of artillery at the disposal of the Second Army is given by the allotment of field guns to the New Zealand Division. Attacking on a front of rather under a mile, the Division was supported by nineteen batteries of eighteen-pounder guns (one hundred and fourteen guns) and six batteries of 4·5-inch howitzers (thirty-six guns). Fifty-six machine-guns also supported the Division's attack. The number of heavy guns under Corps and Army control supporting the Division was in proportion to the number of field guns.

Another feature of the preparations for the attack was the work of the tunnelling companies of the Royal Engineers and Australian Imperial Force, who had been fighting the enemy underground throughout the winter and spring. At zero-hour, twenty-three mines were exploded, which were estimated to contain a million pounds of high-explosive. There were no mines exploded on the territory over which the New Zealand Division fought; but on the Division's left flank a large mine, exploded under Ontario Farm in the enemy's front line, was within six hundred yards of the left flank of the assembly trenches, and considerably closer to them than the first objective.

Finally, thirty-two tanks were ordered to co-operate with the II Anzac Army Corps; and of these, twelve were allotted to the New Zealand Division. As events turned out, their help was not needed, as the few which succeeded in getting across No-Man's-Land were outstripped by the infantry. One tank, however, did very good work on the left flank, and is claimed to have been instrumental in causing the garrison of Swayne's Farm to surrender.

These preparations continued without intermission right up to the very hour of the attack. Meanwhile, on May 22nd, the 2nd Brigade relieved the 3rd (Rifle) Brigade in the line. The 1st Canterbury Battalion, having last had a turn in the line, was in brigade reserve, and relieved the 3rd Battalion of the Rifle Brigade by daylight, taking over huts and tents on the wooded slopes of Hill 63. The 2nd Battalion relieved the 2nd Battalion of the Rifle Brigade in the Douve (or right) sector, at dusk on the same day, the 2nd and 12th Companies being in the line with the 13th Company in support and the 1st Company in reserve. All the troops, except those actually in the line, continued to work in preparation for the attack: casualties were becoming more numerous, but the arrival of reinforcement drafts for both battalions more than made up their strength. On May 30th the

Canterbury Battalions changed places. the 1st Battalion putting the 13th and 2nd Companies in the line, the 12th Company in support, and the 1st Company in reserve. Before the relief, the "B" team from the 1st Battalion was sent back to camp at Morbecque.

The 1st Brigade was due to return from the training area on June 2nd, and was to relieve the 2nd Brigade in the line on the 3rd. In preparation for the relief, the 1st Otago Battalion, which was also in the line, took over the whole of the brigade front on the 2nd, and the 1st Canterbury Battalion marched back to Canteen Corner, a short distance east of the intersection of the Bailleul-Armentières and Neuve Eglise-Steenwerck roads. Here was the bivouac area for the whole brigade : on the morning of the 3rd, the 2nd Canterbury Battalion, which had been relieved early by the 2nd Wellington Battalion, marched in. Tents and tarpaulin shelters were available for use at night, but the troops were not allowed to keep them pitched during daylight, for fear of aeroplane observation by the enemy.

No work was done while the brigade was in bivouacs; the special equipment and materials required for the battle. such as smoke-bombs, flares for signalling to aeroplanes, S.O.S. rockets, picks and shovels and sandbags, were issued to the company commanders, and by them distributed among the men. On the night of the 3rd, the enemy shelled the bivouac area with long range high-velocity guns; but though his shooting was accurate and destroyed a cook-house, it caused no casualties. Otherwise the brigade was undisturbed, and waited for orders to attack.

The "B" team of the 2nd Battalion left for Morbecque on the 4th. On the afternoon of the same day the Brigadier-General held a final conference of all officers of the 2nd Brigade, and, as well as going over the details which were already familiar to all, handed on to them all information which it had been thought advisable to keep confidential up till the last moment, including the date of the attack -- June 7th. The following day the 1st Canterbury Battalion relieved the 1st Auckland Battalion in the tunnels on Hill 63; but the 2nd Battalion remained at Canteen Corner till it moved out on the night of June 6th/7th to its assembly trenches.

Since the return from the training area, the Regiment's casualties had been:—

	Officers.	Other Ranks.
1st Battalion.		
Killed in Action and Died of Wounds ..	–	18
Wounded	1	35
Total	1	53

	Officers.	Other Ranks.
2nd Battalion.		
Killed in Action and Died of Wounds ..	–	4
Wounded	1	51
Total	1	55

Total for both battalions: 22 other ranks killed and 2 officers and 86 other ranks wounded.

CHAPTER IX.

THE BATTLE OF MESSINES.

In the previous chapter it was explained that the British attack on the Messines and Wytschaete Ridges was merely the preliminary to a great attack from the Ypres Salient; and that before any attack could be made from this part of the British line it was essential that these ridges should be taken, because their capture would flatten and secure the right flank of the salient, and would deprive the enemy of much of the high ground from which he obtained his observation on the defences of Ypres. The ridges themselves formed in the German line a salient, which was about as large and deep as our own at Ypres, and the southern flank of which was dominated and protected by the strong defences of the village of Messines. The resemblance between the two salients was only in the matter of size: for the enemy's consisted of strong positions on high ground, which he had deliberately selected on account of their menace to Ypres; whereas the British positions were on low ground, to which our troops had clung desperately, without choice of any other, in spite of the enemy's attempts to drive them out.

It has been seen, too, that the German salient on the ridges ended at St. Yves, on the north-east corner of Ploegsteert Wood. Here the opposing lines, which had been running in a south-easterly direction for about three miles, turned to the south; and running along the eastern edge of the wood, continued in the same direction till they crossed the River Lys at Houplines, east of Armentières. Ploegsteert Wood with its strong defences backed by those of Hill 63, formed the natural southern pivot for the attack on the ridges.

The share in the attack assigned to the II Anzac Army Corps was the capture of the southern flank of the German salient, from St. Yves northwards to the Wulverghem-Wytschaete road, penetrating into the enemy positions to about a mile east of the village of Messines. The Corps' final objective, the "Green Line" and part of the "Black Line," was an almost straight line from the village of St. Yves to the hamlet of Wambeke. The Divisions of this Corps to take part in the first phase of the attack were to be the 3rd Australian Division on the right, the New Zealand Division in the centre, and the 25th Division on the left; which together were to establish a line running north from St. Yves, passing about nine hundred yards to the east of the village of Messines and running through Despagne Farm. This line was known as the "Black Line" and "Dotted Black Line."

Later in the day, the 4th Australian Division was to pass through the portion of this line established by the New Zealand and 25th Divisions, and capture the Corps' final objective from the Messines-Comines road (called on our maps "Hun's Walk") to Wambeke. At the same time, the 3rd Australian Division (which, it was anticipated, would up to then have had a comparatively easy task, and would already, in its first advance, have reached the Corps' final objective in the southern half of its own Divisional frontage*) would advance on the right of the 4th Australian Division, and capture the remainder of the Corps' final objective, from the Douve River to Hun's Walk.

The final objective of the New Zealand Division was, as stated above, a line about nine hundred yards east of the village of Messines. The Divisional and brigade boundaries and objectives are shown on the map at the end of this chapter: it may be broadly stated here that the task of the New Zealand Division was to capture the village of Messines, and to establish and consolidate a temporary defensive position about half a mile to the east of the village, on a frontage of slightly under a mile. This position was to be held as part of the British front line, until the 4th Australian Division had established another line in front of it, on the Corps' final objective.

It will be seen from the map that, on practically the whole of the New Zealand Division's frontage, there was a deep re-entrant in the enemy's front line. On account of this re-entrant,

---

* *i.e.*, the "Black Line." As the part of the German line assaulted was a salient, the early objectives were naturally further to the west than the pivotal point of St. Yves; so that the Black Line, which ran due north till it reached a point opposite the southern end of the village of Messines, from that point began to swing away in a north-westerly direction. At the river Douve, the "Green Line" began; swinging out at first towards the north-east, but eventually running north again.

No-Man's-Land was exceptionally wide on the Division's frontage. Even on the right, where the re-entrant began, the distance to the enemy front line was two hundred yards; and as at this point his trenches ran almost at right-angles to ours, No-Man's-Land quickly widened to five hundred yards, narrowing again, however, to three hundred and fifty yards in the centre. From the centre, our trenches swung further away still, so that, near the left, No-Man's-Land was six hundred yards wide. At this point, which was some three hundred yards from the Division's left boundary for the attack, the British front line turned abruptly at right angles, to face the northern side of the enemy's re-entrant. After this turn, No-Man's-Land narrowed again to two hundred yards, and both the enemy's lines and our own ran west for a quarter of a mile or more. As the enemy had the high ground, the part of the line held by the Division was thus enfiladed to a very serious extent.

The greater width of No-Man's-Land on the left, and the danger of the loss of direction entailed by troops attacking from trenches which did not directly face the objective, made it necessary for assembly trenches to be dug in No-Man's-Land. These trenches were marked out on April 11th by Lieutenant J. Keilar (2nd Field Company New Zealand Engineers), Lieutenant Molloy (1st Otago), and 2nd Lieutenant A. Cracroft Wilson (2nd Canterbury), who were specially complimented by the General Officer commanding the 2nd Brigade for their work. On the night of April 13th, a party of four hundred other ranks of the 1st Otago Battalion, under Major J. Hargest. M.C., dug this trench. A covering party from the 2nd Wellington Battalion, under Captain R. F. C. Scott, protected the working party. The work was carried out without casualties, and reflected great credit on all concerned.

As will be seen from the map, the completion of this trench reduced the width of No-Man's-Land, for the purpose of the attack, to about four hundred yards. Still these preparations could not dispose of the awkward fact that the left Divisional boundary for eight hundred yards ran parallel to the enemy's front line trench, and at a distance of a hundred yards (and under) from that trench. This fact naturally caused a great deal of anxiety prior to the attack; for it was necessary for the attacking troops to assemble, and afterwards attack, with their flank exposed to this trench, in order to take by surprise the front line trench at the base of the re-entrant.

The reserve battalion of the 2nd Brigade was detailed to protect the flank, if required: but as it turned out, no trouble was experienced from this direction on the day of the battle. The credit for this was due: firstly, to the excellence of the 18-pounder barrage, which remained on the trenches on the left flank till it gave place to the infantry who were following it; and secondly, to the fine work of the 25th Division, which had a stiff task on the left, and did it well.

The tasks allotted to the various infantry brigades of the New Zealand Division were as follows:—The 3rd (Rifle) Brigade on the right and the 2nd Brigade on the left were to take the village of Messines, and the German trenches at the rear of the village, which were sited so as to defend the village from the attacks of flanking parties. On the right of the village, the 3rd Brigade was to take the reserve trenches of the enemy front line system (Ulcer Reserve); and on the left the 2nd Brigade was to dig a line a hundred and fifty yards on the enemy's side of the Wytschaete-Messines road.

Except on the extreme left, the whole of these objectives were to be attained in one hour and forty-eight minutes after the attack commenced; and the 1st Brigade was immediately to continue the advance to a line running about five hundred yards east of the village of Messines, but swinging round in a westerly direction north of that village, so as to protect the left flank from counter-attacks from the direction of Wytschaete. The 1st Brigade was to consolidate this line (called the "Black Line"), and then, five and a half hours after the zero hour of the Division's original attack, was to go forward and capture the Division's final objective, the "Black Dotted Line."

The fact that the 25th Division was not timed to come fully up on the left till the 1st Brigade's second attack, delayed the infantry's advance on the left flank; and also made necessary the formation of strong protective flanks on the left, as each successive objective was captured.

Turning now to the 2nd Brigade's share in the attack, the brigade had been allotted the left half of the Division's sector.

The boundary between the 2nd and 3rd Brigades commenced at the point where the River Steenebeek entered our front line, and thence ran in a straight line to the bend of the Gooseberry Farm-Messines road (in No-Man's-Land), and thence up to the left side of that road to its junction with the Wytschaete-Messines road in the village of Messines. From there, the boundary followed the enemy side of the Wytschaete-Messines road in a northerly direction, to an open space in the village, halfway between the Gooseberry Farm-Messines road and the Wulverghem-Messines road: at which point the boundary turned off at right angles, and ran in a straight line to the Chapelle du Voleur, on Hun's Walk.

The 2nd Brigade's share of the Division's objectives was subdivided into the main objective described above, and two sub-objectives, (1) the "Blue Line," *i.e.*, the enemy's front line system as far as and including the support line, with the strongpoint at the Moulin de l'Hospice, and (2) the "Brown Line," *i.e.*, the enemy's reserve trenches, except a portion of those trenches on the left, where the "Brown Line" left the line of the reserve trenches and swung back to the west, thus forming a defensive flank.

On account of the curve of the German salient, and the deep re-entrant opposite the New Zealand Division, the objectives of the 25th Division (on the left), though they were practically in line with those of the New Zealand Division, were some five or six hundred yards further from its jumping-off point than of those of the latter Division. Also, its No-Man's-Land was narrower than that opposite the New Zealand Division; so that the 25th Division had to fight its way over seven or eight hundred yards more than the New Zealanders.

As a result, the plans for the battle involved the New Zealand Division fighting with its flank "in the air," as far as infantry support was concerned, for two hours after the first assault was made. But the flank was not, of course, to be left unprotected: a tremendously heavy artillery barrage was to come down on the whole of the enemy trenches there, and to remain there till the 25th Division had time to fight its way over the intervening ground.

According to the time-table for the attack, nine minutes after zero hour the barrage was to lift off the German front line trenches attacked by the New Zealand Division: and the 25th Division was not timed to arrive level with the same trenches till forty-five minutes after zero. As the 25th Division gradually came up level with the New Zealand Division, the defensive flank on the "Brown Line" (mentioned above) would become unnecessary: so that on the left the 2nd Brigade had a third sub-objective — the "Purple Line" — consisting of that part of the enemy reserve trenches which lay to the north of the "Brown Line." The capture of this third sub-objective would straighten the "Brown Line."

For the same reasons, there was a sub-objective to the 2nd Brigade's main objective, or the "Yellow Line." This "Yellow Line" consisted solely of the German trench (Oxonian Trench) constructed for the defence of the village against attacks from the flanks and rear, and joined the "Brown Line" at the Wytschaete-Messines road, where the "Brown Line" turned towards the west to form the defensive flank. The sub-objective to the main objective was the "Red Line," which ran parallel to and a hundred and fifty yards to the east of the Wytschaete-Messines road. The "Red Line" was to be taken when the 25th Division came up on the left.

The Canterbury Regiment was given the largest share in the capture of the brigade's objectives. The first two sub-objectives were divided among two battalions, the right half being allotted to the 1st Canterbury Battalion, and the left half (together with the third sub-objective) to the 1st Otago Battalion. The whole of the brigade's main objectives were allotted to the 2nd Canterbury Battalion, reinforced by the 10th Company of the 2nd Otago Battalion, which was attached to the 2nd Canterbury Battalion for the operations. The remainder of the 2nd Otago Battalion formed the brigade reserve.

The following transcript of the brigade's Operation Orders shows the tasks allotted to the Canterbury Battalions:—

1ST CANTERBURY BATTALION:

(a) *First sub-objective*: The capture and consolidation of the Blue Line, *i.e.*, Uhlan Trench, Uhlan Support, Uhlan Row.

and Oyster Avenue, from the Gooseberry Farm-Messines road (inclusive) to the Moulin de l'Hospice (exclusive).

(b) *Second sub-objective*: The capture and consolidation of the Brown Line, i.e., the Oyster Reserve [inclusive of the Gooseberry Farm-Messines road and the Wytschaete-Messines road (inclusive)] to the junction of the last named road and the Wulverghem-Messines road (exclusive). This sub-objective also includes the capture of Oyster Avenue, the Strong Works about the Au Bon Fermier Cabaret, and the houses on the northern side of the Gooseberry F̈arm-Messines road, which latter operation is to be allotted to a specially detailed body of troops.

2ND CANTERBURY BATTALION: Brigade Main Objective.

(a) *First sub-objective*: The capture of the Yellow Line (Oxonian Trench) from the right brigade boundary to the Wytschaete-Messines road (inclusive) and the establishment of a bombing post down Unbearable Trench about one hundred yards east of the junction of that trench with Oxonian Trench. The mopping-up of that portion of Messines north of the brigade's right boundary.

(b) *Second sub-objective*: The straightening up of the Yellow Line by capturing the Red Line (October Support) from the Yellow Line to the brigade left boundary.

The 1st Canterbury Battalion had been in the tunnels in Hill 63 since the evening of June 5th. On that evening its Commanding Officer, Lieutenant-Colonel R. Young, who had been attached to the Division for liaison work during the operations, handed over the command to Major A. D. Stitt, who was to lead the battalion in the attack. The second in command of the battalion, Major N. F. Shepherd, left for the transport lines on the same day, to supervise the work of the "Q" branch during the attack.

At 9.30 p.m. on the night of June 6th/7th, the battalion left for its assembly trenches, *via* Plumduff and Calgary Avenues, and was in position by midnight. In the afternoon of that day, one platoon of the 2nd Company and one platoon of the 12th Company had relieved the 2nd Auckland Battalion in the right half of the 2nd Brigade's portion of the front line.

The assembly positions were as follows:—

Battalion Headquarters:
   Auckland Switch.

2nd Company, on right:
   (3 platoons) Advanced Trench (in No-Man's-Land) and
      Front Line.
   (1 platoon) Auckland Switch.

12th Company, on left:
   (2 platoons) Advanced Trench.   .
   (2 platoons) Advanced Travel Trench.

13th Company, in support:
   (2 platoons) Otira Trench, forward of Auckland Switch.
   (1 platoon) Otira Trench, right of Romer Avenue.
   (1 platoon) Otira Trench, left of Romer Avenue.

1st Company, in reserve:
   (2 platoons) Otira Travel Trench, forward of Auckland
      Switch.
   (1 platoon) Otira Travel Trench, right of Romer Avenue.
   (1 platoon) Otira Travel Trench, left of Romer Avenue.

The strength of officers and other ranks taken into action is
not stated in the official reports.

Before moving off for the trenches, the battalion was unfortunate in losing thirty men by shell fire, which caught them di-
viding rations outside the tunnels. The assembly trenches were
not shelled, from the time the battalion arrived in them, till it
moved forward to the assault. Nevertheless, conditions were
rendered very unpleasant by the enemy's copious use of gas, as
appears from the following extract from the Brigadier's Report
on the operations:—

"The move to the assembly trenches was carried out to time,
but under very adverse conditions, owing to the effect of the gas
shells which the enemy kept pouring over our communication
trenches throughout the evening, and the early part of the night.
The effect of these shells is most demoralising and depressing,
and it reflects the greatest credit on the brigade that they succeeded in reaching their assembly trenches in the way they did,
as each man was heavily handicapped by having to wear his box
respirator. Considering the heavy nature of this gas barrage,

the casualties from gas were exceedingly light: the 2nd Otago Battalion suffered the most severely, losing twenty-five men.''

In the meantime, the 2nd Battalion had since the morning of June 3rd been under canvas at Canteen Corner, making final preparations for action. At 9 p.m. on the night of June 6th/7th the battalion left camp for the assembly trenches *viâ* ''Y'' route (a cross country track along the spur which connects Neuve Eglise and Hill 63) and Plumduff and Calgary Avenues. The strength of the battalion was twenty-one officers and six hundred and sixty-nine other ranks, and Lieutenant-Colonel H. Stewart was in command. Major G. C. Griffiths, second in command, remained at the transport lines.

By 1.30 a.m. the battalion was in its assembly positions, which were as follows:—

Battalion Headquarters in Auckland Trench, on the right of Calgary Avenue.

1st Company in Auckland Trench:
    1 platoon on the left of Romer Avenue, 3 platoons between Romer Avenue and the brigade's right boundary.

2nd Company in Auckland Trench:
    3 platoons from Calgary Avenue to Otago Avenue, 1 platoon on the left of Otago Avenue.

12th Company in Auckland Trench:
    On the left of Otago Avenue to Wulverghem-Messines road.

13th Company:
    2 platoons in Auckland Trench between Calgary and Romer Avenues.
    2 platoons in Canterbury Trench between Calgary and Romer Avenues.

Zero hour was fixed for 3.10 a.m. on the 7th. From 12.30 a.m. to that hour the night was fairly quiet, except that one section of machine-guns opened the barrage four minutes before zero. Fortunately this was not sufficient to alarm the enemy; and no great damage was done, beyond the fact that some of the troops in the rear assembly trenches moved forward on hearing the machine-guns open. The morning was very dark, and there was a slight mist in addition, so that it was quite dark when precisely at 3.10 a.m. the mines were exploded at Ontario Farm and our barrage came down.

There was no creeping barrage across No-Man's Land, but there was a stationary 18-pounder barrage on the enemy front line till nine minutes after zero.

At zero hour the leading waves of the 1st Canterbury Battalion (2nd and 12th Companies) left the assembly trench in line in extended order, and advanced across No-Man's-Land till they were checked by our barrage on the enemy front line. They were followed by the 13th Company plus 1 platoon of the 1st Company, and then by the remainder of the 1st Company of the same battalion, extended over the whole of the battalion front, in irregular line of sections in single file, with fifteen yards' distance between companies. On the left, the 1st Otago Battalion moved forward in similar formation.

At thirty yards' distance, these battalions were followed by the 2nd Canterbury Battalion, in four irregular lines of sections with fifteen yards' distance between lines, as follows:—

(1) 2 platoons each of 13th Company (on right) and 2nd Company (on left).

(2) 2 platoons each of 1st Company (on right) and 12th Company (on left).

(3) The remaining platoons of 1st Company and 12th Company.

(4) The remaining platoons of 13th Company and 2nd Company.

The attached company (the 10th North Otago) of the 2nd Otago Battalion formed a fifth line of sections; and immediately behind it came the remainder of that battalion, in similar formation. The last of these troops had passed the forward assembly trench in No-Man's-Land by seven minutes after zero, before the enemy counter-barrage had come down.

Commenting on this the Brigadier says, in his Report on the operations:—

''The rapidity and ease with which the brigade moved out of their assembly trenches and crossed No-Man's-Land, I attribute to the fact that we had already rehearsed this advance six times on a carefully prepared position in the Quelmes area, during the period of training for the offensive, where our own assembly trenches and that of the enemy on the Messines Ridge had been cut as near as possible to scale; and so accurately were they sited

LIEUT.-COLONEL A. D. STITT, D.S.O., M.C

LIEUT.-COLONEL J. G. HUGHES, C.M.G., D.S.O. (D)

and so true was the representation, that when the men came to carry out the actual attack, they found little difficulty in finding their way to their objectives in the German lines.'' It may be added that the darkness of the morning was intensified, not only by the mist, but by the smoke of our guns, and by the clouds of dust raised by the shells.

Immediately the barrage lifted off the enemy front line the 2nd and 12th Companies of the 1st Canterbury Battalion entered it without opposition, and five minutes later the further lifting of the barrage enabled them to capture the support line at 3.25 a.m. The barrage remained stationary on a line two hundred yards in advance of the support line for eleven minutes, during which time the 13th Company and one platoon of the 1st Company of the same battalion moved up to the barrage into position to continue the advance. Twenty-seven minutes after zero (3.37 a.m.) the barrage, which up to this time had conformed to the shape of the front line of the enemy trenches, began to straighten out; and six minutes later the barrage was in a straight line across the whole brigade front, and moving forward at right angles to the line of direction of the advance, at the rate of a hundred yards every three minutes.

The process of straightening out allowed the 1st Company platoon to take the Au Bon Fermier Cabaret, with three machine-guns and seventeen prisoners. The 13th Company followed up the barrage and took the Brown Line at 3.50 a.m.

Immediately after the capture of these objectives, the battalion consolidated in three lines, between the old German front line and the Brown Line. The 13th Company dug a trench fifty to a hundred yards behind Oyster Reserve, from the Wulverghem-Messines road to the Gooseberry Farm-Messines road. About a hundred yards to the rear of the right flank of the 13th Company, the platoon of the 1st Company which had been attached to the 13th Company for the purpose of dealing with Au Bon Fermier Cabaret, dug a strong-point.

Midway between the 13th Company's trench and the Blue Line, the 2nd and 12th Companies dug in, with their flanks resting on the two roads last mentioned above. The remainder of the 1st Company dug a trench under cover of the slope, between the same two roads and from fifty to a hundred yards in advance

of the old enemy front line. At 4.10 a.m., battalion headquarters was established in the ruins of a house, midway between the Au Bon Fermier Cabaret and the Moulin de l'Hospice,
and close to the strong-point garrisoned by the detached platoon
of the 1st Company.

Meanwhile the 2nd Canterbury Battalion had been following
close on the heels of the 1st Battalion. Directly the 1st Battalion
had captured the Brown Line, the 2nd Battalion followed the
barrage into the left portion of the village of Messines. On its
way up the battalion had met with a little opposition from two
machine-guns in shell holes two hundred yards west of the village, which had been passed by the leading troops. These guns
were rushed and the crews killed.

When the barrage was half way through the village, it halted
for fourteen minutes (from 3.52 to 4.06 a.m.). During this time
the 1st Company commenced its work of clearing the dugouts in
the village, to the right of the Wulverghem-Messines road. On
the left, however, the barrage failed to lift, and the 12th Company was thus prevented from entering the northern outskirts
of the village. Two platoons of this company, however, were
worked around to the right flank of the position; and on the barrage lifting, Oxonian Trench was rushed by the whole of the
Company. Many of the enemy were killed, and fifty prisoners
were taken.

Meanwhile the barrage had crossed the remainder of the
village, at the rate of a hundred yards every fifteen minutes,
and was closely followed by two platoons of each of the 2nd and
13th Companies. Very close behind them came the 1st Company,
which in its work of clearing the village met with some resistance
from snipers and bombers. This resistance was quickly overcome; a large number of the enemy were killed, and a hundred
and eighty prisoners were taken. Two machine-guns were captured in the church, by the 1st Company.

On passing through the village, the 13th Company's two
leading platoons (on the right) were held up by a party of the
enemy, which had manned Oxonian Trench and the trenches in
the cemetery to the east of the village. The remaining two
platoons of the Company were immediately brought up, and the
enemy position was rushed. Here a number of the enemy were

killed, and fifty were taken prisoners. On the left. the 2nd Company's two leading platoons met with little opposition, except from a machine-gun, which they captured. The company took its share of Oxonian Trench without much difficulty or resistance.

The 2nd Canterbury Battalion had captured all its objectives by 4.58 a.m., in accordance with the timetable, and without meeting with serious opposition. Of the twenty machine-guns captured by the battalion, only five had been brought into action by the enemy; and these had been rushed before they could do much damage. Practically no artillery fire was encountered till the enemy's support trenches were passed; and no heavy fire until Oxonian Trench was captured.

At 4.12 a.m. Lieutenant-Colonel Stewart had established his battalion headquarters at the Moulin de l'Hospice. After the capture of the final objective, patrols and covering parties were pushed forward as far as the barrage would permit, and the work of consolidation commenced. This consisted of a narrow and deep trench parallel to and about two hundred yards in advance of Oxonian Trench.

At 5 a.m. the enemy began to shell the village very heavily, and this shelling was maintained till the battalion was relieved next day. The digging of the trench proceeded under very heavy shell fire, and it was here that the chief losses of the battalion were incurred. At the same time the 1st Battalion's new trenches came under heavy enfilade fire from the enemy's artillery. This fire continued without intermission until 5 p.m. the following day, and was the main cause of the battalion's casualties in the operations.

At about 5 a.m., Lieutenant-Colonel Stewart, while moving the 2nd Battalion headquarters forward to the village. was dangerously wounded in eight places by a shell. Major J. McCrae, commanding the 2nd Otago Battalion, took over the command, till he was relieved at 8.30 a.m. by Major F. Starnes, D.S.O., who had been sent up from Le Plus Douve Farm. Battalion headquarters was then established by Major Starnes on the south side of the Wulverghem-Messines road, just to the west of the village.

During the clearing of Messines and the capture of Oxonian Trench, our barrage had assumed the nature of a "box barrage"

round the village; while at the same time there was a creeping
barrage through the village, to enable the dug-outs to be cleared
piece-meal. The barrage on the flanks of the village began to
creep forward again at 5 a.m.

By this time the 25th Division was up on the left, and the
1st Brigade came through the 2nd Brigade, and attacked the
Black Line. At 5.20 a.m. (zero plus two hours ten minutes) the
whole of that line had been taken, and a protective barrage established three hundred yards in advance of it. The attack
paused at this point for over three hours, while the artillery
moved up. At 8.40 a.m. (zero plus five hours thirty minutes)
the barrage began to move on again, and nine minutes later the
Black Dotted Line was taken by the 1st Brigade, and posts established there. Shortly after 1 p.m. the enemy were seen massing
on the Green Line for a counter attack. An artillery barrage
was put down, and the attack was broken up before reaching the
Black Dotted Line.

There was still another pause in the attack till 3.10 p.m.
(zero plus twelve hours), when the 4th Australian Division
went through the 1st Brigade, advanced to and captured the
Green Chain Line, and linked up with the Corps on our left.
The reports as to the actual position of the Australians during
the 7th and the night of the 7th/8th are very conflicting, and
the whole matter is obscure: but by 10 a.m. on the 8th, the Green
Chain Line was in the undisputed possession of the 4th Australian Division. Till then the position gave grounds for anxiety,
to the 1st Brigade especially.

The 1st Brigade being firmly established on the Black Dotted
Line, the dispositions of the 1st Canterbury Battalion were altered
slightly. A new trench was dug in front of the Blue Line, and
garrisoned by the 13th Company and three platoons of the 1st
Company, the rest of the battalion remaining in their original
trenches. The change was completed by 4.30 p.m. Half an hour
later, battalion headquarters was moved back to our old front
line, and telephonic communication was established between the
front line companies and battalion headquarters.

Both the Canterbury Battalions spent the rest of the day, and
the night which followed, in improving their positions. During
the night plenty of rations and munitions were brought up; and

though heavy shelling was still maintained by the enemy, the trenches now afforded a good measure of protection against its effects.

The next day (the 8th) the shelling was still continuous and heavy; but the work of improving the trenches went on steadily, and some useful wiring was done, by the 1st Battalion especially. At 6 p.m. on the same day, the 2nd Battalion was relieved by the 1st Wellington Battalion, and moved to Battle Reserve trenches. These trenches consisted of two lines in the right half of the Divisional area, the front line linking up with the 1st Canterbury Battalion's front line. The support line did not join up the 1st Battalion's line, but began at the point where the Blue Line crossed the Messines-Ploegsteert road, and ran parallel to the 2nd Battalion's front line as far as the right Divisional boundary.

On this day the regiment suffered severe loss through the death of the Rev. Father J. J. McMenamin, who was killed while burying the dead. He had been with the 2nd Battalion since it was formed, and was loved and respected by every officer and other rank who had known him.

Rations and a welcome issue of rum came up early in the evening, and with them clean socks for everyone. The night was quiet, and the men had a chance to make up for the previous sleepless nights. Trench improvements continued the following day (the 9th) and at 4 p.m. both battalions moved back to rest, the 1st Battalion to Forfar Camp, Waterloo road, and the 2nd Battalion to Crucifix Camp, on the south-western slopes of Neuve Eglise Hill. Here, on the 10th, Lieutenant-Colonel Young rejoined the 1st Battalion and Major Griffiths took over the command of the 2nd Battalion.

While the casualties may be considered light, when the importance of the operation is taken into account, yet they were heavy enough to reduce the fighting forces of both battalions to much below normal. During the three days they were as under:—

1st Battalion.				Officers.	Other Ranks.
Killed	..	..	..	–	45
Wounded	..	..	..	8	234
Missing	..	..	..	–	8
Total	..	..	..	8	287

		Other
2nd Battalion	Officers.	Ranks.
Killed	5*	38
Wounded	7	270
Missing	—	15
Total	12	323

*Rev. Father McMenamin, Lieutenants F. A. Anderson
and W. P. Thompson, and (Died of Wounds) Lieutenant A. Cracroft Wilson and 2nd Lieutenant P. J.
Palmer.

The missing men were all subsequently accounted for.

Beyond the three machine-guns taken by the 1st Battalion at
Au Bon Fermier Cabaret, there is no record of this battalion's
captures. This is not surprising, when it is remembered that
the battalion's objectives consisted of trenches which had been
under direct observation, and had been so battered by our artillery that it was a difficult matter for the attacking troops to find
where the trenches had been. On the other hand, the 2nd Battalion's final objectives were not under direct observation, and
notwithstanding the terrible bombardment to which the village
had been subject for weeks, many of the underground shelters
remained intact. This battalion's recorded captures were therefore much larger, and comprised:—

Prisoners	350
Machine-guns	20
Trench Mortars, 8-inch	1
9-inch	1
Anti-tank Guns	3
Searchlights	4

The 2nd Brigade remained out of the line till June 12th, the
time being spent in resting and reorganizing. The casualties had
reduced the majority of the platoons below the minimum fighting
strength of twenty-eight laid down by General Headquarters, and
accordingly the companies had to be reorganized on a three platoon basis and in some cases on a two platoon basis. The 2nd
Canterbury Battalion during this period received a reinforcement
of four officers and fifty-two other ranks from its "B" team at
Morbecque.

On June 12th, orders were received to relieve the 9th Australian Brigade in the sector from St. Yves to the River Douve. This was the extreme right of the new line established on June 7th and 8th, the right flank of the brigade being at the junction of the new and old British front lines. The right half of the front line, from St. Yves to Ash Avenue, was allotted to the 2nd Canterbury Battalion, and the left half from Ash Avenue to the Douve to the 1st Otago Battalion. The 1st Canterbury and 2nd Otago Battalions were in reserve at "The Catacombs," a system of deep tunnels in Hill 63, at Hyde Park Corner in Ploegsteert Wood.

These battalions were able to relieve in daylight, and left the rest area early in the afternoon. The 2nd Canterbury Battalion left Crucifix Camp at 7 p.m. and relieved the 35th Battalion Australian Imperial Force, the relief being completed by 1.40 a.m. on the 13th. The companies in the line, from right to left, were the 1st, 2nd, and 12th Companies, with the 13th Company in support. Battalion headquarters was in a deep dug-out underneath St. Yves post office.

Patrols were sent out immediately, but owing to the leaders not having seen the ground in daylight, and the meagre information about the enemy received from the previous garrison, very little ground was covered. After daybreak, patrols were again sent out, and were fired on from Les Trois Tilleuls Farm. Another patrol, working south along the German support line, found the trenches abandoned by the enemy, and met patrols from the 3rd Canterbury Battalion, 4th New Zealand Infantry Brigade, which was holding the old British front line on the eastern edge of Ploegsteert Wood, to the right of the 2nd Brigade. The rest of the battalion spent the day in improving the posts, which had been handed over in poor order.

Late in the afternoon orders were received that the 2nd Brigade was to advance a distance of fifteen hundred yards, and to establish a line of strong-posts from La Truie Farm to a point on the Douve River to the south-west of the Ferme de la Croix. The 3rd New Zealand (Rifle) Brigade on the right, and the 75th Brigade (25th Division) on the left, were to continue the line of posts north and south, the intention being that these posts should be linked up later on, and eventually should become the front line of a new trench system. It was considered by the staff that the enemy had withdrawn his main forces from the objectives, leaving only weak rearguards, and that no artillery barrage to support the attack was necessary.

At the last moment, the 25th Division decided that it would not move forward without a barrage: but the New Zealand Division determined to carry out the original plans. It had been the brigadier's intention to use for this attack the 1st Canterbury and 2nd Otago Battalions, which had suffered less severely than the other battalions of the brigade in the Messines operations. These battalions had therefore been left in the Catacombs, so that they would be kept fresh for the attack, which it was thought would be made early in the morning. The retreat of the enemy upset these calculations; and as the forward movement of the rear battalions in daylight would have warned the enemy of our intended advance, there was nothing to be done but to use the front line battalions.

The ultimate objective assigned to the 2nd Canterbury Battalion was the southern half of the brigade objective, as far north as a road which ran west from Warneton, and passed five hundred yards north of Sunken Farm. The buildings of La Truie and Sunken Farms were accordingly included in the objective; and before these were reached, Fuze Cottage, Thatched Cottage, Flattened Farm, and Au Chasseur Cabaret had to be secured. The advance also involved the capture of a trench system, subsidiary to the old German front line system, and accordingly running north and south. On our maps this trench was called Unchained Trench: it lay two hundred and fifty yards to the west of the Au Chasseur Cabaret.

Orders were received by the company commanders so late that there was barely time to communicate them to the platoon commanders before 9 p.m., the hour fixed for the attack. As the troops were being assembled a large number of low-flying German aeroplanes came over the trenches, and after firing on the troops, returned to give the alarm. Directly the advance began a heavy barrage by artillery and machine-guns came down, and fairly heavy casualties were incurred. The country had been so broken up by artillery fire, that roads and other land-marks were almost unrecognisable, even by day. The night was a very dark one,

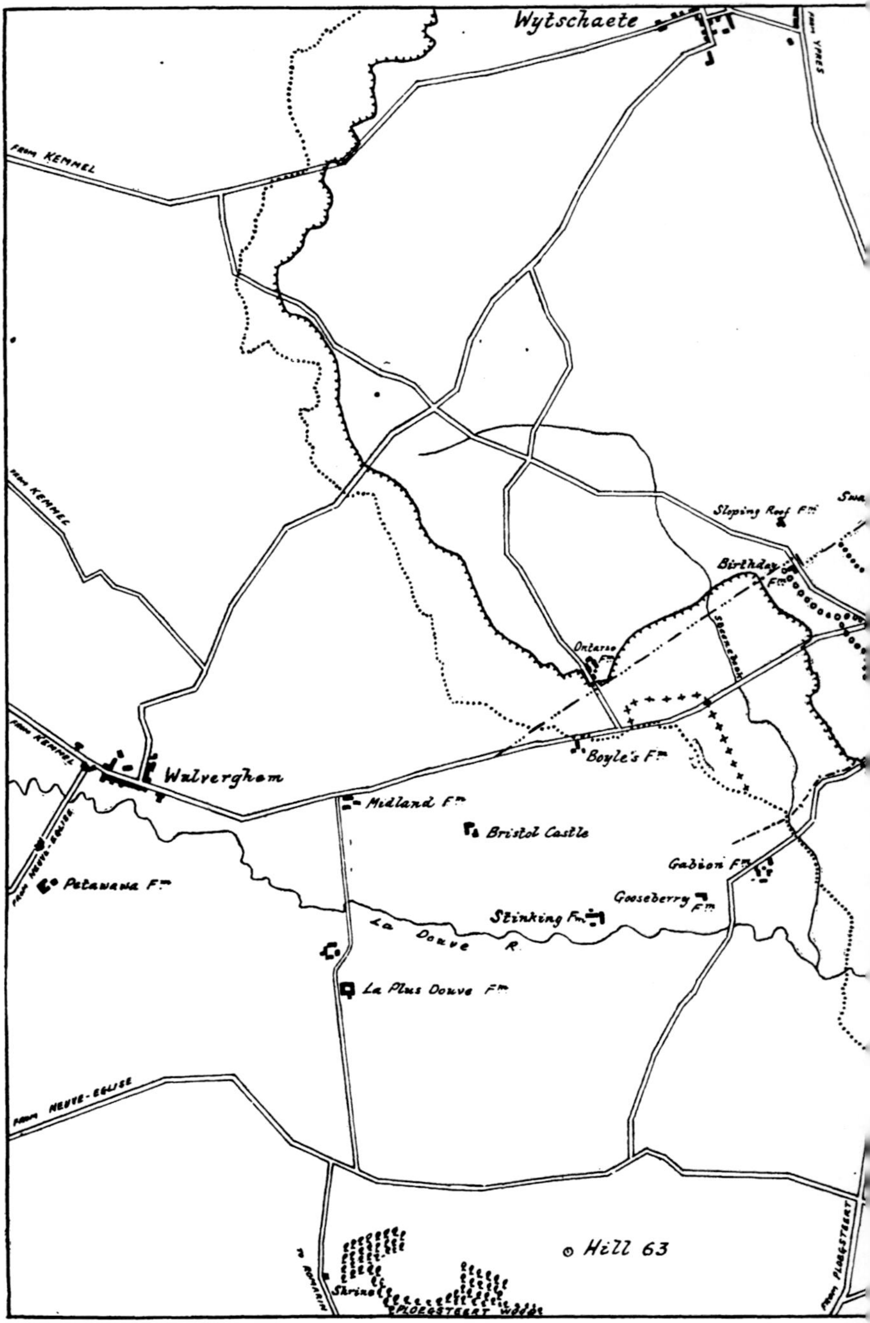

Wytschaete
FROM YPRES
FROM KEMMEL
FROM KEMMEL
Sloping Roof Fm
Birthday Fm
Ontario Fm
Steenebeek
Boyle's Fm
FROM KEMMEL
Wulverghem
Midland Fm
Bristol Castle
FROM NEUVE-EGLISE
Petawawa Fm
Gabion Fm
Gooseberry Fm
Stinking Fm
La Douve R.
La Plus Douve Fm
FROM NEUVE-EGLISE
Hill 63
TO ROMARIN
Shrine
PLOEGSTEERT WOOD
FROM PLOEGSTEERT

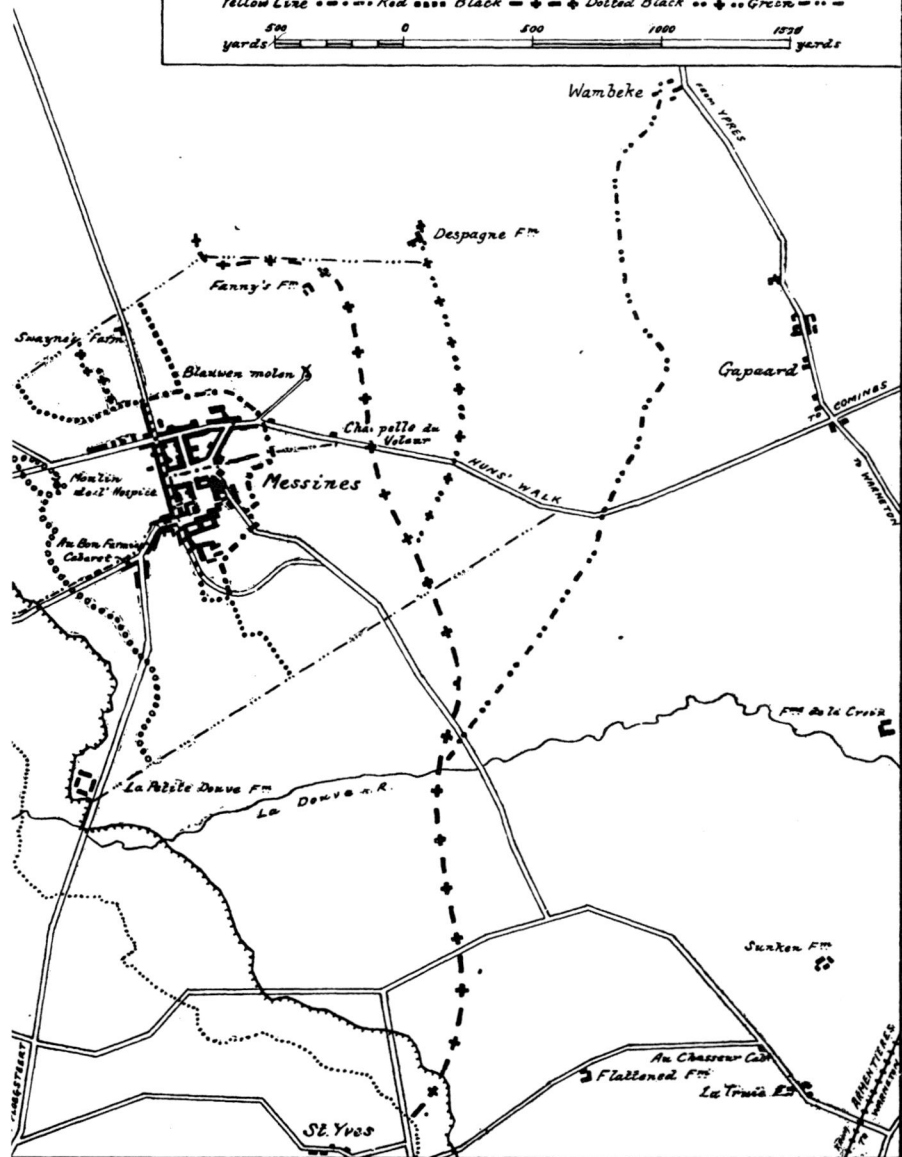

MESSINES

Front Line Trenches, 7th June 1917 : British .... : German ....
N.Z. Division's Assembly Trenches + + + Divisional Boundaries —..—
Inter-Brigade Boundary —..— Blue Line ••••• Brown •••• Purple •+•+
Yellow Line •—•..• Red •••• Black —+—+ Dotted Black •• +•• Green —••—

500   0   500   1000   1500
yards   yards

Wambeke

Despagne Fm

Fanny's Fm

Swayne's Farm

Blauwen molen

Gapaard

Chapelle du Voleur

HUNS' WALK

Moulin de l'Hospice

Messines

Au Bon Fermier Cabaret

Fm de la Croix

La Petite Douve Fm

La Douve a R.

Sunken Fm

Au Chasseur Cab

Flattened Fm

La Truie Est

St. Yves

so that. even with the aid of compasses, it was diffi-ult to keep direction.

On the right of the 2nd Canterbury Battalion was the 1st Company. whose strength was reduced to two platoons by casualties sustained at Messines. To it were attached two platoons of the 13th Company, and the rest of this company was attached to the 2nd Company, in the centre. On the left was the 12th Company.

Flattened Farm and Thatched Cottage were found unoccupied by the enemy; but Unchained Trench was strongly held, and all three attacking companies met with serious resistance at this point. On the right, the bombardment by the 2nd Light Trench Mortar Battery of a strong concrete machine-gun emplacement enabled the 1st Company to eject the enemy from the portion of the trench to the south of the St. Yves-Au Chasseur Cabaret road. The 12th Company, on the left, had lost direction and come too far south. owing to the troops which it had relieved having given incorrect information as to the position of Fuze Cottage. This company drove the enemy from a portion of Unchained Trench to the north of the St. Yves-Au Chasseur Cabaret road.

The 2nd Company had suffered heavily in coming through the barrage: part joined up the 12th Company in Unchained Trench, and one platoon, which had lost direction, dug in two hundred yards south of the 1st Company. One platoon of the 1st Company. which had been detailed to take La Truie Farm, was unable to get any information as to the position of the rest of the battalion, and eventually dug in near the 2nd Company platoon last mentioned, and on the left of the 3rd Brigade.

Meanwhile, in view of the heavy machine-gun fire from the defences of the Au Chasseur Cabaret and La Truie Farm. the company commanders had decided to consolidate the positions they had captured in Unchained Trench. This was reported to battalion headquarters, but as information had been received that the 1st Otago Battalion had taken all its objectives, orders were sent to the company commanders that they were to go on to their final objective. It may be said here that the information as to the Otago Battalion's position was not correct. as the companies of this battalion had "completely lost their way. and came back to their original position with difficulty.''* On receipt of these orders, an assault was made on Au Chasseur Cabaret, but was repulsed by the enemy, with heavy loss to us. However, a concrete observation post, two hundred yards to the north-west of the Cabaret, was captured by the 12th Company.

It was now growing light, so there was no choice but to consolidate the ground already gained. The battalion was in a very exposed position, and movement was difficult, on account of sniping from rifles and machine-guns. During the afternoon of the 14th, the Cabaret and La Truie and Sunken Farms were the targets of a severe and unusually accurate bombardment by our heavy artillery. This reduced the enemy sniping. and enabled the battalion to be reorganised to continue the advance.

It was arranged that the new advance should be made under a creeping barrage: and the 25th Division was also to advance at the same time. Rations and water were brought up during the day with difficulty; and the men were very tired. as they had very little sleep since the night of the 12th. As had happened the previous evening, there was no possibility of bringing up the 1st Canterbury and the 2nd Otago Battalions, which were better fitted to make an attack than the battalions in the line; but it was arranged that these fresh battalions should take over the new line directly it had been consolidated.

The new attack took place at 7.30 p.m. on June 14th. The capture of Sunken Farm was now allotted to the 1st Otago Battalion, and the new inter-battalion boundary ran immediately to the south of the farm. At zero hour, a hurricane bombardment of the Au Chasseur Cabaret was opened by the 2nd Light Trench Mortar Battery. Under cover of the barrage, one platoon (''A'' platoon) of the 1st Company, with fifteen other ranks of the 13th Company attached, worked up the communication trenches, and rushed the Cabaret immediately the barrage lifted. Three machine-guns were taken and their crews killed after some resistance.

The rest of the enemy, in the neighbouring trenches, retreated in the direction of La Basse Ville, but came under heavy enfilade fire from the Lewis-guns of the 12th Company, which was advancing on the left. They also came under heavy fire from the

---

* Brigadier's Report on Operations.

rifles and Lewis-gun of the other platoon ("B" platoon) of the 1st Company, which was advancing on La Truie Farm. This platoon suffered a few casualties from the one machine-gun which was brought into action at the Cabaret; but the prompt capture of the Cabaret enabled it to follow the barrage to the Farm, which was taken without difficulty. The survivors of the garrison, and some of those who had retreated from the Cabaret —twenty-seven in all—were taken prisoners. Over one hundred enemy dead were afterwards counted between the Farm and the Cabaret.

After capturing the Cabaret, the "A" platoon of the 1st Company pushed on, without meeting further resistance; and under cover of the barrage, which was now stationary, dug a strong-point. This was in an avenue of trees, midway between Sunken and La Truie Farms. At the same time, the "B" platoon dug a strong-point a hundred yards to the north of La Truie Farm, under heavy machine-gun and rifle fire from the Warneton-Armentières railway and La Basse Ville, which caused severe casualties. This platoon was joined here by a platoon of the 12th Company, which had been detailed to dig a strong-point further north, but had lost its officer and senior non-commissioned officers before arriving there.

The remainder of the 12th Company dug a support trench in front of Au Chasseur Cabaret. The 2nd Company had been left in reserve in Unchained Trench. This point was on the enemy's barrage line, and the 2nd Company had to sit down under very severe shelling by heavy artillery, and suffered serious casualties.

The 3rd (Rifle) Brigade having attained its objectives the previous evening, did not take part in the advance. The 1st Otago Battalion experienced very little difficulty in attaining its objectives, and on its left the 75th Brigade (25th Division) was equally successful.

During the morning of June 14th, the 1st Company of the 1st Canterbury Battalion had come into support of the 2nd Battalion, and had occupied the front line trenches vacated by that battalion on the night of the 13th. Just before daylight on the 15th, the 2nd Company of the 1st Battalion took over all the 2nd Battalion's posts. The 12th and 13th Companies of the

1st Battalion remained at the Catacombs; but battalion headquarters was moved to the St. Yves post office. The whole of
the 2nd Battalion moved back to the Catacombs, and rested till
the following night. It had suffered very heavy casualties during the operations of June 13th and 14th, having had thirty-one
other ranks killed and three officers and ninety-six other ranks
wounded, out of a total strength of thirteen officers and three
hundred and ninety-eight other ranks engaged.

The two companies of the 1st Battalion at the Catacombs
were engaged in digging new support and travel trenches, on
the nights of the 15th, 16th, and 17th; and on the nights of the
16th and 17th, the 2nd Battalion dug a communication trench,
from the old front line to the German communication trench
which ran beside the St. Yves-Au Chasseur Cabaret road. At
dawn on the 18th, the 2nd Battalion marched out from the Catacombs to its old quarters at Romarin. The night of the same
day, the 1st Battalion was relieved by the 2nd Wellington Battalion, and moved out to Bulford Camp. During the period in
the line this battalion had had two officers and thirty-four other
ranks wounded.

The 3rd Canterbury Battalion (Lieutenant-Colonel R. A.
Row), which had arrived in France at the end of May, took no
part in the actual attack on the Messines Ridge. On June 7th,
when the battle opened, the battalion left its camp near Bailleul
and bivouacked in the neighbourhood of Wulverghem. On the
8th and 9th the battalion was engaged in repairing the Wulverghem-Messines and Birthday Farm-Messines roads, and on
the 10th relieved the 2nd/5th Battalion Loyal North Lancashires
(57th Division) in the old British front line from the Warnave
River to St. Yves. On the 13th, on the evacuation by the enemy
of his old front line and support lines, these lines were occupied
by the battalion on its own front. The same evening the 4th
Battalion of the 3rd New Zealand (Rifle) Brigade continued the
advance, and the 3rd Canterbury Battalion marched back to a
bivouac area near Pont de Nieppe.

Its casualties in the battle had been thirteen other ranks
killed and five officers and forty-four other ranks wounded.

CHAPTER X.

AFTER MESSINES: LA BASSE VILLE: TRAINING FOR PASSCHENDAELE.

On its relief in the line on June 18th, the 2nd Brigade came into Divisional reserve. It had suffered badly during the battle and had worked hard since then, and now was not fit for anything but rest. The remaining officers and men of the "B" teams returned from Morbecque, and with them came reinforcements: in spite of this, however, both the battalions, and especially the 2nd, were much below strength. After a few days' rest, during which the men were re-equipped as well as possible, a programme of training was issued by the brigade commander. On the 21st, Lieutenant-General Sir A. J. Godley, General Officer commanding the II Anzac Army Corps, and two days later, Major-General Sir A. H. Russell, General Officer commanding the New Zealand Division, inspected the brigade.

Meanwhile, the New Zealand Division had been holding a three brigade front from the River Lys to the River Douve (south of Ferme de la Croix). This arrangement had been made possible by the arrival of the 4th New Zealand Infantry Brigade, which had been attached to the Division. On the 30th, the Division was relieved in the line by the 4th Australian Division; and as the latter had only the normal number of brigades, the 4th New Zealand Infantry Brigade, being fresher than any of the other brigades, was detached from the New Zealand Division and temporarily attached to the 4th Australian Division. The 4th New Zealand Infantry Brigade continued to hold the line in the sector between the River Lys (exclusive) and the River Warnave (inclusive).

Later, when the New Zealand Division again went into the line, the 4th Brigade took the place of the 3rd (Rifle) Brigade, which on July 2nd had been detached from the Division, and sent north to work with the 1st French Army in its preparations for the great attack there.

This is a convenient place to record the doings of the 3rd Canterbury Battalion. On being relieved in the line east of Ploegsteert Wood, on June 13th, the battalion marched to a bivouac area near Pont de Nieppe village, on the main road between Armentières and Nieppe. Here it carried on training till the 19th, when it marched to billets at Nieppe. From these billets it supplied working-parties to the line and forward areas, which were not interrupted by a move on the 22nd to billets at Brune Gaye, near Romarin. On June 30th, the battalion relieved the 3rd Otago Battalion in the front line, on the whole of the brigade's sector. Relieved by the 3rd Auckland Battalion on July 8th, the battalion occupied billets at Nieppe, and carried on training there: on the 21st it was inspected by the General Officer commanding the brigade.

On July 20th, the 4th Brigade again became attached to the New Zealand Division, and on the 23rd it was ordered to take over from the 2nd Brigade the portion of the line which lay between the 4th Brigade's existing left flank and a point on the River Lys, half a mile south of the sugar refinery at La Basse Ville. On the date last mentioned, the 3rd Canterbury Battalion relieved the 2nd Otago Battalion in this portion of the line.

To return to the 2nd Brigade: on relief on June 30th, the Division came into Corps reserve, and Divisional Headquarters and the 1st and 3rd Brigades moved to the Berquin area, north-west of Estaires. The 2nd Brigade was left in the Corps area, to carry out certain work that was required in view of a further advance. Both Canterbury Battalions had moved—the 1st to Aldershot Camp, near the Neuve Eglise-Steenwerck road, on June 28th, and the 2nd to Regina Camp, west of the village of Ploegsteert, on the following day.

The work was carried out under the direction of the engineers: the 1st Battalion laid water-pipes and the 2nd Battalion buried telephone cables. The work of the 1st Battalion was at Kemmel, well behind the line, and the parties were not molested even though they did all their work by daylight. The 2nd Battalion parties had quite a different experience: casualties were numerous, for the working areas were well forward, work could be done only at night, and the enemy, being uneasy as to our intentions, shelled everywhere frequently. Lieutenant-Colonel R. Young resumed command of the 1st Battalion on July 1st.

His Majesty the King visited the Messines battle area early in the month, and on the 4th the 2nd Brigade was lined up on the Neuve Eglise-Steenwerck road. and cheered His Majesty as he drove past.

On July 7th the 2nd Battalion was shelled out of Regina Camp, and moved to tents at Canteen Corner. Here it stayed till the 12th, when the brigade had finished its work and rejoined the rest of the Division in the Berquin area. The 1st Battalion was billetted at Doulieu and the 2nd at Neuf Berquin: the mornings were spent in smartening-up drill and training under company commanders' supervision, and the afternoons in games and other forms of recreational training.

On July 18th the 1st Battalion marched back to the Divisional sector, spent the night in the Catacombs (as the deep dug-outs in Hill 63 near Hyde Park Corner were called), and the following day relieved part of the 49th and 50th Battalions of the 13th Brigade of the 4th Australian Division in the front line west of La Basse Ville, from La Truie Farm to a point midway between Trois Tilleuls and Loophole Farms. There was no continuous line of trenches in this sector: the most advanced troops were in small outposts, which consisted of shell-holes connected up and adapted for defence, and which as a rule could not be approached by daylight. The intention was to extend each post from either flank, as time went on, till all met in a continuous line.

The battalion held its sub-sector with the 12th Company in the front line posts, the 13th Company in support, the 1st and 2nd Companies in reserve, and battalion headquarters at Lewisham Lodge. From the evening of the 21st till the 23rd, battalion headquarters was at Laurence Farm, but was forced to return to Lewisham Lodge. as the enemy heavily shelled the farm and set it on fire.

The big attack from the Ypres salient to the sea was fixed for July 31st; and in order to deceive the enemy as to where the real blow was to fall, the II Anzac Army Corps was ordered to take certain steps calculated to lead him to believe that a further advance was intended on the Corps' front — that is, between north-east of Armentières and north-east of Messines. On the

New Zealand Division's front the 2nd Brigade was ordered to establish posts threatening Pont Rouge, a village on the western bank of the River Lys, where the Warneton-Quesnoy road crosses that river: further south, the 4th Brigade was ordered to dig dummy trenches covering other likely bridge-heads on the River Lys; while the 1st Brigade was to capture the village of La Basse Ville.

The operations against Pont Rouge were undertaken by the 3rd Canterbury Battalion, as on June 23rd it had relieved the 2nd Otago Battalion of the 2nd Brigade opposite that village. Operation orders issued to the 3rd Canterbury Battalion on the 22nd gave instructions for two new posts to be established, on the night of July 26th/27th, on the north-east side of the Warneton-Quesnoy road — one a few yards from the road and about seventy yards north-west of the river-bank, and the other about a hundred yards to the west of the first post and about seventy yards north of the river-bank — to command and threaten the bridges over the river.

The orders also laid down that three short dummy trenches were to be dug—two further to the east near the river-bank, and the other between them and our front line—and guiding tapes to be led back to our front line. The object of these and the other operations of the 4th Brigade was to lead the enemy to believe that we contemplated crossing the river at the points opposite the new works.

These operations were duly carried out on the appointed night, when two strong enemy patrols were encountered. These were dispersed, with an estimated loss of fourteen to the enemy, while no casualties were sustained by the battalion.

The 1st Brigade attacked and captured La Basse Ville on July 27th, but was driven out again by an enemy counter-attack. A second attack by the same brigade, on July 31st, was completely successful. Between these two dates the 1st Canterbury Battalion was relieved by the 1st Otago Battalion: battalion headquarters and the 12th and 13th Companies, on relief on the night of the 29th/30th, moved out to Regina Camp (where they joined the 2nd Company, which had been relieved on the 27th) and the 1st Company went to the Catacombs. On August 7th Lieutenant-Colonel Young was appointed temporary brigadier of the 3rd

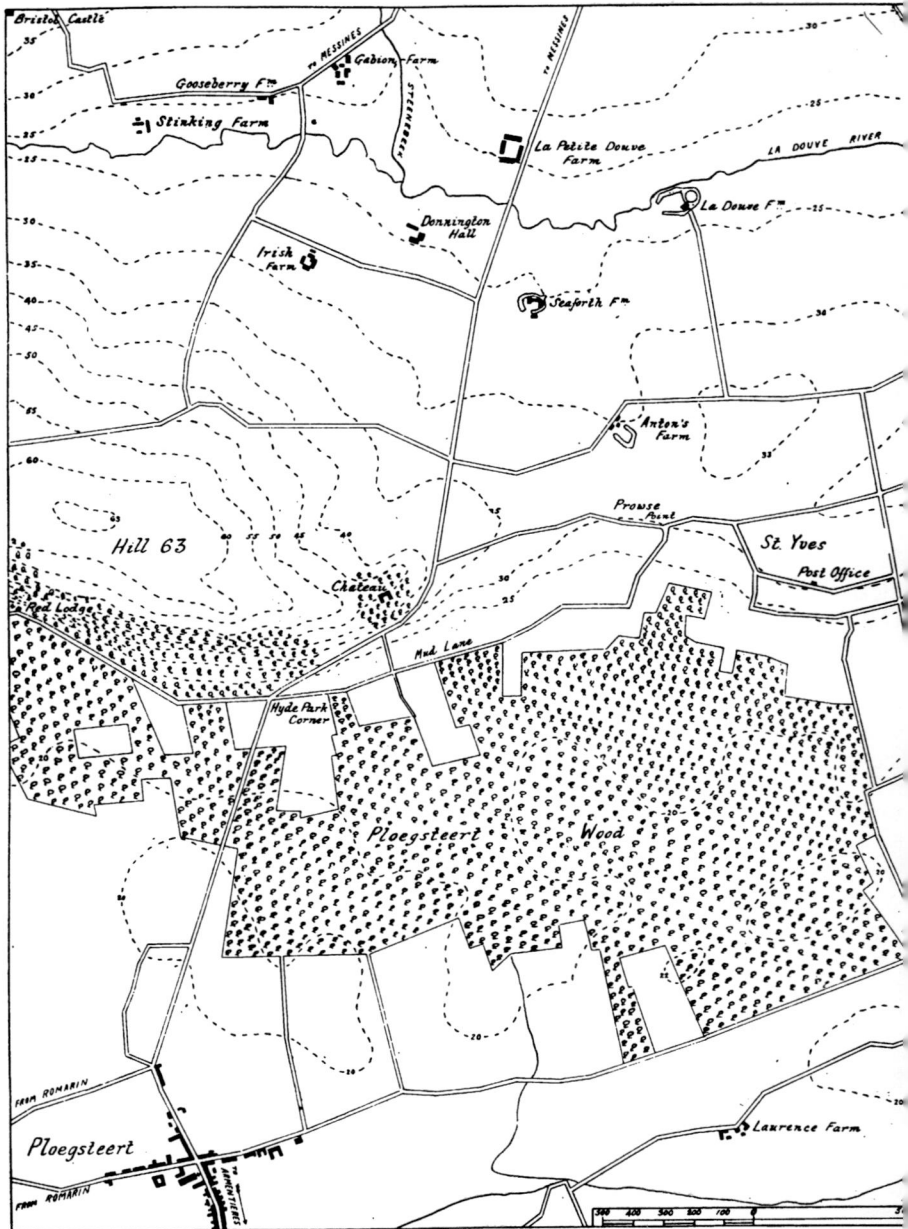

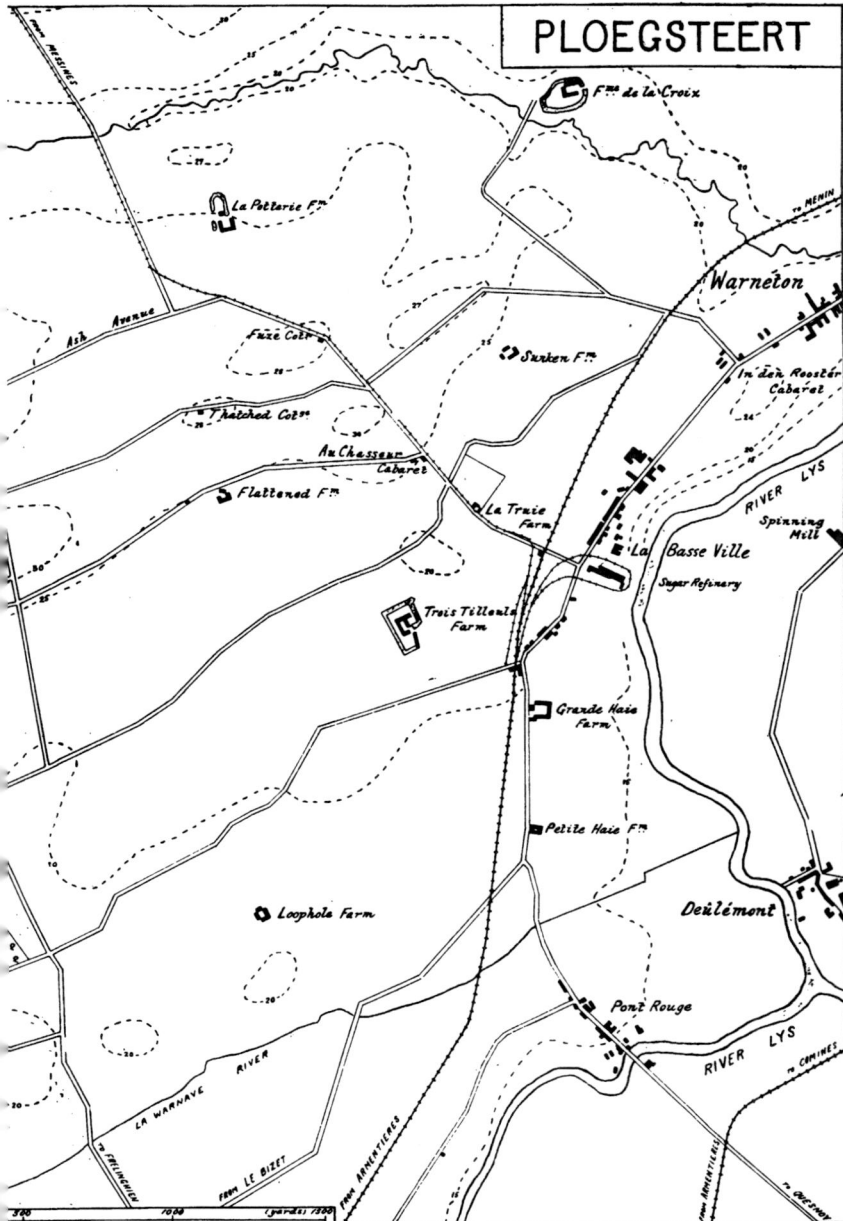

PLOEGSTEERT

Fme de la Croix

La Potterie Fm

Ash Avenue

Fuze Cotᵗ

Thatched Cotᵗ

Au Chasseur Cabaret

Flattened Fm

Sunken Fm

La Truie Farm

Trois Tilleuls Farm

Warneton

In den Rooster Cabaret

RIVER LYS

Spinning Mill

La Basse Ville

Sugar Refinery

Grande Haie Farm

Petite Haie Fm

Loophole Farm

Deûlémont

Pont Rouge

LA WARNAVE RIVER

to FRELINGHIEN

from LE BIZET

from ARMENTIERES

from ARMENTIERES

RIVER LYS

to COMINES

to MENIN

to MENIN

(yards)

MAJOR F. STARNES, D.S.O.

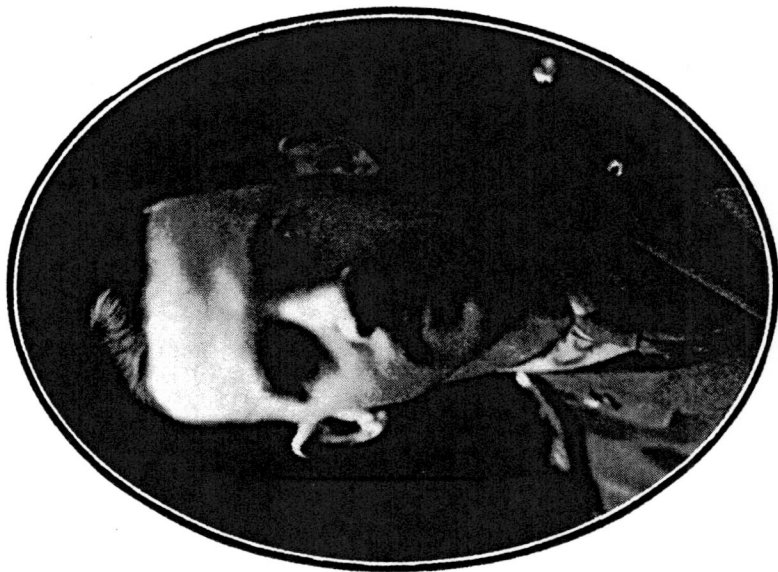

MAJOR N. WILSON, D.S.O, M.C.

(Rifle) Brigade, in place of Brigadier-General F. E. Johnston, C.B., who had been killed that morning; and Major Shepherd took over the command of the battalion. During the night of the same day, the battalion relieved the 1st Otago Battalion in the front line, to the south of La Basse Ville.

The defences here were similar in character to those which the battalion had occupied when last in the line; the 1st Company (on the right) and the 2nd Company (on the left) occupied outposts, the other two companies were in support, and battalion headquarters was again at Lewisham Lodge. The weather was wet, the trenches were very muddy and without duck-walks or any means of drainage, and consequently sickness soon became rife. The enemy's uneasiness made him shell the whole battalion area at all hours of the day and night with high-explosive and gas-shells.

Meanwhile, the 2nd Battalion had left Neuf Berquin on July 19th, and had returned to its old quarters at Romarin, from where it supplied working-parties to the front line. After the capture of La Basse Ville, it carried up the wire and standards required by the Pioneer Battalion for the work of wiring in front of the new positions. On the night of August 5th/6th, the battalion relieved the 2nd Otago Battalion in the outpost line at La Basse Ville and to the left of that village, having the 1st Canterbury Battalion on its immediate right.

The 13th Company occupied the newly established posts to the east and north-east of La Basse Ville, with company headquarters in the village; and on its left the 1st Company held other new advanced posts, with company headquarters in what had been the front line before the capture of the village. The 12th Company was in support, in the neighbourhood of Au Chasseur Cabaret, while the 2nd Company, in reserve, occupied the old German trench-system near St. Yves. Battalion headquarters was still further back, in the deep dug-out underneath St. Yves post office.

The conditions of weather and mud were the same as the 1st Battalion was experiencing, but as the enemy's shelling was concentrated mainly on La Basse Ville and its immediate neighbourhood, the 2nd Battalion's casualties were heavier than those of the 1st Battalion. Inter-company reliefs took place every three days: particulars of these, and the reliefs of the 1st Battalion, will be found in Appendix "B."

In the middle of the spell in the line the enemy's artillery fire slackened considerably on the 1st Battalion's area; but the 2nd Battalion had no respite, and it was the general opinion that this period in the line was the worst in its experience on an inactive front. For the twelve days in the line the casualties were one officer (Captain M. J. Morrison, M.C.) and thirty-three other ranks killed, one officer and one hundred and thirteen other ranks wounded, and thirty-five other ranks evacuated to hospital.

The 1st Brigade took over the line on August 17th, and both Canterbury Battalions were relieved on the night of August 17th/18th by the 2nd Auckland and 1st Wellington Battalions respectively. On relief the 1st Battalion moved back to Bulford Camp, and the 2nd Battalion went to billets at Nieppe. Shortly after arrival there, orders were received that the New Zealand Division would be relieved in the line at the end of the month, and in the meantime the 2nd Brigade would go to the La Motte area for training. The 1st Canterbury Battalion marched out on the 21st, and was followed by the 2nd Battalion on the 22nd. Both battalions were accommodated partly in billets and partly in tents and shelters at Caudescure, on the western outskirts of the forest of Nieppe. The weather was fine, and after three easy days spent in bathing, short route marches and recreational training, the brigade settled down to training under company arrangements.

On the 27th, Lieutenant-Colonel G. A. King, D.S.O., New Zealand Staff Corps, took command of the 1st Canterbury Battalion; and the following day the brigade marched to Caestre, and there entrained for the Lumbres area, west and south-west of St. Omer. Both the Canterbury Battalions detrained at Wizernes that same afternoon, and the 1st Battalion marched to billets for the night at Lumbres, and next day went on to its permanent billets at Coulomby. The 2nd Battalion went all the way to Bayinghem from Wizernes, arriving at its billets there at 2.30 a.m. on the 29th. On September 26th Lieutenant-Colonel G. C. Griffiths left for England on duty, and Major O. H. Mead took command of the 2nd Battalion.

The 3rd Battalion had been relieved in the line by the 3rd Auckland Battalion on July 31st. The battalion now adopted a new arrangement, under which two companies of the battalion were to supply all the working-parties required, and the other two companies were to devote their whole time to training. Accordingly, the 1st and 13th Companies were sent to Support Farm and provided working-parties, while the 2nd and 12th Companies trained at their billets at Brune Gaye. The companies changed places on the 4th, and on the night of the 5th/6th the Battalion relieved the 3rd Auckland Battalion in the same sector as it had previously occupied. There was no offensive action on either side, and the sector was gradually quietening down.

Further reliefs as shown in Appendix ''B'' took place before the end of the month, when the 8th Division relieved the New Zealand Division. On the night of August 31st/September 1st the 3rd Canterbury Battalion handed over its trenches to the 2nd Battalion Devon Regiment, and moved back to Bulford Camp. On September 2nd it marched to Steenwerck and entrained for Wizernes, and thence marched to Coulomby for billets for the night. The following day the battalion moved again by road to its training billets at Surques. All the New Zealand Brigades were now in the training area, excepting the 3rd (Rifle) Brigade, which had been temporarily detached from the Division, and was engaged in burying telephone cables and other work in the Ypres salient.

Besides the casualties suffered in the Battle of Messines, mentioned in Chapter IX, the Regiment had suffered the following casualties while it was holding the trenches in the sector between Messines and the Lys:—

1st Battalion.	Officers.	Other Ranks.
Killed in Action and Died of Wounds ..	–	19
Wounded	1	115
Total	1	134

2nd Battalion.	Officers.	Other Ranks.
Killed in Action and Died of Wounds ..	2*	61
Wounded	1	153
Total	3	214

3rd Battalion.	Officers.	Other Ranks.
Killed in Action and Died of Wounds ..	–	27
Wounded	5	97
Total	5	124

*2nd Lieutenant E. S. Cornford (8th July), and Captain M.G. Morrison, M.C. (Died of Wounds, 15th August).

Total for three battalions: 2 officers and 107 other ranks killed, and 7 officers and 365 other ranks wounded.

These casualties include those mentioned earlier in this chapter.

The training of the Division for the attack east of Ypres differed very little from what had been done before the battle of Messines, except that, as the General Staff hoped to break clean through the enemy's trench systems before the Division was used, more attention was given to open warfare than to trench-to-trench attacks.   The enemy's use of "pill-boxes," or small concrete machine-gun positions, as a substitute for trenches, had evolved a new style of fighting which needed practice: and the possibility of fighting in wooded country made it necessary for all troops to be taught the best means of advancing through woods.   In other respects the training was on much the same lines as before, and there is no need to describe it again in detail.

A good deal of time was devoted to ceremonial drill, in preparation for an inspection of the Division by Sir Douglas Haig, K.T., G.C.B., G.C.V.O., K.C.I.E., Commander-in-Chief of the British Armies in France, which had been fixed for September 14th.   On that date the 1st, 2nd, and 4th Brigades were massed near Harlettes, a mile north of Coulomby, and on the main Boulogne-St. Omer road.   The inspection was a thorough one, and lasted from 10 a.m. till about noon, when the Division marched past the Commander-in-Chief in column of platoons, and returned to its billets.

On September 24th the Division received orders to move the following day, by route march, to the battle area. The 1st Canterbury Battalion left Coulomby early on the 25th, and was billetted that night at Arques, two miles south-east of St. Omer. Marching on again about ten miles the next day, the battalion spent the night at Queue d'Oxelaere, two miles south of Cassel. A march of about the same distance the following day (the 27th) brought the battalion to billets for the night near Watou, five miles west of Poperinghe. The next day the battalion completed its march, and arrived at 4 p.m. in the Ypres North area, to the west of the town and close to the Ypres-Poperinghe railway.

The 2nd Battalion left Bayinghem on the 25th and reached the Watou area on the 27th, spending the night of the 25th at Renescure (on the St. Omer-Hazebrouck road, seven miles west of the latter town), and the night of the 26th at Terdeghem (two miles east of Cassel). From Watou, the battalion was carried on the 28th by motor-bus to Goldfish Chateau, in the Ypres North area; and in the evening marched to the old German front line at Wieltje, two miles north-east of Ypres.

The 2nd Brigade was now ordered to take over from the 59th Division the whole of the New Zealand Division's new sector, and to put all four battalions in the line. Accordingly, on the night of September 29th/30th the 2nd Battalions of the Canterbury and Otago Regiments took over the whole of the left sub-sector of the front line from the 178th Brigade, the 2nd Canterbury Battalion relieving the 2nd/5th Battalion South Stafford Regiment; while the 1st Battalions of the same regiments relieved two battalions of the 177th Brigade in the right of the 59th Division's support lines. The following night the 1st Canterbury and 1st Otago Battalions took over the right sub-sector of the front line, the 1st Canterbury Battalion having its headquarters in Pommern Castle, a thousand yards south of the Wieltje-Gravenstafel road. The order of the four battalions in the line (right to left) was: 1st Canterbury, 1st Otago, 2nd Canterbury, 2nd Otago.

The brigade held the line, with but slight casualties, till the night of October 2nd/3rd, when it was relieved by the 1st and 4th Brigades. The 1st Canterbury and 1st Otago Battalions, on relief by the 3rd Auckland and 3rd Otago Battalions respectively, moved into the old British front line near Wieltje, where they remained in reserve to the 4th and 1st Brigades respectively. The 2nd Canterbury Battalion, on relief by the 1st Wellington Battalion, moved back with the 2nd Otago Battalion to the Ypres North area.

At this stage the movements of the 4th Brigade claim attention, as it was now on the eve of making its first attack. It had left its training area with the rest of the Division on September 25th, to march to the Ypres area. The 3rd Canterbury Battalion moved that day from Surques to Bayinghem; and thence marched successively, on the 26th to Campagne (four miles south-east of St. Omer), on the 27th to Eecke (about midway between Cassel and Bailleul, but north of the main road between those towns), and on the 29th to the Watou area. There the battalion remained till October 1st, suffering several casualties from enemy aeroplane-bombs; and then marched to the Ypres North area, and bivouacked near Goldfish Chateau.

Before going into details of the further movements of the 4th Brigade, it is desirable to begin a new chapter with a review of the general situation at the Ypres salient at this time.

CHAPTER XI.

PASSCHENDAELE.

The third Battle of Ypres had now been raging continuously for nearly two months; but though the first day of the attack had seen the enemy's defences captured to a maximum depth of over two miles on a front of about fourteen miles, the attacks during the rest of the period had advanced our line little over a mile on any part of the battle front. At the date when the New Zealand Division reached the battle area, the British front line ran north from La Basse Ville, passed just east of Gapaard and of Holbeke, crossed the Ypres-Menin canal near Holbeke and the Ypres-Menin road half a mile north-west of Gheluvelt. swept round the eastern side of Polygon Wood. cut through the eastern end of the village of Zonnebeke, and (still running more northerly than westerly) passed to the west of Gravenstafel and midway between the villages of Poelcappelle and Langemarck. Crossing the Ypres-Staden railway about half a mile to the north of Langemarck, the line turned more towards the west and ran in almost a straight line to Drie Grachten, on the Ypres-Yser canal, west of the Forest of Houthulst. This was the northern limit of the battle area at this period.

After his experiences of the effect of artillery concentration on trenches, which he had gained on the Somme and at Messines, the enemy had abandoned continuous lines of trenches for his inner lines of defence, and had substituted groups of small machine-gun posts, which mutually supported each other, and were protected as well by belts of wire. These posts were called "pill-boxes": being constructed of concrete, with overhead cover usually at least three feet thick and not uncommonly six feet thick, reinforced by steel rods, they were indestructible except by direct hits by heavy shells. As a rule, they were not larger than nine feet square, and were thus small targets; and even though their position was betrayed in aeroplane photographs by the tracks leading up to them, they were usually so well camouflaged that it was difficult for artillery observers to see them, or to report whether they had been hit by the shell aimed at them.

Though the attack of July 31st had succeeded in overwhelming the enemy's front line system and the subsidiary line of trenches behind it, the advance had been held up beyond the trenches by the pill-boxes, which had been unharmed by the creeping barrage. From then on, the rate of advance had depended upon the number of pill-boxes which had to be previously dealt with by the heavy artillery; and every attack was ultimately held up by enemy defences of this nature. As a rule, the pill-boxes were scattered in an irregular manner wherever the ground provided suitable sites; but there were also regular defensive lines of pill-boxes sited in positions where, under the old conditions, defensive systems of trenches would have been placed.

In places these lines of pill-boxes were connected by fighting trenches, and the lines were further defended by very strong belts of wire. In the sector to which the New Zealand Division had been sent, a line of this kind ran from south of Potsdam on the Ypres-Roulers railway (close to where the Ypres-Zonnebeke road crosses the railway) north through Zevenkote and Kansas Cross, and skirting to the east of Winnipeg and Vancouver ran round the east and north of Langemarck. Behind this was another strong line of a similar nature, known as the Staden-Zonnebeke line.

A survey of the British advance during the battle up to the end of September shows a fairly substantial gain of ground; but on closer examination it will be seen that the number of strategical positions captured was by no means proportionate to the additional area enclosed in the British lines. In other words, the ridge east of Ypres, which was one of the objectives of the battle, and which, if the original attacks had gone as it was hoped they would, would have been merely the starting point for a shattering blow destined to pierce the whole of the enemy's system of trenches and to destroy all his armies in Belgium — this ridge had fallen into the hands of the British only from east of Zillebeke to Polygon Wood. All the British gains north of the latter point consisted of ground which was still dominated, to a greater or smaller degree, by the ridge.

The newly gained ground gave us. however. jumping-off places for attacks on the rest of the ridge; and although at this late season of the year there was exceedingly little hope of the battle gaining the results for which the Staff had hoped when it began, there seemed no reason why we should not at least take the ridge. Its capture would mean not only dominating positions and trenches which could be easily drained and kept reasonably habitable during the winter, but would also give us a good starting-point for operations in the spring. These were doubtless some of the reasons which led Sir Douglas Haig to persist in the battle: he also suggests in his despatch of 25th December, 1917, that he was anxious to keep the enemy's attention diverted from Cambrai, where his next blow was planned to fall, and from operations in preparation by the French at Malmaison.

The general lie of the main ridge is from north-east to southwest, so that while on the right of the battle front the British line tended to run along the forward (or south-eastern) slopes of the ridge. it crossed the summit at Polygon Wood, and from there descended into the lower ground to the west of the ridge. From Polygon Wood, however, to where the Ypres-Roulers railway crosses the hills, the ridge runs due north, and the Becelaere-Passchendaele road runs along its summit; but half a mile before this road crosses the railway, the ridge turns north-east again. From this point a broad and low spur, two miles long, runs to within a mile to the east of St. Julien: half-way down the spur is the site of Gravenstafel, and south-east of that village, on the upper slopes of the spur, is the low plateau christened "Abraham Heights" by the Canadians in the second Battle of Ypres.

The objectives of a further attack from the line above described naturally included the ridge from Polygon Wood to the Ypres-Roulers railway; but north of the railway the high ground was too far from the front line to be attempted in one day's fighting, and the objective decided on was a straight line from Nieuwemolen, near where the railway crosses the ridge, to Poelcappelle. From this village the line of objectives closed in again towards the front line, which it met at the Ypres-Staden railway, north of Langemarck. The ground to be captured thus included the whole of the spur on which stood Gravenstafel and Abraham Heights.

Accordingly, when the Second and Fifth Armies issued orders for a joint attack on October 4th, the objectives above described were assigned to the various corps to be engaged. The II Anzac Army Corps, the left flank Corps of the Second Army, divided its share of the objectives into two, and ordered the 3rd Australian Division to capture the right portion and the New Zealand Division to take the remainder. On the left of the New Zealand Division the attack was to be carried out by the 48th and 11th Divisions of the XVIII Corps, Fifth Army.

The New Zealand Division's sector was a strip of country about a mile wide running north-east, with the Wieltje-Gravenstafel road sub-dividing it into two almost equal strips. The absence of natural boundaries makes it difficult to describe the limits of the sector, but the boundary lines and objectives are shown on the map at the end of the chapter. The final objective for the day was a line running across the sector, immediately beyond Berlin Copse (or Wood), Waterloo Farm, and Kronprinz Farm.

The attack of the New Zealand Division was to be made by two brigades, the 1st and the 4th: but though, as has been stated, the Wieltje-Gravenstafel road roughly divided the Division's sector into two, it did not form the inter-brigade boundary. This boundary was a straight line drawn through Waterloo and Riverside Farms (both of which were inclusive to the 4th Brigade) and continued on towards the rear, passing to the south-east of the cross roads called Kansas Cross. The British front line in the sector was to the north-east of the Zonnebeke-Langemarck road, Dochy Farm on the right flank being inside our line, while Riverside Farm was in the enemy's territory. The front on which the 4th Brigade was to attack was eight hundred yards in width, and on its left the 1st Brigade was allotted a similar frontage.

The usual creeping and stationary barrages were to support the infantry in the attack, while the heavy guns had been engaged in searching for enemy pill-boxes ever since they had been moved forward to their battle positions. Besides heavy artillery, thirty batteries of 18-pounder guns (one hundred and eighty guns), ten batteries of 4·5-inch howitzers (sixty guns), and sixty-eight machine-guns had been detailed to support the

New Zealand Division alone. The creeping barrage was to move forward by jumps of fifty yards every two minutes for the first two hundred yards, and after that by jumps of fifty yards every three minutes. Twenty-nine minutes after zero, the barrage was to halt for twelve minutes* and then to move on again at the rate of fifty yards every three minutes till the first objective was reached. A hundred and fifty yards past this objective, the barrage was to pause for an hour, and would then move on at the rate of fifty yards every four minutes up to the second (and final) objective. After the final objective was reached, the barrage was to halt a hundred and fifty yards beyond it, to protect the infantry while it consolidated its gains, and was then to die away gradually.

The 4th Brigade's plans for the attack provided that two battalions, the 3rd Auckland on the right and the 3rd Otago on the left, would capture the first objective (or ''Red Line'') which extended along the south-eastern slopes of the Gravenstafel spur, short of Abraham Heights and Gravenstafel village. Immediately after the capture of the first objective, the 3rd Canterbury Battalion on the right and the 3rd Wellington Battalion on the left would pass through the two leading battalions, and form up ready to advance against the second objective (or ''Blue Line'') directly the barrage moved on. On the capture of the second objective, these battalions would establish there a line of posts, and would also dig a continuous support trench across the whole brigade front on the ''Blue Dotted Line,'' three hundred and fifty yards short of the final objective, to link up with trenches dug in like manner by the 10th Brigade of the 3rd Australian Division on the right, and the 1st New Zealand Infantry Brigade on the left.

The 3rd Canterbury Battalion's objective consisted of the portion of the final objective which lay between the intersection of Dagger Trench by the right divisional boundary, and the northern corner of Berlin Copse. In order to reach the objective, the battalion had first to capture Abraham Heights, the highest point in the Division's sector, and then to take Berlin Copse with Dagger Trench leading into it from the south-east. At the

---

*The reason given in orders for this pause was to allow of "leap-frogging" if necessary.

same time, the 3rd Wellington Battalion, on the left, would be occupied with the capture of Gravenstafel village and Berlin and Waterloo Farms.

The assembly for the attack began on the night of October 2nd/3rd, when the 3rd Auckland and 3rd Otago Battalions relieved those troops of the 2nd New Zealand Infantry Brigade who were garrisoning the portion of the front line which lay within the 4th Brigade's boundaries. The same night, two sections from each platoon in the 3rd Canterbury and 3rd Wellington Battalions moved forward to the old German support line in the neighbourhood of Wieltje, battalion headquarters and the rest of the troops of each battalion staying behind at Goldfish Chateau. We will now follow the doings of the 3rd Canterbury Battalion.

The troops of the 3rd Canterbury Battalion who had stayed at Goldfish Chateau left there at 5 p.m. on October 3rd, and joined the rest of the battalion in the old German support trenches east of Wieltje. From there, all officers and non-commissioned officers went forward to reconnoitre the assembly position and the routes to it. Broad white marking tapes were laid on a line running through Zevenkote, Delva Farm, and Elms Corner,* on which the battalion was to assemble later that night; and a similar tape was run forward for about five hundred yards, along the brigade's right boundary, to help the troops to keep their proper direction as they advanced. At 11 p.m. on the night of October 3rd/4th, the battalion moved forward, assembled on the tapes, and bivouacked for the night in shell-holes about the assembly line, with battalion headquarters near Pommern Castle, five hundred yards south-east of Bank Farm. During the night the enemy shelled the assembly area, but caused only two casualties; a light rain also fell.

That the enemy was uneasy was shown by the heavy barrage he put down at 5 a.m. on the 4th, along the whole Divisional front. Zero hour for the attack was fixed for 6 a.m., but before that time the enemy's barrage had died away, enabling the 3rd Canterbury Battalion to leave the assembly line in artillery formation at 5.50 a.m., and to move forward towards the brigade's

---

*So in Battalion Diary. This point is not shown on the map, but is presumably somewhere about Gallipoli.

front line posts,* twelve hundred yards ahead of the battalion's assembly position.

The formation adopted was rather a peculiar one: the two leading companies of the battalion, the 1st on the right and the 2nd on the left, moved in line of platoons in fours, spread over the whole of the battalion frontage of four hundred yards, with fifty yards' interval between platoons. Close on the heels of each platoon came a section either of moppers-up or of carriers (four sections of each), of which one was supplied by each of the leading companies, and the other six came from the remaining companies of the battalion. At a distance of thirty yards behind the leading line of platoons with sections attached, the 12th and 13th Companies followed, also in line of platoons, in fours, in support to the 1st and 2nd Companies respectively. The places of the two platoons which had been detailed for carrying and mopping-up were filled by groups made up of all the stretcher-bearers of the battalion and the battalion signallers, and the line of platoons was closely followed by four carrying sections—two left over from the carrying and mopping-up platoons, and two others supplied by other platoons.

Risky as this formation appears to have been, it was maintained until well after the front line had been passed, and till just before the battalion reached the Red Line, which had meanwhile been captured by the 3rd Auckland Battalion. The 3rd Canterbury Battalion then deployed into extended order, and on passing the Red Line met with some opposition from parties of the enemy in shell-holes with machine-guns. After disposing of these without undue difficulty, the leading troops of the battalion reached the top of the spur (Abraham Heights), and came under direct machine-gun fire from the high ground to the north and north-east.

This was the place where the barrage time-table called for a halt for an hour. During this time the troops lying in the open suffered a good many casualties, nearly all from machine-gun fire. On the barrage moving forward again, however, little resistance was met till the first line reached Berlin Copse. Two pill-boxes held up the 2nd Company here for a short time, until

---

*The leading battalions of the brigade did not begin their advance from the front line posts, but from a taped line between two and three hundred yards behind these posts.

two platoons were detailed to outflank the position, and captured it together with a machine-gun and seventeen prisoners. By 9.10 a.m., (one hundred and ninety minutes after zero) the battalion had captured the whole of its objective, and straightway began to consolidate its gains.

The work of digging a trench on the "Blue Dotted Line" (three hundred and fifty yards behind the final objective) was completed by dusk, in spite of considerable interference by enemy machine-guns and snipers, which were active on Bellevue Spur; and the trench was successfully joined up with the trenches of the Australians and the 3rd Wellington Battalion on the two flanks. This work was done by the 12th and 13th Companies, the leading companies being engaged in digging the front posts. The battalion diary states that the task of these latter companies was increased by the failure of the 3rd Wellington Battalion to come right up to its objectives on its right flank, and that two platoons of the 2nd Company were sent to fill the gap.

It had been the intention of the Commanding Officer of the battalion to hold the line of advanced posts with two platoons of each of the leading companies, and to bring back the remaining platoons to the Blue Dotted Line, but on account of the extra length of the line of posts, and the heavy casualties suffered by the 1st Company, he decided to leave the whole of both companies where they were. Battalion headquarters was established at Boethoek, just behind the centre of the Red Line.

Along the remainder of the battle front the attack had met with equal success: the enemy infantry and artillery both appeared to be thoroughly disorganized,* and the spirits of our troops rose in proportion. Besides inflicting heavy casualties on the enemy, we had taken numerous prisoners and machine-guns, and the 3rd Canterbury Battalion was credited with eighty-six prisoners and eight machine-guns.

Throughout the rest of the day the enemy's shelling was continuous; but as it was scattered over the whole battle area, and was not concentrated as usual on the more advanced troops, it did not cause many casualties in the battalion. The S.O.S.†

---

*Report of the Brigade-Major, 4th Brigade, on operations.
†A signal rocket carried by the front line troops to warn the artillery of an infantry attack by the enemy.

was put up by troops on the right of the battalion at 3 p.m. and again at 6.45 p.m.: our barrage came down immediately on both occasions and no enemy attack was made. Towards the evening the enemy shelling diminished considerably. The night of the 4th/5th passed quietly, though the S.O.S. was again put up on our right, at 9.45 p.m., 12.30 a.m., and 3.30 a.m. Again our artillery put down a protective barrage, and no counter-attack came.

Frequent showers fell on the 5th; but in compensation for the discomforts caused by the rain, the enemy's artillery was not active, and the battalion was able to improve its trenches and bury its dead with little interference. By nightfall on that day the Red, Blue Dotted, and Blue Lines were continuous trenches, traversed and dug to an average depth of four feet six inches.* At 9.30 p.m. on the same date, the 1st/5th Battalion West Riding Regiment relieved the 3rd Canterbury Battalion, which marched back to Goldfish Chateau. The march was a long one and through heavy rain, but at the end of it there was rum and a hot meal, and tents which, though crowded, afforded a place for the sleep which everyone very badly needed. Leaving the chateau at 7.30 p.m. on October 6th, the battalion marched to Vlamertinghe, and from there was carried in motor-buses to Eecke, where it was billetted till the 11th.

During the attack the battalion's casualties had been:—

	Officers.	Other Ranks.
Killed	2*	39
Wounded	9	199
Missing	–	9
Total	11	247

*2nd Lieutenant A. Deans and the Rev. G. S. Bryan-Brown, C.F. 4th class.

The 1st Canterbury Battalion remained in the old German front line, in reserve to the 4th Brigade, during the whole of October 3rd; and early the following morning battalion headquarters and the 2nd and 12th Companies moved forward to Bank Farm. Later in the day, as counter-attacks threatened,

---

*Report of the Brigade-Major, 4th Brigade, on the operations.

the 1st Company also came up from the old German trenches; but the attacks were broken up by artillery fire, and the battalion was not drawn into the fighting. The 2nd Battalion did not move from its quarters near Wieltje, which it had taken up on October 2nd.

On the relief of the New Zealand Division by the 49th Division, on October 5th, the 1st and 2nd Battalions marched to Goldfish Chateau, and from there both battalions were carried by motor-buses to Winnezeele, four miles north-east of Cassel. On the 7th, the 2nd Brigade moved to the Eecke Area, to the west and north-west of the Mont des Cats, where the 1st Canterbury Battalion was billetted at Godewaersvelde, and the 2nd at Eecke. The Division had been ordered to make a further attack, in which the 2nd and 3rd Brigades would be the assaulting brigades, and the period in the back area was spent in organization and preparation for the attack.

Meanwhile, on October 9th, the British had made another attack on a front of six miles extending from a point east of Zonnebeke to the left flank of the Fifth Army, north-west of Langemarck, and in conjunction with operations with the French Army on the left of our Fifth Army. This attack, while fairly successful on the left (in the neighbourhood of the Forest of Houthulst) had been held up practically at its starting point on the right; though the villages of Nieuwemolen and Keerselaarhoek had fallen into our hands. The first orders issued to the New Zealand Division assumed that the attack of October 9th would succeed; and when the attack failed on the Division's frontage, amended orders had to be issued.

The new attack was fixed for October 12th, and the New Zealand Division's sector had been altered slightly: as before, it was about a mile in width, but it lay about a quarter of a mile further to the north-west than the previous area over which the Division had attacked. Across the front ran the Ravebeek, which crossed the Wieltje-Mosselmarkt road about two hundred yards beyond the line established in the attack of October 4th. Before crossing the front, the Ravebeek flowed from east of Passchendaele straight down the valley between the main ridge and the Bellevue Spur, at right angles to the British front line, and

Capt. W. J. Rodger, M.C., D.C.M.

Lieut. J. Vincent, D.C.M., M.M.

2nd Lieut. T. Stockdill, D.C.M

2nd Lieut. W. E. Smith, D.C.M.

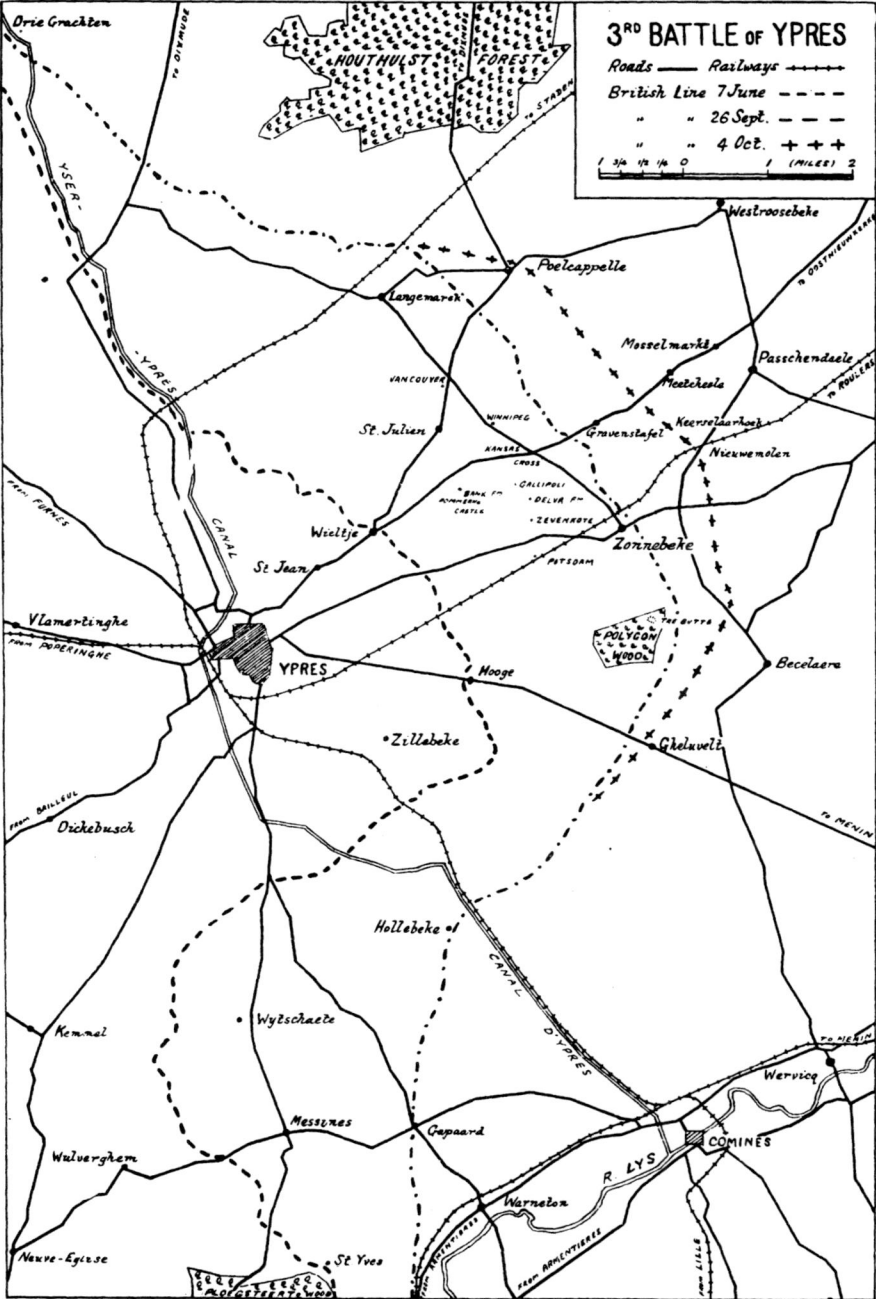

3RD BATTLE OF YPRES

Roads —— Railways +++++
British Line 7 June – · – · –
    "   "   26 Sept. – – –
    "   "   4 Oct. + + +

3/4 1/2 1/4 0   1   (MILES)   2

turned towards the west only on encountering the lower slopes of the Gravenstafel Spur. Under normal conditions this stream would have been a small one, just large enough to drain the valley between Passchendaele on the main ridge and the Bellevue and Gravenstafel Spurs; but now it had been clogged by constant shelling, its waters had been dammed up, and its bed had become a swamp. The rain since October 4th had made the low-lying ground about the stream into a sea of mud, which every shell made more impassable.

The upper course of the Ravebeek (before it took its westward turn) now formed the right Divisional boundary; and when the source of the stream was reached, the boundary continued to run north-east in a straight line roughly parallel to and about six hundred yards to the south-east of the Wieltje-Mosselmarkt road, crossing the Westroosebeke-Passchendaele road about six hundred yards north of the centre of Passchendaele village. The left Divisional boundary was a purely artificial one, that is to say, it did not conform either to roads or to natural features of the country. It was determined simply by a straight line drawn on the map roughly parallel to and distant about a thousand yards to the north-west of the Wieltje-Mosselmarkt road.

As before, the choice of objectives was governed by the position of the main ridge, on which stood the village of Passchendaele. In the attacks of October 4th and 9th, the British line had been advanced to east of the Becelaere-Passchendaele road (which runs along the summit of the ridge) from a point due east of "the Butte" in Polygon Wood to Nieuwemolen, just south of the Ypres-Roulers railway. The object of the forthcoming attack was to establish a new line east of the Becelaerte-Passchendaele road, on the forward slope of the ridge, from Nieuwemolen to east of Passchendaele, and thence round the north-east and north of the latter village, where the ground began to fall again. On the right of the New Zealand Division, the 3rd Australian Division was given the task of capturing Passchendaele, while on the left the Fifth Army was to push forward to work round the southern outskirts of the Forest of Houthulst. The right flank Division of the Fifth Army, the 9th Division, was on the immediate left of the New Zealand Division.

The objectives assigned to the New Zealand Division were four in number:—

1. THE RED LINE: A road running from north-west to south-east across the whole Divisional front and crossing the Gravenstafel-Mosselmarkt road two thousand yards north-east of Gravenstafel village.

2. THE BLUE LINE: A line at an average distance of eight hundred yards in front of the Red Line, crossing the Bellevue spur four hundred yards south-west of Mosselmarkt and then swinging round towards the west.

3. THE GREEN DOTTED LINE: which is more conveniently described by reference to the Green Line (the fourth objective described below).

4. THE GREEN LINE: In the II Anzac Army Corps' area this line began at the Ypres-Roulers railway, two thousand yards north-east of its point of intersection with the Becelaere-Passchendaele road, passed six hundred yards east of Passchendaele church and, curving away towards the west, encircled the village and crossed the Passchendaele-Westroosebeke and Wieltje-Oostnieuwkirke roads about two hundred yards north of their point of intersection. From there it ran almost due west to the left Divisional boundary. The "Green Dotted Line" was a straight line running inside the north-eastern curve of the Green Line, the two lines forming a segment of a circle with the Green Line as the arc and the Green Dotted Line as the chord. The length of the Green Dotted Line was fifteen hundred yards, and its greatest distance from the Green Line was three hundred yards, at the point where the Green Dotted Line crossed the Passchendaele-Westroosebeke road. Half of the Green Dotted Line was in the New Zealand Division's area, and the remainder in the 3rd Australian Division's area.

The 49th Division had attempted to take the Red Line on October 9th, but had been held up by uncut wire, and had advanced its line for a very short distance. The Staden-Zonnebeke

Line, a series of mutually supporting pill-boxes, protected by at least two belts of wire, guarded the western slopes of the main ridge, and crossed the Ravebeek at the point where that stream turns towards the west, as above described. In the attack of October 4th, the right flank of the 3rd Canterbury Battalion's final objective had rested on this line, which, running due north and south, consequently lay diagonally across the uncaptured territory in front of the New Zealand Division on that date. In the same attack, the 3rd Australian Division captured the part of this line which lay to the south of the 3rd Canterbury Battalion's right flank.

The ground gained in the attack of October 9th included the Staden-Zonnebeke Line, as far north as the point at which it crossed the Ravebeek. In ordinary circumstances, the fact that part of the line was in our possession would have enabled attacking troops to work round its flank, and take its defenders in the rear. Now, however, the muddy bed of the Ravebeek protected the uncaptured portion of the line against attacks from flank or rear.

The attack of the New Zealand Division was entrusted to the 2nd Brigade on the right and the 3rd (Rifle) Brigade on the left. The latter brigade had been detached from the Division since the end of August, and had meanwhile been engaged on work under Corps orders, and had not had any rest or training in preparation for the battle. It had returned to the Division early on October 8th, when the 1st Brigade relieved it in Corps employ. The 4th Brigade was held in Divisional reserve.

Each attacking brigade had half the Divisional frontage, and was to attack in depth; that is, one battalion was to take the first objective, a second battalion was then to pass through to take the second objective, and so on till all the objectives had been captured. So, in the 2nd Brigade, the 2nd Otago Battalion was to capture the Red Line, the 1st Otago Battalion the Blue Line, and the 1st Canterbury Battalion the Green Dotted and Green Lines.

The 2nd Canterbury Battalion was held in brigade reserve; however, it was not to be kept intact in the rear till there was occasion for its use, but each company had its own special task allotted it. Thus the 2nd and 12th Companies were to follow the 2nd Otago Battalion, and assist in capturing the Red Line, if their help were to be required; and they would then return immediately and be ready to move to Meetcheele to form a defensive flank, if the Australians on the right were held up. Likewise, battalion headquarters and the 13th Company were to assist the 1st Otago Battalion, and the 1st Company was to move with the 1st Canterbury Battalion; but on these battalions gaining their objectives the headquarters and 1st and 13th Companies of the 2nd Canterbury Battalion were to return to Meetcheele, to form a brigade reserve there ready to repel counterattacks. If necessary, this battalion was to send a company to help the 10th Australian Brigade to capture Passchendaele.

On October 10th the 2nd Brigade concentrated at Eecke, and from there was carried by motor-buses to Ypres, and settled down in "Y" camp. The same day the 1st Canterbury Battalion moved on to bivouacs at Bank Farm, two thousand yards northeast of Wieltje, where it remained till 6 p.m. on October 11th. Then this battalion, with the 1st Company of the 2nd Canterbury Battalion (which with the 13th Company of the same battalion had passed the night of the 10th in the old German front line, south of the Wieltje-Gravenstafel road) moved to its assembly area on the south-east side of the Ravebeek, and by 8.30 p.m. was in position. The 2nd and 12th Companies of the 2nd Battalion went forward on the night of the 10th/11th with the 2nd Otago Battalion to the rear of the latter's assembly area, and dug in near Korek and Boethoek on the Gravenstafel Spur.

The 13th Company joined the 1st Otago Battalion late in the afternoon of the 11th, and moved to its assembly position on the line Delva Farm-Schuler Farm, south-west of the Langemarck-Zonnebeke road. The ground was very heavy after the recent rains and much cut up by shell-fire, and as the night was very dark the journey to the assembly positions was a trying one. Showers fell during the night, and at 3 a.m. a fairly heavy and steady rain came on and lasted till slightly before zero hour. The 1st Canterbury Battalion's assembly area was heavily shelled at 5 a.m.

At 5.25 a.m. our barrage opened on a line behind the forward assembly lines, and continued for four minutes before moving forward. Luckily for the troops under it the barrage was a feeble one; but naturally neither the inaccuracy of the fire nor the scanty sprinkling of shells tended to increase the confidence of the infantry. However. as the barrage moved forward it was followed by the leading troops of the 2nd Otago Battalion, who at once came under very heavy machine-gun fire. An enemy barrage also came down on his edge of the Ravebeek; but it was not a very heavy one, and was not sufficient to prevent our men from crossing the stream. On the other hand, our barrage did very little towards keeping down the enemy machine-gun fire. which was causing such heavy casualties among our leading lines that they soon were unable to keep up with what barrage there was. Immediately after crossing the Ravebeek, the advancing troops found themselves confronted by the Staden-Zonnebeke Line described on page 194.

In the report of the General Officer commanding the 2nd Brigade on the operations. it is stated that a patrol sent out by the 2nd Otago Battalion on the night of October 10th/11th under Sergeant Travis. D.C.M., had discovered that the wire in the Staden-Zonnebeke Line was impassable; and that this was reported to brigade headquarters at 9.30 a.m. on the 11th. The Brigadier goes on to state that the artillery liaison officer at his brigade battle headquarters was requested at about 10 a.m. on that date to arrange for the wire and the pill-boxes to be dealt with by heavy artillery.

The report continues:—"This was not done. Again in the afternoon I requested this same officer to get the heavy artillery to deal with these obstacles: after a long period heavy artillery did open up on the Bellevue Spur, but the damage they did was negligible, and they only tried for a very short time. I do not consider that Major ———— did his best to get a prompt reply from the heavy artillery when my brigade major asked him on the morning of this day. and he did not display much enthusiasm or initiative."

It was these masses of uncut wire, in many cases fifty yards across, and the pill-boxes inside them just beyond the enemy's side of the Ravebeek. which held up the 2nd Otago Battalion; and it was clear by 6 a.m. on the 12th that this battalion could not get on. The artillery barrage, such as it was, had gone on; and there was nothing to hinder the activities of the enemy machine-gunners but the weapons of the infantry. Small parties of Otago men attempted to get at the pill-boxes by crawling under the wire, but all their heroic endeavours were in vain. The 2nd and 12th Companies of the 2nd Canterbury Battalion, attached to the 2nd Otago Battalion, were called up from reserve, and tried to work round the flanks of the pill-boxes at Bellevue, on the Gravenstafel-Mosselmarkt road.

Party after party made the attempt from either flank; and though some got as close as fifteen yards from the pill-boxes, none succeeded in reaching them. There can be no praise too high for these troops, who, with the example of failure after failure before them, undauntedly threw themselves against the impenetrable wire, raked by the heaviest machine-gun fire. Nor did the efforts of the brigade cease with the leading troops: the 1st Otago and 1st Canterbury Battalions, with the remaining companies of the 2nd Canterbury Battalion, now advanced against the wire. Some men got through the first belt, but all were held up by the second belt and by the machine-gun fire from the pill-boxes immediately behind it.

Once the main attack was broken, the task of the enemy defending the line became easier: isolated attempts to advance received the concentrated fire of all machine-guns within reach, and the enemy's snipers became bolder. At last even the smallest movement became impossible, as any man who exposed himself became the target not only of numerous snipers, but even of machine-gun sniping.

With regard to the part played by the Canterbury Regiment in this struggle, the Brigadier makes the following remarks in his report:—

"The 2nd and 12th Companies of 2nd Canterbury Battalion in reserve now pushed up level with the 2nd Otago Battalion, and a party of the 2nd Company under Lieutenant Rawlings also made an attempt by working round to the left; this was also unsuccessful, Lieutenant Rawlings being severely wounded in the attempt.

"Another party from the 13th Company under command [of] Captain Fawcett made an attempt on the right, but was also unsuccessful — Captain Fawcett being severely wounded.

Other parties from these two reserve Canterbury Companies also made attempts, one or two getting within 15 yards of the pill-boxes.

"The bravery and determination of these men were magnificent."

And later on:—

"The remaining battalion, the 1st Canterbury Battalion, followed immediately in rear of the 1st Otago Battalion. As they crossed the Ravebeek they came under heavy shell and machine-gun fire. Lieutenant-Colonel King was killed, and his Adjutant, Captain Dean, wounded within a few minutes of crossing the stream, Colonel King being on the road at the time.

"Captain Dobson then took over command.

"The 1st and 2nd Companies after crossing the Ravebeek moved over the road to the south side to get into their proper position.

"It had been impossible to assemble on the south of the road west of Ravebeek, as the ground was under water.

"The 12th and 13th Companies moved straight ahead across the Ravebeek, and got into line with the 1st and 2nd Companies.

"After crossing the creek the battalion at once saw that both the Otago Battalions in front had been held up. (At this moment Captain Dobson was wounded by a sniper, and Lieutenant Hunter took over command). Thereupon the 1st Canterbury Battalion dashed forward to assist the two Otago Battalions. Some men managed to crawl under the first belt of wire within a few yards of the pill-boxes, but owing to the volume and accuracy of rifle and machine-gun fire, no further progress could be made; the troops were obliged to dig in where they were, close up to the enemy's wire, and wait for the hours of darkness before they could move. The machine-gun fire and sniping was so accurate that anyone showing himself was immediately shot."

The Commanding Officers of all four battalions (with the exception of Lieutenant-Colonel King, of the 1st Canterbury Battalion, who was killed at 5.40 a.m.) were now at Waterloo Farm; and all realized and agreed that it was impossible to advance till the wire had been cut and the pill-boxes destroyed. All communications with brigade headquarters had failed, and after a reconnaissance by Lieutenant-Colonel G. S. Smith, of the

2nd Otago Battalion, the Commanding Officers decided to consolidate where they were, especially as the 10th Australian Brigade and 3rd New Zealand (Rifle) Brigade on the flanks were also held up. At noon the brigade-major arrived at Waterloo Farm, and agreed that the decision of the battalion commanders was the only practical one: Major Stitt arrived at the same time, and took command of the 1st Canterbury Battalion.

At 12.45 p.m. orders were received from brigade headquarters that the battalions were to be re-organized and the attack renewed at 3 p.m. The orders were issued by the General Officer commanding the Second Army, in view of the fact that elsewhere the attack appeared to have succeeded. Both General Godley and General Russell had protested against these orders, but to no purpose. The battalion commanders and brigade-major conferred again, and decided that any attempt to attack would only end in worse disaster: the battalions were mixed up, sniping made re-organization out of the question, and to attempt to attack in their present disorganized state was folly. Apart from these considerations, the men were exhausted by fighting and floundering in the mud, and casualties had been very heavy, especially among officers and non-commissioned officers.

These facts and the opinion of the conference of battalion commanders were submitted to the Brigadier; in the meantime the morning attack had not fulfilled its promise on other parts of the front, and the orders for a further attack were cancelled by Army Headquarters.

In the middle of the afternoon the brigade was ordered to re-organize after dark, and to take up a defensive position with the two Otago Battalions in the front line, and the two Canterbury Battalions in support. The 1st Canterbury Battalion moved back to part of the front line trench established by the 3rd Canterbury Battalion on October 4th, on the forward slopes of Abraham Heights, and was in touch on the right with the 10th Australian Brigade, and on the left, at the Gravenstafel-Mosselmarkt road, with the 2nd Canterbury Battalion. The latter battalion had its 1st and 13th Companies in the same trench line as the 1st Battalion but to the north of the road, and its 2nd and 12th Companies two hundred and fifty yards behind, also to the north of the road. As a great number of the officers

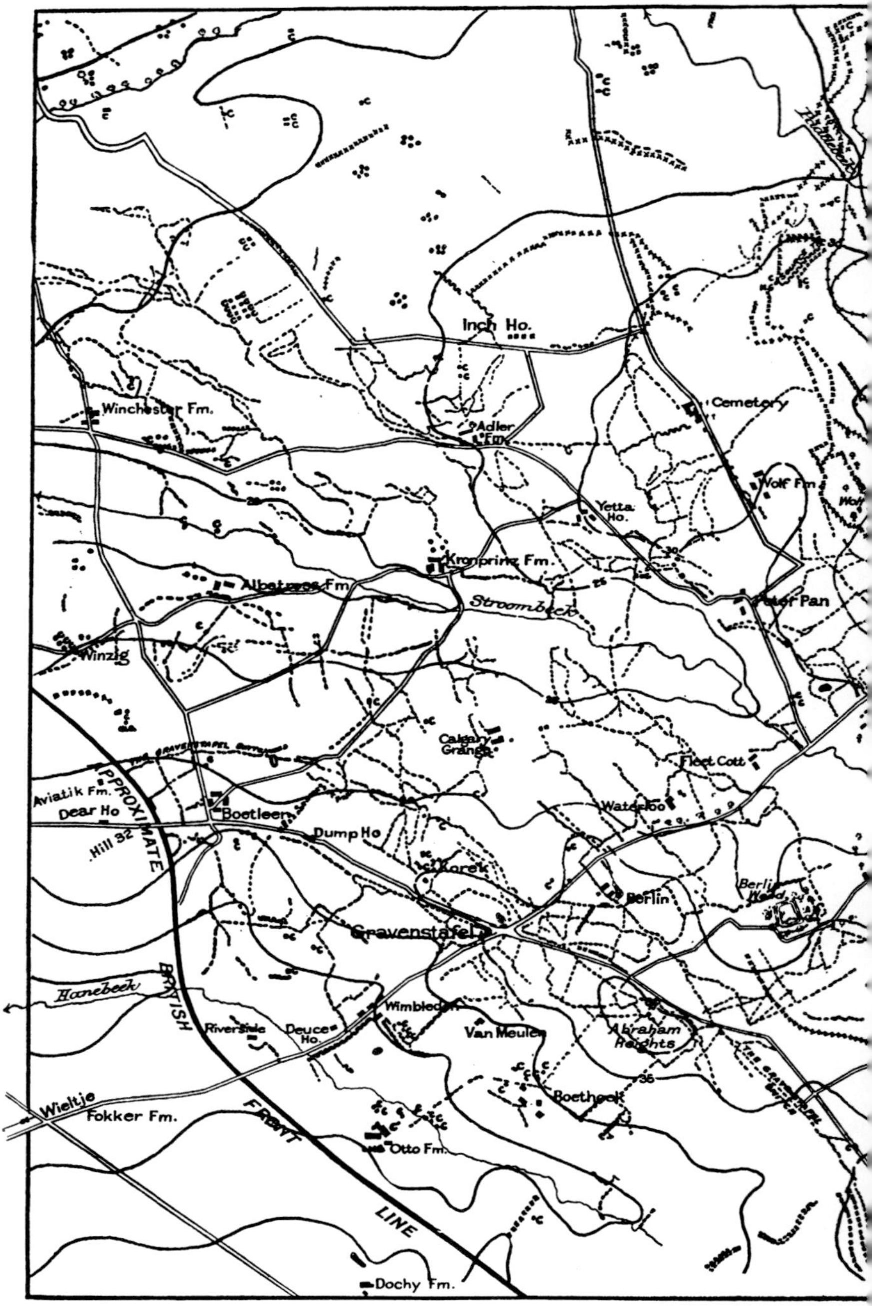

Inch Ho.
Cemetery
Winchester Fm.
Adler Fm.
Wolf Fm.
Yetta Ho.
Kronprinz Fm.
Albatross Fm.
Stroombeek
Peter Pan
Winzig
Calgary Grange
Fleet Cott
Aviatik Fm.
Dear Ho
Boetleer
Waterloo
Hill 32
Dump Ho
APPROXIMATE
Korek
Berlin
Gravenstafel
Hanebeek
BRITISH
Wimbledon
Riverside
Deuce Ho.
Van Meulen
Abraham Heights
Boethoek
Wieltje
Fokker Fm.
FRONT
Otto Fm.
LINE
Dochy Fm.

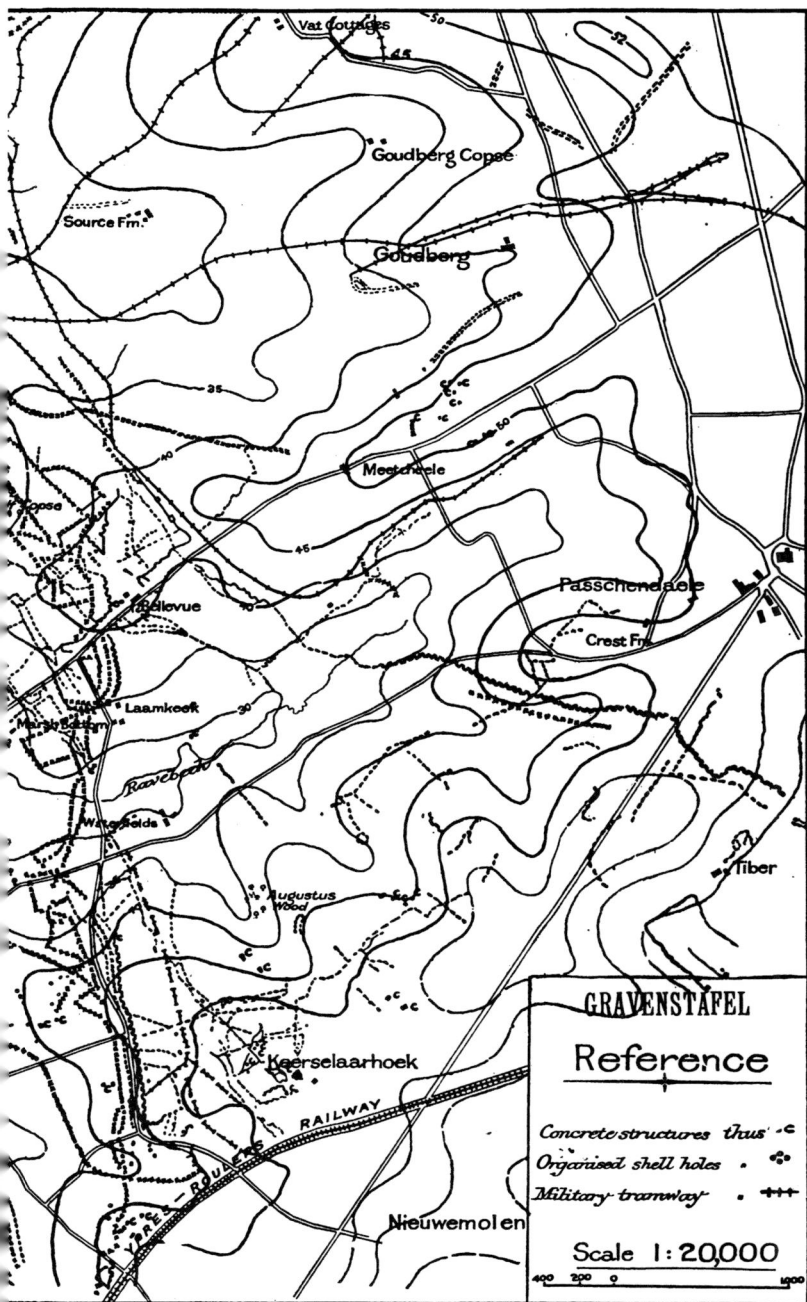

Vat Cottages

Goudberg Copse

Source Fm.

Goudberg

Meetcheele

Bellevue

Passchendaele

Crest Fm.

Laamkeek

Marsh Bottom

Ravebeek

Waterfelde

Tiber

Augustus Wood

Keerselaarhoek

RAILWAY

ROULERS

Nieuwemolen

GRAVENSTAFEL

Reference

Concrete structures thus - c
Organised shell holes . c°
Military tramway . +++

Scale 1 : 20,000

400   200   0   1000

had become casualties, the greatest part of the re-organization was carried out by the surviving non-commissioned officers; and it reflects great credit on them that the work was completed by 9 p.m.

The night of October 12th/13th was quiet, considering that it was the night following an attack, but the weather conditions were exceedingly bad. Heavy rain fell, accompanied by a high cold wind. Yet in spite of the darkness of the night and the desperate weather, and the mud that, if anything, was worse on the road than off it, rations and water were brought up to the men in the trenches.

There was only one road to the rear from the Divisional sector, and it had been a poor one at its best. Up this road had to come all the traffic to the line—troops, guns, ammunition, and supplies of all kinds—and there was no other return route for this traffic. Many of the guns intended to fire the barrage for the attack had become hopelessly bogged on the way up, and could not be extricated in time to be brought into position; and the road was strewn with abandoned ammunition and stores, waggons and dead horses and mules. It was obvious to the enemy that this road was our only means of approach, and he shelled it heavily day and night.

The problem of the collection of the wounded and their conveyance to hospital, which is no light one even in a successful advance, was now a very grave one. The 49th Division had had heavy casualties during its unsuccessful attack on October 9th: and when the New Zealand Division relieved it on the night of October 10th/11th, many of its wounded were still lying in the dressing-station at Waterloo Farm.

Some of these were removed on the night of the 11th by the 3rd Canterbury Battalion: it had arrived from Eecke that day, and had bivouacked at "Y" camp, St. Jean sector; and the 13th Company provided a party of two officers and a hundred other ranks to carry the wounded. On the 12th the battalion moved to the old German front and support lines near Wieltje, and in the afternoon went further forward to Pommern Redoubt (Pommern Castle), and supplied a party of four hundred and fifty other ranks, under Major D. A. Dron, to carry wounded from Waterloo Farm.

In spite of this battalion's work, however, the stretcher cases at Waterloo Farm accumulated, till at one time there were two hundred badly wounded men lying in the open round the dressing-station, besides those inside. This was in addition to the wounded, several hundred in number, who were still lying where they had fallen. Many wounded who might have been saved under better conditions of weather must have died as a result of exposure: and it is to be feared that some were smothered in the mud, from which they were unable to extricate themselves. The ground and road were so heavy that six men were required for each stretcher, and even then their progress was very slow.

On the 13th, parties from the 1st and 2nd Canterbury Battalions were organized as stretcher-bearers, and cleared the ground over which the brigade had advanced the previous day. The enemy was experiencing similar difficulties in collecting his wounded, and refrained from his not unusual practice of firing on our stretcher-bearers. So an informal armistice was observed; though the enemy fired on anyone who appeared without a stretcher. Rain fell at intervals during the day, and hampered the work of rescue.

On the 14th, all the wounded had been removed from the battle-field; but the work was by no means completed, for they all had to be carried from the regimental aid post at Waterloo Farm to the field ambulance's advanced dressing station at Wieltje, the furthest point to which motor ambulances could come. So bad was the road that the carry from the regimental aid post to the advanced dressing-station took from four to six hours, even with six men to a stretcher. By nightfall, however, the regimental aid post had been cleared of wounded.

During the afternoon of October 13th, the 2nd Canterbury Battalion had been ordered to fill a gap in the front line between the 2nd and 3rd Brigades; and after dusk the 12th Company was sent up to establish two strong-points in the neighbourhood of Peter Pan. By 9.30 p.m. this had been done, and the 13th Company had dug and occupied a support line a hundred and fifty yards to the rear of the 12th Company. The rest of the 2nd Battalion and the 1st Battalion remained in the trenches on Gravenstafel Spur. Heavy showers fell at intervals during the night, but it was comparatively quiet.

After another fairly quiet day on October 14th, the 4th Brigade relieved the 2nd and 3rd Brigades at dusk on the whole of the Divisional front, and the 3rd Canterbury Battalion took over the trenches of the 1st and 2nd Battalions on Gravenstafel Spur. The 2nd Brigade became brigade in support, and the 1st and 2nd Canterbury Battalions moved back respectively to Bank Farm and to Capricorn trenches north of Bank Farm. Here the battalions remained during the 15th, resting, re-organizing, drying clothes, and re-equipping themselves from salvage from the battlefield; and moving the following day, the 1st Battalion to the old British and the 2nd Battalion to the old German trenches near Wieltje, spent the rest of that day in a similar way. During the four following days, working-parties were called for from both battalions, and were engaged on different work in the back area, such as burying dead, mending roads, salvaging material, and laying duck-walk tracks. The men were also sent to the baths at Ypres. On the whole the enemy was quiet, but at intervals he shelled the back areas, and his aeroplanes dropped bombs all night and in some places by day also.

The 3rd Canterbury Battalion, on Gravenstafel Spur, suffered from heavy bombardments on October 15th and 16th, and on the 17th relieved the 3rd Auckland Battalion in the right of the line. Here it remained till the evening of October 19th, when the 1st Brigade relieved the 4th Brigade; and the battalion, on handing over its trenches to the 1st Wellington Battalion, moved back to the trenches between Pommern Redoubt and Spree Farm.*

The total casualties for the Regiment in the battle (exclusive of those of the 3rd Battalion mentioned above) had been as follows:—

1st Battalion.	Officers.	Other Ranks.
Killed in Action and Died of Wounds ..	5†	121
Wounded	10	258
Total	15	379

'On the Wieltje road, a quarter of a mile due north of Bank Farm.
†See page 204.

2nd Battalion.	Officers.	Other Ranks.
Killed in Action and Died of Wounds ..	6‡	103
Wounded	10	257
Total	16	360

3rd Battalion.	Officers.	Other Ranks.
Killed in Action and Died of Wounds ..	–	47
Wounded	6	77
Total	6	124

†Lieutenant-Colonel G. A. King, D.S.O. (12th October). Captain L. G. O'Callaghan (12th October), Captain J. Graham (Died of Wounds, 4th October), Lieutenant McK. Gibson (12th October), Lieutenant W. J. Stone (Died of Wounds, 13th October).

‡Major W. H. Meddings (11th October), Captain L. J. Ford and 2nd Lieutenants W. R. Foden, J. L. Green, and A. Talbot (12th October), 2nd Lieutenant M. K. McLeod (Died of Wounds, 13th October).

Total for the Regiment: 11 officers and 271 other ranks killed, and 26 officers and 592 other ranks wounded.

Total (including those of the 3rd Battalion to October 6th) : 13 officers and 310 other ranks killed, and 35 officers and 791 other ranks wounded.

CHAPTER XII.

THE POLYGON WOOD SECTOR:
AND THE POLDERHOEK CHATEAU ATTACK.

On October 21st the 2nd Brigade marched to Ypres, and there entrained for Wizernes, three miles south-west of St. Omer. On detraining, the 1st and 2nd Canterbury Battalions marched the same day to billets at Coulomby and Bayenghem respectively. There they spent the whole of the 22nd in resting and re-equipping, and the following day marched to their permanent billets— the 1st Battalion's at Lottinghem and the 2nd Battalion's at Quesques. Both these villages lie between the St. Omer-Boulogne railway (which runs south of Lottinghem) and the main road between those towns (which runs north of Quesques), and are about fifteen miles east of Boulogne.

Meanwhile, the 4th Brigade had been relieved on the 21st by the 1st Battalion of each of the 8th and 9th Brigades of the 3rd Canadian Division; and after spending the night in bivouacs in the St. Jean area, a mile north-east of Ypres, on the morning of the 22nd marched to Dickebusch, three miles south-west of Ypres, to entrain there on its way to join the rest of the Division. The headquarters and the 1st and 2nd Companies of the 3rd Canterbury Battalion detrained at Nielles, fifteen miles by rail south-west of St. Omer, and marched the same day to their billets at Journy, four miles north-east of Quesques; but the 12th and 13th Companies missed the train, and did not arrive at Journy till the 23rd.

After arrival at their permanent billets, all three battalions were rejoined by their "B" teams, received reinforcements, and began training.

The 2nd Brigade had suffered severely in the attack on Passchendaele; its losses had been greater than in any attack in the Messines or Somme battles, and it had failed for the first time in its history. It is true that the failure carried no disgrace with it, that the brigade had been held up by impassable mud and uncut wire rather than by the enemy's troops: but the fact of the failure was there, and it was some months before the brigade fully recovered its morale.

The lines on which the training was carried on in the rest area showed that the chief aim of the Divisional commander was to re-establish the brigade's self-respect. The hours of the morning, usually strictly reserved for purely military work, were partly devoted to recreational training, and the mental condition of the troops received a large share of the attention which hitherto had rightly been directed mainly to their physical fitness.

In other respects the training was on the usual lines, except that no brigade operations were practised, and even battalion days were not as numerous as usual. The reinforcements received at this time had had very little training: most of them had not fired more than twenty rounds with the short Lee-Enfield rifle, and required special musketry instruction. As usual, also, the specialists, particularly Lewis-gunners and signallers, had suffered severe casualties, and men to take their places had to be specially trained. Wet weather interfered greatly with training during this period.

Early in November, the New Zealand Division received orders to relieve the 21st Division in the line in the Ypres salient, in a sector east of Polygon Wood and south of Zonnebeeke. The right boundary of the sector was a small stream, the Reutelbeek, which, rising on the north of the Ypres-Menin road, near the top of the eastern slope of the ridge, flows into the river Lys at Menin. Months of continual shelling had made the original course of the Reutelbeek unrecognizable and had dammed its flow; and its overflowing waters had converted the low ground about it into an impassable morass.

With its right flank in Cameron Covert protected by the Reutelbeek against the enemy in Polderhoek Chateau, the line crossed the Polygonbeek (a tributary of the Reutelbeek) and ran across the forward slopes of a short spur, at the southern end of which lay the village of Becelaere. At a point about a thousand yards north-west of this village, the line crossed the road leading to Passchendaele, and then ran north, roughly parallel to the road, and at about two hundred yards to the east of it. The

Divisional sector ended east of the scattered hamlet of Molen-aarelsthoek.

The relief was due on November 13th, 14th, and 15th, when the 3rd and 4th Brigades were to take over the front line and the 1st and 2nd Brigades were to remain in reserve. Moving with the 4th Brigade on the 12th, the 3rd Canterbury Battalion marched from Journy to Wizernes, travelled from there by train to Houpoutre on the outskirts of Poperinghe, and the same day marched to a camp at Café Belge, on the Dickebusch-Ypres road, midway between those two places. There it continued training for a few days.

The 2nd Brigade remained at its billets till November 13th, when the 1st Canterbury Battalion left for Coulomby and the 2nd Battalion for Setques. The following day they marched to Wizernes, where they entrained for Houpoutre. Arriving there late in the afternoon, both battalions marched to Reninghelst, three miles south-east of Poperinghe, where they arrived after dark and were accommodated in huts and billets. On this date Lieutenant-Colonel H. Stewart joined the 2nd Battalion for the first time since he was wounded at Messines, and resumed command.

Both battalions remained at Reninghelst till the 16th, and then marched to join the rest of the Division, which had established its headquarters at Chateau Ségard Camp, near Café Belge. The 1st Battalion went into bivouacs at Kruistraathoek, near Divisional headquarters, on a very muddy area which provided damp and uncomfortable quarters. The 2nd Battalion was luckier, as it was sent to Forrester Camp, on the eastern side of the Neuve Eglise-Ypres road, opposite the Chateau Ségard. Both battalions settled down to training at once; but on the 21st the 2nd Battalion was put on to salvage work on a large area between Café Belge and Hell Fire Corner, on the Ypres-Menin road.

On the night of November 14th/15th, the 3rd Wellington and Auckland Battalions of the 4th Brigade relieved the 110th Brigade in the left of the Divisional sector, having the 49th Division on their left; and on the 16th the 3rd Canterbury Battalion, in reserve, took over from the 6th Battalion Leicestershire Regiment the Railway Dug-outs in the embankment of the Ypres-Menin railway line, just east of where it crosses the Ypres-Messines road.

On the night of the 21st/22nd, the battalion relieved the 3rd Auckland Battalion in the left of the brigade sector, with its right flank at the ruined buildings called Joiner's Rest. The trenches were incomplete and unprotected by wire; but before the battalion was relieved it had completed both front line and support trenches, and wired with a single belt the whole of its frontage.

On the night of November 26th/27th, the 4th Brigade took over the whole Divisional front, having the 1st Wellington Battalion attached to it for this purpose. Each of the two battalions already in the line (the 3rd Canterbury and 3rd Otago Battalions) took over an additional length of front line trenches, the 3rd Canterbury Battalion's portion of the line now extending from where the line crossed the Becelaere-Passchendaele road to the left of the Divisional sector. On relief on the night of December 1st/2nd by the 4th Battalion of the 3rd (Rifle) Brigade, the 3rd Canterbury Battalion moved back to billets in Dickebusch Huts, near the Dickebusch-Ouderdom road, and about a mile north-west of Dickebusch.

One of the highest points in the neighbourhood of the New Zealand Division's sector was the spur to the south of the Reutelbeek. Most of this spur was within the British lines; but though the eastern end, on which stood the ruins of the Polderhoek Chateau, had been captured in the advance of October 4th, it had been re-taken by the enemy the same day, and still remained in his hands. The chateau, on account of its high position, gave the enemy excellent observation, not only on the British line and its approaches on the spur itself, but also on the New Zealand Division's sector on the opposite side of the Reutelbeek.

The portions of the Division's front line most seriously affected were the posts in Cameron Covert (between the Reutelbeek and the Polygonbeek) and the right flank of the trenches north of the Polygonbeek; but in addition the chateau enfiladed the depression behind the Division's line, down which the Polygonbeek flowed, and across which was the most direct approach from the reserve positions to the front line. Consequently, the possession by British troops of the Polderhoek Chateau would render easier the defence of the sector: it would also greatly improve our ground observation on Gheluvelt and Becelaere.

POLYGON WOOD

British Line, Nov.ʳ 1917 — — — — —
Duckwalk Tracks ....
500 (yards)   0   500

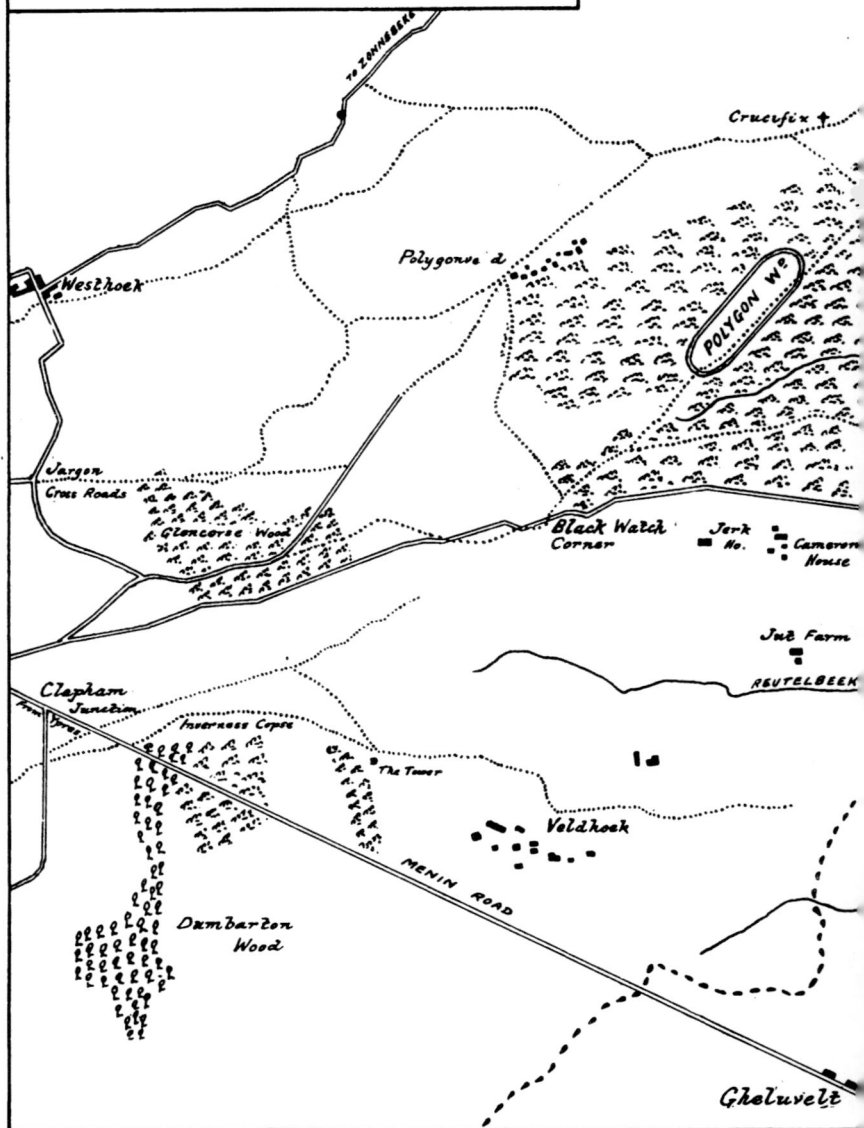

TO ZONNEBEKE

Crucifix †

Westhoek

Polygone d.

POLYGON Wᵉ

Jargon
Cross Roads

Glencorse Wood

Black Watch
Corner

Jerk
Ho.

Cameron
House

Jut Farm

REUTELBEEK

Clapham
Junction

Inverness Copse

The Tower

Veldhoek

MENIN ROAD

Dumbarton
Wood

Gheluvelt

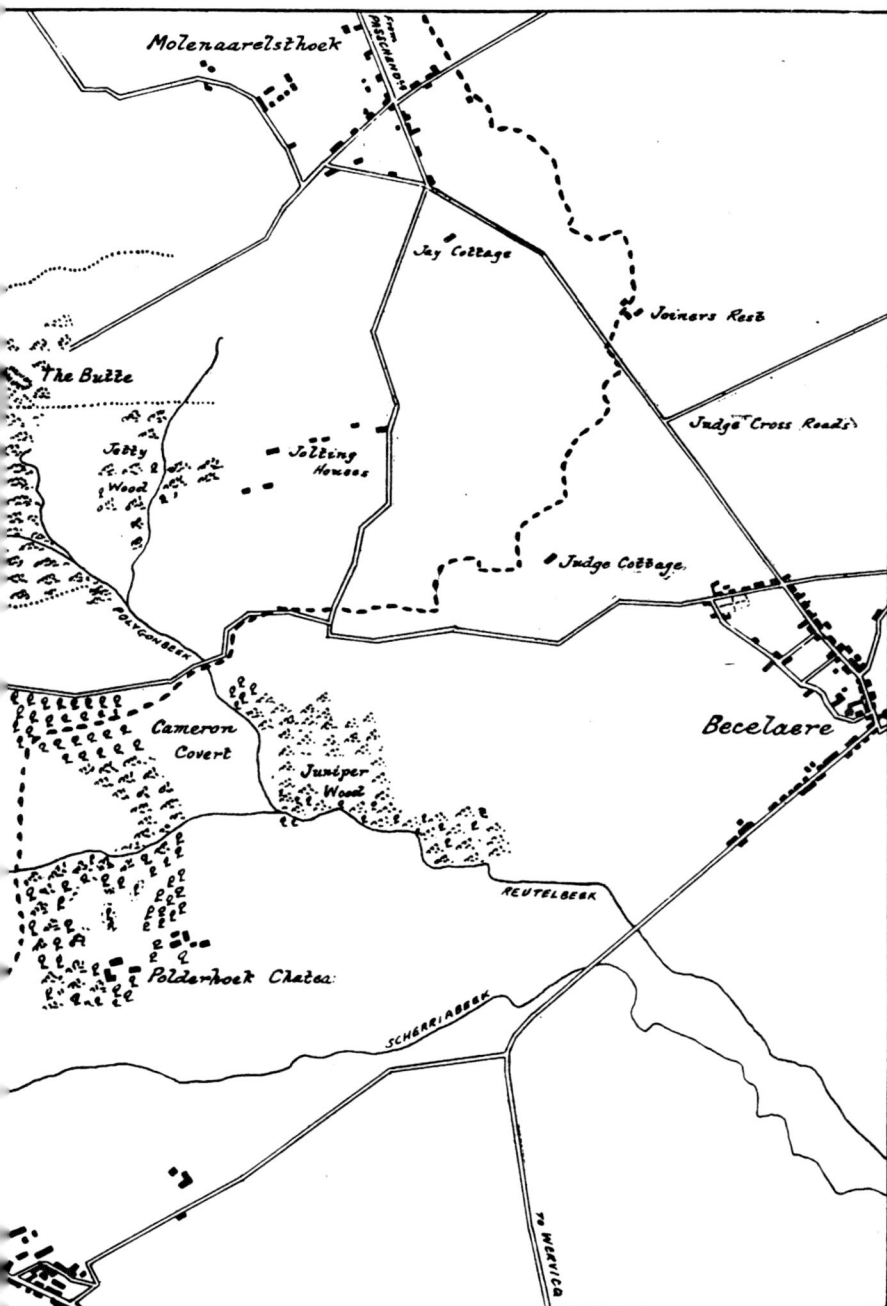

Molenaarelsthoek

From PASSCHENDAELE

Jay Cottage

Joiners Rest

The Butte

Judge Cross Roads

Jetty Wood

Jetting Houses

Judge Cottage

POLYGONBEEK

Cameron Covert

Becelaere

Juniper Wood

REUTELBEEK

Polderhoek Chateau

SCHERRIABEEK

TO WERVICQ

2ND LIEUT. R. C. ECCLESFIELD, D.C.M.

C.S.M. H. PAGE, D.C.M., M.M.

C.S.M. D. M. G. MACKAY, D.C.M.

SERGT.-MAJOR K. B. BURNS, D.C.M.

The British trenches immediately opposite the chateau were not in the New Zealand Division's sector, but were in the sector of the IX Corps, on the right of the New Zealand Division. The consideration that the part of the line held by the latter Division would derive the greater part of the benefit arising from the capture of the chateau, was doubtless the main reason for the decision of the General Officer commanding the Second Army that the II Anzac Corps should undertake the operation. For the same reason, the New Zealand Division was ordered to take over the part of the IX Corps' sector in front of the chateau, and to make the attack. The Divisional Commander detailed the 2nd Brigade for the operation, the assaulting battalions being the 1st Canterbury and 1st Otago Battalions.

These battalions began to train for the assault in the middle of November; but owing to the congestion of troops in the area, the ground available for training was very limited, and wet weather interfered with its progress. On November 18th, Major A. D. Stitt relinquished the command of the 1st Canterbury Battalion and took command of the 2nd Brigade School at Ottawa Camp, Ouderdom, two miles west of Dickebusch, which had been established for the purpose of resting and training a proportion of the officers and other ranks of the front line battalions. Major (temporary Lieutenant-Colonel) O. H. Mead took command of the battalion, which on the 23rd and 24th marched to the Ouderdom-Dickebusch area to continue its training.

On November 25th the battalion moved to Walker's Camp at Dickebusch, where the brigade-major laid out a full scale model of Polderhoek Chateau and its defences. Buildings and pill-boxes were shown in their proper relative positions, and were numbered to correspond with the numbers on the maps which had been prepared for the attack. On the 30th two practice attacks were carried out, in conjunction with the 1st Otago Battalion, and with the co-operation of contact aeroplanes. The General Officer commanding the New Zealand Division watched the morning attack, and in the afternoon the General Officer commanding the II Anzac Corps was present.

The 2nd Canterbury Battalion was to take no part in the attack; nor was it to be held in reserve near the scene of the attack. It was detailed, however, for the important work of

P

digging the assembly trenches and making the reconnaissances of No-Man's-Land for the operation. It has been mentioned that the trenches opposite the chateau were not in the New Zealand Division's sector; on the night of November 25th/26th the 2nd Brigade took over from the 118th Brigade the line from the Reutelbeek to as far south as the Scherriabeek, and the 2nd Canterbury Battalion relieved the 1st/1st Battalion Hertfordshire Regiment and a company of the 4th/5th Battalion Black Watch Regiment. It at once began work on the assembly trenches, which were called Chord and Timaru.

The line was in poor condition, and the wet weather experienced during the spell in the trenches made it an unpleasant one. The enemy's artillery was more active on the areas of the support and reserve companies (the 1st and 2nd Companies) and the overland approaches — there were no communication trenches except in the near neighbourhood of the line — than on the front line trenches. The troops here suffered mainly from the attentions of low-flying aeroplanes, which attacked them with bombs and machine-guns; and from some of our own shells falling short of the enemy's line, which was very close. An inter-company relief took place on the night of November 29th/ 30th, when the 12th Company went into support and the 13th Company to reserve.

The attacking troops had been assigned two objectives. The first, or "Dotted Red" Line, ran roughly north and south at a distance of fifty yards east of the Chateau, extending to the right as far as the road which passes a hundred and fifty yards south of the chateau on its way to join the Ypres-Menin road, and to the left to within fifty yards of the Reutelbeek. The right flank of the final objective, or "Solid Red" Line, rested on the right flank of the Dotted Red Line, and thence ran north-east to include a group of ruins three hundred yards due east of the chateau. Here the line turned and ran practically due north for two hundred and fifty yards, when it turned sharply to the west, and joined the left flank of the Dotted Red Line. The flanks up to the Dotted Red Line had also, of course, to be protected during the advance.

It will be seen that the attack, had it succeeded, would have caused a very narrow and deep salient to project from our line.

A straight line, running also due east, and passing just to the south of the chateau, formed the boundary line between the 1st Canterbury Battalion (on the right) and the 1st Otago Battalion. This meant that the Otago Battalion had a rather larger frontage than the Canterbury Battalion: on the other hand, the outer flank of the Canterbury Battalion was more exposed to attack than that of the Otago Battalion, which was protected to a great extent by the muddy bed of the Reutelbeek.

Each of the two attacking battalions detailed two companies to capture its objectives and a third company to deal with counter-attacks, and kept its remaining company in reserve. The plans of attack prepared by the brigade divided the objectives of each battalion into two, and each of the leading companies was given the task of capturing both objectives on half its battalion's front. Each of the leading companies was to allot the whole of its first objective to two platoons, and the whole of the second objective to its remaining two platoons: all the platoons detailed to capture the first objective on the whole brigade frontage were to assemble and to attack in one "wave," and all the platoons for the final objective were to form a second wave, fifty yards behind the first wave. Each of these waves consisted of two lines of troops: the first, made up of two sections from each platoon, was to make the assault; and the remaining two sections, following close on the heels of their leading sections, were to act as "moppers-up," to deal with any pill-boxes or trenches which the first line would be compelled to leave behind it, in keeping as close as possible to the creeping barrage. On the capture of the first objective by the first wave, it was ordered to consolidate the captured ground, while the second wave was immediately to pass through to continue the advance to the final objective.

On the leading companies leaving their assembly trenches, the counter-attack company was to move up at once and to occupy the positions vacated by them. The reserve companies, it was hoped, would not be called upon till after dark, when they would relieve the companies in the newly established front line, complete its consolidation, and erect wire in front of it.

Directly the advance should begin, the 1st Canterbury Battalion was ordered to commence to form a defensive flank facing south, and to extend this flank as the advance progressed. The

12th Company, the right attacking company of the battalion, was detailed for this duty, and the 1st Company (on the left) was accordingly allotted the whole of the battalion's share of the final objective. This departure from the brigade's plans for the attack was rendered necessary by the nature of the objectives assigned to the 1st Canterbury Battalion, as is readily seen on referring to the map.

The time fixed for the attack was noon on December 3rd. In order to give the attacking troops an opportunity of getting a thorough look at the ground by daylight, two platoons of each of the attacking companies of the 1st Canterbury and 1st Otago Battalions took over the front line on the night of December 1st/ 2nd. Two platoons of the 12th Company (on the right) and two platoons of the 1st Company (on the left) of the 1st Canterbury Battalion relieved the 2nd Battalion in the right half of its frontage, and four platoons of the 1st Otago Battalion took over the rest of the frontage. On relief, the headquarters and 12th Company of the 2nd Battalion went to Walker's Camp by light railway from Birr Cross-Roads (on the Menin road, two miles east of Ypres), and the 1st and 2nd Companies marched to Forrester Camp. The 13th Company was not relieved till the following night, and then moved to Walker's Camp, whither the 1st and 2nd Companies had gone earlier in the day.

The assembly for the attack took place on the night of December 2nd/3rd, which was a quiet one. The remainder of the 1st and 12th Companies of the 1st Canterbury Battalion joined their platoons in the forward assembly trenches, and the 13th Company, in support and as counter-attack company, occupied the trenches to their rear. The 2nd Company was held in reserve, and bivouacked for the night some little distance back, round the old German pill-box known as "the Tower," west of Veldhoek. More than the usual precautions were taken to conceal the relief from the enemy: he gave no sign of having detected it, and the night passed quietly.

At noon on the 3rd the barrage opened erratically, and several shells falling in our own lines caused some confusion.* The

*In justice to the artillery it must be mentioned that at this time of the year the mud was so bad that it was impossible in most places to get stable gun positions. With the guns requiring re-laying after every few shots, a good barrage was out of the question.

leading troops left the trenches as the barrage moved forward. and on topping a slight crest in front of our line were met by heavy machine-gun fire from pill-boxes in the chateau grounds and from Gheluvelt on the right flank. The advance faltered: but the situation was saved by Captain G. H. Gray, commanding the 12th Company, who, accompanied by Lance-Corporal Minnis. went forward and captured a pill-box about a hundred yards east of our front line and north of the road bounding the chateau grounds on the south, taking a machine-gun and eight prisoners. This enabled his company to get forward, in spite of the fact that the intensity of the machine-gun fire had increased very greatly.

Later in the advance, the company was again held up by an enemy strong-point; but Private H. J. Nicholas, by capturing the position single-handed, gained the first Victoria Cross won by a member of the Regiment. The official account of Private Nicholas's gallant action is as follows:—

HONOURS AND AWARDS.

Extract from Sixth Supplement to the *London Gazette* dated 11th January, 1918.

War Office,
11th January, 1918.

"His Majesty the King has been pleased to approve of the award of the Victoria Cross to the under mentioned Officers, Non-commissioned Officers, and Men, for most conspicuous bravery:—

No. 24213 PTE. HENRY JAMES NICHOLAS,
NEW ZEALAND INFANTRY

"For most conspicuous bravery and devotion to duty in attack. Pte. Nicholas, who was one of a Lewis gun section, had orders to form a defensive flank to the right of the advance which was subsequently checked by heavy machine-gun and rifle fire from an enemy strong-point. Whereupon, followed by the remainder of his section at an interval of about twenty-five yards, Pte. Nicholas rushed forward alone, shot the officer in command of the strong-point, and overcame the remainder of the garrison of sixteen by means of bombs and bayonet, capturing four wounded prisoners and a machine-gun.

"He captured this strong-point practically single-handed, and thereby saved many casualties.

"Subsequently, when the advance had reached its limit, Pte. Nicholas collected ammunition under heavy machine-gun and rifle fire.

"His exceptional valour and coolness throughout the oper-ations affording an inspiring example to all."

The company was thus enabled to get forward to within fifty yards of a pill-box (numbered 19 on our maps) due south of the chateau and on the southern edge of the road above referred to, and established a line of posts along the south side of this road, protecting the right flank and facing Gheluvelt. As these posts were established they at once brought rifle and Lewis-gun fire to bear on the enemy defences, and helped the advance materially: in one post a Lewis-gun located and engaged an enemy machine-gun, and put it out of action.

The 1st Company, on the left, had meanwhile advanced under heavy small-arms fire, but was unfortunate in losing, early in the attack, many of its most experienced officers and non-com-missioned officers. Eighty yards short of a pill-box (numbered 18 on the map), which lay about seventy-five yards south of the chateau, and midway between the ruins of that building and pill-box number 19, the 1st Company was held up by mutually supporting fire from machine-guns in the chateau and these two pill-boxes. Here Lieutenant E. G. Bristed was killed, while endeavouring to rush pill-box 18.

It was now about 1 p.m., and the Commanding Officer of the battalion sent forward two strong sections of the 13th Company, to assist the 1st and 12th Companies to capture pill-box number 18; but these sections came under very heavy machine-gun fire on leaving the old front line trenches, and lost so heavily that they were unable to help on the advance. Half an hour later, on this being reported, the Commanding Officer sent up to the firing line a full platoon of the same company, but it could not press the attack any further.

The advance was now definitely held up, as the attacking troops had lost the protection of the creeping barrage, with the result that the enemy machine-gunners were able to continue firing without any interference from our shrapnel. The 1st Canterbury Battalion's firing line now ran about eighty yards west of the chateau and the line of pill-boxes running south from it (Nos. 18 and 19), till it crossed the road on the south of the chateau grounds, and then ran parallel to and about fifty yards to the south of the road till it crossed our old front line. On the left, the 1st Otago Battalion had advanced its line level with the 1st Canterbury Battalion, but was also unable to move any further forward. In order to hold the little ground they had won, both battalions began to dig in on the line reached by their leading companies. The 2nd Company of the 1st Canterbury Battalion was ordered up from the tower to Chord Trench, and came through a heavy barrage of 5·9-inch shells, which, however, fortunately cost the company only one man.

At 2.30 p.m. small parties of the enemy were observed to be moving to the bed of the Scherriabeek, to the south of the front line from which our attack had been made, and to be concentrating there, apparently for a counter-attack. A light trench mortar of the 2nd Battery was promptly brought into position at the right flank of our old front line, and its fire caused the enemy to bolt from their position without waiting to take their rifles or equipment. Our Lewis-guns were trained on the enemy as he fled, and inflicted severe casualties, to judge from the activity of stretcher-bearers for some hours afterwards. About 4.30 p.m. a party of about forty of the enemy approached pill-box 18, but was scattered by Lewis-gun fire.

The work of consolidation was pushed on. During the afternoon, the brigadier sent orders that pill-boxes 18 and 19 were to be captured under cover of darkness: the Commanding Officers of the Canterbury and Otago Battalions had already discussed whether it was advisable to attempt this, and had decided against it, on account of the heavy casualties already sustained, and the risk of losing the few troops now available in reserve. On this being represented to the brigadier, he cancelled his orders. At midnight the two Commanding Officers again discussed the question of attacking the chateau and pill-boxes; but by this time the moon had risen and visibility was good, and the enemy was also very much on the alert. They therefore decided that an attack could result only in additional casualties. Before dawn of the 4th the Canterbury Battalion had dug a continuous line of trenches along its whole front, and had begun a communication trench across the old No-Man's-Land, near the right flank; and this trench also was completed during the day.

Another enemy counter-attack threatened at 8.30 a.m. on the 4th, when his troops were observed massing astride the Becelaere-Gheluvelt road, about a thousand yards east of the Polderhoek Chateau. On the artillery being informed of this, it opened fire and dispersed the enemy troops, who retreated towards Becelaere. Otherwise the day passed quietly, except for an enemy barrage on the left flank at 2 p.m., which was not, however, followed by any infantry action. During the night, the 1st and 12th Companies were relieved by the 2nd Company and a platoon of the 13th Company, and moved back to the old front line and Chord trench. The same night a party from the Pioneer Battalion dug a support trench seventy yards in rear of the new front line.

Next day the enemy began to shell the old front line at 10.30 a.m., and continued to do so all day. During the afternoon the fire increased in volume and extent, and became intense over the whole sector. At 2.10 p.m. abnormal movement was noticed round the chateau, and a counter-attack was expected but did not take place. The enemy's shelling continued, and being well directed at our new positions caused numerous casualties; our artillery's reply could not lessen the enemy's fire, until at 5 p.m. it brought down a heavy barrage on his infantry's positions. After the barrage had lasted an hour and a half, the enemy's fire ceased. From subsequent intelligence reports, it appears that this barrage caught the enemy massing for a counter-attack, caused him heavy casualties, and forced him to retire: but apparently his movements were invisible to the front line troops.

During the night the 2nd Battalion of the Bedford Regiment relieved the two New Zealand battalions, which marched to Birr Cross road and there entrained on light railway trucks. At about 1.30 a.m. on the 6th they arrived at Howe Camp, two miles southwest of Ypres.

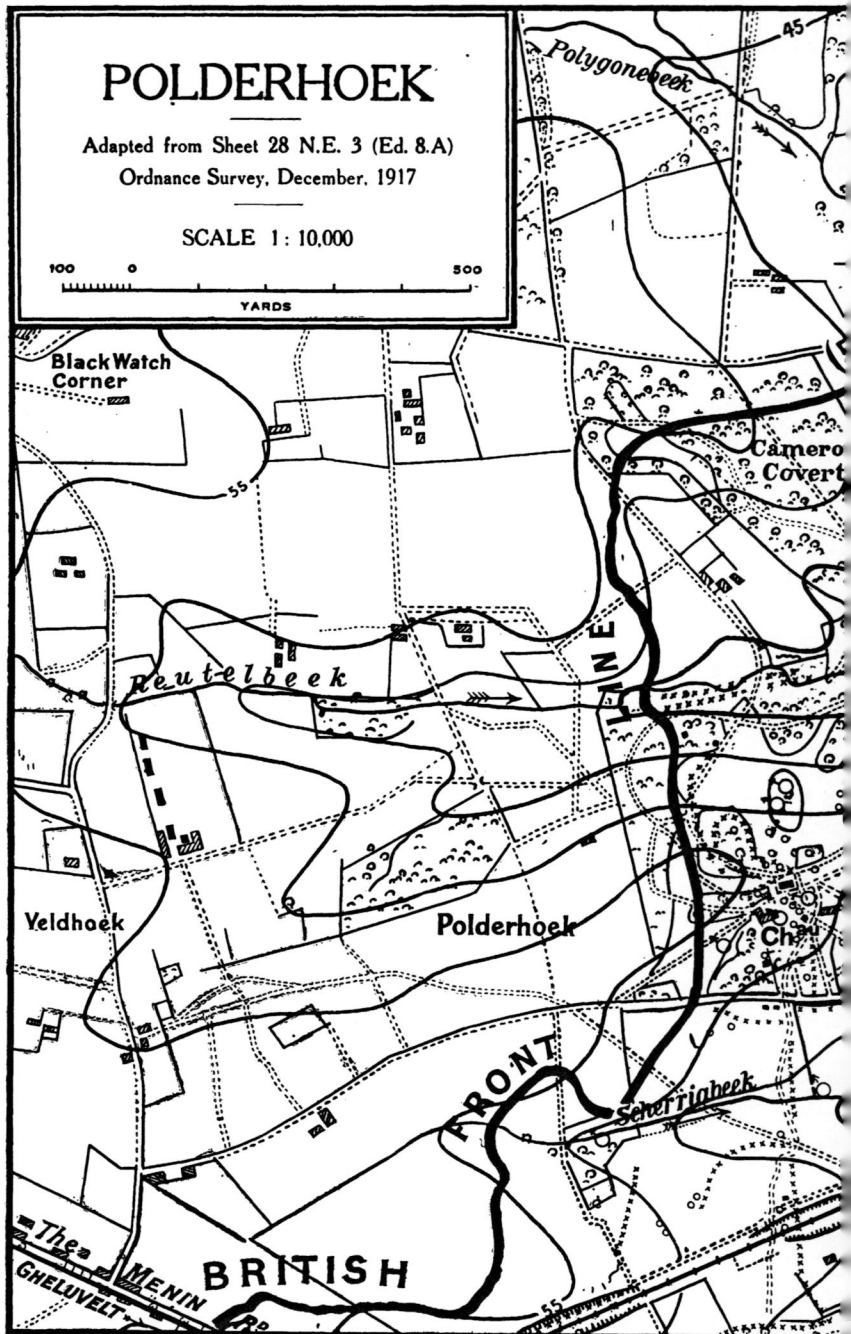

POLDERHOEK

Adapted from Sheet 28 N.E. 3 (Ed. 8.A)
Ordnance Survey, December, 1917

SCALE 1 : 10,000

100   0   500

YARDS

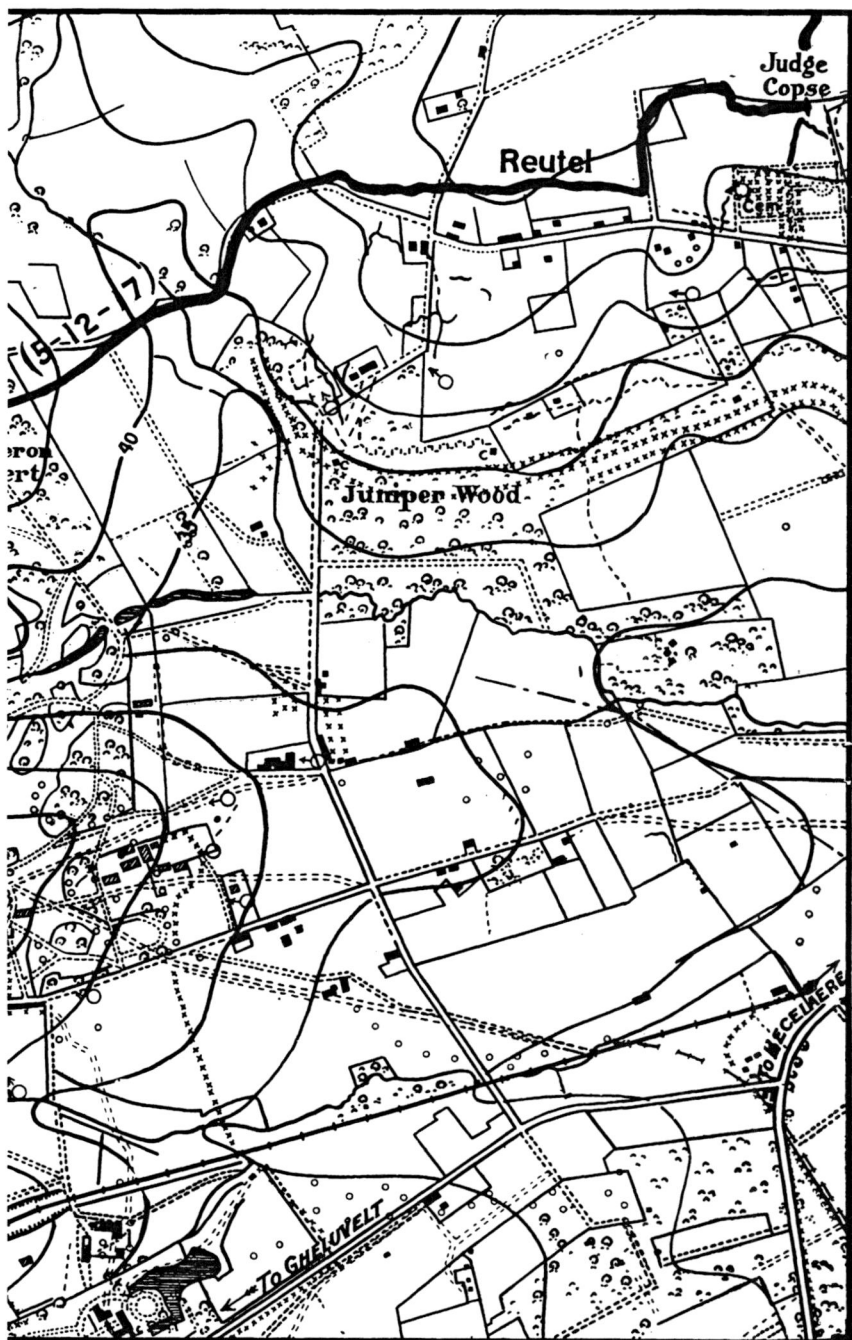

Judge
Copse

Reutel

Cen

(5-12-7)

ron
ert

Jumper Wood

40

TO MECELDERE

TO GHELUVELT

The casualties of the battalion during the attack are not given in its diary, but those for the month of December were as follows:

				Officers.	Other Ranks.
Killed	..	..	..	4*	75†
Wounded	..	..	..	2	163
Missing	..	..	..	–	11
Total	..	..	..	6	249

*Lieutenants W. N. Elliott and E. G. Bristed (on the 3rd), Lieutenant J. A. McQueen, M.C. (on the 11th), and Captain S. L. Serpell, M.C. — Medical Officer — (on the 15th).

†Including eleven died of wounds.

There was no use attempting to disguise the fact that the attack had failed, and that on the whole the opposition encountered, though stiff, was no greater than the opposition which New Zealand troops had successfully overcome on many previous occasions. The attack had been held up neither by mud nor by wire. The 2nd Brigade official report on the operation gives the following reasons for the failure:—

"(a) Inadequacy of training. Though several days (November 27th to 30th, both inclusive) were devoted to practice over ground especially marked out for the purpose, all reports go to show that the men were not 'intensively' trained to the necessary standard. They started off with considerable elan, and there was no lack of natural courage and grit once a line was formed and the course of action obvious. But a large proportion of officers and men were reinforcement drafts quite unfamiliar with hostile shelling or our own barrage fire. When the experienced officers and other ranks became casualties, many falling in the most gallant efforts to push forward, the new hands—already to some extent demoralized by the short shooting of the 18-pounder battery referred to above—were at a loss and failed to show the necessary qualities of dash, determination, and readiness for self-sacrifice which were indispensable factors for success in this operation. A glaring instance was shown by the troops of the right battalion leaving the assembly trenches too soon, by their returning to them, and on their starting forward again by their

pressing into our own barrage. All competent observers lay
stress on this lack of training, and there is no question but that
this is the main reason for the failure.

"(b) The strength of the enemy defences. The mutually
supporting pill-boxes were mostly undamaged by our artillery.
The volume of machine-gun fire from in front and from Gheluvelt
was heavy.

(c) The isolated nature of the attack drew intense artillery
and machine-gun fire, and its limits were still more clearly defined by the smoke barrage. It merits consideration as to whether
a further attempt should not be part of a joint enterprise to
include an attack on Gheluvelt and possibly Becelaere.''

Other critics add the following reasons:—

(1) The only experienced officers and other ranks who took
part in the attack were those who had been in the ''B'' team at
Passchendaele: practically all the survivors of that battle were
sent to the ''B'' team for the Polderhoek attack.

(2) The period allowed for training for the attack was far too
short, and gave neither officers. non-commissioned officers, nor
men a chance to know and feel confidence in each other; and it
had also been interrupted by wet weather.

(3) A strong westerly breeze dissipated the artillery smoke-
screen, which had been put down on the right flank of the attack
in order to hide from enemy observers in Gheluvelt the movements of the assaulting troops. The failure of the smoke-screen
enabled enemy machine-gunners in Gheluvelt to inflict heavy
casualties on the 1st Canterbury Battalion in particular.

It may be noted here that, nine days after the attack, the
enemy re-captured the ground which the 1st Canterbury and 1st
Otago Battalions had taken on December 3rd.

TRENCH WARFARE.

The 2nd Canterbury Battalion remained at Walker's Camp
till December 5th, when the 2nd Brigade came into support to
the Division, and the battalion moved forward to about two miles
east of Ypres. There it was housed in deep dug-outs—battalion
headquarters and the 12th and 13th Companies at Halfway
House Dug-outs, half a mile to the south of Birr Cross-Roads,
and the 1st and 2nd Companies at Railway Wood Dug-outs, the
same distance north of the Cross-Roads.

The Division's sector had now been altered slightly, the northern boundary being moved a quarter of a mile further north, while the Reutelbeek remained the southern boundary.

The area between the Reutelbeek and the Polygonbeek was known as the Cameron Covert sub-sector. It differed from the other sub-sectors held by the Division in that it had no front line or support trenches, but was defended by a series of isolated posts which had not yet been connected into continuous lines. The two streams of the Reutelbeek and the Polygonbeek, converted by shell-fire in fairly wide marshes, flanked Cameron Covert and met in front of it. As the marshes were impassable for large bodies of troops, the sector was secure from attack during the early months of the winter; but later on, when the marshes had frozen, their natural protection disappeared.

The Divisional sector was now too long to be held by one brigade, and there was no accommodation or shelter for two brigades, so an extra battalion was attached to each brigade when it held the line.* The brigade then held the line with four battalions in the front line and one in support. Reliefs took place on the average every six days: the front line battalions then moved to the back areas with the exception of the battalion holding Cameron Covert, which exchanged places with the support battalion. This happened every relief till a brigade went into Divisional reserve, when all four of its battalions were withdrawn from the front area.

On the night of December 9th/10th, the 2nd Brigade relieved the 3rd (Rifle) Brigade in the Divisional front line system between the northern boundary and the Polygonbeek, with three battalions in the line and one in support. The 3rd Battalion of the Rifle Brigade remained in the front line, between the Reutelbeek and the Polygonbeek, and came under the command of the General Officer commanding the 2nd Brigade.

The 1st Canterbury Battalion took over the 2nd Brigade's centre sector, called "Judge Cross Roads," and extending from a point opposite "Judge Cottage," five hundred yards south of the point where our front line crossed the Becelaere-Passchendaele road, to a point just north of "Joiner's Rest," and two

---

*The 1st Brigade had been detached from the Division for work under Corps direction, so that the Division had the normal number of three brigades to hold the line.

hundred and fifty yards north of the same road. It held the line with the 13th Company on the right, the 2nd Company on the left, the 1st Company in support, and the 12th Company in reserve, and with headquarters at "the Butte." This was a large mound of earth about a quarter of a mile north-east of the northern end of the racecourse in Polygon Wood.

The presence of tree stumps on the mound, as well as its distance from the racecourse, showed the unsoundness of the almost universal belief in the New Zealand Division that it formed the foundation of a grand-stand. Colonel H. Stewart has since ascertained, after much research in the British Museum and correspondence with French archæologists, that the mound was constructed about the beginning of the nineteenth century, for the purpose of training in musketry the Belgian infantry stationed at Ypres barracks; and that it had been disused since 1870. It had been extensively tunnelled by the Germans, and was now used as headquarters not only by the brigade in the line, but also by one of its battalions.*

On the right of the 1st Canterbury Battalion was the 2nd Otago Battalion and on its left the 1st Otago Battalion; and the 2nd Canterbury Battalion, in support, occupied bivouacs in Polygon Wood, of which scarcely a stump remained. Much work was required on the front line system, and while the line battalions improved their own trenches, the 2nd Canterbury battalion was set to work on the trenches immediately behind the front line.

Except in a few places close up to the front line, there were no communication trenches in the Divisional sector: and on account of the mud all the traffic in the area was confined to a few duck-walk tracks, the position of which was well known to the enemy, who shelled them constantly. In ordinary circumstances, these tracks would have been exceedingly unsafe; but the mud which rendered them necessary also smothered the enemy shells, and greatly reduced their danger area. However, obviously these tracks were at all times much more unsafe than communication trenches, and when the frosts came, even very badly-aimed shells could cause casualties to troops using the tracks.

---

*After the Armistice the Butte was purchased by the Australian Government, as a site for a memorial to the 5th Australian Division.

On the relief of the 2nd Brigade by the 4th Brigade on the night of December 15th/16th, the 2nd Canterbury Battalion moved from its bivouacs at Polygonveld as battalion in support, and in accordance with the practice mentioned above, relieved the 3rd Battalion of the 3rd (Rifle) Brigade in Cameron Covert, coming under the command of the 4th Brigade. There was very little accommodation near the front line, so while one company held the posts and another was kept in support close up, the two remaining companies were held in reserve close to the bivouacs which they had occupied at Polygonveld when the battalion was in support to the 2nd Brigade. The 1st Canterbury Battalion was relieved by the 3rd Canterbury Battalion, and moving out with the two Otago Battalions, went to Howe Camp, whence it moved on the 21st to the New Hutting Camp, half a mile south of Ypres.

It is not necessary to record here all the reliefs of the three battalions from now on: details are to be found in Appendix "B." The trench warfare in the Ypres salient differed from the Division's earlier experiences at Armentières only by the greater discomforts with which the troops had to contend at Ypres. The trenches were muddy and were as a rule without duck-walks, which meant that the feet of the garrison were almost always wet. There was very little weather-proof sleeping accommodation; and though hot food was sent up from cook-houses behind the line, it usually arrived fairly cold, on account of the long distance it had to be carried.

Snow fell before Christmas, but as it froze it did not add much to the discomforts; though the frozen ground increased the danger zone of shells to as great an extent as the mud had previously reduced it. Later on, when frosty nights were followed by sunny days, numerous casualties were caused in the mornings by the contents of gas-shells fired during the night, which had remained in liquid form till the heat of the sun caused them to evaporate. In this manner the whole of the headquarters of the 2nd Brigade and of the 2nd Canterbury Battalion were gassed in the Butte on the morning of February 18th. The casualties evacuated to hospital from the 2nd Battalion included the Commanding Officer (Major N. R. Wilson),* the adjutant,

---

*Major Wilson had commanded the 2nd Battalion since just before Christmas, when Lieutenant-Colonel Stewart took over the temporary command of the 2nd Brigade. The latter returned to the command of the battalion for a few days in February, leaving on the 15th to go on leave. Major Wilson then again took command of the battalion.

three other officers, and thirty-seven other ranks. None of the cases were serious, and caused more amusement than sympathy in the rest of the battalion, which had just received a severe "strafe" for having had similar casualties.

On January 17th and 18th, the 4th Brigade had relieved the 1st Brigade as Corps working brigade; but now the time had arrived when the supply of reinforcements from New Zealand was insufficient to keep four brigades up to full strength in the field. The actual date of disbandment of the brigade was February 7th: on February 4th its brigadier, Brigadier-General H. E. Hart, D.S.O., took over the command of the 2nd Brigade. The officers and other ranks of the four 3rd Battalions who were not immediately required as reinforcements for the line battalions were formed into four Works (or Entrenching) Battalions, which together made up the New Zealand Works Group, available for work under Corps direction. All reinforcements on being sent from England to France were henceforward sent on by the New Zealand Reinforcement Wing to the Works Group, and there were drafted to their proper works battalion. Demands from the line battalions for reinforcements were supplied by drafts from the corresponding works battalions.

The commanding officer of the 3rd Canterbury Battalion, Lieutenant-Colonel R. A. Row, did not, however, remain with it when it was converted into a works battalion. On February 13th he took over the command of the 1st Battalion from Captain E. M. Cuddon, who was acting Commanding Officer in place of Lieutenant-Colonel O. H. Mead, on leave. On his return, on the 19th, Lieutenant-Colonel Mead took command of the 2nd Battalion, in place of Major Wilson, who had been gassed the previous day. The same day Brigadier-General R. Young (formerly Commanding Officer of the 1st Battalion) took command of the 2nd Brigade, replacing Brigadier-General Hart, who had also been gassed at the Butte.

The New Zealand Division had now been in the line for over three months, and was due and quite ready for its turn in Corps Reserve, when orders came for the relief of the infantry brigades by the 49th Division, between February 21st and 24th. At this time the 2nd Canterbury Battalion was in the line at Judge Cross roads, and the 1st Battalion in brigade reserve with headquarters and two companies at Railway Wood Dug-out, a mile north-west of Hooge, and two companies half a mile to the west, at West Farm Camp. Relieved on the 22nd by a battalion of the 147th Brigade, the 1st Canterbury Battalion moved to Belgian Chateau, a mile and a half south-west of Ypres, where it received reinforcements and was rejoined by details from the brigade school. The 2nd Battalion was relieved in the line by the 1st/6th Battalion West Riding Regiment on the night of the 22nd/23rd, and moved to West Farm Camp, where its strength was increased in the same way as the 1st Battalion's. The following day both battalions marched to Ypres to entrain for the training area.

The following is a summary of the casualties sustained by the Regiment since the return of the New Zealand Division to the Ypres salient in November, 1917, including the casualties suffered in the Polderhoek chateau attack:—

1st Battalion.	Officers.	Other Ranks.
Killed in Action and Died of Wounds .	5*	124
Wounded	7	220
Total	12	344

2nd Battalion.	Officers.	Other Ranks.
Killed in Action and Died of Wounds ..	–	53
Wounded	13	212
Total	13	265

3rd Battalion.	Officers.	Other Ranks.
Killed in Action and Died of Wounds ..	–	49
Wounded	4	91
Total	4	140

*Lieutenant W. N. Elliott (killed 3rd December, 1917), 2nd Lieutenant E. G. Bristed (killed 3rd December,

1917, Lieutenant J. A. McQueen (killed 11th December, 1917), Captain S. L. Serpell, R.M.O. (killed 15th December, 1917), 2nd Lieutenant H. F. Dyer (killed 8th January, 1918).

Total for Regiment: 5 officers and 226 other ranks killed, and 24 officers and 523 other ranks wounded.

SERGT.-MAJOR A. A. ATKINS, D.C.M.

SERGT.-MAJOR J. L. SHACKLETON, D.C.M.

CORPL. HAROLD RHIND, D.C.M

CORPL. F. M. DODDS, D.C.M

CHAPTER XIII.

THE GERMAN OFFENSIVE OF 1918.

On February 23rd the 2nd Brigade entrained at Ypres for
Caestre, a village on the main Cassel-Bailleul road. The brigade
detrained at 9 p.m., and found the Y.M.C.A. waiting with very
welcome hot tea and biscuits. After tea, the battalions marched
to their billetting areas, the 1st Canterbury Battalion to St. Marie
Cappel, and the 2nd Battalion to St. Sylvestre Cappel. The
quarters were good and the weather was fine; and everyone was
relieved to get away from the Ypres Salient, which had not belied
its evil reputation. In these circumstances, the prospect of a
month's spell put all ranks in the highest spirits. The first two
days after arrival were spent in "interior economy," and active
training did not begin until the 26th.

The training was very much on the lines of that done in the
Quelmes area in September, 1917, and at Lottinghem and Quesques at the end of October, 1917, so that no detailed description is necessary. The General Officer commanding the Division
(Major-General Sir A. H. Russell) inspected the Canterbury
Battalions on March 4th, and expressed his satisfaction with the
turn-out and appearance of the men. The maintenance and improvement of morale was achieved by the encouragement of sport
and other recreations. On March 4th the 1st Battalion defeated
the 2nd Battalion at football, by thirteen points to six, and the
following day the 2nd Battalion ran second to the 1st Otago
Battalion, in a brigade cross-country run of three miles. The
same afternoon the 1st Battalion won the brigade football
championship, by defeating the 1st Otago Battalion by six points
to three.

A great deal of time was given to musketry, and on the 8th
the Canterbury Battalions left for a week's shooting in the
Houlle and Moulle area, about six miles to the north-west of
St. Omer. The journey was done in two stages, the 1st Bat-
talion being billeted for the night at Campagne, and the 2nd
Battalion lying at Wardrecques. Both battalions reached their

billets at Houlle the following day, having had splendid weather for the march. In addition to the usual target practice, much time was spent in field practices, under as near an approach to actual service conditions as possible. The battalions left this area on the 16th, and were back in their old billets in St. Marie and St. Sylvestre by the night of the 17th. Training proceeded on the usual lines, and on March 22nd the Corps* Commander (Lieutenant-General Sir A. J. Godley) was present at training operations, and afterwards inspected the battalions. Lieutenant-Colonel H. Stewart had returned from leave on the 20th, and resumed command of the 2nd Battalion.

Meanwhile, the German offensive of March 21st had commenced, and the Otago Battalions, which were at Houlle, were hurriedly recalled. On the 23rd orders were issued for the 2nd Brigade to begin entraining at Caestre the next day. Brigade headquarters and advance parties from the battalions left by the first train, at 3.25 p.m. The 2nd Company of the 1st Canterbury Battalion, which had been detailed as a loading party, also went on this train. The remainder of the 1st Battalion followed in the second train, three hours later; but the third train, with the 2nd Battalion, did not leave till 10.30 p.m. The rest of the brigade entrained the next day.

The railway journey was by way of Calais, Boulogne, and Abbeville, and it was originally intended that the brigade should detrain at Edgehill, a railway siding to the east of Amiens, and about half way between that town and Albert. But when the first train arrived at St. Roch, on the outskirts of Amiens, at 1 a.m. on the 25th, the Brigadier was informed by the French railway officials that the train could go no further, as the track near the town had been destroyed by an enemy aircraft attack. At 4 a.m. orders were received that brigade headquarters was to detrain at St. Roch; and at 7 a.m. motor lorries arrived, and took the troops to Chipilly, a village on the Somme between Corbie and Bray. On arrival there, it was found that no accommodation was available; but orders were received from Division that the brigade group was to go on to Morlancourt and Ville-sous-Corbie, midway between Chipilly and Albert. The Division was now attached to the VII Corps, which formed part of the Third Army.

*The name of the Corps had been changed to XXII Corps as from January 1st, 1918.

On account of the cutting of the railway at Amiens, the de-training point for the remainder of the 2nd Brigade had been altered to Ailly-sur-Somme, five miles west of the town. As the battalions arrived there, they reduced their kits to fighting order. and left their valises and other surplus gear under guard there. The three companies of the 1st Battalion which were on the second train arrived at Ailly at 6.30 a.m. on the 25th. One and a half companies were at once taken by motor lorries to Sailly-Lorrette, a mile west of Chipilly, and the lorries returned for the remainder of the battalion. From Sailly-Lorrette the two parties marched independently to Morlancourt, and the whole battalion (except the 2nd Company, which was still at St. Roch) was in billets there by 11.30 p.m.

Three companies of the 2nd Battalion arrived at Ailly at 9.30 a.m. on the 25th, and bivouacked in a field all day. The service of motor lorries was disorganized; but at 3 p.m. battalion headquarters and the 1st Company and a platoon of the 2nd Company were taken by lorries to Ville-sous-Corbie, where they arrived at 9.30 p.m., and went into billets for the night. Shortly before midnight, orders were received that the Division was to be transferred to the IV Corps (Lieutenant-General Sir G. M. Harper, K.C.B.) and was to concentrate at Hédauville, on the Albert-Doullens road, five miles north-west of Albert.

All troops at Ville-sous-Corbie and Morlancourt immediately began to march to Hédauville; and the motor lorries carrying the 13th Company and the remaining three platoons of the 2nd Company of the 2nd Battalion were diverted to that village, and reached there at 7 a.m. on the 26th. The remaining company of the 2nd Battalion (the 12th Company) had detrained at St. Roch, and had travelled by motor lorry as far as Pont Noyelles, on the Amiens-Albert road; and from there had a twelve miles march to Hédauville, which it reached at 7.45 a.m. By 9 a.m. the 2nd Company of the 1st Canterbury Battalion had come from St. Roch by motor lorry, and the two Canterbury Battalions, with the 2nd Machine-Gun Company and the 2nd Light Trench Mortar Battery, formed the 2nd Brigade Group. The two Otago Battalions were on the march from their detraining points; and the motor lorry service having proved completely inadequate, these battalions did not reach Hédauville till late on the evening of the 26th, and were then put into Divisional reserve.

It is now necessary to examine the general situation on this portion of the British front. Before the German attack of March 21st, the line had run from the Vimy Ridge to a point six miles east of Arras; and after crossing the Arras-Cambrai road had swung south-east, and ran roughly parallel to that road almost to Marcoing, where it turned south again to St. Quentin, forming a wide salient called the Flesquières Salient. About ten miles south of this turning point, the right flank of the Third Army joined the left flank of the Fifth Army.

The success of enemy attacks delivered on March 21st, in a south-westerly direction between the Cambrai-Bapaume road and the Sensée River, and in a westerly direction on the whole front of the Fifth Army, threatened to cut off the troops holding the Flesquières Salient, and made it necessary for the Third Army to withdraw along the whole of its front south of Arras. The withdrawal had been accomplished in an orderly manner, but losses had been heavy; and as the line gradually began to swing back towards Amiens, the front became longer and required more troops to hold it.

The situation on the morning of March 26th was that the Third Army was still retiring, and the IV Corps was falling back to a line Puisieux-Bucquoy-Ablainzeville, where the 62nd and 42nd Divisions had been ordered to make a stand. Further to the south, the 12th Division (V Corps) was moving up to hold the line of the Ancre River from Albert to Hamel. Between the 12th and 62nd Divisions there was therefore a gap of five miles.

This gap between the IV and V Corps had appeared on March 24th, when the Third Army had fallen back to the general line Ham-Longueval-west of Bapaume-Ervillers. From Ervillers the line ran roughly due south for thirteen miles to Hardecourt. Attacks on the 25th caused the two Corps to fall back a distance of about five miles in the centre of this line, while maintaining their positions at Ervillers and Hardecourt; thus lengthening their line to about twenty miles between those places. This operation made a deep re-entrant on the front of the two Corps, and the gap between them naturally had increased greatly at the end of the day—to a width of five miles, as stated above.

It was to fill this gap that the New Zealand Division had been brought in such urgent fashion from the Bray-sur-Somme area;

for though the remnants of the 51st and 19th Divisions were being collected at Sailly-au-Bois, and those of the 25th and 41st Divisions at Gommecourt, none of these troops were sufficiently organized to take such a determined offensive action as was required. The enemy was closely following up the retiring troops of the Third Army, and on the night of the 25th had reached Miraumont and Beaucourt, on the River Ancre. The last-named village was less than two miles from the line which the New Zealand Division had been ordered to take up.

At 2 a.m. on the 26th the first battalion of the Division arrived at Hédauville. This was the 1st Battalion, 3rd New Zealand (Rifle) Brigade, which had marched from Pont Noyelles. After a short rest of four hours, this battalion was sent on to occupy Englebelmer and Auchonvillers and the intervening country, so as to cover the advance of the rest of the Division. There were at this time only four other battalions at the disposal of the General Officer commanding the Division—the 1st Auckland and the 1st and 2nd Canterbury Battalions and the 2nd Battalion of the 3rd New Zealand (Rifle) Brigade. These battalions were formed into two brigade groups, the two Canterbury Battalions forming the 2nd Brigade Group, and the other two battalions the 1st Brigade Group. To each group was attached one machine-gun company. The groups were ordered to move forward at noon, and to fill the gap between Hamel and Puisieux.

Before the battalions moved off that morning. Brigadier-General Young (commanding the 2nd Brigade) appointed Lieutenant-Colonel Stewart (for the time being the senior battalion commander in the brigade) to take command of the transport and "B" teams of the four battalions. The fact that the brigade was engaged in open warfare and the battalions were scattered, necessitated a good deal of separate marching, by the transport especially; and rendered it essential that there should be an experienced senior officer to supervise their work closely. Lieutenant-Colonel Mead took command of the 2nd Canterbury Battalion in place of Lieutenant-Colonel Stewart.

The Division's objectives were divided into two parts, and to the 2nd Brigade group was allotted the southern part, which consisted of practically the old British line, as it existed before the Battle of the Somme in 1916, from west of Hamel to north west of Beaumont-Hamel. The 1st Battalion of the 3rd (Rifle)

Brigade, which had established a line of outposts north and south of Auchonvillers, was now attached to the 2nd Brigade. The two Canterbury Battalions left Hédauville at noon, the 2nd Battalion leading, and advanced along the Mailly-Maillet road, by platoons at one hundred yards distance, with a protective screen of scouts in front.

The 2nd Battalion reached Mailly-Maillet without opposition, but there obtained information from the 3rd (Rifle) Brigade that nothing was known with regard to the situation to the north. One company (the 2nd) was therefore sent along the Serre road, to take up a position on the high ground known as "The Apple Trees," about half a mile north-east of the village, in order to protect the left flank from attack. At the same time the 1st Battalion had assembled in a valley to the south-east of Mailly-Maillet, and patrols had been sent forward to cover the advance of the battalion and to get in touch with the 12th Division on the right.

At about 4 p.m. the 1st Canterbury Battalion, on the right of the brigade frontage, moved forward, by platoons in artillery formation, through the outpost lines held by the 1st Battalion of the 3rd (Rifle) Brigade. The order of battle, from right to left, was 1st, 2nd, 12th, and 13th Companies. The battalion met with no opposition, beyond very light shelling as they crossed the ridge between Englebelmer and Auchonvillers and the ridge to the north of Mesnil, and captured all the brigade objectives from west of Hamel to the south-west of Beaumont-Hamel.

The 2nd Battalion had moved forward in similar formation, rather earlier than the 1st Battalion; and as it approached the western outskirts of Auchonvillers, it came under a certain amount of machine-gun fire and light scattered shelling, which necessitated the platoons deploying into sections. The 2nd Company was kept in its position to the north of the village, to protect the left flank, and the order of battle of the remaining companies (right to left) was 1st, 13th, and 12th. The battalion moved through Auchonvillers at about 3 p.m., and on reaching the eastern outskirts of the village encountered heavy machine-gun fire and considerable shelling. The advance continued, however, and the battalion's objectives were reached and taken by 4.30 p.m.

The battalion was now in the old British trench system to the west of Beaumont-Hamel, and its right was in touch with the 1st Canterbury Battalion, in the same trench system. To the south again, the 1st Battalion was in touch with the 12th Division at Hamel. To the north, however, the situation was not so satis-factory: the 2nd Battalion's left flank was "in the air," and resting on a point due east of the Apple Trees, and the enemy was in possession of One Tree Hill (between Beaumont-Hamel and Colincamps), and was reported to be even in part of Colincamps itself. It was evident that the advance had taken place just in time, for had it been delayed even a few hours, the enemy would have been encountered in force, and would have had to be ejected from trenches lying ready for occupation. The difficulty of capturing these trenches would have been very great, as up till this time the Division had no artillery to support its advance.

During the evening of March 26th the position on the north of the 2nd Brigade was cleared by the advance of the 1st Brigade group, though the left flank of the 2nd Canterbury Battalion was still a considerable distance in front of the 1st Brigade. That Brigade, in its turn, had its left flank "in the air" for some time; but meanwhile other battalions of the Division had arrived, and a 3rd Brigade group, consisting of the 3rd Battalion, 3rd New Zealand (Rifle) Brigade and the 2nd Wellington and the 2nd Otago Battalions, had been formed. This group was sent forward on the left, and closed the gap between the 1st Brigade and the 62nd Division. The New Zealand Division was now holding a line from Hamel to the south of the village of Hébuterne (to which the 62nd Division had retired from Puisieux).

The night of the 26th was a quiet one, and the troops in the line had no interference from the enemy in the work of consoli-dating the position. The trenches found there were in good order, so not much work was required to be done. During the night fighting patrols were pushed out along the whole front and the enemy was found to be in occupation of Beaumont Hamel, and in his front line system of trenches of 1916. Several of these patrols had brushes with the enemy, inflicted casualties on him, and captured machine-guns and prisoners.

About 9 a.m. on March 27th the enemy began to shell the 2nd Brigade's line with field guns and light howitzers. The shelling was light at first, but it gradually increased in intensity, and extended to the battalion in support. By the end of the morning the shelling was heavy, and the enemy had added to its intensity by using light trench mortars and "pine-apple" grenades against the front line trenches. At noon the enemy attacked along the whole brigade front.

The attack was heaviest in the centre, against the 12th and 13th Companies of the 1st Battalion and the 1st and 2nd Comoverland, and others up the communication trenches, but they overland, and others up the communication trenches, but they were beaten off by rifle and machine-gun fire; and although some parties succeeded in getting within bombing range, none reached our trenches, and the surviving attackers retreated to their original position. Several prisoners and three light machine-guns were captured.

During this attack the brigade on the right of the New Zealand Division evacuated Hamel, and fell back till its forward posts were as far back as the 1st Canterbury Battalion's support line. In order to restore the line, the 1st Battalion had to take over another two hundred and fifty yards of trench to its right.

The shelling eased off at 1.30 p.m., and practically ceased at 2 p.m. During the afternoon there was much movement in the enemy back areas: but though a further attack seemed imminent, the remainder of the day passed quietly. The 3rd Brigade of the New Zealand Field Artillery arrived late in the day: and its guns were placed in position that night, and registered at dawn on the 28th. Throughout the day their shooting was excellent, and interfered greatly with the enemy's freedom of movement: and the feeling of confidence, inspired by the knowledge of artillery support, did much to keep up the men's spirits.

There were no further enemy attacks during the rest of the month of March. This was no doubt in part due to the rain, which began to fall on the afternoon of the 28th, and continued over the end of the month. The trenches became in a very bad state, and there was a great risk of trench feet becoming prevalent. The front line troops took advantage of the lull in hostilities to block the saps, up which the enemy had advanced in the previous attacks.

GERMAN OFFENSIVE, 1918

MILES 1 ¾ ½ ¼ 0   1 MILES

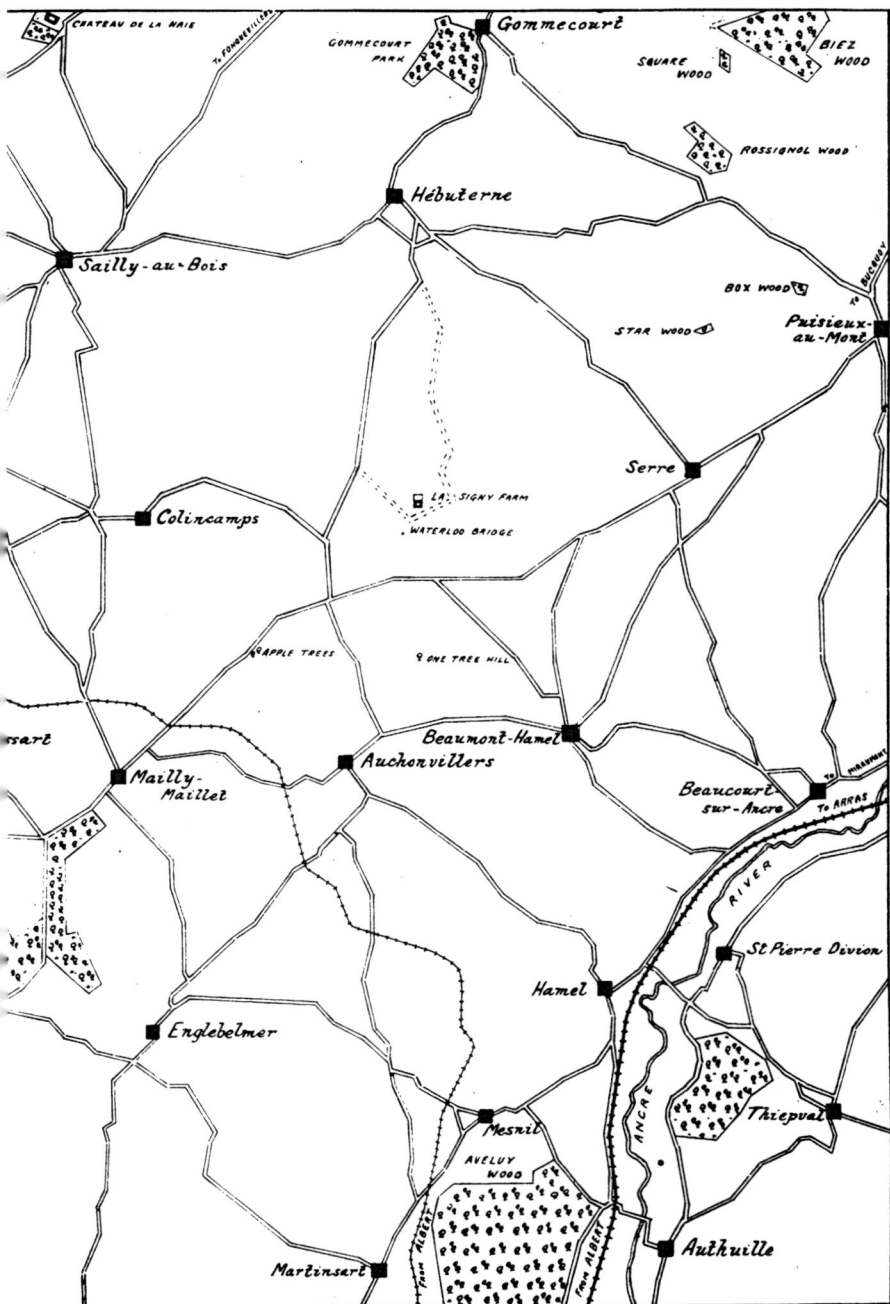

On the night of the 29th/30th the 2nd Canterbury Battalion was relieved by the 1st Otago Battalion, and moved back to the brigade support lines, which extended from the west of Auchonvillers down to Englebelmer. The 1st Battalion remained in the line till the following night, when it was relieved by the 2nd Otago Battalion, and went into bivouacs in Englebelmer, as battalion in reserve of the brigade. The brigade now consisted of its four proper battalions, and the 1st Battalion of the 3rd (Rifle) Brigade had returned to its own brigade.

The casualties in the Regiment in this action had been :—

1st Battalion.		Officers.	Other Ranks.
Killed in Action and Died of Wounds	..	–	15
Wounded	.. ..	3	93
Missing	.. ..	–	1
Total	.. .. ..	3	109

2nd Battalion.		Officers.	Other Ranks.
Killed in Action and Died of Wounds	..	2*	24
Wounded	.. ..	5	53
Missing	.. ..	–	9
Total	.. .. ..	7	86

*2nd Lieutenants J. Sinclair and A. D. Williams (both killed March 27th).

Total casualties for both battalions: 2 officers and 39 other ranks killed, 8 officers and 146 other ranks wounded and 10 other ranks missing.

While the Canterbury Battalions were out of the line, the 1st Brigade advanced its front to level with the left flank of the 2nd Brigade. which consequently was no longer "in the air."

On the night of April 2nd/3rd the 4th Australian Brigade took over five hundred yards of the left flank of the New Zealand Division's frontage, and so reduced the total frontages held by the 1st and 3rd Brigades to the length of the frontage held by the 2nd Brigade. The same night the 2nd Canterbury Battalion relieved the 1st Otago Battalion, in the sector it had previously held. The relief took place in the rain and during the hours of darkness: the order of battle from right to left was 2nd, 13th, and 12th Companies, with the 1st Company in support. The following night the 1st Battalion relieved the 2nd Otago Battalion, under similar conditions, and held the line in the same order of battle as the 2nd Battalion.

Apart from an unsuccessful attempt by the 1st Battalion to establish a post in Hamel, which had been reported as not being occupied by the enemy, but which was found to be held in some force, nothing of importance took place until April 5th. On the night of the 4th/5th the 3rd (Rifle) Brigade had taken over the portion of the Divisional front which was held by the 1st Brigade, and the latter brigade had moved into Divisional reserve. Two of its battalions occupied the "Purple Line," a system of trenches which ran from east of Sailly-au-Bois, and thence south-west, between Courcelles-au-Bois and Colincamps, to the southern end of Beaussart: and the remaining battalions were in bivouacs about a mile behind.

At 5 a.m. on the morning of April 5th the enemy began a heavy bombardment of the Divisional area, as far back as Bus-les-Artois, and launched several attacks on different parts of the front during the day. Only one attack was successful, and in this the enemy overwhelmed the garrison of La Signy Farm, in the 3rd (Rifle) Brigade's sector, and succeeded in holding his gains there.

The 1st Canterbury Battalion was attacked at 9 a.m., the enemy working up the saps leading towards our front line trenches, till the blocks established by us forced him to come into the open. Although our trenches had been badly damaged by the bombardment, and casualties had been rather heavy, the attack was beaten off by fire from rifles, Lewis-guns, and machine-guns, with severe loss to the enemy. The attack was renewed at 2 p.m., but in a half-hearted way: the attackers were again driven off by small-arms fire, and the attack was not pressed.

One party of the enemy succeeded in entering the line, on the front of the brigade on the right flank of the 1st Battalion, where the garrison of a post had withdrawn without giving information of their movement. Corporal White, of the 2nd Company, promptly led a bombing party against this party of the enemy, and drove it out, taking ten prisoners. During the day a Lewis-gun of the 12th Company of this battalion brought down a low-flying enemy aeroplane. which had been obtaining very useful information all the morning, and the pilot and observer were captured. There were no attacks made against the 2nd Battalion during the day.

The attacks of April 5th were the last the Canterbury Regiment was called upon to repel: for though, during the rest of the month (notably on the 13th and 17th), there were several occasions on which the enemy was expected to attack, and all preparations were made to receive him, yet these turned out to be false alarms. On looking back, therefore, the conditions may be said to have returned to those of trench warfare: but of trench warfare where the enemy was in a highly offensive temper. On the night of the 6th/7th the 2nd Canterbury Battalion was relieved by the 1st Otago Battalion, and moved back to its former position in the brigade support lines. Next night the 2nd Otago Battalion relieved the 1st Canterbury Battalion, which went back to its old bivouacs as reserve battalion of the brigade. Typical April weather prevailed, and conditions were little better than in the line, for the enemy artillery was continually searching the back areas for our artillery positions.

To quote Sir Douglas Haig's Despatch of July 20th, 1918:—

"With the failure of his attacks on the 4th and 5th April the enemy's offensive on the Somme battle front ceased for the time being, and conditions rapidly began to approximate to the normal type of trench warfare, broken only by occasional local attacks on either side."

The estimation in which the New Zealand Division and its Commander was held by the French is shown by the following translation of a French Army Order. which was issued shortly after the Armistice of November, 1918. It is quoted here, since it bears particularly on the part which the Division took in holding up the German offensive of 1918.

The translation reads as follows:—

"Minister's Office, Paris, 28th November, 1919. The President of the Council of the Ministry of War mentions in Army Orders the name of the following English Officer: Major General Sir A. H. Russell, New Zealand Division. Has led to countless victories a splendid Division whose exploits had not been equalled, and whose reputation was such that on the arrival of the Division on the Somme Battlefield during the critical days of March, 1918, the departure of the inhabitants was stopped immediately. The Division covered itself with fresh glory during the Battle of the Ancre à la Sambre, at Puisieux-au-Mont, Bapaume, Crèvecour, and Le Quesnoy.—For and by the order of the President of the War Council of the Ministry of War. Boeker, Colonel, Adjutant-General to the Cabinet.''

On April 13th came the turn of the 2nd Brigade to go into Divisional Reserve. Accordingly, at dusk, the 1st Canterbury Battalion moved to the ''Purple Line,'' in front of Bertrancourt and in rear of Courcelles; and the 2nd Battalion went into bivouacs further north, midway between Bus-les-Artois and Sailly-au-Bois. The brigade remained in reserve till the 17th, when it relieved the 1st Brigade in the northern half of the Divisional sector, immediately on the left of the sector which the 2nd Brigade had held when last in the line. The order of battle was now altered, the 1st Canterbury Battalion being in the front line, on the right of the sector, with its left flank at Waterloo Bridge (south of La Signy Farm), with the 1st Otago Battalion on its left, opposite La Signy Farm. The 2nd Canterbury Battalion was in support, in bivouacs to the east of Colincamps, and the 2nd Otago Battalion in reserve.*

Enemy attacks were still expected, and though they did not come, the troops in the line lost no opportunity of undermining the enemy's morale, by active sniping and vigorous offensive patrol work by day as well as by night. The numerous hedges and disused trenches in No-Man's-Land gave good cover for small daylight raids on outlying enemy posts. The fine achievements of Sergeant R. Travis, D.C.M., of the 2nd Otago Battalion, inspired the rest of the Division, and gave the enemy good cause to feel nervous.

On the night of April 22nd/23rd the 1st Canterbury Battalion was relieved by the 2nd Otago Battalion, and moving back to the bivouacs vacated by the latter, became battalion in reserve of the brigade. The same night the 2nd Canterbury Battalion relieved the 1st Otago Battalion in the front line opposite La

---

*The order of battle of the various companies of the two Canterbury Battalions will henceforth be found in Appendix '' C '' till the cessation of trench warfare.

Signy Farm. Two days later the Division "side-slipped" to the north again, the 3rd (Rifle) Brigade being relieved by the 12th Division, on the night of the 23rd/24th, in the southern half of the New Zealand Divisional sector; and the 1st Brigade, on the night of the 24th/25th, taking over from the 4th Australian and 127th Brigades the front line up to and including the village of Hébuterne, with the corresponding support and reserve system.

A relief took place on the night of April 27th/28th, when the 1st Canterbury Battalion relieved the 2nd Otago Battalion in the same sector as before, on the right flank of the Division. The same night the 2nd Canterbury Battalion was relieved by the 1st Otago Battalion, and went back to its former position in support. The 2nd Brigade was relieved by the 3rd (Rifle) Brigade on the night of April 30th/May 1st, and went into Divisional reserve. The 1st Canterbury Battalion was accommo-dated in tarpaulin-covered bivouacs, about a mile to the north-east of Bertrancourt, whilst the 2nd Battalion garrisoned the "Purple Line" forward of Sailly-au-Bois, with battalion head-quarters in the village.

Though, as has been pointed out above, the situation since the 5th of the month had been gradually stabilizing into trench war-fare, the month's casualty lists show the activity of the enemy's artillery and trench mortars. The majority of the casualties tabulated below occurred on days when, from the broad point of view of the General Staff, there was "nothing to report." It is perhaps owing to the undue prominence given by newspapers to the informal truce, on certain portions of the western front, at Christmas, 1915, that there is a wide impression that trench war-fare was governed by a "live and let live" policy. The steady drain of casualties during "quiet" periods show how false is this impression. During April the Canterbury Regiment's losses (apart from casualties incurred by officers and men of the Regi-ment serving with the Entrenching group, no summary of which is available) were as follows:—

	Officers.	Other Ranks.
1st Battalion.		
Killed in Action and Died of Wounds ..	3*	29
Wounded	2	71
Missing	–	1
Total	5	101

*See page 238.

		Officers.	Other Ranks.
2nd Battalion.			
Killed in Action and Died of Wounds	..	2†	18
Wounded	..	5	90
Missing	..	–	8
Total	..	7	116

*Captain R. Harris (Regimental Medical Officer—killed 5th April), Lieutenant W. O. Hastings (killed 5th April), 2nd Lieutenant H. N. Coleman (killed 13th April).

†Lieutenant D. Green (killed 5th April), 2nd Lieutenant M. B. O'Connor (killed 5th April).

Total for both battalions: 5 officers and 47 other ranks killed, 7 officers and 161 other ranks wounded, and 9 other ranks missing.

While the 2nd Brigade was in reserve, much useful work was done on the communication trenches to the front line, and also in improving the reserve line. The 2nd Brigade relieved the 1st Brigade in the left of the Divisional sector, on the night of May 6th/7th, and the 2nd Canterbury Battalion took over from the 2nd Auckland Battalion the right half of the brigade's sector, with its left flank resting on the southern boundary of the village of Hébuterne. The front line trenches were in poor condition, with few duck-walks, and were very wet. But the remainder of the area occupied by the battalion was much better; the country was grassy and not cut up by shell-fire, and movement was possible overland without observation by the enemy. The back part of the battalion's area and its approaches were so free from observation that transport could come up in daylight.

The same night the 1st Canterbury Battalion went into brigade support in Hébuterne village, relieving the 1st Auckland Battalion. The usual relief took place on the night of the 12th/13th, when the 1st Canterbury Battalion relieved the 2nd Otago Battalion on the left flank of the Division, in front of the village; and the 2nd Canterbury Battalion was relieved by the 1st Otago Battalion, and came back into brigade reserve, in and round Sailly-au-Bois. On the 18th/19th the 2nd Brigade came into Divisional reserve again, and the 1st Canterbury Battalion moved back into the "Purple Line," between Hébuterne and

Sailly-au-Bois, with battalion headquarters in the latter. The 2nd Battalion went again to the bivouac area midway between Sailly and Bus.

The brigade held a horse show and military tournament at Vauchelles on May 20th. The 1st Battalion scored more points than any other battalion in the brigade, gaining first places in officers' chargers' jumping (Lieutenant-Colonel Row, on "Britomart"), relay race, hurdle race. travelling kitchens, water carts, pack horses, and mules in G.S. limbers; 2nd places in battalion transport, light draughts in G.S. limbers, officers' chargers ("Britomart"), and non-commissioned officers' riding horses; and 3rd places in officers' chargers (Captain Lascelles' "Esther"), guard mounting, driving competition, pack mules, and maltese carts. The 2nd Battalion was only moderately successful.

On May 24th/25th the 2nd Canterbury Battalion relieved the 2nd Auckland Battalion in the front line, in the sector opposite La Signy Farm, and the 1st Canterbury Battalion became brigade reserve, taking over from the 1st Auckland Battalion in front of Colincamps. A relief on the night of June 1st/2nd sent the 1st Canterbury Battalion into the line to the south of La Signy Farm: the 2nd Battalion coming back into brigade support, to the east of Colincamps, in the same position as it had occupied when acting in the same *rôle* in the previous tour of the brigade in this sector.

The Division was relieved in the line by the 42nd Division on June 7th/8th, and went into Corps reserve. The relief of the 1st Canterbury Battalion by the 1st/5th Battalion East Lancashire Regiment was completed by midnight, and the battalion marched to billets in St. Leger-les-Authie. Earlier in the evening the 2nd Battalion had been relieved by the 1st/8th Battalion Manchester Regiment, and had moved to a camp on the hilltop to the south-west of Authie. Lieutenant-Colonel Stewart resumed command of the 2nd Battalion on the 8th, and on the 21st Lieutenant-Colonel Mead left for England, to take command of the Reserve Battalion, in place of Lieutenant-Colonel Griffiths, who had been appointed to the command of the Base Depôt at Codford.

While the Division was out of the line, four hours in the morning were devoted to training on the usual lines, and there was one hour's recreational training in the afternoon. The rest of the day was free. · A new feature of the training was the practice of tactical schemes, based on the supposition that the enemy had attacked and penetrated our front line. The battalions practised on the actual ground the rôles assigned to them in the defence schemes, in accordance with several imaginary situations. As these movements must have been observed by enemy balloons, no doubt they gave rise to much speculation, and possibly anxiety, behind the enemy's lines.

During this ·period, one brigade of the Division was acting as reserve brigade for the 42nd Division, with two battalions garrisoning the "Purple Line" and the Chateau de la Haie switch line, and the remaining battalions in bivouacs behind those lines. On June 22nd came the 2nd Brigade's turn for this duty: on the afternoon of that day, the 1st Canterbury Battalion moved to the same bivouac area between Sailly-au-Bois and Bus-les-Artois as the 2nd Battalion had occupied in the middle of April. The 2nd Battalion garrisoned the Chateau de la Haie switch, with its right flank in front of the village of Sailly-au-Bois, and battalion headquarters in the village.

The Divisional military tournament and gymkhana was held on June 23rd. The Regiment's representatives were not successful, the only place gained being by the 1st Battalion's team in the relay race, which came third. The Regiment made a much better showing on the 27th, however, when the Divisional band contest and boxing tournaments took place. The band contest was won by the 2nd Battalion's band, which gained 130·5 points (out of a maximum of 150) for its marching, and 110 points (out of the same number) for its music. The heavy-weight championship was won by 10/1199 Private P. L. Caldwell, of the 2nd Battalion, and the light-weight championship by 63755 Private A. Musson, of the 1st Battalion.

At the end of June the New Zealand Division was ordered to relieve the 57th Division and part of the 42nd Division in the line. The sector was practically a new one for the Division, for though the part of the line taken over from the 42nd Division was the northern part of the sector held by the New Zealand Division at the beginning of the month, yet it was only a small portion of the whole of the new sector. In the front line, the

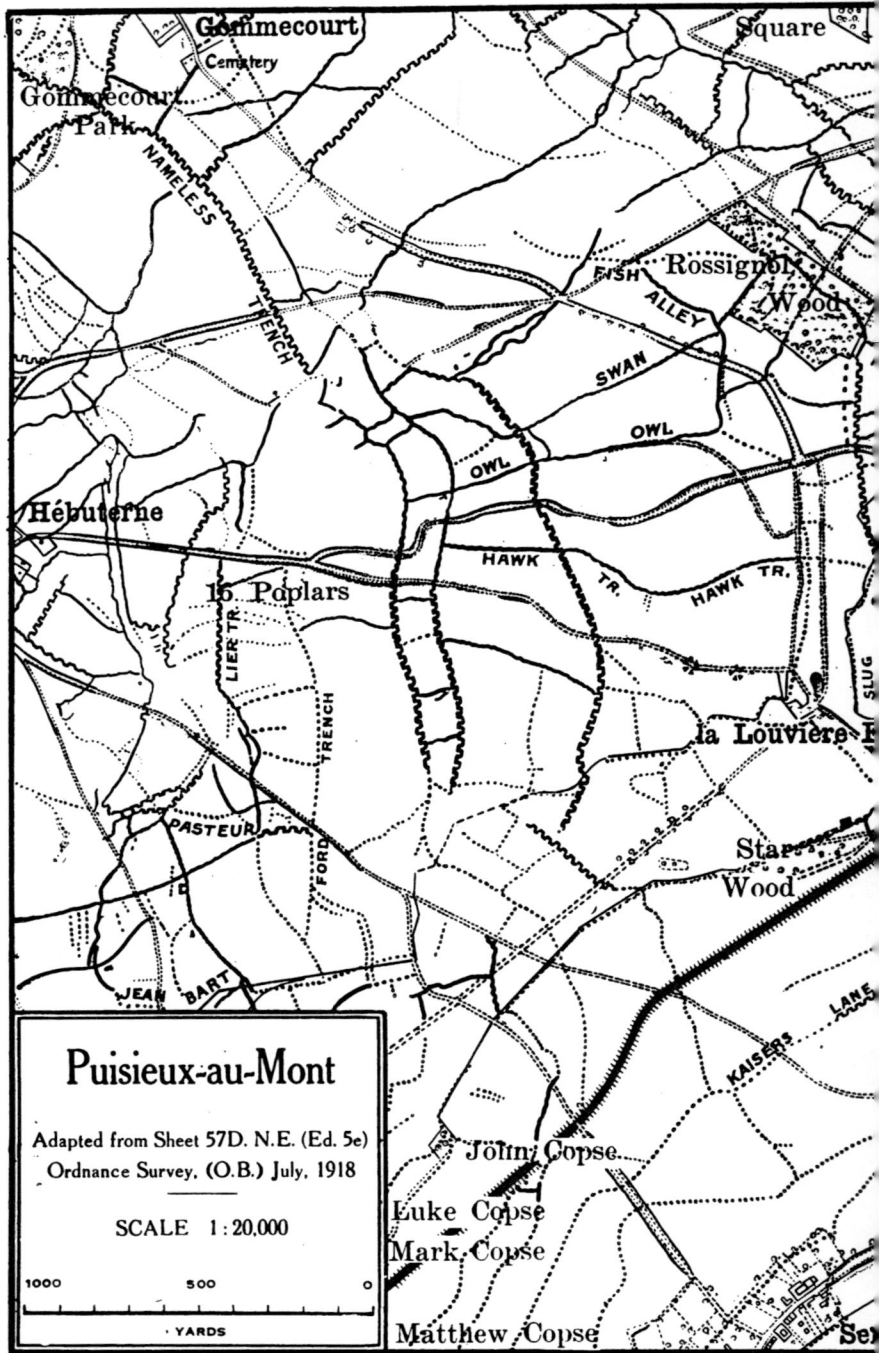

Gommecourt

Cemetery

Gommecourt Park

Square

NAMELESS TRENCH

FISH ALLEY

Rossignol Wood

SWAN

OWL

OWL

Hébuterne

HAWK

15 Poplars

HAWK TR.

LIER TR.

HAWK TR.

SLUG

la Louvière

TRENCH

PASTEUR

FORD

Star Wood

JEAN BART

KAISERS LANE

Puisieux-au-Mont

Adapted from Sheet 57D. N.E. (Ed. 5e)
Ordnance Survey, (O.B.) July, 1918

SCALE 1 : 20,000

1000   500   0

· YARDS ·

John Copse

Luke Copse

Mark Copse

Matthew Copse

Se

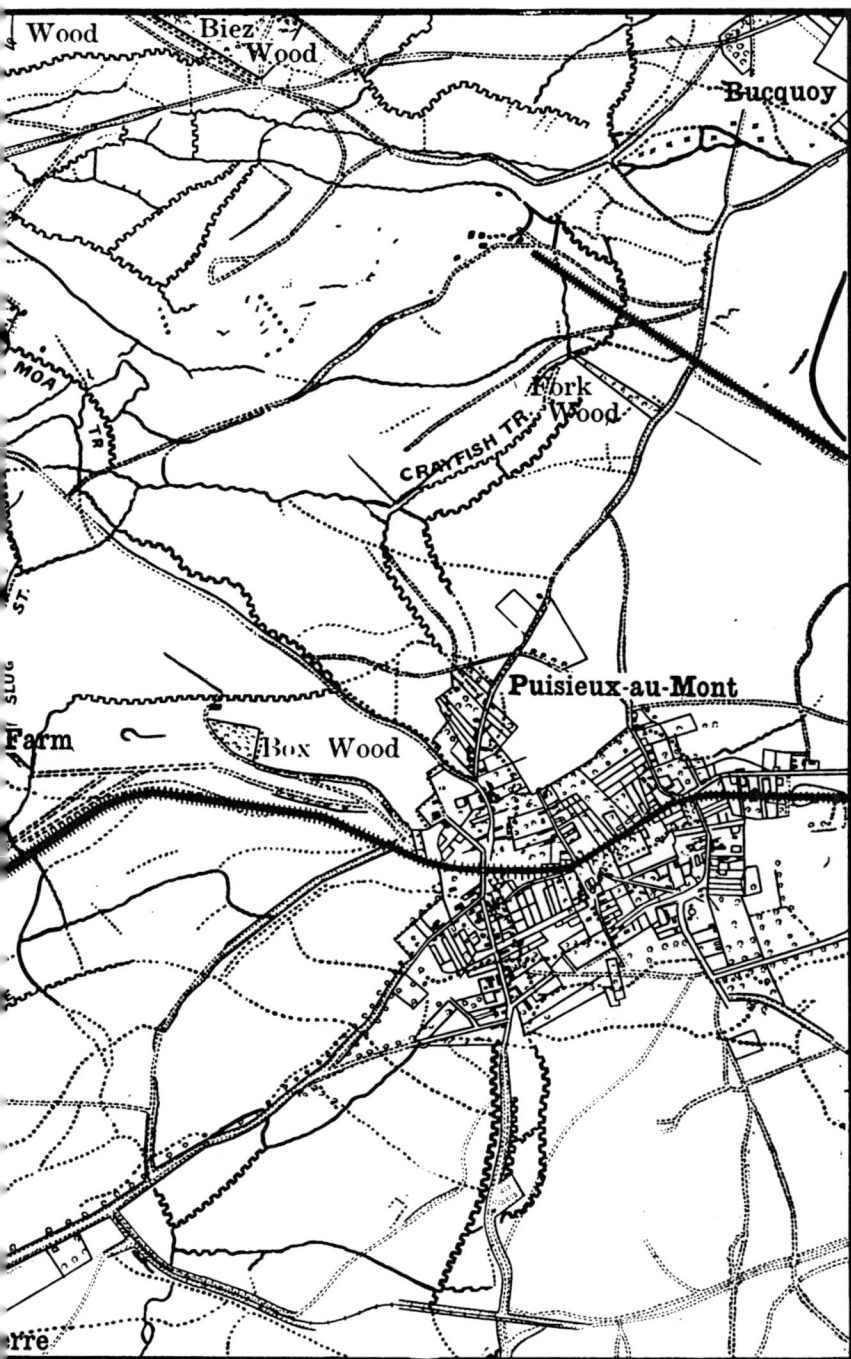

SERGT. C. W. STOBIE, D.C.M.

SERGT. E. E. FAIRHALL, D.C.M.

SERGT. J. P. CUNNEEN, D.C.M.

SERGT. G. HEWITT, D.C.M., M.M

right (or southern) flank of the Division rested on the road which ran from Hébuterne towards La Signy Farm, and its left (or northern) flank rested on the point where the front line was intersected by a prolongation of the south-western boundary of Biez Wood.

In this sector the front line ran for the most part in a north-easterly direction, passing about a quarter of a mile to the south-east of Hébuterne, and rather more than a mile to the south-east of Gommecourt. A mile to the south-east of Gomme-court is Rossignol Wood, about twenty acres in extent. This wood was still held by the enemy, in spite of attempts to drive him out; and though it had been constantly and heavily shelled, there still remained in it many large trees and a good under-growth. Our front line ran parallel to and about two hundred yards distant from the north-western edge of the wood: but, once past the wood, turned at right angles and ran parallel to its north-eastern edge, at about the same distance from it. This turn changed the direction of our line to south-east, and it ran in this direction for over a half mile, before it turned north-east again. As a result, the northern part of the Division's sector was a very nasty salient, against which Rossignol Wood, with its cover for the assembly of attacking troops and its good obser-vation, remained a constant menace.

The relief took place on July 1st, 2nd, and 3rd, the 2nd Bri-gade being in reserve to the Division in its new position. The 1st Canterbury Battalion moved back to Couin Wood, on the night of the 2nd/3rd, and the 2nd Battalion moved to huts on the hill to the south of Coigneux. There the battalions remained engaged in training till the 9th/10th, when the 2nd Brigade re-lieved the 1st Brigade in the northern half of the Divisional sector, with the Puisieux-Gommecourt road as its southern boun-dary. The 1st Canterbury Battalion relieved the 1st Wellington Battalion in the right half of the brigade sector, and the 2nd Battalion relieved the 2nd Auckland Battalion on the left, the point of junction of the two Canterbury Battalions being the angle at Rossignol Wood. An attack by the enemy on a large scale was confidently expected on the morning of the 10th, but did not take place.

The Division now applied itself to the task of gaining possess-ion of Rossignol Wood. On the afternoon and evening of July

15th, the 3rd (Rifle) Brigade, which was in the right half of the Divisional sector, advanced its line by six hundred yards to the east of Hébuterne. On the same evening, the 1st Canterbury Battalion established posts almost on the north-western edge of Rossignol Wood, at its northern corner, and the 2nd Battalion co-operated by establishing posts on the left of the 1st Battalion's new posts, close to the north-eastern edge of the wood. The actual establishment of the posts was done by the 12th Company of each battalion. The casualties in each battalion were light, in spite of fairly heavy machine-gun fire: but the 1st Battalion lost its assistant adjutant (Lieutenant F. Richardson), who was killed while superintending the wiring of the new positions.

The battalions were relieved on the night of July 17th/18th, the 1st Battalion going into brigade reserve, in the old German trenches in and to the west of the village of Gommecourt; and the 2nd Battalion becoming battalion in brigade support, with headquarters in Gommecourt Wood and the companies in the old German trenches between that wood and Pigeon Wood to the north-east. While the battalions were here, the line was pushed still further forward: for on the 20th Rossignol Wood was found to have been evacuated, and was occupied by the 2nd Otago Battalion, which established its front line a quarter of a mile east of the wood. The 1st Brigade, on the right, also moved forward its left flank to conform with the 2nd Brigade, and next day advanced its right flank to a mile beyond Hébuterne.

A further advance by the Otago Battalions, on July 24th, took our front line to the road five hundred yards south-east of Rossignol Wood; and this line was held, in spite of heavy counter-attacks on the 25th. The result of the operations cannot be better summed up than in the words of the congratulatory message received from Sir Julian Byng (commanding the Third Army):—"This operation . . . . has reduced the extent of our front line, and placed the enemy in an extremely difficult position."

It was during this period that United States troops were for the first time attached to the Canterbury Battalions. One or two officers with their "strikers" (batmen), and a few non-commissioned officers were attached to each company; and their keenness and apparent efficiency made a very favourable impression.

The 2nd Brigade came into reserve on the night of July 25th/26th, and the 1st Canterbury Battalion garrisoned the "Purple Line," east of Sailly-au-Bois, the 2nd Battalion returning to its former camp near Coigneux. There they both remained until August 2nd/3rd, when the 2nd Brigade relieved the 1st Brigade in the right half of the Divisional sector. On that night the 1st Canterbury Battalion took over the right of the brigade's sector from the 2nd Auckland Battalion, and the 2nd Canterbury Battalion relieved the 1st Wellington Battalion on the left.

The new sector consisted of derelict enemy trenches, in very bad repair, full of mud, and with very little sleeping accommodation. More United States troops came into the line with the battalions: at first one platoon of Americans was attached to each company, but on the night of August 6th/7th, the 1st Battalion was relieved by the 1st Battalion 317th U.S.A. Regiment (Black Fox). The acting Commanding Officer (Major Stitt), with the assistant adjutant and works officer, four company officers, and a hundred and forty-four other ranks, remained in the line with the Americans; and the rest of the battalion moved back to Sarton, on the Doullens-Albert road, some eleven miles behind the line.

A similar relief of part of the 2nd Battalion (50 men from each company) by the same U.S.A. Regiment was arranged for the same day; but as only half of the American troops arrived the relief was cancelled. On the 6th Lieutenant-Colonel Stewart took over the temporary command of the 2nd Brigade, and Major N. R. Wilson took command of the 2nd Canterbury Battalion.

The 1st Battalion remained at Sarton till August 14th, when it moved to billets in Vauchelles. On the 18th it moved to a canvas camp at Couin; but the following day it was ordered to move again to billets in St. Leger-les-Authie. Lieutenant-Colonel Row returned from Fort Mahon on the 19th, and resumed command of the battalion, which remained at St. Leger till the opening of the final British offensive.

In the meantime, the 2nd Canterbury Battalion had remained in the line till August 10th/11th, and on relief that night by the 1st Otago Battalion had occupied billets in and around Sailly-au-Bois. Working-parties were supplied daily, and while they were out on the morning of the 14th, information came from brigade headquarters that the enemy was withdrawing on the Divisional front, and that the 1st Otago Battalion had moved up to regain touch. At 10 a.m. the Brigadier sent orders that one company of the 2nd Canterbury Battalion was to be sent up, to pass through the outpost line established by the 1st Otago Battalion. As all the men were then still away, it was noon before any company was ready to start. At that hour the 2nd Company, under Major D. A. Dron, left Sailly: it arrived at the outpost line at 3 p.m., and rested there for an hour. Meanwhile, the other companies had been assembled and had left Sailly between 2.30 and 3 p.m.

The outpost line established by the 1st Otago Battalion included the German trench called on our maps "Kaiser's Lane," and ran from there north-east to Box Wood—roughly parallel to, and seven hundred yards north-west of, the Serre-Puisieux road. The enemy's posts were about this road, and on the high ground to the south-east of it.

At 4 p.m. the 2nd Company pushed out fighting patrols from the outpost line, on a frontage of two thousand yards, with the object of capturing an enemy trench running from Serre to Puisieux, and lying to the south-east of the road which connected these villages. The enemy's posts were strongly held, and offered determined resistance, so that by 6 p.m. the 2nd Company had not reached its objectives. The Commanding Officer thereupon decided to put in the 1st Company on the right and the 12th Company on the left; and at 7.50 p.m. these companies left the outpost line, in line of sections in file. A heavy enemy barrage came down between the advancing sections and the Serre-Puisieux road, but it lasted for five minutes only, and caused no casualties.

Meanwhile, the 2nd Company patrols had outflanked the enemy posts, killed or captured the gunners, and were on their objectives. The three companies consolidated on a line from four hundred yards to six hundred yards south-east of the Serre-Puisieux road, and were relieved there, during the night, by the 1st Otago Battalion and the 317th U.S.A. Regiment. Besides pushing the enemy off the high ground, the operation had resulted in the capture of thirty-five prisoners, three machine-guns, and one light minnenwerfer gun, at a cost of five other ranks killed and ten other ranks wounded.

On relief, the 2nd Battalion moved back to trenches a thousand yards east of Hébuterne, till the 18th/19th, when it was relieved by the 3rd Battalion of the 3rd (Rifle) Brigade, and returned to its old huts at Coigneux. The following night, after dark, the battalion moved to tents in the Bois de Warnemont, east of Authie, and remained concealed there the whole of the next day. It was not till then that it became generally known that a great attack had been planned for August 21st.

The total casualties in the Regiment since May 1st had been:

	Officers.	Other Ranks.
1st Battalion.		
Killed in Action and Died of Wounds	2*	28
Wounded	1	51
Total	3	79

	Officers.	Other Ranks.
2nd Battalion.		
Killed in Action and Died of Wounds	3†	32
Wounded	1	67
Total	4	99

	Officers.	Other Ranks.
Canterbury Regiment Details (since the beginning of April—presumably with the Entrenching Group).		
Killed in Action and Died of Wounds	2‡	9
Wounded	–	19
Total	2	28

*2nd Lieutenant R. H. I. Norton (died of wounds 9th May), Lieutenant F. Richardson (killed 15th July).

†2nd Lieutenant D. O'Connor (killed 2nd May), 2nd Lieutenant R. D. Fitch (died of wounds 6th May), 2nd Lieutenant D. C. Griffiths (killed 23rd July).

‡2nd Lieutenant N. R. Harper (died of wounds 15th April), 2nd Lieutenant W. A. Scoullar (killed 6th April).

Total for Regiment: 7 officers and 69 other ranks killed, and 2 officers and 137 other ranks wounded.

CHAPTER XIV

THE BATTLE OF BAPAUME.

The opening of the final Allied offensive had taken place on August 8th, when General Rawlinson's Fourth Army (on a fifteen mile front) and the First French Army (on a five mile front) had attacked east of Amiens. By the 13th that advance had penetrated the enemy lines to a depth of twelve miles, and the attacking troops were temporarily held up by the old Somme defences, on the general line Roye-Chaulnes-Bray. The immediate object of the attack, the freeing of the Paris-Amiens railway from enemy artillery fire, had been attained; and the Commander-in-Chief decided to turn the Somme defences from the north [where the Third (British) Army was already partially across them], rather than make a frontal attack east of Amiens.

The following summary of the strategy of the final British offensive is extracted from Sir Douglas Haig's Despatch of December 21st, 1918:—

"The brilliant success of the Amiens attack was the prelude to a great series of battles, in which, throughout three months of continued fighting, the British Armies advanced without a check from one victory to another. The progress of this mighty conflict divides itself into certain stages, which themselves are grouped into two well-defined phases.

"(a) During the first part of the struggle the enemy sought to defend himself in the deep belt of prepared positions and successive trench systems which extended from the springtide of the German advance, about Albert and Villers-Bretonneux to the Hindenburg Line between St. Quentin and the Scarpe. From these positions, scene of the stubborn battles of the two preceding years, the German Armies were forced back step by step by a succession of methodical attacks which culminated in the breaking through of the Hindenburg Line defences.

"(b) Thereafter, during the second period of the struggle our troops were operating in practically open country against an enemy who endeavoured to stand, on such semi-prepared or natural defensive positions as remained to him, for a period long enough to enable him to organise his retreat and avoid overwhelming disaster. The final stages of our operations, therefore, are concerned with the breaking of the enemy's resistance on these lines.

"Throughout this latter period, the violence of our assaults and the rapidity of our advance towards the enemy's vital centres of communication about Maubeuge threatened to cut the main avenue of escape from the German forces opposite the French and American Armies. The position of the German Armies in Flanders, themselves unable to withstand the attacks of the Allied forces operating under the King of the Belgians, was equally endangered by our progress behind their left flank. To the south and north of the area in which our victorious Armies were driving forward through his weakening defences, the enemy was compelled to execute hasty withdrawals from wide tracts of territory.

"The second phase had already reached its legitimate conclusion when the signing of the Armistice put an end to hostilities. Finally defeated in the great battles of the 1st and 4th November and utterly without reserves, the enemy at that date was falling back without coherent plan in wide-spread disorder and confusion."

Later on in the same despatch, Sir **Douglas Haig** continues:

"In deciding to extend the attack **northwards** to the area between the rivers Somme and Scarpe I was influenced by the following considerations.

"The enemy did not seem prepared to meet an attack in this direction, and, owing to the success of the **Fourth Army,** he occupied a salient the left flank of which was already threatened from the south. A further reason for my decision was that the ground north of the Ancre River was not greatly damaged by shell-fire, and was suitable for the use of tanks. A successful attack between Albert and Arras in a south-easterly direction would turn the line of the Somme south of Peronne, and gave every promise of producing far-reaching results. It would be a step forward towards the strategic objective St. Quentin-Cambrai.

"This attack, moreover, would be rendered easier by the fact that we now held the commanding plateau south of Arras about Bucquoy and Ablainzevelle, which in the days of the old Somme fighting had lain well behind the enemy's lines. In consequence we were here either astride or to the east of the intricate systems of trench lines, which, in 1916, we had no choice but to attack frontally, and enjoyed advantages of observation which at that date had been denied us.

"It was arranged that on the morning of the 21st August a limited attack should be launched north of the Ancre to gain the general line of the Arras-Albert railway, on which it was correctly assumed that the enemy's main line of resistance was sited. The day of the 22nd August would then be used to get troops and guns into position on this front and to bring forward the left of the Fourth Army between the Somme and the Ancre. The principal attack would be delivered on the 23rd August by the Third Army and the Divisions of the Fourth Army north of the Somme, the remainder of the Fourth Army assisting by pushing forward south of the river to cover the flank of the main operation. Thereafter, if success attended our efforts, the whole of both Armies were to press forward with the greatest vigour and exploit to the full any advantage we might have gained."

In the preliminary attacks made on August 21st and 22nd, in order to gain the general line of the Arras-Albert railway, from which the big attack was to be launched, the 3rd New Zealand (Rifle) Brigade, which was in the front line, took part. It also took part in the main attack on the 23rd; but the remainder of the Division did not go into action till the morning of the 24th. In the meantime, the 2nd Brigade, which was in reserve to the Division, had moved forward at daybreak on the 21st and bivouacked in the neighbourhood of Sailly-au-Bois. The 1st Canterbury Battalion's bivouacs were in the Chateau de la Haie Switch, near the Chateau itself, and the 2nd Battalion's in a small valley, on the north-western outskirts of Sailly. Here the brigade remained till the 23rd, when it moved forward, and bivouacked for the night just to the south of the village of Bucquoy. Orders for next day's operations were received by the brigadier at midnight.

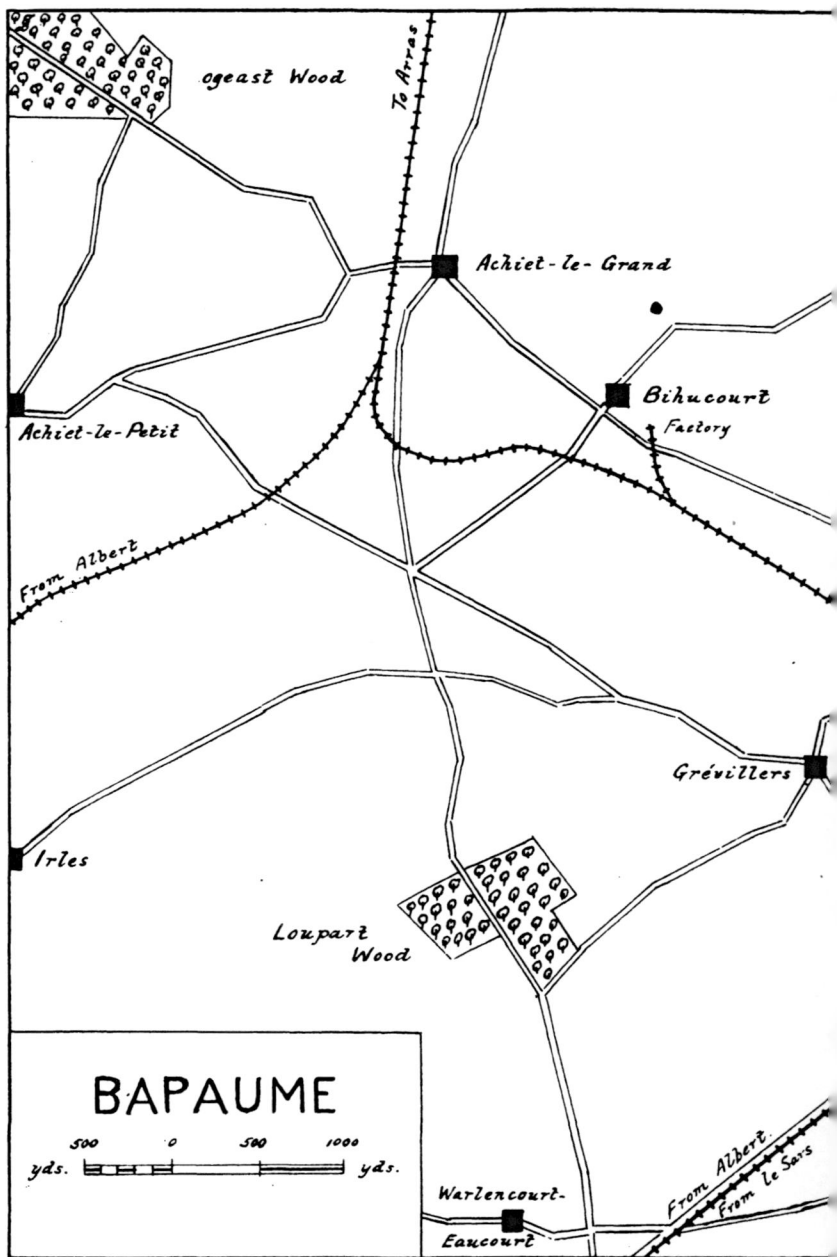

ogeast Wood

To Arras

Achiet-le-Grand

Bihucourt
Factory

Achiet-le-Petit

From Albert

Grévillers

Irles

Loupart
Wood

BAPAUME

500   0   500   1000
yds. ⊨⊞⊞⊞⊟———————⊨ yds.

Warlencourt-
Eaucourt

From Albert
From le Sars

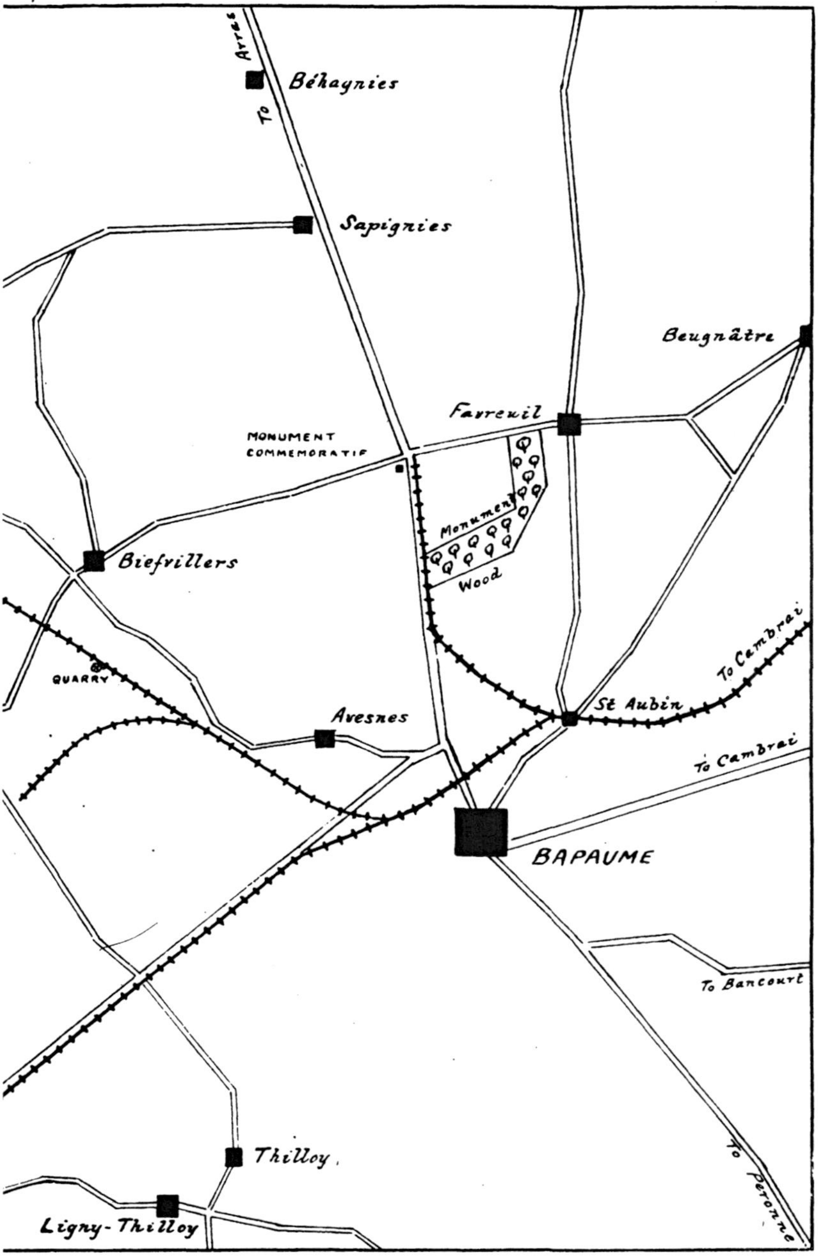

Béhagnies

To Arras

Sapignies

Beugnâtre

Favreuil

MONUMENT
COMMEMORATIF

Biefvillers

Monument
Wood

QUARRY

To Cambrai

St Aubin

Avesnes

To Cambrai

BAPAUME

To Bancourt

Thilloy

To Peronne

Ligny-Thilloy

The 1st and 2nd Brigades were ordered to make the attack on the New Zealand Division's frontage on the 24th. The 1st Brigade's task was to advance as far as a line from the southern corner of Loupart Wood to a quarry on the Bapaume-Achiet le Grand railway between Grévillers and Biefvillers; and included the capture of Loupart Wood and the village of Grévillers. On the left of the 1st Brigade, the 37th Division was to capture Biefvillers. The 2nd Brigade was to pass through the 1st Brigade and the 37th Division, and capture Bapaume and the high ground to the east of that town. Tanks were to take part in the attack; and as, owing to the distance of the advance, no creeping barrage could be provided for the 2nd Brigade, the majority of the tanks were allotted to this brigade.

The 1st Brigade attacked at 4.30 a.m., and by 8 a.m. the 2nd Brigade headquarters received information that Grévillers had been captured. Biefvillers, however, was still in the enemy's hands, and the 2nd Brigade was ordered to capture the village. By 5.30 a.m. the battalions had arrived at their assembly areas, the 1st Canterbury Battalion (on the right) and the 2nd Canter- bury Battalion (on the left) astride the Grévillers-Achiet le Petit road, south-east of the Albert-Arras railway, the 2nd Otago Battalion between the railway and Achiet le Petit, and the 1st Otago Battalion to the north-west of that village. In the 2nd Brigade's attack, the 2nd Otago Battalion replaced the 1st Canterbury Battalion, which remained in its assembly area all day.

The country which now lay in front of the New Zealand Division was part of the area which lay between the British front line of 1916 and the famous Hindenburg Line, to which the Germans had withdrawn in 1917. There had been no heavy fighting on this ground at any time, and consequently it was very little cut up by shell-fire. Before the German offensive of 1918, this part of the country had been used as a British rest and train- ing area: hutted camps abounded, but the villages had been destroyed by the enemy on his retirement in 1917. For many miles in front of the Division the country was open and gently rolling, with small woods here and there.

At 8.30 a.m. the 2nd Otago and 2nd Canterbury Battalions moved forward in lines of sections in file behind a screen of light and heavy tanks. The order of battle of the 2nd Canterbury Battalion, from right to left, was 12th, 13th, and 1st Companies, with the 2nd Company in reserve. The first opposition was en- countered on the high ground between Grévillers and Biefvillers, where the enemy put down a very heavy artillery barrage, and the advancing troops came under heavy machine-gun fire from the Bapaume-Albert road, from Avesnes, and from Biefvillers and the high ground east of that village. The 1st Company was not able to enter Biefvillers, and attempted to work round it from the south, but was held up by machine-gun fire from the trenches east of the village. One platoon, however, succeeded in estab- lishing itself in a trench to the north-east of Biefvillers. The 13th Company had worked further forward almost into Avesnes, while the 12th Company was mixed up with the 2nd Otago Bat- talion, halfway between Avesnes and Grévillers.

The enemy still held Sapignies (to the north) and the high ground between that village and Biefvillers, and were in the sunken road north-east of the latter village. The 2nd Company was therefore ordered to take up a position north-west of the village, to protect the left flank. By noon this company had driven the enemy from the sunken road and a trench to the north-east of it. The German machine-gunners in Biefvillers were now almost cut off, but succeeded in escaping down the trenches to the north-east of the village.

At 2.30 p.m. parties of the enemy were seen assembling in the valley between Biefvillers and the Bapaume-Arras road, but their attempt to work forward was stopped by Lewis-gun and rifle fire, and by the help of the artillery. Further enemy con- centration at Sapignies was reported by aeroplane at 4.30 p.m., but prompt artillery action prevented a counter-attack being delivered from there. During the afternoon the 13th Company was withdrawn from the posts it had established near Avesnes: this step was taken because the posts formed a dangerous salient in our line, and their garrisons were exposed to deadly enfilade rifle and machine-gun fire from close range. The new line ran east of Grévillers and Biefvillers, with the 12th Company south of the Bapaume-Achiet le Grand railway, the 13th Company be- tween the railway and Biefvillers, and the 1st Company east of that village. The 2nd Company remained in its previous position on the left flank.

The advance of the 2nd Brigade was now to be continued by the 1st Canterbury and 1st Otago Battalions. The former left its bivouac area, near the Albert-Arras railway, at 2 a.m. on August 25th, and was assembled in front of Grévillers and Biefvillers by 4.30 a.m. The order of the battle, from right to left, was 1st, 12th, and 13th Companies, with the 2nd Company in reserve. The advance began at 5 a.m., and was helped by sixteen tanks and a creeping barrage. The enemy resisted stubbornly; but a heavy ground mist hid the attackers' movements, and the cover it gave them more than counter-balanced the difficulty it caused them in recognising the lie of the country. The battalion had taken all its objectives by 7 a.m., and had established a line of posts from a point on the Bapaume-Arras road, two hundred yards south of its intersection of the Bapaume-Achiet le Grand railway, to the cemetery on the Bapaume-Arras road.

The 1st Otago Battalion, on the left, had been held up by machine-gun fire after crossing the last-named road, and could not reach its objectives — the south-eastern edge of Monument Wood and the northern edge of the wood lying to the north of Monument Wood. This battalion requested to be allowed to make a further attempt on these objectives and on the enemy trenches south-east of Favreuil. The 2nd Canterbury Battalion was ordered to move up behind the 1st Otago Battalion, and to exploit any success gained by the latter.

The 1st Otago Battalion attacked under a barrage at 6.30 p.m. (August 25th) and gained its objectives. The 1st, 12th, and 13th Companies of the 2nd Canterbury Battalion pushed forward by means of fighting patrols, and gained possession of the high ground to the west of the Bapaume-Beugnâtre road, with some forward posts east of the road. The 2nd Company was employed to protect the right flank of the two attacking battalions, and formed a defensive line facing St. Aubin, and the large dump of timber north of it, both of which were held by the enemy in some force. This company was in touch with the 1st Canterbury Battalion at the cemetery mentioned above.

The 2nd Battalion remained in these positions till the afternoon of the following day. Meanwhile, at dawn on the 26th, the 3rd (Rifle) Brigade had passed through the 2nd Brigade, and had crossed the Bapaume-Beugnâtre road, but had made little progress in front of St. Aubin and beyond Avesnes. That afternoon the 2nd Canterbury Battalion was sent back into bivouacs in and round Biefvillers, where it was engaged on digging trenches for the defence of the village. The 1st Battalion remained in the line till the following night (27th/28th) when it was relieved by the 2nd Wellington Battalion and moved back to trenches south of Bihucourt.

The General Officer commanding the Division had decided to capture Bapaume by enveloping movements from both flanks, but the town was evacuated by the enemy on the night of the 28th/29th. Bancourt, a mile and a half east of Bapaume, fell to the 1st Brigade on the 30th, and on the left of the 1st Brigade the 3rd (Rifle) Brigade was even further to the east. A heavy enemy counter-attack against the whole Divisional front was made at dawn on the following morning; but though it was assisted by tanks it failed at every point, and two tanks were abandoned by the enemy in front of our positions.

In the Despatch already quoted, Sir Douglas Haig states that September 1st marked the close of the second stage of the British offensive, during which the Third and Fourth Armies had driven thirty-five German Divisions from one side of the old Somme battlefield to the other. The disorganisation caused by the British attacks of August 8th and 21st, increasing as the advance was pressed, had resulted in a steady deterioration in the morale of the enemy's troops.

Meanwhile, the battle area had extended further to the north, where the Canadian Corps, the right flank Corps of the First Army, had on August 26th attacked the German positions east of Arras and astride the Scarpe River. Following up the success of this attack, the same Corps, with the XVII Corps (Third Army) co-operating on its right, on September 2nd broke the Drocourt-Queant Line, and captured the Hindenburg Line at the point of junction of those two lines.

Sir Douglas Haig goes on:—

"The result of the Battles of Amiens, Bapaume, and the Scarpe now declared itself.

"During the night of the 2nd/3rd September the enemy fell back rapidly on the whole front of the Third Army and the right of the First Army. By the end of the day he had taken up positions along the general line of the Canal du Nord from Peronne to Ytres, and thence east of Hermies, Inchy-en-Artois, and Ecourt-St. Quentin to the Sensée east of Lécluse. On the following day he commenced to withdraw also from the east bank of the Somme south of Peronne, and by the night of the 8th September was holding the general line Vermand-Epéhy-Havrincourt, and thence along the east bank of the Canal du Nord.

"The withdrawal was continued on the front of the French forces on our right. On the 6th September French troops occupied Ham and Chauny and by the 8th September had reached the line of the Crozat Canal.

"Throughout this hasty retreat our troops followed up the enemy closely. Many of his rear-guards were cut off and taken prisoner; on numerous occasions our forward guns did great execution among his retiring columns, while our airmen took full advantage of the remarkable targets offered them. Great quantities of material and many guns fell into our hands."

Between September 1st and the night of September 2nd/3rd, however, the New Zealand Division did not relax its efforts to drive the enemy from the defensive positions which he had taken up. On September 1st, the 1st and 3rd Brigades continued the advance to east of Bancourt and of Fremicourt. The 2nd Brigade took over the whole Divisional front the same night, with the 2nd Otago Battalion on the right, and the 1st Canterbury Battalion on the left in and in front of Fremicourt. The 2nd Battalion bivouacked west of the same village, on each side of the Bapaume-Cambrai road. On the left, an attack was made at 5.15 a.m. on September 2nd by the 12th Company of the 1st Canterbury Battalion, and after hard fighting all day its left platoons reached almost to the junction of the Fremicourt-Lebucquière and Beugny-Haplincourt roads.

Further south it made little progress, owing to the sunken roads running from Fremicourt to Haplincourt being strongly held by enemy machine-gunners. At 6 p.m., however, a fresh barrage was put down, and with the assistance of a platoon of the 13th Company the enemy positions were taken, with one hundred and fifty prisoners, twenty machine-guns, and a derelict tank.

On the right, the 2nd Otago Battalion had been held up, chiefly owing to the 42nd Division being held up further to the right. By the evening this battalion had reached the Villers au Flos-Haplincourt road, and further north was near the eastern outskirts of Haplincourt; and the 1st Canterbury Battalion was an average distance of three hundred yards west of the Beugny-Haplincourt road.

Early next morning (September 3rd) it became evident from the smoke arising from the villages in the enemy's territory that he was making a further withdrawal. The battalions in the line pushed forward, the 1st and 13th Companies leading the advance of the 1st Canterbury Battalion. By 9.30 a.m. patrols had passed through Vélu Wood, and had reached Bertincourt, after encountering very slight opposition. The battalion, under orders from brigade, halted at and garrisoned an existing line of partially dug trenches, just to the east of the Bapaume-Peronne railway; and the 2nd Company was sent through to establish posts between the railway and the Canal du Nord, which here ran through a tunnel under Ruyaulcourt. The latter village was found to be held by the enemy, but he was apparently not in great strength there.

At nightfall the 1st Battalion was holding the general line of the railway, and was in touch with the 2nd Otago Battalion on the right and the 5th Division on the left; and the 1st Otago and 2nd Canterbury Battalions were ordered to advance through their sister battalions at 7 a.m. on the 4th, with final objectives on the eastern edge of Havrincourt Wood.

To the east of the wood there was a maze of trenches, consisting not only of the famous Hindenburg Line, but also of the British trenches opposite that line before the Battle of Cambrai of 1917. During that battle the British forces had entered the Hindenburg system, and had retained part of it, east of Havrincourt Wood, right up to the retreat of March, 1918. The British defences established after the Battle of Cambrai had again added to the complexity of the system of trenches in this locality. It was therefore certain that the enemy would make a stand on the high ground east of the wood, which might be termed the outpost position of the Hindenburg Line.

The 2nd Canterbury Battalion had remained in its bivouacs near Fremicourt during September 2nd, and on the 3rd had moved up to a system of trenches running north from the Haplincourt-Bertincourt road, midway between those villages. By

7 a.m. on the 4th the battalion had assembled on the railway east of Bertincourt, and the advance was then continued by the 1st Company on the right and the 2nd Company on the left, with the 13th Company in support and the 12th Company in reserve. As the first sections left the railway line they came under artillery fire from field guns, and shortly afterwards came under machine-gun fire from Ruyaulcourt and the high ground to the north and east of the village. The garrisons of some of the enemy posts were captured, but the majority did not wait for our troops.

The advance was continued down into the valley between the village and Havrincourt Wood, and several parties of the enemy were seen coming from the direction of the wood, with the apparent intention of surrendering. Unfortunately our barrage, which had been arranged to deal with the garrisons of the trenches east of Ruyaulcourt, but which had not come down at the proper time, now came down; and our troops were forced to take shelter in the trenches. The enemy took advantage of this respite to garrison the trenches on his side of the valley, a thousand yards west of the wood.

The battalion was held up on the western side of the valley, but late in the afternoon a flanking party of the 2nd Company worked round from the left, and the trenches were rushed. The enemy still held the edge of the wood, and had posts on the right of the 2nd Company; but on the left this company was in touch with the 37th Division. Early in the day battalion headquarters was established at the rear of Ruyaulcourt, and had to move several times, owing to heavy shelling.

Meanwhile, the 1st Otago Battalion had not been able to get forward further than north of Neuville-Bourjonval, owing to heavy machine-gun fire; and the 1st Company of the 2nd Canterbury Battalion was similarly prevented from getting forward further than the trenches east of Ruyaulcourt. The latter battalion dug in for the night, and a hot meal was brought up from the cookers, which were in the neighbourhood of Bertincourt.*

---

*There is no doubt that, during the whole of the existence of the New Zealand Division, its high state of efficiency owed much to the skill and courage of its cooks. Contrary to the practice in the majority of other Divisions, the New Zealand cooks were always with their companies in the line, and shared their hardships and dangers. Napoleon's famous maxim, "An army marches on its stomach," still holds good; and the good effect of hot food on the morale and powers of endurance of troops cannot be easily over-estimated. In particular, the work of the cooks during the open warfare at the end of 1918 calls for special mention. Frequently the travelling cookers were nearer to the enemy than the forward guns of the field artillery; and it was no rare experience for the cooks to prepare meals under shell-fire. Yet never did they fail their comrades in the line.

At 5.30 p.m. on the 5th, with the help of a barrage, the 1st Company advanced to the Hermies-Neuville Bourjonval road, on which the 2nd Company was already established. The advance was made in co-operation with the 1st Otago Battalion on the right. During the night the 2nd Canterbury Battalion "side-slipped" to the right, taking over the line as far as a point due west of the southern edge of Havrincourt Wood, and handing over to the 8th Battalion of the Somerset Regiment the left portion of its line, as far south as a point due east of the northern end of Ruyaulcourt. At the same time an inter-company relief took place, the 12th Company on the right and the 13th Company on the left taking over the front line, with the 2nd Company in support to the east of Ruyaulcourt, and the 1st Company in reserve south of that village.

Heavy shelling during the night of September 5th/6th, followed by a very quiet morning, indicated that the enemy was making a further withdrawal. At mid-day, patrols from the leading companies of the 2nd Canterbury Battalion were pushed forward to Havrincourt Wood, and reported the enemy was still in the western edge, but that parties were moving back, wearing full packs. By 5 p.m. the western edge of the wood had been made good, and patrols were well in advance. The wood here consisted of very large trees, with thick undergrowth, and great caution had to be exercised by the patrols for fear of ambushes. By 7 p.m., however, the battalion was well into the wood and, in close liaison with the units on its flanks, was working forward. At 10 p.m. the leading companies were in touch with the enemy, whose machine-gunners held a line of trenches inside the eastern edge of the wood and west of the Trescault-Metz road.

Owing to company headquarters and two platoons of the 13th Company having lost touch with the remainder of the two leading companies, and touch also having been lost with the unit on the left, the officers in command of the 12th Company and of the remaining two platoons of the 13th Company did not think it advisable to attack in the darkness, and so dug in fifty yards from the enemy and waited for daylight. Battalion headquarters and the 2nd Company had meanwhile moved along the southern edge of the wood, to a point north of Metz, where the 2nd Company covered the edge of the wood, to guard against counter-

SERGT. R. H. HALLIGAN, D.C.M.

SERGT. A. E. DE BOO, D.C.M.

SERGT. B. R. TURNER, D.C.M.

SERGT. N. B. THOMPSON, D.C.M.

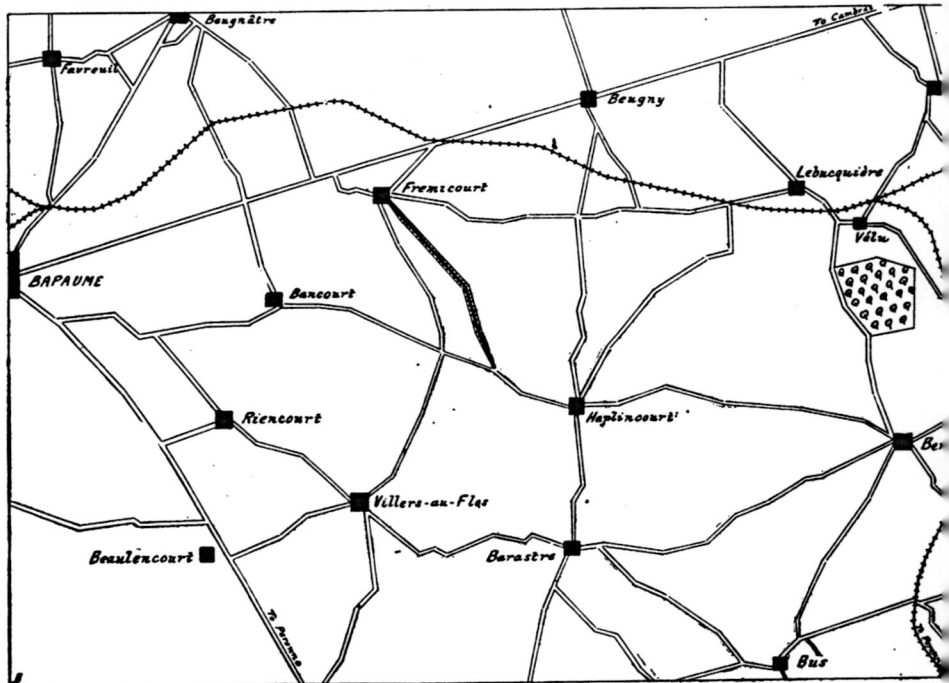

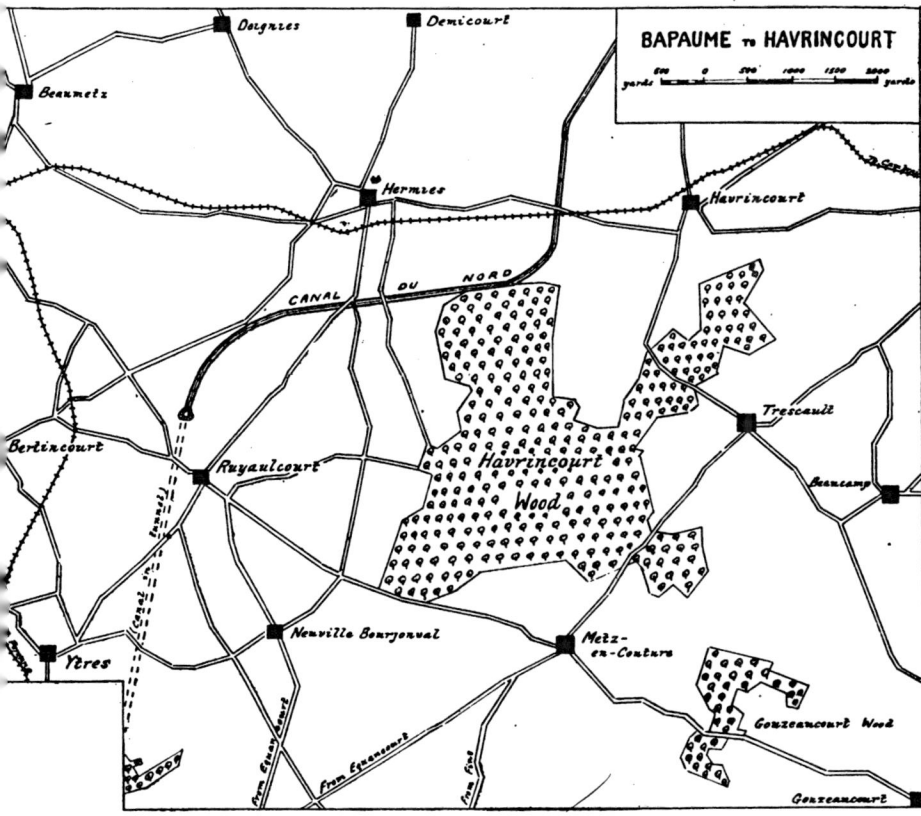

BAPAUME to HAVRINCOURT

yards 500 0 500 1000 1500 2000 yards

Doignies
Demicourt
Beaumetz
Hermies
Havrincourt
CANAL DU NORD
Bertincourt
Ruyaulcourt
Havrincourt Wood
Trescault
Beaucamp
Yeres
Neuville Bourjonval
Metz-en-Couture
Gouzeaucourt Wood
from Equancourt
from Fins
Gouzeaucourt

attacks from the left flank. The 1st Company remained in trenches to the west of the wood.

At daylight on September 7th the 12th Company and the accompanying two platoons of the 13th Company occupied the trenches on the eastern edge of the wood, from which the enemy had withdrawn just before dawn. Shortly afterwards the missing portion of the 13th Company reported to battalion headquarters, but as the troops were very tired no further advance was attempted till noon.

Battalion headquarters was established in a dug-out in the wood. The majority of the dug-outs were mined, and "booby-traps" were everywhere; but no casualties were suffered by reason of any of these devices.

Fighting patrols were pushed forward at noon by the 12th and 13th Companies, and the portion of the wood west of the Trescault-Metz road was secured. During the day the eastern edge of the wood was heavily shelled by big guns, and casualties were numerous. The battalion was relieved by the 4th Battalion of the 3rd (Rifle) Brigade that night, the relief being complete by 12.30 a.m. on the 8th. The battalion moved back to bivouacs, a few hundred yards from its bivouacs of the night of the 3rd/4th, between Haplincourt and Bertincourt. There was little accommodation, and most of the men slept in the open.

To return to the 1st Canterbury Battalion: this unit had remained in its position in front of Bertincourt during the whole of September 4th and the morning of the 5th. The Corps Commander had now been ordered to re-distribute his Divisions, so as to enable them in turn to rest and prepare for the hard work that was anticipated east of Havrincourt Wood; and accordingly the 42nd Division was withdrawn from the front line. The bulk of that Division's frontage was to be taken over by the 1st Canterbury Battalion, and during the afternoon of the 5th the company commanders reconnoitred the new sector. The actual positions could not be inspected, as they were to be captured by the 7th Battalion of the Lancashire Fusiliers at 5.30 p.m. that day.

The relief was commenced at dusk and completed by 3.30 a.m.: the positions taken over were east of Ytres and south-west of Neuville-Bourjonval, and had a frontage of a thousand yards.

The front line was held by the 1st Company on the right and the 2nd Company on the left, with the 13th Company in support and the 12th Company in reserve, and battalion headquarters in Ytres.

At 9 a.m. on September 6th the front line companies, finding no enemy in front of them, moved forward with little opposition. and by nightfall were established in existing trenches on the spur south-east of Metz. The support company (the 13th) was on the Metz-Fins road and in trenches east of that road. and the reserve company (the 12th) was in trenches fifteen hundred yards further to the west. The advance had been rapid, and the 17th Division, on the right, had not kept up with the battalion; the support and reserve companies had therefore to take up positions to defend the flank of the brigade. Battalion headquarters was established in a brick-yard, five hundred yards east of Ytres.

Patrols sent out during the night failed to get touch with the enemy, but on the morning of the 7th they reached Gouzeaucourt Wood, and reported that the southern part of the wood was strongly held. Battalion headquarters was now advanced to the Metz-Equancourt road. In the afternoon the wood was shelled by our artillery, and towards evening the posts of the right company had been moved up to the high ground, close to the western edge of the wood. and patrols had gone through the wood. At 7 p.m. the 2nd Battalion of the 3rd (Rifle) Brigade arrived to take over the line, and the relief was complete by 10.20 p.m. On relief, the battalion bivouacked in and around the village of Ytres.

The regiment's casualties since the opening of the attack had been as follows:—

1st Battalion.	Officers.	Other Ranks.
Killed in Action and Died of Wounds ..	4*	73
Wounded	6	150
Total	10	223

*Captain F. N. Johns, M.C. (Medical officer: killed 25th August), 2nd Lieutenant J. J. L. Pearce (died of wounds 25th August), 2nd Lieutenant A. J. Arnold (died of wounds 27th August), Lieutenant A. T. E. Burnard (killed 2nd September).

2nd Battalion.	Officers.	Other Ranks.
Killed in Action and Died of Wounds ..	4*	78
Wounded	11	279
Total	15	357

*Lieutenant D. L. Kesteven (died of wounds 24th August), 2nd Lieutenant A. Farquhar. M.C. (killed 24th August), Lieutenant J. H. Thomas (killed 4th September), 2nd Lieutenant G. P. Beadel (killed 4th September).

Total for both battalions: 8 officers and 151 other ranks killed, and 17 officers and 429 other ranks wounded.

CHAPTER XV

THE BATTLE OF CAMBRAI AND THE HINDENBURG LINE.

The 2nd Brigade was now brigade in support of the Division, and the Canterbury Battalions remained in their bivouac areas, providing a few parties for burying enemy dead and horses, but for the most part resting. On the 11th the brigade was relieved by the 1st Brigade, and became brigade in reserve. The 1st Canterbury Battalion moved to Haplincourt Wood, and the 2nd Battalion to the north of Villers-au-Flos. There they remained till the 14th, when the New Zealand Division went into Corps reserve.

The 1st Canterbury Battalion was then accommodated in huts to the west of Biefvillers, between the Bihucourt road and the railway, and the 2nd Battalion bivouacked in a trench system a quarter of a mile away, on the southern side of the railway. This area was a peaceful one, out of range of the naval guns which had disturbed everyone's rest at Haplincourt and Villers-au-Flos, and was even left unmolested by the enemy's bombing 'planes. Here the "B" teams rejoined the battalions, reinforcements arrived, and reorganization and training were actively carried out. Lieutenant-Colonel Stewart now resumed command of the 2nd Battalion.

During the period of rest the usual attention was given to games, particularly football. On the 22nd the 1st Battalion defeated the 2nd in an officers' match, by three to nil; and the same day the 1st Battalion's team defeated the 2nd Battalion's in an association game by three goals to two. The following day the 1st Battalion other ranks' team beat the 2nd Battalion's by eight to three.

The brigade was inspected by the General Officer Commanding the Division, the 1st Otago and 1st Canterbury Battalions on the 24th, and the 2nd Otago and 2nd Canterbury on the 25th.

The diarist of the latter battalion expresses the opinion that this was the best inspection parade that the battalion had ever had.

Since the 2nd Brigade had come out of the line on September 8th, the 3rd (Rifle) Brigade had, on the 12th, captured the spur running north-west from the east of Gouzeaucourt Wood to east of Trescault. The northern part of this spur was held by the 3rd Brigade, and later by the 1st Brigade, in spite of many determined counter-attacks; but the former brigade had been unable to hold the southern part of the line established by it on the 12th, and had been pushed down the western slope again. Here the crest of the spur remained No-Man's-Land. On the night of September 14th/15th, the 1st Brigade was relieved by the 13th Brigade (5th Division), and the New Zealand Division came out into Corps reserve as mentioned above. There was no further advance by the IV Corps till the 27th of the month.

On referring again to Sir Douglas Haig's Despatch of December 21st, 1918, we find the following account of the general situation on September 26th :—

"The Battle of Cambrai, which on the 5th October culminated in the capture of the last remaining sectors of the Hindenburg Line, was commenced by the First and Third Armies between the neighbourhood of St. Quentin and the Scheldt. The Fourth, Third and First Armies, in the order named, occupied on the evening of the 26th September a line running from the village of Selency (west of St. Quentin) to Gricourt and Pontruet and thence east of Villeret and Lempire to Villers-Guislain and Gouzeaucourt, both exclusive. Thereafter the line continued northwards to Havrincourt and Moeuvres and thence along the west side of the Canal du Nord to the floods of the Sensee at Ecourt-St. Quentin.

"On the First and Third Army fronts strong positions covering the approaches to Cambrai between the Nord and the Scheldt canals, including the section of the Hindenburg Line itself north of Gouzeaucourt, were still in the enemy's possession. His trenches in this sector faced south-west, and it was desirable that they should be taken in the early stages of the operation, so as to render it easier for the artillery of the Fourth Army to get into position. On the Fourth Army front, where the heaviest blow was to fall, the exceptional strength of the enemy's position made a prolonged bombardment necessary. I therefore decided that a very heavy bombardment, opened during the night of the 26th/27th September along the whole front of all three armies, should be followed on the morning of the 27th September by an attack delivered only by the First and Third Armies. In this way the enemy might be deceived as to the main point of attack, the First and Third Armies would be enabled to get nearer to their final objective, and the task of the Fourth Army artillery would be simplified.''

On September 26th the 2nd Brigade came into immediate Corps reserve, being liable to move at short notice to support the 5th and 42nd Divisions, which were then holding the line. Accordingly the brigade moved to the Bertincourt area. The 1st Canterbury Battalion was billeted at Bus, and the 2nd Battalion at Haplincourt. There they remained all the next day, while the 5th and 42nd Divisions made an attack on the Hindenburg Line, including very strong enemy positions on Welsh Ridge, east of the Cambrai-Peronne railway. It was reported on the afternoon of the 28th that the 42nd Division had taken Welsh Ridge, and was moving east to attack Bonavis Ridge; but this information was subsequently found to be incorrect.

The New Zealand Division was ordered to relieve the 42nd Division, and to continue the advance on September 29th. The object of this attack was to secure the bridge-heads across the Escaut* Canal, between Vaucelles and Crèvecoeur, both inclusive; and to establish posts on the high ground east of the canal. The 5th Division, on the right of the New Zealand Division, was to participate in the attack, which was to be carried out on the New Zealand Division's frontage by the 2nd Brigade on the right and the 1st Brigade on the left. In the 2nd Brigade, the front line battalions, right to left, were the 1st Canterbury and 2nd Otago Battalions, with the 1st Otago and 2nd Canterbury Battalions in support.

The brigade moved from the Bertincourt area on the morning of September 28th to a rendezvous west of Havrincourt Wood, where it remained till dusk. The move forward from the rendezvous was slow and difficult, owing to the amount of traffic on the

---

* The French form of the Flemish word "Scheldt." This Canal is also sometime called " Canal de St. Quentin."

roads; and the assembly positions were not reached till early on the morning of the 29th. The 1st Canterbury Battalion took over the front line at Surrey road, a quarter of a mile east of the Cambrai-Peronne railway, with its right flank a thousand yards north-east of Villers-Plouich. On its left was the 2nd Otago Battalion, and in support to the latter was the 2nd Canterbury Battalion, west of the Villers Plouich-Ribecourt road and north-east of Beaucamp.

The attack was launched at 3.30 a.m., under a creeping bar-rage, and the 1st Canterbury Battalion's objective on Welsh Ridge (the sunken road to the north and south of La Vacquerie) was taken with little difficulty by the 12th Company on the right and the 13th Company on the left. Enemy posts in and round La Vacquerie were still holding out, and caused considerable trouble before they were rushed and captured. The 2nd and 1st Companies were now due to go through, to capture the second objective, to the south-east of La Vacquerie and beyond the Gouzeaucourt-Cambrai road. But as the only troops of these companies to reach the first objective were two platoons of the 1st Company, the 12th Company, after waiting half an hour for the 2nd Company, pushed on, and made good the ridge to the south-east of La Vacquerie but north of the road. The 5th Division had not come up on the right, and the 12th Company's flank was "in the air."

The missing company and a half had lost direction, mainly owing to the darkness, and had swung round to the right. The two 1st Company platoons went astray very badly, and crossed to the right flank of the 2nd Company. Having completely lost touch with the rest of the battalion, they found themselves at daylight in a trench in the neighbourhood of the Gouzeaucourt-Cambrai road, between Gonnelieu and La Vacquerie.

One officer having been badly wounded, the other officer took command of both platoons; and as he knew the attack would be continued during the day, he decided to hold on where he was. His command was then practically surrounded, and was unable to leave its trench on account of heavy machine-gun fire. Between 10 a.m. and 11 a.m. the enemy rushed the trench; and the garrison, the strength of which was reduced to one officer and thirty other ranks unwounded, was captured. The wounded were left by the enemy, and were picked up when the advance was continued.

Meanwhile the 2nd Company, with troops of the Durham Light Infantry, had met strong resistance in the trenches south of La Vacquerie and on the right of the 12th Company, and had taken many prisoners. This company eventually reached the Gouzeaucourt-Cambrai road; but coming under heavy machine-gun fire from both flanks, and the left rear, it was compelled to withdraw again, till it had gained touch on the right with a battalion of the Gloucester Regiment. Later on, it had to withdraw further, to trenches south of La Vacquerie.

When darkness fell, it became possible to advance again, and the remnants of the 1st Company occupied the trenches east of La Vacquerie. The 13th Company, passing through the advanced posts of the battalion, met with fierce opposition, but by dawn had reached the Gouzeaucourt-Cambrai road; while on its right the 12th Company refused the right flank, north-west of the road as far as a point to the south of La Vacquerie. The 5th Division was still behind; but came up under cover of a barrage at 4 a.m. on the 30th, the 1st Canterbury Battalion pausing till then.

Under cover of this barrage the 12th Company pushed out patrols, which met with no opposition on the left, but drove off some enemy parties on the right. These retired towards the south, and the battalion advanced to the banks of the canal without further interference from the enemy's infantry. At 8 a.m. the battalion had reached the approaches to the canal, in the neighbourhood of the Sugar Factory north of Bantouzelle. Enemy transport was seen moving back through the eastern portion of the village, and his infantry was retiring over the slopes east of the canal. Nothing, however, could be seen of the 5th Division; but to the north the 2nd Otago Battalion was also on the line of the canal.

It should be explained that the canal (which is here about thirty yards wide and quite deep) does not follow the exact course of the River Escaut: while the two in many places coincide, yet more commonly the canal runs alongside the river, at a distance varying from fifty yards to a quarter of a mile. Such was the case on the 1st Canterbury Battalion's front, where the river runs about two hundred yards east of the canal.

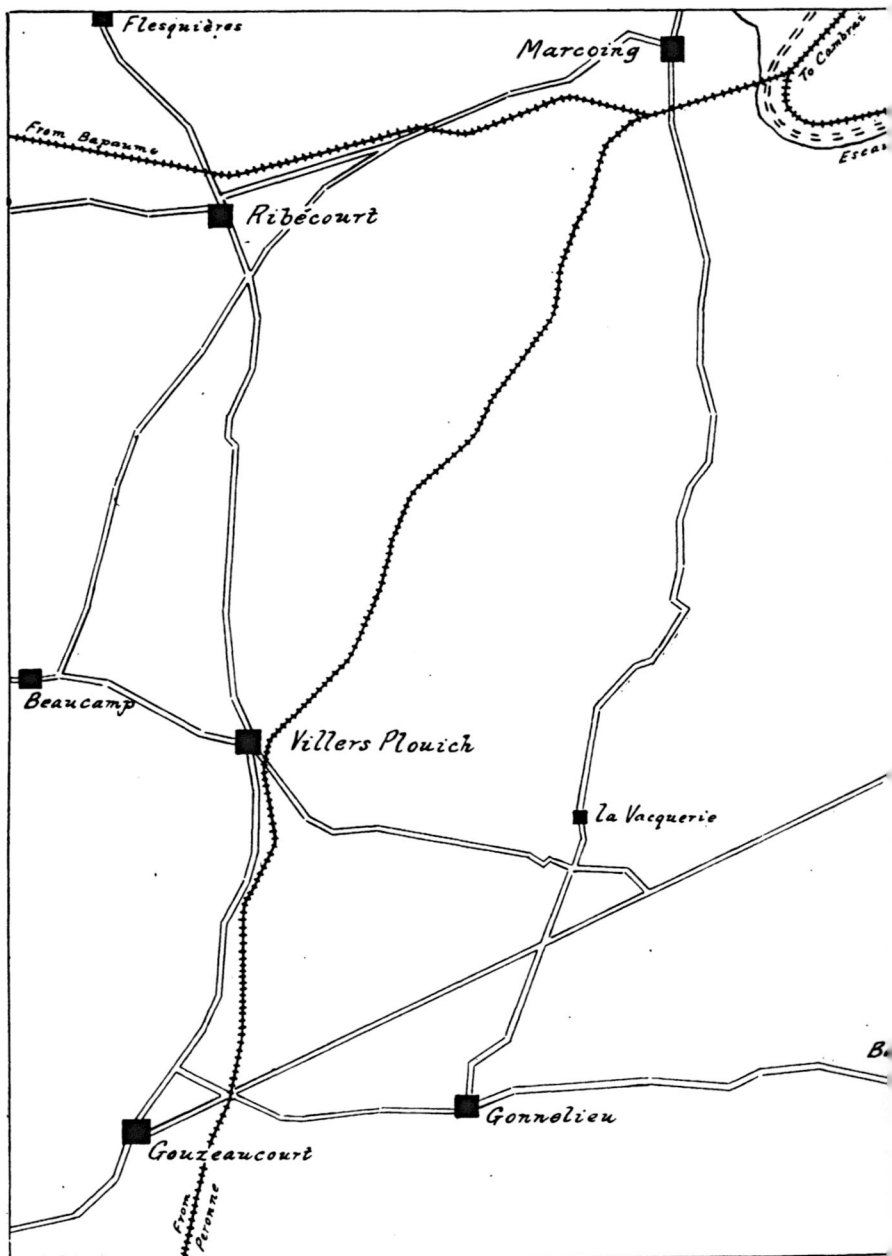

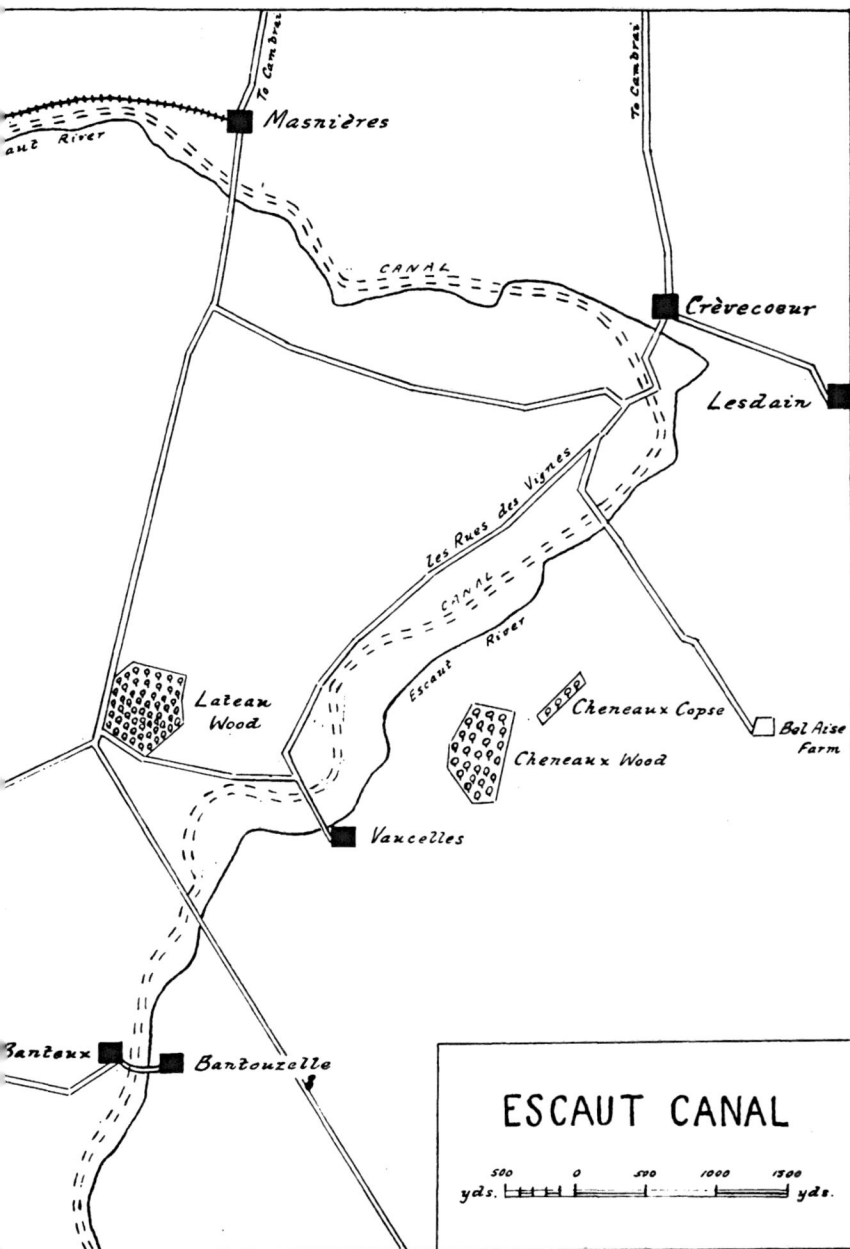

To Cambrai

aut River

Masnières

CANAL

To Cambrai

Crèvecœur

Lesdain

Les Rues des Vignes

CANAL

Escaut River

Lateau Wood

Cheneaux Copse

Cheneaux Wood

Bel Aise Farm

Vaucelles

Banteux

Bantouzelle

ESCAUT CANAL

500   0   500   1000   1500
yds. ⊢⊢⊢⊢⊢ ⊢ — · — ⊢ yds.

On reaching the canal our patrols found the Sugar Factory bridge had been partially destroyed, but that infantry could cross it in single file. Two platoons of the 12th Company crossed the canal and the river, and took up a position two hundred yards to the east of the latter. But at 10.15 a.m., as there was still no sign of the 5th Division on the right flank, and the enemy had begun to dribble back towards the canal and into Bantouzelle, these platoons were withdrawn to west of the canal. An outpost line was established along the west bank, and a defensive flank was formed facing south. This position was eventually consolidated, and was held till the battalion was relieved on the night of October 1st/2nd by the 10th Battalion Royal Fusiliers.

The 2nd Canterbury Battalion had remained in its assembly area till 10.30 p.m. on September 29th when, in accordance with brigade orders, the 13th Company moved up to the La Vacquerie-Masnières road (north of the 1st Battalion) and became attached to the 2nd Otago Battalion, as a counter-attack company. The leading companies of the latter battalion had then reached a point in the Hindenburg Support Line, west of the Gouzeaucourt-Masnières road, two hundred yards to the north-west of Bonavis, and on the western edge of Lateau Wood. Early on the morning of the 30th, the same battalion reached the canal, but finding the bridge at Vaucelles had been destroyed was unable to cross.

The 2nd Canterbury Battalion had been ordered to pass through the 2nd Otago Battalion, in the event of the latter securing bridge-heads over the canal; and early on the morning of the 30th the 1st Company moved foward to trenches of the Hindenburg Support Line, on the south-eastern edge of Lateau Wood, with instructions to seize the high ground a mile to the east of Vaucelles, if the canal could be crossed. The 2nd and 12th Companies moved forward to the east of the La Vacquerie-Masnières road, and battalion headquarters was established east of the same road, on the slope overlooking the canal. By this time it was known that the bridges had been destroyed, and that the village of Vaucelles and the eastern bank of the canal were very strongly held by enemy infantry and machine-guns. It was obvious that a frontal attack on the village, without artillery preparation and support, was out of the question.

The 1st Brigade, on the left, had meanwhile reached the western bank of the canal as far north as Crèvecoeur, and had established a bridge-head in that village; but the eastern bank of the canal was strongly held by the enemy, who prevented a crossing at any other point. At Crèvecoeur the canal turns towards the west, and does not run north again till it reaches Marcoing. At this village the canal had been crossed by the VI Corps, which had captured Masnières, east of the canal, and established another bridge-head there.

The 1st Brigade was now ordered to extend its front, on the night of September 30th/October 1st, to a point on the Rumilly-Crèvecoeur road, about a mile east of Masnières; and the 2nd Brigade "side-slipped" north, as far as the southern outskirts of the village of Les Rues des Vignes. The 2nd Company of the 2nd Canterbury Battalion accordingly relieved troops of the 1st Wellington Battalion, with one platoon in the southern end of the German trench that ran at the rear of the village, and the remainder in a trench that ran north-east from the east of Lateau Wood. Early the same night, the 1st Company relieved all 2nd Otago Battalion troops east of the Bonavis-Masnières road; but next night was relieved by troops of the 37th Division, and moved into the area north of Lateau Wood. At dusk on October 1st the 12th and 13th Companies moved forward to positions about half a mile west of the Bonavis-Masnières road, and battalion headquarters was also moved up to near the road.

The 2nd Canterbury Battalion was now the leading battalion of the brigade, and was holding the whole brigade frontage on the canal. The front extended a mile down the western bank, from the southern end of Les Rues des Vignes. The re-arrangement of brigade areas had given to the 2nd Brigade a strip of country a thousand yards wide, running due east; but the south-western trend of the canal in this locality made the actual front to be guarded slightly over a mile in length. The battalion had now instructions not to attempt to force a passage of the canal in the face of strong opposition; but to keep on the alert so as to miss no opportunity of crossing should one offer. The dispositions of the leading company (the 2nd) were improved, but otherwise the battalion remained where it was till the morning of October 5th.

The 1st Canterbury Battalion, on relief on the night of October 1st/2nd, had moved to trenches north-east of and close to La Vacquerie; and remained there till the evening of the 5th, when it concentrated in an area about two miles to the north-east of that village. On the 1st of the month the 1st Brigade (on the left) had advanced its left flank to the north-east of Crèvecoeur, and gained possession of the western portion of the village. It had been relieved by the 3rd (Rifle) Brigade on the night of October 3rd/4th.

On the morning of October 5th the enemy began to shell Vaucelles and Cheneaux Wood (to its north-east), both of which places had previously been held by the enemy in great strength. A patrol from the 2nd Company of the 2nd Canterbury Battalion found the enemy trenches east of Les Rues des Vignes unoccupied; and a patrol from the 1st Company (under its company commander, Captain L. B. Hutton) crossed the canal at Vaucelles, passed through that village, and penetrated as far as Cheneaux Wood and also to Fox Farm, to the south-east of Vaucelles, without meeting opposition. This patrol on its way out informed the troops on the right flank that the enemy had withdrawn.

Meanwhile, the 12th Company had been ordered to come up through the 2nd Company, and to advance by means of fighting patrols. This company crossed the canal by means of a primitive German raft, composed of a duck-walk supported on four bundles of corks. The raft could carry only three men at a time, but when the time came for the 13th and 2nd Companies to cross, a party of New Zealand Engineers had built a larger and more reliable raft capable of carrying six men. The 1st Company crossed by the bridge at Vaucelles, which was available for infantry only.

The 12th Company met with considerable opposition in a sunken road east of Cheneaux Copse, where it captured five machine-guns, killed numerous Germans, and took fifteen prisoners. As the Division on the right had not yet come up, the Commanding Officer ordered the 12th Company to form a defensive flank facing south, from Cheneaux Wood inclusive and thence east along the high ground to south-west of Bel Aise Farm.

The machine-gun section working with the battalion was also detailed to protect the right flank.

Under this protection the 13th Company moved forward, and late in the afternoon had approached within a short distance of the Masnières-Beaurevoir Line. The most advanced troops of the 12th Company were still further south, and were about seven hundred yards south of the right Divisional boundary. On the north, the 13th Company's left flank was four hundred yards to the right of the inter-brigade boundary, but the 3rd (Rifle) Brigade had extended to its right to cover the gap.

In the afternoon the 37th Division came up on the right; but no further advance was possible, as the leading troops were held up by the Masnières-Beaurevoir system of trenches, which was protected by a very strong belt of wire, fifty yards in depth and unbroken by artillery fire. The 1st Company, in support, was in shelters between Cheneaux Wood and Copse; and after dusk the 2nd Company crossed the canal, and assembled just east of the river. Later in the evening the 1st Company took over the northern four hundred yards of the battalion front, which had been held by the 3rd (Rifle) Brigade.

The Commander-in-Chief summarizes the results of the fighting between September 27th and October 5th as follows:—

"The great and critical assaults in which during these nine days of battle the First, Third, and Fourth Armies stormed the line of the Canal du Nord and broke through the Hindenburg Line mark the close of the first phase of the British offensive. The enemy's defence in the last and strongest of his prepared positions had been shattered. The whole of the main Hindenburg defences had passed into our possession, and a wide gap had been driven through such rear trench systems as had existed behind them. The effect of the victory upon the subsequent course of the campaign was decisive. The threat to the enemy's communications was now direct and instant, for nothing but the natural obstacles of a wooded and well-watered country-side lay between our Armies and Maubeuge."*

---

*Despatch of December 21st, 1918.

CHAPTER XVI.

THE SECOND BATTLE OF LE CATEAU
AND THE BATTLE OF THE SELLE.

The New Zealand Division was now held up by the rearmost trench of the last strong defensive line in the German back area, and beyond this trench lay open country, with only natural obstacles to assist the enemy.

As Sir Douglas Haig puts it, in the Despatch quoted above:—
"The second and concluding phase of the British offensive now opened, in which the Fourth and Third Armies and the right of the First Army moved forward with their left flank on the canal line which runs from Cambrai to Mons and their right covered by the French First Army. This advance, by the capture of Maubeuge and the disruption of the German main lateral systems of communications, forced the enemy to fall back upon the line of the Meuse and realised the strategic plan of the Allied operations.

"The fighting which took place during this period, being in effect the development and exploitation of the Hindenburg Line victory, falls into three stages, the breaks between the different battles being due chiefly to the depth of our advances and the difficulties of re-establishing communications.

"In the first of these stages, the battle of Le Cateau. certain incomplete defences still held by the enemy were captured, and his troops compelled to evacuate Cambrai and fall back behind the line of the Selle River. In the second stage, the Selle River was forced, and by a development of this operation our front pushed forward to the general line Sambre Canal-west edge of the Mormal Forest-Valenciennes, where we were in position for the final assault upon Maubeuge."

The positions reached by the New Zealand Division on October 5th were maintained during the whole of the 6th, when the artillery made an unsuccessful attempt to cut the wire in front of the enemy's trenches. Arrangements were made for the wire to be cut the following day by medium trench mortars.

The Division "side-slipped" to the north again on the 6th, the 2nd Canterbury Battalion's line continuing due north of the front line previously held by the battalion, with the right flank resting on the road from Rues des Vignes to Bel Aise Farm. The left flank platoon of the battalion was in the Masnières line itself, opposite the factory west of Lesdain. This frontage was held by two companies, the 13th on the right and the 1st on the left, each with two platoons in the front line, one platoon in support, and one in reserve. The 12th Company went into reserve on the east bank of the canal, and the 2nd Company remained where it was, but became the support company.

The Third Army was to resume the advance on October 8th. The 2nd and 3rd Brigades were to be the assaulting troops of the New Zealand Division; and the 1st Otago Battalion was ordered to take over the southern half of the 2nd Canterbury Battalion's frontage. As the latter battalion's first objective was now not much wider than five hundred yards, the Commanding Officer decided to use only the 1st Company (with two platoons in the front line) and half of the 13th Company (with one platoon in the front line) to take this objective; the remaining platoons of the 13th Company being retained intact in reserve. The 2nd and 12th Companies remained in support and reserve respectively. Battalion headquarters remained west of the canal till the evening of the 7th, when it moved to a sunken road north of Cheneaux Copse.

The wire in front of the Masnières line was successfully cut by the medium trench mortars on the afternoon of October 7th. This no doubt warned the enemy of the impending attack, as he shelled the assembly areas heavily during the night, and caused numerous casualties. The attack was made at 4.30 a.m. on the 8th, but despite a severe artillery barrage at zero hour, and heavy machine-gun fire from Bel-Aise Farm on the right flank, the attacking troops reached the Masnières line on the right and the factory on the left, in good order. Here they met with considerable resistance, particularly from machine-guns which had been over-run by the first waves.

The first objective, a sunken road running south from the eastern edge of Lesdain, was reached at 6.30 a.m.; but here the resistance was much less vigorous, in spite of the fact that the garrison captured numbered about three hundred. The 2nd Company then passed through, with two platoons covering the whole battalion frontage, and took the sunken road north of Pélu Wood. The remaining platoon of this company at once "leap-frogged" over the leading platoons, and captured the line of trenches west of Le Grand Pont. The 12th Company, coming up close behind, immediately went through the 2nd Company, cleared Le Grand Pont village (which was still being shelled by British "heavies") and Leauette Farm, and passed to the north of the village of Esnes, where touch was gained with the 3rd (Rifle) Brigade on the left at about 8 a.m.

The 12th Company was now on the final objective for the capture of which artillery support was available, though the plans for the attack included a further advance without a barrage later in the morning. The final objective of the 1st Otago Battalion, on the right, ran due south from Le Grand Pont; so that it was necessary for the 12th Company to establish a line facing Esnes, which was still occupied by the enemy. In the meantime, battalion headquarters had been moving up, and by 8 a.m. was established in a dug-out south of Lesdain.

At 9.30 a.m. the 1st Otago Battalion advanced again behind a barrage, and captured the village of Esnes. The 12th Company came under this barrage, but fortunately did not suffer many casualties; and on the 1st Otago Battalion coming up, the 12th Company joined up with it on the west of Esnes. This company pushed on again with the Otago Battalion, and by nightfall had established a line with its right resting due north of the eastern end of Esnes and on the ravine down which flows the stream called the "Torrent of Esnes," and with its left at the cemetery six hundred yards north of the village. To the west of the cemetery the company was in touch with the 3rd (Rifle) Brigade. At the conclusion of the advance the company took possession of three field-guns which had been abandoned by the enemy.

In the course of the afternoon the enemy assembled for a counter-attack in the ravine referred to above, north-east of Esnes; but the Division by then had five brigades of artillery east of the Escaut Canal, and the attack was broken up by artillery fire before it could be launched. Another attempt at a counter-attack was repelled by a 12th Company patrol. Shortly after noon, battalion headquarters moved to a position south of Le Grand Pont, and by 4 p.m. the travelling kitchens were south of Lesdain, preparing the evening meal.

The 1st Canterbury Battalion was reserve battalion of the brigade during the first day's attack, and had moved early in the morning to trenches east of the Bonavis-Masnières road. At 4 p.m. it moved again, to the Masnières line, and the Commanding Officer and company commanders went forward to reconnoitre the 2nd Battalion's positions, preparatory to the advance planned for the next day. At midnight the 1st Battalion moved to its assembly positions; the attacking companies, the 2nd on the right and the 13th on the left, being on the Selvigny-Longsart road, north-west of Haucourt, and the 12th (in support) and the 1st (in reserve) north-west of Esnes.

The advance was continued on October 9th at 5 30 a.m.. under a barrage. The 3rd Battalion of the 3rd (Rifle) Brigade had been temporarily attached to the 2nd Brigade and advanced on the 3rd Brigade's former frontage; and on the right of the 1st Canterbury Battalion the 2nd Otago Battalion covered the southern half of the 2nd Brigade's frontage. No opposition was encountered at first, and it soon became clear that the enemy had retired during the night. The barrage therefore became rather a hindrance than a help, especially as there were many complaints of short shooting, and as the barrage halted for half an hour a mile short of the first objective—the Ligny-Wambaix road.

The direction of the attack had become slightly more northward, and the villages of Fontaine-au-Pire and Beauvois-en-Cambresis were in the direct line of the battalion's advance. The artillery barrage covered the advance only as far as the Cambrai-Caudry railway, which was reached at 9 a.m. without opposition, and without casualties beyond those caused by our own shells. When the barrage died away, two troops of the 3rd Hussars crossed the railway and endeavoured to capture Fontaine, but were driven back by machine-gun fire. During the afternoon, patrols made good the road which ran half a mile beyond and parallel to the railway; but heavy machine-gun fire prevented any further advance till after 4 p.m.

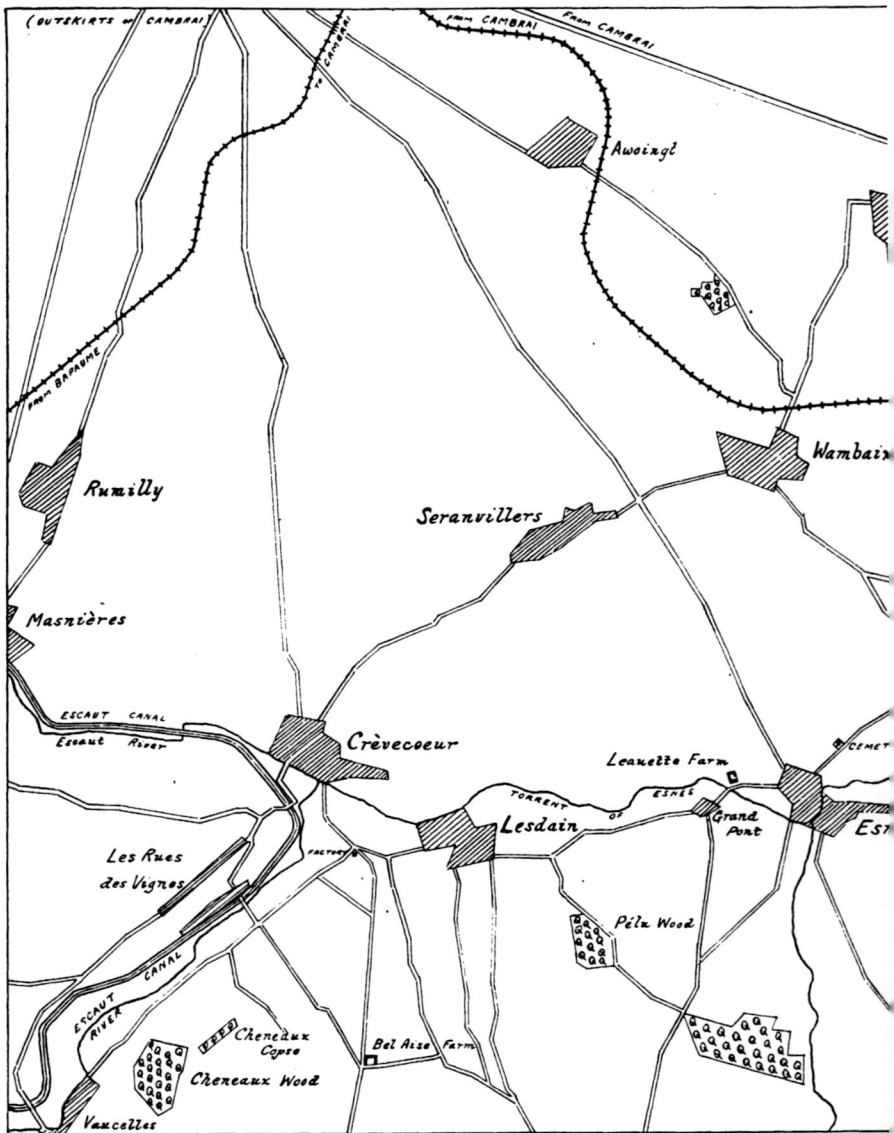

Boussières

Quiévy

Bévillers

Herpigny Farm

Aulicourt Farm

Estourmel

To Quievy

Cattenières

Beauvois-en-Cambresis

To Le Cateau

aix

Fontaine-au-Pire

Caudry

Longsart

To Le Cateau

METERY

Esnes

Haucourt

Ligny

Montigny

Caullery

Selvigny

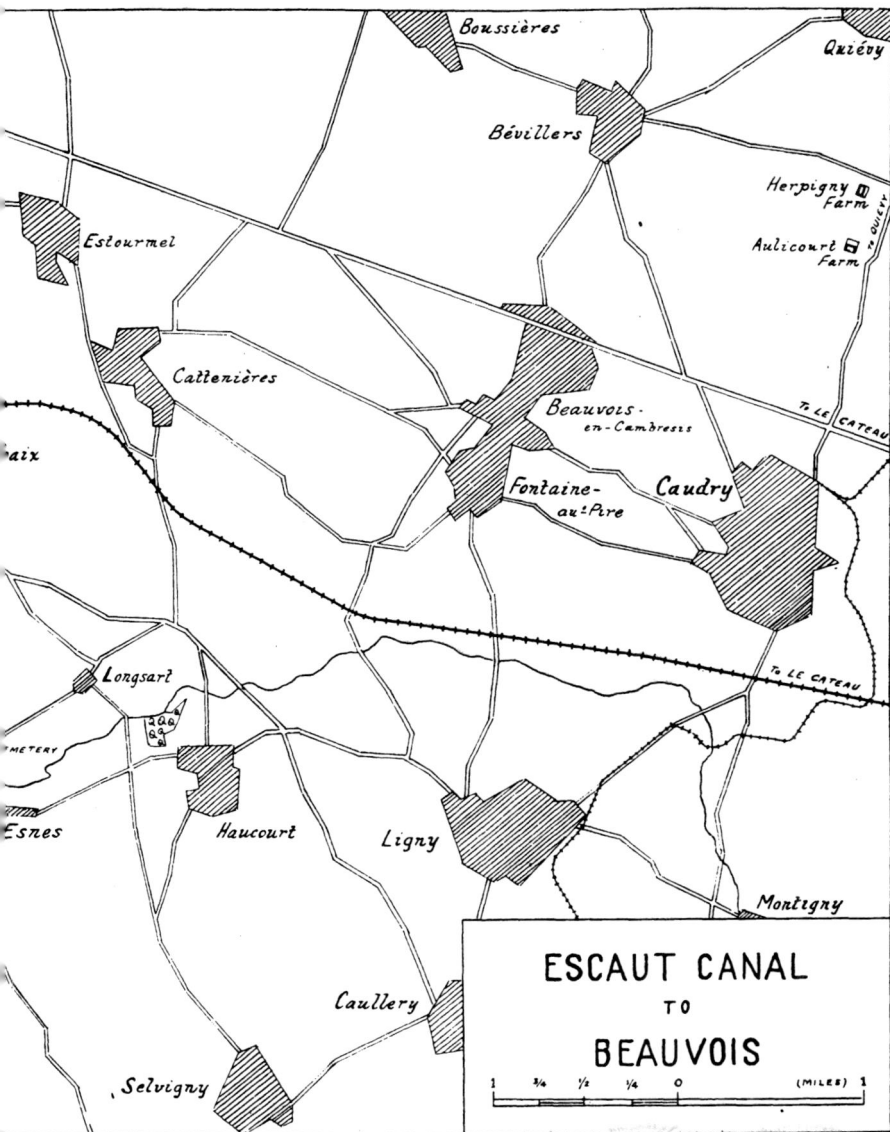

ESCAUT CANAL
TO
BEAUVOIS

1   ¾   ½   ¼   O   (MILES) 1

L/Corpl. M. H. Coppell, D.C.M.

Pte. F. White, D.C.M.

Pte. A. J. Findlay, D.C.M

Pte. D. P. Lloyd, D.C.M.

The 1st and 12th Companies then moved up to the road, and a patrol of the 1st Company succeeded in entering Fontaine and reaching the Caudry-Cattenières road. On the left, however, the 12th Company patrols, attempting to pass to the west of Fontaine, were held up by machine-gun fire from the large factory on the western edge of Beauvois. It was unfortunate that the forward section of artillery was at this juncture out of touch with the battalion, as its aid would probably have enabled the infantry to advance.

The main outpost line was now in touch on both flanks; but the 1st Company's advanced patrol in Fontaine was "in the air" altogether, and returned to the road during the night to avoid being cut off. The 2nd Brigade was still performing the *rôle* of the advanced guard of the Division, and on the night of October 9th/10th the 3rd Battalion of the 3rd (Rifle) Brigade ceased to be attached to the 2nd Brigade. The 1st Canterbury Battalion, during the night, "side-slipped" to the left, relieved the 3rd Battalion of the Rifle Brigade, and gained touch with the Guards Division; and the 2nd Otago Battalion took over a portion, on the right, of the 1st Canterbury Battalion's line. Forward battalion headquarters moved up close to the railway.

Next morning (October 10th) the enemy was found to have made a further withdrawal, and the 2nd and 13th Companies continued the advance from the Cambrai-Le Cateau road, meeting little opposition till they reached Herpigny Farm, which the 2nd Company took shortly after 10 a.m. The 13th Company met with resistance from Aulicourt Farm and the road east of it, but captured the farm. Battalion headquarters moved to a house in Beauvois, on the Cambrai-Le Cateau road.

The 1st Battalion had now made good the road between Herpigny and Aulicourt Farms, and from this line the Brigadier had ordered the 2nd Battalion to lead the advance. This battalion had been close on the heels of the 1st Battalion, and had spent the night of the 9th/10th in the ravine south of Longsart. On the morning of the 10th the Commanding Officer rode to Beauvois to get in touch with the Commanding Officer of the 1st Battalion. The battalion followed, and was assembled in the valley a quarter of a mile north-east of Beauvois by 1 p.m.

T

The Guards Division, on the left, had been held up west and south-west of Quievy. The Commanding Officer accordingly decided to advance on a two-company frontage, with the 1st Company on the right and the 13th Company on the left, and made the 2nd Company, in support, especially responsible for the protection of the left flank. The 12th Company was kept in reserve. On the right the 1st Otago Battalion had two hours earlier passed through the 2nd Battalion of the same regiment, and was well forward.

The front line and support companies of the 2nd Canterbury Battalion moved forward at 2 p.m. (10th October), directly information came through that the 1st Canterbury Battalion was on its final objective. The 2nd Battalion crossed the Caudry-Quievy railway and advanced towards Viesly; and was on the approaches of the village by 5.30 p.m. No resistance had been met with, but the enemy was in strength in Fontaine-au-Tertre Farm, two thousand yards north of Viesly. On this account, and as the Guards were still well behind, the battalion could not catch up with the advance of the 1st Otago Battalion, which, with its earlier start, had passed through Viesly and by 9.30 p.m. was only five hundred yards west of Briastre.

The high ground north of Viesly was occupied, however, by the 2nd Canterbury Battalion, and touch had been obtained with the left of the 1st Otago Battalion, when the 2nd Brigade was relieved by the 1st Brigade at 10 p.m. The 2nd Brigade marched back to comfortable and commodious billets in Beauvois. Here the brigade remained till the 22nd, engaged in refitting and training, but having plenty of rest and recreation. Vegetables were plentiful, and were highly appreciated after the scant supply of the past three or four months.

Since going into action on September 29th the Regiment's casualties had been:—

1st Battalion.	Officers.	Other Ranks.
Killed in Action and Died of Wounds	–	48
Wounded	6	111
Total	6	159

| | | Other |
2nd Battalion.	Officers.	Ranks.
Killed in Action and Died of Wounds ..	4*	38
Wounded	4	121
Total	8	159

*Major D. A. Dron (killed 8th October), Lieutenant G. B. L. Porter (killed 8th October), 2nd Lieutenant D. M. Moriarty (killed 8th October), 2nd Lieutenant E. A. Price (died of wounds 10th October).

Total for both battalions: 4 officers and 86 other ranks killed, and 10 officers and 232 other ranks wounded.

The enemy made a stand on the high ground east of the River Selle, so that, in comparison with the extent of the advance of October 8th, 9th, and 10th, little progress was made by the 1st Brigade before it was relieved by the 42nd Division on the night of October 12th/13th. In spite of determined resistance, however, the 1st Brigade crossed the river on the 11th; and the following day crossed the Solesmes-Le Cateau railway. After this brigade had been relieved, there was no further advance till the 20th, when the Third Army crossed the Selle and gained the high ground two thousand yards east of the railway; and further north penetrated the enemy defences to a point a mile east of Solesmes. The village of Romeries, to the north-east of Solesmes, still remained in the enemy's hands.

These operations of October 20th were carried out with the object of obtaining suitable starting points for an attack on a large scale on the 23rd, to be made by the Third and Fourth Armies on a fifteen-mile front from Mazinghien, south-east of Le Cateau, to Maison Bleu just south of the Cambrai-Bavai road. The following day two Corps of the First Army extended the attack for another five miles on the left, to the Scheldt River, south of Valenciennes.

The leading troops of the New Zealand Division in the attack of the 23rd were those of the 2nd Brigade. The brigade accordingly left its billets at Beauvois on the afternoon of October 22nd to march to its concentration area. There were few roads in the district, and they were crammed with traffic; so that the march

was very slow and tedious. The 1st Canterbury Battalion
(under Major A. D. Stitt, in the absence of Lieutenant-Colonel
Row on leave) was settled in its area, midway between Solesmes
and Belle Vue, by 7 p.m., with two companies on the railway,
battalion headquarters a hundred yards behind, and the remaining companies in a quarry east of the railway. The 2nd Battalion
(under Major N. R. Wilson, in the absence of Lieutenant-Colonel
Stewart on duty in England) reached its concentration area,
immediately to the south of Solesmes, at 5.30 p.m. All the companies bivouacked for the night in the railway triangle south
of the town, with battalion headquarters in a house on the
northern side of the triangle.

Orders were received early in the evening that at 3.20 a.m.
the following day the 42nd Division, with the 5th Division on
its right and the 3rd Division on its left, would attack Romeries
and the ridge west of Beaurain. An hour later, the 42nd and
5th Divisions would capture Beaurain, and straighten out the
line between that village and Romeries. The 37th and New
Zealand Divisions were ordered to pass through the 5th and 42nd
Divisions respectively at 8.40 a.m.; and at the same time the 3rd
Division was to continue its advance on the left.

The advance of the 2nd Brigade was made with the 1st Otago
Battalion on the right and the 2nd Canterbury Battalion on the
left, with the remaining battalions in support to their sister
battalions. The 2nd Canterbury Battalion left its concentration
area at dawn, and moved to a ploughed field south of the
Solesmes-Vertigneul road. There it remained till 7.15 a.m., when
a smoke barrage was brought down to cover the advance of the
2nd Brigade to its starting point for the attack. Meanwhile, the
42nd and flanking Divisions had taken their objectives; and
directly the smoke barrage came down the 2nd Brigade moved
up to the 42nd Division's front line.

The attacking companies of the 2nd Canterbury Battalion
(from right to left) were the 2nd and 12th Companies, with the
13th Company in support and the 1st Company in reserve.
Practically no resistance was met in the first stage of the attack,
and before 10 a.m. the leading troops had captured the first
objective, the Escarmain-Vendegies au Bois road. Here a halt
was made while the 1st Canterbury Battalion assembled on the

Vertain-Neuville road, and at 12.12 p.m. passed through the 2nd Battalion and continued the advance, with the 2nd Otago Battalion on its right and the 3rd Division on its left. The front line companies of the battalion were the 1st Company (right) and 2nd Company (left), the 12th and 13th Companies being respectively in support and reserve.

Half a mile beyond the starting point the attacking troops passed over the top of the spur which runs from Neuville down to Escarmain, and came under heavy artillery fire. This continued as they advanced down the slope to the St. Georges river; and they also came under machine-gun and rifle fire from the high ground on the north-east of the stream.

Our barrage here was rather a disadvantage to the attackers, as it prevented them from crossing quickly the zone of the enemy's fire. But after our barrage had died away the leading companies pushed on, and captured prisoners, machine-guns, and artillery at the river. The bridge at Pont-à-Pierres had been destroyed by the enemy; but the river was small and presented no formidable obstacle. Little resistance was encountered beyond the river, and the battalion's objectives, on the high ground a thousand yards to the north-east of the river, were taken without difficulty at about 2.30 p.m.

The front line of the battalion was now out of touch on both flanks, and the leading companies therefore consolidated the ground already gained. Battalion headquarters was established on the Beaudignies road, close to Pont-à-Pierres. Patrols were pushed forward by the leading companies, and reached the southern edge of Beaudignies without meeting any of the enemy. The Commanding Officer therefore decided to occupy Beaudignies, to prevent the demolition of the bridges of the River Ecaillon, which flows through the village. The 12th Company was detailed for the operation, and one platoon of the 13th Company was attached to it. These troops moved forward at 5 p.m. from their position near Pont-à-Pierres, the 12th Company working round the south-east side of the village, while the platoon of the 13th Company made its way down the main street.

Though no opposition was met, the greatest caution was necessary, so that it was 9 p.m. before the bridges were safe in our hands. A quarter of an hour later a party of the enemy attacked the 13th Company patrol at the northern bridge-head, but was repulsed. The village was now under heavy machine-gun fire from the high ground east of Le Quesnoy, but later in the evening our patrols worked up the Le Quesnoy road and drove the enemy from his positions. During the fight for the bridge-heads Sergeant J. H. Nicholas, V.C., M.M., was killed.

In the meantime, the 2nd Battalion had concentrated in the neighbourhood of Pont-à-Pierres, and at 9.30 p.m. received orders from the Brigadier that two companies were to establish a line on the Ruesnes-Ghissignies road, north-east of Beaudignies. An hour later the 1st Company (on the right) and the 13th Company (on the left) moved forward. A request had been made for a barrage to be put down on the objectives, and the attacking troops had been instructed to wait for the barrage. The arrangements fell through, and the messages sent to the companies, informing them of this change of plan, did not reach them till 12.30 a.m. By this time the enemy had come back to the objectives; but the attack was pushed home at 1 a.m and the enemy driven out.

The advanced troops were now in touch with the 1st Otago Battalion on their right, but the Division on the left was not up, and a further advance was thought inadvisable. Patrols sent out by the support company (the 12th) discovered enemy posts to the west of Beaudignies, and a defensive flank facing that direction was formed by this company. Further north the 12th Company of the 1st Battalion had been left to protect the left flank of the front line companies. Headquarters of the 2nd Battalion had meanwhile moved from the farm-house at Pont-à-Pierres to a farm-house a quarter of a mile south of Beaudignies; but the 2nd Company remained at Pont-à-Pierres till next day, when it moved close to battalion headquarters.

At 4 a.m. on October 24th the 3rd Division advanced on the left under a barrage. This barrage came down also on the rear of the sunken road occupied by the 2nd Battalion's front-line companies, and compelled the garrison to fall back to cover. On the barrage moving forward the line was re-established; and by 9 a.m. the left was advanced to the high ground six hundred yards north-east of the road. Throughout the day the line crept gradually forward; until at nightfall it ran parallel to, and twelve hundred yards in advance of, the Ruesnes-Ghissignies road. At 6.45 in the morning advanced battalion headquarters had been established in the north of the village.

The 3rd (Rifle) Brigade relieved the 2nd Brigade before midnight on the 24th, and the 1st Canterbury Battalion moved back into billets at Vertigneul. The 2nd Battalion went back to Le Mesnil and Pont-à-Pierres Farms, battalion headquarters being in the latter. On the afternoon of October 27th, however, the enemy began to shell the bridge and farm buildings at Pont-à-Pierres, with blue-cross gas-shells. No casualties were caused, but it was thought advisable to abandon the farm; and battalion headquarters was moved to near Le Mesnil Farm, while the 2nd Company bivouacked in the open between the two farms. Next day the battalion was ordered back to Romeries, where it was accommodated in tents and a chair factory.

CHAPTER XVII.

THE BATTLE OF THE SAMBRE.

The 2nd Brigade remained in the neighbourhood of Vertigneul, in support to the Division, till November 4th. During this time the line was advanced by "peaceful penetration," till the left flank of the 3rd (Rifle) Brigade, which was holding the line on the whole Divisional front, rested at the point where the Beaudignies-Orsinval road crosses the Valenciennes-Le Quesnoy railway. From there the line ran south, parallel to the Solesmes-Le Quesnoy railway, and about a quarter of a mile west of it. Further south, in the sector of the adjoining Division, the front line crossed the railway east of Ghissignies, and swung towards the south-east.

Meanwhile, Valenciennes had fallen to the Canadians on November 1st. The Allied Command had anticipated that directly this town fell the time would be ripe for a decisive attack, which would deprive the enemy of the power to withdraw to a shorter front for the winter. There were already indications of an early withdrawal by the enemy, particularly on the northern and southern portions of the front, so that it was necessary that the attack should be made without delay. This attack was made on November 4th, by the British Fourth, Third, and First Armies, on a thirty mile front from Oisy, on the Sambre River, to Valenciennes.

The British attacks in the latter part of October had been in a north-easterly direction, their object being to outflank Valenciennes from the south, and so to compel the enemy to evacuate this town. As a result of these tactics, the left flank of the Third Army bent back towards the west; but the advance of the XVII Corps and the First Army through Valenciennes, on November 1st and 2nd, had resulted in the establishment of a line running practically due north and south, with its northern flank protected by the marshes north-east of Valenciennes. The attack of the 4th was accordingly directed due east again.

BEAUVOIS TO BRIASTRE

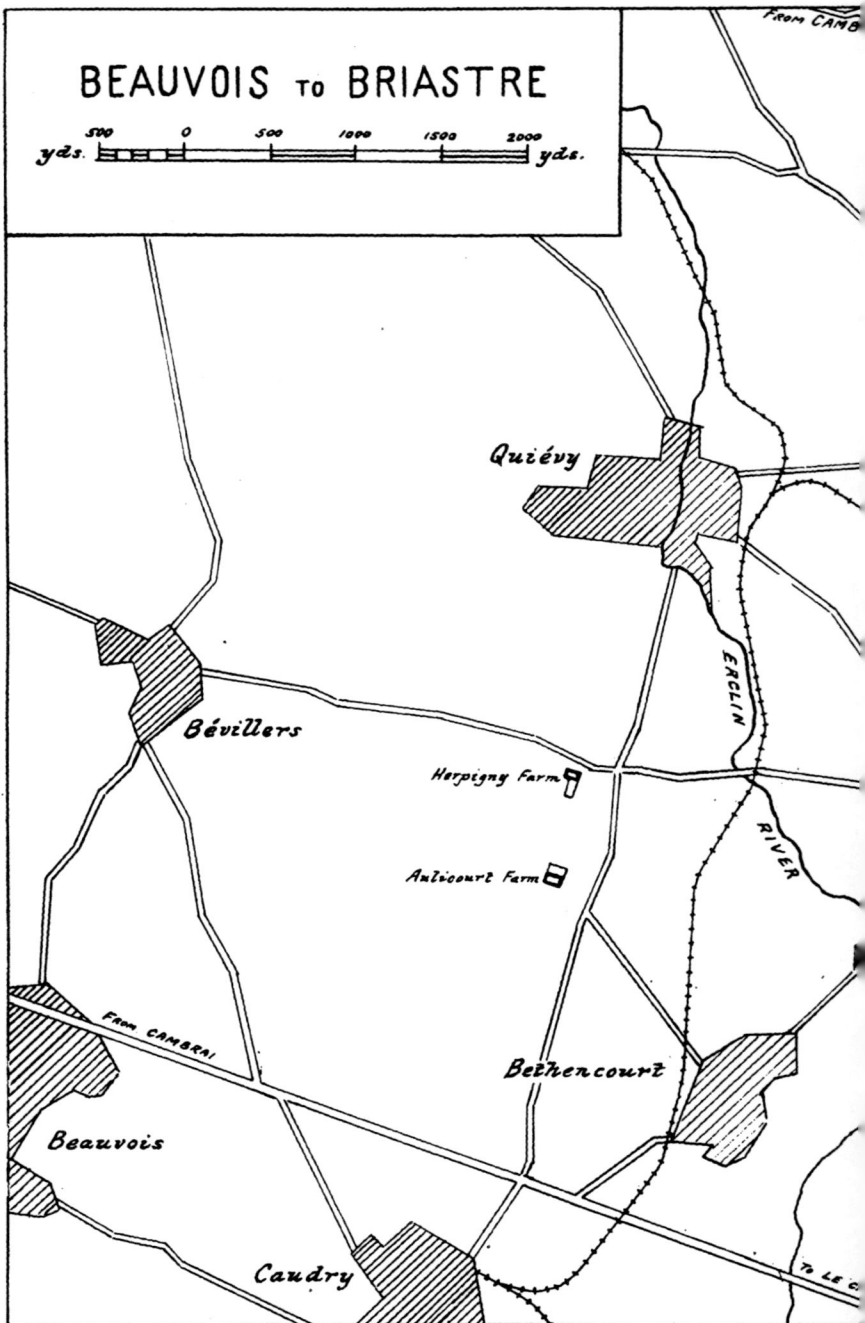

yds. 500 0 500 1000 1500 2000 yds.

FROM CAMB

Quiévy

ERCLIN

RIVER

Bévillers

Harpigny Farm

Anticourt Farm

FROM CAMBRAI

Bethencourt

Beauvois

Caudry

To LE C.

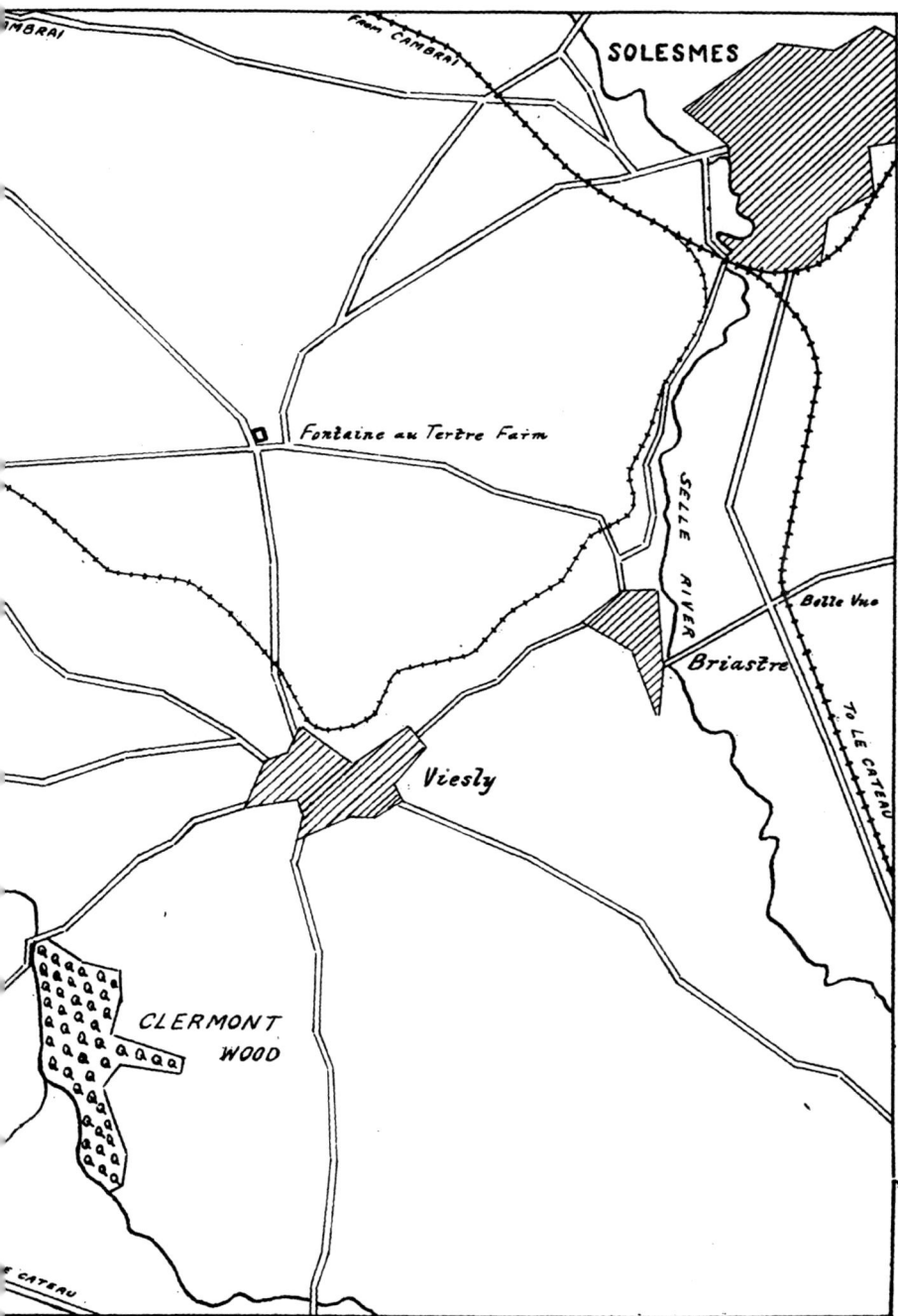

SOLESMES

From CAMBRAI

CAMBRAI

Fontaine au Tertre Farm

SELLE RIVER

Belle Vue

Briastre

To LE CATEAU

Viesly

CLERMONT
WOOD

LE CATEAU

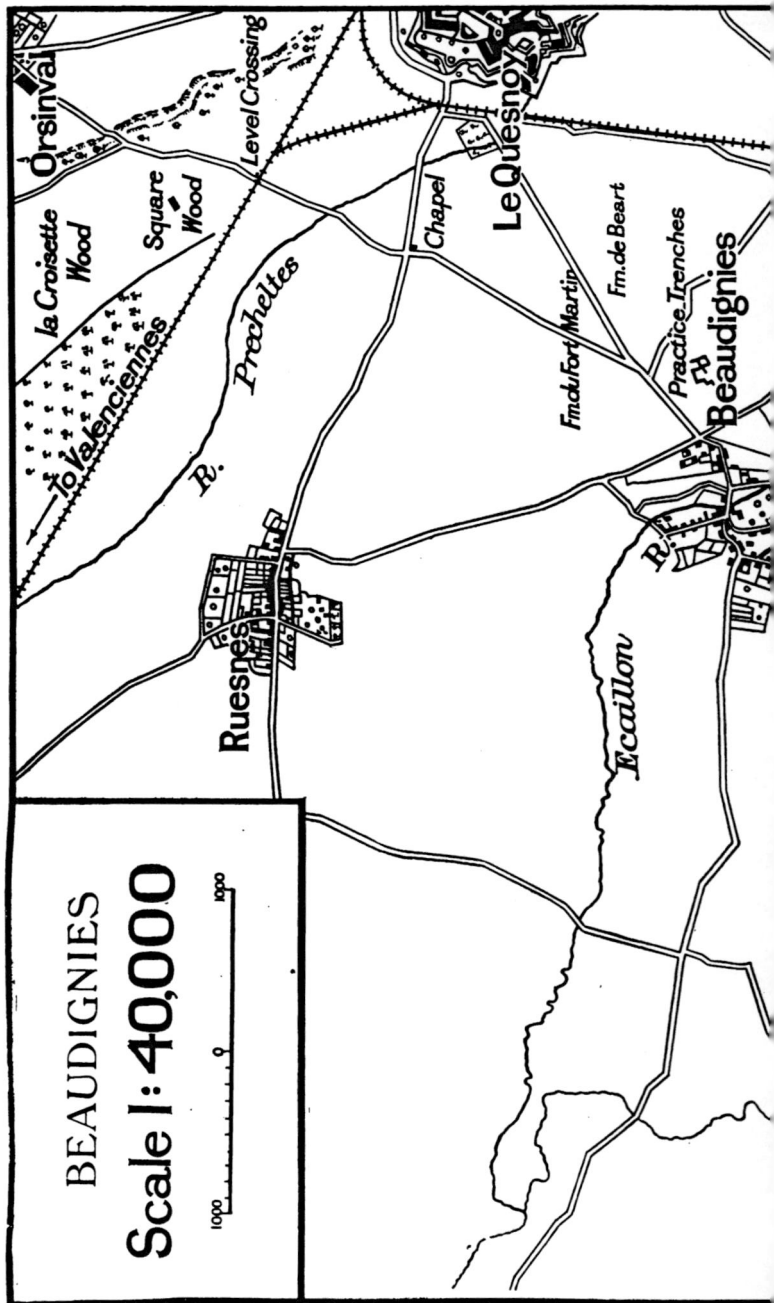

BEAUDIGNIES

Scale 1: 40,000

Orsinval

la Croisette Wood

Square Wood

Level Crossing

To Valenciennes

Precheltes

R.

Le Quesnoy

Chapel

Fm. de Beart

Fm. du Fort Martin

Practice Trenches

Beaudignies

R.

Ruesnes

Ecaillon

R.

1000

0

1000

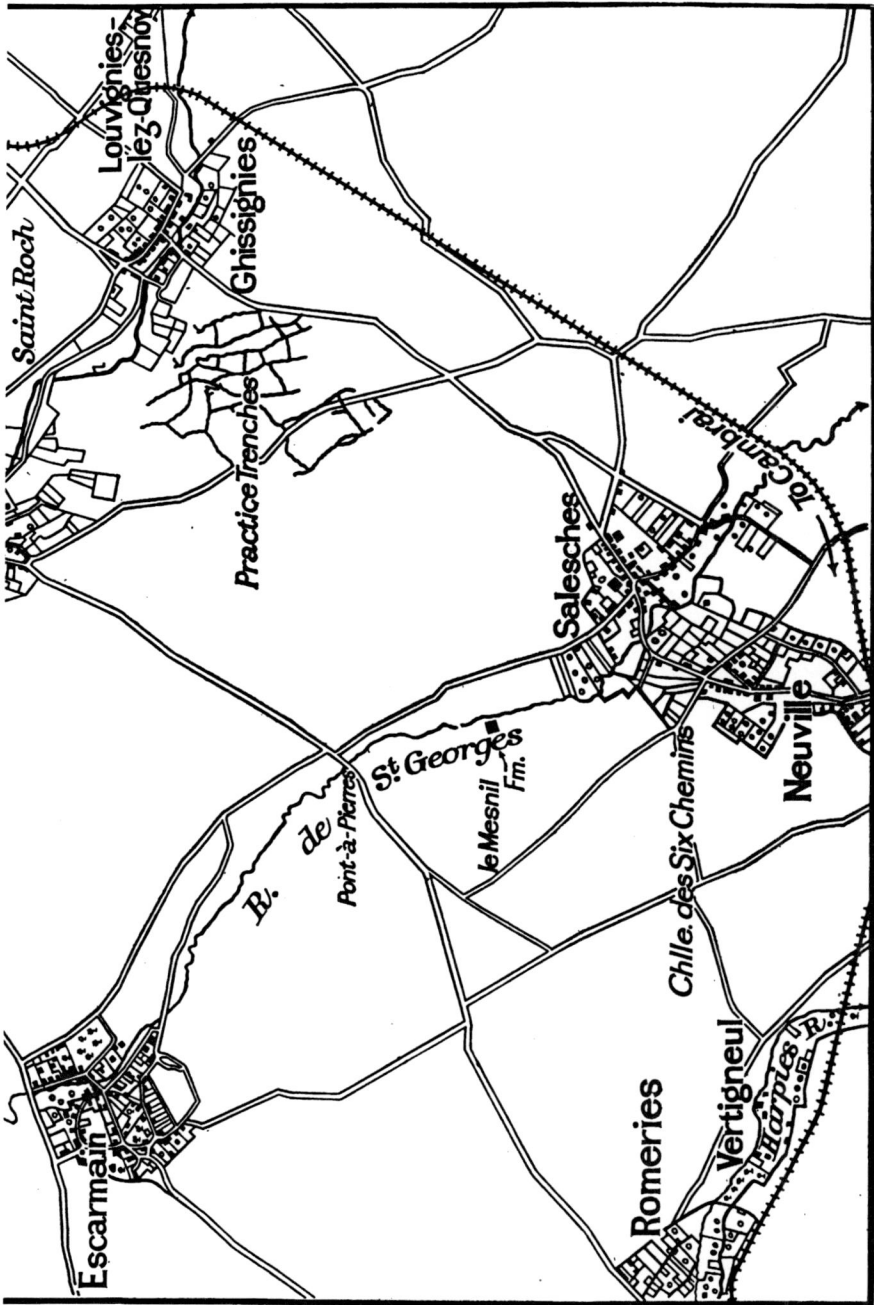

Louvignies-lez-Quesnoy

Saint Roch

Ghissignies

Practice Trenches

Salesches

St Georges

le Mesnil Fm.

R. de Pont-à-Pierres

Neuville

To Cambrai

Chlle. des Six Chemins

Escarmain

Romeries

Vertigneul

R. Harpies

To quote again from Sir Douglas Haig's Despatch of December 21st, 1918:—

"The nature of the country across which our advance was to be made was most difficult. In the south the river had to be crossed almost at the outset. In the centre the great Forest of Mormal, though much depleted by German wood-cutting, still presented a formidable obstacle. In the north the fortified town of Le Quesnoy, and several streams which ran parallel to the line of our advance, offered frequent opportunities for successful defence. On the other hand our troops had never been so confident of victory or so assured of their own superiority."

The length of the front to be attacked by the New Zealand Division was two thousand five hundred yards; and six hundred yards from the starting point was the town of Le Quesnoy, occupying almost half the Divisional frontage. The town was protected by a double moat and rampart; and although its fortifications were of little use against modern siege artillery, they were a formidable obstacle to infantry. Our natural reluctance to bombard the town, seeing that it was occupied by French civilians, made easier the task of its defenders. Rather than sacrifice lives in an assault on the town, the General Officer Commanding the Division decided to hold the enemy from the front, and to send troops round on both flanks, to meet at the back of the town and cut off the garrison.

The 3rd (Rifle) Brigade attacked at 5.30 a.m., and advanced to the Orsinval-Le Quesnoy road, north of the town, and to Cantiane, on the Le Quesnoy-Englefontaine road, south of the town. Between these points it reached a line running in a semicircle round Le Quesnoy, and almost on the edge of the moat on the western side of the town.

In the second stage of the attack the 1st Brigade took part. As there was no room to manoeuvre on the Divisional front north of Le Quesnoy, this brigade advanced in a south-easterly direction from the area of the 62nd Division, on the left of the 3rd (Rifle) Brigade, and established a line on the north and north-east of the town, with its left flank at Ramponeau. At the same time, the 3rd (Rifle) Brigade advanced its right flank in a north-easterly direction, till the right portion of its line ran parallel to, and a quarter of a mile south-west of, the Le Quesnoy-Jolimetz road.

The third stage of the attack saw the two brigades linked up on the "Green Line" (north of Jolimetz-Potelle-Villereau) and in touch with the 37th and 62nd Divisions on the right and left respectively. Le Quesnoy was now completely surrounded and cut off, and the 1st Brigade took over the whole of the Divisional front, the 3rd (Rifle) Brigade being left to deal with Le Quesnoy, which was still holding out.

At 10.30 a.m. the 1st Brigade made a further advance, and by noon had reached a line running north and south through Herbignies, with its right flank close to the Forest of Mormal. Patrols were pushed forward into the forest, and by midnight the brigade had reached its final objective, having penetrated three thousand yards into the forest on the right, and reached Sarloton on the left. At Le Quesnoy the garrison, numbering about a thousand, had held out until about 4.30 p.m., when the 3rd (Rifle) Brigade stormed the ramparts and entered the town, after strenuous and picturesque fighting.

The 2nd Brigade, in Divisional support, had concentrated early on the morning of November 4th in the fields to the south-west of Beaudignies. There it remained till two in the afternoon, when it was ordered to move up, so as to be ready to pass through the 1st Brigade and resume the advance on the morning of the 5th. Le Quesnoy was at this time still holding out, so that a lengthy detour through Ghissignies and Louvignies was necessary to avoid machine-gun fire from the town. The 1st Canterbury Battalion was commanded by Major A. D. Stitt, as Lieutenant-Colonel Row had been attached to brigade headquarters for liaison duties. The battalion halted for tea at Moulin Goffart, north-west of Jolimetz, and spent the night in Herbignies. The 2nd Battalion (under Major N. R. Wilson) marched across country from Louvignies to the Le Quesnoy-Jolimetz road, and by way of the last named village to its bivouac area west of Herbignies. The march was a very trying one for all battalions of the brigade.

The attack of the 2nd Brigade on November 5th was carried out, on the whole Divisional frontage of two thousand five hundred yards, by the 2nd Otago Battalion on the right and the 1st Canterbury Battalion on the left. The latter battalion moved forward at 3.30 a.m. to its assembly positions on the Bavai-

Englefontaine road, on the edge of the forest of Mormal. At this place the trees had been cut, but from half a mile forward of the left flank, and a mile and a half forward of the right flank, the whole of the country over which the advance had to be made was covered either with forest of tall trees or else with very tall and dense undergrowth.

The order of battle, from right to left, was the 12th and 13th Companies, with the 2nd Company in support and the 1st Company in reserve. On the left flank was the 62nd Division. The attack was made at 5.30 a.m. under a creeping barrage, and little serious resistance was met with before Forester's House, on the road which runs north through the forest to Obies and Bavai. Here the advance was held up till the leading companies had worked round from the flanks; this manoeuvre was completed about 9 a.m., when the house was taken, with five machine-guns, one minnenwerfer, and numerous prisoners.

In spite of the fact that the 2nd Otago Battalion was held up on the right, and that the left flank was two thousand five hundred yards in advance of the 62nd Division, the battalion pushed on another fifteen hundred yards to its final objective. This was captured after heavy fighting. Battalion headquarters was established at Forrester's House shortly after its capture; and during the day this, and the forest generally, was heavily shelled by the enemy.

After capturing the final objective, the companies advanced another half a mile, to a line fifteen hundred yards west of the eastern edge of the forest. Here they were held up on the western edge of a wide clearing, by machine-gun fire from both flanks; and particularly from the standing forest on the right. The 2nd Otago Battalion was now coming up on that flank, but had not advanced as far as the 1st Canterbury Battalion. The position on the left flank, which now ran along the northern edge of the forest, was very dangerous; for the 62nd Division was still far behind, and the enemy could be seen in considerable numbers a long way behind the flank of the leading troops.

The 2nd Canterbury Battalion had moved from its bivouac area just before daylight, and advanced through the forest in close support to the 1st Battalion. At 2 p.m. the Brigadier, having not yet received the report that the 1st Battalion's final objective had been taken, ordered the 2nd Battalion to pass through and continue the advance on the left flank. In the meantime, the 1st Battalion had already passed beyond its objective, and was approaching the clearing near the eastern edge of the wood.

Owing to the density of the wood, and the length of the front, the companies of the 2nd Battalion found difficulty in keeping in touch with battalion headquarters, which was continuously changing its location as the battalion advanced. The leading companies were therefore in better touch with the 1st Battalion companies than with their own battalion headquarters, and were earlier in hearing of the 1st Battalion's advance beyond its final objective than was the Commanding Officer of the 2nd Battalion.

When the orders to go through the 1st Battalion reached the leading companies, the 1st Battalion had already advanced to take the objective assigned by the Brigadier to the 2nd Battalion. It was not until the 1st Battalion had been held up, and Major Wilson had come forward to confer with Major Stitt, that the position was cleared up. The two Commanding Officers then arranged that the 2nd Battalion should relieve the 1st, which was to leave one company to protect the left flank.

By 4 p m. the relief was complete, and the 2nd and 12th Companies of the 2nd Battalion were holding the western edge of the clearing, with the 1st Company on the northern edge of the wood, on the left flank. The 13th Company and battalion headquarters were half a mile further back. Patrols were sent out, and the enemy was reported holding the other side of the clearing, while no touch could be gained with either of the Otago Battalions on the right flank. Later on, it was reported that the 2nd Otago Battalion had cleared the wood on the right, and a fighting patrol sent out by the 2nd Company established a post on the road on the eastern edge of the forest. The enemy, how-ever, was still holding in strength part of the wood on the left of and behind this post, and was also reported to be three hundred yards east of the edge of the wood. It was now quite dark, and no further advance could be attempted.

The brigade was relieved during the night by a brigade of the 42nd Division. The 1st Canterbury Battalion marched at

8 p.m. direct to the barracks at Le Quesnoy; but the 2nd Battalion was not relieved till after midnight, and so halted at dawn at Herbignies for a hot meal. Rain had begun to fall early on the morning of the 5th, and continued all day, so that everybody was very wet, and the going through the forest was very difficult. Altogether, the 5th/6th was one of the most exhausting days of the last phase of the war; for the advance in the rain all day—long though it was—was shorter than the march back to Le Quesnoy. Both battalions were dead tired when they reached Le Quesnoy, but there they found comfortable billets, with fires to warm themselves and dry their clothes.

The Regiment's casualties from October 23rd (inclusive) had been as follows:—

1st Battalion.	Officers.	Other Ranks.
Killed in Action and Died of Wounds ..	2*	25
Wounded	8	116
Total	10	141

2nd Battalion.	Officers.	Other Ranks.
Killed in Action and Died of Wounds ..	2†	24
Wounded	2	100
Total	4	124

*2nd Lieutenants T. Bell and A. H. W. Ell (both killed 23rd October).

†Lieutenant H. G. McNiven (killed 24th October), 2nd Lieutenant L. W. P. Reeve (died of wounds 13th November).

Total for both battalions: 4 officers and 49 other ranks killed, and 10 officers and 216 other ranks wounded.

The following is the official summary of the total casualties of the Canterbury Regiment from the formation of the New

Zealand Expeditionary Force up to and including January 5th, 1919:—

	Officers.	Other Ranks.
Killed	57	1,530
Died of Wounds	24	527
Died of Disease	6	155
Dead, Cause Unknown	2	50
Drowned	–	2
Wounded	220	5,633
Total	309	7,897

CHAPTER XVIII.

THE MARCH TO GERMANY
AND GARRISON DUTY IN COLOGNE.

The 2nd Brigade rested in Le Quesnoy till November 11th, and on the 10th provided a guard of honour for M. Poincaré, President of the French Republic, on the occasion of his visit to the town. The following afternoon the brigade began to march to the Beauvois area, news of the Armistice having been received during the morning. The night of the 11th was spent in billets at Quievy, and the march was resumed next morning.

The time in Beauvois was spent at first in light training and recreation; but later on a good deal of attention was paid to route marching, in preparation for the march to Germany. During this period Lieutenant-Colonel Stewart left the 2nd Battalion, to take up the duties of Director of Education to the New Zealand Expeditionary Force. Major N. R. Wilson assumed command until December 4th, when Lieutenant-Colonel Stitt was transferred from the 1st Battalion to the 2nd.

On November 28th the march began; and as the brigade passed through the area occupied by the 37th Division, the latter's bands played the column through the villages, and its troops lined the streets to give our men a hearty send-off — a compliment that was much appreciated by everyone.

Lack of space prevents a detailed account of the march, but a list of the billetting areas of the Canterbury Battalions will be found in Appendix "E." The weather was wonderful for the time of the year, and there were only four actual marching days that were wet. The roads were for the most part good, but the boots worn by the men were not good enough to stand a long march; and as supplies of new boots and materials for repairs were a long time in arriving, a good deal of discomfort was suffered by many of the men.

The issue of rations, though no smaller than usual, proved insufficient to sustain the men on a lengthy march. It is suggested that the explanation is that men engaged in trench warfare, which is more or less sedentary, do not require as much to eat as men who are expending their energy in marching long distances. Fortunately, potatoes and other vegetables could be bought in many of the villages, and the regimental funds provided by the people of Canterbury enabled the rations to be substantially increased.

The long stay of the New Zealand Division in Flanders had given its members a rather poor opinion of the Belgians; but its march to Germany caused that opinion to be altered. The New Zealanders were greeted with enthusiasm, and met with the greatest kindness and hospitality; this was particularly marked in the district round Charleroi, at Auvelais, and at Verviers, the last large town through which the Division passed.

The 2nd Brigade crossed the German frontier on December 20th, entrained at Herbesthal and reached Ehrenfeld, a suburb of Cologne, the same day. The Y.M.C.A., working at both ends of the train journey, showed once again its energy and enterprise by providing hot drinks and food for the troops. The 1st Canterbury Battalion was the first battalion of the Division to reach Germany, as it left its last billets in Belgium at 1.30 a.m. on the 20th, entrained early in the morning, and arrived at Ehrenfeld at 10 a.m.

The brigade was stationed at Mülheim, on the right bank of the Rhine; and the route taken from Ehrenfeld skirted the town of Cologne, and crossed the river by the bridge of boats at Mülheim. The 1st Canterbury Battalion marched into the barracks of the German 16th Infantry Regiment, where it was very comfortably quartered. The 2nd Battalion arrived at Ehrenfeld just after dark the same day, and began to march to Mülheim at 6 p.m. It had been intended that this battalion should also be quartered in the barracks, but the space allotted to it was occupied by English troops. After three uncomfortable days in temporary quarters, the battalion was accommodated in two large schools, near the barracks. It was, however, several weeks before anything approaching barrack-room conditions was attained.

The duties of the 2nd Brigade, in its capacity of part of the Army of Occupation, were chiefly to provide numerous isolated guards over enemy munitions of war. A whole company was

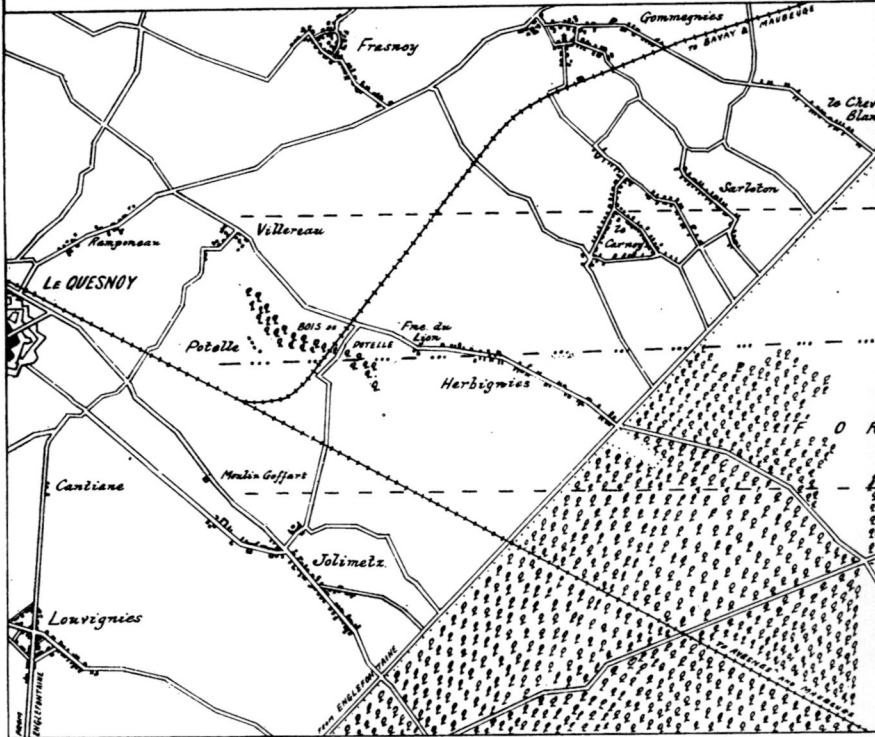

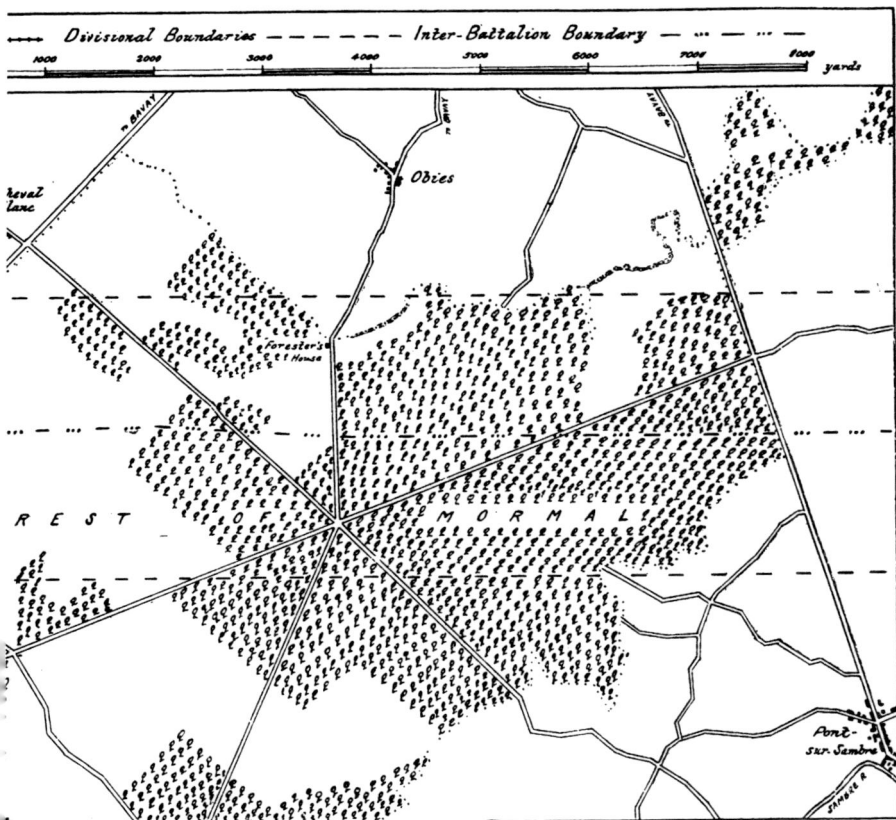

Obies

Cheval
Blanc

Forester's
House

F O R E S T   O F   M O R M A L

Pont-
sur-Sambre

permanently stationed at the dye-works at Leverkusen, four miles north of Mülheim, to provide guards over a large store of high-explosives there. The 13th Company of the 2nd Canterbury Battalion was detailed to perform this duty when the brigade arrived at Mülheim; and was afterwards relieved by a company of the 1st Battalion.

The smaller permanent guards and the usual battalion and company guards and fatigue parties, provided by the remaining companies of the two battalions, kept the majority of the men fully employed. In addition there was drill, physical training, and route marching in the mornings. In the afternoons leave was granted to all ranks to be absent from barracks; this leave extended at first to Cologne, but later on only a limited number of men were allowed passes to the city.

A special trip by steamer, up the Rhine as far as Königs-winter, took place on January 2nd; and small parties with guides were daily taken to Bonn, and round the sights of Cologne.

Christmas was celebrated by both battalions with as near an approach to festivity as was possible, though transport difficulties had prevented the arrival of the turkeys ordered months before. These arrived in time for the New Year, when the real Christmas dinner was held. Meanwhile, Lieutenant-Colonel Stitt had returned to the 1st Battalion as Commanding officer, on Lieutenant-Colonel Row's departure to a course at Camberley; and Major N. R. Wilson resumed command of the 2nd Battalion, with the temporary rank of Lieutenant-Colonel.

On January 4th and 6th the 2nd Brigade practised the action to be taken by it, as laid down by Division, in the event of rioting by civilians. The battalions marched out in battle order, and took possession of the telegraph offices, railway stations, and other points of strategic importance. As a demonstration of strength, the practice made an obvious impression on the people of the district.

The educational classes promoted by the New Zealand Expeditionary Force began on January 17th, and thenceforward all ranks, when not engaged in purely military duties, were given the opportunity of preparing themselves for their return to civil life. The aims of those responsible for the educational scheme

w

were unfortunately frustrated, to a great extent, by the rapidity of the demobilisation of the Division.

January 18th and 19th were notable by reason of a visit by His Royal Highness the Prince of Wales. On the afternoon of the 18th all the officers of the two battalions were present at the 1st Battalion's Officers' Mess, when the Prince paid an informal visit and took tea with the officers. The following day His Royal Highness, accompanied by the Divisional and Brigade Commanders, attended Church Parade at the 1st Battalion's barracks, and afterwards inspected the brigade in the barrack square.

The beginning of the end of the Canterbury Regiment of the New Zealand Expeditionary Force came on December 26th, when the first draft for demobilisation marched out from the 1st Battalion. A small draft from the 2nd Battalion followed on January 6th, and drafts from both battalions left on the 14th and 28th. Men on leave from the New Zealand Division were retained in England, and further reduced the strength of the battalions.

In accordance with the scheme of demobilisation, the two Canterbury Battalions were amalgamated on February 3rd, their strength at that date being: — 1st Battalion, thirty-two officers and five hundred and eighty-seven other ranks; 2nd Battalion, thirty-two officers and six hundred and thirty-six other ranks. The new battalion was lodged in the barracks formerly occupied by the 1st Battalion, and was commanded by Lieutenant-Colonel A. D. Stitt, with Major N. R. Wilson as Second in Command, and Captain M. R. Walker* as Adjutant.

During the month of February large drafts marched out, on the 4th, 11th, 18th, and 25th, so that on the 27th the battalion strength was reduced to twenty-nine officers and four hundred and ninety-nine other ranks. On this date the battalion amalgamated with the Otago Battalion to form a South Island Battalion, under the command of Lieutenant-Colonel Stitt. Further large drafts left during the month of March, on the 4th, 11th, and 18th; and on March 25th the final draft left for England.

---

* This officer had been Adjutant of the 2nd Battalion since the Somme, 1916, continuously, except for a break at the beginning of 1918, when he was in hospital owing to the effect of gas poisoning. He had thus filled the office of Battalion Adjutant for a longer period than any other officer in the Division.

The end of the Canterbury Regiment as a unit of the New Zealand Expeditionary Force may therefore be said to have arrived on February 27th, though the infantry battalions were not officially disbanded till March 25th. On reaching England the men of the Regiment were drafted to various camps, according to their ports of disembarkation in New Zealand, but the Regiment was represented in the march of the Overseas troops through London on May 3rd, when a draft of two hundred men from Number 1 Camp, Sling, was on parade.

APPENDIX "A."

THE CANTERBURY REGIMENT AT SLING.

[Based on material contributed by Major R. A. R. Lawry, O.B.E. (Canterbury Regiment) Staff Captain 4th New Zealand Infantry (Reserve) Brigade].

When in April, 1916, the New Zealand Division was transferred from Egypt to France, there was left behind in Egypt, with a specially selected staff of officers and non-commissioned officers, the nucleus of a Training Battalion for each Infantry Brigade. The 1st and 2nd Brigade training battalions each consisted of Auckland, Canterbury, Otago, and Wellington companies, each company to supply reinforcements for the corresponding service battalion. The 3rd Brigade Training Battalion consisted of New Zealand Rifle Brigade personnel only.

In order to facilitate administration, it was decided to transfer the Base and Training Depôt to England. Sling Camp, near Bulford, Salisbury Plain, where the British section of the New Zealand Expeditionary Force was encamped in 1914, was allotted for this purpose; and the training battalions, together with other arms of the service, numbering in all forty-one officers and seven hundred and four other ranks, left Alexandria on May 31st, 1916, disembarked at Plymouth on June 10th, and arrived the same day at Sling, where each unit was accommodated in a separate hutted camp. The Canterbury companies of the 1st and 2nd Brigade Training Battalions were commanded by Captain A. F. R. Rohloff and 2nd Lieutenant C. F. Carey respectively.

Next day Colonel V. S. Smyth, N.Z.S.C., took command of the Depôt, which was thereafter known as the New Zealand Reserve Group. Training under unit commanders began at once, and arrangements were made for the training of infantry officers and non-commissioned officers at various schools of instruction in the Southern Command. Those who obtained first-class passes were appointed instructors at Sling in their respective subjects.

A few days later the 1st and 2nd Brigade Training Battalions were re-organized—the former to consist of North Island troops and the latter of South Island troops. The South Island Battalion, under the command of Major G. Mitchell, Otago Regiment, was known in future as the 3rd (Reserve) Battalion Canterbury-Otago Regiments, and comprised two companies for each of those Regiments.

On August 12th the strength of the Group having increased, owing to the arrival of the 12th and 13th Reinforcements and sundry drafts from the New Zealand Command Depôt at Codford, to over one hundred and sixty officers and three thousand six hundred other ranks, the reserve companies for each Infantry Regiment were re-organized into separate Reserve Battalions, the 3rd (Reserve) Battalion Canterbury Regiment being under the command of Colonel G. J. Smith, T.D., Canterbury Regiment.

Reinforcements at the rate of approximately one thousand per month continued to arrive from New Zealand, where they had received from eight to sixteen weeks' elementary training. On arrival at Sling a reinforcement lost its identity as such, and was absorbed into the various Regiments of the New Zealand Expeditionary Force, as far as possible in accordance with the districts in New Zealand where the men normally resided. They immediately commenced a course of training, the duration of which varied according to the urgency of the demand from France.

Men from New Zealand or from hospital who had had previous service overseas were posted to their original regiments, and received a short refresher course, chiefly in musketry and trench warfare. All troops were graded in platoons according to the degree of efficiency attained, backward men being set back into less advanced platoons. The training was severe, lasting from 6.30 a.m. until 9 p.m., often seven days a week, but the health of the troops was excellent.

Good rifle ranges, a live bombing ground, and a gas chamber were available in the immediate vicinity, and the large areas of undulating War Department land alongside the camp were eminently suitable for training in field operations by day and by night. Large vehicle sheds and gutted stables and three covered miniature ranges were used for indoor instruction in wet weather.

Owing to the heavy casualties to the Division during the Battle of the Somme, 1916, the demand for reinforcements during this period was very great, and training was reduced to an intensified course covering from eight to twenty-eight days, according to the demand. To economise in administrative staffs, the double-battalion organisation was soon resumed, Colonel G. J. Smith, T.D., commanding the Canterbury-Otago Battalion. When the demand for reinforcements again became normal, each draft arriving from New Zealand was given four weeks' training at Sling.

On March 29th, 1917, Colonel G. J. Smith was appointed Officer in Charge of Administration, New Zealand Reserve Group, and Major J. L. Saunders, D.S.O., Otago Regiment, succeeded him as Commanding Officer of the 3rd (Reserve) Battalion Canterbury-Otago Regiments.

In April, 1917, the 4th New Zealand Infantry Brigade was formed for service in France, and the creation of a 3rd Service Battalion for each Infantry Regiment necessitated that the 3rd (Reserve) Battalion should in future be known as the 4th (Reserve) Battalion.

On July 30th, 1917, Major J. L. Saunders was appointed G.S.O. of the New Zealand Reserve Group, and Major C. B. Brereton (Canterbury Regiment) assumed command of the 4th (Reserve) Battalion Canterbury-Otago Regiments. In August of that year separate Reserve Battalions for each of the four Regiments were again established; and Major Brereton remained in command of the Canterbury Battalion until succeeded by Lieutenant-Colonel G. C. Griffiths on October 6th, 1917.

It had always been held that the four weeks' course of training at Sling was not sufficient to produce the standard of efficiency required in France. Owing to the great distance of New Zealand from the theatre of war, the training there was as not up-to-date and complete as it would otherwise have been, and much of the training at Sling was necessarily of an elementary nature. Towards the end of 1917, therefore, the course was lengthened to eight weeks, with very satisfactory results.

At the beginning of 1918 a system of exchange of officers between the service and reserve battalions was brought into force. Instead of the company commanders at Sling being selected from officers who were passing through the reserve battalion on their way to rejoin their service battalions, they were now sent over from the service battalions on a four months' tour of duty with the reserve battalion. By this means, the latest ideas in the field reached the reserve battalion more quickly than had hitherto been the case.

Lieutenant-Colonel O. H. Mead succeeded Lieutenant-Colonel Griffiths as Commanding Officer of the Canterbury Battalion on July 5th, 1918, on the latter being appointed Commanding Officer of the New Zealand Command Depôt at Codford.

On January 1st, 1919, the Canterbury Battalion was reorganized into the Canterbury District Repatriation Detachment for all arms of the service, Lieutenant-Colonel Mead remaining in command until August 14th, when the detachment was disbanded, the final details being transferred to other detachments.

APPENDIX "B."

Showing the dispositions of the Canterbury Battalions when in the front line trenches, from the arrival of the New Zealand Division in France to the end of the winter of 1917-1918.

Battalion.	Date in.	Relieved.	Date Out.	Relieved by.
2nd	1916. 15/16 May	9th Northumb F.	23/24 May	2/3/N.Z. (R.) B. *
1st	20/21 May	1/W.I.R. †	25/26 May	(inter-coy.)
1st	25/26 May	(inter-coy.)	28/29 May	1/W.I.R.
2nd	2/3 June	2/3/N.Z. (R.) B.	20/21 June	2/A.I.R. ‡
1st	9/10 June	1/A.I.R.	20/21 June	1/W.I.R.
1st	3/4 July	{ 1/W.I.R. { 1/W.I.R.	15/16 July	1/A.I.R. (partial)
1st	15/16 July	——	7/8 Aug.	1/W.I.R.
1st	5/6 Aug.	1/A.I.R.	7/8 Aug.	1/W.I.R.
2nd	8/9 July	2/A.I.R.	16/17 July	2/A.I.R.
2nd	27/28 July	2/A.I.R.	8/9 Aug.	2/A.I.R.
1st	13 Oct.	60th Batn. A.I.F.	25 Oct.	1/A.I.R.
1st	4 Nov.	1/A.I.R.	12 Nov.	1/A.I.R.
1st	20 Nov.	1/Auck. I.R.	28 Nov.	1/A.I.R.
1st	6 Dec.	1/Auck. I.R.	14 Dec.	1/A.I.R.
2nd	20 Oct.	2/Auck. I.R.	26 Oct.	2/A.I.R.
2nd	1 Nov.	2/Auck. I.R.	7 Nov.	2/A.I.R.
2nd	13 Nov.	2/Auck. I.R.	19 Nov.	2/A.I.R.
2nd	25 Nov.	2/Auck. I.R.	30 Nov. & 1 Dec.	37th Bn. A.I.F.

*King's Liverpool Regiment.   †Royal Irish Rifles.   ‡3rd Battalion, Otago Infantry Regiment.

Note.—A change from one sector to another is indicated by a horizontal line across the page. The various sectors were as follows :—

Armentières, May to August, 1916.
Messines to the River Lys—March to August, 1917.
Sailly, October, 1916, to February, 1917.
Ypres Salient—September, 1917, to February, 1918.
Armentières—(2nd Battalion only), October to December, 1916.

The dispositions for subsequent trench warfare will be found in Appendix " C."

1st.	2nd.	12th.	13th.
Vancouver and S.P.Z.	R. Front Line (Pont Ballot 78 & 79)	L. Front Line (Pont Ballot 80 & 81)	Subsidiary
R. Front line (68, 69, & parts 67) & R. and Cent. Support	L. & Cent. Front (70, 71 & 72) & L. Support	Subsidiary	Subsidiary
Subsidiary	Subsidiary	R. Front & R. & Cent. Support	L. & Cent. Front & L. Support

(No record ; on 7th frontage extended to north by addition of Trenches 82 and 83)

(No record)

R. Front (No. 1 & 2 Localities) & Right Suppt.	R. Cent. Suppts.	L. Centre Front (No. 3 Local.) & L. Cent. Sup.	L. Front (Nos. 4 & 4a Localities) & L. Support
R. Front (No. 1 & 2 Localities) & R. Support	R. Cent. Suppts.	Battaln Reserve (Subsidiary)	Brigade Reserve (Subsidiary)
R. Front (No. 1 & 2 Localities) & R. Support	R. Cent. Suppts.	L. Centre Front (No. 3 Local.) & L. Cent. Sup.	L. Front (Nos. 4 & 4a Localities) & L. Support

(No record)

(No record)

R. Front & Support lines	C. Front & Support lines	L. Front & Supt.	Reserve
Reserve	C. Front & Support lines	L. Front & Support lines	R. Front & Supt.
L. Front & Supt.	C. Front & Support lines	Reserve	R. Front & Supt.
L. Front & Supt.	Reserve	C. Front & Supt.	R. Front & Supt.

Vancouver and S.P.Z.	R. Front line	Cent. Front line	L. Front line
R. Front line	Cent. Front line	L. Front line	Vancouver and S.P.Z.
Cent. Front line	Left Front line	Vancouver and S.P.Z.	R. Front line
L. Front line	Vancouver and S.P.Z.	R. Front line	Centre Front line

Battalion.	Date in.	Relieved.	Date Out.	Relieved by.
2nd	1917. 1 Jan.	2/Auck. I.R.	9 Jan.	1/C.I.R.
1st	9 Jan.	2/C.I.R.	17 Jan.	2/C.I.R.
2nd	17 Jan.	1/C.I.R.	23 Jan.	1/3/N.Z.(R.)B.
1st	26/27 Jan.	16th Royal Scots	3/4 Feb.	2/C.I.R.
2nd	3/4 Feb.	1/C.I.R.	11/12 Feb.	1/C.I.R.
1st	11/12 Feb.	2/C.I.R.	19 Feb.	2/C.I.R.
2nd	19 Feb.	1/C.I.R.	26 Feb.	2/10/K.L.R. *
1st	12 Mar.	9th Bn.R.I.R.†	20 Mar.	2/C.I.R.
2nd	20 Mar.	1/C.I.R.	28 Mar.	1/C.I.R.
1st	28 Mar.	2/C.I.R.	{ 6 Apr. { 6/7 Apr.	1/W.I.R. (L) } 1/A.I.R. (R) }
2nd	22 May	2/3/N.Z.(R.) B.	30 May	1/C.I.R.
1st	30 May	2/C.I.R.	2 June	1/O.IR.
3rd	10/11 June	2/5 Lyl. N. Lanc.	13/14 June	2/C.I.R. 4/3/N.Z.(R.)B.
3rd	30 June/ 1 July	3/O.I.R. ‡	8 July	3/A.I.R.
3rd	23/24 July	2/O.I.R.	31 July/ 1 Aug.	3/A.I.R.
3rd	6/7 Aug.	3/A.I.R.	16/17 Aug.	3/A.I.R.
3rd	24/25 Aug.	3/A.I.R.	31 Aug./ 1 Sept.	2nd Bn. Devon. Regt.
1st	19/20 July	Pts. 49th & 50th Bns. A.I.F.	29/30 July	1/O.I.R.
2nd	5/6 Aug.	2/O.I.R.	8/9 Aug.	(inter-coy.)
2nd	8/9 Aug.	(inter-coy.)	10/11 Aug.	(inter-coy.)
2nd	10/11 Aug.	(inter-coy.)	11/12 Aug.	(inter-coy.)
2nd	11/12 Aug.	(inter-coy.)	13/14 Aug.	(inter-coy.)
2nd	13/14 Aug.	(inter-coy.)	14/15 Aug.	(inter-coy.)
2nd	14/15 Aug.	(inter-coy.)	16/17 Aug.	(inter-coy.)

*2nd Battalion 3rd N.Z. (Rifle) Brigade.   †1st Battalion, Wellington Infantry Regiment.   ‡1st Battalion, Auckland Infantry Regiment.

1st	2nd	12th	13th
Reserve	R. Front & Supt.	C. Front & Supt.	L. Front & Supt.
R. Front & Supt.	C. Front & Supt.	L. Front & Supt.	Reserve
R. Front & Supt.	C. Front & Supt.	L. Front & Supt.	Reserve
Subsidiary	R. Front & Supt.	C. Front & Support (moved to Posts on 31st Jan.)	L. Front & Supt.
L. Front & Supt.	Posts (Res.)	Subsidiary	R. Front & Supt.
R. Front & Supt.	Subsidiary	L. Front & Supt.	Posts (Reserve)
Posts (Res.)	L. Front & Supt.	R. Front & Supt.	Subsidiary
Reserve	Right Front	Support	Left Front
Right Front	Right Support	Left Support	Left Front
Right Front	Left Support	Left Front	Right Support
Reserve	Right Front	Left Front	Support
Support	Left Front	Reserve	Right Front
(No details)			
Reserve	Right	Centre	Left
Right Front	Reserve	Support	Left Front
Support	Right Front	Left Front	Reserve
Right Front	Support	Reserve	Left Front
Subsidiary	Subsidiary	Front line posts	Supports
Left Front	Reserve	Support	Right Front
Support	Right Front	Left Front	Reserve
Left Front	Right Front	Support	Reserve
Left Front	Reserve	Support	Right Front
Support	Reserve	Left Front	Right Front
Support	Right Front	Left Front	Reserve

Battalion.	Date in.	Relieved.	Date out.	Relieved by.
2nd	16/17 Aug.	(inter-coy.)	17/18 Aug.	1/W.I.R.
1st	7/8 Aug.	1/O.I.R.	12/13 Aug.	(inter-coy.)
1st	12/13 Aug.	(inter-coy.)	17/18 Aug.	2/A.I.R.
2nd	29/30 Sept.	2/5 South Staffs.	2/3 Oct.	1/W.I.R.
2nd	25/26 Nov.	1/1/ Herts.	29/30 Nov.	(inter-coy.)
2nd	29/30 Nov.	4/5/ Blk. Watch (inter-coy.)	1/2 Dec.	{ 1/O.I.R. 1/C.I.R. }
3rd	21/22 Nov.	3/A.I.R.	1/2 Dec.	4/3/N.Z.(R.)B.
1st	9/10 Dec.	{ 1/3 N.Z. (R) B. 4/3 do. } pts.	12/13 Dec.	(inter-coy.)
1st	12/13 Dec.	(inter-coy.)	15/16 Dec.	3/C.I.R.
2nd	15/16 Dec.	3/3/N.Z.(R.)B.	18/19 Dec.	(inter-coy.)
2nd	18/19 Dec.	(inter-coy.)	22/23 Dec.	3/O.I.R.
3rd	15/16 Dec.	1/C.I.R.	22/23 Dec.	1/C.I.R.
1st	22/23 Dec.	3/C.I.R.	27/28 Dec.	3/C.I.R.
3rd	27/28 Dec.	1/C.I.R.	1918. 2/3 Jan.	3/3/N.Z.(R.)B.
1st	1918. 8/9 Jan.	3/3/N.Z.(R.)B.	14/15 Jan.	3/3/N.Z.(R.)B.
2nd	14/15 Jan.	1/3/N.Z.(R.)B.	20/21 Jan.	2/A.I.R.
1st	20/21 Jan.	3/3/N.Z.(R.)B.	23/24 Jan.	(inter-coy.)
1st	23/24 Jan.	(inter-coy.)	26/27 Jan.	1/W.I.R.
2nd	26/27 Jan.	2/A.I.R.	1/2 Feb.	2/A.I.R.
1st	8/9 Feb.	1/3/N.Z.(R.)B.	12/13 Feb.	(inter-coy.)
1st	12/13 Feb.	(inter-coy.)	15/16 Feb.	2/C.I.R.
2nd	15/16 Feb.	1/C.I.R.	18/19 Feb.	(inter-coy.)
2nd	18/19 Feb.	(inter-coy.)	22/23 Feb.	1/6/West Riding

1st.	2nd.	12th.	13th.
Left Front	Reserve	Support	Right Front
Left Front	Right Front	Support	Support
Support	Support	Left Front	Right Front
(No details)			
Support	Reserve	Right Front	Left Front
Right Front	Left Front	Support	Reserve
(No details)			
Support	Left Front	Reserve	Right Front
Right Front	Reserve	Left Front	Support
Front	Support	Reserve	Support
Reserve	Support	Front	Support
Reserve	Right Front	Left Front	Support
Support	Left Front	Reserve	Right Front
1918. Right Front	Support	Reserve	Left Front
Support	Left Front	Reserve	Right Front
R. Front & Supt.	L. Front & Supt.	Reserve	Reserve
R. Front & Supt.	L. Front & Supt.	Support	Reserve
Reserve	Support	Left Front	Right Front
Reserve	Reserve	Right Front	Left Front
Support	Left Front	Reserve	Right Front
Right Front	Reserve	Left Front	Support
Right Front	Left Front	Support	Reserve
Support	Reserve	Right Front	Left Front

APPENDIX " C."

Dispositions of the Canterbury Battalions when in the front line trenches, from April, 1918 to the final offensive.

Battn.	Date in	Date out	Companies in Line		Coy. in Support	Coy. in Reserve
			Right	Left		
	1918	1918				
1st	17/18 April	22/23 April	1st	12th	13th	2nd
2nd	22/23 April	27/28 April	2nd	1st	13th	12th
1st	27/28 April	30 Apr./1 May	13th	2nd	1st	12th
2nd	6/7 May	9/10 May	12th	13th	{ 2nd (R) { 1st (L)	
2nd	9/10 May	12/13 May	2nd	1st	{ 12th (R) { 13th (L)	
1st	12/13 May	15/16 May	1st	12th	2nd	13th
1st	15/16 May	18/19 May	13th	2nd	12th	1st
2nd	24/25 May	1/2 June	13th	12th	2nd	1st
1st	1/2 June	7/8 June	1st	12th	13th	2nd
1st	9/10 July	14/15 July	2nd	13th	12th	1st
1st	14/15 July	17/18 July	1st	12th	13th	2nd
2nd	9/10 July	17/18 July	12th	13th	2nd	1st
1st	2/3 August	6/7 August	2nd	13th	1st	12th
2nd	2/3 August	10/11 August	1st	2nd	13th	12th

APPENDIX "D."

Locations of Battalions when out of the line in France.

Arrived.	Battalion.	Place.	Left.
1916.			
15 April	1st	Morbecque	9 May
12 April	2nd	Roquetoire	1 May
1 May	2nd	Neuf Berquin	14 May
14 May	2nd	Armentières	15 May
9 May	1st	Estaires	13 May
13 May	1st	Armentières	20 May
23 May	2nd	Armentières	2 June
28 May	1st	Armentières	9 June
27 June	1st	Armentières	3 July
16 July	2nd	Armentières and Houplines ..	27 July
15 Aug.	1st	Armentières	16 Aug.
17 Aug.	2nd	Armentières	18 Aug.
16 Aug.	1st	Wardrecques	20 Aug.
18 Aug.	2nd	Blaringhem	21 Aug.
21 Aug.	1st	Merelessart	2 Sept.
21 Aug.	2nd	Allery	2 Sept.
2 Sept.	1st	Airaines	3 Sept.
3 Sept.	1st	La Chaussée	7 Sept.
7 Sept.	1st	Coisy	8 Sept.
8 Sept.	1st	Dernancourt	10 Sept.
10 Sept.	1st	Fricourt	14 Sept.
2 Sept.	2nd	Le Mesge	3 Sept.
3 Sept.	2nd	Picquigny	7 Sept.
7 Sept.	2nd	Cardonette	8 Sept.
8 Sept.	2nd	Camp south of Lavieville ..	10 Sept.
10 Sept.	2nd	Fricourt Wood	12 Sept.
4 Oct.	1st	Pommiers Redoubt	7 Oct.
8 Oct.	1st	Longpré	11 Oct.
12 Oct.	1st	Estaires	13 Oct.
3 Oct.	2nd	Fricourt	6 Oct.
6 Oct.	2nd	Bailleul-sur-Somme	11 Oct.
11 Oct.	2nd	Strazeele	14 Oct.
14 Oct.	2nd	Armentières	14 Oct.
25 Oct.	1st	Rue des Fiefs	4 Nov.
26 Oct.	2nd	Armentières	1 Nov.
12 Nov.	1st	Rue des Fiefs	20 Nov.
28 Nov.	1st	Rue des Fiefs	6 Dec.
30 Nov.	2nd	Armentières (½ battalion) ..	1 Dec.
1 Dec.	2nd	Estaires	23 Dec.
14 Dec.	1st	Rue des Fiefs	23 Dec.
23 Dec.	1st	Estaires	1 Jan. 1917
23 Dec.	2nd	Rue des Fiefs	1 Jan.

Arrived.	Battalion.	Place.	Left.
1917.			
1 Jan.	1st	Rue des Fiefs	9 Jan.
9 Jan.	2nd	Rue des Fiefs	17 Jan.
17 Jan.	1st	Rue des Fiefs	24 Jan.
24 Jan.	1st	Estaires	26 Jan.
24 Jan.	2nd	Estaires	26 Jan.
26 Jan.	2nd	Rue Delpierre and Erquinghem ..	3 Feb.
3 Feb.	1st	Rue Delpierre and Erquinghem ..	11 Feb.
11 Feb.	2nd	Rue Delpierre and Erquinghem ..	20 Feb.
20 Feb.	1st	Rue Delpierre and Erquinghem ..	25 Feb.
25 Feb.	1st	Estaires	26 Feb.
26 Feb.	1st	Nieppe	12 March
26 Feb.	2nd	Sailly (Rue des Fiefs) ..	5 March
5 March	2nd	Romarin	14 March
14 March	2nd	Red Lodge	20 March
20 March	1st	Red Lodge	28 March
28 March	2nd	Red Lodge	5 April
5 April	2nd	Romarin	16 April
6 April	1st	Nieppe	16 April
16 April	1st	Pradelles	17 April
16 April	2nd	Grand Sec Bois ..	17 April
17 April	1st	Wallon Cappel ..	18 April
17 April	2nd	Lynde	18 April
18 April	1st	Tatinghem	1 May
18 April	2nd	Setques and Quelmes ..	1 May
1 May	1st	Wallon Cappel ..	2 May
1 May	2nd	Lynde	2 May
2 May	1st	Pradelles ..	3 May
2 May	2nd	Grand Sec Bois ..	3 May
3 May	2nd	Romarin	22 May
3 May	1st	Bulford Camp, Neuve Eglise ..	10 May
10 May	1st	Nieppe	22 May
22 May	1st	Hill 63	29 May
29 May	2nd	Red Lodge	2 June
29 May	3rd	Sanvic, Le Havre ..	30 May
30 May	3rd	Ballieul	6 June
2 June	1st	Canteen Corner ..	5 June
3 June	2nd	Canteen Corner ..	6 June
5 June	1st	Hill 63	6 June
7 June	3rd	Kandahar Farm ..	10 June
9 June	1st	Forfar Camp, Neuve Eglise ..	12 June
9 June	2nd	Crucifix Camp, Neuve Eglise ..	12 June
12 June	1st	Catacombs, Hill 63 ..	15 June
13 June	3rd	Pont de Nieppe ..	19 June
15 June	1st	(12th and 13th Coys.) Hill 63 ..	18 June
15 June	2nd	Catacombs, Hill 63 ..	18 June
18 June	1st	Bulford Camp ..	28 June
18 June	2nd	Romarin	29 June
19 June	3rd	Nieppe	22 June
22 June	3rd	Brune Gaye	30 June
28 June	1st	Aldershot Camp, Neuve Eglise ..	12 July
29 June	2nd	Regina Camp	7 July
7 July	2nd	Canteen Corner ..	12 July
8 July	3rd	Nieppe	23 July
12 July	1st	Doulieu	18 July
12 July	2nd	Neuf Berquin	19 July
18 July	1st	Catacombs	19 July

Arrived. 1917.	Battalion.	Place.	Left.
19 July	2nd	Romarin	5 Aug.
29 July	1st	Regina Camp (1st Co. at Catacombs)	7 Aug.
31 July	3rd	Support Farm and Brune Gaye ..	8 Aug.
16 Aug.	3rd	Support Farm and Brune Gaye ..	24 Aug.
17 Aug.	1st	Bulford Camp	21 Aug.
17 Aug.	2nd	Nieppe	22 Aug.
21 Aug.	1st	Caudescure	28 Aug.
22 Aug.	2nd	Caudescure	28 Aug.
28 Aug.	1st	Lumbres	29 Aug.
29 Aug.	1st	Coulomby	25 Sept.
29 Aug.	2nd	Bayenghem	25 Sept.
31 Aug.	3rd	Bulford Camp	2 Sept.
2 Sept.	3rd	Coulomby	3 Sept.
3 Sept.	3rd	Surques	25 Sept.
25 Sept.	1st	Arques	26 Sept.
26 Sept.	1st	Queue d'Oxelaere	27 Sept.
27 Sept.	1st	Watou	28 Sept.
28 Sept.	1st	Goldfish Chateau	29 Sept.
25 Sept.	2nd	Renescure	26 Sept.
26 Sept.	2nd	Terdeghem	27 Sept.
27 Sept.	2nd	Watou	28 Sept.
28 Sept.	2nd	Old German Front line near Wieltje	29 Sept.
25 Sept.	3rd	Bayenghem	26 Sept.
26 Sept.	3rd	Campagne	27 Sept.
27 Sept.	3rd	Eecke	29 Sept.
29 Sept.	3rd	Watou	1 Oct.
1 Oct.	3rd	Goldfish Chateau	2 & 3 Oct.
2 Oct.	1st	Old German Front line near Wieltje	4 Oct.
2 Oct.	2nd	Wieltje	5 Oct.
4 Oct.	1st	Bank Farm	5 Oct.
5 Oct.	1st	Winnezeele	7 Oct.
7 Oct.	1st	Godewaeresvelde	10 Oct.
5 Oct.	2nd	Winnezeele	7 Oct.
5 Oct.	3rd	Goldfish Chateau	6 Oct.
6 Oct.	3rd	Eecke	11 Oct.
7 Oct.	2nd	Eecke	10 Oct.
10 Oct.	1st	"Y" Area, Ypres	10 Oct.
10 Oct.	2nd	"Y" Area, Ypres	10 Oct.
10 Oct.	1st	Bank Farm	11 Oct.
10 Oct.	2nd	(less 2 coys.) Old German Front line south of Wieltje Road ..	11 Oct.
10 Oct.	2nd	(2 coys.) near Korek & Boethoek ..	11 Oct.
11 Oct.	3rd	"Y" Camp St. Jean Sector ..	12 Oct.
12 Oct.	3rd	Pommern Redoubt	14 Oct.
14 Oct.	1st	Bank Farm	16 Oct.
14 Oct.	2nd	Capricorn Trenches	16 Oct.
16 Oct.	1st	Old British Front Line	21 Oct.
16 Oct.	2nd	Cambrai Support	21 Oct.
19 Oct.	3rd	Pommern Redoubt—Spree Farm ..	21 Oct.
21 Oct.	1st	Coulomby	23 Oct.
21 Oct.	2nd	Bayenghem	23 Oct.
21 Oct.	3rd	St. Jean Area	22 Oct.
22 Oct.	3rd	Journy	12 Nov.
23 Oct.	1st	Lottinghem	13 Nov.
23 Oct.	2nd	Quesques and Verval	13 Nov.
12 Nov.	3rd	Chateau Belge	16 Nov.

Arrived.	Battalion.	Place	Left.
1917.			
13 Nov.	1st	Coulomby	14 Nov.
13 Nov.	2nd	Setques	14 Nov.
14 Nov.	1st	Reninghelst	16 Nov.
14 Nov.	2nd	Reninghelst	16 Nov.
16 Nov.	1st	"A"Camp, Kruisstraathoek ..	25 Nov.
16 Nov.	2nd	Forester Camp	25 Nov.
16 Nov.	3rd	Railway Dugouts	21 Nov.
25 Nov.	3rd	Walker Camp	1 & 2 Dec.
1 Dec.	3rd	Dickebusch Huts	15 Dec.
1 Dec.	2nd	(Bn. H.Q. & 12th) Walker Camp ..	5 Dec.
1 Dec.	2nd	(1st & 2nd Coys.) Forester Camp	2 Dec.
2 Dec.	2nd	(1st, 2nd & 13th) Walker Camp ..	5 Dec.
5 Dec.	2nd	Halfway House and Railway Wood Dugout	9 Dec.
6 Dec.	1st	Howe Camp	9 Dec.
15 Dec.	1st	Howe Camp	20 Dec.
20 Dec.	1st	New Hutting Camp	22 Dec.
22 Dec.	3rd	Warrington Hutments	27 Dec.
27 Dec.	1st	Howe Camp	8 Jan. 1918
27 Dec.	2nd	Dickebusch Huts	8 Jan.
1918			
2 Jan.	3rd	Warrington Camp	8 Jan.
8 Jan.	3rd	Dickebusch Huts	not recorded
14 Jan.	1st	Manawatu Camp	20 Jan.
not recorded	3rd	Belgian Chateau	not recorded
26 Jan.	1st	Halfway House and Railway Wood Dugouts	1 Feb.
1 Feb.	1st	Howe Camp	8 Feb.
1 Feb.	2nd	Dickebusch Huts	8 Feb.
8 Feb.	2nd	Railway Wood Dugouts and Otago Camp	15 Feb.
15 Feb.	1st	Hussar Camp East & Sapper Camp	21 Feb.
21 Feb.	1st	Railway Wood Dugouts and West Farm Camp	22 Feb.
22 Feb.	1st	Belgian Chateau	23 Feb.
22 Feb.	2nd	West Farm Camp	23 Feb.
23 Feb.	1st	St. Marie Cappel	8 March
23 Feb.	2nd	St. Sylvestre Cappel	8 March
8 March	1st	Campagne	9 March
8 March	2nd	Wardrecques	9 March
9 March	1st	Houlle	16 March
9 March	2nd	Houlle	16 March
16 March	1st	Campagne	17 March
16 March	2nd	Wardrecques	17 March
17 March	1st	St. Marie Cappel	24 March
17 March	2nd	St. Sylvestre Cappel	24 March
25 March	1st	Morlancourt	25 March
25 March	2nd	Ville-sous-Corbie	25 March
26 March	1st	Hédauville	26 March
26 March	2nd	Hédauville	26 March
29 March	2nd	Bde Support line—Auchonvillers Englebelmer	2 April
30 March	1st	Bde. Res. Englebelmer	3 April
6 April	2nd	Bde. Support line—Auchonvillers-Engelbelmer	13 April
7 April	1st	Bde. Res. Englebelmer	13 April

Arrived.	Battalion.	Place.	Left.
1918.			
13 April	1st	Purple Line—Bertrancourt ..	17 April
13 April	2nd	Between Bus-les-Artois and Sailly-au-Bois	17 April
17 April	2nd	Bde. Support east of Colincamps ..	22 April
23 April	1st	Bde. Res., near Colincamps ..	27 April
28 April	2nd	Bde. Support east of Colincamps ..	30 April
1 May	1st	N.E. of Bertrancourt	6 May
1 May	2nd	Sailly-au-Bois	6 May
6 May	1st	Hébuterne	12 May
13 May	2nd	Sailly-au-Bois	18 May
19 May	1st	Purple Line between Hébuterne and Sailly	24 May
19 May	2nd	Between Bus and Sailly	24 May
24 May	1st	Bde. Reserve in front of Colincamps	1 June
1 June	2nd	Bde. Suport, east of Colincamps ..	7 June
8 June	1st	St. Leger-les-Authie	22 June
8 June	2nd	Authie	22 June
22 June	1st	Between Bus and Sailly	2 July
22 June	2nd	Sailly & Chateau de la Haie switch	2 July
3 July	1st	Couin Wood	9 July
3 July	2nd	Coigneux	9 July
17 July	1st	Bde. Res. Gommecourt	25 July
17 July	2nd	Bde. Supt. Gommecourt-Pigeon Wd.	25 July
25 July	1st	Purple Line east of Sailly ..	2 Aug.
25 July	2nd	Coigneux	2 Aug.
7 Aug.	1st	Sarton	14 Aug.
11 Aug.	2nd	Sailly	14 Aug.
14 Aug.	1st	Vauchelles	18 Aug.
15 Aug.	2nd	Bde. Support east of Hébuterne..	18 Aug.
18 Aug.	1st	Couin	19 Aug.
18 Aug.	2nd	Coigneux	19 Aug.
19 Aug.	1st	St. Leger-les-Authie	21 Aug.
19 Aug.	2nd	Bois de Warnemont	21 Aug.
21 Aug.	1st	Chateau de la Haie Switch ..	23 Aug.
21 Aug.	2nd	Sailly	23 Aug.
23 Aug.	1st	Bucquoy	24 Aug.
23 Aug.	2nd	Bucquoy	24 Aug.
26 Aug.	2nd	Biefvillers	1 Sept.
27 Aug.	1st	Bihucourt	1 Sept.
1 Sept.	2nd	Fremicourt	3 Sept.
3 Sept.	1st	Bertincourt	5 Sept.
8 Sept.	1st	Ytres	11 Sept.
8 Sept.	2nd	West of Bertincourt	11 Sept.
11 Sept.	1st	Haplincourt Wood	14 Sept.
11 Sept.	2nd	Villers au Flos	14 Sept.
14 Sept.	1st	Biefvillers	26 Sept.
14 Sept.	2nd	Biefvillers	26 Sept
2 Oct.	1st	Neighbourhood of La Vacquerie ..	5 Oct.
10 Oct.	1st	Beauvois	22 Oct.
10 Oct.	2nd	Beauvois	22 Oct.
24 Oct.	1st	Vertigneul	4 Nov.
24 Oct.	2nd	Le Mesnil & Pont-à-Pierres Farms	28 Oct.
28 Oct.	2nd	Romeries	4 Nov.
5 Nov.	1st	Le Quesnoy	11 Nov.
5 Nov.	2nd	Le Quesnoy	11 Nov.
11 Nov.	1st	Quievy	12 Nov.
11 Nov.	2nd	Quievy	12 Nov.
12 Nov.	1st	Beauvois	28 Nov.
12 Nov.	2nd	Beauvois	28 Nov.

APPENDIX "E."

Showing the places at which the 1st and 2nd Canterbury Battalions were billetted on their march from Beauvois to the German frontier.

Date.		1st Battalion.			2nd Battalion.
Nov.	28	Vendegies-sur-Ecaillon		..	Vendegies-sur-Ecaillon
Nov.	29	Villers-Pol	..	..	Villers-Pol
Nov.	30 }	Hergies	..	..	Houdain
Dec.	2 }				
Dec.	3	Rousies	..	..	Cerfontaine
Dec.	4	Erquelinnes	..	..	Erquelinnes
Dec.	5 }	Thuin	..	..	Thuin
Dec.	6 }		..		
Dec.	7	Montignies-sur-Sambre		..	Montignies-sur-Sambre
Dec.	8	Auvelais	..	..	Auvelais
Dec.	9 }	Flawinne	..	..	Temploux
Dec.	10 }				
Dec.	11	Vedrin ..	..	..	Champion
Dec.	12	Bierwart	..	..	Waret-L'Evecque
Dec.	13 }	Ampsin	..	..	Amay
Dec.	16 }				
Dec.	17	Ougree (Liège) ..		..	Sclessin (Liège)
Dec.	18	Pepinster	..	..	Nessonvaux
Dec.	19	Baelen ..	..	..	Bilstain

APPENDIX "F."

HONOURS AND AWARDS.

Conferred on members of the Canterbury Regiment of the New Zealand Expeditionary Force.

Note.—This list was compiled by the Base Records Office, Wellington. The letters "L.G." followed by a number and date indicate the issue of the "London Gazette" in which the award is officially gazetted. The date has no reference to the date of the act for which the honour was awarded: no complete record of such dates has been kept in New Zealand.

Victoria Cross.

Rank and Name.	Authority.
24213 Private Nicholas, H. J.	L.G. 30471, 11/1/18

Commander of the Order of the Bath.

Lieutenant-Colonel Young, R., C.M.G., D.S.O.	L.G. 31370, 3/6/19

Commander of the Order of St. Michael and St. George.

Lieutenant-Colonel Griffiths, G. C.	L.G. 31377, 3/6/19
Lieutenant-Colonel Hughes, J. G., D.S.O.	L.G. 29438, 11/1/16
Lieutenant-Colonel Stewart, H., D.S.O., M.C.	L.G. 31370, 3/6/19
Lieutenant-Colonel Young, R., D.S.O.	L.G. 29438, 11/1/16

Bar to Distinguished Service Order.

Lieutenant-Colonel King, G. A., D.S.O.	L.G. 30450, 1/1/18)
Lieutenant-Colonel Stewart, H., D.S.O., M.C.	L.G. 30450, 1/1/18)

Distinguished Service Order.

Captain Critchley-Salmonson, A. C. B.	L.G. 29202, 3/7/15
Lieutenant-Colonel King, G. A.	L.G. 29608, 3/6/16
Lieutenant-Colonel Mead, O. H.	L.G. 31370, 3/6/19
Lieutenant-Colonel Row, R. A.	L.G. 30450, 1/1/18
Captain Starnes, F.	L.G. 29824, 14/11/16
Lieutenant-Colonel Stewart, H., M.C.	L.G. 30111, 4/6/17
Major Stitt, A. D., M.C.	L.G. 30450, 1/1/18
Major Wilson, N. R., M.C.	L.G. 31092, 1/1/19
Lieutenant-Colonel Young, R.	L.G. 29357, 5/11/15

Officers of the Order of the British Empire.

Major Lawry, R. A. R.	L.G. 31097, 1/1/19
Captain McGowan, H. E.	L.G. 31097, 1/1/19
Major Starnes, F., D.S.O.	L.G. 31210, 3/3/19

Members of the Order of the British Empire.

Honorary Lieutenant Osborne, W. H.	L.G. 31377, 3/6/19
Lieutenant West, T. S.	Cable, 3/2/20

Bar to Military Cross.

Lieutenant Johnston, H., M.C.	L.G. 31219, 8/3/19
Lieutenant McLeod, J. M. C., M.C.	L.G. 30901, 16/9/18

Military Cross.

Second Lieutenant Allen, J. E., M.M.	L.G. 31158, 1/2/19
Second Lieutenant Barton, J. M.	L.G. 30234, 16/8/17
Second Lieutenant Bennett, P. L.	L.G. 31183, 15/2/19
Lieutenant Bristol, I. A.	L.G. 30234, 16/8/17
Captain Brooker, S. W. B.	L.G. 30399, 26/11/17
Second Lieutenant Burt, H. D.	L.G. 31183, 15/2/19
Captain Campbell, H.	L.G. 31183, 15/2/19
Lieutenant Chisholm, J. S.	L.G. 31370, 3/6/19
Captain Dailey, G. C.	L.G. 30234, 16/8/17
Lieutenant Dean, A. G.	L.G. 30450, 1/1/18
Captain Dobson, D.	L.G. o f 1/1/17
Second Lieutenant Farquhar, A.	L.G. 30507, 4/2/18
Captain Fawcett, E. J.	L.G. 30399, 26/11/17
Lieutenant Ferguson, D.	L.G. 31043, 2/12/18
Lieutenant Fraser, J. W.	L.G. 31370, 3/6/19
Captain Free, C. W.	L.G. 30234, 16/8/17
Captain Fryer, H.	L.G. 31043, 2/12/18
Captain Gabites, H. S.	L.G. 30716, 3/6/18
Captain Gibbs, L. J.	L.G. 30716, 3/6/18
Lieutenant Gillies, T. S.	L.G. 30399, 26/11/17
Second Lieutenant Gray, C. A.	L.G. 30507, 4/2/18
Captain Gray, G. H.	L.G. 30507, 4/2/18
Second Lieutenant Gray, R. N.	L.G. 30507, 4/2/18
Captain Harley, H. S.	L.G. 29837, 25/11/16
Second Lieutenant Harper, N. R.	L.G. 30901, 16/9/18
Second Lieutenant Hartshorn, G.	L.G. 31158, 1/2/19
Lieutenant Hind, C. A. S.	L.G. 30813, 26/7/18
Second Lieutenant Holmes, C. H.	L.G. 30399, 26/11/17
Lieutenant Hunter, A. C. C.	L.G. 30507, 4/2/18
Captain Hutton, L. B.	L.G. 31183, 15/2/19
Second Lieutenant Iverach, J. A. D.	L.G. 31043, 2/12/18
Lieutenant Johnston, H.	L.G. 30507, 4/2/18
Captain Jones, L. F.	L.G. 31043, 2/12/18
Lieutenant McLeod, J. M. C.	L.G. 30716, 3/6/18
Second Lieutenant McQueen, J. A.	L.G. 30111, 4/6/17
Captain Merton, J. L. C.	L.G. of 1/1/17
Second Lieutenant Mitchell, J.	L.G. 31183, 15/2/19
Captain Morrison, M. J.	L.G. 30234, 16/8/17
Captain Natusch, S.	L.G. 30234, 16/8/17
Lieutenant Ponder, A. O.	L.G. 31183, 15/2/19
Lieutenant Rawlings, C. R.	L.G. 30399, 26/11/17
Lieutenant Rodger, W. J., D.C.M.	L.G. 31219, 8/3/19
Captain Rohloff, A. F. R.	L.G. 30399, 26/11/17
Captain Rutherfurd, T. W. L.	L.G. 30450, 1/1/18
Second Lieutenant Sinclair, F. J	L.G. 31119, 10/1/19
Captain Smith, S. G.	L.G. 31183, 15/2/19
Captain Stewart, H.	L.G. 29438, 11/1/16
Captain Stitt, A. D.	L.G. of 1/1/17
Captain Tonkin, J. F.	L.G. 30716, 3/6/18
Second Lieutenant Tremewen, W. B.	L.G. 31158, 1/2/19
Lieutenant Wales, J. G. C.	L.G. 30716, 3/6/18
Lieutenant Walker, M. R.	L.G. 30111, 4/6/17
Second Lieutenant Wilson, F. W.	L.G. 30399, 26/11/17
Captain Wilson, N. R.	L.G. 30450, 1/1/18

Distinguished Conduct Medal.

6/884	Sergt.	Atkin, A. A.	L.G. 29384, 26/11/15
15545	Corpl.	Auld, J. A.	L.G. 31186, 18/2/19
6/194	Private	Barlow, H.	L.G. 29286, 3/9/15
6/2960	L.-Cpl.	Burns, K. B.	L.G. 30601, 2/4/18
40191	L.-Cpl.	Coppell, M. H.	L.G. 31186, 18/2/19
22419	Sergt.	Cunneen, J. P.	L.G. 31225, 12/3/19
26253	Sergt.	De Boo, A. E.	L.G. 31370, 3/6/19
33705	Corpl.	Dodds, F. M.	L.G. 30983, 30/10/18
6/625	Sergt.	Ecclesfield, R. C.	L.G. 31186, 18/2/19
6/628	Sergt.	Fairhall, E. E.	L.G. 31011, 15/11/18
6/227	Private	Findlay, A. J.	L.G. 29286, 3/9/15
6/1031	C.S.M.	Godfrey, J. A. (M.M.)	L.G. 30601, 2/4/18
6/3335	Sergt.	Halligan, R. H. (M.M.)	L.G. 30716, 3/6/18
6/4053	Private	Hammond, A. J.	N.Z.E.F. Orders, 31/8/17
9/1438	L.-Cpl.	Hewitt, G. (M.M.)	N.Z.E.F. Orders, 31/8/17
24/2026	Sergt.	Livingstone, B. V. (M.M.)	L.G. 31182, 14/1/19
6/1097	Corpl.	Lloyd, D. P.	N.Z.E.F. Orders, 31/8/17
6/4318	Sergt.	McCall, J. J.	N.Z.E.F. Orders, 31/8/17
24381	C.S.M.	MacKay, D. M. G.	L.G. 30879, 3/9/18
6/3817	Corpl.	O'Brien, J. H.	N.Z.E.F. Orders, 31/8/17
25299	Sergt.	O'Grady, M.	L.G. 31182, 14/1/19
6/524	Sergt.	Page, H.	N.Z.E.F. Orders, 31/8/17
32378	Corpl.	Putnam, P. S.	L.G. 31182, 14/1/19
6/1129	Corpl.	Rhind, H.	L.G. 29631, 20/6/16
6/978	Sergt.	Rodger, W. J.	L.G. 29286, 3/9/15
32923	Private	Shakleton, J. L.	L.G. 31182, 14/1/19
6/549	C.S.M.	Smith, W. E.	L.G. 30399, 26/11/17
6/2764	Sergt.	Stobie, C. W.	L.G. 31186, 18/2/19
6/1156	Private	Stockdill, T.	L.G. 29202, 3/7/15
6/157	Sergt.	Tavender, B. N.	L.G. 29438, 11/1/16
8/859	Sergt.	Thompson, N. B.	L.G. 31092, 1/1/19
6/804	Corpl.	Turner, B. R.	L.G. 30716, 3/6/18
6/1128	Sergt.	Vincent, J.	L.G. 30399, 26/11/17
23/1861	Sergt.	Walker, W. R.	L.G. 30601, 2/4/18
6/2005	Private	Ward, J.	L.G. 31370, 3/6/19
6/3924	Private	White, F.	N.Z.E.F. Orders, 31/8/17
6/3199	L.-Cpl.	White, W.	L.G. 30879, 3/9/18
6/741	Private	Wilson, C. M.	L.G. 29252, 3/8/15

Bar to Military Medal.

15493	Sergt.	Clark, A. S. (M.M.)	L.G. 31338, 14/5/19
6/1574	L.-Cpl.	Howie, W. D. (M.M.)	L.G. 30940, 7/10/18
6/2285	L.-Sgt.	Stevenson, F. W. (M.M.)	L.G. 31173, 11/2/19

Military Medal.

26233	Private	Adams, W. C.	L.G. 31138, 21/1/19
47660	Corpl.	Adlam, V. J.	L.G. 31173, 11/2/19
26975	Private	Allen, H. C.	L.G. 31173, 11/2/19
6/2344	Sergt.	Allen, J. E.	L.G. 30498, 28/1/18
55386	Private	Alley, R.	L.G. 31138, 21/1/19
6/2034	Private	Anderson, H.	N.Z.E.F. Ords., 13/10/16
6/1447b	Sergt.	Anderson, J. A.	L.G. 30431, 17/12/17
6/3984	Corpl.	Armstrong, J. W.	L.G. 31138, 21/1/19
5/27a	Private	Archer, W.	L.G. 31227, 13/3/19
31455	Corpl.	Arthur, E. W.	L.G. 30873, 29/8/18
11598	L.-Cpl.	Atkinson, V.	L.G. 30476, 14/1/18
29214	Private	Baigent J. T.	L.G. 30476, 14/1/18

58136	Private	Bannatyne, N.	L.G. 31173, 11/2/19
34609	Private	Barker, T. A.	L.G. 31173, 11/2/19
14193	Private	Barnett, P. E.	L.G. 31173, 11/2/19
6/1464	Sergt.	Bell, T.	N.Z.E.F. Ords, 15/11/16
6/3247	Sergt.	Berney, G. R. B. B.	L.G. 31173, 11/2/19
64612	Private	Berridge, F.	L.G. 31405, 17/6/19
7/2360	Sergt.	Bigham, H.	L.G. 30431, 17/12/17
26240	Corpl.	Black, R. I.	L.G. 30797, 16/7/18
14930	Se-gt.	Blakemore, J. F.	L.G. 31061, 11/12/18
52563	Private	Blomkvist, H. H. A.	L.G. 31142, 21/1/19
6/4588	Private	Bower, H. R.	N.Z.E.F. Orders, 30/6/17
6/3628	Private	Bradley, A.	N.Z.E.F. Orders, 30/6/17
44437	Private	Brailey, E. S.	L.G. 31142, 21/1/19
22225	L.-Sgt.	Breslin, J.	L.G. 31227, 13/3/19
6/1785	Sergt.	Brien, W. S.	L.G. 30573, 13/3/18
6/15	Sergt.	Brister, S. G.	L.G. 29758, 21/9/16
6/4207	L.Cpl.	Bromell, M. C.	L.G. 30476, 14/1/18
6/943	Sergt.	Brothers, W. F.	L.G. 29780, 11/10/16
26547	Private	Brown, N. G.	L.G. 31142, 21/1/19
59599	Private	Bryant, W. H.	L.G. 31405, 17/6/19
57469	Private	Buller, R. C.	I.G. 31338, 14/5/19
33688	Private	Burnett, W. H. J.	L.G. 31173, 11/2/19
29140	Sergt.	Cain, R. H.	L.G. 31227, 13/3/19
10/1199	L.-Cpl.	Caldwell, P. L.	L.G 31173, 11/2/19
6/3270	Corpl.	Cameron, R. B.	L.G. 31227, 13/3/19
14398	Private	Capon, M.	L.G. 30573, 13/3/18
6/2971	Sergt.	Carter, F. D.	L.G. 30476, 14/1/18
23797	L.-Cpl.	Chalmers, C.	L.G. 30573, 13/3/18
6/1807	L.-Cpl.	Childs, R. A.	L.G. 31338, 14/5/19
6/3653	Private	Churchill, J. L.	L.G. 30431, 17/12/17
15493	Sergt.	Clark, A. S.	L.G. 30962, 21/10/18
13/981	Corpl.	Clark, M.	N.Z.E.F. Ords., 31/10/16
6/2385	C.Q.M.S.	Cody, J. F.	L.G. 30431, 17/12/17
44092	L.-Cpl.	Cole, F. C.	L.G. 31227, 13/3/19
6/1490	Private	Coles, T.	L.G. 29780, 11/10/16
7/543	Private	Coley, J. B.	L.G. 30431, 17/12/17
15498	Private	Columbus, L. H.	L.G. 30573, 13/3/18
6/4232	L.-Sgt.	Cooper, G. B.	L.G. 31227, 13/3/19
6/2369	Sergt.	Couling, J.	N.Z.E.F. Orders, 30/6/17
37770	L.-Cpl.	Cree, J.	L.G. 31227, 13/3/19
26997	Corpl.	Cribb, W. H.	L.G. 30797, 16/7/18
57487	Private	Crossen, W. J.	L.G. 31338, 14/5/19
6/2105	Private	Cruickshank, A.	L.G. 30431, 17/12/17
6/1825	Private	Curry, D. W.	N.Z.E.F. Ords., 10/10/16
30912	Sergt.	Cusack, J. W.	L.G. 31405, 17/6/19
6/891	Corpl.	Cutts, T.	L.G. 30873, 29/8/18
6/3293	Sergt.	Dagnall, W.	L.G. 31142, 21/1/19
6/2590	Sergt.	Dartnell, C. A.	N.Z.E.F. Ords., 31/10/16
47318	Private	Dawson, C. R.	L.G. 31227, 13/3/19
18284	Corpl.	Day, H. N.	L.G. 31338, 14/5/19
62269	Private	Dean, E. M.	L.G. 31405, 17/6/19
6/863	Corpl.	Denne, A. E.	L.G. 30498, 28/1/18
6/3681	Sergt.	Dixon, W. B.	N.Z.E.F. Orders, 30/6/17
6/218	Sergt.	Dodd, A. J.	L.G. 29827, 15/11/16
7/1453	L.-Sgt.	Donaldson, G. A. H.	L.G. 31227, 13/3/19
6/2599	Corpl.	Douglas, K. W.	L.G. 31512, 20/8/19
6/1516	Private	Doyne, J. D.	L.G. 31405, 17/6/19
15507	Private	Dron, T.	L.G. 30476, 14/1/18

35451	Sergt.	Edgecombe, F. C.	L.G. 31405, 17/6/19
6/2041	Sergt.	Ellen, H.	N.Z.E.F. Ords., 31/10/16
38945	Private	Emery, O.	L.G. 31338, 14/5/19
6/3312	L.-Cpl.	Erikson, A. G.	L.G. 30476, 14/1/18
6/3313	Private	Everett, P.	L.G. 30476, 14/1/18
19134	Corpl.	Eyles, H. P.	L.G. 31142, 21/1/19
6/451	Private	Fairbrother, R. E.	N.Z.E.F. Ords., 31/10/16
6/1838	L.-Cpl.	Farrell, G.	N.Z.E.F. Ords, 31/10/16
6/3314	L.-Cpl.	Feathers, T. E.	L.G. 30873, 29/8/18
6/3702	Sergt.	Fenemor, R. C.	L.G. 30830, 6/8/18
38948	Private	FitzSimmons, A. J.	L.G. 30797, 16/7/18
27005	Private	Flood, J.	L.G. 30962, 21/10/18
6/1844	Private	Flynn, E. J.	L.G. 30498, 28/1/18
57211	Private	Foley, P.	L.G. 31142, 21/1/19
27261	Private	Foster, G. A. W.	L.G. 31405, 17/6/19
49530	Corpl.	Foster, R.	L.G. 31405, 17/6/19
6/2622	C.S.M.	Fraser, A. H.	L.G. 31405, 17/6/19
7/1845	Private	Gaffney, P. J.	L.G. 31142, 21/1/19
41528	C.Q.M.S.	Galvin, F. G.	L.G. 31405, 17/6/19
21671	Private	Garlick, R. T.	L.G. 30234, 16/8/17
6/2627	Sergt.	Garrett, W. E.	L.G. 30573, 13/3/18
23/1639	Private	George, B.	L.G. 31405, 17/6/19
27271	Private	Gillon, J.	L.G. 30476, 14/1/18
6/3329	Private	Glassey, J.	L.G. 30476, 14/1/18
36967	Corpl.	Gledhill, G. L.	L.G. 31227, 13/3/19
6/1031	Sergt.	Godfrey, J. A.	N.Z.E.F. Orders 30/6/17
14969	L.-Cpl.	Godsiff, G. F.	L.G. 30573, 13/3/18
28462	Sergt.	Goldfinch, S.	L.G. 31061, 11/12/18
3/2752	Private	Graham, A. C.	L.G. 30476, 14/1/18
6/242	Sergt.	Grindley, A. J.	L.G. 29893, 6/1/17
36346	Sergt.	Gulliver, E. L.	L.G. 31405, 17/6/19
21677	L.-Cpl.	Hailes, W. J.	L.G. 31338, 14/5/19
6/3335	L.-Cpl.	Halligan, R. H.	L.G. 30431, 17/12/17
6/2651	Private	Hammill, A.	N.Z.E.F. Ords., 13/10/16
6/3341	L.-Cpl.	Harper, L. A.	L.G. 30797, 16/7/18
47671	Private	Harper, T. S.	L.G. 31338, 14/5/19
6/3728	Sergt.	Harrington, T. W.	L.G. 30476, 14/1/18
27285	Private	Harris, H.	L.G. 31173, 11/2/19
6/4054	Private	Harris, J.	N.Z.E.F. Ords., 31/10/16
52606	Corpl.	Hearn, F. W.	L.G. 31227, 13/3/19
15076	Sergt.	Henderson, C. I.	L.G. 31227, 13/3/19
21681	Private	Heslop, J. W.	L.G. 31227, 13/3/19
9/1438	Private	Hewitt, G.	N.Z.E.F. Ords., 31/10/16
15540	L.-Cpl.	Hewitt, J. E.	L.G. 31338, 14/5/19
6/1566	Corpl.	Hinton, C. F. V.	L.G. 30476, 14/1/18
6/266	Sergt.	Hopkins, E. A.	L.G. 30962, 21/10/18
11670	Private	Hough, R.	L.G. 30001, 26/3/17
23/1685	Sergt.	Howden, J. A.	L.G. 31338, 14/5/19
6/1574	Private	Howie, W. D.	N.Z.E.F. Ords., 31/10/16
6/66	Sergt.	Howlett, D.	N.Z.E.F. Ords., 31/10/16
40750	Corpl.	Hurley, D.	L.G. 31227, 13/3/19
33727	Corpl.	Idle, S.	L.G. 31173, 11/2/19
25/1641	Sergt.	Irvine, G. W. M.	L.G. 30431, 17/12/17
6/3364	C.S.M.	Johnsen, F. W.	L.G. 31227, 13/3/19
15457	Corpl.	Johnston, T. O.	L.G. 30476, 14/1/18
45282	Private	Kearney, J. J.	L.G. 31142, 21/1/19
32349	L.-Cpl.	Kelliher, J.	L.G. 30431, 17/12/17
24178	Corpl.	Kelly, J. J.	L.G. 31405, 17/6/19

6/836	L.-Sgt.	Kember, R. H.	L.G. 29780, 11/10/16
6/3061	Corpl.	Kennedy, H.	L.G. 30573, 13/3/18
6/3370	Private	Kenrick, M. M.	L.G. 31142, 21/1/19
6/3377	Private	Laing, J. F.	L.G. 30498, 28/1/18
31862	Private	Lambert, W. A.	L.G. 31227, 13/3/19
24/2018	Private	Langvard, W.	L.G. 31227, 13/3/19
21592	Private	Leshke, A.	L.G. 30573, 13/3/18
24/2026	Sergt.	Livingston, B. V.	L.G. 30797, 16/7/18
6/87	L.-Cpl.	Loader, C.	L.G. 30431, 17/12/17
6/4299	Sergt.	Lowe, F. T.	L.G. 31405, 17/6/19
37933	Private	McAlinder, C. R.	L.G. 31173, 11/2/19
21708	Private	McBeath, A. D.	L.G. 31227, 13/3/19
15012	Private	McColgan, W.	N.Z.E.F. Ords., 30/6/17
6/1909	L.-Cpl.	McDougall, C. M.	L.G. 30962, 21/10/18
26301	Corpl.	McDowell, R.	L.G. 30476, 14/1/18
21705	Private	McGowan, D. L.	L.G. 31227, 13/3/19
15458	Sergt.	McKinley, R.	L.G. 30431, 17/12/17
6/3806	Private	McLachlan, L. D.	N.Z.E.F. Ords., 31/10/16
57238	Private	McLean, J. H.	L.G. 31227, 13/3/19
6/4108	Private	McLeely, J. W. J.	L.G. 31142, 21/1/19
6/3391	Sergt.	McMahon, A. E.	L.G. 30234, 16/8/17
6/2703	Private	McMillan, G. R.	L.G. 31227, 13/3/19
6/1666	Private	McRohan, J.	L.G. 30476, 14/1/18
46599	Private	Malloch, R. T.	L.G. 31142, 21/1/19
6/3778	L.-Cpl.	Manning, C. J.	L.G. 29854, 9/12/16
7/1866	Corpl.	Marshall, G. L.	L.G. 31173, 11/2/19
33255	Private	Mason, F. C.	L.G. 31405, 17/6/19
11069	Private	Melgren, R. F.	L.G. 30476, 14/1/18
6/2708	Private	Messenger, W.	N.Z.E.F. Ords., 30/6/17
39619	L.-Cpl.	Michau, L. J.	L.G. 30573, 13/3/18
27340	Private	Miller, L. P.	L.G. 31227, 13/3/19
27343	Private	Millington, W.	L.G. 31227, 13/3/19
32958	Sergt.	Mills, S. R.	L.G. 31405, 17/6/19
6/2709	L.-Cpl.	Minnis, H. W.	N.Z.E.F. Ords., 30/6/17
6/2204	L.-Cpl.	Molloy, J.	N.Z.E.F. Ords., 31/10/16
26293	Private	Morris, J. H.	L.G. 30476,, 14/1/18
6/1346	Private	Munro, R.	L.G. 31173, 11/2/19
7/754	L.-Cpl.	Murdock, R. J.	N.Z.E.F. Ords., 31/10/16
27348	Private	Nelsen, M. L.	L.G. 30476, 14/1/18
32372	Private	Nichol, A. B.	L.G. 31227, 13/3/19
24213	Sergt.	Nicholas, H. J. (V.C.)	L.G. 31227, 13/3/19
23420	Corpl.	Nield, A. H.	L.G. 30476, 14/1/18
21722	Private	Noonan, D. P.	L.G. 30476, 14/1/18
27036	Corpl.	Noonan, W. S.	L.G. 31173, 11/2/19
11923	Private	O'Brien, T.	L.G. 30431, 17/12/17
49512	Sergt.	Odell, L. M.	L.G. 31405, 17/6/19
6/3819	L.-Cpl.	Oliver, E. E.	L.G. 31227, 13/3/19
6/3820	L.-Cpl.	Osborne, D. S.	N.Z.E.F. Ords., 30/6/17
6/3821	L.-Cpl.	Osborne, S. K.	N.Z.E.F. Ords., 13/10/16
6/524	Private	Page, H.	L.G. 29780, 11/10/16
43925	L.-Cpl.	Palmer, P. J. L.	L.G. 31227, 13/3/19
6/2044	Sergt.	Parton, R. A.	L.G. 30476, 14/1/18
32380	L.-Cpl.	Paterson, D. T.	L.G. 31227, 13/3/19
27356	Sergt.	Pearce, A. J. B.	L.G. 31405, 17/6/19
6/3127	Private	Pearcy, G. H.	L.G. 29981, 9/3/17
6/118	C.Q.M.S.	Perkins, H. A.	L.G. 29780, 11/10/16
32461	Private	Perry, J.	L.G. 31173, 11/2/19
15601	Private	Phillips, D. R.	N.Z.E.F. Ords., 30/6/17

27041	Private	Pitcher, G. J.	L.G. 31142, 21/1/19
6/4127	L.-Cpl.	Poultney, S.	L.G. 30797, 16/7/18
41662	Private	Proud, G. O. D.	L.G. 31142, 21/1/19
46075	Private	Quinn, P.	L.G. 31142, 21/1/19
14151	Private	Ralph, W. A.	L.G. 30431, 17/12/17
6/3842	L.-Cpl.	Rennie, J. W.	N.Z.E.F. Ords,. 30/6/17
6/3845	Sergt.	Rigby, J. H.	L.G. 30573, 13/3/18
24/1792	Private	Ritchards, W.	L.G. 31142, 21/1/19
6/2839	Sergt.	Robertson, L.	L.G. 30573, 13/3/18
64719	Private	Robson, R.	L.G. 31405, 17/6/19
11731	Private	Ross, J. D.	N.Z.E.F. Ords., 13/10/16
24226	Private	Rowe, G. L.	L.G. 30476, 14/1/18
6/3151	Corpl.	Russell, R. D.	L.G. 31142, 21/1/19
6/2745	Corpl.	Sands, L. R.	N.Z.E.F. Ords., 30/6/17
6/539	C.Q.M.S.	Scott, D. C.	L.G. 29893, 6/1/17
6/1191	L.-Cpl.	Simpson, C. E.	L.G. 30873, 29/8/18
23/1809	Sergt.	Simpson, F. W. P.	L.G. 30476, 14/1/18
45149	Private	Smith, A. R.	L.G. 30797, 16/7/18
31360	Private	Smith, G. T.	L.G. 31173, 11/2/19
27972	Corpl.	Smith, R.	L.G. 30476, 14/1/18
6/2290	Private	Smith, W. A.	N.Z.E.F. Ords., 30/6/17
6/1725	Private	Stainton, T.	L.G. 30573, 13/3/18
6/2285	L.-Cpl.	Stevenson, F. W.	L.G. 30476, 14/1/18
15621	Corpl.	Stewart, R.	L.G. 31173, 11/2/19
6/3884	L.-Cpl.	Stiles, R. W.	N.Z.E.F. Ords., 30/6/17
24238	Private	Stubbington, F. C.	L.G. 30797, 16/7/18
6/3891	Corpl.	Taylor, G. S.	L.G. 31173, 11/2/19
6/4362	Private	Tennant, J. W.	N.Z.E.F. Ords., 30/6/17
9/524	Private	Templeton, T.	L.G. 31142, 21/1/19
6/366	Private	Tetley, C. A.	L.G. 31227, 13/3/19
6/2299	L.-Cpl.	Thomas, H. A.	L.G. 30573, 13/3/18
26206	Corpl.	Thomas, S. A.	L.G. 30873, 29/8/18
6/2776	C.Q.M.S.	Thompson, A. C.	L.G. 30431, 17/12/17
10282	C.Q.M.S.	Thompson, H. C.	L.G. 31512, 20/8/19
6/370	Sergt.	Thompson, S. G.	N.Z.E.F. Ords., 30/6/17
6/1131	Private	Thomson, A. F.	L.G. 29893, 6/1/17
6/4161	Sergt.	Tillman, A. N.	L.G. 30573, 13/3/18
40258	Private	Tod, C.	L.G. 30797, 16/7/18
6/3489	Sergt.	Tomes, J.	L.G. 30573, 13/3/18
6/3905	Sergt.	Turner, H. H.	L.G. 30476, 14/1/18
23904	Corpl.	Verity, S. N.	L.G. 31173, 11/2/19
6/1128	L.-Cpl.	Vincent, J.	N.Z.E.F. Ords., 31/10/16
32413	Private	Wade, E.	L.G. 30431, 17/12/17
63458	Private	Wade, W. M.	L.G. 31173, 11/2/19
32263	Sergt.	Wagg, W. J. K.	L.G. 31405, 17/6/19
24257	Private	Watson, W. L.	N.Z.E.F. Ords., 30/6/17
29566	Private	Webb, S. H.	L.G. 31405, 17/6/19
46657	Sergt.	Weir, G. H.	L.G. 31338, 14/5/19
28245	Private	Wells, K. C.	L.G. 30431, 17/12/17
30329	Sergt.	Whittington, W. C.	L.G. 31142, 21/1/19
63461	L.-Cpl.	Wilkinson, S.	L.G. 31173, 11/2/19
29606	Private	Williams, E.	L.G. 30498, 28/1/18
40856	Private	Wilson, J. J.	L.G. 31173, 11/2/19
23912	Private	Wilson, J. T.	L.G. 31061, 11/12/18
6/1202	Corpl.	Wilson, W. A.	L.G. 31227, 13/3/19
32488	Corpl.	Wright, L.	L.G. 31430, 3/7/19

Mentioned in Despatches.

Lieutenant Birdling, A. J. W.	L.G.	30107, 1/6/17
Lieutenant Campbell, H.	L.G.	29890, 2/1/17
Lieutenant Conway, A. E.	L.G.	29455, 28/1/16
Captain Critchley-Salmonson, A. C. B. (D.S.O.)	L.G.	29251, 3/8/15
Captain Dailey, G. C.	L.G.	29890, 2/1/17
Lieutenant Duncan, A. W.	L.G.	30107, 1/6/17
Captain Fraser, D. P.	L.G.	30107, 1/6/17
Lieutenant Fraser, J. W.	L.G.	31089, 31/12/18
Captain French, F. W.	L.G.	31448, 11/7/19
Second-Lieutenant Gabites, H. S.	L.G.	29890, 2/1/17
Lieutenant Gibbs, L. J.	L.G.	29354, 5/11/15
Major Griffiths, G. C.	L.G.	30107, 1/6/17
Lieutenant Hind, C. A. S.	L.G.	30706, 28/5/18
Lieutenant Hocking, W. M.	L.G.	30706, 28/5/18
Major Hughes, J. G. (D.S.O.)	L.G.	29455, 28/1/16
Lieutenant Jerred, H. V.	L.G.	31089, 31/12/18
Captain Jones, L. F.	L.G.	30448, 28/12/17
Lieutenant-Colonel King, G. A. (D.S.O.)	L.G.	30448, 28/12/17
Second-Lieutenant Le Mottee, J. B.	L.G.	29354, 5/11/15
Lieutenant Loudon, J. R.	L.G.	30107, 1/6/17
Second-Lieutenant Manby, W. L.	L.G.	31448, 11/7/19
Captain Mead, O. H.	L.G.	29890, 2/1/17
Lieutenant-Colonel Mead, O. H.	L.G.	31448, 11/7/19
Second-Lieutenant Monson, H. F. J.	L.G.	30107, 1/6/17
Second-Lieutenant Natusch, S.	L.G.	30107, 1/6/17
Second-Lieutenant Ponder, A. O.	L.G.	30448, 28/12/17
Major Row, R. A.	L.G.	30107, 1/6/17
Lieutenant-Colonel Row, R. A.	L.G.	30448, 28/12/17
Lieutenant-Colonel Row, R. A. (D.S.O.)	L.G.	31089, 31/12/18
Captain Shepherd, N. F.	L.G.	29890, 2/1/17
Second-Lieutenant Smith, P. W.	L.G.	29890, 2/1/17
Captain Starnes, F. (D.S.O.)	L.G.	29890, 2/1/17
Major Starnes, F. (D.S.O.)	L.G.	31318, 30/4/19
Lieutenant-Colonel Stewart, D. McB.	L.G.	29251, 3/8/15
Captain Stewart, H. (M.C.)	L.G.	29455, 28/1/16
Lieutenant-Colonel Stewart, H. (M.C.)	L..	29890, 2/1/17
Lieutenant-Colonel Stewart, H. (D.S.O., M.C.)	L.G.	30107, 1/6/17
Lieutenant-Colonel Stewart, H. (D.S.O., M.C.)	L.G.	30448, 28/12/17
Lt.-Col. Stewart, H. (C.M.G., D.S.O., M.C.)	L.G.	31448, 11/7/19
Major Stitt, A. D. (M.C.)	L.G.	30448, 28/12/17
Captain Tonkin, J. F. (M.C.)	L.G.	31089, 31/12/18
Captain Wakelin, W. R.	L.G.	31448, 11/7/19
Captain Wellsted, A. W.	L.G.	31448, 11/7/19
Second-Lieutenant Weston, G. T.	L.G.	30706, 28/5/18
Second-Lieutenant Wilson, F. W.	L.G.	30448, 28/12/17
Lieutenant Wilson, R. L.	L.G.	30706, 28/5/18
Major Wilson, N. R. (M.C.)	L.G.	31089, 31/12/18
Lieut.-Colonel Young, R. (C.M.G., D.S.O.)	L.G.	29890, 2/1/17
T.-Brig.-General Young, R. (C.M.G., D.S.O.)	L.G.	31089, 31/12/18
T.-Brig.-Gen. Young, R. (C.B., C.M.G., D.S.O.)	L.G.	31448, 11/7/19
6/403 Private Auld, W.	L.G.	31448, 11/7/19
6/2936 Sergt. Black, P.	L.G.	31089, 31/12/18
6/2380 Sergt. Cade, P. M.	L.G.	30706, 28/5/18
15097 Private Clemett, C. E.	L.G.	30448, 28/12/17
52782 Sergt. D'Arcy, J. P.	L.G.	31448, 11/7/19
6/2597 L.-Cpl. Derrett, L. W.	L.G.	30448, 28/12/17
6/625 Sergt. Ecclesfield, R. C.	L.G.	31089, 31/12/18

6/227	Private	Findlay, A. J.	L.G. 29251, 3/8/15
6/227	Private	Findlay, A. J. (D.C.M.)	L.G. 29455, 28/1/16
6/2615	Private	Finn, R.	L.G. 30448, 28/12/17
6/234	Sergt.	Gill, D. D.	L.G. 29354, 5/11/15
6/4048	Private	Grooby, G. H.	L.G. 31448, 11/7/19
6/244	C.S.M.	Guy, A. H.	L.G. 30448, 28/12/17
6/472	Private	Head, A. E.	L.G. 31448, 11/7/19
14997	Corpl.	Keeper, B. E.	L.G. 31448, 11/7/19
6/3372	T.-Cpl.	Killoh, L. W.	L.G. 30107, 1/6/17
26296	Sergt.	McCann, W.	L.G. 30706, 28/5/18
6/1651	L.-Cpl.	McClelland, W. T.	L.G. 29890, 2/1/17
15458	Sergt.	McKinley, R.	L.G. 30448, 28/12/17
6/109	Sergt.	Natusch, S.	L.G. 29664, 13/7/16
21604	C.Q.M.S.	Niven, J. W.	L.G. 31448, 11/7/19
6/1681	C.Q.M.S.	Owen, A.	L.G. 30448, 28/12/17
6/1688	L.-Cpl.	Peake, W.	L.G. 30107, 1/6/17
6/1690	Corpl.	Pegler, J. A.	L.G. 30107, 1/6/17
6/1129	Sergt.	Rhind, H. (D.C.M.)	L.G. 29664, 13/7/16
27043	L.-Cpl.	Riley, W. H.	L.G. 30448, 28/12/17
31548	Private	Simpson, G. H.	L.G. 31448, 11/7/19
31540	Corpl.	Stackhouse, E.	L.G. 30706, 28/5/18
28636	R.S.M.	Stewart, L.	L.G. 31448, 11/7/19
6/2764	Corpl.	Stobie, C. W.	L.G. 30107, 1/6/17
6/1156	Private	Stockdill, T.	L.G. 29251, 3/8/15
6/770	L.-Cpl.	Studley, W. H.	L.G. 29455, 28/1/16
6/157	L.-Cpl.	Tavender, B. N. (D.C.M.)	L.G. 29455, 28/1/16
6/1126	Sergt.	Teague, J. A.	L.G. 30448, 28/12/17
6/1131	Private	Thomson, A.	L.G. 29455, 28/1/16
11969	Private	Thompson, G. R.	L.G. 30448, 28/12/17
6/3188	Corpl.	Tyler, E. H.	L.G. 30448, 28/12/17
14725	Sergt.	Warner, A.	L.G. 30448, 28/12/17
6/879	R.S.M.	West, T. S.	L.G. 30448, 28/12/17
6/1434	C.Q.M.S.	Willcox, E. F.	L.G. 31448, 11/7/19

Meritorious Service Medal.

32421	S-Sgt.	Albiston, C.	L.G. 31132, 17/1/19
6/3239	Sergt.	Annand, W. J.	L.G. 31370, 3/6/19
6/14	C.Q.M.S.	Barnes, G.	Cable, 3/2/20
6/2939	S.-Sgt.	Boundy, H. H.	**L.G.** 30750, 17/6/18
6/2982	Sergt.	Commons, T. F.	L.G. 31132, 17/1/19
6/2624	S.-Sgt.	Fraser, C.	L.G. 31370, 3/6/19
20917	Sergt.	Gentles, J. A.	L.G. 31377, 3/6/19
6/3023	Private	Gillespie, H. H.	L.G. 31370, 3/6/19
6/23	S.S.M.	Glanville, W. L.	Cable, 3/2/20
6/1545	C.S.M.	Grant, G.	L.G. 30750, 17/6/18
6/244	C.S.M.	Guy, A. H.	L.G. 30450, 1/1/18
6/648	C.Q.M.S.	Head, W. A.	L.G. 31370, 3/6/19
21586	Private	Jeffries, H. T.	L.G. 30750, 17/6/18
6/1599	S.Q.M.S.	Kitson, H.	Cable, 3/2/20
6/495	S.S.M.	Lovell, G. E.	L.G. 30450, 1/1/18
24668	S.-Sgt.	McLachlan, B. G.	Cable, 3/2/20
28628	C.S.M.	Nuttal, H.	Cable, 3/2/20
6/1690	C.Q.M.S.	Pegler, J. A.	L.G. 30750, 17/6/18
6/2246	C.S.M.	Price, W.	Cable, 3/2/20
6/709	Sergt.	Quintrell, S. B.	L.G. 31132, 17/1/19
6/330	S.-Sgt.	Radd, E.	Cable, 3/2/20
6/126	Sergt.	Rennie, J.	L.G. 30750, 17/6/18

27043	C.Q.M.S. Riley, W. H.	L.G 31132, 17/1/19
53525	S.-Sgt. Rogers, W. J.	L.G. 31370, 3/6/19
6/3162	C.Q.M.S. Smith, J.	L.G. 31132, 17/1/19
28236	Corpl. Thomas, R. W.	L.G. 31370, 3/6/19
36373	L.-Cpl. Tonks, A. B.	L.G. 30750, 17/6/18
6/985	C.Q.M.S. Waddington, G.	L.G. 31370, 3/6/19
29201	Sergt. Williams, H. R.	L.G. 31370, 3/6/19
6/179	R.Q.M.S. Woods, S.	L.G. 31132, 17/1/19
6/1435	Private Worgan, J. R.	L.G. 30750, 17/6/18

Royal Red Cross (2nd Class).

12/3065	Corpl.	Kelly, E.	L.G. 31092, 1/1/19

Mentioned for Home Service.

			W.O. Communiqué
	Capt.	Foord, F. J.	27/3/19
	Lieut.	Hutton, L. B.	13/3/18
	Major	Lawry, R. A. R.	13/8/18
	Capt.	McGowan, H. E.	27/3/19
6/945	S.-Sgt.	Buddle, F. L.	13/8/18
20917	S.-Sgt.	Gentles, J. A.	27/3/19
6/268	C.S.M.	Hugo, V.	13/8/18

FOREIGN DECORATIONS.

FRENCH.

Croix de Chevalier (Legion of Honour).

Lt.-Col. Young, R. (C.M.G., D.S.O.)   L.G. 29486, 24/2/16

Croix de Guerre.

	Capt.	Stewart, H.	L.G. 29486, 24/2/16
23797	Sergt.	Chalmers, C. (M.M.)	L.G. 31150, 29/1/19
6/1618	C.Q.M.S.	Mason, A.	L.G. 30792, 12/7/18
6/126	Sergt.	Rennie, J.	L.G. 30792, 12/7/18
27987	L.-Cpl.	Teahan, J.	L.G. 30945, 10/10/18
6/1128	Sergt.	Vincent, J.	L.G. 30792, 12/7/18
6/4170	Sergt.	Watchman, R.	L.G. of 3/10/19
6/879	R.S.M.	West, T. S.	L.G. 30792, 12/7/18
6/936	Sergt.	Wheeler, E. A.	L.G. 30792, 12/7/18

BELGIAN.

Decoration Militaire.

6/3817	L.-Sgt.	O'Brien, J. H.	L.G. 30290, 17/9/17

Croix de Guerre.

	Lieut.	Lumley, J.	L.G. 31275, 5/4/19
11653	L.-Cpl.	Gambirazzi, J.	L.G. 31275, 5/4/19
13/3200	Private	Park, J.	L.G. 31275, 5/4/19
6/1387	R.S.M.	Robertson, H.	L.G. 31275, 5/4/19

RUSSIAN.

Medal of St. George (2nd Class).

6/15	Sergt.	Brister, S. G.	L.G. 29945, 15/2/17

SERBIAN.

Gold Medal.

6/732   Private Soutar, W. J.   L.G. 29945, 15/2/17

ITALIAN.

Silver Medal.

2nd Lt. Walker, M. R.   L.G. 30096 25/5/17

ROUMANIAN.

Medaille Barbatie si Credinta (1st Class).

26296   C.S.M.   McCann, W.   L.G. of 19/9/19

APPENDIX "G."

——— ———

Casualty list (deaths only) up to the arrival of the New Zealand Expeditionary Force in France :—

Note.—This list was compiled by the author from the official lists issued by the New Zealand Defence Department. The dates shown are not those on which the casualties occurred, but the dates of the cabled casualty lists on which the deaths were reported to the Base Records Office at Wellington.

Killed in Action.

Regtl. No.	Rank.	Name.	Date Reported.
	Lieut.-Col.	Stewart, D. McB.	4th May, 1915.
	Major	Grant, D.	12th June, 1915.
	Captain	Goulding, J. H.	9th June, 1915.
	Lieutenant	Ffitch, H. H.	17th May, 1915.
	Lieutenant	Forsythe, A. E.	17th May, 1915.
	Lieutenant	Wright, H. M.	11th August, 1915.
	2nd Lieut.	Blake, V.	14th December, 1915.
6/2012	R.Q.M.S.	Wilson, E. D.	26th August, 1915.
6/623	Sgt.-Major	Dunleavy, T.	26th August, 1915.
6/1445	Sergeant	Addison, L. J.	7th September 1915.
6/758	Sergeant	Corbett, L. G.	12th June, 1915.
6/1001	Sergeant	Currie, A.	25th January, 1916.
6/440	Sergeant	Davey, O. E.	12th June, 1915.
6/443	Sergeant	Dewhirst, E.	12th June, 1915.
6/830	Sergeant	Haher, O. L.	13th June, 1915.
6/1061	Sergeant	Humpherson, B. A.	26th August, 1915.
6/1638	Sergeant	Mortimore, A. E.	27th August, 1915.
6/333	Sergeant	Rees, D. L.	17th June, 1915.
6/979	Sergeant	Ross, J. W. T.	12th June, 1915.
6/151	Sergeant	Steven, W. J.	18th September, 1915.
6/551	Sergeant	Stevens, T. H.	25th January, 1916.
6/2049	Sergeant	Vere, H. E.	27th August, 1915.
6/568	Sergeant	Wallace, J. H.	26th August, 1915.
6/738	Sergeant	Williams, H. E.	26th August, 1915.
6/467	L./Sergeant	Hamilton, W. A.	12th June, 1915.
6/518	L./Sergeant	McInnes, A.	12th June, 1915.
6/506	L./Sergeant	Miles, E. G.	26th August, 1915.
6/390	L./Sergeant	White, H. W. W.	26th August, 1915.
6/807	Corporal	Brass, W.	23rd May, 1915.
6/639	Corporal	Grace, F.	25th January, 1916.
6/57	Corporal	Hawke, E.	23rd May, 1915.
6/1886	Corporal	James, J. S.	31st July, 1915.
6/1351	Corporal	Macdonald, T.	12th June, 1915.
6/967	Corporal	Maber, G. F.	25th January, 1916.
6/1680	Corporal	Olsen, G. H.	15th September, 1915.

Regtl. No.	Rank.	Name.	Date Reported.
6/119	Corporal	Petre, R. J.	17th June, 1915.
6/1183	Corporal	Woods, S. E.	17th June, 1915.
6/1076a	L./Corporal	Codyre, A. E.	26th August, 1915.
6/433	L./Corporal	Cogan. E. D.	12th June, 1915.
6/2377	L./Corporal	Colley, W. L.	16th December, 1915.
6/1117	L./Corporal	Halkett, W. J.	25th January, 1916.
6/1088	L./Corporal	Johnson, S. F.	12th June, 1915.
6/114	L./Corporal	Olds, J.	15th September, 1915.
6/121	L./Corporal	Pierce, C.	12th June, 1915.
6/260	Bugler	Heenan, T.	26th August, 1915.
6/744	Bugler	Woolhouse, G. M.	12th June, 1915.
6/2050	Private	Alborough, D. B.	26th August, 1915.
6/580	Private	Anderson, J.	22nd November, 1915.
6/11	Private	Bain, A. C. W.	25th January, 1916.
6/411	Private	Barnett, H. T.	23rd May, 1915.
6/1140	Private	Bergh, H. L.	12th June, 1915.
6/588	Private	Blake, S. C.	22nd November, 1915.
6/885	Private	Boland, F.	12th August, 1915.
6/589	Private	Bonar, H. G.	12th June, 1915.
6/190	Private	Bond, P. R.	17th June, 1915.
6/1018	Private	Bowen, A. C.	23rd May, 1915.
6/169	Private	Boyd, D. P.	12th June, 1915.
6/591	Private	Breeze, G. P.	26th August, 1915.
6/203	Private	Brooks, J. V.	12th June, 1915.
6/595	Private	Brown, S. G.	12th June, 1915.
6/1794	Private	Budd, H. G.	26th August, 1915.
6/19	Private	Burns, T. L.	23rd May, 1915.
6/2019	Private	Cameron, J. C.	6th August, 1915.
6/888	Private	Campbell, E. J. C.	27th June, 1915.
6/425	Private	Campbell, H. M.	27th June, 1915.
6/2384	Private	Campbell, W.	26th August, 1915.
6/1256	Private	Cardno, W.	25th January, 1916.
6/1257	Private	Carmine, F.	26th August, 1915.
6/23	Private	Chapman, L. T.	23rd May, 1915.
6/427	Private	Cheyne, L. N.	25th January, 1916.
6/1485	Private	Clark, F. A.	26th August, 1915.
6/1263	Private	Clark, S.	29th August, 1915.
6/2093	Private	Clarke, A. P.	26th August, 1915.
6/25	Private	Cochrane, E. G.	12th June, 1915.
6/1074a	Private	Codling, T.	26th August, 1915.
6/1000	Private	Cogle, R.	12th August, 1915.
6/1489	Private	Cole, F. T.	25th January, 1916.
6/1264	Private	Collins, B.	27th June, 1915.
6/1268	Private	Cookes, C. C.	26th August, 1915.
6/1022	Private	Coote, P. S.	27th June, 1915.
6/602	Private	Corrie, H. W.	12th August, 1915.
6/604	Private	Cottle. G. S.	26th August, 1915.
6/435	Private	Crawford, N.	12th June, 1915.
6/608	Private	Currie, R. H.	23rd May, 1915.
6/2112	Private	Davey, A. O.	26th August, 1915.
6/441	Private	Davis, W.	17th June, 1915.
6/1509	Private	Daynes, C. E.	12th June, 1915.
6/444	Private	Dick, A. S.	6th December, 1915.
6/446	Private	Dove, W. E.	23rd May, 1915.
6/1832	Private	Duncan, V.	26th August. 1915.
6/1276	Private	Dundon, W. T.	17th June, 1915.
6/1520	Private	Earnshaw, J. E.	7th August, 1915.
6/225	Private	Eyles, T.	25th January, 1916.

Regtl. No.	Rank.	Name.	Date Reported.
6/1443	Private	Farrell, J. J.	17th June, 1915.
6/36	Private	Feldwick, R.	23rd May, 1915.
6/226	Private	Fellowes, A. R.	23rd May, 1915.
6/1842	Private	Fitzgerald, P. G.	26th August, 1915.
6/39	Private	Foote, A. A.	25th January, 1916
6/1536	Private	Fraser, A. E.	17th June, 1915.
6/895	Private	Fraser, J.	12th June, 1915.
6/631	Private	French, A.	12th June, 1915.
6/43	Private	French, F.	17th June, 1915.
6/2134	Private	Furness, L. T.	23rd September, 1915.
6/459	Private	Gardiner, A.	28th August, 1915.
6/1077	Private	Garforth, W.	23rd May, 1915.
6/633	Private	Garland, A. G.	23rd May, 1915.
6/897	Private	Gibbs, C. C.	27th June, 1915.
6/49	Private	Glen, J. S.	1st July, 1915.
6/1540	Private	Gold, R. H.	25th January, 1916.
6/1302	Private	Gudgeon, R. F.	23rd May, 1915.
6/1552	Private	Hall, W. E.	25th January, 1916.
6/2154	Private	Hanton, E.	6th September, 1915.
6/1558	Private	Harsant, C. B.	25th January, 1916.
6/470	Private	Harte, W.	12th June, 1915.
6/1309	Private	Hayes, G. T.	23rd May, 1915.
6/647	Private	Hazeldine, J.	12th June, 1915.
6/1095	Private	Highsted, A. B.	12th June, 1915.
6/184b	Private	Holmes, P. E.	4th February, 1916.
6/267	Private	Hughes, R. F. A.	12th June, 1915.
6/963	Private	Jameson, K. S.	12th June, 1915.
6/271	Private	Jarman, J. S.	12th June, 1915.
6/1582	Private	Jesson, L.	21st January, 1916.
6/485	Private	Johnson, J. W.	12th June, 1915.
6/486	Private	Kappely, W.	25th January, 1916.
6/1592	Private	Kelly, J.	26th August, 1915.
6/1894	Private	Kelly, T.	27th August, 1915.
6/666	Private	Kjaer, J. A.	1st August, 1915.
6/278	Private	Knight, C.	17th June, 1915.
6/1203	Private	Lambert, T.	15th June, 1915.
6/2685	Private	Lane, E. H.	15th January, 1916.
6/1533a	Private	Langridge, F. B.	12th June, 1915.
6/80	Private	Lattimore, G. P.	17th June, 1915.
6/84	Private	Lindsay, G. L.	12th June, 1915.
6/285	Private	Littlejohn, E. G.	29th August, 1915.
6/2021	Private	Lodge, A.	21st February, 1916.
6/2192	Private	Logan, T. S.	26th August, 1915.
6/1333	Private	Lydster, W. O.	15th September, 1915.
6/1612	Private	Lyndhurst, J.	27th June, 1915.
6/683	Private	McIntyre, A. F.	23rd May, 1915.
6/499	Private	Mackie, R. C.	23rd May, 1915.
6/796	Private	Mahalm, T. P.	26th August, 1915.
6/99	Private	Mansell, W. J.	26th August, 1915.
6/670	Private	Manson, S.	12th June, 1915.
6/671	Private	Marr, H.	27th June, 1915.
6/1925	Private	Marsh, J. B.	26th September, 1915.
6/2389	Private	Mein, G. F. C.	26th August, 1915.
6/1627	Private	Milburn, E. K.	6th August, 1915.
6/505	Private	Milburn, J. T.	31st July, 1915.
6/2373	Private	Miles, I.	23rd September, 1915.
6/105	Private	Milne, C. J.	25th January, 1916.
6/1106	Private	Mitchell, E. W.	26th August, 1915.

Regtl. No.	Rank.	Name.	Date Reported.
6/1342	Private	Moore, J. R.	25th January, 1916.
6/678	Private	Moriarty, T.	12th June, 1915.
6/1936	Private	Mullany, L.	26th August, 1915.
6/315	Private	Nilsen, H. W.	26th August, 1915.
6/1221	Private	Norris, O. M.	23rd May, 1915.
6/1676	Private	O'Connor, J. J.	25th January, 1916
6/1219	Private	O'Reilly, E.	25th January, 1916.
6/1060	Private	Orme, W.	12th June, 1915.
6/925	Private	Pacey, C. R.	26th August, 1915.
6/116	Private	Parson, L. H.	3rd July, 1915.
6/526	Private	Patching, W. G.	12th June, 1915.
6/1952	Private	Pattrick, A. E.	10th July, 1915.
6/1372	Private	Paul, W. J.	17th June, 1915.
6/323	Private	Penny, S. M.	26th August, 1915.
6/120	Private	Phelan, E.	31st January, 1916.
6/1376	Private	Pickles, I.	12th June, 1915.
6/1066	Private	Pink, H. F.	23rd May, 1915.
6/816	Private	Porter, G. G.	27th June, 1915.
6/2245	Private	Price, R. L.	26th August, 1915.
6/1961	Private	Purcell, E. E.	26th August, 1915.
6/1696	Private	Queenan, J.	20th November, 1915.
6/530	Private	Radcliffe, H. J.	23rd May, 1915.
6/1971	Private	Robinson, J. E.	26th August, 1915.
6/535	Private	Robinson, S.	12th June, 1915.
6/715	Private	Rose, C.	27th June, 1915.
6/928	Private	Rostrom, J.	12th June, 1915.
6/137	Private	Sapsford, F. L.	23rd May, 1915.
6/1396	Private	Scott, C. E.	25th January, 1916.
6/1082	Private	Scott, J. A.	23rd May, 1915.
6/540	Private	Scoullar, J. L.	23rd May, 1915.
6/1401	Private	Semple, W.	12th June, 1915.
6/1124	Private	Shaw, B. W. B.	17th June, 1915.
6/1980	Private	Sherman, A. J.	26th August, 1915.
6/345	Private	Sigglekow, N. H.	26th August, 1915.
6/1011	Private	Sime, N. R.	3rd July, 1915.
6/349	Private	Simpson, M. A.	26th August, 1915.
6/1403	Private	Smith, A. H.	12th June, 1915.
6/546	Private	Smith, S.	26th August, 1915.
6/2295	Private	Sneyd, A. R.	15th September, 1915.
6/1984	Private	Spence, W.	26th August, 1915.
6/554	Private	Stevenson, C. E.	12th June, 1915.
6/1734	Private	Talbot, B. H.	27th August, 1915.
6/1997	Private	Thompson, A.	15th September, 1915.
6/852	Private	Turner, J.	26th August, 1915.
6/773	Private	Twidle, C. F.	3rd July, 1915.
6/1237	Private	Verey, W. H.	26th August, 1915.
6/378	Private	Wall, R.	25th January, 1916.
6/567	Private	Wall, W. A.	12th June, 1915.
6/2023	Private	Ward, C.	26th August, 1915.
6/570	Private	Watkins, R. E.	27th June, 1915.
6/571	Private	Watson, A.	12th June, 1915.
6/176	Private	Whitcombe, D. J. A.	26th August, 1915.
6/1759	Private	Willcocks, A. J.	26th August, 1915.
6/737	Private	Willetts, G. C.	20th May, 1915.
6/576	Private	Woodside, A. W.	26th August, 1915.
6/939	Private	Wootton, W. C.	12th August, 1915.
6/1059	Private	Wotton, H. E. J.	26th August, 1915.
6/578	Private	Yates, F. G.	25th January, 1916.
6/988	Private	Yorke, C. C.	27th August, 1915.

Died from Wounds.

Regtl. No.	Rank.	Name.	Date Reported.
	Major	Cribb, C. W. E.	13th August, 1915.
	Captain	Houlker, J.	2nd October, 1915.
	Lieutenant	Burnard, E. M.	11th May, 1915.
	Lieutenant	Maurice, F. D.	10th May, 1915.
	Lieutenant	Priest, A. F. L.	3rd January, 1916.
6/413	Sergeant	Bennington, A. J.	25th June, 1915.
6/1526	Sergeant	Evans, E D.	3rd June, 1915.
6/1007	Sergeant	MacMullen, C. F.	3rd July, 1915.
6/983	Sergeant	Stocker, I. P. D.	16th June, 1915.
6/156	Sergeant	Tait, A.	20th January. 1916.
6/1083	Sergeant	Wood, B. B.	14th May, 1915.
6/1049	L./Sergeant	Wyatt, H. L.	4th July, 1915.
6/13	Corporal	Ballantyne, C. H.	25th January, 1916.
6/753	L./Corporal	Bishop, G. H.	25th June, 1915.
6/835	L./Corporal	Joslen, H. W.	15th September, 1915.
6/371	L./Corporal	Thwaites, R.	29th June, 1915.
6/2	Private	Adcock, L. D.	6th August, 1915.
6/4	Private	Aitken, J. H.	4th May, 1915.
6/2057	Private	Anderson, N. W. H.	20th September, 1915.
6/1453	Private	Auld, W.	9th May, 1915.
6/1442	Private	Bird, E.	13th July, 1915.
6/1470	Private	Bottle, H.	30th May, 1915.
6/187	Private	Boyce, J. S.	30th September, 1915.
6/18	Private	Burnett, N. F.	27th December, 1915.
6/1267a	Private	Collins, R. W.	13th December, 1915.
6/31	Private	Constance, J. E.	15th September, 1915.
6/2495	Private	Costello, P.	19th September, 1915.
6/30	Private	Couchman, V. R.	29th August, 1915.
6/1100	Private	Deacon, J. M.	1st July, 1915.
6/1836	Private	Edgar, C.	4th July, 1915.
6/626	Private	Elcock, C.	26th August, 1915.
6/1839	Private	Fauchelle, H.	14th September, 1915.
6/1285	Private	Forbes, R. L.	11th June, 1915.
6/1848	Private	Fox, J.	30th October, 1915.
6/1539	Private	Gill, E.	18th August, 1915.
6/2140	Private	Ginders, J. E.	15th September, 1915.
6/2149	Private	Haining, G. O.	28th September, 1915.
6/246	Private	Ham, W. A.	6th February, 1915.
6/1555	Private	Handley, H.	5th June, 1915.
6/2155	Private	Hardie, S.	4th November, 1915.
6/1565	Private	Herring, F. W.	3rd June, 1915.
6/832	Private	Hewitt, J. A.	6th August, 1915.
6/1036	Private	Huffam, W. C.	14th May, 1915.
6/1585	Private	Johnston, J. W.	17th June, 1915.
6/1588	Private	Jones, D. J.	14th September, 1915.
6/1593	Private	Keith-Murray, W. H.	28th June, 1915.
6/2184	Private	Lee, E. I. W.	6th September, 1915.
6/283	Private	Lewis, T. E.	1st September, 1915.
6/2189	Private	Lively, J.	30th September. 1915.
6/88	Private	Lockwood, W. A.	8th June, 1915.
6/1647	Private	McArthur, J.	6th June, 1915.
6/1354	Private	McCoy, A. H.	10th May, 1915.
6/1656	Private	McGregor, P. D.	6th September. 1915.
6/665	Private	Machray, T. J. B.	28th April, 1915.
6/2444	Private	McIntosh, J.	24th November, 1915.
6/519	Private	McKay, D.	22nd August, 1915.
6/2225	Private	McLauchlin, P.	9th October, 1915.
6/1099	Private	Mann, A. C. D.	7th October, 1915.

Regtl. No.	Rank	Name.	Date Reported.
6/98	Private	Manning, H. D.	8th June, 1915.
6/1155	Private	Mills, D. C.	7th September, 1915.
6/1177	Private	Morrison, W. B.	28th May, 1915.
6/698	Private	Noble, C. C.	12th May, 1915.
6/1670	Private	Nolan, J. P.	7th June, 1915.
6/1675	Private	O'Connor, J.	1st September, 1915.
6/924	Private	O'Donnell, W. H.	26th September, 1915.
6/2237	Private	Orton, L.	5th September, 1915.
6/527	Private	Patterson, A. F.	30th May, 1915.
6/1375	Private	Peacock, H.	21st May, 1915.
6/2463	Private	Phillips, F. S.	18th August, 1915.
6/1377	Private	Piper, G.	10th May, 1915.
6/1381	Private	Pullinger, J.	19th September, 1915.
6/1041	Private	Quigley, R.	26th August, 1915.
6/128	Private	Richards, F. L.	9th May, 1915.
6/338	Private	Robb, T. J. G. B.	13th July, 1915.
6/2390	Private	Robertson, A.	6th September, 1915.
6/136	Private	Roxburgh, M.	12th September, 1915.
6/1043	Private	Scanlon, J.	1st September, 1915.
6/1979	Private	Senior, F.	12th August, 1915.
6/140	Private	Sherring, L. S.	16th May, 1915.
6/143	Private	Smith, E. G.	11th May, 1915.
6/1986	Private	Spring, M.A.	6th September, 1915.
6/1989	Private	Stevens, R.	27th September, 1915.
6/729	Private	Stitchbury, N. C.	18th September, 1915.
6/1169	Private	Stodart, J. H.	3rd September, 1915.
6/1733	Private	Swift, H.	7th July, 1915.
6/2357	Private	Talbot, F. W.	21st February, 1916.
6/372	Private	Toms, A.	3rd June, 1915.
6/1420	Private	Tuckwell, G. T.	28th May, 1915.
6/164	Private	Turner, A. H.	28th May, 1915.
6/1425	Private	Valieres, P.	30th May, 1915.
6/1744	Private	Waghorn, F. G.	8th June, 1915.
6/389	Private	White, G. H.	12th May, 1915.
6/2327	Private	Willis, S. R.	23rd August, 1915.
6/938	Private	Wilson, A. G.	3rd June, 1915.
6/393	Private	Wilson, P.	28th September, 1915.
6/747	Private	Wylde, A. T.	25th January, 1916.
6/181	Private	Yeoman, G. F.	10th July, 1915.
6/750	Private	Ziegler, J. L.	18th June, 1915.

Died from Disease.

Regtl. No.	Rank	Name.	Date Reported.
	Lieutenant	Stead, O. V.	25th September, 1915.
	2nd Lieut.	Griffiths, G.	21st February, 1916.
6/1084	Sergeant	Baker, L. F.	31st August, 1915.
6/1524	Corporal	Ellis, R. W.	3rd August, 1915.
6/1200	Corporal	Kelly, P. J.	7th October, 1915.
6/2055	Private	Adams, J. H.	29th September, 1915.
6/2527	Private	Appleton, L.	29th November, 1915.
6/883	Private	Arnold, R.	25th September, 1915.
6/1462	Private	Barry, F.	2nd October, 1915.
6/2395	Private	Bridle, F. W.	19th September, 1915.
6/2077	Private	Brown, A.	27th July, 1915.
6/1789	Private	Brown, E.	25th August, 1915.
6/1795	Private	Burgess, A. C.	2nd November, 1915.
6/2562	Private	Burnett, J. R.	30th December, 1915.
6/2102	Private	Coumbe, F.	19th November, 1915.
6/213	Private	Cresswell, R.W.	24th October, 1915.
6/2409	Private	Dobson, J.	7th September, 1915.

Regt. No.	Rank.	Name.	Date Reported.
6/217	Private	Doidge, A. B.	16th July, 1915.
6/2124	Private	Eyes, C. E.	4th October, 1915.
6/1534	Private	Frame, D.	29th November, 1915.
6/41	Private	Franklin, G. S.	27th September, 1915.
6/1543	Private	Gow, J. M.	9th October, 1915.
6/2142	Private	Gregory, W.	17th November, 1915.
6/1081	Private	Hardy, J.	17th January, 1916.
6/2156	Private	Harrison, I. J.	22nd December, 1915.
6/1562	Private	Henderson, W. H.	28th July, 1915.
6/1882	Private	Hunt, K. N.	12th August, 1915.
6/1888	Private	Johnston, G.	20th September, 1915.
6/1896	Private	King, A. N.	3rd April, 1916.
6/1120	Private	Lockwood, A. W.	4th October, 1915.
6/1610	Private	Lukey, F. W.	29th August, 1915.
6/1648	Private	McAuley, J. A.	6th July, 1915.
6/2219	Private	McIntosh, J. D.	14th September, 1915.
6/686	Private	McKain, T.	25th July, 1915.
6/1616	Private	Marshall, T. C. W.	29th September, 1915.
6/2200	Private	Miller, W.	15th November, 1915.
6/1347	Private	Mustarde, W. J.	21st September, 1915.
6/845	Private	Patterson, J. R.	6th October, 1915.
6/1955	Private	Pearse, J. H.	15th September, 1915.
6/1708	Private	Senior, H.	3rd January, 1916.
6/561	Private	Talke, A.	28th January, 1916.
6/——	Private	Wall, J.	19th January, 1915.
6/1048	Private	Whiffen, F.	5th September, 1915.
6/391	Private	Williams, D.	8th October, 1915.
6/2018	Private	Young, C.	11th October, 1915.

Died — Cause Unknown.

Regt. No.	Rank.	Name.	Date Reported.
	2nd Lieut.	Barclay, C. C.	25th January, 1916.
	2nd Lieut.	Skelton, W. G.	25th January, 1916.
6/1860	Sergeant	Greenwood, E.	23rd March, 1916.
6/656	Sergeant	Ingram, E. A.	25th January, 1916.
6/990	Sergeant	Robbins, E. L.	25th January, 1916.
6/652	L./Sergeant	Hogben, G. McL.	23rd March, 1916.
6/1865	L./Corporal	Hansen, O.	23rd March, 1916.
6/1111	Private	Ayre, C.	25th January, 1916.
6/1450	Private	Batchelor, H. T.	23rd March, 1916.
6/1468	Private	Blatherwick, G.	1st April, 1916.
6/1223	Private	Bourk, A. D.	25th January, 1916.
6/946	Private	Campbell, G. S.	1st April, 1916.
6/1821	Private	Coull, J.	23rd March, 1916.
6/872	Private	Diamond, B.	23rd March, 1916.
6/1027	Private	Fitchett, A. V.	23rd March, 1916.
6/785	Private	Geary, H. S.	24th January, 1916.
6/1551	Private	Hall, A.	23rd March, 1916.
6/2175	Private	Jones, J. A.	23rd March, 1916.
6/277	Private	King, W.	23rd March, 1916.
6/1901	Private	Lockett, T.	23rd March, 1916.
6/1357	Private	McGregor, S. McK.	23rd March, 1916.
6/2022	Private	McGuire, P. F.	23rd March, 1916.
6/1916	Private	McLagan, J.	1st April, 1916.
6/101	Private	Marshall, W. R.	23rd March, 1916.
6/712	Private	Reid, T.	23rd March, 1916.
6/1413	Private	Sutton, B.	18th March, 1916.

Drowned.

Regt. No.	Rank.	Name.	Date Reported.
6/1444	Private	Alexander, J.	31st January, 1916.

Died from other Causes.

6/642	Private	Green, T. F. H.	17th June, 1915.
6/1581	Private	Jackson, A. E.	20th June, 1915.
6/1891	Private	Joyce, P. J.	28th January, 1916.
6/1439	Private	Ludlow, O. J.	30th June, 1915.
6/125	Private	Rayfield, H. C.	15th January, 1915

APPENDIX "H"

CASUALTY LIST (deaths only) after the arrival of the New Zealand Expeditionary Force in France.

Note.—This list was compiled from lists supplied by the Base Records Office, Wellington. The dates shown are in most cases those on which the casualties occurred.

It will be noticed that a few names have no battalion numbers marked against them. The probable explanation is that these casualties occurred either in the Reserve Battalion at Sling, or at the New Zealand Base Depôt or the Entrenching Group in France.

KILLED IN ACTION.
Officers.

Number.	Rank.	Name.	Battalion.	Date.
6/941	2nd. Lieut.	Allen, R. H.	2nd	2/10/16
15445	Lieutenant	Anderson, F. A.	2nd	7/6/17
36305	2nd Lieut.	Beadel, G. P.	2nd	4/9/18
6/1464	2nd Lieut.	Bell, T.	1st	23/10/18
7/1195	Lieutenant	Birdling, A. J. W.	2nd	20/9/16
6/1786	2nd Lieut.	Bristed, E. G.	1st	3/12/17
41286	Rev.	Bryan-Brown, G. S.	3rd	4/10/17
27214	2nd Lieut.	Burnard, A. T. E.	1st	2/9/18
36739	2nd Lieut.	Coleman, H. N.	1st	13/4/18
6/3212	Lieutenant	Cormody, A F.	1st	8/7/16
6/2099	2nd Lieut.	Cornford, E. S.	2nd	8/7/17
27693	2nd Lieut.	Deans, A.	3rd	4/10/17
6/1053	2nd Lieut.	Donn, J. M.	2nd	2/10/16
6/1517	Major	Dron, D. A.	2nd	8/10/18
6/2605	2nd Lieut.	Dyer, H. F.	1st	8/1/18
11635	2nd Lieut.	Ell, A. H. W.	1st	23/10/18
11572	Lieutenant	Elliott, W. N.	1st	3/12/17
6/452	2nd Lieut.	Farquhar, A.	2nd	24/8/18
23/1047	2nd Lieut.	Foden, W. R.	2nd	12/10/17
6/2027	Captain	Ford, L. J.	2nd	12/10/17
6/408	Captain	Fraser, D. P.	2nd	20/9/16
6/635	Lieutenant	Gibson, McK.	1st	12/10/17
6/3962	2nd Lieut.	Gowdy, H.	2nd	20/9/16
3/324	Lieutenant	Green, D. B.	2nd	5/4/18
6/239	2nd Lieut.	Green, J. L.	2nd	12/10/17
11583	2nd Lieut.	Griffiths, D. C.	2nd	23/7/18
7/2019	Captain	Harley, H. S.	2nd	2/10/16
3/3071	Captain	Harris, R. (R.M.O.)	1st	5/4/18
45314	Lieutenant	Hastings, W. O.	1st	5/4/18
6/65	2nd Lieut.	Herman, R. P.	1st	8/7/16
6/3961	2nd Lieut.	Hickmott, R. G.	2nd	16/9/16
3/1113	Captain	Johns, F. N (R.M.O.)	1st	25/8/18
6/836	Captain	Kember, R. H.	2nd	22/9/16
11/680	Lieut.Col.	King, G. A.	1st	12/10/17
6/2895	Lieutenant	Lavie, G. S.	2nd	11/6/16

Number.	Rank.	Name.	Battalion.	Date.
6/308	2nd Lieut.	McKee, F. G.	2nd	20/9/16
6/1215	Maj. (Chap.)	McMenamin, J. J.	2nd	8/6/17
24384	Lieutenant	McNiven, H. G.	2nd	24/10/18
8/602	Lieutenant	McQueen, J. A.	1st	11/12/17
6/3214	Lieutenant	Marriott, W. J.	2nd	20/9/16
48142	Major	Meddings, W. H.	2nd	11/10/17
10/3405	2nd Lieut.	Monson, H. F. J.	2nd	20/9/16
6/3224	2nd Lieut.	Moriarty, D. M.	2nd	8/10/18
24291	Captain	O'Callaghan, L. G.	1st	12/10/17
24397	2nd Lieut.	O'Connor, D.	2nd	2/5/18
18582	2nd Lieut.	O'Connor, M. B.	2nd	5/4/18
6/122	Lieutenant	Porter, G. B. L.	2nd	8/10/18
8/3843	Lieutenant	Richardson, F.	1st	15/7/18
7/1801	Lieutenant	Riley, H. B.	2nd	2/10/16
24/946	2nd Lieut.	Scoullar, W. A.	—	6/4/18
3/2874	Captain	Serpell, S. L. (R.M.O.)	1st	15/12/17
36761	2nd Lieut.	Sinclair, J.	2nd	27/3/18
8/116	2nd Lieut.	Swinard, N. C.	2nd	20/9/16
14037	2nd Lieut.	Talbot, A. E.	2nd	12/10/17
14903	Lieutenant	Thomas, J. H.	2nd	4/9/18
6/854	2nd Lieut.	Upton, F. C. R.	2nd	2/10/16
24119	2nd Lieut.	Watt, W. F.	2nd	2/10/16
32555	2nd Lieut.	Williams, A. D.	2nd	27/3/18

Other Ranks.

Number.	Rank.	Name.	Battalion.	Date.
46161	Private	Adair, J. M.	1st	3/12/17
47296	Private	Adam, D. N.	2nd	5/4/18
11588	Private	Adams, F. B.	1st	17/9/16
61120	Private	Adams, J.	1st	2/9/18
62222	Private	Addison, J. B.	1st	20/4/18
24527	Private	Affleck, H. D. B.	1st	14/10/17
30154	Private	Aiken, H. C.	3rd	22/11/17
6/3979	Private	Aitken, J.	2nd	5/11/18
14044	Private	Aitken, R. F.	1st	5/4/18
6/1445	Sergeant	Alexander, T. H.	2nd	16/9/16
65648	Private	Allan, A.	2nd	4/9/18
38925	Private	Allan, W.	1st	12/10/17
25/928	Private	Allen, A. D.	2nd	21/9/16
43934	Private	Allen, A. E.	1st	26/8/18
33995	Private	Allen, H. S.	1st	23/10/18
6/3599	Private	Allen, R. A.	2nd	16/9/16
6/3982	Private	Allen, S.	1st	8/10/18
33997	Private	Allerby, O. R.	3rd	25/7/17
70923	Private	Allfrey, G. A.	1st	23/10/18
27191	Private	Amyes, A. C.	2nd	12/10/17
6/3237	Private	Anderson, D. A.	1st	17/9/16
6/3601	Private	Anderson, G.	2nd	21/9/16
6/2034	Private	Anderson, H.	2nd	1/10/16
43936	Private	Anderson, J.	2nd	12/10/17
10135	Private	Anderson, W. A.	2nd	16/9/16
6/3604	Private	Andrew, W. J.	2nd	21/9/16
6/3602	Private	Andrews, H. F.	2nd	30/11/17
7/2226	Private	Annand, S. G. W.	2nd	1/10/16
56127	Private	Archer, F.	1st	30/11/17
6/2389	Private	Archer, F. J.	2nd	21/9/16
21638	Private	Archibald, J. F.	2nd	7/6/17

Number.	Rank.	Name.	Battalion.	Date.
11597	Private	Ardley, C. L.	1st	7/6/17
12958	Private	Armstrong, A.	1st	3/12/17
27156	Private	Armstrong, B.	3rd	4/10/17
39628	Private	Armstrong, J. E.	1st	24/12/17
25/932	Corporal	Armstrong, T.	3rd	19/10/17
6/1233	Private	Arnold, L. G.	1st	10/8/17
51967	Private	Arnst, J.	1st	25/8/18
6/3610	L.-Corporal	Arthur, J.	2nd	1/10/16
26979	Private	Ash, R.	1st	25/8/18
7/1586	Private	Ashbolt, V.	2nd	21/9/16
21640	Private	Askew, L. M.	1st	23/4/18
24124	Private	Atkinson, H. H.	1st	2/10/17
6/3613	L.-Corporal	Atkinson, M. B.	2nd	6/6/16
6/2922	Private	Atkinson, R. S.	1st	17/9/16
6/1454	Private	Austin, A. H.	2nd	28/3/18
23/1930	Private	Avery, J. L.	2nd	14/6/17
32426	Private	Bachelor, E. W.	1st	7/6/17
46221	Private	Baigent, J. W.	2nd	29/3/18
29206	Private	Bailey, S.	3rd	12/10/17
44991	Private	Bainbridge, A.	1st	3/12/17
14050	Private	Baird, A.	2nd	6/5/17
6/12	Sergeant	Baker, A. K.	1st	9/7/16
11580	Sergeant	Baker, A. S.	1st	7/6/17
11602	Private	Baker, J.	2nd	21/9/16
55393	Private	Baker, L. J.	1st	29/9/18
24125	Private	Ballagh, S.	1st	12/10/17
6/3965	Sergeant	Banks, S. W. M.	1st	12/10/17
57456	Private	Barclay, G.	1st	2/2/18
6/4198	Private	Barden, H. W.	1st	21/9/16
6/2062	Private	Barltrop, F.	1st	17/9/16
6/2063	Private	Barltrop, H. C.	1st	27/9/16
22182	Corporal	Barnett, A. J.	2nd	7/7/17
38255	Private	Barnett, F. J.	1st	3/12/17
49503	Private	Barnett, G. H. S.	1st	27/3/18
38796	Private	Barr, W. R. R. L.	1st	25/8/18
6/3617	L.-Corporal	Barrett, F.	2nd	1/10/16
31768	Sergeant	Barrett, G. A.	2nd	28/3/18
2/1460	Private	Barrett, R. E.	2nd	16/9/16
6/1777	L.-Sergeant	Barry, F. G.	1st	4/7/16
24126	Private	Barry, G.	1st	12/10/17
11607	Private	Barter, L. S.	2nd	16/9/16
15470	Private	Bartley, G.	2nd	7/6/17
33677	Private	Bartlett, C. M.	3rd	15/12/17
51145	Private	Baskin, J.	2nd	7/9/18
21642	Private	Batchelor, H. W.	1st	7/6/17
6/2535	Private	Batstone, B.	1st	28/9/16
6/2392	L.-Corporal	Batty, W.	1st	12/10/17
29138	Private	Baxter, O. J.	2nd	7/6/17
6/2537	L.-Corporal	Beal, G.	1st	17/9/16
49587	Private	Bean, J.	3rd	18/10/17
40763	Private	Beaton, J.	2nd	24/4/18
6/2538	Private	Beatty, E. J.	1st	16/9/16
24127	L.-Sergeant	Beaumont, E. H.	2nd	12/10/17
23/1945	L.-Corporal	Beavis, W. D.	2nd	16/8/17
29726	Private	Beckett, O. W. M.	2nd	7/6/17
34011	Private	Bedford, E. J.	3rd	12/10/17
34012	Private	Bee, A. W.	3rd	28/12/17

Number.	Rank.	Name.	Battalion.	Date.
51257	Private	Bell, J. McP.	2nd	25/8/18
27203	Private	Bell, S. F.	1st	7/6/17
38256	Private	Benbow, P. J.	1st	12/10/17
61028	Private	Bennett, J.	1st	10/10/18
6/3990	Private	Bennington, E. G.	1st	12/10/17
26980	L.-Corporal	Benson, F.	1st	6/4/17
6/3622	Private	Benson, J. H.	2nd	22/9/16
3/7	Corporal	Benton, A.	1st	7/6/17
33679	Private	Berg, F. L.	1st	23/10/18
6/2541	Private	Berry, I.	1st	21/9/16
59589	Private	Bidwell, E.	1st	31/5/18
27205	Private	Billing, P. H.	2nd	12/10/17
32291	L.-Corporal	Birmingham, W.	3rd	15/10/17
28960	Private	Bisman, C.	3rd	4/10/17
28851	Private	Black, D. A.	3rd	19/10/17
6/2545	Sergeant	Black, G.	2nd	14/8/18
9/2048	Private	Black, R. S.	2nd	21/9/16
32430	Private	Blackett, P. L.	3rd	4/10/17
6/3626	Private	Blackwell, A. A.	2nd	16/9/16
63283	Private	Blanchard, A.	1st	7/9/18
28576	Private	Blunden, L. W.	3rd	4/10/17
6/3993	Private	Blunt, A. A.	1st	6/7/16
6/2452	Private	Bollard, I. H. A.	1st	25/9/16
24528	Private	Boon, H. L.	1st	15/6/17
14053	Private	Borthwick, W.	1st	7/6/17
7/819	L.-Corporal	Boucher, F.	2nd	12/10/17
45974	Private	Bovey, W. S.	1st	12/10/17
29144	Private	Bowkett, H.	2nd	13/6/17
6/1471	Private	Box, E.	1st	9/7/16
64262	Private	Boyd, J. G.	1st	23/10/18
42781	Private	Boyd, R.	3rd	4/10/17
7/454	Private	Boyland, J. R.	2nd	19/9/16
6/188	L.-Corporal	Boyle, N. A.	1st	16/9/16
46547	Private	Bradbury, W. E.	1st	3/12/17
57016	Private	Braddick, A. L.	1st	29/9/18
61511	Private	Brady, J.	1st	29/9/18
54634	Private	Bramley, H. A.	1st	28/4/18
61513	Private	Brassett, B. W.	1st	25/8/18
39595	Private	Breeze, W. H.	—	17/4/18
29145	Private	Bremner, W. L.	2nd	13/6/17
6/1785	Sergeant	Brien, W. S.	2nd	13/12/17
15485	Private	Briggs, J.	1st	13/6/17
6/3634	Private	Bristow, D. C.	2nd	21/9/16
63549	Private	Brooker, P. A.	1st	2/9/18
6/3637	Private	Brooks, N. A.	2nd	21/9/16
36308	Private	Broome, F. F.	1st	29/9/18
31460	Private	Broomfield, R. C.	2nd	14/6/17
6/3639	Private	Brosnahan, T. J.	2nd	16/7/16
35494	Private	Brougham, A. W.	1st	12/10/17
33687	Private	Brown, F.	3rd	5/7/17
61035	Private	Brown, F. A.	2nd	27/3/18
7/1974	Private	Brown, F. G.	2nd	1/10/16
27209	L.-Corporal	Brown, G. A.	2nd	7/6/17
6/3263	L.-Corporal	Brown, G. A. C.	1st	27/9/16
68507	Private	Brown, H. S.	2nd	8/10/18
21559	L.-Corporal	Brown, J.	2nd	7/6/17
29202	Private	Brown, J. C. P.	2nd	7/6/17

Number.	Rank.	Name.	Battalion.	Date.
51259	Private	Brown, L. T.	2nd	2/7/18
6/2366	L.-Corporal	Brown, N. E.	2nd	14/6/17
33736	Private	Brown, W. L.	2nd	15/8/18
6/2489	L.-Corporal	Browne, W. H.	1st	5/12/17
43948	Private	Brunt, H. J.	1st	12/10/17
55415	Private	Bryant, W. H.	1st	9/2/18
49594	Private	Bryden, W. P.	1st	3/12/17
6/4589	Private	Buchler, J. W.	1st	17/9/16
47310	Private	Buckley, B. A.	1st	12/10/17
43950	L.-Corporal	Bufton, S. L.	1st	18/4/18
6/2561	Private	Bunny, H. W.	1st	9/7/16
7/625	Private	Burge, J. E.	2nd	21/9/16
46168	Private	Burke, I. E.	1st	12/10/17
42786	Private	Burrough, A. T. W.	3rd	14/12/17
19/31	Private	Burson, A. E.	1st	3/12/17
46550	Private	Burt, L. C.	1st	12/10/17
6/4004	Private	Burton, A.	2nd	12/8/17
32415	Private	Bussell, W. S.	1st	7/6/17
40185	Private	Butt, E. W.	1st	3/12/17
6/2564	Corporal	Buttle, H. N.	1st	9/7/16
2/1479a	Private	Caddigan, E. W.	2nd	21/9/16
14071	Private	Cairns, J.	2nd	6/7/17
49599	Private	Caldwell, C.	2nd	13/12/17
29672	L.-Corporal	Caldwell, J.	1st	13/6/17
10/1199	L.-Corporal	Caldwell, P. L.	2nd	1/10/18
6/4006	Corporal	Cameron, D.	1st	6/4/17
43951	Private	Campbell, A.	3rd	16/8/17
58197	Private	Campbell, A. N.	1st	21/8/18
7/2369	Private	Campbell, F.	2nd	15/9/16
20/8	Corporal	Campbell, P.	1st	5/12/17
23795	Private	Campbell, T.	2nd	1/10/16
34625	Private	Canavan, A. B.	3rd	29/11/17
6/205	Sergeant	Cannington, H. W.	1st	9/7/16
10215	Private	Carey, H. O.	1st	27/9/16
15699	Private	Cargill, W.	2nd	7/6/17
6/825	Sergeant	Carter, M. D.	1st	3/12/17
32432	Private	Carter, W.	2nd	6/8/17
6/3649	Private	Cassin, G. G.	2nd	16/9/16
11622	Private	Cassin, J. M.	1st	11/12/17
6/4008	Private	Caswell, G. A.	2nd	16/9/16
6/2572	Corporal	Catley, H.	1st	2/9/18
7/1829	Private	Catlow, T.	2nd	14/6/17
6/1258	C.S.M.	Cavanagh, W.	2nd	15/8/17
6/4217	Sergeant	Caygill, L. A.	1st	3/12/17
13422	Private	Chalmers, D. R.	2nd	1/10/18
6/1804	Private	Chambers, R. C.	2nd	7/6/17
6/1805	Private	Chambers, T. J.	1st	9/7/16
6/2972	Private	Chamings, S. R.	1st	25/9/16
34631	Private	Chaney, G.	3rd	29/11/17
43955	Private	Charles, I. M.	3rd	12/10/17
6/3651	L.-Corporal	Charleston, A. D.	2nd	1/10/16
35495	L.-Corporal	Charters, R.	3rd	11/8/17
6/1483	Private	Cheeseman, L.	1st	7/6/17
55423	Private	Childs, E.	1st	13/12/17
21655	Private	Ching, A. B.	2nd	24/8/18
6/3652	Private	Chisnall, C.	2nd	16/9/16
6/2092	Corporal	Chivers, A. R.	1st	25/9/16

Number.	Rank.	Name.	Battalion.	Date.
24138	Private	Claridge, I. E.	1st	12/10/17
29747	Private	Clark, J.	2nd	16/8/17
6/3655	Private	Clark, J. G.	2nd	26/12/16
51337	Private	Clarke, A. C.	1st	3/12/17
23/1592	Private	Clarke, J. C.	2nd	12/8/17
23/2161	Private	Clarke, T. C.	1st	7/9/18
14944	Corporal	Clarkson, B.	2nd	7/6/17
57478	Private	Clarkson, W. C.	1st	3/12/17
6/2107	L.-Corporal	Clarkson, W. F.	1st	12/3/18
6/1811	Sergeant	Clarry, C.	1st	3/12/17
49526	Private	Cleere, R.	1st	5/4/18
6/1143	L.-Sergeant	Clements, A. E.	3rd	18/12/17
15495	Private	Clements, E.	1st	25/8/18
15097	Private	Clemmett, C. E.	2nd	29/11/17
46954	Private	Clough, F. O.	2nd	11/12/17
32124	Private	Clulow, R.	3rd	22/11/17
33695	Private	Coffey, C. E.	3rd	4/10/17
6/4221	Private	Cogdale, C. W.	1st	13/7/16
64303	Private	Coker, A.	2nd	27/5/18
29148	L.-Corporal	Cole, D.	2nd	28/3/18
63560	Private	Cole, R. H.	1st	29/9/18
24140	Private	Coleman, E. A.	2nd	24/8/18
52156	Private	Collett, C. H.	1st	3/12/17
21656	Private	Collings, F. E.	2nd	4/6/17
6/3276	Private	Collins, E. J. F.	1st	21/9/16
47313	Private	Collins, M.	2nd	30/11/17
6/3279	Private	Collins, W.	1st	9/7/16
6/3281	L.-Corporal	Colman, W.	2nd	29/9/16
24/1620	Private	Colville, C. F.	2nd	28/11/16
6/3282	Private	Comport, W. C.	1st	16/9/16
6/871	Sergeant	Compton, A. G.	2nd	21/9/16
6/2984	L.-Corporal	Connell, H.	1st	12/3/18
6/4223	Private	Cook, A.	1st	12/10/17
6/3662	Private	Cook, G. W.	2nd	14/6/17
6/2581	Private	Cook, L.	1st	7/6/17
12107	Private	Cooke, C. B.	2nd	1/10/16
7/1709	Private	Cooke, C. H.	2nd	8/6/17
6/1494	Private	Cookson, C. F.	3rd	18/10/17
6/28	Corporal	Cookson, W. E.	1st	19/7/16
6/2987	Private	Coombs, J. F. H.	1st	16/9/16
6/4014	Private	Cooper, J.	2nd	21/9/16
48174	Private	Cooper, M. J.	2nd	29/3/18
49604	Private	Corbett, A.	1st	29/9/18
36319	Private	Corbett, T. H. L.	3rd	4/10/17
32938	Private	Corcoran, M.	3rd	29/11/17
14070	Private	Corry, E.	1st	6/9/18
59618	Private	Cossey, E.	1st	7/6/18
14948	L.-Corporal	Costello, F.	2nd	1/10/16
24/1962	Private	Cotter, H.	2nd	5/4/18
57485	Private	Cotton, A. A.	1st	3/12/17
6/1822	Private	Coumbe, L. J.	2nd	6/7/17
6/3667	Private	Coup, G. H.	2nd	29/9/16
6/2405	Private	Cowan, T. W.	1st	16/9/16
11591	Sergeant	Cox, B. S. K.	3rd	4/10/17
49504	Private	Cox, J. H.	3rd	21/1/18
6/1023	Private	Cox, R. G.	1st	28/9/16
29222	Private	Cozens, W. W.	1st	7/6/17

Number.	Rank.	Name.	Battalion.	Date.
6/3669	Private	Cracknell, L.	3rd	17/12/17
6/4226	L.-Sergeant	Craighead, G. M.	1st	15/7/18
40193	Private	Crawford, R.	2nd	12/10/17
34638	Private	Crawford, R.	3rd	15/12/17
53906	Private	Crawshaw, E. E.	1st	9/10/18
29224	Private	Crean, T.	3rd	15/10/17
21663	Private	Creed, T. R.	2nd	8/6/17
6/1500	Private	Creswell, A. E.	1st	17/9/16
53904	Private	Crichton, J. W.	1st	26/12/17
6/1502	Private	Crimmins, J. P.	1st	12/10/17
30909	Private	Crisp, B. R.	1st	7/6/18
6/4598	Private	Croft, A. J.	2nd	13/6/17
6/4017	Private	Crompton, J. J.	1st	1/10/17
11625	Private	Crone, J. J.	2nd	1/10/16
55436	Private	Cronin, J. M.	1st	26/12/17
28306	Private	Cross, A. W.	1st	3/12/17
46558	Private	Cross, E. C.	1st	12/10/17
29226	Private	Cross, G. H.	1st	14/6/17
15489	Private	Cross, G. H.	1st	7/6/17
6/2588	Private	Cross, H. H.	2nd	8/6/17
6/4228	Private	Crossen, H. S.	1st	25/9/16
24/1630	Private	Crossen, L.	2nd	13/6/17
46559	Private	Crossen, R. J.	1st	3/12/17
57197	Private	Crouch, A. E.	1st	27/12/17
54121	Private	Cuff, R. W.	1st	5/4/18
6/3291	Private	Cullen, P. O.	1st	16/6/16
21665	Private	Culpitt, H. W.	2nd	12/10/17
32436	Private	Cuming, R. A.	1st	12/10/17
6/2994	Private	Cummins, D. H.	1st	28/8/18
43958	Private	Cummins, F. R.	1st	23/4/18
23/1605	Private	Curline, H. J.	2nd	16/8/18
6/3292	Private	Curnick, J.	1st	12/10/17
6/3672	Sergeant	Currie, G.	2nd	21/9/16
45834	Private	Curry, J. H.	1st	12/10/17
14951	Corporal	Curtis, H. E.	2nd	14/11/16
6/2995	Private	Dale, A. E.	1st	16/9/16
27238	Private	Dalley, J. T.	2nd	7/6/17
24/2571	Private	Dalley, R. W.	2nd	12/10/17
14952	L.-Corporal	Dalley, S. M. C.	2nd	5/4/18
29228	Private	Dalton, J.	1st	13/1/18
14953	Private	Dalton, R.	2nd	13/6/17
44997	Private	Daly, M.	1st	12/10/17
29150	Private	Daly, P. J.	2nd	14/6/17
33700	Private	Dann, C. R.	3rd	16/12/17
39476	Private	Darby, J. H.	1st	25/8/18
6/2591	Private	Davern, T.	1st	27/9/16
6/4233	Private	Davey, W. J.	1st	27/9/16
6/2113	Private	Davidson, A.	1st	26/9/16
6/4021	L.-Corporal	Davidson, M.	2nd	8/10/18
29152	Private	Davidson, M. F.	2nd	7/6/17
10221	Private	Davies, J.	1st	7/6/17
6/3674	Private	Davies, J. J.	2nd	16/9/16
29229	Private	Davies, M. W.	2nd	27/3/18
57043	Private	Davies, W. D.	1st	29/9/18
37784	Private	Davis, B. C.	1st	2/10/17
62268	Private	Davis, W. J. S.	1st	25/8/18
6/4020	Private	Davison, C. H.	1st	6/5/17

Number.	Rank.	Name.	Battalion.	Date.
6/3676	Corporal	Dawe, L. G.	2nd	16/9/16
57489	Private	Dawson, J.	1st	29/9/18
70094	Private	Dawson, W. J.	1st	9/10/18
47866	Private	Dean, A. E.	1st	3/12/17
29230	Private	Debenham, H. E.	1st	12/10/17
46564	Private	Delamain, C. W.	2nd	27/5/18
49562	Private	Delaney, M. P.	1st	3/12/17
46565	Private	Dennehy, T.	1st	12/10/17
40782	Private	Dennis, J. C.	1st	10/8/17
6/2999	Private	Dent, J.	1st	27/9/16
41507	Private	Derby, J. W.	2nd	12/10/17
6/4022	Private	Derungs, L. R.	2nd	1/10/16
14956	Private	Devereux, J. P.	2nd	12/10/17
6/2498	Private	Devine, P. J.	1st	9/7/16
57492	Private	Dickson, A.	1st	3/12/17
25150	Sergeant	Dighton, L. P.	2nd	9/6/17
14404	Private	Dimsdale, C.	2nd	12/10/17
6/3299	L.-Corporal	Dixon, T. H.	1st	12/10/17
44578	Private	Doak, S. W.	1st	12/10/17
6/3682	Private	Dobier, A. R.	2nd	16/9/16
64300	Private	Dobson, J. T.	1st	3/9/18
6/218	Sergeant	Dodd, A. J.	2nd	15/9/16
39964	Private	Dodds, C. W.	1st	16/8/17
6/3683	Private	Dodson, S. R.	2nd	14/6/17
6/4025	Private	Dohrmann, E. W.	1st	20/9/16
14080	Private	Donnan, T.	1st	5/6/17
14079	Corporal	Donohue, A. T.	2nd	12/10/17
35195	Private	Donohue, L. G.	3rd	3/12/17
23/1972	Private	Donovan, J. S.	2nd	19/9/16
34651	Private	Dorreen, L.	3rd	10/6/17
29234	Private	Drabble, W. T. H.	2nd	12/10/17
29235	Private	Drummond, M. C.	1st	7/5/17
6/3302	L.-Sergeant	Dryburgh, A.	2nd	4/9/18
6/2120	Private	Dryburgh, W.	1st	15/12/17
14957	Private	Dryden, E. J.	1st	7/5/17
6/3303	Corporal	Duckmanton, H.	1st	7/6/17
54240	Private	Due, C. F.	1st	2/9/18
6/1518	Sergeant	Duff, R.	2nd	30/11/17
6/3002	Private	Dunckley, R.	2nd	11/7/16
55455	Private	Dunn, A.	1st	22/1/18
6/3306	L.-Sergeant	Dunn, C.	1st	13/12/17
6/3691	Private	Durie, H.	2nd	1/10/16
32510	Corporal	Duvall, V. H.	1st	12/10/17
55457	Private	Dyson, C. F.	1st	26/12/17
6/1519	Private	Dyson, O.	1st	16/9/16
26255	Private	Eaglesome, J. M.	2nd	12/10/17
14958	Private	Earl, P.	2nd	6/11/16
32150	Private	Eaton, T.	1st	12/10/17
24147	Private	Eggleston, P. D.	2nd	1/10/16
6/4600	Sergeant	Elliott, C. C.	1st	23/10/18
6/3696	Private	Elliott, J. A.	2nd	1/10/16
40789	Private	Ellis, A. W.	3rd	16/12/17
27252	Private	Ellis, H. H.	1st	12/10/17
6/2607	Corporal	Ellison, M. H.	1st	16/9/16
28994	Private	Elvy, C. D.	1st	23/10/18
37793	Private	Elworthy, W. D.	1st	3/12/17
23/128	Private	Eriksen, J. J.	2nd	21/9/16

Number.	Rank.	Name.	Battalion.	Date.
6/3009	Private	Espley, H.	1st	17/9/16
28995	Private	Evans, F. L.	3rd	18/10/17
57499	Private	Evans, G. L.	1st	25/8/18
6/224	Private	Eyles, L. W.	3rd	11/8/17
51157	Private	Fabrin, P. H. J.	1st	27/4/18
6/451	Sergeant	Fairbrother, R. E.	2nd	16/8/17
15890	Private	Farac, M.	3rd	11/8/17
59883	Private	Faul, M. J.	2nd	27/3/18
39973	Private	Faulknor, J. D.	2nd	15/8/17
46177	Private	Favell, E. S.	3rd	22/11/17
55462	Private	Feather, W. H.	1st	12/3/18
6/3700	Private	Ferguson, W.	2nd	21/9/16
6/1529	L.-Corporal	Ferguson, W. A.	1st	26/7/17
74426	Private	Ferriman, G. D.	2nd	24/10/18
29239	Private	Field, A.	2nd	7/6/17
38143	Private	Field, M. S.	1st	29/9/18
46573	Private	Fife, W. J.	1st	12/10/17
15512	Private	Findlay, R.	1st	7/6/17
26256	Private	Finlay, J.	2nd	12/10/17
6/4246	L.-Corporal	Finlay, W. J.	1st	3/12/17
27869	Private	Finlayson, H. J.	2nd	12/10/17
62802	Private	Fisher, C. F.	1st	5/4/18
32154	Private	Fisher, F. S.	2nd	7/6/17
55467	Private	Fitzgibbon, E.	2nd	5/4/18
39468	Private	Fitzpatrick, M. B.	1st	18/4/18
15078	Private	Fleming, W.	2nd	16/8/17
42797	Private	Flowers, W.	3rd	22/11/17
60928	Private	Foley, D. J.	1st	3/9/18
62042	Private	Ford, C.	1st	3/9/18
23/1630	Private	Forde, H.	2nd	16/9/16
6/3318	Private	Foreman, H. T.	1st	17/9/16
6/3320	L.-Corporal	Foster, A.	1st	12/10/17
6/3321	Private	Foster, C. J.	1st	14/8/16
15456	Private	Foster, T. D.	2nd	7/6/17
6/2414	Private	Foster, T. G.	2nd	19/2/18
31485	Private	Fountain, C. W.	2nd	24/10/18
23/1632	Private	Frandsen, A.	2nd	15/9/16
21573	L.-Corporal	Frankish, C. R.	2nd	7/6/17
30197	Private	Fransden, R. P.	3rd	9/8/17
53959	Private	Frew, J.	1st	5/12/17
6/4037	Private	Fridd, P.	2nd	21/9/16
31486	Private	Frost, W. G.	2nd	7/6/17
62295	Private	Frost, W. J.	1st	30/9/18
6/45	Private	Gale, E. L.	1st	16/9/16
10421	Private	Gallagher, M. J.	1st	18/2/17
6/3020	Private	Gallagher, P.	1st	27/9/16
48786	Sergeant	Garland, G. A.	2nd	8/10/18
9/2070	Private	Garrett, J. J.	2nd	15/9/16
6/3708	Sergeant	Garrett, L. C.	2nd	15/9/16
11644	Private	Gaskell, C.	1st	29/9/16
6/4248	Private	Gason, W. H.	1st	12/10/17
37805	Private	Geange, G. A.	2nd	12/10/17
11865	Private	Gee, R. H. St. C.	2nd	21/9/16
23/1638	Private	Gee, W. J.	2nd	21/9/16
15528	Private	Gibb, B. S.	2nd	6/8/17
6/3710	Private	Gibbs, J. I.	2nd	14/6/17
6/3711	Private	Gibbs, M. J.	2nd	7/6/17

Number.	Rank.	Name.	Battalion.	Date.
14968	Private	Gibson, G.	2nd	24/10/18
6/2629	Private	Gibson, L.	1st	11/7/16
46578	Private	Gibson, S.	1st	11/12/17
10226	Private	Gibson, W.	1st	11/7/16
46182	Private	Gifford, A. H.	1st	23/4/18
60931	Private	Gilham, W. C.	2nd	29/3/18
70266	Private	Gillard, C. E.	1st	10/10/18
6/2630	Corporal	Gillespie, D. T.	2nd	7/7/17
29962	Private	Gills, C.	1st	3/12/17
6/3327	L.-Corporal	Gilmour, A. M.	1st	17/9/16
57821	Private	Girdwood, A.	2nd	8/10/18
70856	Private	Girvin, W. J.	1st	23/10/18
35481	Private	Glendinning, H.	3rd	4/10/17
47324	Private	Glennie, C.	1st	12/10/17
6/3330	Private	Glink, F.	1st	9/7/16
14969	Sergeant	Godsiff, G. L.	2nd	24/8/18
6/2633	Private	Godsiff, J. C. H.	1st	11/7/16
34663	Corporal	Godwin, J. J.	3rd	26/11/17
23/1991	Private	Goodall, E.	2nd	28/8/16
34664	Private	Goodwin, F. G.	3rd	16/8/17
23/1643	Private	Goodwin, F. G.	2nd	15/9/16
23/2565	Private	Goodwin, L. C.	2nd	16/9/16
69787	Private	Gordon, J.	2nd	1/10/18
63332	Private	Gough-Gubbins, G.	2nd	27/8/18
27276	Private	Gould, E. J.	2nd	4/9/18
6/3024	L.-Sergeant	Goyen, R.	1st	16/8/17
34054	Private	Gradwell, A. E.	1st	17/10/17
39987	Private	Graham, C.	2nd	5/9/18
6/3718	Private	Gray, C. D.	2nd	21/9/16
15527	Private	Gray, E. A.	1st	12/3/18
11651	Private	Gray, G.	1st	3/12/17
6/238	L.-Corporal	Gray, J.	1st	16/9/16
11656	Private	Gray, J.	2nd	21/9/16
39799	Private	Greeks, C. P.	2nd	6/8/17
44934	Private	Green, C. H.	1st	29/9/18
58519	Private	Green, F.	1st	2/9/18
61612	Private	Green, V. L.	1st	6/9/18
65514	Private	Greenhow, A.	1st	25/8/18
44367	Private	Gregory, S. V.	1st	25/8/18
47326	Private	Greygoose, J.	2nd	24/10/18
45002	Private	Griebel, G. J.	1st	5/4/18
39590	Private	Griffen, J.	1st	12/10/17
30203	Private	Griffiths, J. E.	1st	12/6/17
60933	Private	Griffiths, M. T. W.	1st	23/10/18
51161	Private	Grove, R. W.	1st	26/8/18
34667	Private	Gudsell, J. T.	1st	4/10/17
6/2418	Sergeant	Gunderson, R. W.	1st	3/12/17
6/3723	Sergeant	Guthrie, L.	2nd	27/3/18
6/244	C.S.M.	Guy, A. H.	1st	12/10/17
25996	Corporal	Guy, W. A. C.	1st	27/3/18
6/466	L.-Corporal	Gynes, D. J.	2nd	7/6/17
6/1151	Private	Haase, O. L.	1st	19/9/16
61136	Private	Hagen, E.	2nd	1/6/18
59641	Private	Haggart, G.	1st	30/9/18
58524	Private	Hall, A.	1st	9/2/18
6/1553	Sergeant	Hall, W. G.	2nd	13/6/17
6/4256	Private	Halliday, J.	2nd	21/9/16

Number.	Rank.	Name.	Battalion.	Date.
23386	Private	Hallmond, P. C.	2nd	1/10/16
6/3725	Private	Halpin, P.	1st	25/9/16
48855	Private	Halstead, C. C.	1st	10/2/18
6/3336	Private	Hamilton, A.	1st	14/7/16
6/2152	Private	Hamilton, C. H. T.	1st	20/2/18
27281	Private	Hamilton, J.	2nd	7/6/17
44107	Private	Hamilton, J.	1st	23/10/18
47328	Private	Hamilton, M.	2nd	24/8/18
6/4053	Sergeant	Hammond, A. J.	2nd	13/12/17
12106	Private	Hammond, L. B.	1st	5/4/18
14977	Private	Hampton, D.	1st	6/11/16
23/1654	Private	Hands, B.	1st	16/9/16
24111	Private	Hanna, J. R.	1st	12/10/17
43972	Private	Hannah, R.	2nd	31/7/17
6/3726	Private	Hansby, A. J.	2nd	12/10/17
71599	Private	Hansen, A. O.	2nd	8/10/18
10196	Private	Hardie, L. F.	2nd	27/7/16
6/3338	Private	Harding, A. E.	1st	12/10/17
31498	Private	Harding, S. G.	2nd	12/10/17
45863	Private	Hare, H. W.	2nd	12/10/17
11658	L.-Corporal	Harkess, B. H. V.	1st	5/12/17
29165	Private	Harney, T.	2nd	13/6/17
14981	Private	Harper, G.	2nd	7/6/17
33719	Private	Harris, C. D.	3rd	4/10/17
32176	Private	Harris, G. B.	3rd	11/8/17
40210	Private	Harris, J. H.	2nd	12/10/17
45864	L.-Corporal	Harris, W. E.	2nd	24/8/18
25240	Private	Harrison, E. E.	2nd	1/10/16
6/2655	Sergeant	Harrison, G. J. C.	1st	3/12/17
38281	Private	Harrison, T. A.	1st	12/10/17
40808	Private	Harry, W.	3rd	16/12/17
6/3730	Private	Hart, A. B.	2nd	24/8/18
32448	Private	Hartley, E.	1st	7/6/17
6/3342	Private	Harvey, F.	1st	6/11/16
6/2425	Corporal	Hastedt, R. C.	1st	15/12/17
4/132	Private	Hatwell, F. A. L.	1st	24/4/18
6/3731	Private	Havill, J. A.	2nd	21/9/16
24/1999	L.-Corporal	Hawke, C. J.	2nd	12/10/17
6/3733	L.-Corporal	Hawkes, V. E.	2nd	29/9/16
6/3734	Private	Hawksworth, F.	2nd	22/5/16
6/58	Sergeant	Hay, G.	1st	18/2/17
58527	Private	Hay, R. E.	1st	3/12/17
6/3344	Private	Hay, W.	1st	17/9/16
11661	Private	Haycock, L. R.	2nd	12/10/17
27798	Private	Hayes, F. W.	2nd	5/9/18
6/3736	Private	Hayman, L.	2nd	1/10/16
6/2568	Private	Head, H.	1st	9/7/16
34676	Private	Heap, T.	2nd	14/8/18
35204	Private	Hearle, W. W.	2nd	19/10/17
27290	Private	Hearn, J. T.	2nd	13/6/17
11663	Private	Hearn, V. J.	1st	27/9/16
62309	Private	Hemsley, A. H.	1st	5/11/18
48876	Private	Henderson, W. A.	2nd	5/4/18
21680	Private	Henderson, W. C.	2nd	20/5/17
6/4267	Private	Hendry, W.	1st	25/9/16
43976	Private	Henery, A. T. C.	2nd	12/10/17
23179	Private	Hennessy, J.	1st	12/10/17

Number.	Rank.	Name.	Battalion.	Date.
6/3038	Private	Herring, H.	2nd	6/7/17
6/2913	Corporal	Heslop, W.	2nd	15/7/16
6/4268	Private	Hessell, H. O.	1st	25/9/16
10077	Corporal	Hewin, W. H.	3rd	17/12/17
6/3743	Corporal	Heywood, I. M.	2nd	20/12/17
6/1871	Private	Hibbitt, C. C.	1st	26/9/16
27012	Private	Hibell, G. G.	2nd	7/6/17
11667	Sergeant	Hickenbottom, B. G.	1st	23/4/18
6/4617	Private	Higgins, A. H.	2nd	16/9/16
6/3744	Private	Higgins, C. W.	1st	6/6/17
51392	Private	Higgins, D.	1st	23/10/18
21682	Private	Higgins, W. H.	2nd	20/5/17
30224	Private	Hill, A. F.	3rd	4/10/17
6/3348	Private	Hill, A. G.	1st	16/9/16
6/3042	L.-Corporal	Hill. H.	2nd	19/2/18
7/2269	Private	Hill, L. W.	2nd	1/10/16
6/3350	Corporal	Hindmarsh, R. St. J.	1st	25/9/16
14104	Private	Histen, T. J.	1st	12/10/17
28144	Private	Hodgkins, T. E.	1st	7/6/17
62313	L.-Corporal	Hogben, H. McL.	2nd	27/3/18
6/264	Private	Hollis, A. W.	1st	16/9/16
65399	Private	Hollis, S. R.	1st	27/8/18
49543	Private	Honey. W. R.	2nd	5/4/18
6/4061	Private	Hooper, R. B.	2nd	12/10/17
30225	Private	Hopkins, J.	3rd	12/10/17
6/3045	Private	Horgan, C.	1st .	26/7/17
14914	Private	Horgan, J.	1st	3/12/17
6/4062	Private	Horne, G.	2nd	28/11/17
6/2669	Private	Hornsby, A. J.	1st	25/9/16
14986	Private	Horsfield, J. K.	1st	12/10/17
6/1570	Private	Horsman, G.	1st	16/9/16
40812	Private	Horwell, C. F.	2nd	26/8/18
62321	Private	Houlihan, T.	2nd	5/10/18
28883	Private	Houston, D.	2nd	29/3/17
6/3047	Private	Houston, R. J.	1st	16/9/16
7/1079	Private	Howard, J. N.	2nd	6/7/17
6/4064	L.-Corporal	Howatson, D.	2nd	17/7/18
31504	Private	Howells, J. J.	1st	2/10/17
62322	Private	Howie, C.	2nd	8/10/18
37817	L.-Corporal	Hubbard, R. E.	3rd	4/10/17
6/2671	Sergeant	Hudson, G.	1st	27/9/16
35086	Private	Hudson, G. A.	3rd	18/10/17
38960	Private	Hughan, T. L.	1st	10/10/18
70814	Private	Hughes, F. A.	2nd	8/10/18
47336	Private	Hullen, H. C.	2nd	13/12/17
6/903	Private	Hulls, A. H.	1st	27/12/17
6/3355	Private	Hume, J. A.	1st	27/9/16
49627	Private	Humphrey, S. P.	2nd	4/9/18
6/1575	Private	Humphreys, F. J.	1st	16/9/16
32173	Private	Humphries, L. G.	1st	3/12/17
46187	Private	Humphries, O. E.	2nd	12/10/17
6/480	Private	Hunt. H.	2nd	1/10/16
23/2008	Private	Hunt, J.	2nd	21/9/16
40815	Private	Hurse, L. B. E.	1st	12/10/17
6/2429	Private	Husband, H. A.	1st	25/9/16
47338	Corporal	Hutt, W. F.	2nd	28/3/18
6/4065	Private	Hyde. E. J.	2nd	21/9/16

Number.	Rank.	Name.	Battalion.	Date.
23/2009	Private	Illston, H. D.	3rd	12/6/17
6/1883	Private	Ingle, T.	1st	18/2/17
15547	Private	Inglis, J.	2nd	14/6/17
6/3050	L.-Corporal	Inns, W.	2nd	21/9/16
23/2010	Private	Irwin, A.	1st	3/9/18
27017	Corporal	Jackson, A. E.	2nd	2/4/17
6/2673	Private	Jackson, F.	2nd	16/9/16
64311	Private	Jackson, G.	2nd	26/8/18
6/3361	Private	Jackson, J. W.	2nd	21/9/16
6/3052	Private	Jackson, L. V.	1st	16/9/16
33729	Private	Jackson, P. H.	3rd	5/10/17
14990	Private	Jackson, W.	2nd	7/6/17
51219	Private	Jacobs, J.	1st	25/8/18
26268	Private	James, E. R.	1st	2/10/18
53024	Private	James, H. A.	2nd	25/12/17
23/1697	Private	Jameson, P. McF.	2nd	21/9/16
38289	L.-Corporal	Jarman, H. N.	1st	25/8/18
6/4071	L.-Corporal	Jay, J. E.	2nd	12/10/17
6/1887	Sergeant	Jennings, A. C.	2nd	7/6/17
27906	Private	Jensen, W. F.	2nd	12/10/17
6/3757	Private	Johns, L. E.	2nd	1/10/16
6/4276	Corporal	Johnson, C. A.	1st	12/10/17
27300	Private	Johnston, C.	1st	29/9/18
23/1700	Corporal	Johnston, D.	2nd	21/9/16
32343	L.-Sergeant	Johnston, H. A.	3rd	19/12/17
14995	Private	Johnston, H. M.	2nd	8/6/17
29170	Private	Johnston, J. E.	1st	1/10/18
6/2174	Private	Jolly, J. J.	2nd	21/9/16
40817	Private	Jones, A. R.	1st	3/9/18
11677	Private	Jones, D.	1st	12/10/17
25/987	Private	Jones, J. C.	2nd	1/10/16
6/4618	Private	Jones, L. J.	2nd	7/6/17
6/273	Sergeant	Jones, M.	1st	15/12/17
14993	Private	Jones, W. E.	2nd	7/6/17
11048	Private	Jonkers, S. F.	2nd	1/10/16
31511	Private	Jordan, G.	2nd	8/6/17
6/4279	Corporal	Jory, P. J.	1st	14/2/18
6/3057	Private	Judge, G.	2nd	6/8/17
6/2675	Private	Julian, E. A.	1st	27/9/16
6/3368	Private	Julian, H.	1st	16/7/16
44384	Private	Julian, M. D.	2nd	12/10/17
30377	Private	Julian, S. H.	3rd	22/11/17
27908	Private	Juno, W. H. P.	1st	27/3/18
16894	Private	Kane, A. M.	3rd	19/12/17
15559	Private	Kearns, J.	2nd	7/6/17
24/2011	Private	Keating, J.	2nd	21/9/16
27307	Private	Kelland, C. C.	1st	28/4/18
38290	Private	Kelly, R. D.	1st	5/11/18
42807	Private	Kemp, W. H.	3rd	11/8/17
35091	Private	Kennedy, J.	3rd	18/10/17
43989	Private	Kerr, J.	3rd	4/10/17
6/3761	Private	Kerr, W. E.	2nd	21/9/16
17927	Private	Kilminster, H. M.	1st	8/6/17
6/78	Sergeant	Kilpatrick, R.	2nd	23/3/17
58545	Private	King, A. F.	1st	28/3/18
6/3064	Private	King, R. L.	1st	27/9/16
6/3764	Private	King, V. B.	2nd	15/9/16

Number.	Rank.	Name.	Battalion.	Date.
6/3765	L.-Corporal	Kingsbury, R.	2nd	29/9/16
6/3374	Private	Kingsley, D. C.	1st	8/6/17
6/2434	Private	Kinsella, W.	1st	6/9/18
15558	Private	Kinzett, P.	2nd	14/12/17
55509	Private	Kirby, M.	1st	13/1/18
24181	Private	Kitching, J. A.	2nd	12/10/17
62339	Private	Knight, J. H.	2nd	24/8/18
6/3767	Private	Knuckey, W.	2nd	13/6/17
58548	Private	Lahman, S.	1st	29/9/18
6/3377	Private	Laing, J. F.	3rd	28/11/17
33135	Sergeant	Lake, A. E.	1st	22/12/17
10239	Private	Lamonte, J. D.	1st	27/9/16
38966	Private	Lane, T.	1st	12/10/17
29265	Private	Lang, J. F.	3rd	16/12/17
10240	Private	Larsen, A.	2nd	21/9/16
42809	Private	Lash, H. S.	2nd	12/10/17
26282	Private	Laugesen, L. V.	2nd	15/6/17
36338	Private	Law, W. L.	3rd	4/10/17
24183	Private	Lawn, B. W.	1st	27/9/16
55512	Private	Lawrence, S. E.	1st	31/5/18
6/3772	Private	Lawton, W.	2nd	1/10/16
6/3069	Private	Leckner, T. E.	1st	12/10/17
24/2021	L.-Corporal	Le Cren, E. A.	2nd	21/9/16
64646	Private	Lee, J.	1st	30/9/18
46195	Private	Leece, C.	2nd	12/10/17
47676	Private	Le Mottee, A. M.	2nd	12/12/17
38968	Private	Lennon, G. E.	1st	22/12/17
21701	L.-Corporal	Lennox, E.	1st	23/4/18
6/2185	Private	Letchford, G.	2nd	8/8/17
38046	Private	Letford, F. E.	1st	12/10/17
6/3379	Private	Levy, H.	1st	17/9/16
6/3071	Private	Le Warne, F. J.	2nd	6/6/17
46958	Private	Lilley, C. D.	2nd	12/10/17
39440	Corporal	Lindbom, A. W.	2nd	14/4/18
15561	Corporal	Lindsay, D. J.	1st	2/9/18
6/2383	Private	Little, G.	1st	17/9/16
63006	Private	Livingstone, E. J.	1st	23/10/18
11062	Private	Llewell, A. T.	2nd	12/10/17
46960	Private	Lloyd, J. O.	2nd	29/9/17
23/2025	Private	Lloyd, W. J.	2nd	1/10/16
32196	Private	Lobley, W.	2nd	8/6/17
21702	Private	Locker, R. J.	2nd	7/6/17
40224	Private	Logan, J. R.	2nd	12/10/17
34697	Private	Long, H. A.	2nd	12/1/18
6/2194	Private	Loomes, W. G.	1st	12/10/17
23/196	Private	Lott, T.	2nd	21/9/16
27023	Corporal	Lowe, P. J. S.	1st	29/9/18
62350	Private	Lucas, C.	1st	5/11/18
13048	Private	Luis, G.	2nd	1/10/16
32193	Private	Luker, E.	3rd	5/10/17
6/2195	Private	Lumsden, R. D.	2nd	15/9/16
6/4622	Private	Lunn, F.	2nd	1/10/16
38294	Private	Lusty, F. M.	—	14/4/18
27024	Corporal	Lutton, E. E.	2nd	27/8/18
45009	Corporal	Lyon, E.	1st	29/9/18
60954	Private	Lyons, J. M.	2nd	28/3/18
44006	Private	McAdam, G.	2nd	12/10/17

Number.	Rank.	Name.	Battalion.	Date.
36348	Private	McAleer, J. C.	1st	3/12/17
6/4100	Private	McAllister, P.	1st	15/10/17
40230	L.-Corporal	McArtney, R. D.	2nd	12/10/17
6/3791	Private	MacAuley, A. H.	2nd	15/9/16
6/4317	Sergeant	McBeath, J.	1st	27/9/16
30258	Private	McBride, J. C.	1st	31/5/18
42813	Private	McBride, J. J.	2nd	4/9/18
1/259	Private	McCallum, J.	3rd	16/8/17
6/1649	Private	McCann, P.	1st	25/9/16
25279	Private	McCarthy, E. F.	2nd	7/6/17
6/4634	Corporal	McCarthy, H.	2nd	26/3/18
39479	Private	McCarthy, J.	2nd	6/7/17
24663	Corporal	McCarthy, L. I. J.	2nd	17/2/18
26297	Private	McCauley, A. B.	2nd	24/8/18
53931	Private	McClelland, J. J.	2nd	17/7/18
6/1651	Sergeant	McClelland, W. T.	2nd	14/8/18
25280	Private	McClintock, A. S.	2nd	1/10/16
11706	Private	McCloy, C. J.	1st	18/8/17
51661	Private	McConnon, E.	2nd	25/12/17
27330	Private	McCrea, R.	1st	12/10/17
6/3797	L.-Corporal	McCree, H.	2nd	30/11/17
58568	Private	MacDonald, A.	1st	3/12/17
29275	Private	MacDonald, C.	3rd	12/6/17
11704	Private	McDonald, C.	1st	25/9/16
14132	Private	McDonald, G.	1st	7/6/17
23/1748	Private	MacDonald, H.	2nd	1/10/16
29276	Private	McDonald, H.	2nd	24/10/18
7/927	Sergeant	McDonald, J.	2nd	1/10/16
32457	Private	McDougall, A.	1st	12/10/17
23013	Private	McDowall, J.	2nd	16/8/17
16224	Private	McDowell, D.	2nd	7/6/17
60972	Private	McFarlane, L. G.	2nd	11/5/18
27331	Private	McFarlane, S. M.	1st	12/10/17
4/1684	Private	McGeady, J.	1st	5/11/18
5/171	Private	McGee, S. G.	1st	3/12/17
29176	Private	McGee, W.	3rd	4/10/17
58572	Private	McGough, P.	1st	27/3/18
6/3800	Corporal	McGuigan, S.	2nd	1/10/16
70177	Private	McGuinness, B.	2nd	24/10/18
29177	Private	McGuinness, J. O.	2nd	27/3/18
6/1658	Private	McGuire, P.	1st	17/9/16
44066	L.-Corporal	McHarg, L. H.	2nd	25/8/18
6/3801	L.-Corporal	McIlroy, V. A.	2nd	6/8/17
70114	Private	McIndoe, F.	1st	1/10/18
32959	L.-Sergeant	McIndoe, G. F.	2nd	5/4/18
23861	Private	McInnes, H. A.	2nd	1/10/16
54145	Private	McIntosh, J.	2nd	29/3/18
39442	Private	McIntyre, F.	2nd	6/8/17
22442	Private	McJennett, F. J.	2nd	13/6/17
24/1731	Private	McKay, E. A.	2nd	15/9/16
7/1877	Private	McKay, G.	2nd	14/6/17
48878	Private	McKay, G. G.	2nd	24/1/18
24455	Private	McKay, J. A.	3rd	4/10/17
11703	Private	Mackay, N.	1st	3/12/17
58576	Private	Mackay, R.	1st	5/4/18
10175	Private	McKee, J. S.	2nd	5/2/17
57241	Private	McKeeman, J. M.	1st	29/9/18

Number.	Rank.	Name.	Battalion.	Date.
29930	Private	McKelvy, J. G.	3rd	4/10/17
32212	Private	Mackenzie, J.	3rd	28/12/17
6/3805	L.-Corporal	McKenzie, W.	2nd	12/10/17
30621	Private	McKeown, C.	3rd	18/10/17
21594	Corporal	Mackie, B.	1st	8/5/18
54147	Private	McKinnon, J.	1st	13/1/18
26/1654	Private	McKinnon, J. G.	2nd	1/10/16
68643	L.-Corporal	Mackintosh, C. N.	2nd	24/8/18
51285	Private	Mackintosh, N. J.	1st	28/3/18
29274	Private	Mackintosh, R. M.	3rd	4/10/17
47354	Private	McKnight, H.	1st	25/8/18
30271	Private	McKnight, W. R.	2nd	5/10/18
48249	Private	MacLean, J.	2nd	12/10/17
53511	Private	McLeary, A. L.	2nd	25/12/17
6/1662	Private	McLellan, A. J. C.	1st	16/9/16
6/2223	Private	McLeod, A.	1st	27/9/16
6/3231	Corporal	McLeod, J. D.	1st	27/9/16
14137	Private	McMillan, J. S.	1st	7/6/17
6/3809	Sergeant	McNeil. J. S.	2nd	16/9/16
51223	Private	McNicol, A.	2nd	12/10/17
6/2229	Private	McPhee, D.	1st	16/9/16
27328	Private	McQuilken, A.	2nd	7/6/17
51286	Private	MacRae, A.	2nd	27/3/18
40831	L.-Corporal	McRae, J.	2nd	8/10/18
6/1666	Sergeant	McRohan, J.	1st	25/5/18
11709	Private	McVicker, J.	2nd	1/10/16
6/3394	Private	McWha, D. W.	1st	18/4/18
40824	Private	Machu, N. J.	3rd	15/10/17
47557	Private	Mackle, J. J.	2nd	1/6/18
6/4090	Private	Mahon, F.	2nd	6/6/16
34524	Corporal	Mahoney, J. G.	1st	12/10/17
27334	Private	Maidens, J.	2nd	13/6/17
6/3397	Private	Maidment, A. C.	1st	9/7/16
46055	Private	Mainman, E. R.	2nd	12/10/17
27335	Private	Maister, R. O.	1st	9/2/18
32359	Private	Maitland, A.	3rd	4/10/17
29042	Private	Makeig, F.	2nd	7/7/17
6/1334	Private	Male, F.	1st	18/7/16
6/3777	Private	Malmanche, H. S.	2nd	24/8/18
40825	Private	Manhire, E. A. D.	3rd	4/10/17
60958	Private	Mann, G.	2nd	24/8/18
23/1726	Sergeant	Manning, P.	2nd	12/10/17
6/1614	Sergeant	Manson, A.	2nd	13/12/17
33740	Private	Manson, L.	1st	29/9/18
63629	Private	Mardon, L. A. J.	2nd	25/8/18
26288	Private	Marshall, A.	1st	12/10/17
23/1727	Private	Marshall, H.	1st	2/9/18
6/4304	Private	Marshman, S. W.	1st	17/6/17
27337	Private	Martin. J. W.	2nd	26/3/18
61700	Private	Martin, L.	1st	27/4/18
6/1929	Private	Martin. R. W.	1st	12/10/17
11900	Private	Martin, W.	3rd	28/11/17
6/2442	Private	Maslin, G. F.	2nd	1/10/16
51990	Private	Mason, V. J.	2nd	6/9/18
44132	Private	Matheson, A.	1st	12/10/17
6/3401	L.-Sergeant	Matheson. K. M.	2nd	1/10/16
6/3095	Private	Mathews, T. F.	1st	27/1/17

Number.	Rank.	Name.	Battalion.	Date.
31519	Private	Mathieson, J. McA.	2nd	31/7/17
6/915	Private	Mattson, J. A.	1st	21/9/16
24205	Private	Mattson, L.	1st	12/10/17
63193	Private	Maulseed, W. J.	2nd	8/10/18
6/841	Private	Mawson, E.	2nd	17/9/16
58555	Private	Maze, N.	1st	29/9/18
15575	Private	Mead, H. S.	2nd	7/6/17
6/2707	Private	Mears, W. W.	1st	11/7/16
6/3409	Corporal	Meek, P.	1st	19/7/17
6/104	Sergeant	Mein, W. H. R.	1st	7/6/17
28897	Private	Mellon, H.	1st	7/6/17
6/1621	Private	Mellon, O.	1st	2/10/17
46654	Private	Menzies, W. R.	1st	5/4/18
47504	Private	Mercer, E. J.	—	14/4/18
27341	Sergeant	Merrett, C. S.	3rd	18/12/17
15566	Private	Middleton, A.	1st	3/12/17
20189	Private	Middleton, J. B.	1st	3/12/17
44000	L.-Corporal	Miles, H. E. O.	2nd	5/4/18
6/675	L.-Corporal	Miller, A.	1st	16/9/16
10/3652	Private	Miller, R. G.	2nd	1/10/16
64316	Private	Miller, T. E.	2nd	29/5/18
6/4308	Private	Mills, A.	2nd	21/9/16
47914	Private	Mills, R.	2nd	5/4/18
6/3098	Private	Milne, G. R.	1st	9/7/16
6/2709	L.-Corporal	Minnis, H. W.	1st	3/12/17
56984	Private	Mitchell, D. C.	1st	11/1/18
32202	Private	Moje, G. H.	2nd	12/10/17
51660	L.-Corporal	Moore, A. C.	3rd	12/10/17
14465	Private	Moore, A. G.	2nd	28/5/17
40600	Private	Moore, C.	2nd	4/9/18
37838	Private	Moore, J. A.	2nd	6/8/17
6/3785	L.-Corporal	Moore, W. H.	2nd	21/9/16
29282	Private	Moorfoot, T.	1st	25/8/18
2/1633a	Private	Morey, F.	1st	12/10/17
6/4630	L.-Corporal	Morgan, A.	2nd	1/10/16
60966	Private	Morgan, J. M.	1st	26/8/18
6/1344	Private	Morgan, W. S.	2nd	4/9/18
6/3104	Private	Morganti, C. V.	2nd	21/9/16
47679	Private	Moriarty, J.	2nd	12/10/17
6/3406	Private	Morris, H.	1st	25/9/16
6/4654	L.-Corporal	Morrison, J.	2nd	21/9/16
24/2041	Private	Morrison, T. C.	2nd	24/8/18
22426	Private	Mortimer, F.	1st	3/12/17
10246	Private	Morton, J.	1st	3/12/17
37840	Private	Moulder, H.	2nd	7/7/17
44981	Private	Muir, J.	3rd	4/10/17
7/2083	Private	Munro, C. V.	2nd	13/6/17
63370	Private	Munro, W. G.	2nd	5/9/18
38078	Private	Murphy, A. M.	2nd	8/10/18
6/2107	Private	Murphy, E.	1st	26/9/16
39480	Private	Murphy, E.	2nd	12/8/17
21047	Private	Murphy, W.	1st	1/6/17
32205	Private	Murray, J. J.	1st	7/6/17
63646	Private	Murray, J. J. H.	2nd	10/7/18
27940	Private	Murray, T. J.	2nd	7/6/17
23855	Private	Mustchin, R.	2nd	12/10/17
23/1744	L.-Corporal	Myer, H.	2nd	12/10/17

Number.	Rank.	Name.	Battalion.	Date.
6/2823	Private	Myhill, E. J.	1st	9/7/16
6/2230	Private	Nacey, M.	1st	22/12/17
29186	Private	Naish, F. G.	2nd	6/7/17
15587	Private	Napier, J.	2nd	13/6/17
15109	Private	Napper, A. W.	2nd	7/6/17
6/3410	Private	Naughton, M. J.	1st	25/9/16
63398	Private	Neill, A.	2nd	4/9/18
6/3411	Corporal	Neilson, E.	1st	12/10/17
6/3813	Private	Nelson, C.	2nd	21/9/16
6/3413	Private	Nelson, G. A.	1st	27/9/16
10145	Private	Nelson, H.	1st	6/4/18
15015	Private	Nelson, J.	2nd	30/11/17
34718	Private	Nelson, P. S.	3rd	10/6/17
15588	Private	Nelson, R. P.	2nd	7/2/17
41927	Private	Neville, P.	3rd	4/10/17
21601	Private	Newcombe, H. W.	2nd	7/6/17
40234	Private	Newlove, E.	2nd	12/10/17
31530	Private	Newlove, L. M.	2nd	12/10/17
24779	Private	Newman, J. W.	1st	3/9/18
32459	Private	Newman, R. M.	1st	12/10/17
52099	Private	Newnham, T.	1st	27/3/18
54385	Private	Newport, H. C.	1st	29/9/18
15585	L.-Sergeant	Newport, J. H.	2nd	5/4/18
6/3114	Private	Newport, N.	2nd	12/10/17
15/71	Sergeant	Newton, G.	2nd	12/10/17
24213	Sergeant	Nicholas, H. J.	1st	23/10/18
23084	Private	Nicholls, O. A.	2nd	12/10/17
46200	Private	Nicol, A.	2nd	12/10/17
6/3116	Private	Ninnes, A. E.	1st	27/9/16
34124	Private	Noble, W. J.	3rd	22/11/17
24214	Private	Nordstrom, A. W.	1st	12/10/17
6/3118	Private	Nordstrom, H. A.	1st	7/6/17
40236	Private	Norton, H.	2nd	24/8/18
6/3816	L.-Corporal	Nottage, D. B.	2nd	15/9/16
21606	Private	Oates, W. H.	2nd	12/10/17
25295	Private	O'Berg, J. A.	2nd	26/3/18
44143	Private	O'Boyle, J.	1st	1/10/17
7/2112	Private	O'Boyle, J. J.	2nd	15/9/16
34126	L.-Corporal	O'Brien, J. J.	2nd	26/8/18
11923	Corporal	O'Brien, T.	2nd	26/11/17
6/1673	Private	O'Carroll, J.	2nd	16/9/16
47543	Private	O'Connell, M.	2nd	20/11/17
6/4119	Private	O'Connor, T. A.	2nd	21/9/16
6/3419	Private	O'Donnell, F. J.	1st	11/7/16
16786	Private	O'Donoghue, D.	3rd	4/10/17
33054	Private	Ogilvie, G. E.	1st	25/9/18
25299	Sergeant	O'Grady, M.	2nd	8/10/18
30275	L.-Corporal	Oldfield, S. A.	1st	2/9/18
37479	Private	O'Leary, H. H.	2nd	24/8/18
15017	Private	O'Leary, T. J.	2nd	14/6/17
9/1342	Private	Oliver, H.	2nd	21/9/16
36355	Private	Olsen, N. C.	3rd	27/7/17
48258	Private	Olsen, R. B.	2nd	12/10/17
7/2115	L.-Corporal	O'Neill, A. J.	2nd	14/9/17
27350	Private	O'Neill, J. B.	3rd	28/9/17
29065	Private	O'Neill, T.	1st	5/4/18
40837	Private	Orange, R. L.	2nd	5/4/18

Number.	Rank.	Name.	Battalion.	Date.
6/3821	Private	Osborne, S. K.	2nd	3/8/17
7/2116	Corporal	O'Shaughnessy, B. J.	2nd	1/10/16
6/3122	Private	O'Shea, C.	1st	15/3/17
27353	Private	Overend, W. A.	3rd	22/11/17
62376	Private	Oxley, H. K.	2nd	5/10/18
44146	Private	Oxnam, J. T.	1st	12/10/17
69280	Private	Packer, D. B.	2nd	15/7/18
6/1683	Private	Page, F. J.	2nd	29/9/17
42818	Private	Page, J. R.	2nd	12/10/17
68844	Private	Page, L. H.	2nd	24/8/18
6/115	Private	Page, R.	2nd	1/10/16
73445	Private	Painter, P. E.	2nd	5/11/18
6/319	L.-Corporal	Palin, H. W.	1st	27/9/16
32463	Private	Pannell, E. D.	1st	12/10/17
49651	Private	Panton, P. J.	1st	9/1/18
15597	Private	Parker, N. S.	1st	7/6/17
46072	Private	Parkman, W.	3rd	5/10/17
6/3824	Private	Parris, B.	2nd	15/9/16
30635	Private	Paterson, A. McL.	1st	27/3/18
6/3126	Private	Patterson, W.	2nd	21/9/16
24/1163	Private	Pauling, E. J.	2nd	1/10/16
27954	Private	Pell, A. J. T.	2nd	12/10/17
8/3730	Private	Pennal, W.	2nd	16/9/16
28913	Private	Pennie, W.	1st	25/8/18
59712	Private	Penzer, E. J.	2nd	5/4/18
40244	Private	Pepperell, A. H. B.	2nd	24/8/18
13/3064	Private	Percy, G. M.	1st	17/9/16
7/2123	Private	Perrett, C. R.	2nd	21/9/16
48261	Private	Perry, 'D.	2nd	12/10/17
29190	Private	Perry, E. W.	1st	12/10/17
32461	L.-Corporal	Perry, J.	1st	23/10/18
28912	Private	Perry, T. J.	1st	3/12/17
6/4125	Private	Petersen, J.	2nd	12/10/17
7/1885	Sergeant	Peterson, W. C.	2nd	30/11/17
52006	Private	Phelps, E. E.	1st	18/4/18
41616	Private	Philips, E. M.	2nd	12/10/17
10/1618	Private	Phillips, H. A.	3rd	11/8/17
24221	Private	Pifford, H. R. G. S.	2nd	7/6/17
44151	Private	Pilcher, W. H.	1st	1/10/17
25/231	Sergeant	Pilcher, W. T.	3rd	4/10/17
6/3432	L.-Corporal	Pittick, A.	1st	5/12/17
6/3433	Private	Plank, E.	1st	15/6/17
60986	Private	Plaskett, W.	2nd	29/3/18
51189	Private	Plumridge, D. H.	1st	3/12/17
14144	Private	Polaschek, W.	1st	12/10/17
40841	Private	Polson, J.	2nd	6/8/17
32462	Private	Postgate, A. B.	1st	7/6/17
6/4342	Private	Potts, C. E.	2nd	15/9/16
6/1694	Private	Poulter, G. J.	1st	20/9/16
49052	Corporal	Pound, A. E. J. W.	2nd	8/10/18
47682	Private	Powell, J.	2nd	12/10/17
29292	L.-Corporal	Powell, L.	1st	25/12/17
6/328	Private	Power, J.	1st	16/9/16
6/2046	Sergeant	Prattley, H. J.	2nd	1/10/16
6/3131	Private	Preece, E. E.	1st	27/9/16
28941	Corporal	Preston, F. H. C.	3rd	25/7/17
32229	L.-Corporal	Preston, T. R.	2nd	24/8/18

Number.	Rank.	Name.	Battalion.	Date.
61150	Private	Price, W. N.	2nd	4/9/18
44413	Private	Prince, H.	2nd	27/8/18
33437	Corporal	Pringle, A. M.	—	14/4/18
29859	Private	Proctor, G. H.	3rd	4/10/17
25/1008	Sergeant	Proctor, J.	3rd	4/10/17
30285	Private	Purser, C. E.	3rd	22/11/17
32378	L.-Corporal	Putnam, P. S.	1st	5/11/18
36486	Private	Quaid, W. S.	2nd	5/4/18
64346	Private	Quill, T. E.	1st	25/8/18
24/2126	Private	Quinn, B. G.	1st	4/6/18
34143	Private	Radcliffe, P. N.	2nd	12/10/17
27367	Private	Rae, W. J.	1st	7/5/17
21610	L.-Corporal	Ralph, C. R.	2nd	4/9/18
14151	L.-Corporal	Ralph, W. A.	1st	3/12/17
31534	Private	Rapley, H. L.	2nd	7/6/17
12/1490	Sergeant	Rawlings, J. L.	2nd	1/10/16
6/1964	Private	Rayment, J. W.	1st	9/7/16
6/531	Private	Raymond, C.	1st	25/9/16
31535	Private	Rayner, J.	2nd	7/6/17
27959	L.-Corporal	Read, J. B.	1st	7/6/17
29295	Private	Reader, F. D. M.	1st	7/6/17
6/3135	Private	Redmond, F.	2nd	21/9/16
74494	Private	Reed, A. E.	2nd	23/10/18
38981	Private	Reed, S. H.	1st	4/4/18
36248	Private	Reese, A. D.	2nd	14/6/17
26315	L.-Corporal	Reeves, A.	1st	3/12/17
24104	Sergeant	Reid, E. D.	1st	13/12/17
6/3841	Private	Reid, H.	2nd	21/9/16
58597	Private	Reid, S. P.	1st	25/8/18
11736	Private	Reilly, F.	1st .	16/6/17
52280	Private	Renals, W. T.	3rd	28/12/17
60990	Private	Rennett, A. D.	2nd	25/8/18
6/3842	Sergeant	Rennie, J. W.	2nd	5/4/18
46082	Private	Revill, M.	—	14/4/18
40057	Private	Reynolds, D. G.	2nd	28/3/18
29297	Private	Reynolds, T. F.	2nd	24/10/18
6/3140	S.-Sergeant	Rhind, E. J.	1st	15/12/17
6/1967	Corporal	Rhind, H.	2nd	16/9/16
11724	L.-Corporal	Rhodes, F. T. S.	1st	27/12/17
23/1790	Private	Richards, R.	2nd	1/10/16
62387	Private	Richards, W. J.	2nd	7/9/18
6/3843	Private	Richardson, A.	2nd	24/8/18
11725	Private	Richardson, W.	2nd	1/10/16
14723	L.-Sergeant	Richmond, C.	2nd	7/6/17
21735	Corporal	Ricketts, P. C.	2nd	12/10/17
10148	Private	Rider, C. W.	2nd	16/9/16
53968	Private	Rides, A.	2nd	29/1/18
67850	Private	Riley, K.	2nd	24/10/18
24268	Private	Riley, L.	2nd	7/7/17
49846	Private	Rimmer, J.	2nd	12/10/17
21736	Private	Rinaldi, S. T.	2nd	7/4/17
6/802	Private	Riordan, J. J.	1st	16/9/16
15416	Private	Ripley, P. A.	2nd	8/8/17
62390	Private	Ritchie, P.	1st	25/8/18
13/3237	Private	Rix, A. J.	2nd	21/9/16
21737	Private	Robb, W. J.	2nd	12/10/17
6/337	Private	Roberts, S. W.	2nd	6/8/17

Number.	Rank.	Name.	Battalion.	Date.
29300	Private	Robertshaw, W.	2nd	14/6/17
55546	Private	Robertson, W. G.	2nd	24/8/18
6/2533	Private	Robinson, A. G.	1st	7/6/17
53611	Private	Robinson, J. H.	1st	5/4/18
29301	Private	Robinson, R. E.	2nd	12/10/17
19/234	Private	Robinson, R. T.	2nd	7/6/17
13/3072	Private	Rogers, H.	2nd	7/5/17
26177	Private	Rolfe, A.	1st	25/8/18
31538	Private	Rolfes, H. J.	2nd	24/8/18
27143	T.-Corporal	Rollinson, G. O.	3rd	11/6/17
7/1281	Private	Ronan, H.	2nd	14/6/17
6/3853	Private	Roper, L. B.	2nd	1/10/16
48273	Private	Rosanoski, G.	2nd	25/8/18
6/3146	Corporal	Rose, L. H.	1st	7/6/17
39447	Private	Rosenberg, C.	2nd	12/12/17
22372	Private	Rosie, R. H.	2nd	16/8/17
21612	Private	Ross, A.	2nd	7/6/17
55545	Private	Ross, A. G.	3rd	16/12/17
6/2258	Sergeant	Ross, D.	2nd	24/8/18
6/3147	Private	Ross, J.	2nd	16/9/16
37864	Private	Ross, S. M.	2nd	12/10/17
56994	Private	Ross, W.	1st	28/3/18
6/2469	Private	Ross, W. J.	1st	7/6/17
44021	Private	Roud, W.	3rd	5/10/17
6/3449	Corporal	Rowe, M. W.	1st	27/3/18
32541	Corporal	Russell, J. L.	3rd	11/6/17
6/2260	Private	Russell, W. G.	1st	26/9/16
24/2561	Private	Ryan, F. J.	2nd	14/6/17
6/1705	Private	Ryan, J.	2nd	24/8/18
13/3076	Private	Ryan, L. P.	2nd	15/9/16
6/3454	L.-Corporal	Sanders, H.	2nd	12/10/17
6/1706	Private	Sanderson, V. R.	1st	3/12/17
23259	Private	Sandiforth, F.	1st	12/10/17
6/2746	Private	Sangwell, W. H. P.	1st	5/4/18
38853	Private	Satchell, W. E.	3rd	22/11/17
53534	Private	Satherley, E.	2nd	17/5/18
6/3860	Private	Saunders, A. E. B.	2nd	7/6/17
5/728	Private	Saville, P. A.	1st	25/8/18
22427	Private	Scannell, M. J.	1st	7/6/17
33772	Private	Scarlett, N. W.	2nd	30/9/17
11737	Corporal	Scarr, A. G.	2nd	14/6/17
39450	Private	Schmidt, E. T.	3rd	28/12/17
23/1800	Private	Schroder, W. F.	2nd	1/10/16
32472	Private	Schumacher, G. J.	1st	12/10/17
48413	Private	Schwass, L. P.	2nd	15/7/18
32391	Private	Scoltock, W.	3rd	4/10/17
38612	Private	Scott, A. J.	3rd	11/8/17
6/3862	Private	Scott, J.	2nd	30/11/17
6/2905	Sergeant	Scott, R. H.	2nd	1/10/16
21614	Private	Scott, W.	2nd	7/6/17
6/3863	Sergeant	Scrimgeour, R.	2nd	14/6/17
6/2750	L.-Corporal	Scrimshaw, R. A.	1st	27/9/16
23896	Private	Scrivener, L. R.	2nd	29/9/16
37015	Private	Sears, H. J.	2nd	8/10/18
44599	Private	Seaward, H.	1st	7/6/18
49552	Private	Sexton, J.	1st	28/3/18
24/1808	Private	Seyb, W.	2nd	21/9/16

Number.	Rank.	Name.	Battalion.	Date.
59731	Private	Shadwell, E.	2nd	9/5/18
6/929	Private	Shand, D. L.	1st	23/9/16
37104	Private	Shannon, P.	2nd	8/10/18
46618	Private	Sharman, J.	3rd	16/10/17
6/2266	Private	Sharpe, T.	1st	7/6/17
64363	Private	Sharratt, E. T.	2nd	24/8/18
41114	Private	Shaw, E.	1st	12/10/17
63432	Private	Shaw, R. C.	2nd	24/8/18
6/3866	Corporal	Shaw, W.	2nd	21/9/16
34738	Private	Shepherd, B. A.	3rd	4/10/17
27720	Private	Sheridan, T. H.	1st	7/6/17
6/1192	Private	Sherwood, V. E.	1st	25/9/16
32245	Private	Shirley, W.	3rd	20/10/17
39640	Private	Shore, N.	3rd	12/10/17
6/3461	Sergeant	Simmers, W. W.	2nd	13/6/17
40252	Private	Simmons, A. J.	2nd	6/8/17
29308	Private	Simmons, H. S.	2nd	13/6/17
6/3463	Private	Simpson. F.	1st	9/7/16
33968	Private	Simpson, W.	3rd	4/10/17
22410	Private	Slattery. J. P.	1st	12/10/17
6/4644	Act.-Sergt.	Smale, A. D.	1st	27/9/16
48864	Private	Small, A. E.	—	14/4/18
9/1737	Private	Small. D. L.	2nd	19/6/16
38986	L.-Corporal	Small. F. W.	3rd	4/10/17
15619	Private	Smart, R.	2nd	7/7/17
6/726	Sergeant	Smith, A. L.	1st	16/9/16
57276	Private	Smith, B.	2nd	24/8/18
10/3741	Sergeant	Smith, B. A.	1st	11/12/17
15624	Corporal	Smith, C. C. J.	2nd	7/6/17
7/2153	Private	Smith, E. G.	2nd	21/9/16
31546	Private	Smith. E. R.	2nd	7/7/17
39609	Private	Smith, F. A.	2nd	31/7/17
59741	Private	Smith. F. B.	2nd	24/8/18
24230	Private	Smith, F. C.	2nd	1/10/16
46621	Private	Smith, F. C.	3rd	5/10/17
46208	Private	Smith, G.	3rd	4/10/17
34741	Private	Smith, J. A.	3rd	4/10/17
6/2279	Private	Smith, R.	1st	17/9/16
6/4145	Private	Smith, S. R.	2nd	16/9/16
6/3473	Private	Smith. W. S.	1st	9/7/16
47367	Private	Smithies, F.	1st	12/10/17
39474	Private	Smyth, J. G.	2nd	12/8/17
24232	Private	Smyth, W.	2nd	8/10/18
6/4147	Private	Snell. C.	2nd	1/10/16
6/3474	Private	Somerville, J. E.	2nd	7/6/17
17110	Private	Somerville, W. A.	2nd	26/11/17
44603	Private	Soper, N.	2nd	26/5/18
9/1240	Sergeant	Souness, L. W.	1st	15/12/17
24/2095	L.-Sergeant	Souter, P.	2nd	5/4/18
32242	Private	Sowry, L. H.	3rd	11/8/17
45966	Private	Spencer, E.	2nd	26/11/17
13/2921	Private	Squinobal, A. G.	2nd	21/9/16
39483	Private	Stannard, H. E.	2nd	6/8/17
6/3166	Sergeant	Stanton. J. R.	1st	25/8/18
64930	Private	Stanton, R. J.	2nd	8/10/17
26329	Private	Stapleton, G.	2nd	13/6/17
32475	Private	Stapleton, J.	1st	7/6/17

Number.	Rank.	Name.	Battalion.	Date.
6/2762	Private	Stapleton, J. A.	1st	25/9/16
12/4095	Private	Steeds, P. M.	2nd	12/10/17
6/3879	L.-Sergeant	Steel, H. W.	2nd	16/9/16
63778	Private	Steel, J. D.	2nd	24/8/18
48289	Private	Steel, M.	2nd	5/4/18
7/1006	Private	Steele, J. G.	2nd	28/6/16
10179	Private	Stenson, N. R.	1st	12/10/17
13479	Private	Stevens, A.	2nd	1/10/16
6/3480	Private	Stevens, J. J.	2nd	5/4/18
6/3170	Private	Stewart, D.	3rd	15/12/17
42825	Private	Stewart, R. J.	3rd	21/11/17
21900	Private	Stewart, W. G.	2nd	14/6/17
61113	Private	Stirling, E. G.	2nd	8/10/18
24236	Private	Stocker, L.	1st	29/5/17
40256	Private	Stocks, J.	2nd	8/8/17
6/850	Private	Stokes, G. R.	1st	19/7/16
64373	Private	Stone, J.	2nd	27/8/18
24117	Corporal	Strachan, F. A.	1st	12/11/16
6/2909	Sergeant	Strange, D. W.	2nd	21/9/16
32239	Private	Stratford, L. J.	1st	2/9/18
6/3485	Private	Stuart, G.	1st	24/9/16
59750	Private	Stubbington, C. G.	2nd	24/8/18
28601	Private	Sturges, A.	3rd	5/10/17
63782	Private	Sullivan, M.	2nd	24/8/18
6/2292	Private	Sutherland, H.	2nd	21/9/16
26331	Private	Sutherland, R.	2nd	12/10/17
64722	Private	Swiney, F. A. E.	1st	8/5/18
40083	Private	Symonds, R.	3rd	5/10/17
21749	Private	Taiaroa, G.	2nd	7/6/17
27983	Private	Tarbard, G.	1st	2/10/17
51450	Private	Tarleton, J. B.	2nd	17/5/18
15042	Private	Tarrant, A. H. S.	2nd	12/10/17
11978	Private	Tarrant, H.	2nd	12/10/17
23/1841	L.-Corporal	Tassie, A. G.	2nd	21/9/16
27047	Private	Tavender, N. F. H.	1st	7/6/17
21750	Private	Taylor, B. W.	2nd	7/6/17
14166	Private	Taylor, J.	1st	6/5/17
63448	Private	Taylor, J.	2nd	27/8/18
6/4157	Private	Taylor, J. L.	2nd	15/7/16
15452	L.-Corporal	Taylor, N. O.	2nd	7/6/17
46624	Private	Taylor, R.	1st	13/5/18
63689	Private	Taylor, S.	2nd	8/10/18
48296	Private	Taylor, W. J.	2nd	24/8/18
6/2774	Private	Teague, J. D.	1st	7/6/17
30015	Private	Telford, G. W.	3rd	24/11/17
38815	Private	Tennent, K. W.	3rd	4/10/17
6/1416	L.-Corporal	Terris, W. G.	1st	13/8/17
7/2162	L.-Corporal	Thatcher, H. L.	2nd	16/8/17
24/1839	Private	Thew, R. F.	2nd	30/9/16
6/368	Private	Thomason, B. V.	2nd	29/9/16
55564	Private	Thompson, A. C.	2nd	25/12/17
6/3895	Private	Thompson, B.	2nd	16/9/16
30318	Private	Thompson, E.	3rd	11/6/17
11969	Private	Thompson, G. R.	1st	8/6/17
47946	Private	Thompson, J.	1st	23/10/18
62413	Private	Thompson, O. McM.	2nd	24/8/18
6/772	C.S.M.	Thompson, R.	1st	9/7/16

Number.	Rank.	Name.	Battalion.	Date.
6/3182	Private	Thompson, R. W.	2nd	1/10/16
23900	Private	Thompson, V. A.	2nd	7/6/17
10405	Private	Thoumine, D. E.	2nd	1/10/16
34174	Private	Tidswell, D. F.	1st	3/9/18
62415	Private	Tiller, S. J.	2nd	28/3/18
24/1840	Private	Tilson, C. J.	2nd	23/10/18
14168	Private	Tilson, L. G.	2nd	14/6/17
44609	Private	Todd, E. A.	1st	6/4/18
15046	Private	Todd, J.	2nd	7/6/17
31553	Private	Tomlinson, J. D. B.	1st	12/10/17
6/3490	Private	Tonkin, P.	1st	27/9/16
15047	L.-Corporal	Townsend, S. H.	2nd	12/10/17
74243	Private	Trail, A.	1st	10/10/18
37891	Private	Trott, A.	2nd	12/10/17
40087	Private	Trubshoe, G.	2nd	5/4/18
45041	Private	Tubb, E.	2nd	8/10/18
6/2305	Private	Tulley, C.	1st	27/9/16
34754	Private	Tulloch, J. C.	3rd	4/10/17
15626	Private	Tunmer, E. P.	1st	3/12/17
29318	L.-Corporal	Turner, A.	1st	15/5/18
54172	L.-Corporal	Tweed, D. H.	2nd	8/10/18
6/2361	L.-Corporal	Tyree, W. A.	3rd	4/10/17
6/3190	Sergeant	Varney, J. F.	1st	12/10/17
46810	Private	Vesey, R.	2nd	13/12/17
34756	Private	Vincent, A. E.	2nd	6/8/17
32259	Private	Vincent, A. L.	3rd	10/6/17
15049	Private	Vincent, L. McD.	2nd	14/6/17
59763	Private	Vincent, P. D.	2nd	24/10/18
28927	L.-Corporal	Vincent, S. V. C.	2nd	12/10/17
44038	Corporal	Waddell, G. H.	2nd	23/4/18
34757	Private	Waine, F. J. W.	2nd	12/10/17
27998	Private	Waite, W. F.	1st	14/6/17
6/1747a	Private	Waldron, G. E.	1st	9/7/16
31557	Private	Walker, A. R.	1st	5/12/17
30325	Private	Walker, J.	3rd	5/10/17
6/2789	Private	Walker, J. J.	1st	25/9/16
36375	Private	Wallace, H. J.	3rd	5/10/17
44039	Private	Wallace, S.	2nd	16/8/17
44040	Private	Wallis, C.	3rd	18/10/17
9/1755	L.-Corporal	Wallis, E. T. B.	1st	12/10/17
6/3912	Private	Walsh, J.	2nd	27/7/16
6/3911	Private	Walsh, J.	2nd	16/9/16
15051	Corporal	Walsh, P.	1st	3/12/17
51669	Private	Walsh, T. J.	3rd	16/10/17
38324	Private	Ward, T. F.	1st	5/11/18
63797	Private	Wareham, W. H.	1st	29/9/18
27050	Private	Wark, T.	2nd	6/8/17
14725	Sergeant	Warner, A.	2nd	12/10/17
24446	Private	Warner, C.	2nd	7/6/17
6/2006	L.-Corporal	Warner, F.	2nd	16/9/16
6/381	Sergeant	Warnock, H. D.	1st	7/6/17
42828	Private	Waterhouse, T. E.	2nd	8/10/18
44177	Private	Waters, G. W.	1st	29/9/18
6/1750	L.-Corporal	Waterson, H.	1st	9/7/16
63799	Private	Waterson, H. R.	2nd	26/8/18
11140	L.-Corporal	Watkinson, P.	2nd	12/10/17
44044	Private	Watson, C. L.	2nd	12/10/17

Number.	Rank.	Name.	Battalion.	Date.
34181	Private	Watson, G. E.	3rd	28/7/17
22179	Private	Watson, J. R.	2nd	8/6/17
6/2798	Private	Watson, L. J.	1st	25/9/16
14171	Private	Watson, W.	2nd	14/6/17
64688	Private	Watt, J.	1st	30/9/18
15056	L.-Sergeant	Watts, F. J.	2nd	12/10/17
32976	Private	Waugh, J.	2nd	30/5/18
41683	Private	Way, E. J.	2nd	31/7/17
26350	Private	Weastell, S. D.	1st	1/6/17
6/1753	Private	Webb, H. C.	1st	9/7/16
63978	Private	Weeds, A. E.	1st	15/7/18
7/1929	Private	Weenink, R. F.	2nd	21/9/16
32407	Private	Weir. J. G. H.	3rd	4/10/17
6/2801	Private	Weir, P.	1st	16/6/16
11751	Private	Wellings, W.	1st	12/10/17
7/289a	Private	Wells, A. E.	2nd	5/8/17
6/3918	Corporal	Wells, W. W.	2nd	21/9/16
34763	Corporal	Welsh, A. D.	1st	29/9/18
6/3919	Private	Welsh, W. H.	2nd	1/10/16
6/4373	Private	Welshman, W.	1st	27/9/16
56494	Private	Wenzlick, G.	1st	3/9/18
38326	Private	West, L. B.	2nd	30/11/17
32481	Private	Westenra, F. A.	3rd	16/10/17
63802	Private	Weyergang, O. P. A.	1st	4/6/18
61012	Private	White, H. J.	1st	25/8/18
7/1157	Private	White, T. P.	2nd	17/5/16
11/2003	Corporal	White, W.	2nd	26/11/17
21628	Private	Whiteside, J.	2nd	7/6/17
44614	Private	Whitfield, P. P.	3rd	9/10/17
58635	Private	Whitley, A. V.	2nd	20/12/17
6/3507	Private	Whitmore, J. E.	1st	27/9/16
6/4376	Private	Whitteker, A. E.	2nd	7/6/17
32980	Private	Whittem, J. H.	3rd	9/8/17
14174	Private	Whyte, R. H.	1st	12/10/17
37904	Private	Wickens, F. G.	2nd	29/3/18
28055	Sergeant	Wigzell, J. O. F.	1st	5/4/18
24259	Private	Wild, H.	1st	12/10/17
6/3201	Private	Wildman. F. C.	2nd	21/9/16
6/2324	Private	Wilkes, O. G.	1st	22/1/17
6/3508	Private	Wilkinson, H. A.	1st	17/9/16
6/1760	Private	Willey, G.	1st	9/7/16
41692	Private	Williams, A. O.	2nd	29/3/18
6/2326	L.-Corporal	Williams, F. J.	1st	11/7/16
58638	Private	Williams, J. R.	1st	31/5/18
13/970	Private	Williams, S.	1st	27/9/16
40755	Private	Williams, W. J.	1st	5/12/17
29118	L.-Sergeant	Williams, W. R.	1st	31/5/18
55025	Private	Williamson. P. C.	1st	5/4/18
6/2811	L.-Corporal	Willis, F.	1st	27/9/16
6/2812	Corporal	Willoughby, S.	1st	7/6/17
6/3204	Private	Wills, A. V.	1st	25/9/16
70579	Private	Wills, W. F.	1st	9/10/18
34766	L.-Corporal	Willstead, C. E.	3rd	4/10/17
34767	Private	Wilson, A. B. D.	2nd	6/8/17
32491	Private	Wilson. A. J.	1st	12/10/17
6/3510	Private	Wilson. C. E.	2nd	21/9/16
46635	Private	Wilson. G. C. L.	1st	14/12/17

Number.	Rank.	Name.	Battalion.	Date.
24447	Private	Wilson, H. H.	1st	7/6/17
6/4651	Private	Wilson, J.	1st	12/10/17
53950	Private	Wilson, J.	1st	2/6/18
28929	Private	Wilson, K. D.	2nd	14/6/17
6/3515	Private	Wilson, R. H.	1st	30/7/16
40267	Private	Windleborn, L. H.	2nd	13/12/17
6/2334	Corporal	Winter, L. G.	2nd	12/10/17
45291	Private	Winter, W.	1st	12/10/17
15628	L.-Corporal	Withers, H.	1st	3/12/17
23/2597	Private	Witting, C. W.	2nd	16/9/16
6/2329	Private	Wood, T H.	1st	27/9/16
6/4653	Private	Woodberry, S. O.	2nd	21/9/16
23914	L.-Corporal	Woods, V. F.	2nd	13/6/17
8/3798	Private	Wooldridge, F. A. C.	2nd	1/10/16
42841	Private	Woolford, F. J.	1st	25/8/18
6/3935	Private	Woolhouse, E. J.	2nd	21/9/16
46970	Private	Wornall, W.	1st	13/10/17
32489	Private	Wright, S. E.	1st	2/10/17
28928	L.-Sergeant	Wright, T. H.	1st	25/8/18
27412	Private	Wright, W.	1st	18/6/17
51464	Private	Wright, W.	1st	3/12/17
32977	Private	Wrobleske, F.	3rd	28/12/17
6/2969	Private	Wylie, F.	2nd	15/9/16
23/985	L.-Corporal	Yardley, H. H.	2nd	16/9/16
25/921	Sergeant	Yarrall, H. S.	3rd	11/6/17
62472	Private	Yeates, F. F.	2nd	4/9/18
46217	Private	Young, C. A. M.	2nd	7/9/18

ACCIDENTALLY KILLED.
Officers.

Number.	Rank.	Name.	Battalion.	Date.
6/1104	Major	Brown, F. B.	2nd	7/3/17
	Lieut.	Carey, C. F.	Reserve	7/11/16
6/1109	Major	Jordan, B. S.	2nd	24/5/18

Other Ranks.

6/1782	Private	Booker, T. E.	1st	8/3/17
44354	Corporal	Crombie, A. J.	1st	12/12/17
9/1280	Private	Donaldson, J.	2nd	26/6/16
34114	Private	McGinley, J.	3rd	3/7/17
7/2122	Corporal	Pawsey, A. A.	2nd	26/11/17

DIED OF WOUNDS.
Officers.

Number.	Rank.	Name.	Battalion.	Date.
40744	2nd Lieut.	Arnold, A. J.	1st	27/8/18
23924	2nd Lieut.	Bowden, J. D.	2nd	10/10/16
22186	2nd Lieut.	Fitch, R. D.	2nd	6/5/18
39730	Captain	Graham, J.	1st	4/10/17
6/645	2nd Lieut.	Harper, N. R.	—	15/4/18
6/2091	Lieut.	Joyce, N. S.	2nd	8/6/16

2 A

Number.	Rank.	Name.	Battalion.	Date.
44189	Lieut.	Kesteven, D. L.	2nd	24/8/18
22439	2nd Lieut.	MacLeod, M. K.	2nd	13/10/17
7/2072	Captain	Morrison, M. G.	2nd	15/8/17
6/2448	2nd Lieut.	Norton, R. H. I.	1st	9/5/18
5/118a	Lieut.	Palmer, P. J.	2nd	7/6/17
38867	2nd Lieut.	Pearce, J. J. L.	1st	25/8/18
32226	2nd Lieut.	Price, E. A.	2nd	10/10/18
33072	2nd Lieut.	Reeve, L. W. P.	2nd	13/11/18
6/1990	Lieut.	Stone, W. J.	1st	13/10/17
15468	Lieut.	Thompson, W. P.	2nd	7/6/17
15448	Lieut.	Wilson, A. C.	2nd	12/6/17

Other Ranks.

Number	Rank	Name	Battalion	Date
14043	Corporal	Absolom, M.	1st	3/12/17
62221	Private	Ackroyd, A.	1st	17/8/18
48149	Private	Adair, V. H. S.	2nd	9/5/18
11589	Private	Adams, T. C.	2nd	7/2/17
6/2520	Private	Adamson, M. I.	2nd	30/3/18
44332	Private	Adkin, G. D.	1st	10/9/18
14916	Private	Affleck, D.	2nd	25/4/18
56997	Private	Alding, J. W.	1st	2/9/18
6/2388	Private	Allan, J. E. W.	1st	23/9/16
29203	Private	Allan, R. B.	3rd	17/10/17
10200	Private	Allen, C. B.	2nd	15/9/16
6/2052	Private	Allington, S.	1st	21/11/16
38254	Private	Amos, C. A.	1st	12/10/17
15460	Private	Amos, E.	1st	6/6/17
43935	Private	Anderson, C. R.	2nd	14/10/17
32931	Private	Anderson, W.	3rd	5/10/17
11594	Private	Andrews, A. H.	2nd	21/9/16
24/2513	L.-Sergeant	Andrews, J.	2nd	11/6/17
11595	Private	Annand, F.	1st	22/10/17
33671	Private	Anstiss, W. T.	3rd	29/7/17
6/584	L.-Corporal	Armitage, J.	1st	2/10/16
44570	Private	Armstrong, M. J.	1st	5/9/18
6/3609	Private	Arrowsmith, A.	2nd	21/9/16
31455	L.-Sergeant	Arthur, E. W.	2nd	8/4/18
27197	Private	Ashton, G.	2nd	28/3/18
59580	Private	Astbury, H. V.		29/4/18
34608	Private	Attewell, A. J.	3rd	20/12/17
6/585	Corporal	Avent, F. R.	1st	30/9/16
6/10	Sergeant	Bailey, W. W.	1st	6/6/17
7/1440	L.-Corporal	Baird, H. J.	2nd	1/11/16
64842	Private	Baker, J.	2nd	8/10/18
41067	Private	Barber, E. A. B.	1st	22/1/18
36303	Private	Barker, J. L.	2nd	28/3/18
41466	Private	Barnard, J. C.	2nd	8/4/18
29208	Private	Barratt, G. W. F.	1st	25/12/17
41469	Private	Batten, L. C.	3rd	6/10/17
6/1778	Private	Bazett, G. K.	2nd	7/6/17
57458	Private	Beckett, J. E.	2nd	6/2/18
6/2932	Private	Beddis, W. J.	2nd	30/9/16
36306	Private	Begg, A.	3rd	14/8/17
67621	Private	Bell, D. L.	2nd	9/10/18
23/2542	Private	Bell, J. S.	2nd	17/10/17
6/3991	Private	Berry, A. F.	1st	6/9/18
38257	Private	Biggs, F. A.	3rd	29/10/17

Number.	Rank.	Name.	Battalion.	Date.
11611	Private	Biggs, F. A. E.	2nd	17/9/16
45982	Private	Bird, H. R.	1st	29/10/17
6/2546	Private	Blackburn, A.	1st	18/6/16
6/1466	Private	Blackburn, W.	1st	3/4/17
6/2069	L.-Corporal	Blair, A. C.	2nd	25/9/16
62487	Private	Bland, R. W.	2nd	7/9/18
59591	Private	Blunden, R. P.	1st	27/8/18
62693	Private	Bohringer, H. E.	1st	12/11/18
47037	Private	Boughton, T. G. J.	1st	22/12/17
6/2071	Corporal	Boulton, P. R.	2nd	7/6/17
24134	L.-Corporal	Bradley, J.	1st	22/10/17
43677	Private	Brew, D.	2nd	12/12/17
38931	Private	Briggs, J.	1st	28/8/18
6/2945	L.-Corporal	Brighting, L. C.	1st	6/11/16
61198	Private	Brock, W. S.	1st	25/8/18
47065	Private	Brouard, D. W.	1st	22/12/17
13406	Private	Brown, F. H.	1st	16/10/17
47309	Private	Brown, R.	2nd	24/4/18
6/2954	Corporal	Brown, S.	1st	21/10/17
6/1476	Private	Browne, C. H. O.	1st	18/9/16
6/2079	Private	Brownlee, R.	1st	14/6/16
6/2080	Private	Bruce, W. S.	1st	14/10/17
6/3265	Private	Burke, H. J.	2nd	31/5/16
25186	Private	Bush, L. A.	2nd	8/8/17
6/2563	Private	Butler, A.	1st	19/9/16
6/2565	Private	Byron, C.	1st	16/7/16
22769	Private	Cairns, J.	1st	23/10/17
21562	Private	Campbell, J. B.	2nd	8/6/17
44574	Private	Campbell, P. D.	1st	2/10/17
6/3647	Private	Campbell, R. A.	2nd	3/12/17
6/2400	Private	Carlyon, S. J.	1st	11/7/16
7/1981	L.-Corporal	Carter, R. C.	1st	27/8/18
6/2825	L.-Corporal	Carver, L. T.	2nd	12/10/18
59606	Private	Cate, A. A.	1st	15/9/18
14940	Private	Cate, H. A.	2nd	16/11/16
6/2090	Private	Chapman, A.	1st	10/7/16
15490	L.-Corporal	Chapman, G. J.	2nd	29/8/18
6/4009	Private	Chapman, N. F.	1st	17/9/16
14941	Private	Chapman, W. J.	1st	17/10/18
45998	Private	Christophers, J. A.	1st	5/12/17
6/3653	L.-Corporal	Churchill, J. L.	2nd	14/12/17
15500	Private	Claridge, B. S.	2nd	9/6/17
6/3657	Private	Clark, D.	2nd	17/9/16
6/3275	Private	Cleworth, J. H.	1st	12/7/16
31470	Private	Clive, P. D.	2nd	14/4/18
6/3659	Private	Clough, E. E.	1st	17/10/17
34032	Private	Collins, M.	3rd	12/8/17
70247	Private	Cooke, D. A.	1st	30/9/18
7/1602	Private	Cooke, R. G.	2nd	4/7/16
40192	Private	Coppell, J. H.	1st	26/10/17
34639	Private	Crawford, R. A.	3rd	8/10/17
26997	Corporal	Cribb, W. H.	2nd	27/5/18
6/3219	Private	Cronin, F. D.	1st	7/10/16
27229	Private	Cronin, T. J.	1st	13/12/17
6/2105	Sergeant	Cruickshank, A.	1st	26/5/18
6/3177	Private	Crum, G. D. J.	1st	17/9/16
13425	L.-Corporal	Cunningham, F. J.	1st	31/3/18

Number.	Rank.	Name.	Battalion.	Date.
61222	Private	Currie, W. R.	2nd	10/10/18
6/3294	Private	Dansie, T.	1st	4/10/16
46562	Private	Darby, W. D.	1st	15/10/17
6/1826	Private	Davis, C. H.	1st	30/7/16
33701	Private	Davis, H. S.	3rd	20/10/17
34646	Private	Dean, W. H.	1st	16/10/17
34647	Private	Delaney, E.	3rd	6/10/17
6/2597	L.-Corporal	Derrett, L. W.	1st	14/10/17
6/809	Private	Dick, J. A.	1st	17/12/17
64299	Private	Dixon, J.	1st	17/5/18
6/3300	Private	Dobbie, P. F.	1st	7/6/17
55450	Private	Dobby, A. J.	1st	9/1/18
38943	Private	Dobby, G. T.	2nd	17/8/17
40194	Private	Docksey, A. H.	1st	17/12/17
41512	Private	Doyle, P. E.	3rd	20/10/17
6/621	Private	Doyle, W. J.	1st	29/5/16
5/41a	Private	Duke, J. M.	2nd	19/5/18
23/1038	Private	Duncan, N.	2nd	30/7/16
6/1277	Sergeant	Dwyer, T. B.	1st	7/4/18
6/3007	Private	Edman, H. L.	2nd	11/11/16
27766	Private	Eggeling, H. F.	1st	3/10/17
42795	Private	Eginton, C.	3rd	22/11/17
6/3008	L.-Corporal	Elderton, A.	1st	10/7/16
38511	Private	Elliot, J. C. M.	3rd	6/10/17
24149	L.-Corporal	Ellis, H.	2nd	12/10/17
6/4603	Private	Ettles, W. A.	2nd	21/9/16
41519	Private	Farrelley, J. W.	1st	3/12/17
7/1355	Private	Faville, C. E.	2nd	26/9/16
62284	Private	Finn, P.	1st	2/6/18
6/3315	Private	Fisher, R. P.	2nd	31/10/18
6/3316	Private	Fitzgerald, T.	1st	20/10/16
73013	Private	Foote, W. E.	2nd	11/10/18
24154	Private	Ford, J.	1st	19/5/18
21669	Private	Foster, L.	2nd	22/10/17
24157	Private	Fraser, A. D.	2nd	8/12/17
14408	Sergeant	Fraser, W. M.	2nd	15/8/18
23/1635	Private	Freeman, H. G.	2nd	15/9/16
38950	Private	Frew, A.	1st	13/12/17
6/2135	Private	Frickelton, W. T.	1st	28/9/16
23821	Private	Galbraith, W. McA.	2nd	30/9/16
23/1637	L.-Corporal	Gardner, A. P.	2nd	22/9/16
48193	Private	Gavigan, O. D.	2nd	30/1/18
6/231	Private	Geary, T. F.	1st	12/10/17
32163	Private	Gibbons, G. W. T.	2nd	8/6/17
27164	Corporal	Gibson, H. H. W.	2nd	6/2/17
58509	Private	Gidley, R. N.	1st	2/9/18
29244	Private	Gill, F. B.	2nd	14/4/18
6/3022	Private	Gill, G.	2nd	17/9/16
62300	Private	Gill, H. H.	2nd	2/10/18
40747	Corporal	Glover, C. J.	1st	9/1/18
6/1031	C.S.M.	Godfrey, J. A.	1st	26/12/17
7/2012	Private	Gosling, C. W.	2nd	15/9/16
22401	Private	Gospodnetich, S. A.	1st	7/12/17
58514	Private	Gourlay, A. V.	1st	30/8/18
6/1300	Private	Graham, P. J.	1st	6/12/17
12/3030	Corporal	Grant, W.	1st	23/1/18
6/3717	Sergeant	Grantley, E.	2nd	15/8/18

Number.	Rank.	Name.	Battalion.	Date.
37801	Private	Greeks, R. S.	1st	17/10/17
6/2143	Private	Greer, S.	1st	2/10/16
6/3334	Private	Griffin, R. W.	1st	29/5/16
57069	Private	Guerin, J.	—	23/3/18
6/4049	Private	Gummow, E.	2nd	7/6/17
38280	Private	Gunn, A. E.	1st	12/10/17
6/2642	Private	Gunning, R. J.	1st	18/6/17
62304	Private	Hall, H. W.	2nd	8/10/18
14976	Private	Halliday, R.	2nd	8/7/17
6/2651	Private	Hammill, A.	2nd	22/9/16
7/54	Private	Hampton, J. M.	1st	5/10/16
14978	Private	Hancock, J.	2nd	24/11/16
6/248	L.-Corporal	Hannen, S.	2nd	17/8/18
46582	Private	Hansen, J.	2nd	12/10/17
14979	Private	Hardy, E. L. G.	3rd	19/10/17
24102	Private	Hardy, J.	1st	28/7/17
6/3729	Private	Harris, A. L.	2nd	17/10/16
40211	Private	Harris, J.	1st	12/10/17
15538	Private	Harris, R. F. W.	2nd	12/6/17
10230	Private	Harrison, W. J.	2nd	5/10/16
24/1996	Private	Hartnett, J.	2nd	23/9/16
43974	Private	Harry, B.	3rd	14/5/18
26266	Private	Harvey, A. P.	2nd	10/10/18
23/1661	Corporal	Harvey, C.	2nd	14/12/17
23/1999	Private	Harvey, L. G.	1st	29/11/16
7/209	Private	Harvey, P.	2nd	28/9/16
34068	L.-Corporal	Hawthorne, N.	3rd	21/12/17
32565	Sergeant	Hedges, A. E.	1st	13/12/17
58529	Private	Hegarty, G. T.	1st	11/1/18
66167	Private	Henderson, D.	1st	6/11/18
36811	L.-Corporal	Hendry, W. E.	1st	24/12/17
64708	Private	Henessey, C.	2nd	4/9/18
44582	Private	Heslop, G. W.	2nd	24/10/17
6/4058	Private	Hiddleston, A. H.	1st	15/9/16
24/2532	Private	Hill, E. T.	2nd	22/9/16
47331	Private	Hillock, T.	1st	29/3/18
30061	Corporal	Hind, W. E. R.	2nd	6/10/17
62871	Private	Hitch, G. E.	1st	24/10/18
41551	Private	Hodgson, G. H.	2nd	13/10/17
27166	Private	Hoffman, W.	2nd	28/11/17
6/2666	Private	Hollis, D. E.	1st	27/7/16
73502	Private	Hood, W. R. E.	2nd	7/11/18
6/2501	Private	Hooper, T. H.	1st	7/8/16
24/2006	Private	Hosie, A. J.	2nd	16/7/17
6/2670	Corporal	Hoskins, W. W.	1st	1/5/18
47838	Corporal	Hubbard, E. B.	1st	12/3/18
41557	Private	Hudson, G. H.	2nd	28/3/18
40216	Private	Hughes, M. J.	2nd	19/8/17
6/3356	L.-Corporal	Hume, R. A.	1st	14/10/17
7/2331	Private	Hunter, F. T.	2nd	15/9/16
24/2010	Private	Illingworth, W. L.	3rd	13/8/17
29260	Private	Inglis, L.	3rd	18/6/17
6/3755	Private	Ingram, F. C.	1st	8/6/17
6/4273	Sergeant	Ireland, A. E.	1st	12/8/16
6/2170	Corporal	Israel, L. L.	3rd	5/10/17
7/2190	Private	Ivey, F. A.	2nd	13/8/17

Number.	Rank.	Name.	Battalion.	Date.
63744	Private	Jakins, E. C.	2nd	25/8/18
7/1851	Private	James, A. G.	2nd	29/11/16
23/1699	Private	Jennings, W.	2nd	21/9/16
26269	L.-Corporal	Johnson, G. A.	1st	18/9/18
40012	Private	Johnstone, W. W. E.	2nd	16/10/17
21694	Private	Jones, F.	3rd	30/10/17
29264	Corporal	Jones, W. G. H.	2nd	22/10/18
14996	Private	Kavanagh, J. J.	2nd	14/10/17
29172	Private	Kay, A. I. W.	1st	14/10/17
26274	Private	Kean, C.	2nd	14/6/17
6/4076	Private	Kearton, R. D.	2nd	18/6/16
36919	Private	Kelly, S. T.	3rd	14/8/17
15557	Corporal	Kelly, W. J.	1st	27/8/18
55505	Private	Kennedy, A. F.	2nd	5/4/18
6/1595	L.-Corporal	Kerridge, G. W.	2nd	3/7/16
6/4080	Private	Kimber, G.	3rd	27/12/17
37195	Private	King. C. W. J.	2nd	24/10/17
7/221	L.-Corporal	Kinzett, L. J.	2nd	26/9/16
6/3065	Private	Kirdy, J. A.	1st	8/6/17
7/1372	Private	Kirk, E. W.	2nd	7/4/18
48223	Private	Kirkland, J.	3rd	20/10/17
6/2683	Private	Knowles, C. L.	1st	12/10/17
26280	Private	Kohlies, W. G.	2nd	10/6/17
13/3181	Private	Laing, A. M.	1st	31/7/16
24/2019	Private	Lankey, C. J.	2nd	22/10/16
29036	Private	Legh. W. A.	2nd	8/10/18
11688	Private	Lewis, B.	2nd	8/6/17
6/4291	Private	Lewis, S.	1st	5/12/17
6/3072	Private	Lewis, T. W.	1st	30/9/16
6/4088	Private	Lindsay. J. W.	2nd	1/10/16
26122	Private	Little. J. R.	1st	10/6/17
67809	Private	Lowe, J. A.	2nd	8/10/18
54374	Private	Lowe, S. C.	1st	25/5/18
29040	Private	Lunt. F. W.	3rd	30/9/17
10/4471	Private	Lusty, O.	2nd	2/10/16
64650	Private	Lynch. P.	1st	27/8/18
15583	Private	McAllister. G. B.	1st	5/11/18
6/1905	Private	Macann. G.	1st	9/7/16
60969	Private	McAulay, A.	2nd	28/4/18
6/4101	Private	McCarthy, J.	2nd	20/9/16
70176	Private	McClung, G. E.	2nd	5/11/18
15012	Private	McColgan. W.	2nd	9/6/17
6/2213	Private	McCool. P.	1st	9/6/17
6/3798	Private	McDonald. H. D.	2nd	1/10/16
40042	Private	McEwen, C. C.	1st	2/9/18
7/2103	Private	McGill, G.	2nd	23/9/16
26302	Private	McGowan, C.	2nd	5/6/17
6/4300	Private	McGregor. E. E.	2nd	11/7/16
6/307	L.-Corporal	McIsaac. S. R.	1st	11/10/16
6/4106	Private	McIven, R. C.	2nd	6/10/16
44139	Private	McKay, W.	1st	27/8/18
6/1915	Private	McKenzie, H. G.	2nd	10/10/18 (N·Z.)
32365	Private	McLaren, R. E.	2nd	8/10/18
48250	Private	McLean, J. D.	1st	8/6/18
44591	Private	McManus, J. B.	2nd	12/10/17
6/4303	Private	Marks, T.	1st	10/7/16
34700	Private	Marshall. J. B.	3rd	13/10/17

Number.	Rank.	Name.	Battalion.	Date.
6/3779	Private	Marshall, V. S.	2nd	21/9/16
72075	Private	Martin, A.	2nd	8/11/18
6/4305	Private	Martin, H. H.	1st	13/3/17
16484	Private	Mathews, P. J.	3rd	5/10/17
49638	Private	Maylen, W.	2nd	28/3/18
49828	Private	Maynard, A.	2nd	23/10/17
15004	L.-Corporal	Mead, E. W. L.	2nd	12/10/17
6/2708	Private	Messenger, W.	1st	22/7/17
6/1625	L.-Corporal	Mewton, R.	1st	16/6/16
38973	Private	Mills. S. C.	2nd	23/12/17
32356	Private	Mitchell, J.	3rd	18/10/17
24207	Private	Mockett, J. J.	1st	31/3/17
26291	Private	Moody, H.	1st	16/6/17
24/2038	Private	Moores, H. H.	2nd	16/9/16
25/1781	Private	Moores, P. A.	2nd	2/10/16
45891	Private	Morgan J. S.	1st	31/3/18
6/2206	Private	Morgan, R. H.	1st	11/9/16
52688	L.-Corporal	Moyna, E. T. J.	2nd	21/10/18
69968	Private	Muir. A.	2nd	23/10/18
34708	Private	Munro, C.	3rd	22/10/17
6/1346	L.-Corporal	Munro, R.	2nd	8/9/18
24209	Corporal	Murdoch. C. G.	1st	3/9/18
7/754	Sergeant	Murdoch, R. J.	1st	7/6/17
25137	Private	Murfitt, J. S. H.	2nd	12/10/17
64318	Private	Myers, F.	1st	30/9/18
6/1668	L.-Corporal	Napier, P. J.	1st	20/9/16
6/4111	Private	Naughton, R.	1st	16/10/16
24211	Corporal	Neal, H.	1st	29/9/18
49647	Private	Nelson, T.	2nd	10/1/18
7/2300	Private	New. J. C.	2nd	21/9/16
13082	Private	Nichols, J. C.	2nd	4/10/16
6/316	Private	Ninnes, T.	1st	17/10/17
6/3415	Private	Norris, S.	1st	24/5/16
28909	Private	Nutsford, H. G.	2nd	11/6/17
23868	L.-Corporal	O'Connell, J.	2nd	29/9/17
63764	Private	O'Grady, E. W.	1st	1/10/18
6/2719	Private	O'Shea, D.	1st	21/9/16
6/318	L.-Sergeant	Owen. H. F.	2nd	8/8/17
6/3123	C.S.M.	Page. W. E.	2nd	10/6/17
6/1949	Private	Paget, E. C.	2nd	16/6/17
60982	Private	Paget. F. H.	2nd	30/5/18
6/1951	Private	Parsons, J.	1st	13/7/16
6/1686	Private	Patchett, S.	1st	10/7/16
28914	Private	Paterson, G. H.	1st	7/6/17
33761	Private	Pavelka E.	3rd	20/6/17
6/1688	Corporal	Peake, W.	1st	1/6/17
21730	Private	Pearce. G.	1st	15/10/17
21162	Sergeant	Pearson. J.	2nd	4/9/18
59711	Private	Penn. T. L.	2nd	24/10/18
6/2242	Private	Peters. A.	2nd	30/5/16
39472	Private	Phillips, H.	2nd	8/8/17
46203	Private	Philpot. H. G.	2nd	12/1/18
64342	Private	Phinix, J.	2nd	26/5/18
40243	Private	Pitcher. A. J.	2nd	12/1/18
7/2126	Corporal	Pluck. J. T.	2nd	12/10/17
6/1692	Private	Pollard. F.	2nd	22/9/16
6/2728	L.-Corporal	Pollard. L. N.	1st	28/7/17

Number.	Rank.	Name.	Battalion.	Date.
45614	Private	Pritchard, H. N.	2nd	30/8/18
32723	Private	Proctor, W.	2nd	8/10/18
6/2904	Sergeant	Ramsay, R. G.	2nd	20/9/16
34730	Private	Rankin, E. J.	3rd	21/12/17
6/3440	Private	Rankin, J. J.	1st	10/7/16
29294	Private	Rasmussen, J.	3rd	1/1/18
34731	Private	Raxworthy, J. R.	3rd	4/10/17
6/4642	Private	Reeves, A.	1st	16/9/16
6/1700	Private	Reid, J.	1st	14/7/16
6/127	Sergeant	Rennie, R.	1st	20/7/16
27362	Private	Ritchie, H. S.	1st	17/10/17
37863	Private	Ritchie, T.	2nd	20/2/18
33769	Private	Robinson, F. G.	2nd	7/4/18
6/3852	Private	Rodda, B. B.	2nd	3/10/16
11729	Private	Roding, D.	2nd	19/9/16
24227	Private	Rogers, A. E.	1st	2/2/17
48276	L.-Corporal	Russell, H. S.	2nd	8/11/17
46096	Private	Salamonson, A. J.	3rd	15/10/17
37890	L.-Corporal	Sammett, J.	2nd	7/9/18
21613	Private	Sandford, W.	2nd	22/6/17
55550	Private	Schumacher, F. W.	2nd	14/4/18
10151	L.-Corporal	Seymour, G. A.	1st	3/12/17
5/178	Private	Shanks, R. S.	1st	26/9/16
46921	Private	Shearer, T. G.	3rd	20/12/17
1/397	Sergeant	Shelley, P. B.	1st	26/8/18
34740	Private	Shepherd, W. H.	3rd	29/7/17
11579	Sergeant	Sheppard, J. C.	1st	20/9/16
6/1713	Private	Shirley, S.	2nd	21/10/17
64671	Private	Simpson, W. H.	1st	24/4/18
11738	Private	Singleton, M.	1st	22/4/17
6/2345	Private	Skilton, J. J.	3rd	16/12/17 .
7/2313	Private	Sleeman, E. A.	2nd	4/11/16
32240	Private	Smail, W. J.	1st	3/4/18
9/1137	L.-Corporal	Small, F. J.	2nd	9/6/17
27169	Private	Smee. F. F.	1st	9/6/17
55553	Private	Smith, A. A.	1st	27/3/18
34153	Private	Smith, A. O. R.	3rd	26/10/17
72680	Private	Smith, D. McK.	1st	1/10/18
27971	Private	Smith, E. P.	3rd	6/10/17
15039	Private	Smith, R.	1st	8/6/17
30300	Private	Smith, W. A. W.	1st	5/12/17
63683	Private	Smith, W. H.	1st	5/9/18
24106	Sergeant	Sotheran, O.	2nd	14/10/17
6/3165	Private	Stade, M. A.	2nd	21/9/16
21743	Private	Stagg, L. T.	1st	7/12/17
6/2283	Private	Stephen, D.	2nd	25/8/18
62405	Private	Stewart, H.	2nd	24/10/18
74239	Private	Stewart. R.	1st	27/10/18
19/266	Private	Stocks. R.	1st	16/10/18
6/3483	Private	Stowell. A. P.	1st	6/6/17
34746	Private	Styles, W. J. M.	1st	27/3/18
40081	Private	Sullivan, J.	2nd	8/10/18
11743	Private	Sutcliffe. W. H.	2nd	25/9/16
6/2768	Private	Sutton. F.	1st	23/7/17
38992	Private	Tapp. J.	3rd	8/10/17
62464	Private	Tarbutt. E. B.	2nd	3/9/18
6/2339	Private	Tate. C.	1st	5/10/16

Number.	Rank.	Name.	Battalion.	Date.
56198	Private	Taylor, J.	2nd	24/10/18
32256	Private	Taylor, R.	2nd	21/9/18
6/2775	Private	Terrill, E.	1st	16/7/16
44033	Private	Terry, J. McL.	2nd	28/3/18
27393	Private	Thomas, A.	2nd	17/8/18
15627	Private	Thomas, W.	2nd	16/11/16
6/3894	Private	Thompson, A.	2nd	23/9/16
40851	Private	·Thompson, R. W.	2nd	27/8/18
44035	Private	Thyne, G.	2nd	13/8/17
6/4365	Private	Tincler, C. K. K.	1st	11/6/17
46212	Private	Tombs, W. H.	3rd	6/12/17
6/3901	Private	Townshend, A. W.	2nd	6/2/17
37894	Private	Tremain, H.	1st	16/5/18
45024	Private	Turnbull, A. C.	1st	5/12/17
6/3187	Corporal	Twidle, J. V.	1st	10/8/17
29321	L.-Sergeant	Ure, J. H.	—	29/4/18
46214	Private	Verrall, V. E.	1st	21/1/18
6/1426	L.-Corporal	Wade, H.	1st	24/5/16
6/2311	L.-Corporal	Wakelin, L.	1st	18/8/17
21624	Private	Walker, A.	1st	6/9/18
42829	Private	Walker, F.	3rd	18/10/17
6/3910	L.-Corporal	Walker, G.	2nd	1/10/16
51295	Private	Walker, W.	1st	19/10/17
23/1861	Sergeant	Walker, W. R.	2nd	20/12/17
21754	Corporal	Wanden, H. W.	2nd	27/3/18
58632	Private	Warn, F.	2nd	26/4/18
18516	Private	Warren, E. L.	2nd	14/10/17
68807	Private	Warren, I.	2nd	25/8/18
58633	Private	Watkins, E.	2nd	13/7/18
51204	Private	Watson, R.	1st	12/10/17
53849	Private	Watt, W. J.	1st	20/9/18
46630	Private	Webley, H.	3rd	6/11/17
6/2322	Private	Wells, J.	2nd	11/6/17
63697	Private	Westwood, F.	1st	26/8/18
6/388	R.S.M.	Wheway, A.	2nd	19/6/17
29328	Private	White, J.	2nd	11/6/17
6/3198	Private	White, T. H.	2nd	12/10/16
6/2010	Private	Whiteford, J.	1st	5/12/17
53724	Private	Wilds, J. E.	2nd	22/4/18
6/3202	Corporal	Wilkinson, F.	2nd	20/9/16
6/1762	L.-Corporal	Williams, E. P.	1st	29/12/17
11586	Corporal	Williams, J. J.	2nd	9/6/17
10260	Private	Williams, P. E.	1st	11/7/16
24/2567	Private	Williamson, J.	2nd	15/6/17
6/3929	Private	Willoughby, W. G.	2nd	13/7/16
24261	L.-Corporal	Wilson, A. E.	1st	27/5/18
41167	Private	Wilson, F. A.	2nd	12/6/17
34198	Private	Wilson, R. A.	3rd	2/10/17
6/2962	Private	Wilson, R. W. L.	1st	28/9/16
64400	Private	Wilson, W. F.	2nd	23/10/18
6/3932	L.-Corporal	Wing, W.	2nd	17/9/16
6/2014	L.-Corporal	Winter, G. E.	1st	23/9/16
11764	Private	Wood, C. L.	1st	11/6/17
63077	Private	Woodward, H. C.	1st	27/8/18
51205	Private	Wright, C. W.	1st	29/9/18
44054	L.-Corporal	Wright, H. T. A.	2nd	24/10/18
29332	C.S.M.	Wright, O. G.	2nd	1/9/18

DIED OF DISEASE.

Officers.

Number.	Rank.	Name.	Battalion.	Date.
6/718	Captain	Rutherfurd, T. W. L.	1st	19/10/18
		(detached on special duty).		
6/2590	2nd Lieut.	Dartnall, C. A.	1st	15/11/18(N.Z.)

Other Ranks.

70898	Private	A'Court, F. A.	Reserve	14/10/18
6/3592	L.-Corporal	Adam, J. J.	2nd	15/5/17 (N.Z.)
31453	Private	Allen, W.	1st	23/2/17
58657	Private	Anderson, A. E.	2nd	31/10/18
6/3983	Private	Anderson, J.	1st	27/4/17
11603	Private	Barbour, J.	Reserve	18/8/16
23/1547	Private	Bartlett, A. W.	2nd	10/8/16
6/3989	Private	Bell, S.	2nd	24/1/18 (N.Z.)
21649	Private	Benson, A.	2nd	5/11/18
11610	Private	Best, S.	2nd	2/1/17
14932	Private	Blick, T. G.	2nd	19/8/18
72870	Private	Bowles, J.	—	7/10/18
15475	Private	Boyce, E.	1st	26/2/17
27158	Private	Bryant, F. C.	1st	26/11/18
6/2556	Private	Bryant, J. W. H.	1st	24/11/16
6/2958	L.-Corporal	Bunyard, W. J.	1st	3/7/18
39452	Private	Burrough, J.	2nd	24/6/17
6/1487	Private	Clements, P.	1st	29/6/16 (N.Z.)
43136	Private	Cochrane, J. G.	1st	13/11/18
29149	Private	Considine, P.	2nd	6/5/18
28087	Private	Cook, C. H.	Reserve	14/3/18
6/3297	Private	Dawson, J. A.	1st	8/5/16
38266	Private	Debenham, C.	3rd	17/6/17
26254	Private	Dukes, W. H.	2nd	4/11/18
73157	Private	Duncan, A. P.	2nd	25/11/18
72769	Private	Duxfield, L. A.	1st	16/12/18
40791	Private	Elstob, J.	3rd	9/8/17
46179	Private	Flower, F. G.	1st	22/10/17
6/3704	Private	Fox, J. S.	2nd	29/8/16
64762	Private	Gavin, J.	2nd	7/5/18
61132	Private	Gibbs, W. I.	Reserve	20/2/18
51716	Private	Ginders, G. P.	—	15/3/18
11649	Private	Goss, W.	1st	11/12/16
59638	Private	Griffin, J.	Reserve	22/2/18
43971	Private	Guy, T.	1st	16/10/18
38282	Private	Harris, S.	1st	6/2/18
40212	Private	Harvey, C. J.	2nd	7/5/18
5/271	Private	Harvey, T. S.	2nd	27/5/16
6/2173	Private	Jeffries, J.	2nd	12/2/17
28889	Private	Kane, J. A.	2nd	14/11/18 (N.Z.)
26273	Private	Kearns, D.	2nd	4/5/17
6/2382	Private	Kearse, T. W.	1st	25/10/17
57229	Private	Kessell, W. H.	3rd	15/1/18
70824	Private	Lander, G. K.	Reserve	12/9/18
6/490	C.Q.M.S.	Latimer, L. V.	2nd	14/11/18 (N.Z.)
6/4292	Private	Lilley, D.	1st	15/11/17
6/2689	Private	Linford, H. J.	1st	22/11/18 (N.Z.)
64657	Private	McCracken, C. A.	Reserve	23/2/18

Number.	Rank.	Name.	Battalion.	Date.
17806	Private	McDonnell, J. W.	1st	18/11/18
58133	Private	Mapp, R. W.	Reserve	18/2/18
34703	Private	Martin, E.	3rd	30/1/18
70915	Private	Mitchell, A. C.	Reserve	13/10/18
62358	Private	Moody, F. R.	Reserve	22/2/18
64330	Private	Nelson, A.	Reserve	11/2/18
24215	Private	O'Connor, H.	1st	6/1/17
6/2460	Private	Parker, E. H.	3rd	15/9/17
53520	Private	Perkins, J.	2nd	27/10/18
6/1953	Corporal	Pickering, J.	1st	16/6/16 (N.Z.)
63415	Private	Poynter, W. D.	Reserve	27/2/18
11728	Private	Roberts, C. L.	2nd	25/11/18
57838	Private	Rowse, W. H..	2nd	18/6/18
43929	Private	Sager, G.	Reserve	13/9/17
27966	Private	Shaw, A.	Reserve	15/1/17
48283	Private	Simpson, A. F.	1st	6/12/17
47688	Private	Smith, P. H.	Reserve	14/8/17
36370	Private	Stephens, N. H.	2nd	4/11/18
6/3888	Private	Summerville, H. H.	2nd	12/5/17
61158	Private	Syder, H. C.	Reserve	9/2/18
15040	Private	Tait, J.	2nd	15/9/17
73202	Private	Tarrant, F. I.	1st	12/12/18
55562	Private	Tarrant, L. A. B.	Reserve	15/12/17
6/157	Sergeant	Tavender, B. N.	1st	16/11/18 (N.Z.)
10403	Private	Thompson, G. W.	1st	6/3/17
36373	L.-Corporal	Tonks, A. B.	3rd	31/3/18
63790	Private	Treleaven, R. R.	Reserve	20/2/18
6/2308	Private	Vercoe, P. R.	1st	8/3/17
61006	Private	Wade, J.	Reserve	23/8/18
58629	Private	Walker, D. J.	Reserve	3/11/17
74137	Private	Walker, V.	Reserve	14/10/18
79934	Private	Warner, A. H.	Reserve	20/10/18
31568	Private	Watson, W. R.	Reserve	20/3/17
10134	Private	Weld, J. E.	1st	17/10/18
37903	Private	Whitelaw, A. G.	3rd	10/1/18
31558	Private	Winter, H.	Reserve	4/2/17
59780	Private	Wood, C. M.	2nd	24/9/18
70960	Private	Woodham, J. C.	Reserve	17/8/18

FOUND DEAD.

61149	L.-Corporal	O'Connor, J.	2nd	6/8/18

KILLED.

24/2008	Private	Hughes, F.	2nd	25/8/16
6/1598	Private	King, J.	1st	19/8/17

DIED OF INJURIES ACCIDENTALLY RECEIVED.

44967	Private	Clinton, T.	1st	28/10/17
21664	Private	Cross, W.	Reserve	1/3/17
36363	Private	Sampson, D.	1st	25/6/18

DIED AS A RESULT OF A MOTOR ACCIDENT.

Number.	Rank.	Name.	Battalion.	Date.
15006	Private	Mitchell, H. T.	2nd	9/10/17

DROWNED.

63622	Private	Knox, J. J.	2nd	3/8/18

MEMBERS OF "C" COMPANY OF VARIOUS REINFORCEMENTS WHO DIED ON THE VOYAGE TO ENGLAND.

69830	Private	Burke, E. P.	3/9/18
79320	Private	Ferguson, J.	5/9/18
11640	Private	Frasi, J. G.	22/6/16
76332	Private	Hansen, L. G.	11/9/18
79450	Private	Hansen, W. J.	2/9/18
73406	Private	Hawker, C. A.	6/9/18
79396	Private	Hocken, H.	6/9/18
79264	Private	Hoddle, W. J.	5/9/18
70865	Private	Hood, H. V.	4/9/18
79461	Private	Laurenson, G. S.	4/9/18
78248	Private	McLean, A. A.	27/8/18
11692	Private	Marshall, H. J.	24/7/16
79406	Private	Power, J.	5/9/18
79473	Private	Rowson, S.	5/9/18
79477	Private	Smith, A.	4/9/18
72083	Private	Stevenson, T. J.	7/9/18
31552	Private	Tombs, C.	17/2/17